Introduction to
Administrative Office Management

INTRODUCTION TO ADMINISTRATIVE OFFICE MANAGEMENT

Zane K. Quible

Michigan State University

Winthrop Publishers, Inc.

Cambridge, Massachusetts

Library of Congress Cataloging in Publication Data

Quible, Zane K
  Introduction to administrative office management.

  Includes index.
  1. Office management.   I. Title.
HF5547.05   651'.3   76-55770
ISBN 0-87626-400-3

To my wife, Pat

Interior design and cover design by Harold Pattek

© *1977 by Winthrop Publishers, Inc.*
  17 Dunster Street, Cambridge, Massachusetts 02138

10 9 8 7 6 5 4 3 2 1

Contents

Contents

Preface

Administrative office management, which is primarily concerned with the processing of information, is currently receiving considerable attention. The most significant reason for such increased attention is the awareness that the efficiency with which information is processed is very likely to have a pronounced impact on the profit picture of the organization.

The processing of information can become exceedingly complex because of the involvement of three components: employees, equipment, and work processes. If the processing of information is to be done in a systematic, efficient manner, the interrelationships among employees, equipment, and work processes must be closely scrutinized.

Each chapter in this text is concerned with one or more of the three components involved in information processing. When a chapter is concerned with two or three of the components, the interrelationships are described in detail.

The chapters concerned with the employees component contain many suggestions for helping employees—both supervisory and non-supervisory—to become more effective and efficient in performing their jobs. The major thrust of these chapters is the administrative office manager's involvement in this vital component.

The chapters concerned with the equipment utilized in the processing of information discuss the various functions of the equipment. Much of the equipment utilized in information processing is multifunctional. This component, of the three, is the most rapidly changing. Almost daily a new piece of equipment is introduced on the market. The administrative office manager is likely to spend a considerable amount of time investigating the various types of equipment in order to obtain the most appropriate piece of equipment for the work processes for which it will be used.

The third component—work processes—is a special feature of this text. In the discussions that deal with some of the more complex work processes, carefully outlined steps are identified. Thus, inexperienced as well as experienced individuals can easily follow the steps that make up these work processes. The development of efficient work processes is another crucial function of the administrative office manager.

The new developments and concepts in administrative office management are given full coverage in this text. One whole chapter is devoted to word processing, which is perhaps the most significant new development in administrative office management. Less significant developments and concepts are included as major sections of the appropriate chapters.

This text, although primarily written for college-level administrative office management courses, is also very useful as a reference manual for administrative office managers. The "how to" approach contained throughout the text makes it especially useful as a reference manual.

Several unique features have been incorporated into the text to aid the student in the learning process. At the beginning of each chapter, a topical outline of the chapter is presented. In addition, chapter aims and chapter terms are included for each chapter. At the end of each chapter, review questions, two minicases, and one comprehensive case are included. A *Student Guide*, which contains an application problem for each chapter, as well as a comprehensive in-basket simulation, is available to accompany this text.

The author is indebted to many individuals who helped in the development of this text. For their constructive and helpful reviews, the author thanks Dr. David Hyslop, Bowling Green State University; Dr. Marjorie Kinney, Massachusetts Bay Community College; Dr. Max McKitrick, Western Michigan University; and Dr. Dennis Mott, Oklahoma State University.

The author also appreciates the assistance provided by James Curran, James Russell, Ronald Soltis, Ronald Ward, and Mary Jo Westgate. Their assistance made significant improvements in several of the chapters.

The author also appreciates the support and encouragement provided by various individuals at Michigan State University. These individuals enabled the text to become a reality more rapidly than it might have without their help.

In addition, the author wishes to acknowledge and thank his parents for instilling in him at an early age the need to persevere and "stick with it."

And lastly, the author wishes to acknowledge his wife, Pat, whose patience and understanding were invaluable in the preparation of this text. Without her support, the task would have been much more difficult.

Part
1
The
Function

The Managerial Process

Chapter
1

Evolution of Management Theory
    Scientific Management Movement
    Administrative Movement
    Human Relations Movement
    Modern Movement
    Summary

The Functions of Management
    Planning Function
    Organizing Function
    Staffing Function
    Directing Function
    Controlling Function

The Administrative Office Management Function
    Objectives
    Emerging Concepts
    The Administrative Office Manager
        Qualifications
        Professionalism
        Background

A Career in Administrative Office Management

Management Information Systems
    Characteristics of Management Information Systems
    Objectives of Management Information Systems
    Advantages of Management Information Systems
        Information center
        Greater efficiency
        Greater effectiveness
        Reduction of operating costs
        Better control

Chapter Aims   After studying this chapter, the student should be able to:

1. Explain the significance of each of the following four movements in the development of management theory: scientific management movement, administrative movement, human relations movement, and modern movement.

2. Discuss the nature of the various functions of management and identify typical activities involved in each.

3. Identify the areas involved in administrative office management.

4. Explain the emerging concepts that have added responsibility and prestige to the administrative office management function.

5. Identify the qualifications of an administrative office manager.

6. Discuss the nature of the management information system concept, including the characteristics and advantages of the concept.

Chapter Terms   *Functional areas:* the various functions that comprise an organization. Examples are sales, marketing, finance, and accounting.

Management: the process of managing people, which involves getting things done through and with others.

Scientific management: the first phase in the development of management theory, which was begun by Frederick Taylor and was popular during the late 1800s and early 1900s. Scientific management made extensive use of time and motion study.

Administrative movement: the second phase in the development of management theory, popular during the 1930s. The movement viewed the organization as consisting of a total entity rather than as comprising isolated functions.

Human relations movement: the third phase in the development of management theory, popular during the 1940s and 1950s. This movement focused primarily on small groups and individuals.

Modern movement: the fourth phase in the development of management theory, which had its beginnings in the 1950s. This movement consists of operations research and behavioral science elements.

Operations research: the technique in which a model for problem solving is frequently utilized.

Behavioral science research: the scientific study of observable and verifiable human behavior.

Managerial functions: includes the functions of planning, organizing, staffing, directing, and controlling. Each function comprises several activities.

Management information system: the concept in which the computer is used to obtain desired information in the desired format at the desired time. Although each of the functional areas puts information into the system, other functional areas can access the information for use in decisionmaking.

In any formally organized unit—for example, an organization or a department within an organization—one or more individuals in the unit must be responsible for the planning, organizing, staffing, directing, and controlling activities of the unit. These individuals are generally known as *managers*, and they are responsible for performing the managerial functions within their respective units.

Collegiate-level study of managerial processes and techniques has expanded rapidly during the last three to four decades. During this time, there has been a solidification of managerial objectives and principles common to the different types of organizations: for example, profit and nonprofit, public and private, large and small, manufacturing and retail, and so forth. Since the **functional areas**—production, sales, accounting, finance, marketing, as an example—within organizations have become more specialized, the study of these specific areas has also expanded rapidly during this time. It is not uncommon to find collegiate-level courses dealing with such functional areas as financial management, sales management, personnel management, marketing management, institutional management, purchasing management, and administrative office management.

Management has been defined as the process of getting things done through and with people.[1] Therefore, management in one form or another has existed since the creation of humans. Historians believe that effective management of social groups has now existed for more than 6000 years and that without the well-developed operations and procedures characteristic of the early Egyptian, Greek, and Roman Empire civilizations, their existence would have been quite short-lived.

Evolution of Management Theory

The industrial revolution of the 1800s resulted in more effective utilization of production equipment and centralized production and is largely responsible for the creation of the efficient industrial organization. For many years these new industrial organizations, while making mass production possible, were not well understood, especially in terms of the effect that mass production processes had on employees.

The evolution of management theory has progressed through four rather distinct phases, beginning with the **scientific mangement movement** in the early 1900s, and including the **administrative movement** of the 1930s, the **human relations movement** of the 1940s and 1950s, and the current **modern movement.**

Scientific Management Movement

The work of Charles Babbage in the 1830s is considered by many to have been the forerunner of what was later to develop as scientific management. Many organizations during the last half of the nineteenth

---

1 Harold Koontz and Cyril O'Donnell, *Principles of Management: An Analysis of Managerial Functions*, 5th ed. (New York: McGraw-Hill Book Company, 1972), p. 43.

century placed a considerable amount of emphasis on production processes. Babbage developed several production-oriented concepts that are still widely used today. For example, he was concerned with dividing and assigning labor on the basis of skill, the feasibility of replacing manual operations with automatic equipment, work measurement, cost determination, and wage incentive plans.

Frederick W. Taylor, generally regarded as the founder of scientific management, was also greatly concerned with the emphasis that organizations placed on production during the late 1800s and early 1900s. Taylor believed that a major problem being experienced by industrial organizations could be resolved if management would determine the expected level of output of employees and then communicate these expectations to the employees. Scientific management, as conceived by Taylor, was to solve two major problems: to increase the output of the employees and to improve the operating efficiency of management.

Taylor viewed each worker as a separate economic entity whose motivation to work stemmed from the worker's financial needs. Therefore, Taylor believed that workers had to overcome the fear of being replaced by a machine or by an automated process. To do this, Taylor believed that workers had to produce more at a lower cost and that they should be paid on a piecework basis so that they could earn more money.

The cornerstone of scientific management as formalized by Taylor was the use of time and motion study to increase workers' efficiency in using machines. Time study is concerned with the amount of time a task takes for completion, while motion study is concerned with the efficiency of the motion involved in performing the task. Taylor's scientific management philosophy was based on the following principles:

1. *The development of one best method.* Each job had to be analyzed to determine the most efficient processes.

2. *The selection and development of workers.* For any specific job, care had to be exercised to select the best worker.

3. *Bringing together of the best methods and the selected workers.* Because of increased earnings, workers will support improved work processes.

4. *Close cooperation of managers and employees.* Although there must be a division of labor between managers and workers, close cooperation is essential.

Taylor and his followers, who believed that there was one best way to do a job, emphasized the mechanical and physiological aspects of work, which in many cases were detrimental to the workers' psychological and social needs. As management theory progressed through the evolutionary stages, Taylor's philosophy was often challenged and frequently attacked.

Administrative Movement

The administrative movement, popular during the 1930s, focused on the firm as a whole or total entity rather than on certain isolated functions. During this stage managerial processes were thought to consist of planning, organizing, commanding, coordinating, and controlling functions.

Henri Fayol, a French geologist and engineer, was one of the more important proponents of the administrative philosophy. Fayol and his followers believed in the universality of managerial principles. The following list of fourteen principles characterizes Fayol's philosophy:

1. Division of labor
2. Authority
3. Discipline
4. Unity of command
5. Unity of direction
6. Subordination of the individual interest to the general interest
7. Remuneration
8. Centralization
9. Scalar chain (line of authority)
10. Order
11. Equity
12. Stability of tenure of personnel
13. Initiative
14. Esprit de corps[2]

In addition to formulating the management principles, Fayol also believed that all organizational activities could be divided into six groups:

1. Technical (production)
2. Commercial (buying, selling, and exchanging)
3. Financial (search for and optimum use of capital)
4. Security (production of property and persons)
5. Accounting (including statistics)
6. Managerial (planning, organizing, commanding, coordinating, and controlling)[3]

Human Relations Movement

The human relations movement, taking place during the 1940s and 1950s, was largely in response to organizations' failure to treat their em-

---

2 Henri Fayol, *General and Industrial Management* (London: Sir Isaac Pitman and Sons, Ltd., 1949), pp. 19–42.
3 Ibid., p. 3.

ployees as humans. Rather than focusing on the whole organization, as was true of the administrative movement, the human relations movement was primarily concerned with individuals and small groups. The relationship between the superior and subordinate was stressed, particularly in terms of interpersonal relations and communication. Much of the work that evolved out of the human relations movement was concerned primarily with the lower levels of management. The human relations movement may have had a greater impact on the evolution of management theory had the behavioral scientists used the findings of their research to further the development of management theory. Instead, they used their research to develop a science of human relations.

One of the primary proponents of the human relations movement was Elton Mayo. The now famous Hawthorne Studies conducted by Mayo and other researchers from Harvard University provided the primary impetus for the development of the human relations movement. The Hawthorne Studies, which took place at Western Electric's Hawthorne, Illinois, plant, were concerned with determining the effects that such factors as lighting, heat, fatigue, and layout had upon productivity.

One phase of the study determined the relationship between the illumination level of the work area and the output of the plant workers. As the illumination level was increased, the output also predictably increased. But unexpectedly, the output continued to increase even when the illumination level was decreased. The researchers concluded, on the basis of the research, that the human element had a greater impact in determining output and reaction to change than did the technical factor. Those advocating human relations strongly believe, therefore, that treating humans as humans has a greater effect on operating efficiency and output than do any of the technical factors.

Modern Movement

The fourth phase in the evolution of management theory, the modern movement, began in the early 1950s. Since many of the proponents of this movement received their formal education during the time of the human relations movement, the modern movement is to a certain extent influenced by the human relations movement.

The modern movement consists of two approaches—the quantitative approach and the nonquantitative approach. The quantitative approach involves what is known as **operations research**, while the nonquantitative approach is frequently called **behavioral science research.**

Operations research, as part of the modern movement, is concerned primarily with the making of decisions, specifically with deciding which operations should be undertaken and how they should be undertaken. Operations research frequently requires the use of a model for problem solving.

Systems analysis is closely related to operations research, with the following basic differences: systems analysis depends more heavily on judgment and premonition, whereas operations research depends more heavily on quantitative methods. Put another way, systems analysis is more subjective, while operations research is more objective.

Behavioral science research, being nonquantitative, is the scientific study of observable and verifiable human behavior. The effects of behavioral science research can be observed at three levels in organizations—individual, group, and organizational. While the individual level is concerned with such factors as motivation, attitudes, and personality, the group level is concerned with interactions, group norms, and group leadership. The behavioral science research that takes place at the organizational level has been concerned with such areas as bureaucracy and the effect that the design of the total system has on behavior.

Some interesting comparisons can be made of behavioral science research and operations research. Behavioral science research is for the most part inductive and operations research is deductive. Behavioral science research is concerned with the manner in which decisions are made, while operations research is concerned with how they ought to be made. Behavioral science research uses psychology, sociology, and anthropology as its base, but operations research is more concerned with mathematics, computer science, and statistics.

Summary

The scientific management movement was production-oriented and therefore was greatly concerned with efficiency and its effect on production. The administrative movement, credited with viewing the firm as a total entity, is largely responsible for categorizing various managerial functions. The human relations movement, on the other hand, viewed management as a small-group, worker-centered process. It was during this movement that a considerable amount of research was conducted within organizations. The present modern movement is using more behavioral and quantitative analysis tools in conducting research. The research presently being conducted is more experimental and inductive than the research conducted during any of the preceding movements.

Some of the theories that grew out of each movement are still widely practiced today. Because of this "hybridization," the movements are not mutually exclusive of one another.

The Functions of Management

The managerial process involves several different **managerial functions.** For example, a portion of the manager's time will be consumed by planning activities. Organizing activities will also consume a portion of the manager's time, as will staffing, directing, and controlling activities. The portion of time that each of the five managerial functions consumes depends on several factors. For example, if an individual other than the manager is responsible for supervising employees, the manager will spend less time with the directing function. If the organization has a fairly comprehensive employee selection process, the manager perhaps will not have to spend as much time with the staffing function. The more important factors that determine the amount of time that each function will consume include (1) the size of the organization; (2) the hierarchical level of the manager; (3) the organizational structure of the organization; and (4) the number of employees directed by the manager.

Planning Function

Many of the activities characteristic of the planning function can be categorized as short-range activities, long-range activities, or both short- and long-range activities. For example, budgeting, an important activity in the planning function, is primarily a short-range activity, but it is also a long-range activity. Determining or setting goals and objectives are both short-range and long-range activities. Other activities that are characteristically part of the planning function are: determining future manpower requirements, scheduling work to meet completion deadlines, determining need for automating processes or procedures, determining need for additional equipment, determining expansion possibilities, and determining space needs.

Organizing Function

Many of the activities in the organizing function become necessary because of the planning function. For example, an organization that is attempting to achieve a short-range objective of increasing production by 5 percent will ultimately have to organize its resources in such a way that the objective can be obtained. Therefore, many of the activities of the organizing function are concerned with determining what has to be done and how it should be done. Another important activity of the organizing function is determining the hierarchical relationship between employees, which is usually depicted on an organizational chart. The organizing function is also concerned with efficiently organizing the organization's processes and procedures.

Staffing Function

The activities in the staffing function are primarily concerned with making sure the organization has the best qualified employees obtainable within the constraints of the organization's financial resources. The staffing function of most organizations consists of determining job requirements, duties, and responsibilities. The staffing function is also concerned with selecting new employees, orienting new employees, and developing training programs so that present employees can maintain a high level of effectiveness or so new employees can become more competent in their positions.

Directing Function

Depending upon the nature of a manager's job, a considerable amount of time may be spent in the daily direction and supervision of employees. While some managers are fairly far removed from daily supervision activities, others spend a sizeable portion of each day supervising employees. Determining horizontal and vertical lines of communication is another activity of the directing function. Although determining lines of communication is primarily a directing function, adequate lines of communication have a definite impact on the organizing function. Without adequate communication and supervision, work processes and procedures are likely to be somewhat inefficient.

Controlling Function

The controlling function is primarily concerned with determining how well an actual operation conforms with expected results. If results fail to meet expectations, an attempt should be made to determine the reasons expectations were not met. Consequently, functions that can be positively identified as being responsible for the operation's failure to meet expected results should be carefully evaluated.

If the planning, organizing, staffing, and directing functions are properly carried out, the controlling function is simplified to a great extent.

The Administrative Office Management Function

The administrative office management function is primarily supportive in nature. This means that many of the activities of the administrative office management function support individuals throughout the organization by freeing them of the responsibility for such activities. For example, a centralized records management program is an important activity of the administrative office management function. By making the administrative office manager responsible for maintaining records, other individuals have more time to perform their designated duties. Many of the activities of the administrative office management function involve providing individuals with accurate information and data in the form they request and when they request it. Other activities of the administrative office management function involve helping individuals in the various units of the organization to achieve their objectives effectively and efficiently. Still other activities help to make the organization a physically and mentally attractive place in which to work.

The present trend toward centralizing many of the office functions and services has added a new dimension to the administrative office management function. When only a few of the office functions and services were centralized, office management (as it was then called) was rather isolated and involved only a few of the individuals within organizations. Because of the present trend toward centralization, most individuals in organizations are affected in one way or another by the administrative office management function. The fact that so many of the functions and services of administrative office management have become so specialized also adds a new dimension to this rapidly growing area.

In organizations that have not yet centralized the administrative office management function, each unit manager is generally responsible for organizing and directing the unit's office activities. In many cases, this results in duplication of effort, duplication in the type of information created, and general inefficiency.

A fundamental purpose of the administrative office management function is to centralize control of the office activities and services. In some instances physical centralization and functional centralization will occur, although it is possible to have physical centralization without functional centralization and vice versa.

Objectives

Administrative office management, like any other area of management, has a common core of objectives. Some of the more common objectives are:

1. To coordinate the activities of the administrative office management function with the activities of other organizational functions.

2. To maintain reasonable quantity and quality standards so that satisfactory levels of production are possible.

3. To develop efficient work procedures and processes in order to increase the organization's profit margin.

4. To provide a satisfactory physical and mental working environment for the organization's employees.

5. To enhance the effective supervision of office personnel.

6. To make information available when needed and where needed.

7. To help define duties and responsibilities of employees within the unit and to develop satisfactory lines of communication among these employees and among other employees in the organization.

8. To schedule work properly so that all jobs are completed on time.

9. To develop procedures to help select the right person for the right job.

10. To provide ample opportunities for helping employees maintain a high level of work effectiveness.

11. To make sure that specialized equipment is efficiently and properly utilized.

12. To provide ample security for materials and information that falls under the jurisdiction of the administrative office manager.

Emerging Concepts

Two rather significant concepts have added responsibility and stature to the administrative office management function. Many organizations are using a rather sophisticated systems approach for carrying out many of their various functions. One type of system, the management information system, is discussed later in this chapter. Systems analysis and design is frequently the responsibility of administrative office management. Another significant concept is the widespread use of automated equipment and procedures wherever possible. The data processing area is also frequently the responsibility of the administrative office manager. Basically, systems analysis and data processing are closely related, and in some cases are even interrelated.

Systems analysis refers to the study, analysis, and improvement of the organization's systems that are designed to coordinate the operations found throughout the organization. The systems found in many organizations are interrelated and are built around the computer and other automated processes. Before many of the organization's procedures can be automated, a thorough systems analysis needs to be undertaken. Because of concern for productivity and efficiency, an organization must determine which operations can be simplified or consolidated if automation is utilized. By interrelating the operations, efficiency is enhanced, and automation can be used to a great extent in carrying out the operations.

The Administrative Office Manager

The role of the administrative office manager has become much broader during the last few years. The individual responsible for the office function used to be called the office manager. The role of the office manager was somewhat limited, and in most cases the manager was primarily concerned with supervising employees who performed office-type activities. Today, the individual responsible for the office function is more appropriately called the administrative office manager. The functions of the administrative office manager have expanded to include much more than mere supervision of office employees. The position of administrative office manager is very broad, and in all probability, no two managers perform identical functions and duties.

The role of the administrative office manager is becoming more challenging because of rapid advances in technology, new equipment, and work processes. The contemporary office employee is also providing new challenges for the administrative office manager, especially in organizations whose office employees belong to a union or to some collective bargaining unit.

Qualifications. Expanding job duties have resulted in today's administrative office manager's needing different qualifications than his predecessor, the office manager, needed. The qualifications needed for the administrative office manager are broader but also are more intensive than were those needed for the office manager.

In terms of educational preparation, a thorough understanding of various business functions is very important. Since administrative office management is primarily supportive in nature and is designed to help other units to achieve goals and objectives, the administrative office manager needs a solid background in such functional areas as accounting, marketing, sales, management, and so forth. Furthermore, administrative office managers are frequently responsible for systems analysis and design. Therefore, in order properly to integrate functional areas, the administrative office manager needs a thorough understanding of the functional areas. A specialized knowledge of the following areas is also important: work simplification, work measurement, work standards, records management, forms design, electronic data processing, job analysis, job evaluation, office layout, office equipment, cost control, performance appraisal, and employee selection.

Another important qualification is the ability to provide adequate leadership for subordinates. Depending on the size of the organization, leadership may include supervising subordinates. In large organizations, supervision will most likely be the responsibility of supervisors rather than of the administrative office manager. Leadership also includes the ability to inspire and to motivate employees. Another important function of leadership is the ability to instill in subordinates the desire to act in the best interests of the organization, to be loyal to the organization, and to be cooperative. The ability to work well with others and human relations skills are also crucial for the administrative office manager.

The ability to delegate responsibility is another important qualification of the administrative office manager, as well as the ability to make decisions effectively and to communicate with others. The administrative office manager must also be able to accept the viewpoint of others and must exercise good judgment. Furthermore, the administrative office manager must have initiative and the desire to continue to learn and to develop professionally through organization memberships, participation in seminars and conferences, and assimilation of the contributions of pertinent literature.

Professionalism. Administrative office managers can become more professional by being active members in professional organizations. Perhaps the most important organization is the Administrative Management Society, which is an international organization with chapters located in various cities throughout the United States, Canada, and Jamaica. The monthly meetings of AMS chapters are primarily designed to disseminate information on new technology, trends, and work processes. The international headquarters of AMS are located at Willow Grove, Pennsylvania.

The Certified Administrative Manager (C.A.M.), a program sponsored by the Administrative Management Society, is another means for the administrative office manager to become a more professional manager. Individuals who meet the requirements for the C.A.M. program become members of the Academy of Certified Administrative Managers. Certification requirements are:

1. Passing the C.A.M. examination, which covers personnel management, financial management, control and economics, systems and information management, and administrative services.
2. Two years of administrative management experience.
3. Proof of high standards of personal and professional conduct.
4. Evidence of communication ability.
5. Evidence of leadership ability.

Other professional organizations of interest to administrative office managers are American Records Management Association, Association for Systems Management, Data Processing Management Association, National Microfilm Association, International Word Processing Association, and the Business Forms Management Association.

An abundance of professional literature of interest to administrative office managers also exists. Some of the better known periodicals include *Administrative Management, Management World* (the official magazine of AMS), *Modern Office Procedures, The Office,* and *Word Processing World.*

Background. To be successful as an administrative office manager, certain minimum educational requirements are needed, coupled with appropriate work experience. Although an individual may have the needed educational requirements for being an administrative office manager, the individual may not be successful without first having some work experience. It is for this reason that many administrative office managers have "come up through the ranks." Many have previously served as a supervisor of employees in one of the functional areas of administrative office management—for example, data processing.

Some of the college-level courses that administrative office managers find helpful are accounting, economics, business law, finance, statistics, and oral and written communication, as well as administrative office management.

A Career in Administrative Office Management

The rapid growth of information processing in organizations is increasing the number of career opportunities in administrative office management. An increasing number of organizations are discovering that one way to improve their profits is to scrutinize closely the cost of their office operations. Such organizations have also discovered that their profits can be improved by concentrating on the efficiency of the office operations. For these two reasons, many organizations are placing increasing emphasis on administrative office management. In turn, the number of opportunities for those wishing to pursue a career in administrative office management has greatly increased.

FIGURE 1–1

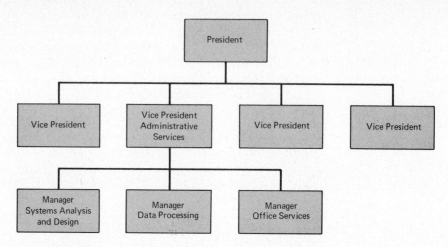

Administrative office management is generally considered to be within the middle-management level of organizational hierarchy. In some organizations, especially larger ones, administrative office management is likely to be an important component of one of the functional areas of the organization. The name of the functional area is likely to be administrative services, and a vice president of administrative services (or a vice president with some other similar title) is likely to be responsible for the area. Within the functional area, several middle-level managers are likely to report to the vice president for administrative services. A typical organization pattern is to have a manager responsible for systems analysis and design, another manager responsible for data processing, and a third manager responsible for office services or information processing. In organizations that utilize the word processing/administrative support concept, which is discussed in Chapter 8, the individual responsible for office services or information processing is more likely to be called a manager of word processing/administrative support rather than a manager of office services or information processing. Figure 1–1 illustrates this organizational pattern.

The organization pattern illustrated above has also made available a new career opportunity for the middle-level managers. This career opportunity is vice president of the functional area, which in the illustration is administrative services. It is now possible for an individual who started in a low-level office job to become a vice president for administrative services. Such opportunities make a career in administrative office management not only desirable but also very rewarding.

The opportunities for individuals' choosing a career in administrative office management generally increase as the demand for clerical workers increases. The Bureau of Labor Statistics, U.S. Department of Labor, has projected that between 1972–1985 the number of clerical workers will increase nearly 40 percent.[4] On the basis of this statistic, the opportunities in the field of administrative office management look exceedingly bright.

The only significant change in the characteristics of administrative office managers projected to take place during the next decade is the number of women who will choose administrative office management as a career. Although administrative office management is still a male-dominated field, especially in larger organizations, the male-female ratio is expected to become more balanced in years to come. An increasing number of women are starting their management careers as administrative office managers.

More and more, administrative office managers are assuming important roles in management and policymaking, with accompanying increases in authority and prestige. Administrative office management has become an important mechanism for integrating major information systems within an organization. Therefore, administrative office management is likely to encompass and direct the total information and communication processes of the organization.

Management Information Systems

Because of rapid growth in size and complexity, many organizations were being confronted with vastly increasing volumes of paperwork. Many organizations were finding it increasingly difficult to obtain the desired information in the desired format at the desired time. Although the computer has helped solve these problems to a large extent, there is also ample evidence that the computer has added to the problem by helping to generate the vast volume of paperwork. To overcome some of these problems, many organizations have developed **management information systems.** The computer is the hub or at the center of these well-designed systems. In this sense, the computer provides a very valuable function as an information center, and each of the organizational functions feeds data through the computer into the information center. This concept is illustrated in Figure 1–2. The result is that managers now have at their disposal a wide variety of information that facilitates their decisionmaking. Before the development of organizationwide integrated management systems, data was fragmented; and in many cases, tedious clerical operations had to be mechanically performed on the data before it could be put in usable form.

The management information system was developed when many or-

---

4 U.S. Department of Labor, Bureau of Labor Statistics, "Employment Outlook for Tomorrow's Jobs," *Occupational Outlook Handbook,* 1974–75 ed. Reprint Bulletin 1785–1 (Washington, D.C.: U.S. Government Printing Office, 1976), p. 6.

FIGURE 1–2   Management Information System

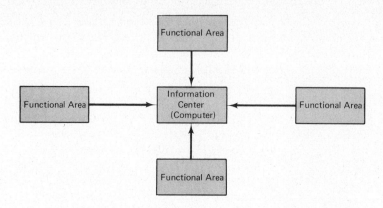

ganizations found it impossible to manage or control their information needs and requirements. The scope of the concept is quite broad, since the information cycle involves creating, processing, storing, retrieving, transmitting, and destroying activities. Without proper managerial controls applied to each of these activities, problems will likely surface.

Information is needed by managers to assist them in making decisions regarding internal and external situations. Depending upon the extent to which managers have available appropriate information, their jobs can be made much easier. Internal situations requiring the use of information include making decisions about the organization's productivity, manpower requirements, employee security, and the like. External situations require completely different types of information. For example, managers need to have available information pertaining to the activities of competing organizations. Without this information, an organization will not be able to maintain a competitive position for a very long period of time. Other external information is needed regarding the financial picture of the environment in which the organization exists. Unless this information is available, managers will likely make some unsatisfactory financial decisions.

Characteristics of Management Information Systems

A well-developed management information system possesses readily identifiable characteristics:

1. Management information systems involve the total organization —not fragmented or isolated activities.

2. The framework of the management information system is determined by the functional areas of the organization.

3. The elements that make up the system involve interrelated functional areas of the organization.

4. Routine processes are performed mechanically, thus reducing errors.

Objectives of Management Information Systems

As is true of any important system in an organization, objectives become very important. Without well-defined objectives, individuals associated with the system have considerable difficulty determining the system's scope of activities. Without properly defined objectives, the effectiveness of the system will be difficult to determine.

Some of the more common objectives of a management information system are:

1. To make information available when needed, where needed, and in the format needed.

2. To supply accurate information.

3. To use the most efficient methods for processing data.

4. To provide requested information at a reasonable cost.

5. To provide necessary security for important and/or confidential information.

6. To keep the information function up to date by incorporating feasible technological advances in the management information system. When properly developed and implemented, the system will assist the organization to increase its service function and its profitability.

Advantages of Management Information Systems

Using a management information system results in significant advantages, including the following:

Information center. One of the characteristics of the management information system concept is the utilization of an integrated information center that contains data from each of the major functional areas of the organization. The information center results in many clear-cut advantages for the organization. Since the hub of this information center is the computer, data can be readily manipulated and produced in many different formats, thus making the managers' jobs much easier. Prior to the time that management information systems were utilized by organizations, the information created by the various functional areas was so fragmented that it was often useless to other functional units, and thus, the information could never be utilized to the fullest extent.

Greater efficiency. Because so many of the procedures of a management information system are mechanically performed, greater efficiency can be accomplished. Machines are able to perform mechanical operations more rapidly, more efficiently, and more accurately than humans are able to perform. Since machines free humans of many of the mechanical operations, they can be more appropriately used to perform the functions that machines cannot perform. The result is that both humans and machines are more efficiently utilized, and in many cases the efficiency level is almost optimum. Since inadequately utilized resources become very obvious in a management information system, the system assists management in developing procedures that properly utilize the resources of the organization.

Greater effectiveness. In many cases, management information systems enable organizations to improve operations that are already being performed well. In this light, the utilization of a system will greatly enhance operating efficiency. Organizations become more effective because information is available much more rapidly and in a more usable format. Management information systems have frequently enabled organizations to detect "early warning signals" so that changes can be made before serious problems arise. Management information systems also provide information that enables organizations to take advantage of many unique opportunities that may not be so obvious in a more traditional operating approach.

Reduction of operating costs. For many organizations, the utilization of management information systems has significantly reduced operating costs in a variety of ways. For example, by electronically storing a large amount of data in the information center, multiple "hard copies" of documents can be destroyed. This helps lower costs by reducing the amount of storage space that is needed, in addition to speeding up the amount of time that it takes to retrieve information. Utilizing information systems can also help reduce operating costs by providing more accurate information than is generally possible when information is compiled by employees. Other costs can also be significantly reduced by combining forms, or in some cases, by completely eliminating forms.

Better control. Since an integrated management information system is composed of the various functional areas in an organization, better control can be exerted over work processes. Before the functions were combined and integrated into one system, they were in many cases fragmented and operated independently of one another. But by constructing an integrated system from the various functional areas, greater control over the organizational processes is a natural result.

Many of the activities for which the administrative office manager is responsible are directly related to the functions of a management information system. Typical systems consist of three components—employees, equipment, and forms—and the administrative office manager is responsible for numerous activities that involve one or more of these components. For example, work simplification, concerned with determining the simplest way for employees to perform work, is one of the important elements of a management information system. In many organizations, the administrative office manager is responsible for work simplification. Other activities for which the administrative office manager is responsible that are related to the management information system are records management, information retrieval, forms design and control, and equipment utilization.

Review Questions

1. What impact did the industrial revolution of the 1800s have on evolution of management theory?

2. Who is generally considered to be the founder of scientific management?

3. What technique or process was used during the scientific management movement to help increase workers' efficiency in using machines?

4. How does the scientific management movement differ from what is known as the administrative movement?

5. What is the significant impact of the Hawthorne Study?

6. What are the basic differences between systems analysis and operations research, the two approaches of the modern movement?

7. What educational qualifications are needed by an administrative office manager?

8. How might an administrative office manager become more professional?

9. What conditions have brought about the need for management information systems?

Minicases

Mr. David Johnson, the administrative office manager of Madison Corporation, recently retired after having worked for the company for twenty-three years. Mr. Johnson was very traditional and had very little interest in some of the emerging concepts of administrative office management. Upon his retirement, the vice president to whom the administrative office manager is responsible suggested that the office employees prepare for him a list of the characteristics they would like the new administrative office manager to possess. What characteristics would you like the new administrative office manager to have?

*   *   *

Recently, several employees in the Dumand Company were discussing the scientific management concept and its role in the development of management theory. Mary Jackson said that she was under the impression that scientific management was a scheme to get employees to produce more without showing much concern for the welfare of the employees. Nancy Brown indicated that scientific management was basically concerned with improving efficiency at the expense of all other considerations. Another employee, Carol Wilcox, indicated that both Mary and Nancy were somewhat incorrect in their statements because scientific management was fundamentally concerned with assuring management that it got its fair share of work from each employee. Assess the accuracy of each of the statements made by the three employees in the Dumand Company.

Case

The Quincy Manufacturing Corporation, a manufacturer of replacement auto parts, has grown rapidly during the last ten years. The net profit of the firm has expanded nearly 300 percent, while the number of employees in the firm has more than doubled.

Until approximately one year ago, the firm hired an external computer service to perform all of its data processing functions. About two years ago, a management consultant firm was hired to conduct a feasibility study to determine if the firm should have its own computer system. The result of the feasibility study indicated that the Quincy Manufacturing Corporation should install its own computer system, primarily for two reasons: greater efficiency and greater utilization of computer applications.

The computer system is under the jurisdiction of the administrative office manager, who is directly responsible to the vice president for corporate relations. Although the personnel who work with the computer system are directly responsible to the administrative office manager, they are supervised by the data processing supervisor.

At this point, the data processing personnel are still developing various applications. The organization's accounting and payroll functions are the only ones that are totally operational.

You, the administrative office manager, recently received a memorandum from the vice president for corporate relations regarding management information systems. The vice president indicated in his memo that he knew nothing about the concept but now that the firm has the computer system, he feels the concept should be thoroughly investigated. He asked you, as the manager responsible for the computer system, to prepare a report for him explaining the management information system concept.

1. What information do you think should be contained in your report to the vice president for corporate relations? Why?
2. Prepare the report.

The Organizing Process

Chapter
2

Organizational Principles

No. 1—Definition of Objectives
No. 2—Span of Control
No. 3—Interrelated Functions
No. 4—Chain of Command
No. 5—Designated Supervisors
No. 6—Commensurate Authority and Responsibility
No. 7—Work Assignment
No. 8—Employee Participation
No. 9—Overall Level of Responsibility

Organizational Structures

Line Structure
Advantages of line structure
Disadvantages of line structure
Line and Staff Structure
Advantages of line and staff structure
Disadvantages of line and staff structure
Functional Structure
Advantages of functional structure
Disadvantages of functional structure
Committee Structure
Advantages of committee structure
Disadvantages of committee structure
Product Structure

Centralization versus Decentralization

Factors that Determine the Feasibility of Centralization
Nature of the organization
Size of the organization
Diversification of organization
Conformity to standardized processes
Quality of personnel
Distribution of operating processes
Attitude of personnel
Advantages of Centralization
Disadvantages of Centralization

The Organization Chart

Chapter Aims   After studying this chapter, the student should be able to:

1. Explain why objectives should be clearly defined.
2. Explain what is meant by span of control.
3. Explain what is meant by interrelated functions and why functions are becoming increasingly related.
4. Explain chain of command.
5. Explain why subordinates should be responsible to only one supervisor.
6. Explain why authority and responsibility must be commensurate.
7. Explain why employee participation is advantageous.
8. Identify the advantages of employee participation in decisionmaking processes.
9. Explain the factors that determine whether centralization of a function or area is desirable and/or feasible.

Chapter Terms   *Organizational principles:* a set of conditions that enable an organization to maximize its operating effectiveness. Examples include definition of objectives, span of control, interrelated functions, and so forth.

Span of control: the number of subordinates a supervisor can effectively supervise. The span of control is determined by several factors, including the nature of the work being performed by the subordinates, the capability of supervisors and subordinates, and the nature of other responsibilities of supervisors.

Chain of command: the formal lines of authority in an organization. Chain of command identifies who reports to whom.

Employee participation: the practice of seeking and utilizing employee participation in the decisionmaking process.

Line Structure: the type of organizational structure in which direct authority is vertical in nature, flowing from the top of the organization to the bottom of the organization.

Line and staff structure: the type of organizational structure in which staff employees support and assist the line employees. While the line employees are directly concerned with the primary attainment of the organizational objectives, the staff employees support and assist the line employees.

Functional structure: the type of organizational structure in which a functional area manager has line authority over subordinates in his or her functional area and has functional authority over certain employees in other functional areas.

Committee structure: the use of a formally organized group of employees to perform either in a managerial capacity or in an advisory capacity.

Product structure: the organizational structure in which an organization's products provide the basis for the structure of the organization.

Centralization: a situation in which one person, rather than several, is made responsible for a particular activity or function.

Decentralization: a situation in which two or more people are equally responsible for a particular activity or function.

Organization chart: the graphic illustration that depicts the formal relationships between individuals and units or departments within an organization.

Chapter 1 examined the relationships between the planning, organizing, staffing, directing, and controlling functions. The organizing function, which gets its thrust from the planning function, is the focus of this chapter. Enterprises must organize their resources to achieve the objectives formulated during the planning function. The organizing function helps to assure the efficient utilization of the enterprise's resources.

The organizing function should receive adequate consideration in order to achieve the following: efficient utilization of resources of the organization; adequate consideration for the functional areas in the organization; a better understanding by employees of their duties and responsibilities; and a satisfactory employee morale level.

Although giving adequate consideration to the organizing function will not necessarily provide success in each instance, the odds for success are considerably higher than if the organizing function is not given adequate consideration.

Throughout the years, **organizational principles** have evolved that greatly facilitate the organizing function. These principles provide basic guidelines for employees who are concerned with the organizing function. When the organizational principles are utilized in designing activities for the organizing function, the enterprise's objectives can be achieved much more readily.

Organizational Principles

The following organizational principles are applicable for any type of enterprise and for nearly any activity that is designed to help achieve objectives. Adherence to the principles provides a much more enjoyable working environment for both subordinates and superiors.

No. 1—Definition of Objectives

Before objectives can be achieved, they must be clearly defined, understood, and accepted by each individual who is concerned with the achievement of the objectives. Without clearly defined or clearly understood objectives, appropriate courses of action are difficult to determine. Objectives that are well formulated during the planning function enable the organization to use its resources properly, which is necessary if the objectives are to be achieved. Objectives should be stated in such a way that it is easy to determine when they have been achieved. Objectives are, therefore, frequently stated in numerical terms, perhaps most often involving quantity or time elements. Objectives can be either short- or long-range and might involve only a few or all of the organization's employees. It is also important that the objectives be realistic, attainable, and consistent with the basic philosophy of the organization.

In many instances, the functions of a group are determined by the objectives of that group. Therefore, if the group is part of a larger group, the objectives of both groups must be compatible and consistent. Unless the objectives of the two groups are compatible, the value and worth of the objectives should probably be questioned.

No. 2—Span of Control

Span of control refers to the number of subordinates a supervisor is able to supervise effectively. Although no formula exists that can be used to determine an appropriate span of control, several important factors should be considered. For example, the nature of the work being performed is an important factor. The nature of some office activities requires a greater amount of supervision than that required for other activities. Another factor is the capability of supervisors and subordinates. Skillful supervisors are able to supervise more subordinates than supervisors who are not as skillful. Likewise, if subordinates are well trained, the supervisor will not have to do as much supervising. The nature of the responsibilities of the supervisor can also be significant in determining the span of control. If the supervisor has many responsibilities in addition to supervising subordinates, the span of control will have to be somewhat limited. The hierarchical level of the supervisor is also an important determinant. Generally, as the supervisor rises higher in the hierarchical structure, the span of control must be more limited.

There appears to be a trend toward increasing the span of control. The computer is probably largely responsible for this trend since many of the mechanical activities that were formerly performed by employees are now performed by automation. Therefore, the supervisor no longer has to supervise closely employees who perform such mechanical activities.

No. 3—Interrelated Functions

Because organizations are no longer composed of mutually exclusive functions but rather comprise interrelated functions, the functional areas —for example, sales, production, finance, marketing, and personnel— are interrelated.

In many instances, when one of the functional areas is experiencing difficulty, one or more of the other functional areas is also likely to experience difficulty. For example, if the marketing function is experiencing difficulty, the sales function will likely in time also experience difficulty. Because of the interrelationships between the functions, therefore, the objectives of one function must be consistent with the objectives of the other functions. Furthermore, similarities between various activities should be used as the basis for determining in which function each activity belongs. Otherwise, coordination between the activities is seriously hampered.

Since many of the activities for which the administrative office manager is responsible are found within each of the major functions, the administrative office manager is in a unique position. It is for this reason that the office manager needs a general knowledge of each of the major functions.

The computer has also had a significant impact on the degree to which the various functions are interrelated. As was discussed in the preceding chapter, the computer is the mechanism through which the various functional areas are frequently interrelated.

No. 4—Chain of
Command

Chain of command refers to the formal specification of who reports to whom within the organization. Every employee within an organization should be familiar with the chain of command as it affects him or her. Once the chains of command have been established, every effort should be made to adhere to the command; otherwise, communication between individuals is likely to become ineffective. Simple chains are generally more effective than complex chains, perhaps because they are more readily understood. In addition, communication requires less time to move through a simple chain than through a complex chain. Finally, simple chains are more clear-cut and definitive than are complex chains.

No. 5—Designated
Supervisors

Closely related to the chain of command principle is the principle that states that an employee should be directly responsible to only one supervisor. This is also known as unity of command. When an employee is responsible to more than one supervisor, the employee is likely to be subjected to undesirable circumstances. For instance, expecting an employee to take conflicting orders from several persons puts the employee in a very undesirable situation. Confusion also arises when each supervisor simultaneously makes a request of the employee. It is not uncommon for employees to also frequently experience loss of morale and unnecessary confusion when they are directly responsible to more than one supervisor.

No. 6—Commen-
surate Authority
and Responsibility

Another organizational principle states that when an individual is responsible for a certain task, that individual must also be given the authority to carry out the task. Without commensurate authority and responsibility, the individual cannot be held accountable for the successful completion of the task since the individual has very little control over the situation.

A common problem for some supervisors is the inability to delegate authority. In fact, inability to delegate authority is perhaps one of the most frustrating experiences for many supervisors. This means that the supervisor has to perform many duties that could be performed by subordinates. The supervisor is, therefore, unable to perform at an optimum level, while the morale level of subordinates declines because the supervisor has not delegated a sufficient amount of authority and responsibility. The following identifies some of the reasons supervisors fail to delegate authority: (1) lack of confidence in subordinates; (2) lack of technical competence; and (3) feeling that unless the supervisor does the work, the supervisor will not be familiar with what took place.

Some supervisors allow their subordinates to assume too much authority, which tends to result in subordinates' assuming too much control or taking excessive liberties. Although this does not occur as frequently as the supervisor's failure to delegate authority, the results may be just as disastrous. Usually, when subordinates are allowed to assume too much authority, the work group lacks cohesiveness, which results in very little cooperation among the work groups.

No. 7—Work Assignment

The work assignment for each individual should take into consideration the special strengths and talents of the individual. This means that an individual should be given an assignment commensurate with his or her ability and interests. A clear definition of the individual's duties and responsibilities is also very important. An individual cannot be held accountable for his or her performance without clearly defined duties and responsibilities.

In some instances, an individual's work assignment is determined after the individual is hired. This is not recommended because it is not always possible to revise a job to accommodate the job holder.

No. 8—Employee Participation

Employees should be encouraged to participate as much as possible in the decisionmaking process. A growing number of managers are realizing the advantages of **employee participation.** In many cases, the employees who work most closely with the situation under consideration are much more familiar with the situation than is a manager or supervisor. Therefore, the employee's insight and suggestions are very valuable in the decisionmaking process. Another advantage of using participation is that employees receive recognition from the participation process, and thus, they are motivated to work harder. Even though employees are given an opportunity to participate in the decisionmaking process, ultimate responsibility for the decisions must rest with the manager or supervisor.

No. 9—Overall Level of Responsibility

An individual's overall level of responsibility should be determined by his or her position in the organizational hierarchy. Therefore, individuals in the upper hierarchical levels have a greater amount of responsibility than do those individuals at the lower levels. Whereas individuals at lower levels have less responsibility, they are generally more concerned with performing operational tasks than are the individuals in the upper hierarchical levels.

Organizational Structures

The internal organizational structure determines authority relationships among employees. Several different organizational structures are utilized by organizations. The more common ones are **line structure, line and staff structure, functional structure,** and **committee structure.** Although not as commonly used perhaps as the others, some organizations utilize the **product structure.** Many organizations utilize a combination of two or more organizational structures.

Line Structure

The line structure, the oldest and simplest organizational structure, refers to the type of structure in which direct authority flows vertically from the top hierarchical levels, through the middle levels, and on to the bottom levels. Line structure is also generally thought to consist of those activities directly associated with the attainment of the primary objectives of the organization. Line organization is sometimes called military or scalar organization.

Because of the growing complexity of most organizations, the line structure is primarily restricted to use in small organizations or recently founded organizations. Owners or managers of such organizations have time to perform duties directly related to the primary objectives of the organization, as well as time to perform other duties. However, when the organization increases in size and the duties of the owners and managers become more complex, additional support staff becomes necessary. When support staff is utilized, line structure no longer exists.

Because of the direct authority characteristic of the line organizational structure, each employee is directly responsible for the performance of designated duties. In other words, the duties of each employee are clearly defined. Line authority, therefore, gives the superior the right to take disciplinary action against subordinates who fail to carry out reasonable orders or directions. Line structure, however, does not give supervisors direct authority over individuals in other units or departments.

Advantages of line structure. Several distinct advantages result from using the line organizational structure. For example, because of the direct authority and clearly defined areas of responsibility, employees are fully aware of the boundaries of their jobs. Decisionmaking is expeditious with this structure because the direct lines of authority eliminate a considerable amount of bureaucratic buckpassing. Also, because the line organizational structure is simple, it is clearly understood by each employee. Since employees are familiar with the duties and responsibilities expected of them, they can be held directly accountable for failure to perform at acceptable levels.

Disadvantages of line structure. Perhaps the most serious disadvantage of line structure is its failure to provide the specialization needed in organizations when they become more complex. The line structure provides no specialized staff assistance to the line managers; therefore, the line managers have to perform the specialized activities themselves. If the managers' duties continue to expand, some duties will eventually be slighted, and thus, the effectiveness of the manager could be hampered. Another disadvantage of the line structure results from its occasional failure to provide for the adequate replacement of key managerial personnel. In line organizations, the duties of most employees are so limited that they are not able to gain the broad experiences needed for assuming managerial positions.

**Line and Staff
Structure**

When the line and staff organizational structure is used, the direct authority that is characteristic of line structure is still present, as are the line activities that are concerned with the attainment of the primary objectives of the firm. Staff activities, which are specialized and support line activities, add a new dimension to the organizational structure. Since staff employees assist the line, the staff activities are designed to help facilitate the attainment of the primary objectives of the organization.

It should be pointed out that what are considered to be line activities in one organization may be considered as staff activities in other organizations. The two can be differentiated by answering the following question: Do the activities contribute directly to the attainment of the primary objectives of the organization? If the activities do make a direct contribution, they are line activities. If not, they are staff activities. The manager of the unit or department that performs staff activities will, however, need some line authority. For example, the office services area of most organizations is considered to be a staff unit, but unless the administrative office manager is given line authority to issue orders, the work in the office services department will perhaps be very inefficient. In the example above, the administrative office manager has line authority only over the subordinates in the office services department. The administrative office manager's relationship to all other employees within the organization is strictly a staff or advisory relationship.

An organization chart depicting line and staff organizational relationships is illustrated in Figure 2–1.

In the illustration, the vice presidents for production and sales are line managers (their activities contribute directly to the attainment of the primary objectives of the organization) and the vice presidents for finance and corporate affairs perform supportive staff activities.

Advantages of line and staff structure. The most distinctive advantages of the line and staff organizational structure result when line employees are freed from having to perform the specialized activities that can be assigned to staff employees. Thus, line managers have more time to perform activities that contribute directly to the attainment of the organization's objectives. The line managers can also take advantage of the specialized assistance of the staff personnel. Staff units are usually sufficiently flexible to efficiently undertake and successfully complete new projects within a minimum amount of time. Such flexibility is often not possible in pure line organizational structures. Staff positions are also used by many individuals as preparation for moving into a line position.

Disadvantages of line and staff structure. Conflict between line and staff employees may result in some serious disadvantages. For example, since staff employees perform primarily only in supportive or advisory capacities, line employees in some instances choose to ignore the advice of staff

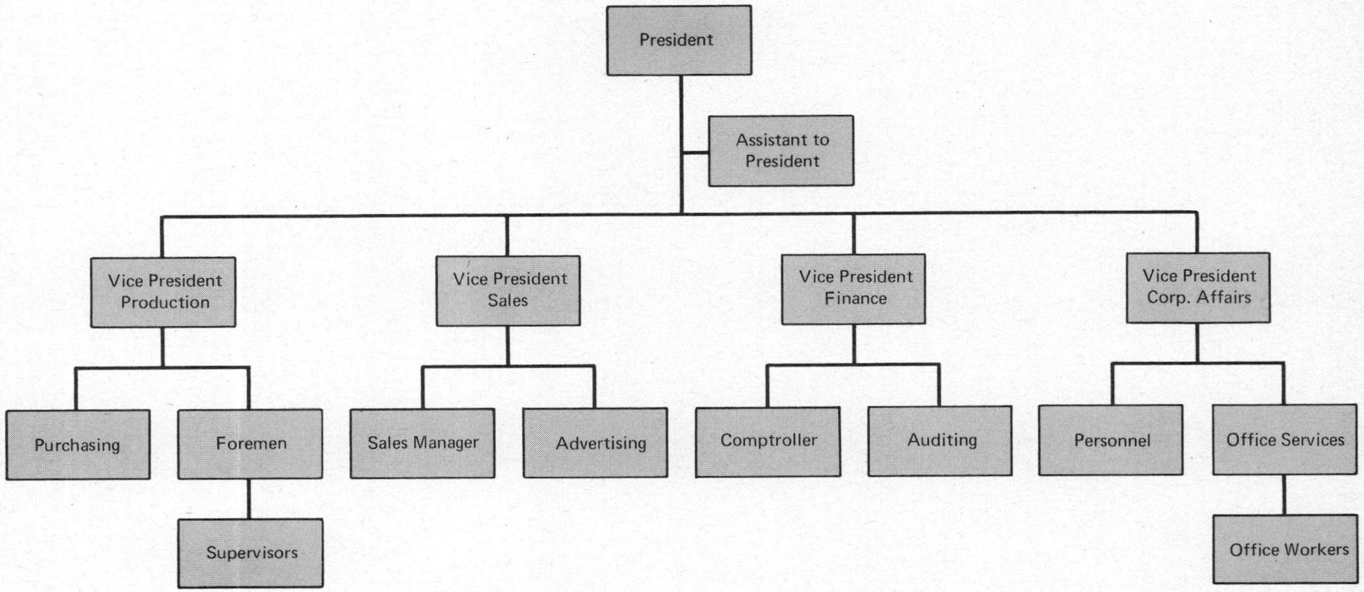

FIGURE 2-1 Partial Organization Chart Depicting Line and Staff Organization

employees. In other instances, staff employees have usurped some of the authority of line managers, which adds to the conflict between line and staff employees. In addition, some line managers never allow the talents of very capable staff employees to be fully utilized because the line managers question the value of the staff employees.

Functional Structure

The use of functional organizational structure means that the various specialized areas of an organization determine its structure. For example, in a manufacturing organization, the specialized functional areas might be production, sales, marketing, finance, and corporate affairs. Each functional area is managed by a specialist, who in many cases has the title of vice president. The manager of the functional area has *line authority* over the subordinates in the functional area. The manager also has *functional authority* over activities in other functional areas that pertain to his or her functional area. Therefore, the manager of a functional area possesses both line authority and functional authority. This concept is illustrated in Figure 2–2.

For example, in the partial organization chart in Figure 2–2, the administrative office manager has line authority over the office workers in the office services department. But since the organization utilizes the

FIGURE 2–2 Partial Organization Chart Depicting Functional Organization

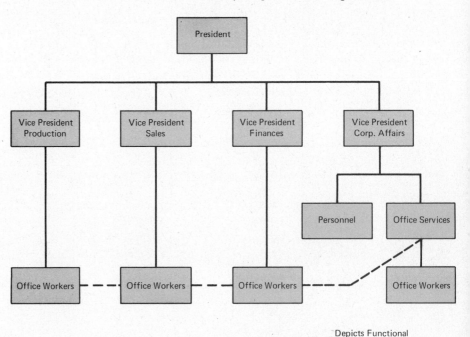

functional organizational structure, the administrative office manager also has functional authority over the office workers found in the other functional areas. With line authority, the manager has the right to issue orders and to take disciplinary action against individuals over whom line authority exists. Functional authority, on the other hand, gives a manager the right to issue orders and to make suggestions to, but not to take disciplinary action against, individuals over whom only functional authority exists. With functional organizational structure, it is possible for an employee to have two or more supervisors.

Advantages of functional structure. The most distinct advantage of using functional organizational structure is the expertise provided by the functional specialists. Because of their expertise, these specialists are able to contribute a considerable amount of specialization in solving complex problems occurring within their specialized areas. With other types of organizational structures, some of the functional areas may be slighted. But with the functional organization, such problems are not likely to be the case.

Disadvantages of functional structure. A distinct disadvantage of functional structure occurs when employees have two or more supervisors, which can result in considerable confusion for some employees. Another potential disadvantage of the functional organizational structure is the tendency for some managers to evade areas in which they have functional authority, thus resulting in some problems with coordination of activities.

Committee Structure

Although not everyone agrees that committees should be one of the organizational structures, the use of committees serves an important function in many organizations. Some committees perform important managerial functions, while others are simply advisory in nature. The purpose for which a particular committee is formed has a significant bearing on the perceived importance of the committee. This type of organizational structure is appropriately used in conjunction with any of the three types of organizational structures previously discussed. It is doubtful that an organization would have a very long existence if committees were used as the primary organizational structure. While some committees within organizations have perpetual existence, others are organized to perform one function, and when that function has been performed, the committee is dissolved.

Advantages of committee structure. The recommendations of a committee are frequently accepted more readily than are the recommendations of one individual. Because of the widely varying views of the committee members, their recommendations have a broader base and thus are likely to be more acceptable to others. Another advantage of committee organization is that decisions are made on the basis of several individuals' judgments—not on the basis of only one individual's judgment. Hence, there is less chance that a wrong decision will be made. The use of committees is also advantageous since group deliberations are apt to be more complete than would be true with one individual's deliberations.

Disadvantages of committee structure. Committees are often characterized as requiring a considerable amount of time to function properly. In many cases the time-consuming nature of committees is regarded as a primary disadvantage. Other disadvantages are low productivity in terms of the time consumed by the committee and the possible domination of the committee by certain individuals.

Product Structure

The product organizational structure is found when an enterprise utilizes its products as the basis for organization. Each major product might have its own division, with a top-level official—usually a vice president or general manager—being responsible for each of the organization's divisions. Within the structure of each of the divisions, line and staff organization is also commonly used.

The product organizational structure functions well when the various divisions of an organization are located throughout a broad geographical area. This means that each division is basically an autonomous unit. In most cases, each division has its own functional areas, such as production, marketing, finance, personnel, and corporate affairs.

The concept of product organization is illustrated in the organization chart in Figure 2–3. In the illustration, each of the major products is placed in a separate division, with a vice president being in charge of each division. The vice presidents for finance and corporate affairs basically perform staff activities.

The primary advantage of product structure is that as divisions grow in size and complexity, they function more efficiently as autonomous units. This also can result in a serious disadvantage. Unless the organization's headquarters provide adequate coordination of the various divisions, the goals and objectives of the total organization may become impossible to achieve.

Centralization versus Decentralization

There appears to be a trend for organizations to centralize many activities that were formerly decentralized. **Centralization** means that similar activities found throughout the organization are placed under the jurisdiction of one individual, although the activities may or may not be performed in one central location. With **decentralization,** individuals located throughout the organization have jurisdiction over various activities. To illustrate, many organizations utilize a centralized records management program. This means that one individual within the organization is responsible for the program and that the records of the various func-

FIGURE 2–3 Partial Organization Chart Depicting Product Organization

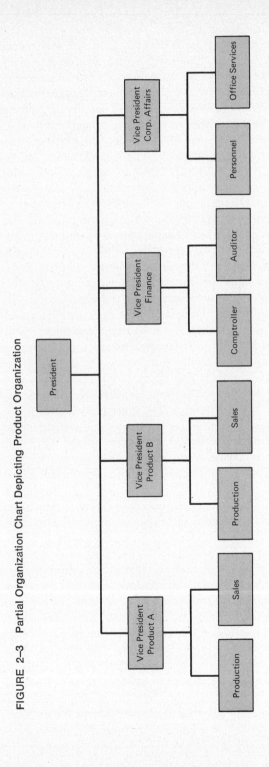

tional areas are most likely stored in one central location. If the records management program is decentralized, the managers of each unit are responsible for the maintenance of the records in their respective departments. In addition to centralized records management programs, other office activities that are frequently centralized include the following: incoming and outgoing mail, printing and duplicating, and wood processing.

True centralization of the office function means that all office work is concentrated in one physical location and that one individual is designated as having responsibility for supervising office employees. Several alternatives of varying degrees of centralization are also found. One alternative is for each of the departments or units in the organization to be responsible for carrying out its own office activities, although one individual in the organization has primary responsibility for coordinating the activities of each of the departments or units. Another alternative, which is quite widely used, centralizes certain office activities, while other office activities remain under the jurisdiction of the individual departments or units. An administrative office manager is typically responsible for the centralized office activities, while the department or unit managers are responsible for any office activities that are performed in their respective units or departments. In many cases, the managers of the other departments or units utilize the expertise of the administrative office manager for solving office-related problems found in their departments.

The computer has had a large impact on the centralization of all types of activities in the organization. The management information system that was discussed in the preceding chapter makes centralization entirely feasible. Without computer facilities, centralization would not in many cases be practical or even possible. Although the computer has done much to make the centralization of many activities possible, some activities can be centralized without using computer facilities.

Factors that Determine the Feasibility of Centralization

Several factors determine the extent to which centralization of office activities is desirable and in some cases feasible. Each is discussed in the sections that follow:

Nature of the organization. The greater the volume of office work and paper-processing activities found in the organization, the greater is the desirability of centralizing office activities. Two types of organizations—financial institutions and insurance companies—have centralized office activities because of the vast amount of paper work processed within the organization. Other organizations whose nature does not result in the creation of vast quantities of paper work may not have as great a need for centralizing their office activities.

Size of the organization. As organizations grow in size, the need for centralized control becomes increasingly important. Without the coordination that results from centralized control, a considerable amount of inefficiency is likely to occur. Centralized control also frequently results in centralized location. However, in very large organizations that occupy a large amount of space, decentralized location of certain office activities may actually be more advantageous. It appears that until organizations reach a particular size, centralized location of office activities is desirable, but when organizations grow beyond a certain size, decentralized location of various office activities is more advantageous.

Diversification of organization. Organizations that are widely diversified in terms of products, operating processes, and personnel frequently find centralization to be a difficult process. It is for this reason that only a minimum number of office activities and even fewer other activities will be centralized in many widely diversified organizations. The coordination that results from centralization can produce many beneficial results if widely diversified organizations can overcome the difficulties brought on by centralization.

Conformity to standardized processes. One of the by-products of centralization is the degree to which activities begin to conform to standardized processes. With centralization, standardized processes are developed, and employees are expected to utilize the standardized processes when performing their job duties. Standardization and centralization are essentially interdependent upon one another.

Quality of personnel. Most organizations find that in order for decentralization to be successful, higher quality employees are needed than is the case when office activities are centralized. This is because activities are usually overseen by a specialist who is able to provide closer direction of employees. With decentralization, on the other hand, the unit or department manager may know little or nothing about specialized office activities. This means that the employees themselves must be sufficiently trained to perform the specialized activities.

Distribution of operating processes. When the operating processes of an organization are distributed over a wide geographical area, physical centralization may not be possible. Depending on the situation, however, it may be possible for an organization to centralize control over the activities while allowing the activities to be decentralized in location. This frequently happens in large organizations that conduct business over a wide geographical area. Some organizations also centralize certain of their activities within regional centers or areas, and control over the regional centers or areas is then centralized through the main headquarters of the organization.

Attitude of personnel. No matter how much effort, cost, and planning takes place in centralization of office activities, centralization will not be successful unless existing personnel resistance to change is overcome. Unless there is some assurance that the centralization of office activities will be generally accepted by personnel, the efforts, costs, and planning involved will perhaps be of little value.

Advantages of Centralization

The following advantages result from centralizing the control and/or location of the performance of office activities:

1. Greater uniformity of work methods and procedures.
2. Less duplication of effort and equipment.
3. Fewer duplicate copies of documents to be stored.
4. Greater standardization of work processes.
5. Better utilization of employees, since they can perform duties in their specific areas of specialization.
6. Employees who are not well trained or who have limited qualifications can be trained to function well in a centralized unit.
7. Peak work loads in a centralized unit can be efficiently handled, since all employees within the unit can be assigned to help with the peak work.
8. Work is performed more continuously and is not affected by the absence of an employee.
9. Salaries are more equitable, since it is easier to determine which employees are performing comparable jobs and thus who should receive comparable salaries.

Disadvantages of Centralization

The disadvantages of centralization include:

1. Excessive time may be consumed by employees going to and from the location of the centralized activities.
2. Widely dispersed centralized activities may not be equally accessible to all personnel.
3. The technical nature of some work is such that the work might be better performed in some department other than the centralized unit.
4. Confidentiality of some materials necessitates that these materials cannot be processed through a centralized unit or department.
5. Assigning work to be performed according to its priority is not always possible.

The Organization Chart

The **organization chart** depicts an organization's formal structure by illustrating the formal relationships between various individuals and departments or units. The chart is also useful for illustrating lines of authority and responsibility, work flow, and span of control. In essence, the organization chart illustrates who reports to whom. The organization chart does not illustrate employees' interactions that are not officially recognized by the organization. Even though the interactions are not formally recognized by the organization, such interactions are very important.

Since the organization chart illustrates hierarchical relationships, the chart is most logically constructed by starting at the top and working downward. Therefore, the major functions of the organization must be identified. Secondary functions within each of the major functions must also be identified. If the secondary functions consist of other subfunctions, these must also be identified.

Specific guidelines useful for preparing organization charts include:

1. Hierarchical relationships should be considered, so that individuals or departments of similar hierarchical importance are placed on the same horizontal level.

2. Vertical and horizontal authority is identified with solid lines.

3. Functional authority is illustrated with dotted lines.

4. Vertical and horizontal lines should intersect the boxes at the centers of the boxes but should not be drawn through the boxes.

5. Each horizontal row of boxes should be the same size.

6. The titles illustrated on the chart should be complete. This means that the functional area for which an individual is vice president, for example, should be identified.

7. The chart should include the name of the organization and the date of its preparation.

Organization charts are advantageous in that they illustrate formal lines of authority. Thus, individuals know who reports to whom. By being familiar with the lines of authority, employees have a better understanding of the formal structure of the organization, which in many cases is essential for smoothly functioning managerial processes. Organization charts are also useful for identifying the existence of overlapping responsibility that needs to be eliminated. The chart is also useful for identifying where voids exist in authority relationships. Furthermore, the chart is useful for illustrating promotion opportunities to job applicants and new employees and also assists in identifying areas suitable for training and orientation.

The most significant disadvantage of the organization chart results from its failure to illustrate informal interaction between employees that is necessary for their carrying out day-to-day activities. Such informal organization cannot be illustrated on the organization chart. Another disadvantage of the organization chart is that it gives the impression that all departments or units can be well defined and distinguished from one another, which may not always be the case.

Review Questions

1. Review the advantages that result from giving adequate consideration to the organizing function.

2. Why should objectives be clearly defined?

3. What factors determine an appropriate span of control for a supervisor?

4. Why should an employee be responsible to only one supervisor?

5. Why is line structure not feasible in large organizations?

6. Review the basic differences between line structure and line and staff structure.

7. What are the basic concepts involved in functional structure?

8. What is meant by centralization and decentralization in terms of the organizational process?

9. What is meant by informal organization and why can it not be depicted on an organization chart?

Minicases

A frequent complaint among the supervisors in the Bailer Corporation is that they are unable to do an effective job of supervising their subordinates because (1) the subordinates are not carefully selected for the positions in which they are placed, and (2) the supervisors have too many subordinates for effective supervision. The basis for the first complaint is that some subordinates have special training or skills that are not utilized in their jobs. The basis for the second complaint is that some supervisors have as many as twenty to twenty-five subordinates to supervise. What organizational principles are apparently being violated in this corporation? What factors should be considered in determining the number of subordinates that the supervisor can effectively supervise?

*   *   *

Mary Brown is a secretary in a large doctor's office in the Philadelphia area. She is responsible for the secretarial activities of three of the fifteen doctors in the office. Her work is becoming increasingly frustrating because in many instances, when the doctors give her work to do, they put a high priority on the work. When the jobs are not completed as rapidly as they would like them to be, she is frequently reprimanded. When she explains that she had other high priority work to be completed, the doctors get very upset with her. What organizational principle is violated in this instance? What suggestions do you have to remedy the situation?

Case

The Trust Life Insurance Company, whose customers are located primarily in the southwest area of the United States, is a full-line insurance company. The company's growth record during the past ten years has been considerably above average, primarily because of the foresight of corporate management.

The company recently purchased a fifteen-story office building in downtown Albuquerque. At the present time, the company occupies the first four stories and leases the remaining floors. The clerical function of each of the six major departments is presently decentralized. This means that each department is responsible for its own typing, records management, copying, and mailing activities. Employees who perform these activities in each department are supervised by the department's office supervisor.

Two of the six office supervisors recently attended a one-day conference and heard a presentation concerned with the centralizing of office activities. The two supervisors were fascinated with the concept and decided to talk with their managers about centralizing various office activities. These two supervisors have become quite concerned about recent inefficiency in work processes, duplication of work, duplication of equipment, and lack of coordination between the office activities of various departments.

You are to assume the role of one of the office supervisors.

1. Describe the concept of centralization as you would explain the concept to the manager of the department in which you work.

2. What office activities do you think the company should centralize?

3. What reasons are you going to use as justification for centralizing office activities identified in No. 2?

Part

2

The
Office

Selecting an Office Location

Chapter

3

Conducting the Feasibility Study

Factors to Consider in Selecting a Building Site
Financial Factors
Operational Factors
Employee Factors

Making the Decision

New Developments in Building Site Location
The Office Park
The Self-contained Urban Complex
The Specialty-Professional Building
The Office Condominium Complex

Making the Move
Procedures for Getting Ready to Move
Preliminary-stage activities
Intermediate-stage activities
Final-stage activities

The Move and Public and Employee Relations

Chapter Aims After studying this chapter, the student should be able to:

1. Discuss the financial factors that should be considered in selecting a building site.

2. Identify the advantages and disadvantages of ownership, leasing, and sale-leaseback.

3. Explain what is meant by operational factors and identify those that should be considered in selecting a building site.

4. Explain what is meant by employee factors and identify those that should be considered in selecting a building site.

5. Identify the characteristics of an office park, a self-contained urban complex, a specialty-professional building, and an office condominium, and identify the characteristics of each.

6. Identify ways to lessen the impact of an organization's move out of a community.

Chapter Terms *Feasibility study:* a study that is conducted when an organization is considering a change in its location. The study is designed to gather information about many different factors that should be considered when making the decision whether or not to move to a new location.

Sale-leaseback: a situation in which an organization sells its building to an investor who then gives the organization a long-term lease on the building.

Office park: a complex of offices that are typically housed in one or more buildings, resembling a college campus.

Self-contained urban complex: a complex that contains office space, housing, shopping, recreational, cultural, and entertainment facilities.

Office condominium: an arrangement in which office space is sold to an organization but ownership of the common areas (corridors, rest rooms, etc.) of the building is retained by the original owner of the building.

Specialty-professional building: the arrangement in which individuals of the same profession occupy the entire building. An example is a medical building.

Few decisions have a greater effect upon the success or failure of an organization than the decision of selecting an appropriate building site. Although it is a decision not often made during the life of an organization, it is rare that a more permanent or irreversible decision is made.

A considerable amount of effort is expended to make the environment of the office a pleasant place in which to work. But this effort will have little significance if care is not also taken to select a suitable building location—a location not only suitable in the near future but also in the years to come. The location of an individual's job may affect the mode of transportation in getting to and from work as well as the location of the individual's residence. The location of the individual's job may also have an effect on the lifestyle of the individual, especially from the time the individual leaves home in the morning until the return home in the evening.

Conducting the Feasibility Study

More and more organizations are having professional consultants conduct **feasibility studies** to determine whether or not the organization should move to a new location, and if so, what alternatives are available. The use of professional consultants is desirable for several reasons. If the move involves a manufacturing plant and its general offices, the complexity of factors increases considerably. Professional consultants have expertise in areas in which company personnel may be deficient.

In many cases, a feasibility study can be conducted more quickly and more objectively by professional consultants than by company personnel. When professional consultants conduct the feasibility study, there is less chance of a premature information leak about the possible move.

Small organizations employing only a few individuals may find the use of consultants unjustifiable in terms of cost and need. In such cases, the factors discussed in the next section are of great importance.

Factors to Consider in Selecting a Building Site

Most of the important factors to consider in selecting a building site tend to fit into one of three categories: *financial factors, operational factors,* and *employee factors.* Because of the nature of several of the factors, there is a tendency for some overlapping, especially between the financial and operational factors.

Financial Factors

Perhaps the most important financial factor to consider is which of the following alternatives provides the organization with the best return on its building investment: ownership, leasing, or **sale-leaseback.** Each has distinct advantages and disadvantages that must be considered.

The ownership alternative (which includes building a new facility or remodeling an existing facility) enables an organization to have a building designed to meet its specific needs and objectives. Other advantages of this alternative are: having a permanent location, gaining the prestige inherent in ownership, having the opportunity to rent unused portions of a building, naming a building after the organization for greater publicity, and being able to remodel the building when changes must be made. Disadvantages characteristic of ownership include a large capital investment in the building and the chance that the location may become less desirable in the future.

Leasing also offers distinct advantages for some organizations. For example, the landlord, rather than the tenant, is usually responsible for building maintenance and repair. The organization's management is also freed of problems inherent in ownership. Other advantages include financial flexibility, since large amounts of capital do not have to be allocated for the building and changes in office location are more easily made than when the organization owns the building. The two most serious disadvantages of the leasing alternative are having nothing tangible to show for the lease payments and the possibility of being unable to remodel when the facility no longer meets the needs of the organization.

The sale-leaseback alternative refers to a situation in which an investor purchases a building from an organization and the organization is then given the option to lease the building from the investor. In some cases, the building will be an existing facility, while in other cases the organization will build a new facility to meet its specifications and will then sell the facility to an investor who leases the building to the organization. With sale-leaseback, the organization has the advantage of occupying a building designed to meet its needs but not having to invest a large amount of capital in the building. The organization is also freed of the responsibility of building maintenance and repair. In addition to the disadvantages inherent in leasing, the sale-leaseback arrangement may result in some inconvenience to an organization should the original investor sell the building to a second investor.

When the decision is made to build a new facility, land and construction costs must also be considered. In most cases, these costs vary considerably between urban, suburban, and outlying areas, with costs generally being lower in suburban and outlying areas. In addition to the cost of constructing a new facility, there is always the possibility of a major delay in building construction. The result is a considerable amount of inconvenience if a commitment has been made to vacate the premises at a specific time.

Other important financial factors of a recurring nature are the tax and insurance rates in the area. Like land and construction costs, tax rates are generally lower in suburban areas than in downtown areas. However, as more businesses move to suburban communities, more extensive services (police and fire protection, street maintenance, utilities, and schools) have to be provided, and higher taxes are usually levied to pay for these services. In some suburban areas, business enterprises are given special tax advantages to make the move to the suburban location more attractive. On the other hand, because of the emphasis on social responsibility, some businesses are given special tax rates when constructing new facilities in metropolitan areas.

Depending upon the distance of the move, transfer and termination allowances for employees may involve a considerable amount of money. Many organizations pay moving expenses for those employees who decide to move to the new location, and it is not uncommon for an organization to reimburse an employee for expenses incurred in visiting the new community before the employee decides whether to move with the organization or to terminate employment. Most organizations also feel compelled to give a termination allowance to senior employees who do not wish to make the move, and in many cases employees are given help in finding new jobs. Each of the above-mentioned situations costs money—but because of public and employee relations, it is to the organization's advantage to be concerned about transfer and termination allowances.

A business enterprise must also be concerned with factors that may have financial implications as a result of a loss in sales. Of concern is the effect a move may have on the present clientele. An effort should be made to determine how many of the present clientele will no longer do business with an organization if its location is changed. An organization should also make an attempt to determine to what extent a particular address may affect its financial status. For this reason, some organizations are greatly concerned about address prestige. Furthermore, most organizations generally tend to stay in close proximity to the location of their competitors. As an example, most large cities have an area known as the financial district. Finally, when a building is occupied by more than one enterprise, some organizations are concerned about the character and stability of the other occupants of the building.

Operational Factors

Operational factors refer to those factors that have an impact upon the efficient operation of the organization. As was mentioned in the previous section, some operational factors may also have financial implications.

The building is a significant factor in determining the efficiency of an organization's operations. When a building is purchased, considerable effort should also be made to determine how well the facilities will meet the needs of the organization. If extensive remodeling is required, perhaps it would be more economical to build a new structure. Also of concern is the feasibility of building expansion should the need arise. The office environment and the layout also have a great effect upon the efficiency of the operation of the organization. This area will be thoroughly discussed in Chapter 5.

The quality of the labor force obtainable at the price the organization is willing to pay is also important. Generally, the labor force tends to follow the sources of employment. As more organizations move to the suburbs, for example, so do those seeking employment. This factor has financial implications in cases in which the needed labor force is not readily available and therefore higher salaries have to be paid to attract employees to the new area. Since professional and technical employees may not be as readily available, these two classifications of employees tend to cause more concern than do the clerical and secretarial classifications.

Adequate parking, transportation, and eating facilities may also affect the efficient operation of an organization—either directly or indirectly. Insufficient facilities in any of the three areas may cause the employees to be late to work. If adequate parking and eating facilities are not available, the organization may find that it has to provide such facilities.

Although perhaps affecting the efficient operation of an organization only indirectly, the following items also should be considered: banking, hotel, airport, and mail facilities, and the availability of public transportation.

Employee Factors   Employee factors concern the relationships that exist between the world in which the employees work and the world in which they live. Available transportation to and from work is of great importance to the employee. When an organization is considering the alternatives, great care should be taken to select a location that will not result in considerable travel stress and strain, which tends to lower employee productivity and efficiency. When an organization is faced with the problem of relocation, it may be wise to determine the geographical areas in which the employees live and then use this information in making the location decision. Organizations not sensitive to this factor may be confronted with high employee attrition, resulting in considerable expense to the company in terms of hiring and training new employees.

Another factor to consider is the availability of adequate housing for those employees who wish to reside near their jobs. This factor is perhaps of greater concern for individuals who will be hired in the future than for present employees, since only a small percentage of employees tend to move to a new residence when an organization relocates in the same geographical area.

To some employees, facilities for shopping and banking during the lunch hour are also very important. Adequate facilities are usually available in downtown areas, but in suburban and outlying areas these may not be as plentiful.

A comparison form, similar to the one shown in Figure 3–1, is helpful when weighing the merits of the alternative sites. Column A on the form lists the factors to be considered. Column B identifies by numerical code the relative importance of each factor. For each of the alternative locations, two columns are used: Column C (and C1, C2, etc.) is used to identify by numerical code the relative desirability of each factor, while

Column D (and D1, D2, etc.) is used to record the weighted value of each factor (arrived at by multiplying the importance of factor code by the desirability of factor code). For example, in Figure 3–1, the cost of land was judged to be a very important factor (code of 5) in weighing the various alternative sites. For Alternative 1, the land costs are judged to be of average desirability (code of 3), which results in a weighted value of 15 (arrived at by multiplying 5 by 3). For Alternative 2, the cost of land was judged to be very desirable (code of 5), resulting in a weighted value of

FIGURE 3–1   Comparison Form for Selecting a Building Site

Importance of Factor Code	Desirability of Factor Code
5—Very important	5—Very desirable
4—Fairly important	4—Fairly desirable
3—Average importance	3—Average desirability
2—Not very important	2—Not very desirable
1—Unimportant	1—Undesirable
0—Not appropriate	0—Not appropriate

Factors (A)	Importance of Factor (B)	Alternative 1		Alternative 2	
		Desirability of Factor (C)	Weighted Value (D)	Desirability of Factor (C1)	Weighted Value (D1)
Cost of land	5	3	15	5	25
Cost of building					
Cost of construction					
Physical features of building					
Condition of building					
Feasibility of building expansion					
Office environment					
Availability of supplies					
Availability of materials					
Availability of parking facilities					
Availability of eating facilities					
Availability of banking facilities					
Availability of postal facilities					

FIGURE 3–1   (Continued)

Availability of transportation					
Availability of housing					
Availability of shopping					
Adequacy of utilities					
Adequacy of police protection					
Adequacy of fire protection					
Tax rates					
Insurance rates					
Cost of fringe benefits					
Cost of labor					
Effect of move on clientele					
Importance of address prestige					
Location of competitors					
Character of other tenants					
Nature of schools					
Nature of streets					
Other					
TOTAL					

25. After all the factors for each alternative site have been assessed, the weighted factor values can be summed, thus arriving at a numerical total with which to compare the desirability of the various sites. The higher the total, the more desirable the site is as an alternative.

Making the Decision

Needless to say, making an incorrect decision about the appropriateness of a site can be very costly to the organization. A managerial team can, at best, strive only to make the optimum decision on the basis of the facts. In most cases, there is a certain amount of trade-off between some of the factors. The financial factors generally receive more emphasis than do the operational or employee factors. There is always the possibility, however, of placing too much emphasis on economics, with the result of poorly constructed facilities, poorly maintained facilities, or poorly designed facilities. As managerial teams become more employee-oriented in the future, perhaps the operational and employee factors will receive more emphasis.

**New Develop-
ments in Building
Site Location**

Three rather recent developments in office site location are the **office park,** the **self-contained urban complex,** and the **office condominium** complex. Although not necessarily a new development, the **specialty-professional** building is also currently receiving much attention.

The Office Park

An office park is a complex of offices typically housed in one or more buildings. The parks, frequently resembling a college campus, are usually located in a suburban or outlying area and are owned by real estate developers. In many ways, the characteristics of the office park are similar to the characteristics of an industrial park. Since the parks are usually located in suburban areas, space is less costly to rent than comparable space in an urban setting.

The developers claim the following advantages for the office park: rents are lower, more parking space is available, a greater amount of space is available, customers are located nearby, and problems of pollution, crime, and traffic congestion will likely be reduced. Furthermore, the developer is usually responsible for maintenance and repairs, thus freeing tenants of this responsibility.

Developers have found that office parks are most ideally located near a shopping center, thus providing employees with easy access to shopping, banking, and eating facilities.

Several disadvantages of the concept have emerged. Among these are such disadvantages as considerable intermingling of those individuals employed in the park.[1] When employer-employee relations become somewhat strained, the word spreads very rapidly. The word also spreads very rapidly when an enterprise is not competitive in terms of salary or fringe benefits.

When business enterprises are considering the possibility of moving into an office park, the lease covenants should be thoroughly studied. An investigation should also be made of such factors as tenant turnover, the financial situation of the park, and the background of other tenants.

An artist's rendition of an office park appears in Figure 3–2.

**The Self-
contained Urban
Complex**

Unlike the office park concept, the self-contained urban complex is a phenomenon of the urban setting. The complex is basically a "city within a city" and consists of office space, housing, shopping, recreational, cultural, and entertainment facilities. Perhaps the most significant advantage of the self-contained urban complex is its impact on reducing crime in the area surrounding the complex. The fact that the complex is commercially active around the clock serves as a crime deterrent. The complex also provides an impetus for rebuilding deteriorating urban areas, thus

[1] Excerpted from *Administrative Management,* copyright © 1970 by Geyer-McAllister, Publications, Inc., New York.

FIGURE 3–2   Artist's Rendering of Office Park

Reprinted, Courtesy of The Chicago Tribune

revitalizing downtown areas of cities. Providing employees with the opportunity to live and work in the same complex is also considered by some to be a distinct advantage.

On the negative side is the characteristically high turnover of business tenants. Without continuous and positive public relations, its attractiveness is often diminished.

Figure 3–3 illustrates the self-contained urban complex.

The Specialty-Professional Building

The specialty-professional building may also be a phenomenon of the urban setting, but such buildings are also found in suburban areas. The concept is characterized as having professional individuals, such as doctors or lawyers, housed in one building for the primary convenience of clients. Tenants of specialty-professional buildings also enjoy the prestige of close association with other tenants who have common interests.

Professional buildings for doctors, for example, are frequently lo-

FIGURE 3–3   Self-Contained Urban Complex

Courtesy, Renaissance Center Partnership

cated near a hospital, and in many cases, a pharmacy is also located near or even within the building. Medical professional buildings also facilitate patient referral services since doctors of all specializations are frequently housed in the building.

In the case of legal professional buildings, many times the developer will provide tenants with rather extensive library facilities within the building. Such conveniences are often very enticing to new tenants.

The Office Condominium Complex

Of rather recent origin is the office condominium complex. Such complexes are usually developed by real estate firms who then sell office space to various organizations. Corridors, elevators, public restrooms, and other structural features used in common by the office occupants are often retained by the real estate firm. The office occupants are usually required to belong to an owners' association, thus giving them some governing power. By purchasing an office condominium, occupants have many of the advantages of building ownership, in addition to the advantage of being relieved of maintenance and upkeep responsibility in certain areas of the building. Certain restrictions imposed upon the occupants, however, may be viewed as a disadvantage, as may the required association membership and association dues.

Making the Move

Moving to a new location does not have to be anticipated with visions of chaos and total disruption. With proper preplanning and organization, the move can actually be accomplished with a minimum of expense and time.

Procedures for Getting Ready to Move

Moving to a new location will be accomplished more easily if employees are kept informed about the progress of the project. The chief executive officer of the organization should officially notify the employees as soon as the decision has been made to move to a new location. Once the decision is made, it is very difficult to keep the pending move from being "rumored," and employees will generally have better feelings toward the organization if they learn of the move through official channels.

Many company officials feel that it is advantageous to charge a committee with the responsibility of keeping the employees informed. Bulletins are frequently prepared describing such items as drawings of the new facility, layout, nearby shopping and eating facilities, and decor arrangements within the building. To facilitate the transition, some organizations set up mock offices so the employees will be able to see the new environment. Adequate communication will also help maintain employee morale and motivation between the time the move is announced and the time the move is made.

The following represent factors that should be considered in preparing for the move. The factors are arranged in categories: preliminary-stage activities, intermediate-stage activities, and final-stage activities.

Preliminary-stage Activities

1. *Appoint a moving coordinator and a moving committee.* The moving coordinator is responsible for organizing the move in its entirety. Because of the nature of these duties, the individual will undoubtedly have to be relieved of all other job duties until the move is completed.

The moving committee consists of individuals from each of the departments. Companies with numerous departments may find it more convenient to have an individual represent two or three departments.

2. *Select a moving company.* Organizations frequently ask for bids on the moving job prior to selecting the moving company. When submitting a bid, the moving company should be asked to supply the following information: type of moving vehicles to be used, description of moving equipment to be used, applicable tariffs, number of employees to help with the move, services—either general or specialized—to be provided by the moving company, insurance coverage, warehouse facilities in the event that storage is important, and names of other clients of the moving company (for reference purposes).

3. *Prepare and award the contract.* When all bids have been received and the moving company is selected, the contract between the two parties should be signed. The contract should specify who is responsible for packing and coding and tagging the moving containers.

4. *Arrange for additional insurance.* Many companies prefer to take out insurance in excess of that provided by the mover.

5. *Determine the monetary provisions for transfer and termination.* Many employees will want to have this information available before deciding whether it would be economically advantageous to transfer or to terminate their employment.

6. *Determine which employees wish to move to the new location.* It is important that some early planning take place so the organization will not experience a personnel shortage once the move is completed. It is also important that this be done so a cost estimate of employee transfer can be made.

7. *If applicable, assist employees in finding new employment.* If the distance of the move is considerable, some employees will elect to terminate employment. Good public relations result from assisting these employees in finding new employment.

Intermediate-stage Activities

1. *Prepare moving instructions.* Specific written instructions should be prepared for each individual involved in the actual moving.

2. *Provide for security of valuable and/or confidential materials.* Special care has to be taken to protect and secure valuable and/or confidential materials. Generally, the individuals who normally have access to these materials should be responsible for the materials en route to the new building.

3. *Prepare a scale layout.* Each department should prepare a layout of the new facilities showing where the items are to be placed, thus simplifying the unpacking and organizing process.

4. *Arrange for special workers.* Because of the nature of some equipment, electricians and plumbers may be needed to disconnect or reconnect the equipment.

5. *Request new paper supplies.* Paper supplies with the new address should be available at the time the company moves into the new building.

6. *Provide for data processing equipment.* Because of its sensitivity, special care has to be taken in moving the data processing equipment. In some cases, the equipment vendors will be able to provide valuable assistance.

7. *Notify customers, insurance companies, governmental agencies, and post office of date of move.* Of all those to notify, the customers' list is the most extensive. Companies frequently notify their customers by enclosing notification in a monthly mailing, such as a statement.

8. *Notify vendors and interior decorators of desired delivery date.* When substantial amounts of new equipment and furniture are desired, it is most convenient to have the items delivered and in place after the interior decorator finishes the decorating but before the actual moving date.

9. *Determine types and numbers of new employees that will be needed at the new site.* If many new employees are needed at the new location, it may be advantageous to do some hiring before the move is made. If the organization is unable to do its own hiring, local personnel agencies are sometimes used.

10. *Make provisions for maintaining the old building.* In cases where an organization owns the premises just vacated and the premises are not immediately reoccupied or sold, provisions have to be made for building maintenance, insurance coverage, security, and utilities.

11. *Prepare a time schedule of crucial dates.* For the greatest amount of control over the moving process, a time schedule should be developed and adhered to as closely as possible. An example of such a schedule appears in Figure 3–4.

Once the time schedule is drawn up, the moving coordinator should prepare a detailed, step-by-step checklist of tasks to be completed. In

FIGURE 3–4

June   8—Notify vendors of dates to deliver new equipment and furniture
     15—Order new paper supplies
     30—Notify customers of change of address
      —Notify insurance agency, post office, governmental agencies of change of address

July   7—Have telephone, electrical, and water connections transferred
     8—Code and tag items
     9—Code and tag items
    10—Start packing
    11—Finish packing
    12—Move

---

addition to listing the tasks, the checklist should also specify who is responsible for each task, the date by which the task is to be completed, and a column to indicate that the task has been completed. A sample checklist is illustrated in Figure 3–5.

FIGURE 3–5

Tasks to do	Responsibility of	Date to be completed by	Date completed

Final-stage Activities

1. *Arrange for utilities in new location.* Telephone, electrical, water, and gas connections should be made in the new building before the move gets underway. Most companies wait until the moving is completed before having any of the utilities in the old building disconnected.

2. *Provide for equipment and furniture no longer used.* Several alternatives are available, including holding an auction by the organization, commissioning a secondhand store to sell the items, or selling directly to employees.

3. *Arrange for news release of pending move.* If the organization is large enough to have a public relations director, responsibility for the news release is frequently assigned that individual.

4. *Make an inventory of what is to be moved.* An inventory of every item that is to be moved should be prepared before any items leave the premises. The same inventory can be used at the new location to determine if any missing items are misplaced in the new building or are still at the old location.

5. *Arrange for postmoving inspection of the premises.* This inspection serves several purposes: to determine whether items on which insurance can be collected were damaged, to determine whether any equipment is malfunctioning, and to determine what unfinished work has yet to be completed.

The Move and Public and Employee Relations

When an organization moves from one location to another, the move can create a variety of employee and public relations problems. Of special significance is the organization that employs a large portion of the local work force. The move most likely will result in substantial unemployment, as well as eliminate a major contributor to the community tax base. An organization can do much to alleviate the ill feelings in such instances. There may also be some community resistance when a major enterprise moves into a new community, especially if it is perceived that the enterprise will have a negative effect on local environmental conditions.

The following are suggestions for improving public and employee relations when an organization decides to move. First and foremost, if the move will result in substantial unemployment within the community, much goodwill can be created if the organization makes an extensive effort to find new employment for those employees wishing to stay behind. If it is possible for the organization to sell the facilities to a similar employer, not only will the tax base of the community perhaps remain relatively stable but also the employment problem will be solved to a great extent. For this reason, when many socially responsible organizations move to a new location, they spend large sums of money to underwrite industrial surveys as a means of attracting new employers into the community.

Other ways to overcome poor relations are to continue to support and participate in the community until the day of the move, to provide employees with adequate termination allowances, and to assist employees in selling their homes if they decide to move with the organization.

An organization can do much to gain a positive image in the new community. Keeping the new community up to date on the progress of the project is considered to have significant advantages. Meeting with lay groups, the chamber of commerce, and governmental agencies can also produce much goodwill. If the organization makes an industrial survey of prospective locations, making the findings of the survey available to the community provides evidence of a willingness to cooperate.

Some organizations feel the necessity of hiring a community relations manager just as soon as the decision has been made to move to a new location. The main function of this individual is to serve as a liaison between the organization and the new community. Hiring the liaison person from the new community is generally viewed as evidence of good faith on the part of the organization. Finally, hiring new employees from within the community is viewed more favorably than is recruiting new employees from some other geographical area.

Review Questions

1. What are the advantages of having professional consultants conduct the feasibility study?

2. What is meant by sale-leaseback?

3. Compare and contrast the office park, self-contained urban complex, specialty-professional building, and office condominium complex in terms of the following:

   a. Typical location
   b. Advantages
   c. Disadvantages
   d. Special characteristics

4. Consider each of the following factors and identify those that you consider to be crucial in moving to a new location. Then arrange the factors in a logical sequence in order that the move can be made more efficiently.

a. Provide for security of valuable and/or confidential materials
b. Arrange for utilities in new location
c. Prepare and award the moving contract
d. Notify vendors and interior decorators of desired delivery dates
e. Appoint a moving coordinator and moving committee
f. Make an inventory of what is to be moved
g. Determine the monetary provisions for transfer and termination
h. Arrange for postmoving inspection of the premises
i. Determine the types and numbers of employees that will be needed at the new site
j. Make provisions for the maintenance of the old building
k. Provide for equipment and furniture no longer used
l. Provide for data processing equipment

Minicases

The Quindel Corporation built a new office building approximately ten years ago. At the time the building was built, it was not anticipated that the firm would expand much more in terms of the products manufactured or the volume produced. About four years ago, the firm had to use a considerable amount of its reserve capital to avoid going bankrupt during an industrywide recession. Recently, the firm developed a new product that is very promising financially, but a considerable amount of capital is needed to get the product on the market. The company's ability to secure a loan for the manufacture of the product is out of the question. To obtain the needed capital, the corporation has a choice of sale-leaseback or of selling its building and leasing another building somewhere else. Which of the two alternatives do you feel is more realistic for the Quindel Corporation? Why? What are the advantages and disadvantages of the alternative you selected?

*   *   *

The Bronson Corporation, which is located in a downtown area of Omaha, has grown so much that its present building is no longer adequate. There is no room to expand the present premises as the buildings on both sides are large office buildings. Therefore, no more space is available. The managers of the corporation are considering moving to a building in a suburban area about twenty-five miles from downtown Omaha. A quick check of the residential addresses of the employees of Bronson revealed that less than 10 percent of the employees live in the suburban area that is being considered by Bronson. In fact, about 70 percent of the employees live from fifteen to twenty miles south of the suburban area being considered. Discuss the impact that a move to the suburban area would have on the present employees. How might the impact of the corporation's move to the suburban area be lessened for the present employees?

Case

The Weber Manufacturing Corporation, which designs and manufactures replacement parts for American automobiles, has experienced tremendous growth during the last ten years. The corporation presently rents office space on two floors of a twenty-year-old building in New York City. Inasmuch as no more space is available for rental purposes, the problem of relocation is readily apparent. The manufacturing plant was relocated in an industrial area of Newark, New Jersey, about ten years ago.

The corporation employs approximately 300 people in the home office. Because of the tremendous growth of the corporation during the past few years, additional equipment and furniture were placed in the offices with little or no regard to work flow and efficiency of operation. A study also revealed that the air conditioning, lighting, and heating systems are now inadequate for the number of people employed by the corporation. Different brands of equipment and furniture have been purchased, resulting in a very uncoordinated appearance. The corporation also found that major structural changes would have to be made to install needed data processing equipment.

The management has decided that it would be more feasible to move the offices to new premises.

1. What are some of the problems the corporation is likely to experience in its pending move?

2. What additional information will an outside consulting firm need to assist the corporation in selecting a new location?

3. What factors should be considered in selecting a new building site?

4. What suggestions might be made for the individual who will be assigned the responsibility of coordinating the move to the new premises?

The Layout of the Office

Chapter
4

Goals of Office Layout

Factors in Office Layout
    The Feasibility Study
    The Work Flow
    The Organization Chart
    Projection of Employees Needed in the Future
    The Communication Network
    Departmental Organization
    Private and General Offices
    Space Requirements
    Specialized Areas
        The reception area
        The board/conference room
        The computer room
        The administrative service center
        The mailroom
        The duplicating room
        The central records area
    Safety Considerations
    Expansion
    Environmental Conditions
    Equipment and Furniture

New Developments in Office Layout
    Office Landscaping
    Movable Partitions
    Modular Furniture

Principles of Effective Office Layout

Preparing the Layout
    Templates
    Cutouts
    Plastic Models
    Magnetic Boards

Chapter Aims After studying this chapter, the student should be able to:

1. Identify the items that are included in a feasibility study and explain why attention must be given to the various items.
2. Explain how a major source document is used to analyze the work flow.
3. Explain why an organization chart should be considered in planning office layout.
4. Explain how a communications matrix is used to analyze the communication network in an organization.
5. Discuss the purpose of an administrative service center and identify the characteristics of such a center.
6. Explain the features of the office landscaping concept.
7. Identify the characteristics of movable partitions and modular furniture.

Chapter Terms *Work flow:* the movement of information through a given department or organization. The information frequently involves forms.

Communication network: the face-to-face contact and phone conversations between individuals. An analysis of such communication is necessary in determining the appropriate geographical location of departments and individuals.

Administrative service center: a centralized area in a building that is responsible for several different functions, including storage of stationery and supplies, mail and communication services, filing and records management, secretarial and clerical assistance, informational retrieval, and library facilities.

Office landscaping: the open planning of office space that is free of traditional permanent walls, corridors, private offices, and the row-after-row arrangement of desks.

Movable partitions: a partition device used in place of permanent walls. Such partitions are easily movable.

Modular furniture: self-contained furniture units comprised of desk space, file space, and storage space.

The layout of an office may have a greater effect upon the operating efficiency of an organization than any other factor. Since layout is affected by the interrelationships among *equipment, information,* and *personnel,* considerable attention has to be focused upon these three components if operating efficiency, production, and coordination are to be optimized. Office layout involves more than simply placing personnel and installing equipment in a given space. It also has to be concerned with the management of office space, attempting to maximize effectiveness with a minimum cost.

Office layout is important for several reasons. To a great extent, layout determines whether or not floor space is effectively utilized. Layout also has an impact upon the impression one may get of the premises and may be a significant determinant of the overall job satisfaction of employees. In addition, efficient layout helps to eliminate bottlenecks in the flow of work as well as to maximize profit.

Goals of Office Layout

Office layout has several goals with which the administrative office manager should be concerned. One significant goal is to create efficient **work flow.** Another goal is systematically to allocate and to utilize floor space. Layout also helps to create an office environment that contributes to the satisfaction of office employees and that has a positive effect on the clients of the organization. Other goals are the following: to provide efficient employee work areas, to provide sufficient flexibility for future expansion when the need arises, and to provide conditions that facilitate employee supervision.

Factors in Office Layout

If the layout of an office is to be effective, basic factors must be considered during the planning stages of the layout project. The factors discussed below are among the most important.

The Feasibility Study

The feasibility study is a useful tool in planning and designing office layout. Before an organization can objectively weigh the available alternatives and options, the findings of the feasibility study should be thoroughly analyzed. In many cases, the feasibility study will be directed by a management consultant firm that specializes in office planning services. Such a study will outline the needs of the organization and will serve as a basis for determining which alternatives best meet the needs of the organization.

Items to be considered in the feasibility study include:

1. The financial growth of the organization during the last ten years and the anticipated growth during the next ten and twenty years.

2. The classifications and numbers of present employees and a projection of employees needed in the future.

3. An analysis of present space requirements and an analysis and projection of future space requirements.

4. A study of the systems and procedures and work flow patterns of the organization.

5. The interrelationships between each of the departments.

6. An analysis of the communication patterns between individuals and groups.

The report that summarizes the findings of the feasibility study usually consists of a complete analysis of the data and a set of guidelines. With this information available, the organization is able to select the most appropriate alternatives on the basis of the facts that were gathered.

The Work Flow

The flow of work, which is very crucial in determining the efficiency of office layout, refers to the movement of information either vertically (between superiors and subordinates or vice versa) or horizontally (between employees with the same responsibility level).

For the most efficient work flow, personnel and equipment should be arranged in such a way that the information moves in as straight a line as possible to avoid backtracking and crisscrossing patterns. To accomplish the straight-line flow, the duties, responsibilities, and activities of each employee must be thoroughly studied. When little or no attention is given to the work flow, delays in the flow of information are common, documents may have to be handled excessively, and personnel have to exert needless effort.

The work flow of most departments usually involves a major document, typically a form. For example, in a credit department, the major document may be the credit application; in an accounts payable department, the payment voucher; in a purchasing department, the purchase order. A most effective means of studying the work flow is to follow the movement of the document through the department. The movement may be traced in either of two ways: (1) by preparing and analyzing a flow chart (see Figure 21–6), or (2) by actually charting or diagraming the movement of the document through its work flow patterns (see Figure 21–7). Because effective layout takes into consideration the interrelationships among equipment, paper, and personnel, an analysis must be made of the effect that the equipment component has on the movement of paper between employees. More and more, the equipment component is concerned with the computer and other data processing facilities.

The Organization Chart

Closely related to the study of the work flow is the analysis of the organization chart. In situations in which work flow is primarily vertical in nature (superior-subordinate), the organizational chart clearly depicts the lines of authority. The organization chart also identifies job relationships between employees of similar hierarchical rank. So that future needs of the organization will be met, the anticipated number of employees should also be projected. If a comprehensive feasibility study has been made, these projections are usually readily available.

Projection of Employees Needed in the Future

If an organization is going to have space and facilities suitable for the future, the projection of employees needed in the future has to be carefully and accurately made. To make this projection, the following should be considered: the potential for developing new products or services that will require large increases in the number of office employees, the yearly rate of growth of the firm as measured by profit, the yearly increase in the number of employees, and possible changes in office operations that will require new employees. Unless these factors are given careful consideration, the organization may find its premises to be totally unsatisfactory after a short period of time.

The Communication Network

In addition to studying the flow of work between individuals and departments, it is also vitally important to analyze the nature of phone and face-to-face contact between individuals and departments. If the work flow, the organization chart, and the **communication network** indicate that certain individuals and departments have a considerable amount of contact, it is logical to group the individuals and departments in close proximity to one another.

To summarize data on phone and face-to-face contacts, a chart similar to Figure 4–1 is useful. This is a summary of tally sheets kept by each employee over a period of at least two weeks; the time period should be representative and void of any unusual fluctuations. For example, the data in Figure 4–1 indicate that forty phone contacts were made between the president and the assistant to the president, while sixty face-to-face contacts were made between these two individuals.

The communications matrix is useful for clearly illustrating which individuals have frequent contact with one another and, consequently, which individuals should be located near one another.

Departmental Organization

While recent developments, such as widespread use of the computer, have brought about some changes in the organizational structure of the typical business enterprise, most enterprises are still organized by functions—specifically, by departments or areas. In deciding upon the location of each department, consideration should be given to the flow of work between the various departments. Closely related departments, such as accounting and data processing, should be located near one another. Likewise, departments with frequent public contact (purchasing and personnel) should be located near the entrance or reception area of the building. Departments characterized as producing considerable noise, such as receiving or printing and duplicating, should be located near one another. Areas that cut across all departments (central records area and the word processing center) should be centrally located for purposes of convenience and accessibility to other departments. Individuals or departments with a minimum of public contact, such as the president and other execu-

FIGURE 4–1 Communication Matrix

	President	Assistant to President	Tax and Legal Advisor	V.P. Corporate Relations	V.P. Finances	V.P. Production	Administrative Office Manager	Central Records Supervisor	Data Processing Supervisor	Sales Manager
President	■	40 / 60	10 / 17	18 / 10	20 / 7	10 / 12	3 / 0	0 / 0	3 / 0	1 / 0
Assistant to President		■	30 / 25	20 / 16	18 / 18	7 / 3	10 / 8	5 / 0	18 / 4	15 / 10
Tax and Legal Advisor			■	20 / 19	8 / 12	3 / 0	0 / 1	4 / 7	0 / 0	7 / 12
V.P. Corporate Relations				■	17 / 23	15 / 12	5 / 9	0 / 0	4 / 2	1 / 0
V.P. Finances					■	14 / 16	5 / 3	3 / 1	15 / 21	5 / 8
V.P. Production						■	5 / 3	4 / 1	10 / 5	18 / 23
Administrative Office Manager							■	19 / 27	15 / 13	5 / 9
Central Records Supervisor								■	21 / 18	5 / 8
Data Processing Supervisor									■	15 / 18
Sales Manager										■

The intersection of the rows and columns is coded as follows:

upper number — number of phone contacts between individuals

lower number — number of personal contacts between individuals

tive officers, should be located in a less heavily traveled area of the building.

Private and General Offices

There seems to be a trend toward using more general offices and fewer private offices. In the past, private offices were used for reasons of prestige and status. They were also used by employees who had need for a quiet area in which to concentrate and for those individuals who were working with confidential materials.

Reasons frequently cited for doing away with private offices include the following: the cost of private offices is considerably greater than the comparable space in a general office; private offices complicate the supervision of employees; the permanent walls surrounding private offices make layout changes difficult; heating, cooling, and lighting are more difficult than in an open area; and private offices impede communication.

Some of the newer developments in layout—office landscaping, modular equipment and furniture, and the use of movable partitions—have further decreased the need for private offices. Each of these developments is discussed in another section of this chapter.

Space Requirements

Minimum space requirements are affected by a variety of factors. For example, employees who use equipment to carry out the functions of their jobs will need more space than employees whose jobs do not require the use of equipment. Other factors affecting the space allocation are nature and type of furniture, structural pillars and columns, windows, and nature of work.

Figure 4–2 identifies minimum space requirements for various individuals and rooms. Using the figures given in Figure 4–2, the total amount of space required for an organization can be approximated.

FIGURE 4–2   Minimum Space Requirements

Individual/Room	Space Requirements
Top-level executives	425 square feet
Middle-level executives	350 square feet
Supervisors	200 square feet
Office employees	75–100 square feet
Modular work station	100 square feet
Conference room	25 square feet per person
Reception room	35 square feet per person
Main corridor	6–8 feet wide
Secondary corridor	4–5 feet wide
Cross aisles (every 25–30 feet)	3–4 feet wide

Specialized Areas

There are a variety of specialized work areas that should be considered in planning office layout. The type of specialized areas that an organization will want to consider are dependent upon the nature of the organization. A discussion of some of the most common areas follows.

The reception area. In many ways, the reception area and the first chapter of a book are similar in that both determine what kind of first impression is likely to be created. Good first impressions of the office building certainly affect public relations and are apt to result in increased profit for the organization.

As far as the size of the reception area is concerned, thirty-five square feet of space should be allowed for each individual that may be in the reception area at any one time. For example, if the maximum number of people that will be in the reception area at the same time is ten, a space allocation of 350 square feet would be appropriate.

In addition to planning the appropriate size of the reception area, consideration should also be given to flow of traffic through the area. The layout should facilitate the movement of people through the area without bothering those that remain in the reception area. Other important considerations include the choice of furniture, color scheme, lighting, the individual responsible for receptionist duties, and the location of other rooms in relation to the reception area. To avoid distracting employees, it is generally thought that the reception area should not be in view of office areas.

Some manufacturing organizations use the reception area to display the company products, provided that such a display does not detract from the appearance of the area. Some organizations also display a map that identifies the location of branch offices and plants. Other organizations provide short film presentations informing visitors about various aspects of the organization.

The board/conference room. Since the cost of office space is increasing, few organizations can afford the luxury of an elaborately designed board room that will be used only infrequently. For this reason, organizations design rooms that are multipurpose in nature. Rooms are designed that are sufficiently elaborate to serve as the board room, yet functional enough to serve as a conference room. This results in maximizing the efficient use of expensive office space. Depending on the size of the organization and the nature of layout, additional smaller conference rooms may be located throughout the organization.

When it is intended that the board/conference room will serve in a dual capacity, the room is typically designed with built-in soundproof dividers that permit the area to be divided into two or three smaller rooms so that more than one meeting can be in session simultaneously.

As a means of making the board/conference room more versatile, many organizations are installing the most modern audiovisual and communications equipment. In large board rooms, microphones are sometimes installed in the ceiling for voice amplification, while other rooms are wired for portable telephones in order to facilitate the making and receiving of important phone calls during meetings.

In some board rooms, cathode ray tubes are installed to facilitate the immediate accessing of information stored in the computer. Commonly found in most board rooms are chalkboards, projector screens, and recording equipment. Some organizations also install limited kitchen facilities adjacent to the board/conference room to facilitate the serving of food and refreshments.

The computer room. The computer room represents a considerable invest-ment to the organization. No other room within an office building has en-vironmental requirements as strict as those of the computer room. Because of strict installation requirements, computer manufacturers stress the importance of a considerable amount of preplanning. Inasmuch as computer hardware changes so rapidly, it is important that space needs be projected for several years hence. It is also important that the physical specifications of the computer equipment be thoroughly analyzed and taken into consideration before determining the size of the computer room.

A most fundamental requirement in planning the computer room is to locate the installation in a fireproof, noncombustible building. The walls, floors, and ceiling of the computer room also need to be constructed of noncombustible materials. It is vitally important that the room be pro-tected from water damage—either coming up through the floor or down through the ceiling.

For most efficient computer operation, strict temperature and humid-ity levels must be maintained. A temperature of 75° F. and a relative humidity level of 50 percent are recommended. It is generally recom-mended that the computer installation have its own air conditioning sys-tem rather than being dependent upon the air conditioning facilities of the building.

Computer equipment is usually installed on a raised platform above the regular floor. This permits future layout changes with minimum structural changes, and the raised floor protects the interconnecting cables between the various pieces of equipment. In some installations, the space between the two floors is used to supply cool air to the equipment.

Because of the noise generated by some of the eqiupment in the computer room, extensive acoustical control may be necessary, including the installation of acoustical ceiling panels. Other factors to consider in designing computer facilities include providing suitable office space for the computer personnel (programmers, supervisors, and technicians), providing suitable storage vaults for tapes, and allowing for auxiliary equipment, such as the keypunch equipment.

The administrative service center. More and more organizations are in-stalling **administrative service centers** throughout the building. When the centers are linked to one another and to a central administrative service center, the administrative function then becomes centralized throughout the organization. Service centers frequently provide the following kinds of administrative services: stationery and supplies storage, mail and communications services, filing and records management, secretarial and clerical assistance, information retrieval, and library facilities.

A major objective of the administrative service center is to handle a greater work load with the same number of people—primarily by upgrading present personnel.[1] Administrative service centers were originally developed to eliminate inefficiency in office operations. For example, in many instances, filing space is not appropriately utilized, supplies are not appropriately dispersed throughout the office area, and copy equipment is inefficiently used. The centralized control characteristic of the service center helps to eliminate many areas of inefficiency.

The service centers should be located close to the users of the centers. The nature of the work being performed determines the type of services provided by the center. Since services can be added or dropped as the need arises or diminishes, the service center provides much flexibility in the administrative function of the office.

Figure 4–3 illustrates the layout of an administrative service center.

The mailroom. As a communication center, the mailroom has a significant impact on the efficiency with which information moves in and out of the organization. To a great extent, mailroom efficiency can be enhanced by

FIGURE 4–3   Administrative Service Center

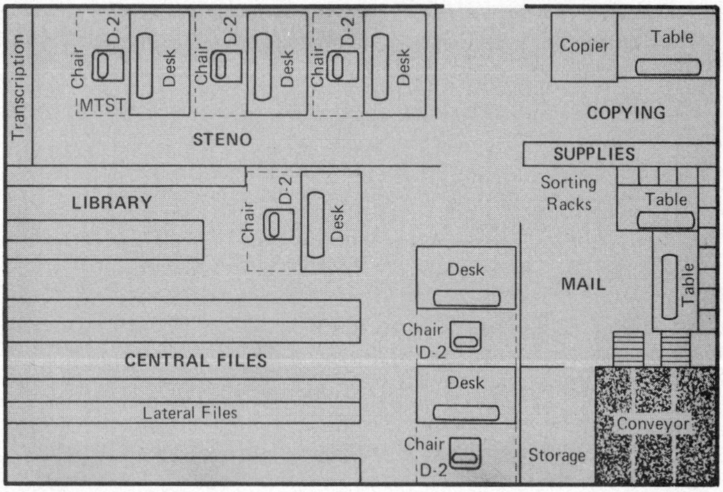

Courtesy, Geyer-McAllister Publications Inc.

[1] Excerpted from *Administrative Management*, copyright © 1969 by Geyer-McAllister, Publications, Inc., New York.

proper layout. The mailroom should be located near the receiving area of the building, but it should also be located as centrally as possible. The following three areas are those that frequently comprise the mailroom:

Incoming area—where incoming mail is received and placed in dumping bins.

Sorting area—where mail is sorted and readied for distribution throughout the organization.

Outgoing area—where outgoing mail is stamped, sealed, and readied for mailing.

The flow of mail through the mailroom should be considered when deciding on the appropriate location of the various pieces of equipment.

The duplicating room. In terms of layout, the duplicating room should be centrally located, so that it is easily accessible to the organization's employees. For this reason, duplicating rooms are frequently located near the physical center of the building. Noise made by some of the printing equipment can be controlled by special acoustical construction materials. The room should also be properly ventilated, since some printing materials produce unpleasant fumes. Other special features that are desirable are darkroom, washing, and storage facilities, as well as adequate counter space.

The central records area. For the greatest amount of convenience, the central records area needs to be located centrally within the organization. Special provisions may also need to be made for fire protection, proper atmospheric conditions, and security to prevent unauthorized entry of individuals. Because of the extreme weight of materials stored in the central records area, certain structural requirements may have to be considered in the construction process.

Safety Considerations

The design and layout of the office should not impede the movement of employees from one area to another area. The layout should enable employees to move easily through the aisles rather than take shortcuts through the work areas, and the aisles and corridors should not be obstructed by equipment and furniture. Doors should not swing open into aisles, and stairwells and exits should conform with guidelines established by the National Fire Protection Association Code No. 101.

Expansion

Each time the layout is changed, the possibility for expansion must be considered. Many organizations, in order to maintain flexibility, prepare a yearly space analysis in much the same way that the yearly budget is prepared. A space analysis is usually made for each of the next five consecutive years, for the tenth year, and for the fifteenth year hence.

When preparing a space analysis, a chart similar to Figure 4–4 may be used as a guideline.

FIGURE 4–4 Space Analysis

	Number of People	Square Feet of Space Required per Person	Total
CORPORATE OFFICES			
President	—	—	—
Vice Presidents	—	—	—
Treasurer	—	—	—
MIDDLE MANAGERS			
Administrative Office Manager	—	—	—
Systems and Procedures Manager	—	—	—
OPEN OFFICE SPACE			
Accounting Department	—	—	—
Sales Area	—	—	—
SPECIAL AREAS			
Conference Room	—	—	—
Computer Room	—	—	—
Reception Room	—	—	—
Word Processing Center	—	—	—
Mailroom	—	—	—
Duplicating Room	—	—	—
Central Records Area	—	—	—
STORAGE			
Centralized File Area	—	—	—
File Cabinets	—	—	—
Storage Closets	—	—	—
TOTAL SPACE REQUIRED			

Environmental Conditions

Environmental conditions, including color, lighting, air conditioning, and noise control, are also important factors to consider in designing the layout of an office. Each of these is covered in Chapter 5.

Equipment and Furniture

Inasmuch as equipment and furniture have an effect on space requirements, decor, and noise, these two factors must also be considered in designing the layout of an office. The topic of equipment and furniture is discussed in Chapter 6.

**New Develop-
ments in Office
Layout**

Office
Landscaping

Of the new developments in the design and layout of the office, **office landscaping, movable partitions,** and **modular furniture** are among the most important.

Office landscaping, developed by the Quickboner Team in Germany, was implemented in that country for the first time in 1960 and is now being used in the United States with increasing frequency. The office landscape concept refers to the planning of office space free of the traditional permanent walls, corridors, and private offices, and of the row-after-row arrangement of desks and other furniture. The concept is also characterized as having a considerable amount of open space partitioned into work areas by using movable partitions, modular furniture, and in some cases plants and foliage. To accomplish the partitioning of work areas, furniture is arranged in clusters and at various angles as opposed to the traditional rows.

In conventional layout, the private office is often used as a status symbol. Landscaping, in its pure form, uses no private offices. Individuals receive status through their work assignments, by their location and amount of space within the work area, and from the type and amount of furniture they are given.

Landscaping is based on the cybernetics of the organization, which means that information flows or processes are considered when planning a landscaped office. The information flow of the organization typically consists of paper flow, telephone communications, and personal visits. For this reason, systems and procedures analysts and communications consultants should work closely with the architects and interior designers in planning the landscaped office.

Among the special features of landscaping are the following:

1. Landscaping utilizes only a minimum number of permanent walls. Large open areas with approximately 10,000 square feet of space are most desirable for developing the landscape concept. By utilizing a floor grid system (five feet by five feet, for example) for electrical and telephone connections, individual work stations can be conveniently placed at any location and at any angle.

2. The location of each work station is crucial in determining the efficiency of work flow. Work stations should be located in such a way as to facilitate a smooth flow of work, so work will not pile up, and so there will be a minimum of crisscrossing and backtracking.

3. To provide a suitable work environment, special attention may have to be given to acoustics and noise control. The type of acoustical devices used for a conventional office may not be sufficient for the large open areas characteristic of landscaping. Sound-absorbing walls, ceilings, partitions, and carpeting may have to be utilized. Acoustical conditioning is sufficient when sounds are no longer disturbing at a distance of fifteen feet from the source.

4. Uniform air conditioning and humidity control in the large open areas are easily accomplished, although the installation appropriate for conventionally designed office areas may not be appropriate for the large open areas characteristic of landscaping.

5. Since desks are no longer arranged in rows along windows, adequate artificial lighting must be provided.

6. The color scheme and furniture arrangement must provide a pleasant working atmosphere for the employees. The use of partitions, modular furniture, and planters provides privacy while adding to the atmosphere of the surroundings.

7. The furniture used in a landscaped office is often designed to facilitate worker efficiency. If, for example, a portion of an individual's work is better performed in a standing position, the furniture can be designed to conveniently accommodate the employee in a standing position. Furthermore, the amount of storage space given each employee is kept to a minimum.

8. Because of the emphasis on rapid transfer of inactive materials to another storage area, new filing systems may have to be utilized, thus facilitating continuous flow of inactive materials from the office area to more appropriate storage facilities.

There are several benefits that result from using the office landscape concept, including:

1. Significant cost savings result when changes in layout are required by expansion and organizational changes.

2. The initial cost of installing a landscaped office may be as much as 10–25 percent less than the cost of conventional office space.

3. Since a minimum number of permanent walls and private offices are used, the amount of usable floor space is considerably greater.

4. Moving a square foot of landscaped office space is considerably less than the cost of moving a square foot of conventional office space (35 cents per square foot compared with $2 to $15 per square foot).[2]

5. Landscaping is apt to result in significant improvements in office productivity because of greater efficiency in work flow, improved communication channels, improved worker morale, and a greater feeling of worker involvement.

Figure 4–5 illustrates the landscape concept.

Movable Partitions

The use of movable partitions in office design and layout is rapidly increasing, perhaps because they are significantly less costly than per-

---

[2] Excerpted from *Administrative Management*, copyright © 1969 by Geyer-McAllister, Publications, Inc., New York.

FIGURE 4–5   Office Landscaping

Courtesy, Vogel-Peterson Company, Elmhurst, Illinois

manent walls. Partitions are available in a variety of sizes and shapes, and several different types of outer surfaces, including wood, metal, plastic, glass, and carpet, are available. Partitions may be prewired with telephone and electrical connections as well as constructed with special sound-absorbing materials. Figure 4–6 illustrates a movable partition.

FIGURE 4–6 Movable Partitions

Courtesy, Steelcase Inc.

Modular Furniture   Most modular furniture is self-contained, since the unit consists of desk space, file space, and storage space. Modular units can be specially designed to meet specific needs of employees, resulting in greater worker productivity and efficiency. Modular units most likely use less space than conventional furniture, and in some cases, the modular furniture and movable partitions can be purchased as a single component. Figure 4–7 illustrates modular furniture.

FIGURE 4–7   Modular Furniture

Courtesy, Steelcase Inc.

Principles of Effective Office Layout

The following principles of effective layout are important considerations in the design and layout of office space. The list is perhaps most effectively used as evaluative criteria.

1. The interrelationships between equipment, information, and personnel in the flow of work should be determined.

2. The work flow should move in as straight a line as possible. Crisscrossing and backtracking should be avoided.

3. The work flow should revolve around the major source document.

4. The organization chart should be used to determine the hierarchical relationships between individuals.

5. For most effective layout, communication patterns between individuals must be determined.

6. Work groups performing similar or related duties should be located near one another.

7. Individuals or work groups with frequent public contact should be located near the entrance to the premises.

8. Individuals or work groups whose work requires considerable concentration should be placed in a low traffic, quiet area of the building.

9. Space allocation should be based on the position of the individual, the nature of the work being performed, and the amount of special equipment required.

10. Groups or individuals providing specialized services should be located near those who use the specialized services.

11. Furniture and equipment should meet the needs of the individuals using the furniture and equipment.

12. Aisles should be sufficiently wide to accommodate the rapid, efficient movement of employees.

13. Safety considerations are of utmost importance.

14. Large open areas are more efficient than smaller enclosed areas.

15. Adequate provisions have to be made for lighting, decor, air conditioning, humidity control, and noise control.

16. Concern for future expansion is important.

17. The work should come to the employee—not vice versa.

Preparing the Layout

After each of the important design and layout factors has been studied and analyzed, a scaled model of the floor plan should be prepared. To facilitate the development of the model, the construction blueprint is useful in drawing the floor areas, since it identifies the location of support pillars, doors, windows, stairwells, and other structural characteristics.

Once the floor plan model has been drawn, the exact location of each piece of furniture and equipment should be determined. Tools available for preparing the layout are templates, cutouts, plastic models, and magnetic boards. To assure accurate space relationships, the layout and the various scaled versions of furniture and equipment must use the same scale.

Templates

Templates consist of scaled versions of furniture and equipment and are typically constructed of cardboard or plastic. The template is used in tracing the various items on the layout. A template is illustrated in Figure 4–8.

Cutouts

Cutouts are purchased in sheets, and illustrations of individual furniture and equipment items are removed from the sheets by cutting. Cutouts are of two types: paper and self-adhering Mylar.

Plastic Models

Plastic models are scaled versions of various pieces of office furniture and equipment. Since the plastic models can be easily repositioned on the floor plan, their use facilitates exploring various layout possibilities. Figure 4–9 illustrates plastic models positioned on a layout board.

Magnetic Boards

Magnetized models of furniture and equipment are another frequently used tool for preparing layouts. While a magnetic field readily

FIGURE 4–8   Office Layout Template

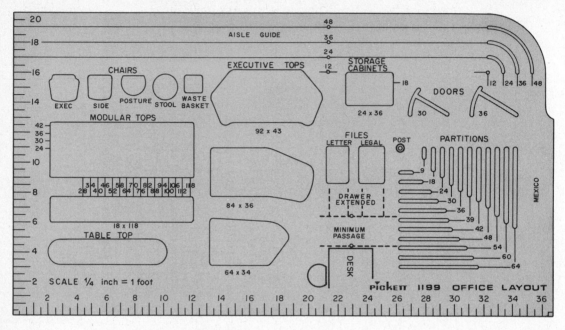

Courtesy, Pickett Company

adheres the models to the board, they can be easily repositioned. A lay-out using the magnetic board is illustrated in Figure 4–10.

Review Questions

1. Discuss the importance of effective office layout.

2. List and discuss some of the important factors to consider in office layout.

3. Why is it important to study the work flow in an organization? How might the work flow be studied?

4. Why is there a trend away from using private offices in office buildings?

5. What factors determine the amount of space allocated each individual within the organization?

6. Review the characteristics of office landscaping.

7. What are the benefits of office landscaping?

8. Discuss five principles of effective layout and give or cite examples where you have seen these principles violated.

9. Identify the tools available for preparing office layout diagrams.

Minicases

You are one of the consultants for Modern Office Interiors, a company that specializes in designing office interiors. As a consultant, you are

FIGURE 4–9   Plastic Models

Courtesy, A'D'S' Company, Indianola, Pennsylvania 15051

responsible for analyzing your client's present situation, for determining what the future needs of the client may be, and for making recommendations to the client. You recently had a call from a prospective client who thought office landscaping primarily involved distributing a few plants around the office. As a professional consultant, you feel compelled to ex-

FIGURE 4–10   Magnetic Boards

Courtesy, Magna Visual Inc.

plain to the prospective client that landscaping involves more than the mere distribution of plants. Outline the information about landscaping that you plan to provide the prospective client.

*   *   *

The purchasing department of the Anderson Electronics Company has been given approval to update and modernize the department. The equipment now contained in the department is up to date, but most of the employees feel that the layout is quite unreasonable. Although procedures have changed from time to time, the layout has not changed in the last ten years. Employees in the purchasing department have frequently complained that the layout is inefficient. For example, two employees who work closely together in the processing of purchase orders are located across the room from one another. Two other employees who also work closely together are located quite a distance from one another. In designing the new layout for the purchasing department, what devices would you use to analyze the two examples cited above? What other factors would you want to consider in analyzing the present layout in order to make the layout more efficient?

Case

John Allen and Frank Smith are partners in a law office. Because their present office has become inadequate, the lawyers have rented office space in a new office building presently being constructed. You have been hired to help them design the layout of the new premises. The owner of the building has agreed to construct permanent walls where you believe they should be placed.

The personnel consists of the following individuals:

2 attorneys
1 executive secretary
1 receptionist
1 clerk typist
1 law clerk (compiles briefs and researches cases for attorneys and is in charge of the law library for the lawyers)

The equipment and furniture consists of the following items:

6 desks
12 four-drawer file cabinets
4 tables (one for each attorney, one for the executive secretary, and one for the law clerk)
6 four-shelf bookcases (one for each of the attorneys and the remainder for the law books)
4 sofas (one for each attorney and two for the reception area)
1 conference table (to be used jointly by the attorneys)
16 chairs
1 automatic typewriting console (for use by the executive secretary and the clerk typist)

In designing the layout, the attorneys have expressed an interest in keeping the construction of permanent walls to a minimum—specifically, permanent walls are to be used only to enclose their individual offices and the restrooms. Privacy for the others is to be achieved through the installation of modular furniture and/or movable partitions.

Using the diagram on the opposite page, prepare the new layout showing the location of the permanent walls, the location of the equipment and furniture, and the location of any modular furniture or movable partitions.

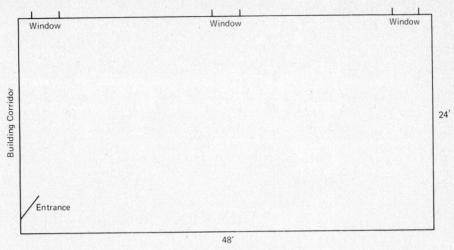

Scale $\frac{3}{8}$ inch = 4 feet

The Environment of the Office

Chapter
5

The Effect of the Office Environment on the Employee

Lighting
> Characteristics of Adequate Lighting Systems
>> Sufficient quantity of light
>> Brightness of light
>> Contrast of light
>> Reflectance of light
>> Absence of glare
>> Uniformity of light
> Types of Lighting Systems
>> Direct
>> Semidirect
>> Indirect
>> Semi-indirect
>> General diffuse
> Kinds of Lighting
>> Natural light
>> Fluorescent lighting
>> Incandescent lighting

Color
> Color Considerations
>> Color combination
>> Effect of light on color
>> Reflectance value of color
>> Impact of colors
>> Guiding principles
> Floor Coverings
> Color of Furniture
> Recommended Color Schemes for Specific Office Areas
>> Corridors
>> General offices
>> Conference room

Noise Control
> Control of Office Noise
>> Proper construction
>> Sound-absorbing materials
>> Sound-absorbing devices
>> Masking

Conditioning the Air
Temperature of Air
Humidity Level
Circulation of Air
Cleanliness of Air

Music

Chapter Aims   After studying this chapter, the student should be able to:

1. Discuss the impact of an unsatisfactory office environment on employees.

2. Explain the following characteristics of good lighting systems: quantity of light, brightness of light, contrast of light, reflectance of light, absence of glare, and uniformity of light.

3. Explain why the indirect lighting system is the most desirable type of lighting system for office areas.

4. Explain why fluorescent lighting is generally preferred to incandescent lighting for office lumination.

5. Explain each of the following considerations for developing a color scheme in an office: color combination, effect of light on color, reflectance value of color, and impact of color.

6. Explain the various ways in which noise in an office can be controlled.

7. Identify the acceptable temperature, humidity, and circulation standards for an office environment.

8. Explain the reasons for installation of a music system in an office.

Chapter Terms   *Office environment:* the lighting, color scheme, noise level, and condition of the air in an office.

Foot-candle: the standard for measuring the quantity of light. It is the amount of direct light a distance of one foot from a standard candle.

Foot-lambert: the standard for measuring the brightness of light. It is approximately equal to one foot-candle of either direct or reflected light.

Primary colors: the colors red, yellow, and blue.

Secondary colors: colors that are made by mixing two primary colors.

Tertiary colors: colors that are made by combining two parts of one primary color and one part of another primary color.

Decibel: the standard for measuring sound. It is the smallest change in sound that can be detected by the human ear.

Masking sound: a technique of controlling noise in an office. It involves the use of a sound that masks out unwanted noise.

The environment of the office has a significant impact on employees' performance. Since the effect of the environment on employees' performance can often be measured in terms of dollars and cents, particular attention should be paid to the environment of the office and its effect on employees. In addition to the layout of the office, which was discussed in the preceding chapter, and the efficient utilization of furniture and equipment, which is discussed in the subsequent chapter, the **office environment** is affected by such factors as lighting, color scheme, noise level, and the overall condition of the air. Each of these factors, therefore, may have either a positive or negative effect on employees' performance. The installation of music systems in many offices has also had the effect of improving the environment in which employees work.

The Effect of the Office Environment on the Employee

Social scientists are conducting an increasing amount of research to identify factors that have an effect on employees' performance. In conducting this research, the social scientists have assessed such characteristics as the abilities and attitudes of employees, their training, and their cultural background. But these are characteristics that employees bring with them into the organization. The social scientists have also conducted research to assess the various office environmental factors over which the employees have very little control. The outcome of this research has caused management and supervisors to be more responsive to the needs of employees. In the long run, everyone within the organization gains when there is a responsive attitude toward the needs of employees.

Failure to give proper consideration to the environment of the office is reflected in several ways. A poor office environment often results in decreased levels of production and employee morale. Absenteeism and tardiness are apt to increase, as are the number of errors made by employees. In extreme cases, the employee's physical well-being may actually be hampered.

Lighting

One of the most important facets of the office environment is the lighting system. As is also true of the other environmental factors, lighting can affect the employees both physically and psychologically. A common physical effect of inadequate lighting is increased fatigue from excessive eye strain. Psychologically, inadequate lighting results in loss of morale, which will eventually cause a decrease in the quantity and quality of work performed.

Characteristics of Adequate Lighting Systems

Adequate lighting systems possess certain well-defined characteristics. Among these characteristics are the following: quantity of light, brightness of light, contrast of light, reflectance of light, absence of glare, and uniformity of light.

Sufficient quantity of light. The **foot-candle,** the unit measure of light, is defined as the amount of direct light a distance of one foot from a standard candle. One watt of light per square foot produces approximately fifteen foot-candles. Between 100 and 150 foot-candles are recommended for most types of office work. Therefore, in a room containing 200 square feet, 2000 watts are needed to provide 150 foot-candles.

Brightness of light. The unit measure of brightness of light is the **foot-lambert,** which is approximately equal to one foot-candle of either direct or reflected light. The brightness of light in a given area should not exceed 350–400 foot-lamberts. Light that exceeds these levels will result in considerable eye fatigue.

Contrast of light. The contrast of light between two surfaces can also be measured in terms of foot-lamberts. When the contrast between two surfaces is excessive, eye fatigue results from the frequent dilation and contraction of pupils of the eyes. An acceptable range for contrast of light is a three to one ratio. This means that the brightness of the surface on which a task is being performed should be no greater than three times the brightness of the background. Therefore, if a task is being performed on a surface reflecting sixty foot-lamberts, the background of the surface must have a brightness of approximately twenty foot-lamberts if the three to one ratio is to be maintained.

Reflectance of light. The reflectance of light is the ratio between the amount of light reflected from a surface and the amount of light striking the surface. Since light colors have a higher reflectance value than do darker colors, light colors reflect more light than do darker colors. A reflective value of 80–90 percent is recommended for ceilings; 25–50 percent for floors; 50–60 percent for walls; 25–40 percent for furniture; and 20–60 percent for desk tops.

Absence of glare. An efficient lighting system is completely void of any surface glare. Direct glare, which results from sunlight or ceiling light, can be eliminated by such mechanical devices as shades and appropriate light fixtures. Reflected glare is caused by light striking shiny or highly polished surfaces. Reflected glare can be eliminated by using a lighting system in which very little direct light strikes shiny or highly polished surfaces.

Uniformity of light. Although the lighting system must supply an adequate and uniform amount of light when and where needed for the tasks being performed, uniform levels of light throughout the entire office area become monotonous and uninteresting. To eliminate the monotony, the amount of light in nonworking areas can be either increased or decreased in comparison to the amount of light needed in the working areas.

Types of Lighting Systems

Lighting systems consist of the following types: direct, semidirect, indirect, semi-indirect, and general diffuse.

Direct. Lighting systems of this type direct approximately 90–100 percent of the lighting downward to the working surface. The result is that direct and reflected glare are likely to be bothersome. Since very little of the light is diffused, shadows are created. Unless the light fixtures are quite close together, the working areas will most likely not be uniformly illuminated.

Semidirect. With semidirect lighting, 60 to 90 percent of the light is directed downward, with the remainder of the light directed upward and reflected from the ceiling. Thus, some of the shadows that are characteristic of the direct lighting system are eliminated.

Indirect. The indirect lighting system is the recommended system for most types of office tasks. With indirect lighting, 90 to 100 percent of the light is first directed upward to the ceiling and walls. The light then becomes diffused and is reflected downward to the working area. Since the ceiling becomes the source of light for the working area, it needs to be of a sufficiently light color to reflect light. Because most of the light is diffused before it strikes the working surface, shadows and glares for the most part are eliminated.

Semi-indirect. With semi-indirect lighting, 60 to 90 percent of the light is directed toward the ceiling and walls and is then reflected downward. The remainder of the light is immediately directed downward. As was the case with indirect lighting, the ceiling provides the major light source for this lighting system. Although the semi-indirect lighting system may produce a greater amount of light for the same wattage level than does the indirect system, shadows and glare may also be a greater problem with semi-indirect lighting.

General diffuse. This lighting system directs 40 to 60 percent of the light directly to the working surface with the remainder of the light reflected downward from the ceiling and walls. Although this system produces more light for the same wattage than does the semi-indirect system, shadows and glare are also more noticeable than when semi-indirect lighting is used.

Kinds of Lighting

The three most commonly used kinds of office lighting are natural daylight, fluorescent lighting, and incandescent lighting.

Natural light. Natural or daylight is a very efficient lighting system, but because of its lack of dependability, other lighting sources also have to be installed. In addition to its efficiency, natural light often provides psychological advantages for employees. Natural light does not have the capability of penetrating very far into enclosed areas. On extremely bright days, the brightness of natural light has to be controlled.

Many newer buildings are being constructed with glass-enclosed courtyards at the center of the buildings. Such courtyards serve several purposes, one of which is to provide a greater amount of working area along walls with windows. The result is that more employees can take advantage of natural light.

Employees whose work areas utilize natural light should be situated in such a way that the light comes over their left shoulders if they are right handed but over their right shoulders if they are left handed. Under no circumstances should employees in their normal working positions have to face windows.

Fluorescent lighting. The use of fluorescent lighting in office buildings continues to increase. It is the most commonly used kind of lighting system found in offices. The illumination produced by fluorescent lighting closely resembles natural light. Although fluorescent lighting is initially more expensive to install than is incandescent lighting, fluorescent lighting offers several advantages over incandescent lighting. Fluorescent lighting produces less heat and less glare. Fluorescent tubes last considerably longer than filament bulbs. It consumes less electricity; and the lighting is more evenly distributed.

Many buildings today are being constructed with luminous ceilings similar to the one illustrated in Figure 5–1. One of the most significant advantages of the luminous ceiling is the efficiency with which it eliminates shadows and glare on working surfaces. Because of uniformity produced by luminous ceilings, several different lighting techniques are being utilized in office areas as a means of providing variation. One such device is the small, strategically placed spotlight.

Incandescent lighting. This type of light is produced by filament bulbs and is the type of light most commonly found in homes. Although fluorescent lighting is generally regarded as the most efficient light for office areas, incandescent lighting can also be used effectively. One common use of incandescent lighting is to break up the monotony of lighting panels. Incandescent lighting can also be used very effectively for emphasis purposes.

Initially, the installation of incandescent lighting is less expensive than is the cost of installing fluorescent lighting. This is about the only advantage incandescent lighting enjoys in comparison to fluorescent lighting. Incandescent lighting does not last as long, the colors are less natural, it consumes more electricity, and it is apt to produce greater amounts of glare and shadow.

Incandescent lighting can also be used to provide heat for office buildings. This technique is discussed more thoroughly in another section of this chapter.

FIGURE 5–1   Illuminated Ceiling

Courtesy, Armstrong Cork Company

Color

Since people find color either pleasant or unpleasant, color in an office can make a significant impact. Although most people are aware of the physical impact of color in an office, most people are not aware of the psychological impact of color. For example, the psychological impact of color has either a positive or negative influence on production, fatigue, morale, attitude, and tension. Color in an office, therefore, provides not only an aesthetic value but also a functional value.

Color Considerations

There are several important color considerations in developing a color scheme in an office. Among these important considerations are the following: color combination, effect of light on color, reflectance value of color, and impact of color. Each is discussed in the following section.

Color combination. Combining the three **primary colors**—yellow, red, and blue—produces **secondary colors.** For example, mixing red and yellow makes orange, yellow and blue makes green, and blue and red makes violet. **Tertiary colors** are made by combining two parts of one primary color and one part of another primary color. This concept is illustrated in

FIGURE 5–2   Color Chart

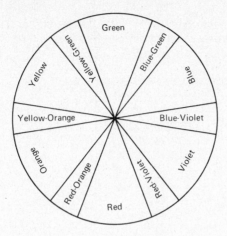

Figure 5–2. The tertiary colors are yellow-orange, yellow-green, blue-green, blue-violet, and so forth. The twelve colors in Figure 5–2 provide the foundation for color coordination. The colors are coordinated by selecting colors according to their positions on the color chart illustrated in Figure 5–2. Some acceptable color coordination schemes are:

1. Complementary colors—opposite each other on the color chart. For example, red-green, violet-yellow, and blue-orange.

2. Split complementary colors—the colors on either side of a complementary color. For example, blue-violet and blue-green are the split complementary colors of orange.

3. Triad colors—the three colors equally distant from one another on the color chart. For example, triad colors are orange, green, violet, or yellow-orange, blue-green, and red-violet.

Effect of light on color. The type of lighting system used in an office is also apt to have a significant effect upon the color scheme. This is true because the various types of artificial light have different color spectrums. Thus, the light source will enhance only those colors within the office that are also within the spectrum of the light source. To illustrate, fluorescent lighting is generally void of red and orange colors, while incandescent lighting is void of purple-blue combinations. Therefore, fluorescent lighting will not enhance red and orange colors and incandescent lighting will not enhance purple-blue color schemes.

Reflectance value of color. As was mentioned in the lighting section of this chapter, the various colors possess different reflectance values.

Lighter colors reflect a greater percentage of light than do the darker colors. Certain areas of the office require colors with higher reflectance values than do other areas. The ceiling, for example, requires a color with a higher reflectance value than does the floor. Figure 5–3 illustrates the reflectance value for various colors.

FIGURE 5–3   Reflectance Values of Colors

Color	Reflectance Value (Percent)
White	86
Light Green	67
Light Yellow	64
Light Blue	58
Light Gray	54
Medium Yellow	47
Orange	35
Medium Red	23
Dark Blue	17
Dark Red	13
Dark Green	10

Impact of colors. Each color has a distinct impact on the mood that it creates. Colors regarded as cool—blue, green, and violet—create calm and retiring moods. The warm colors—red, orange, and yellow—on the other hand, create warm and cheerful moods. The natural tints, including beige, buff, and off-white, are mildly stimulating, while deep purple and pale violet are considered to create depressing moods. Gray tends to have a sleep-inducing effect.

Guiding principles. The following principles should be considered in designing a color scheme for an office area:

1. Color cannot be considered by itself, but must be considered in terms of its impact on the total environment of the office.
2. Black and white colors can be used to influence other colors. Black will influence another color by making it lighter and more distinctive. White will influence another color by making it darker.
3. Any color used against a darker color will appear lighter, while any color used against a lighter one will appear darker.
4. Colors lose their brilliance and "wash out" in bright light, but they darken and lose their intensity in dim light.
5. Warm colors are considered to advance, while cool colors recede.

6. Two colors with greatly contrasting values have the effect of tiring eyes rather quickly.

7. Small areas of bright, secondary colors that are in balance with large areas are often useful.

8. Light colors will make a small room look larger.

9. A narrow area can be made to appear wider by making the end walls a brighter color than the side walls.

10. Deep brown is the most preferred dark color in an office.

11. A low ceiling will appear to be higher if the ceiling is a lighter color than are the walls.

12. In working areas, floors should be darker than walls, and the walls should be darker than the ceiling.

13. Because of excessive contrast, dark colors should not be used on walls with windows.

14. In work areas in which the natural light is from the north or east, a warm color should be used on the wall opposite the window, but when the natural light is from the south or west, a cool color should be used on the wall opposite the window.

15. Window coverings, such as drapes and other kinds of shades, should be functional as well as aesthetic.

Floor Coverings

The color of walls and ceilings are just one part of the color scheme in an office. The type and color of the floor covering is also very important. Although tile and other floor finishes are still widely used, carpet is being used with increasing frequency. Nowadays, since there are nearly as many colors of carpet as there are paint colors, color coordination is very simple. Carpet provides several significant advantages. It is useful for noise control. Its maintenance is often less expensive than maintaining other types of floor coverings. And, it is more comfortable and less tiring for employees who spend a substantial portion of each day in a standing position.

Since some carpeting creates electrostatic charges, special provisions may have to be made so that such charges do not interfere with the operation of some types of sensitive electric office equipment.

Color of Furniture

For an office to have an appropriate color coordination scheme, consideration must also be given to the colors of the furniture. Since most furniture is used for a longer period of time than the walls remain the same color, alternative color schemes should be considered at the time the initial color scheme is planned. Floor and furniture colors that permit only one wall color do not provide a sufficient amount of flexibility.

There seems to be a trend toward selecting furniture colors that are in contrast to wall colors. Not only is this useful because of greater flexibility in the color scheme, but such a practice also helps to eliminate some of the monotony of having similar colors.

When selecting furniture, care should also be given to the contrast value, as well as the reflectance value of the working surfaces of such furniture. If the contrast and reflectance values are too great, undue eye strain will occur. Shiny and highly polished surfaces on furniture should also be avoided if the lighting system produces an appreciable amount of either direct or reflected glare.

Recommended Color Schemes for Specific Office Areas

The nature and uses of specific office areas should be considered in selecting an appropriate color scheme.

Corridors. Since corridors are typically not very well lit, light colors can be utilized to take advantage of their reflectance value. Washable wall coverings are being used in many instances because painted surfaces are difficult to maintain.

General offices. The type of lighting system, the directional location of any natural lighting in the given work area, the color of the floor covering, the nature of the work being performed, and the color of the furniture are all factors that should be taken into consideration when selecting an appropriate color for a general office area. It may be most advantageous to select the color favored by the majority of the employees in a given work area.

Conference room. Most conference rooms favor a rather neutral color combination. Such a color combination is often used to produce a cordial working atmosphere.

Noise Control

The noise level in an office is another of the environmental factors that must be considered. When noise reaches a level where it becomes unpleasant, various physical and psychological conditions occur. For example, continued high noise levels can cause employees to experience permanent hearing loss. High noise levels are also the cause of fatigue and low levels of production, as well as nervous conditions and tension.

The **decibel**, the unit measure of sound, is the smallest change in sound that can be detected by the human ear. The faintest sound that the human ear can detect is zero decibels. Therefore, other sounds with greater intensity have decibel values higher than the zero value. Figure 5–4 illustrates the decibel values for some common office sounds. Office noises typically range in intensity from twenty to ninety decibels with fifty being the decibel value for the average office.

The following example illustrates the benefits of controlling office noise: The Aetna Life Insurance Company undertook a two-year study of the impact that noise conditioning had on its employees. The efficiency of the employees increased 8.8 percent, machine operator errors decreased 52 percent, turnover decreased 47 percent, and typists' errors decreased 29 percent.

FIGURE 5–4   Decibel Levels of Office Sounds

Office Area	Decibels
Loud Office Machines Room	90
Noisy Office	70
Average Office	50
Quiet Office	30
Sound-Proof Office	10

Source: Adapted from "Stop, Look, and Listen to Your Office Environment," *Modern Office Proce-dures*, March, 1970, p. 18. Copyright, 1970, by Industrial Publishing Company.

Control of Office Noise

Office noise can be controlled by various means, including proper construction, utilization of sound-absorbing materials and devices, and installation of a **masking system** designed to make noise levels less noticeable.

Proper construction. A considerable amount of office noise can be controlled by proper construction of the premises. Sound moves either through the air (called airborne sound) or through structural facilities (structural sound) prior to becoming airborne. Examples of airborne sound are conversation and sounds generated by various pieces of equipment. An example of structural sound is equipment vibration (which means that before becoming airborne, vibration sounds travel through a structural feature in the working area).

To help eliminate airborne sounds, several construction techniques are available:

1. Attaching a network of feeder ducts to the main ducts in the air conditioning system. A system using only main ducts allows considerable noise to be carried through the ducts.

2. Windows and doors that seal properly.

3. Building into the structural features dead airspace, which helps to decrease the amount of noise that travels from one area to another.

4. Use of construction materials that prohibit vibration noises from occurring.

Sound-absorbing materials. Many different types of sound-absorbing materials suitable for use in offices are being manufactured. Many sound-absorbing materials, which include such items as ceiling, walls, and floor coverings, have a functional as well as an aesthetic value. Drapes are also often used to absorb sounds.

Nowadays, many of the ceiling systems integrate light, noise control devices, and air conditioning features into one unit. Although the initial cost of such a system may be higher, the overall efficiency provided by such a system will most likely justify its cost. To help control noise, several different wall coverings are available. Soft, porous materials—for example, cork—are used. More common, perhaps, is the use of carpet as a wall covering. Several different companies are also manufacturing permanent, full length, sound-absorbing wall panels.

If the ceiling and floor coverings are adequate in terms of noise control, special wall coverings are not needed in most cases. In offices in which a high concentration of noise exists, special ceiling, wall, and floor materials may be needed.

The most efficient sound-absorbing floor covering is carpet. Special consideration may have to be given to the installation of carpet that is static free because of its effect on some types of equipment.

More extensive sound-absorbing materials may be needed in offices that utilize the office landscaping concept. Landscaping, which we discussed in the preceding chapter, utilizes only a minimum number of permanent walls. Because of this characteristic, special ceiling, wall, and floor materials may be needed.

For maximum benefit, materials used for noise control should possess three characteristics or qualities:

1. Absorption—the degree to which noise is absorbed within materials.

2. Reflection—the degree to which sound is not absorbed by various materials but is reflected back into space.

3. Isolation—the degree to which materials prevent sounds from passing through them. To eliminate a "dead" sound, a proper balance between reflection and absorption is needed. As noise levels increase, absorption needs to be increased and reflection decreased. Materials with hard surfaces—metal, glass, plastic—reflect a greater amount of noise than do surfaces with soft finishes—draperies, carpet, porous ceiling tiles, and the like. Isolation of noise depends on the airtightness, weight, and stiffness of materials.

Sound-absorbing devices. Several sound-absorbing devices are frequently used in controlling office noise. The most frequently used device is sound-absorbing padding placed under certain kinds of office machines—for example, the typewriter. Another device used frequently in many offices is a sound-absorbing cover placed over a piece of equipment, such as a typewriter or keypunch machine. Figure 5–5 illustrates one of the various types of sound-absorbing covers that are available.

Certain types of movable partitions (see page 87), which are often used to achieve privacy, are also frequently used to absorb sound.

FIGURE 5–5 Typewriter Cover for Noise Control

Courtesy, Jensen Engineering Inc., Santa Rosa, California

Masking. Another method many offices use as a means of controlling noise is the masking technique. Masking means that office noise blends in with low level, nondisturbing background sounds. Thus, in effect, masking drowns out various noises. Masking noise, also known as white noise, is very comparable to the sound produced by air moving through a duct or tunnel. The masking sound is transmitted throughout the premises by means of a speaker system.

Conditioning the Air

Another of the environmental factors having a physical and psychological impact on employees is the air in which the employees must work. In addition to the temperature of the air in an office, other important components are humidity, ventilation, and cleanliness of the air.

Most new office buildings located in areas with varied climates are constructed with a year-round, integrated air conditioning system. This means that the atmospheric condition of the office is very constant day after day. Integrated systems are comprised of two or more of the air conditioning components.

The benefits of having properly conditioned air in an office will in many cases more than pay for the cost of the system. For example, since the comfort of the employees is improved, greater levels of productivity and efficiency can be expected. Absenteeism and tardiness are reduced, and in some cases employees' health is improved. Furthermore, cleaning and redecorating costs can be reduced by utilizing an integrated air conditioning system.

Temperature of Air

When the humidity level is within the proper range, the ideal working temperature in an office is 68 degrees. An energy consciousness may result in lowering the temperature a few degrees below the ideal temperature.

In office buildings that contain a considerable amount of glass, solar heat can be utilized as a source of heat. Depending on the type of lighting systems and the characteristics of the local climate, the lighting system might also be used to help provide some of the temperature needs of the premises. Some lighting systems are constructed with ducts serving a dual purpose: (1) to cool the luminaires as a means of prolonging their life, and (2) to draw off and either distribute the warm air throughout the premises or direct the warm air outside the building when it is not needed for heating purposes. In warmer climates, the heat generated by the lighting system is often sufficient to warm the premises.

Units to cool the air consist of two types: central units found in most new office buildings, and self-contained units that are often installed in buildings that were not constructed with centralized air-cooling units. One means of determining whether or not the installation of an air-cooling system can be justified in relation to its cost is to determine the anticipated increase in worker efficiency. The services of professional consultants are recommended when the installation of an air-cooling system is being considered.

Humidity Level

For the maximum comfort, the humidity level in an office should range somewhere between 40–60 percent, with the optimum humidity level somewhere around 50 percent. A year-round air conditioning system humidifies the air in the winter and dehumidifies it in the summer.

The humidity level has an impact on the temperature level. If the humidity level is within the recommended range, the actual temperature in an office can be decreased and still be comfortable. If the humidity level is less than the recommended range, the temperature will have to be increased to achieve the same degree of comfort.

Circulation of Air

The air in working areas must be properly circulated if an air conditioning system is to have its maximum impact. Without some air circulation, the temperature of the air that surrounds an individual tends to increase, thus causing a certain amount of discomfort. An adequate circulation standard is approximately twenty-five cubic feet of air per person per minute. Air that is being circulated at too fast a rate becomes noticeable because of the draft that it creates. An acceptable standard for air circulation is approximately fifty feet per minute. Circulation of air is very necessary in certain office areas. For example, circulation helps remove the unpleasant odors produced by the ink required by some printing processes.

Cleanliness of Air   Devices designed to cleanse the air are being installed with increasing frequency in office buildings. These devices cleanse the air of germs, as well as of dust and dirt. While ultraviolet lights are useful for killing germ-laden bacteria, mechanical filters are used to remove dust and other foreign particles. Because of the sensitivity of data processing equipment, a dust-free atmosphere is essential in the data processing center.

Music   The use of music in offices is very widespread and appears to be on the increase. There are several beneficial results of installing a music system. Music helps to relieve the job boredom and monotony that cause a decrease in productivity and job satisfaction. Music also has the general effect of relieving mental and physical fatigue and reducing nervous tension and strain. Depending on the type of music being played, it can also have a stimulating effect on employees. Music also has a positive effect on employees' attitudes, which results in their making fewer errors and their being absent and tardy less often.

Several different alternatives are possible for developing a music system. One commonly used system is the purchase of music from a service vendor who specializes in programming music for offices. One such vendor is Muzak. Organizations that adopt a service vendor for a music system are typically charged according to the number of employees in the organization.

Other alternatives are to use a local FM radio station as the music source. When a radio station is employed, special auxiliary equipment can be obtained that shuts the system down during the time that commercials and news broadcasts are being transmitted. A third alternative is for an organization to provide its own music source—through either tapes or records. In most cases, conventional public address systems satisfactorily accommodate each of the alternatives discussed above.

Much of the success of a music system depends greatly upon the nature of the music programming. For example, the kind of work being performed should be used to determine the types of music—show tunes, classical numbers, semiclassical numbers, and popular tunes—that should be played. Employees whose work requires a high degree of concentration should be subjected to nothing but the most subdued music.

Another factor to consider in music programming is the time of the work day that the music will be played in relation to its intended impact on the employees. It is psychologically advantageous to play more stimulating music during the time of day when employees' efficiency is not up to par because of fatigue and boredom. Fatigue is generally most noticeable midway through the morning and afternoon work periods and just before the lunch hour and quitting time.

Research has also shown that when music is played continuously, it soon loses its full impact because employees are no longer conscious of its presence. Therefore, short breaks in the music program will tend to cause employees to be more conscious of its presence. An on-for-fifteen-minutes, off-for-fifteen minutes cycle is generally recommended.

Review Questions

1. As measured in foot-candles, what is an adequate amount of light for most office work?

2. What is the maximum amount of light, as measured by brightness, recommended for an office area?

3. When the contrast of light exceeds a three to one ratio, what is the effect on humans?

4. Compare and contrast the five different kinds of lighting systems. What are the advantages and disadvantages of each?

5. What is meant by complementary colors, split complementary colors, and triad colors? How is each used in developing a color scheme?

6. As a measure of noise, what is the average decibel level in most offices?

7. Review the characteristics that sound-absorbing materials should possess.

8. What are the desirable temperature, humidity, and circulation levels for most offices?

9. What is the principal factor used to determine the nature of the music that is most appropriate for different times during the day?

Minicases

The Garner Insurance Company leases office space in a seventy-year-old building in downtown Peoria, Illinois. The lessor, in order to keep the building occupied, has given the various tenants a "good deal" on the rent. Because of the low rent, the lessor has always said "no" when a tenant has asked that the environment of the premises be improved. The employees of the Garner Insurance Company have frequently complained to the owners of the company about the poor environment of the premises. Because the lessor refuses to improve the premises, the insurance company offsets the poor environment with fairly liberal fringe benefits for its employees. The fringe benefits tend to appease the employees for a short period of time, but after a few months, they again ask that something be done about the environment. Describe the effect that the poor environment is likely to have over a period of time on the employees. Do you think the company is justified in using fringe benefits to appease its employees? Why or why not?

*   *   *

Various individuals in the Ramsey Hospital Supply Company have long felt the need for a music system in the building. You, the administrative office manager of the company, have been made responsible for drawing up a set of guidelines for the design of the music system. It is felt that over the long run, it would probably be less expensive for the company to develop its own system than to use a music vendor. The switchboard operator is to be responsible for operating the system, which will use the public address system that is already in the building. What guidelines can you suggest for designing the format of the music that will be used in the new system? How might the value of the system be assessed once it has been functioning for severals months?

Case

The Kermit Insurance Corporation, an independent agency, is located in an Illinois town of 75,000 residents. The fact that the corporation represents twelve different insurance companies makes it the largest independent agency in the city.

The corporation owns the small building in which it is located. The building, now about thirty-five years old, is in good condition but lacks some of the conveniences of newer buildings. Because of the ideal location of the building, the corporation is reluctant to move.

Several years ago, small window air-cooling units were installed in the ten agents' offices. The units are so small that no significant cooling takes place in the general office area of the six office employees.

The corporation has been plagued by excessive turnover in recent years. Many of the office employees who leave state that the unpleasant conditions of the office play a significant part in their decision to seek employment elsewhere. The office supervisor also frequently states that she feels productivity would increase if the environment of the office were more suitable during the warm weather.

Mr. Kermit recently had a building contractor make an estimate of the cost of installing a centralized air conditioning system. The estimate was $21,000. The contractor suggested that the annual cost of operating the system could run as high as $700, but this could be partially offset by the increased productivity of the employees, perhaps as much as 10–15 percent. In other words, the same amount of work could be performed by fewer employees. The average weekly payroll of the six office employees is $710.

1. Assuming that the installation of an air conditioning system would increase productivity by 15 percent during the five months that it would be used, how long will it take for the system to pay for itself?

2. On this basis, do you think the system can be justified? Why or why not?

3. What other benefits besides reduced turnover and increased productivity might result from the installation of such a system?

Office Equipment and Furniture

Chapter
6

Office Equipment
> Planning Considerations
>> Equipment considerations
>> Vendor considerations
>> Maintenance considerations
> Leasing Considerations
> Equipment Maintenance Considerations
>> Service contract
>> Call basis
>> In-house service
> Replacement Considerations
> Inventory Control Considerations

Office Furniture
> New Developments in Office Furniture
>> Modular design
>> Portable design
>> Functional design
> Advantages of New Developments

Chapter Aims   After studying this chapter, the student should be able to:

1. Identify and discuss several of the factors that must be considered in the selection of office equipment.

2. Identify the factors that should be considered when determining which of the following alternatives is more advantageous: leasing or purchasing office equipment.

3. Explain the differences between true leases, leases with the option to purchase, and sale-leaseback.

4. Identify the advantages and disadvantages of the following methods of equipment maintenance: service contracts, call basis, and in-house maintenance department.

5. Identify the types of information that should be kept on each piece of equipment for inventory control purposes.

6. Identify and discuss some of the factors that should be considered in selecting office furniture.

7. Explain modular design, portable design, and functional design as these characteristics relate to the design of modern office furniture.

Chapter Terms   *True lease:* a type of lease in which the lessee never intends to purchase the equipment or furniture being leased.

Lease with the option to purchase: the type of lease in which the lessee may exercise the option to purchase at some time in the future.

Office equipment and furniture represent a significant investment for any organization. The selection of such equipment and furniture is likely to be either partially or wholly the responsibility of the administrative office manager. Because of the vast number of products now available and because of the amount of the organization's investment, extreme care must be taken if the organization is to receive an adequate return on its investment. Without exercising a sufficient amount of care in selecting the equipment and furniture, one or more of the following are likely to result: the equipment fails to meet the needs for which it was obtained; the furniture is not sufficiently functional; the organization is unable to receive an adequate return on its investment; or the equipment or furniture, although adequate at the time it was purchased, is no longer adequate.

Office Equipment

The process of selecting new office equipment is frequently a very time-consuming process, especially if the amount of equipment to be selected represents a major investment to the organization. If only a small amount of equipment is being selected, the process may not consume as much time.

Planning Considerations

A variety of factors needs to be considered in selecting new office equipment. The number of factors to be considered and their importance are likely to be determined by the type of equipment and it uses. While some types of office equipment require the consideration of only a minimum number of factors, other types of office equipment require the consideration of all factors.

In many instances, it is possible to undertake comparative analyses of the various brands of equipment being considered. The various equipment brands are often compared on the basis of the functions of the equipment, the equipment manufacturers, and the equipment vendors.

The following provides a discussion of the factors that should be considered in selecting new office equipment. Each factor is classified as an equipment consideration, a vendor consideration, or a maintenance consideration.

Equipment considerations include:

1. *Needs of the equipment.* Before a new piece of equipment can be selected, the needs of the equipment must be determined. The needs of the equipment can be either partially or wholly determined by the work that is to be processed by the equipment. Too often organizations either purchase or lease equipment that is more sophisticated than is needed for processing work. Therefore, those equipment functions that are never used add to the cost of the equipment and lower the organization's return on its investment. If the piece of new equipment is to be used to process

work that is part of the organization's operating systems, it is advisable to have someone who is familiar with the operating systems determine the needs of the equipment. One of the most frequent reasons equipment fails to meet the needs for which it was obtained is that the needs of the equipment were not accurately or completely determined.

2. *Determination of appropriate equipment.* Once the needs of the equipment have been determined, it is now possible to determine which pieces of equipment most appropriately meet these needs. Since it is very likely that the equipment needs can be adequately met by several different pieces of equipment, a fairly comprehensive search of appropriate equipment should be undertaken. One of the most commonly used means of determining the appropriate equipment is to provide the equipment vendors with detailed descriptions of the types of work that the equipment will be used to process. The vendors can then determine which equipment is appropriate. This step is generally not as important with low cost, nonspecialized equipment as with high-cost, specialized equipment.

3. *Dependability of equipment.* Once the various pieces of appropriate equipment have been identified, the dependability of the equipment has to be assessed. While some equipment manufacturers have reputations for producing dependable office equipment, others do not enjoy the same reputation. Several different means are used to determine the dependability of equipment. One means is to contact other organizations who utilize the same type of equipment. Although most equipment vendors very willingly provide the names of their most satisfied customers, other users of the same equipment should also be contacted, if possible. The names of other users of the same equipment can usually be readily obtained. In some instances, nonreferred users may provide a more realistic evaluation than those users referred by equipment vendors. Another means of determining the dependability of the equipment is to read equipment reports compiled by such independent organizations as Buyers Laboratory, Inc., a New York–based testing firm. A final means of determining the dependability of equipment, although not always completely reliable, is to evaluate the dependability of other equipment of the same brand that is already being used in the organization.

4. *Specifications of the equipment.* Although not important for all types of equipment, the specifications of certain types of equipment are very important. The specifications, as used in this chapter, refer to such items as equipment size, electrical requirements, installation requirements, and special structural requirements. Some equipment, although suitable in all other respects, has to be eliminated from consideration because of inappropriate specifications.

5. *Cost of the equipment.* The cost of the equipment has a significant impact on the organization's return on its investment. While the cost of the equipment is very important, some organizations place too much emphasis on this factor. The result is the selection of equipment

that is less expensive than competitors' equipment. If the selected equipment fails to perform as well as competitors' equipment or is less efficient than competitors' equipment, the result may be a lower return on the investment.

6. *Operational processes of the equipment.* Some specialized office equipment requires the use of certain supplies for the operation of the equipment. For example, certain copying machines and printing equipment require the use of specialized supplies (fluids, inks, toners, and so forth). The necessity of such specialized supplies should be determined, as well as the interchangeability of supplies. Some organizations eliminate from consideration the purchasing of equipment that requires the use of supplies restricted to certain brands of equipment.

7. *Safety features.* The safety features of office equipment should be a primary consideration when selecting the equipment. While most routine types of office equipment are not hazardous, certain types of equipment used in printing and duplicating processes are not as safe when employees are careless. Therefore, the nature of the safety features on the equipment should be evaluated.

8. *Flexibility of equipment.* More and more equipment is being manufactured that is capable of being modified with add-on attachments. These attachments are frequently added as the need arises. Although such attachments may not be needed at the time of the purchase of the equipment, consideration should be given to the possibility of future need. It is, therefore, important to give this factor adequate consideration at the time the equipment is purchased. Another dimension of the flexibility of the equipment is its possible use for a variety of work processes. Since some equipment can be used for a wider variety of work processes than can other equipment, the extent of the flexibility of the equipment should be thoroughly evaluated.

9. *Ease of equipment operation.* Another of the factors to consider when selecting equipment is the ease with which the equipment is operated. Some of the more specialized office equipment is easier to operate than is other equipment. One of the more efficient means of determining the ease with which the equipment is operated is to seek input from individuals who operate the various types of equipment being considered. To make a comparative analysis, it may also be possible to have the equipment vendors outline in detail the steps involved in using the equipment to perform various work processes.

10. *Speed of equipment operation.* In some instances, the operational speed of the equipment is a very important consideration. If this is the case and if the operating speeds are quite variable, the different pieces of equipment being considered should be compared in terms of operating speed.

11. *Cost of equipment operation.* The per-unit cost of producing work is especially important when selecting equipment that is to be used

in high-volume operations. Although the per-unit cost may be quite similar for the various pieces of equipment being considered, over a period of time the differences in per-unit costs may be quite significant. The per-unit cost is especially important when selecting printing, duplicating, and copying equipment since the various operating processes are quite variable, thus significantly affecting the per-unit cost.

12. *Equipment operator input.* The employees who will be responsible for operating the equipment are often given an opportunity to provide input into deciding which piece of equipment to select. Not only is this advantageous for selecting equipment that will satisfy the employees but it also gives employees a feeling of recognition. It should be pointed out that unless employees are satisfied with the operation of a particular piece of equipment, there is a chance that they will not use the equipment as efficiently as it might otherwise be used.

13. *Standardization of equipment.* Most organizations find it advantageous to have as few different brands of equipment as possible. The result is standardization of equipment. Several advantages result from this practice. The organization may be able to take advantage of quantity purchasing as well as to reduce its service costs because of having fewer brands of equipment to maintain. Another advantage is the ease with which various employees can operate the similar pieces of equipment.

Vendor considerations include:

1. *Reputation of the equipment vendor.* Because most office equipment is obtained through equipment vendors, the reputation of the vendors must be considered. Factors that determine the vendor's reputation include: age of the vendor firm, size of the firm, services provided by the firm, financial stability of the firm, range of equipment sold by the firm, and community attitude toward the firm. Most organizations are more concerned about the reputation of the vendor firm when purchasing specialized, high-cost equipment than when purchasing low-cost nonspecialized equipment.

2. *Training provided by the manufacturer or equipment vendor.* Because of the specialized nature of many of the new types of office equipment, employee training on the equipment may be necessary. The quality of the training experiences provided by the various manufacturers or vendors are not equal in all instances. Whereas some vendors provide training only at the time the equipment is installed, others will provide training whenever a new operator uses the equipment. Thus, if the original equipment operator leaves the organization, the vendor will provide training experiences for the replacement operator. When specialized equipment is being considered, it is important to investigate the nature of the training experiences that are provided by the manufacturer or vendor.

3. *Purchasing options.* Some vendors only sell certain types of equipment, while others lease as well as sell equipment. If an organization is interested only in purchasing or leasing equipment, this factor needs to be considered early in the selection process. The advantages and disadvantages of purchasing and leasing are discussed in detail in another section of this chapter.

4. *Delivery of the new equipment.* The timing of equipment purchase or replacement cannot always be planned. Because of circumstances over which the organization has no control, the immediate delivery of new equipment may be very important. Therefore, equipment that is not available for immediate delivery may have to be eliminated from consideration.

Maintenance considerations are:

1. *Servicing the equipment.* The ability to obtain fast, reliable service on the equipment is another factor that should be considered in selecting equipment. This is especially true in situations when no backup equipment is available to perform crucial work processes. Since some equipment vendors do not provide the same quality of equipment servicing as others, this factor should be carefully weighed, especially when purchasing expensive, intricate equipment. In addition, the geographical location of the vendor may be important. Vendors who are located quite a distance from the organization may not be able to provide rapid service.

2. *Equipment maintenance.* Another factor to be considered is the routine equipment maintenance required of the equipment operator. This factor is important to consider because some equipment requires more routine maintenance than comparable equipment. An investigation of the nature of equipment maintenance is especially important when purchasing printing, duplicating, and copying equipment since the maintenance of such equipment varies considerably.

Leasing Considerations

Some organizations find it more advantageous to lease various pieces of office equipment than to purchase the equipment. The decision of leasing versus purchasing should be carefully thought out. When one of the two alternatives is clearly an advantage, that alternative should be chosen. The factors that should be considered in determining whether leasing or purchasing is more advantageous are summarized as follows:

1. *How rapidly are new technological developments occurring in the type of equipment being considered?* If the type of equipment is characterized as changing significantly because of technological developments, it may be advantageous to lease the equipment. Thus, the organization is able continually to update its equipment.

2. *What is the purchase cost of the equipment?* Some of the more expensive office equipment is leased rather than purchased. When equipment is obtained in this way, capital that may be more urgently needed for other uses is not tied up in expensive equipment.

3. *What leasing arrangements are equipment vendors willing to provide?* Although most equipment vendors in a given geographical area are quite competitive in terms of the leasing arrangements, some vendors may provide conditions that make leasing more advantageous than purchasing. In such cases, leasing should be given serious consideration.

4. *What special provisions are made available when leasing equipment?* In some instances, the lessor is responsible for equipment maintenance. Some organizations find this to be a very significant cause for leasing rather than purchasing office equipment.

5. *How stable are the various work processes for which the equipment is needed?* If it is anticipated that the work processes will change significantly during the life of the equipment, leasing should be given serious consideration. Thus, the organization does not have the responsibility of trying to sell a piece of equipment that is no longer needed or that does not adequately meet its work-processing requirements.

6. *What is the per-unit cost of work when leasing equipment as opposed to purchasing equipment?* When the equipment is to be used for high-volume operations, the per-unit cost of each of the two alternatives should be determined. If the leasing alternative is considerably less costly over a period of time, leasing may be more desirable than purchasing the equipment.

Several different alternatives exist for leasing office equipment. Leases consist of two types: **True leases** and **leases with the option to purchase.** A true lease is one in which the lessee never intends to purchase the equipment being leased. A lease with an option to purchase is one in which the lessee may exercise an option to purchase at some point in the future. A true lease may be obtained for a short period of time or for a longer period of time with an option to renew. Short-term leases are frequently used for obtaining equipment when the organization's work load is especially heavy for a short period of time. Thus, rather than having to pay on a lease for a long period of time or having to purchase the additional equipment, it can be obtained for a short period of time. Another type of true lease, the long-term with option to renew, is used for leasing equipment that will be needed for a period of several years. At the end of the initial lease period, some lessors give lessees a lower cost lease upon renewal.

A lease with the option to purchase is also used for obtaining office equipment. At the end of the lease period, or at any point during the time that the lease is in effect, the lessee has an option to purchase the equipment. The amount that the lessee has paid on the lease is usually applied to the cost of purchasing the equipment. Some organizations use this alternative to determine how well the equipment will meet its needs before purchasing the equipment.

Another alternative, although not too commonly used for obtaining office equipment, is sale-leaseback. This alternative involves the organization's purchase of the equipment, which is then sold to a lessor, who then gives the organization a lease on the equipment. This alternative is advantageous to organizations that need capital in a short period of time.

Although some use the terms *equipment leasing* and *equipment rental* synonymously, differences between the two terms are likely to exist. Leasing frequently involves a contract clearly stipulating the length of time the lease is in effect. Rental, on the other hand, may not require the lessee to use the equipment for a specified period. Thus, the equipment can be returned to its owner at any time with no additional financial obligations.

Leasing office equipment results in several advantages:

1. Leasing conserves capital that may be needed for other purposes. Because the organization does not invest its working capital in leased equipment, this capital is available for other uses, such as expansion, construction, and so forth.

2. The organization is able to obtain up-to-date equipment. When an organization leases equipment, the financial cost of exchanging obsolete equipment for new equipment is less than the cost of purchasing new equipment.

3. Lease payments are tax deductible if the lessee holds a true lease rather than a lease with the option to purchase. A lease with an option to purchase is considered to be a conditional sales contract and, thus, is not deductible.

4. Leasing equipment enables an organization to more effectively utilize its financial resources. A short-term lease is advantageous for obtaining equipment that is needed for only a short period of time each year. An organization that purchases equipment for such purposes is unable to maximize the return on its investment.

While leasing office equipment results in several advantages, several distinct disadvantages also result. The disadvantages of leasing office equipment include:

1. Leased office equipment is frequently more costly than purchased equipment. The total lease payments frequently exceed the purchase price of the piece of equipment.

2. The lease may stipulate that the lessee is responsible for equipment maintenance and repairs. If this is the case and if the piece of equipment has a higher-than-average service record, the leased equipment may become very costly.

3. Most leases stipulate that the lessee keep detailed records on the leased equipment. If this is the case and if the organization leases a considerable amount of equipment, the paperwork may become quite burdensome.

4. If the lease gives the lessee an opportunity to purchase the equipment, the lease payments are not tax deductible. The payments are deductible only if the lease is classified as a true lease.

A fairly new development in leasing office equipment is the emergence of leasing companies. Rather than lease equipment from an equipment vendor or from the equipment manufacturer, some organizations extensively employ the services provided by leasing companies. When equipment is leased from a leasing company, the company acts as a third party between the lessee and the manufacturer. Thus, the leasing company purchases the desired equipment from the manufacturer and then leases the equipment to the lessee. One desirable characteristic of leasing companies is the flexibility of the leasing arrangements they provide.

Equipment
Maintenance
Considerations

Because of the mechanical nature of most types of office equipment, maintenance is a very important function, not only because of the detrimental effect of improper maintenance on equipment, but also because of the cost of equipment maintenance. The life of office equipment is often affected by the quality of the maintenance given the equipment. Day-by-day operator maintenance is also very important for increasing the longevity of equipment and for decreasing the number of equipment repairs.

Equipment maintenance is typically provided by one or more of the following three methods: service contract with a representative of the equipment manufacturer or service agency; service on a call basis with a representative of the equipment manufacturer or service agency providing the service; and an in-house service department. Some organizations put a portion of their equipment on a service contract and the remainder of the equipment is maintained on a call basis. Each of the three methods is explained in the following paragraphs.

Service contract. This method of equipment maintenance involves a service contract with a representative of the equipment manufacturer or with a service agency. Most contracts are valid for a period of one year. During the term of the contract, the representatives of the equipment manufacturer or service agency are responsible not only for equipment repairs but also for routine maintenance, such as cleaning and lubrication. Some service contracts specify that the equipment will receive a thorough cleaning and lubrication once a year, in addition to a specified number of routine inspections during the year. Thus, a distinct characteristic of this method is the preventive maintenance that it provides. Depending upon the nature of the contract, the cost of minor replacement parts may be covered by the contract, while the owner of the equipment may be responsible for the cost of major replacement parts.

Service contracts provide some important benefits. Perhaps the most important is the provision of preventive maintenance that is a characteristic of the system. Another advantage is the reduction of paperwork that is involved. If maintenance is provided on a call basis, the amount of paperwork involved in preparing vouchers and checks is quite extensive over a period of time. When a service contract is used, the paperwork is processed once a year.

The most significant disadvantage of service contracts is their cost. Depending on the provisions of the contract and the type of equipment covered by the contract, the cost may range from $30 to $40 per year. Thus, equipment that needs no repairs will cost as much in terms of maintenance as equipment that needs frequent repairs. Although service contracts may be quite costly, their cost can be partially offset in a variety of ways, thus making their use more feasible. Because of preventive maintenance, equipment may last longer, which helps to offset the cost of the contract. The cost can also be partially offset by the reduced amount of paperwork.

Call basis. When equipment is maintained on a call basis, the representative of the equipment manufacturer or service agency is called each time the equipment needs to be repaired. Unless special provisions are made, the equipment does not receive the yearly cleaning and lubrication that is provided by service contracts. The owner of the equipment, therefore, pays only for services performed.

In comparison to a service contract, this method of equipment maintenance appears on the surface to be less costly. But when the cost of preparing payment invoices and checks and the lack of preventive maintenance are considered, the call basis may be more expensive than having a service contract on the equipment.

In-house service. Large organizations frequently have their own in-house service departments. This means that they employ individuals trained to service the equipment. Because of frequent changes in equipment technology, these employees have to periodically receive additional training. Therefore, in addition to the salaries of these individuals, the organization must consider the fringe benefits as well as the cost of retraining. It is for these reasons that this method of equipment maintenance is frequently feasible only for larger organizations. When an organization has its own in-house service, the different brands of equipment are frequently kept to a very minimum number. Thus, the organization may not be able to achieve the flexibility that is possible when a greater number of brands of equipment are utilized.

When an in-house service department is utilized, equipment can frequently be repaired more rapidly than is possible with either of the other two methods. This has a significant impact on equipment downtime. When the service department is not busy with equipment repair, preventive maintenance on equipment can be performed. In addition to the cost of staffing the in-house service department, equipment parts and tools must be considered.

When deciding which of the three methods of equipment maintenance to utilize, several variables should be considered:

1. The cost and provisions of a service contract.
2. The frequency of equipment repair.
3. The impact of preventive maintenance on increasing the life of the equipment.
4. The availability of and expense incurred in employing trained service employees.
5. The number of different brands of office equipment owned by the organization.
6. The type of equipment to be maintained.
7. The cost of paperwork associated with equipment maintenance.
8. The speed with which the equipment must be repaired.

Replacement Considerations

Another concern of the administrative office manager is equipment replacement. The efficiency of equipment replacement is greatly determined by the replacement procedures followed by the organization. The useful life of office equipment is frequently determined by the amount of usage the equipment receives, as well as by the nature of the equipment. Thus, equipment that receives a high degree of usage or that tends to become obsolete quite rapidly may be depreciated over a shorter period of time than other types of equipment. For example, a typewriter that is used most of each work day may be depreciated over a five-year period, while an adding machine that is seldomly used may be depreciated over a ten-year period. At the end of the depreciation period, the equipment is traded in for new equipment.

It is not always financially feasible to keep office equipment for the length of time the equipment is being depreciated. Perhaps technology or work processes change, thus making the present equipment inefficient. Perhaps a particular piece of equipment has a very frequent breakdown record. The organization may consider accelerating the trade-in time. In other instances, some equipment may be in excellent condition and have a good repair record at the time it is to be traded in. In such instances, some organizations keep this equipment for a longer period of time.

Systematic replacement procedures facilitate the yearly budget-preparation process. By knowing which equipment is to be replaced each year, the replacement costs can be accurately reflected in the budget.

Thus, the organization is able to more accurately predict its financial needs.

Inventory Control Considerations

Another important function typically delegated to the administrative office manager is equipment inventory. Without accurate inventory records, control over expensive office equipment is difficult to obtain. Inventory control involves keeping detailed records on each piece of equipment. Such information might include:

1. The serial number of each piece of equipment owned, leased, or rented by the organization.
2. The date the equipment was purchased, leased, or rented.
3. The purchase cost of the equipment.
4. The life of the equipment (either actual life or lease life).
5. The yearly depreciation of the equipment.
6. The book value of the equipment.
7. The location of each piece of equipment.
8. The organization's identification number assigned to the equipment.
9. The costs involved in servicing the equipment.

For control purposes, it is important that the equipment inventory records be kept up to date. Otherwise, little will be gained by maintaining an equipment inventory. Most organizations undertake a detailed equipment inventory on a yearly basis. The inventory is undertaken to determine whether or not the equipment is located where its record indicates that it is located and to make sure that all equipment can be accounted for.

Office Furniture

The selection of office furniture should receive the same amount of attention that the selection of office equipment receives. The effect of improperly selected office furniture may be felt for a long period of time because furniture, being typically owned rather than leased, is not easily disposed of. In addition, the fact that the life of office furniture is quite long makes its proper selection even more critical.

The selection of office furniture should be guided by several factors. The impact of these factors should be thoroughly determined before office furniture is selected.

1. *The intended use of the furniture.* Before the appropriate furniture can be selected, the intended use of the furniture must be thoroughly analyzed. To select furniture without first considering the intended use often results in inappropriately selected furniture.

2. *The appropriateness of the furniture in relation to the decor of the office.* The coordination of the office furniture with the decor of the

office significantly determines the appropriateness of office furniture. Since most offices are redecorated several times during the life of office furniture, the adaptability of the furniture should also be considered. To select office furniture that is only appropriate for the present decor is a questionable practice.

3. *The suitability of the furniture for the individuals who will use the furniture.* A considerable amount of employee fatigue can be eliminated if the various pieces of furniture can be adjusted to meet the needs of the employees who use the furniture. Much of the office furniture presently manufactured is adjustable in a variety of ways in order to compensate for the variability of physical characteristics of employees.

4. *The versatility of the furniture.* It is not uncommon for most types of office furniture to have more than one purpose. It is therefore important when selecting office furniture to investigate the versatility of the furniture. To select office furniture that serves only one purpose is questionable if more versatile furniture is available and feasible.

5. *The durability of the furniture.* The durability of the furniture is determined by the construction process and the materials used in the construction process. For example, metal furniture is generally considered to be more durable than wooden furniture. The durability of the furniture is likely to have a direct impact on the length of life of the furniture.

6. *The hierarchical level of the individual for whom the furniture is being purchased.* Because certain types of office furniture are more prestigious than other types, the prestige of the furniture should be matched with the hierarchical level of the individual who will be using the furniture. Thus, employees at higher hierarchical levels should have more prestigious furniture, while employees at lower hierarchical levels should have less prestigious furniture. Prestige of the furniture is frequently determined by the materials used in the construction process, the size of the furniture, and the special design characteristics of the furniture.

7. *The size of the furniture in relation to room or area size.* When selecting new office furniture, the size of the area or room in which the furniture is to be placed must be considered. Selecting furniture that is too large for the area causes several problems. A safety hazard is likely to be created, since sufficient aisle or corridor space may not be possible. In addition, the aesthetics of the area may not be maximized.

New Developments in Office Furniture

Over the years, new developments in office furniture have been quite substantial. Many of the developments can be characterized as possessing one or more of the following characteristics: modular design, portable design, and functional design. Each of these three characteristics is discussed in the following sections.

Modular design. This characteristic refers to the design of office furniture that provides many variations in the furniture components and variation in the arrangement of the components. In many instances, a modular unit consists of several different components, including desk or working space, storage space, file space, and shelf space. In order to determine the components that are needed in the modular unit, the nature of the employee's job duties are considered. Thus, those employees whose jobs require greater amounts of working space and less storage space are given sufficient working space. In many cases, modular design results in self-contained work stations, such as illustrated in Figure 4–7. The self-contained work stations, in addition to containing the necessary working and storage space areas, also contain electrical and telephone connections.

Portable design. The increasing utilization of open space planning in office layout has increased the need for portability of office furniture. One of the characteristics of open space planning is the ease with which office areas can be rearranged. To facilitate the rearrangement of an office area, portable office furniture is very desirable. Movable partitions, such as those illustrated in Figure 4–6, are an example of portable office furniture. Movable partitions, which are used to accomplish the same purposes as permanent walls, are advantageous since extensive remodeling is not required when there is a need to rearrange office space. Thus, office space can be easily rearranged when certain functional areas need greater amounts of space while other functional areas need less space.

Functional design. This characteristic refers to the design of office furniture based on individual needs. The design of much of the new office furniture is based on an analysis of work processes and employees' effort in the performance of their jobs. Much of the new office furniture has a research base. To illustrate, if the employee is able to perform job duties more effectively in a standing position than in a sitting position, furniture is readily available to accommodate the user. Office furniture with functional design is made possible to a great extent because of the considerable number of modular furniture components that are now on the market.

Figure 6–1 illustrates the three design characteristics of new developments in office furniture.

Advantages of New Developments

The use of office furniture that incorporates the three design characteristics discussed in the section above results in significant advantages:

1. The furniture takes into consideration user needs, thus improving employee morale and production levels.

2. The cost of changing office layout is considerably less than when permanent walls have to be moved.

3. Office space can be completely reorganized in one or two days' time, thus significantly reducing downtime.

FIGURE 6–1   Line Drawing Showing New Developments in Office Furniture

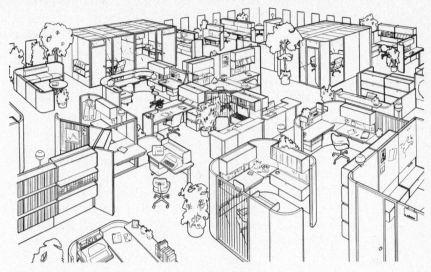

Courtesy School Arts Magazine, *Davis Publications, Inc.*

4. Depending upon the circumstances, the furniture may be considered as office equipment rather than real estate, thus resulting in faster depreciation and lower taxes.

5. Lighting, heating, and air conditioning facilities are more efficiently utilized, thus conserving energy requirements.

6. The furniture, being portable, can be easily removed from one building location to another, thus simplifying office moves.

Review Questions

1. How can the dependability of equipment be determined?

2. Why is the ability to obtain fast, reliable service on equipment an important factor to consider when selecting new equipment?

3. Why is the flexibility of equipment an important factor to consider when selecting new equipment?

4. If a particular line of equipment is experiencing rapid technological advancements, is purchasing or leasing generally more advantageous? Why?

5. In what ways do equipment leasing and equipment rental differ?

6. What advantages and disadvantages result from equipment leasing?

7. What services are provided by leasing companies?

8. What factors should be considered when determining

whether service contracts, call basis, or an in-house maintenance department would be most advantageous for equipment maintenance?

9. How do functional design and modular design of office furniture differ from one another?

Minicases

The Danielson Company, which was founded nearly fifteen years ago, is a full-line paper supplier. At the time the company was founded, only minimum attention was given to its equipment. The company has no regular replacement policy, nor does the company have an equipment inventory control plan. During the last several months, several pieces of equipment have been misplaced for a period of time. Several managers feel that if the company had an equipment inventory control program, misplaced equipment or stolen equipment would be more easily found. In developing an inventory control program, what information should be kept on each piece of equipment? Besides helping locate misplaced or stolen equipment, how else might this information be used?

*   *   *

Several administrators of the Douglas Corporation are at the present time giving thought to putting each of the firm's typewriters on a service contract, which costs $35 per year per typewriter. At the present time, the corporation uses the "call basis" method of equipment maintenance. The firm trades in typewriters on a seven-year rotation plan. In deciding whether a service contract method or call basis would be more advantageous for this organization, what factors are you going to consider? On the basis of the cost of the equipment maintenance, how might you determine which of the two methods of maintenance would be more advantageous?

Case

The Thomas Bakery Company provides about 70 percent of the bakery goods for food stores in the western and northern suburbs of Chicago. The firm, which has been in existence for only ten years, experienced very rapid growth during the first five years of existence. The firm is still increasing its market but not as rapidly as the first few years of its existence.

Because of the near phenomenal growth of the firm in its first years of existence, many of its management practices were hastily carried out. More emphasis seemed to be placed on getting a task completed than on the efficiency with which a task was completed. A good example of this situation involves the purchasing and/or leasing of a variety of pieces of office equipment. While some of the equipment can be obtained only through a purchase option, other equipment can be obtained through either a purchase or a lease option. In the last several months, several instances have been discovered in which equipment was purchased when a lease arrangement would have been more advantageous and vice versa. The result is increased costs for the firm, which has had a negative impact on the firm's financial picture.

Because of the firm's recent problems with purchasing and leasing office equipment, several of the firm's managers have suggested that a set of guidelines be developed to determine whether a specific piece of equipment should be purchased or leased.

1. What guidelines should be used to determine whether equipment should be purchased or leased?

2. How might the effectiveness of your guidelines be evaluated once they are being utilized?

Office Communication Services and Devices

Chapter
7

The Mailroom
   Mailroom Personnel
   Mailroom Layout
   Mailroom Equipment
      Addresser-printer equipment
      Opening equipment
      Stamping-sealing equipment
      Automatic envelope emptiers
      Label preparation equipment
      Inserting equipment
      Bundling equipment
   Use of Alternative Delivery Methods

Mechanical Devices for Transportation of Internal Correspondence
   Pneumatic tubes
   Conveyor systems

Telephone Service and Devices
   Telephone Systems
      PBX
      PAX
      CENTREX
   Alternative Telephone Services
      WATS
      Telpak
      Wideband Data Service
   Grade of Service
   Special Telephone Services and Devices
      Dial intercoms
      Manual intercoms
      Line illumination
      Voice amplifiers
      Automatic dialers
      Answering devices
   Other Devices Using Telephone Lines
      Facsimile devices
      Teletypewriter devices
      Picturephone
      Data-Phone
   Telephone Interconnect Equipment

Telegraph Services and Devices
   Telex
   TWX
   WIREFAX

Intraorganizational Communication Devices
TELautograph
Intrafax
Closed-circuit television
Paging systems

Chapter Aims   After studying this chapter, the student should be able to:

1. Identify and discuss the factors that determine the personnel, layout, and equipment requirements of the mailroom.
2. Identify the working areas that must be contained in a large mailroom.
3. Explain the differences between PBX, PAX, and CENTREX telephone systems.
4. Discuss Telpak and Wideband Data Service.
5. Explain the meaning of telephone grade of service.
6. Explain how a dial intercom device functions.
7. Explain the differences between Telex and TWX.
8. Explain the uses of TELautograph and Intrafax equipment.

Chapter Terms   *PBX (Private Branch Exchange):* a telephone system that has a switchboard or console for incoming and outgoing calls. Interoffice calls can be dialed by the employee.

PAX (Private Automatic Exchange): a telephone system that has a switchboard or console for incoming calls. Outgoing calls and interoffice calls can be dialed by the employee.

CENTREX (Central Exchange): a telephone system that does not require a switchboard or console. Employees have individual telephone numbers that enable them to receive incoming calls without going through the switchboard or console. Employees can dial their own outgoing and interoffice calls.

WATS (Wide Area Telephone Service): a billing method for long distance telephone service. For a flat monthly toll, subscribers can use the WATS line either for an unlimited amount of time each month or for a limited number of minutes, depending upon the billing plan.

Telpak: a service provided by American Telephone and Telegraph that enables a subscriber to lease on a full-time basis telephone lines between two specific locations.

Wideband Data Service: a system that selects the proper width band for the type of data being transmitted through telephone lines. The faster that data is transmitted through the lines, the wider the band has to be.

Grade of service: the leasing of an adequate number of telephone circuits to handle an organization's telephone service.

Facsimile devices: a mechanical device that uses telephone lines to transmit a reproduction of a document from one location to another.

Data-Phone: a device that is used to transmit and receive coded data for input into a computer.

Telephone interconnect service: a service that enables an organization to either purchase or lease its telephone equipment from a private manufacturer. Telephone lines are leased from the telephone company.

Office employees spend a considerable portion of their working time utilizing the various communication services and devices found in offices. The managers and executives of organizations are also very likely to spend a sizeable portion of their working time using such communication services and devices. Because of their integral function in any organization, an understanding of the various communication services and devices is vital.

The communication services and devices with which this chapter is concerned include the following: the mailroom, mechanical devices for transporting internal correspondence, telephone services and devices, telegraph services and devices, and intraorganizational communication devices.

The Mailroom

The mailrooms found in organizations located throughout the country are very diverse. In fact, of all the functions of administrative office management, greater diversity may be found in the mailroom than in most of its other functions.

The structure of the mailroom is significantly determined by the size and needs of the organization. Smaller organizations are generally able to function with one individual who has other responsibilities in addition to processing incoming and outgoing mail and delivering internal correspondence. In larger organizations, one or more employees are responsible on a full-time basis for the mail function. The personnel, layout, and equipment requirements of the mailroom are determined by several different factors, including the following:

1. The number of employees in the organization.
2. The correspondence volume of the organization. (The nature of some organizations results in considerably greater volumes of incoming and outgoing correspondence than that of other organizations.)
3. The speed with which the mail must be handled. (Organizations which receive a considerable amount of money through the mails each day may require faster mail-handling procedures than organizations that do not receive large amounts of money.)
4. The nature of the outgoing mail that is processed in the mailroom. (Correspondence mailed in standard-sized envelopes that does not need to be weighed requires less processing time than materials that must be weighed or that require special handling because of the size of the mailing container).

Some of the typical functions of mailrooms are the processing of incoming and outgoing mail, the internal pickup and delivery of mail, distribution of internal correspondence, and the receipt and shipment of parcels. The extent to which each of these functions is performed in the mailroom partially determines the number and type of personnel needed in the mailroom, as well as the amount and type of equipment needed to perform the various functions.

Mailroom Personnel

The type and number of personnel required in the mailroom is determined by the size of the organization and the variety of functions provided by the mailroom. When one or more full-time employees are needed in the mailroom, the mailroom supervisor is typically responsible for the day-to-day operations, while the administrative office manager is most likely to be ultimately responsible for the operation of the mailroom. Some of the other types of employees found in mailrooms include the following: senior mail clerk, mail clerk, delivery clerk, and messenger.

The senior mail clerk may be responsible for opening and routing to the appropriate individuals mail that is addressed to the organization rather than to a specific individual within the organization. This individual needs to have a thorough understanding of the various operational functions of the organization, as well as familiarity with the individuals who work in each of the functions. In addition, the senior mail clerk may be responsible for other routine duties commonly performed in the mailroom.

The mail clerk is primarily responsible for rough sorting the incoming mail according to predetermined categories, such as by floor or by department. The mail clerk is also frequently responsible for operating the various mailing machines, in addition to performing other routine duties.

The delivery clerk is generally responsible for the mail for a specific area or group of departments in the organization. The delivery clerk may also be responsible for pickup and delivery of internal correspondence as well as for sorting outgoing mail.

The messenger is typically responsible for delivery of materials and mail on a special request basis. In some instances, the messenger may be responsible for transporting the rough-sorted mail from the mailroom to the appropriate delivery clerks. In addition, the messenger may, upon request, be responsible for running errands either inside or outside the organization.

Mailroom Layout

Because of the amount of physical activity involved in the mailroom, its layout can have a direct bearing on the efficiency of its operation. For this reason, special consideration needs to be given to the layout of the mailroom.

The functions performed by the mailroom determine the areas that should be considered in planning the layout of the room. For example, space needs to be provided for dumping the mail out of the mail sacks. The dumping table typically has raised sides and may be higher than a normal table in order to accommodate those who wish to work in a standing position. After the mail is dumped, the next process may be to align the various envelopes so they can be run through the mail opener. Mail that is marked "personal" or "confidential" has to be removed before the mail is run through the opener. In some organizations, the envelopes are not opened until they are delivered to the individuals to whom they are addressed.

Another area that needs to be considered in designing the layout of the mailroom is the sorting area. If the mailroom is responsible for the rough sorting of incoming mail, but not for the final sorting, less space is needed than if the mailroom is responsible for both sortings. Pigeonhole racks are frequently used for this phase.

In addition to the areas needed for the processing of incoming mail, space also has to be provided for determining the appropriate recipient of mail that is addressed only to the organization. Additional space is also needed for packing and wrapping parcels, in addition to stamping, sealing, and sorting outgoing mail.

When designing the layout of the mailroom, special consideration should be given to the flow of work. The processing of mail should move from one phase to the next with a minimum amount of physical effort and distance. The efficiency of the design of the mailroom greatly determines the speed and accuracy with which the mail is processed. Figure 7–1 illustrates a well-designed mailroom.

FIGURE 7–1 Mailroom Layout

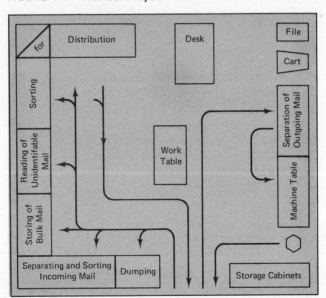

Courtesy, Pitney-Bowes

**Mailroom
Equipment**

Much of the new equipment being manufactured for processing incoming and outgoing mail greatly reduces the amount of physical effort involved in processing the mail. Some of the new developments in equipment design combine several functions into one piece of equipment. For example, equipment is available that performs all the following functions: stamping, postmarking, sealing, counting, and stacking.

Several different categories of equipment may be found in the modern mailroom. These include the following:

Addresser-printer equipment. This type of equipment is used to print mailing addresses on envelopes and other types of mailing containers. Addresser-printers vary considerably in terms of their mechanical operation. While some addresser-printers are manually operated, most are electrically operated. All addresser-printers require the use of data plates, which are about the size of a plastic credit card. The data plates, which are made of metal, plastic, or foil, are capable of holding at least 320 characters. To

FIGURE 7–2   Addressing Machine

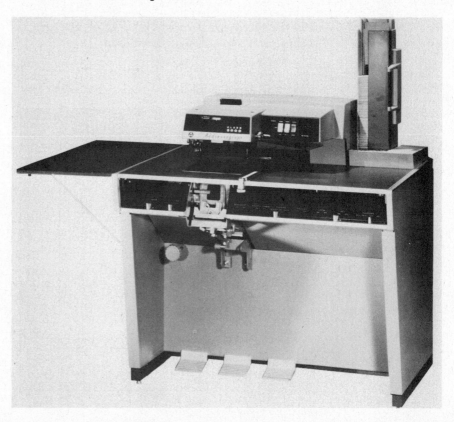

Courtesy, Addressograph Multigraph, Multigraphics Division

imprint names and addresses on mailing containers, a tray containing the data plates is inserted into the addresser-printer. As the data plate comes in contact with the mailing container, the impression on the envelope is made by a ribbon inserted between the raised characters on the data plate and the envelope. Figure 7–2 illustrates an addresser-printer device.

Opening equipment. A considerable amount of employee time can be saved by utilizing automatic opening equipment. The opener trims off a very small part of the envelope. Care has to be taken to make sure that the opener does not also trim the contents of the envelopes, thus cutting the contents of the envelopes into two or more sections. A device for opening mail is illustrated in Figure 7–3.

Stamping-sealing equipment. A wide variety of stamping-sealing equipment is now available. While some of the equipment only stamps and

FIGURE 7–3   Opening Equipment

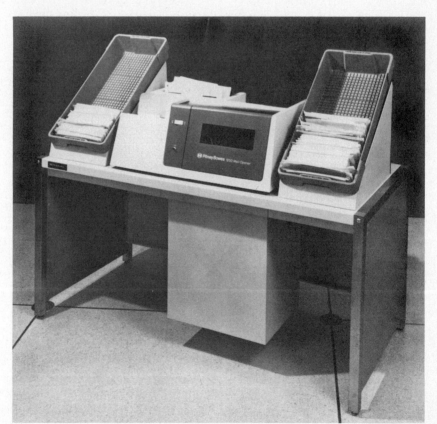

Courtesy, Pitney-Bowes

seals envelopes, other more sophisticated equipment performs the following additional functions: postmarking envelopes, stacking of envelopes,
recording the amount of postage used, and counting the number of envelopes processed. In addition, some postage meters can be equipped with
attachments for check signing and backstamping.

Stamping-sealing equipment typically consists of the mechanical devices, in addition to the postage meter which is detachable. The postage
meter can only be leased from an authorized manufacturer. The meter
is taken to a U.S. Post Office where, upon purchasing postage, the meter
is reset and resealed. The capacity of some postage meters is as high as
$9,999.99. Each time an envelope is processed through the meter, the
amount of the postage affixed to the evelope is subtracted from the meter.

In addition to reducing the amount of physical effort involved in
preparing outgoing mail, the use of stamping-sealing equipment is advantageous for another reason. When such equipment is used, envelopes
that require more than the minimum amount of postage are generally
weighed, thus assuring the accuracy of the amount of postage affixed to
the envelope.

Figure 7–4 illustrates a stamping-sealing device.

FIGURE 7–4   Stamping-Sealing Equipment

Courtesy, Pitney-Bowes

Automatic envelope emptiers. Equipment is also available that is designed
to remove automatically the contents of envelopes. In addition to removing the contents of the envelopes, the devices are also capable of automatically disposing of empty envelopes. The devices are adjustable so
that envelopes of different sizes can be processed through the device.

Label preparation equipment. Another type of equipment often found in
the mailroom is equipment used for the rapid preparation of labels. The

printing mechanism of the label preparation equipment is typically activated by magnetic tape, such as that used by data processing equipment, or punched cards. Names and addresses are contained on the medium, and as the medium is fed through the equipment, names and addresses are printed on labels. Pressure sensitive labels are frequently used, and equipment can be obtained that affixes the labels automatically.

Inserting equipment. This type of equipment is used to stuff inserts into envelopes. Some of the inserting equipment being manufactured is also capable of folding up to six sheets of paper before inserting the material into an envelope. An inserter is illustrated in Figure 7–5.

Bundling equipment. The purpose of this equipment is to tie and bundle packages and bundles. Since this equipment is capable of performing at a much faster rate than are humans, the utilization of such equipment should enable an organization to save a considerable amount of time in preparing the outgoing mail. A tyer-bundler is illustrated in Figure 7–6.

FIGURE 7–5 Inserting Equipment

Courtesy, Pitney-Bowes

Use of Alternative Delivery Methods

Because of the increased costs of using services provided by the U.S. Postal Service, many organizations have found the use of alternative delivery methods for packages and parcels to be not only less expensive but also faster. The services provided by United Parcel Service (UPS) and Greyhound Package Express are found by many to be distinctly advan-

FIGURE 7–6   Bundling Equipment

Courtesy, National Bundle Tyer Company

tageous over the use of the U.S. Postal Service. Another alternative is the private delivery companies that are found in some cities. The supervisor of the mailroom needs to be familiar with the services provided by each of the alternative delivery methods. This helps assure that the appropriate method is used for the circumstances of each situation.

Mechanical Devices for Transportation of Internal Correspondence

A considerable amount of the correspondence generated by an organization stays within the organization. While some of the correspondence stays within the department in which it is generated, other correspondence must be transported to other departments in the organization. In addition to using mechanical devices, a messenger service is often used for the transportation of internal correspondence. Two of the more common types of mechanical devices used for transportation of internal correspondence are pneumatic tubes and conveyor systems.

Pneumatic tubes. The use of a pneumatic tube system requires a network of pneumatic tubes located throughout the building. To install a pneumatic tube system after a building has been erected adds greatly to the cost of the system. To transport documents from one department to another department, the documents are placed in special carriers that travel through the network of tubes. Less sophisticated tube systems generally have a central receiving-distribution point that connects all the departments in the organization to the tube network. More sophisticated pneumatic systems incorporate an automatic dialing tube unit. To use the system, an employee dials the destination point and inserts the carrier into the tube. The carrier is automatically switched from one tube to another until it reaches the proper destination. Such a system eliminates the need for the central receiving-distribution point needed in less sophisticated pneumatic tube systems.

Conveyor systems. An effective mechanical device for transporting documents from one location to another location on the same floor is the conveyor system. These systems consist of a continuous conveyor belt on which several multilength channels are placed. Each work station has its own channel. To transport a document to a specified location, the document is placed in the appropriate channel. The document is then moved by the conveyor belt to the desired work station. At the end of its destination, the document hits the block at the end of the channel and falls into a receiving tray. The number of work stations that can receive documents by this system is limited to the number of upright channels that are contained in the system.

Telephone Service and Devices

Many of the communication devices used in the business world use the telephone and/or telephone lines. While the telephone is still most often used for audio communication, its use for transmission of written communication, data, and facsimile materials is increasing.

Telephone Systems

Several different telephone systems are found in organizations. Each of the systems has special characteristics and uses. The types of telephone systems include the following: **PBX, PAX,** and **CENTREX.**

PBX. This system, which is the acronym for private branch exchange, requires the use of a switchboard or console for incoming and outgoing calls. A PBX system does not require the use of an operator for making interoffice calls.

PAX. The PAX system, or private automatic exchange, also utilizes a switchboard or console. The operator receives the incoming calls and connects the calling party with the appropriate individual in the organization. With a PAX system, employees dial their own outgoing and inter-office calls.

CENTREX. The CENTREX system, the acronym for central exchange, does not require the use of a switchboard or console for the completion of calls. Each employee in the organization is assigned a seven-digit telephone number. Thus, neither incoming or outgoing calls have to go through a switchboard or console. Employees also make their own inter-office calls, typically by dialing the last four or five digits of the telephone number of the individual or department they wish to contact. With a CENTREX system, employees may also be able to dial their own long distance calls without the use of an operator. Of the three systems, CENTREX is the most private, because it is impossible for someone to listen to another person's call. In addition, it is possible to obtain an itemized telephone bill for each of the telephones in the building. Thus, fewer long distance nonbusiness telephone calls are likely to be made because of the individual telephone bills. Because employees have their own telephone numbers, an operator will most likely be needed to provide number information service.

Alternative Telephone Services

During the last few years, several telephone service alternatives have been developed. These services include the following: **WATS** (wide area telephone service); **Telpak**; and **Wideband Data Service.**

WATS. The use of WATS has resulted in substantial cost reductions for many organizations. Before WATS is installed, it is important that the need and use for such a system be accurately determined. To install WATS without first determining the need may result in considerably more expensive telephone costs.

WATS lines are available on an inward or outward basis. An inward WATS line can only be used to call the organization that rents the line. Many organizations rent inward WATS lines as a service to their customers or to provide telephone service between a home office and its regional branches. Any telephone number with an "800" area code is an inward WATS lines.

Outward WATS lines, on the other hand, can only be used for making outward calls and cannot be used for inward calls. If the organization uses a telephone system that requires a switchboard or console, the WATS line frequently originates at the switchboard or console. Thus, the operator is responsible for dialing WATS line calls and for keeping a user waiting list when several employees wish to use the line when it is already in use. It is also possible to rig employees' telephones so they can access the WATS line without using the switchboard or console operator.

WATS lines are rented on a full-time basis and on a measured-time basis. When rented on a full-time basis, for a flat monthly toll, the WATS line can be used as many hours each month as the user wishes. WATS lines are rented on the basis of bands. The country is divided into six bands, and each band services specific area codes. To be able to use the WATS line for coast-to-coast coverage, Band 6 must be rented, which also entitles the user to Bands 1–5. Rental of Band 3 entitles the user only to Bands, 1, 2, and 3. The costs of WATS lines varies from state to state. Separate WATS lines are used for interstate and intrastate calls. An intrastate call may not be made on an interstate WATS line.

The measured-time basis for renting a WATS line entitles the user to 600 minutes of talking time per month. When a line is used for more than 600 minutes a month, the user is charged for the excess minutes at a lower rate and in units of tenths of hours. No refunds are made for using the line less than 600 minutes per month.

Telpak. Telpak, a service of American Telephone and Telegraph, provides on a full-time basis leased telephone lines between two specific locations. Rather than lease a number of individual telephone lines for the transmission of data, audio communication, and so forth, Telpak provides a group of leased lines on a full-time basis. It is generally much less costly to lease the lines on a group basis than to lease the same number of lines on an individual basis.

Wideband Data Service. Wideband Data Service takes into consideration the type of data being transmitted through telephone lines, and thus enables one to select the most appropriate band width for the type of data being transmitted. For example, the slower that words are being transmitted through the lines, the narrower the band can be, while the faster the transmission rate, the wider the band has to be. Thus, rather than renting a band sufficiently wide to handle the transmission of all types of data, Wideband Data Service provides several different width bands, and the user can select the appropriate band for the type of data being transmitted. To illustrate, computers that are communicating with one another at rates of 200,000 words per minute need a wider band than teletypewriters transmitting at 100 words a minute. The wider the band that is needed, the more costly that band is.

Grade of Service

Grade of service refers to having telephone circuits available when needed. When an organization's grade of service is not sufficient, callers will frequently get busy signals because there is not an adequate number of trunk lines into the organization. If not more than three busy signals are heard in 100 call attempts, the grade of service is generally considered to be sufficient.

Grade of service not only applies to incoming calls but also to outgoing and interoffice calls. For example, if busy signals are frequently heard when the outgoing call access (usually 9) is dialed, the organization may have to consider the installation of more outgoing trunk lines.

On telephone systems other than CENTREX, an insufficient number of talking paths or links will also frequently result in a busy signal when attempting to make interoffice calls. When all the interoffice talking paths or links are busy, it is impossible to make an interoffice call until one of the paths is freed. When the number of talking paths is insufficient, consideration should be given to adding more paths to the system.

When an organization is concerned about the adequacy of its grade of telephone service, the telephone company can attach meters to the organization's lines to determine how many busy signals are heard during a certain period. To make the study more valuable, it is also helpful if the telephone company monitors the number of calls that were completed. Thus, the ratio of busy signals to completed calls can be calculated as a means of determining the adequacy of the grade of service.

Special Telephone Services and Devices

Several different special telephone services and devices are available at fairly reasonable rental rates: dial intercoms, manual intercoms, line illumination, voice amplifiers, automatic dialers, and answering devices.

Dial intercoms. For some executives the dial intercom is an especially useful device. The dial intercom is a device that provides a special connection between the executive's and subordinates' telephones. If the executive places a call to a subordinate and the subordinate's phone is already in use, the dial intercom can be used. By dialing the appropriate one- or two-digit special number, the intercom buzzes in the subordinate's phone, which signals the subordinate that the executive wishes to talk with the subordinate. The subordinate thus interrupts or terminates the in-progress conversation. This device saves the executive a considerable amount of time since the subordinate's number only has to be dialed one time in order to communicate with the subordinate.

Manual intercoms. Manual intercoms provide a telephone connection between an executive and the secretary who answers the executive's telephone. Both the executive's telphone and the secretary's telephone have a push botton identified as "local." When either the secretary or the executive depresses the "local" button, they can communicate with one another without first having to dial a number. The manual intercom is especially useful as a device for screening calls. If the secretary and the executive wish to communicate with one another about the party who is calling, the calling party is put on "hold" and the two can talk with one another on the "local" line without the calling party's hearing the conversation.

Line illumination. When a secretary is responsible for answering the telephone for several different individuals, it may be desirable to install a line illumination system on the secretary's telephone. Each line for which the secretary is responsible has a button on the secretary's phone that lights up when an incoming call is received on that line. Thus, the secretary knows which line to answer as well as the individual to whom the call is being made. When the secretary is responsible for answering the phones for only one or two individuals, a bell system may be used. Each line has a different bell that differentiates the various lines.

Voice amplifiers. This device provides a hands-free approach to using the telephone. The device amplifies the call originator's voice so it can be heard throughout a small room. It also amplifies the call recipient's voice. Thus, the call recipient can be a distance from the phone and can hear and can be heard. The device is especially useful when several individuals wish to hear what the call originator has to say or wish to communicate with the call originator.

Automatic dialers. These devices are used primarily for speed and accuracy purposes. Not only is dialing completed more rapidly, but the dialing of a wrong number is eliminated. Some of the automatic dialers use plastic cards with punched holes while others use magnetic tape. The punched card devices, which are part of the telephone, require a punched card for each of the numbers that are to be automatically dialed. The card is inserted into a slot on the telephone, the receiver is lifted, and the start button depressed. The number is thus automatically dialed.

The device that uses magnetic tape is self-contained rather than being part of the telephone. The device holds up to 1,000 numbers on the magnetic tape. To use the device, the name of the party being called is located on the dial register, the telephone receiver is lifted, and a button is depressed that activates the automatic dialing process.

Answering devices. Many organizations, especially smaller ones, have installed answering devices that are activated when no one is available to answer the telephone. They are frequently used before opening hours, during the lunch hour, and after hours. The answering device, which contains a tape on which a prerecorded tape is inserted, asks the caller to leave a message, such as the caller's name and telephone number. The appropriate individual can then return the call.

Other Devices Using Telephone Lines

In addition to telephones, several other communication devices used in organizations also require the use of telephone lines. While some of the devices utilize "voice grade" lines, others require the use of lines capable of transmitting fast-rate communication. The following are the devices that utilize telephone lines: **facsimile devices,** teletypewriter devices, Picturephone, and **Data-Phone.**

Facsimile devices. Telephone lines are also used to transmit impulses for making facsimile reproductions. Facsimile devices, which are useful for sending identical duplicates of documents from one location to another location, require facsimile devices in both locations. The document that is to be transmitted is placed on the facsimile equipment. The sending party then calls the receiving party who switches on the facsimile device at the receiving end. After the sender's telephone receiver and the receiver's telephone receiver are connected to their respective facsimile devices, the transmission of the document begins. A facsimile device is pictured in Figure 7–7.

FIGURE 7–7   Facsimile Device

Credit, Xerox Corporation

Teletypewriter devices. Another of the devices that utilizes telephone lines is the teletypewriter. Whereas the telephone is used for audio communication, the teletypewriter is used for transmitting written communication between two locations. A teletypewriter is required at both the sending and receiving locations. To transmit written communication, the telephone number of the receiving party is dialed, which activates the receiver's teletypewriter. As the sender types the material on the teletypewriter keyboard, impulses carried through the telephone lines reproduce the same material on the receiver's teletypewriter. The teletypewriter can be equipped with an attachment for preparing perforated tape used for the input of data into a computer system.

Picturephone. Another of the devices that utilizes telephone lines and that is most likely to be the telephone of the future is the Picturephone. The Picturephone, which incorporates a televisionlike screen and a telephone, enables the caller and receiver of the call to see and hear one another. The Picturephone is illustrated in Figure 7–8.

FIGURE 7–8   Picturephone

Courtesy, American Telephone and Telegraph Company

Data-Phone. The Data-Phone is used for transmitting and receiving coded data for input into a computer. The Data-Phone is capable of transmitting data recorded on the following three mediums: punched cards, perforated tape, and magnetic tape. The Data-Phone converts the data into tones that are suitable for telephone transmission between two points. At the receiving end, the tones are converted back to data signals that are compatible with the computer equipment.

To transmit data by means of a Data-Phone, the sender calls the receiver. If the computer equipment is ready to receive data, proper identification is given, the sender fastens the telephone receiver to the Data-Phone device, and the transmission begins. Data-Phones are capable of

FIGURE 7–9   Data-Phone

Courtesy, American Telephone and Telegraph Company

transmitting at rates of 3,000 words a minute. The Data-Phone is illustrated in Figure 7–9.

Telephone Interconnect Equipment

A court decision in 1968 gave customers the right to obtain equipment from sources other than a telephone company. This means that organizations may either lease or purchase telephone equipment from an equipment supplier rather than lease the equipment from a local telephone company. This is referred to as **telephone interconnect.** The telephone lines to which the interconnect equipment is attached are still leased from the telephone company.

When selecting interconnect devices, it is important to consider the reliability of the equipment supplier and the quality of equipment and service the supplier is able to provide. The system can be no better than the equipment obtained from the supplier or the service provided by the supplier.

Telephone interconnect provides several important advantages for the organizations who utilize the system:

1. Over a period of time, the organization may be able to save a significant amount of money when using interconnect equipment rather than leasing comparable equipment from a telephone company.

2. Because of the possibility of ownership, interconnect can be used

to hedge against inflation. (When leasing equipment from the telephone company, lease rates are frequently increased from time to time.)

3. Interconnect equipment can be depreciated over a period of time, which means that tax writeoff is possible.

4. Interconnect equipment is often more flexible than the equipment leased from a telephone company, thus increasing the organization's efficiency.

The disadvantages of using interconnect equipment can be summarized as follows:

1. When purchasing the interconnect equipment, the service provided by some suppliers tends to decrease, thus most likely resulting in a less-than-optimum situation.

2. Purchased equipment may be difficult to dispose of if the equipment is made obsolete by more sophisticated equipment.

3. The service provided by some interconnect equipment suppliers compares very poorly to the service that a telephone company is able to provide.

Telegraph Services and Devices

While most of the communication devices involve telephone lines, several use telegraph lines. Such devices, although probably not as commonly used in organizations, do serve a purposeful function. The devices that utilize telegraph lines are Telex, TWX, and WIREFAX.

Telex. The use of Telex requires a tape-oriented teleprinter. The perforated tape is prepared off-line, which means that the impulses are not transmitted through the telegraph lines at the time the tape is prepared. After the message has been completed and its accuracy has been verified, the tape is inserted in the machine, and the receiver's number, which connects the sender's and the receiver's teleprinters, is dialed. The message is transmitted through the telegraph lines at sixty-six words per minute. Telex charges are based on the amount of time and the distance the message is transmitted. Telex costs are approximately one-half the cost of telephone calls.

TWX. The process and application of Telex and TWX are similar in many respects. The equipment used in TWX and Telex systems is similar except for the following: TWX accommodates an eight-level code perforated paper tape whereas Telex utilizes a five-level code tape. For data transmission methods requiring the eight-level code tape, Telex cannot be used. Another difference between TWX and Telex is the method of charging or billing. Telex charges are made in increments of six seconds, whereas one minute is the minimum TWX charge. Whereas Telex transmits at a rate

FIGURE 7–10   TWX

Photo courtesy of Western Union

of sixty-six words a minute, TWX transmits at a rate of one hundred words a minute. Figure 7–10 illustrates a TWX device.

WIREFAX. Another of the facsimile devices is the WIREFAX. This particular device utilizes telegraph lines. The WIREFAX is capable of transmitting any document on which printing or drawing appears. WIREFAX transmission is restricted to documents not larger than seven and one-half by nine and one-half inches.

Intraorganizational Communication Devices

Several different devices are used for information or data transmission within an organization. Although the devices are vastly different from one another, they do have the common characteristic of facilitating communication.

TELautograph. This device, which uses telephone lines, is used for transmitting handwritten messages between two points. Whereas most of the telephone devices discussed earlier in this chapter are used for external communication, the TELautograph is used almost exclusively within the organization. It is especially useful for transmitting messages between an office area and the warehouse area of manufacturing firms.

As the words are written on the sending unit, the receiving unit of the TELautograph simultaneously records the same words. The sending unit converts the written word to electrical impulses. As the currents are received on the receiving unit, the electrical currents cause the writing mechanism to duplicate the writing. Figure 7–11 illustrates the TELautograph device.

Intrafax. The intrafax is also a facsimile system used internally within an organization. It can be used to transmit duplicate copies of all kinds of forms, letters, drawings, and other kinds of documents between various offices in an organization.

Closed-circuit television. The use of closed-circuit television is increasing in organizations. Not only is closed-circuit television being used for the transmission of information, but it is also used by organizations for security purposes. When used to transmit information between two points in the organization, the information to be transmitted is placed in front of the closed-circuit camera. The image is transmitted instantly to the television monitor at the receiving end.

FIGURE 7–11   TELautograph Device

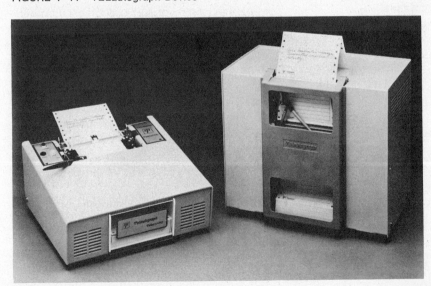

Courtesy, Telautograph Corporation

Paging systems. A variety of paging systems are used extensively in many organizations. One type of paging system utilizes the organization's public address system. When an employee is being summoned, the employee's name or code is amplified through the public address system. The employee is generally asked to call the switchboard operator or some other employee in order to obtain the message.

Another of the paging systems also utilizes the telephone switchboard. Each of the highest level executives is given a code that is signaled through the premises when the executive has an important message. Upon hearing the signal, the executive calls the switchboard operator for the message.

A third type of paging system uses portable pocket-size paging devices. While some of the portable paging devices only buzz, others permit either one- or two-way audio communication. The portable paging devices can be used at distances of several miles from the location of the base paging device.

Review Questions

1. In what ways are the duties of the senior mail clerk, the mail clerk, the delivery clerk, and the messenger likely to vary?
2. In a PBX and a PAX system, what functions does the switchboard or console operator perform?
3. How do the various billing plans of WATS lines differ from one another?
4. What is the purpose of a manual intercom?
5. What is the purpose of a facsimile device?

Minicases

The administrators of Central States Lumber Company, which is located in Davenport, Iowa, have decided to investigate the possibility of using telephone interconnect equipment. Their primary reasons for thinking that interconnect equipment may be advantageous is because of equipment flexibility and reduced telephone costs. Because the administrators are not very well informed about the interconnect system, they have asked you, the administrative office manager, to explain the concept in detail. Identify the points about telephone interconnect that you plan to present to the administrators.

*   *   *

Several of the high-level administrators of the Donald Alexander Corporation complain about their frequent inability to contact their subordinates by phone because the subordinates' phones are already in use. This means that the administrator or an assistant has to keep dialing the subordinates' numbers until their phones are no longer in use. In some instances this consumes a considerable amount of time. One of the administrators was talking with a client about this problem not too long ago, and the client suggested that the administrator have a special attachment installed on the phone that would enable the administrator to signal the subordinate when the subordinate's phone is already in use. What is this device called? How does it work?

Case

The Jaymar Corporation, which is located on the west side of Chicago, is a manufacturer of sporting goods. The firm employed around fifty people until about seven years ago. The firm, which now employs nearly 250 people, has grown rapidly under the administration of the current president, who has held this position for about eight years.

When the company was still quite small, its mailing needs could be adequately handled by one postage meter, which was located in the accounting department. From time to time, additional postage meters have been placed throughout the company. It is now quite obvious that a centralized mailroom facility is needed. At the present time, one of the most inefficient functions of the organization is its incoming and outgoing mail procedures.

Since you are the administrative office manager for Jaymar, the responsibility for the mailroom will be yours. The vice president to whom you are responsible has asked for your help in this matter. He would like for you to "brief" him about the centralized mailroom concept. In your briefing, you should be able to discuss with the vice president the following items:

1. Factors that have a significant bearing on the personnel, layout, and equipment requirements of the mailroom.
2. The type of personnel needed in the mailroom.
3. The layout of the mailroom.
4. The functions of the various types of equipment typically found in centralized mailrooms.

Word
Processing

Chapter
8

The Word Processing Concept Illustrated

Determining the Need for Word Processing
First Stage of the Study
Second Stage of the Study

Making the Decision

Equipment Used in Word Processing
Automatic Typewriters
Recording Equipment
Transcription Equipment
Copy Equipment

Advantages and Disadvantages of Word Processing
Advantages of Word Processing
Disadvantages of Word Processing

Effect of Word Processing on Secretarial Personnel

Data Processing and Word Processing

Chapter Aims   After studying this chapter, the student should be able to:

1. Explain the word processing concept in terms of the equipment, personnel, and procedures that are involved in the concept.

2. Explain how the need for a word processing center is determined.

3. Identify the types of information that are collected during the first and second stages of the feasibility study.

4. Explain the advantages and disadvantages of word processing.

5. Explain the differences between administrative secretaries and correspondence secretaries in relation to the types of tasks they perform.

6. Explain the techniques that are frequently used for motivating correspondence secretaries to maintain an interest in their jobs.

Chapter Terms   *Word processing:* a mix of people, equipment, and procedures used to transform ideas and thoughts into printed copy.

Automatic typewriters: a category of typewriters frequently used in word processing. In addition to being used for typing the first draft of a document, they are also used to automatically type the needed number of final copies of a document. As material is typed the first time, it is stored in coded form, usually on a magnetic card, disk, or cassette, for subsequent use.

Feasibility study: the study, which consists of two stages, that is used to determine the need for the installation of a word processing center.

Recording equipment: equipment used by word originators to record their dictation, which is later transcribed.

Transcription equipment: equipment used to play back the dictation recorded by word originators on the recording equipment. The playback of the dictation takes place when the dictation is being transformed into typewritten copy.

Administrative secretaries: secretaries who perform nontyping functions in an organization that utilizes word processing. Examples include such tasks as answering the telephone, performing administrative tasks for word originators, filing, and so forth.

Correspondence secretaries: the secretaries in the word processing center whose jobs consist primarily of typing and proofreading tasks.

Of all the recent developments in administrative office management, **word processing** is perhaps the most revolutionary. Its impact is felt at all levels of the organization. By definition, word processing refers to the mix of people, equipment, and procedures used to transform ideas and thoughts into printed copy. Word processing, which involves specialized employees, equipment, and procedures, differs markedly from some of the more traditional approaches of transforming ideas and thoughts into printed copy.

The Word Processing Concept Illustrated

An effective means of presenting the word processing concept is first to illustrate a word processing system. After the system is illustrated, the concept is discussed in detail.

When an organization utilizes a word processing system, the transformation of the ideas and thoughts into printed copy is performed by expert typists whose primary job function is typing. The expert typists are typically not responsible for performing other traditional secretarial or clerical duties such as filing, answering the telephone, receiving office callers, and so forth. In many organizations, the expert typists are centrally located. The nontyping secretarial and clerical duties are performed by other employees who do very little if any typing.

In addition to using specialized personnel, word processing also utilizes specialized equipment. For example, **automatic typewriters** are used that are capable of storing in coded form all material that is produced on the typewriter. The material is frequently stored in coded form on cards containing strips of magnetic tape, on magnetic disks, or on magnetic tape cassettes. Material is manually typed the first time but is automatically typed thereafter. To do this, the appropriate magnetic card, disk, or cassette is inserted into the machine, which then automatically types the material stored on the magnetic medium. Unless there is a need to revise, add to, or delete material stored on the magnetic medium, it is used to activate the typewriter to automatically type as many additional copies of the material as are needed. When revisions are necessary, the magnetic card, disk, or cassette is still used to activate the typewriter to type the nonrevised portion of the material, but the typist has to manually type the revised portion. Some of the automatic equipment now available also records the revisions on the magnetic card, disk, or cassette as they are being typed. Therefore, the revised material can also be automatically typed once the material is recorded on the magnetic medium.

In addition to using automatic typewriters, word processing also utilizes machine dictation equipment. The word originator dictates the material into the equipment, which stores the material on a recording medium. The expert typist uses the automatic typewriter to transcribe the material that has been stored on the recording medium contained in the dictation equipment.

The third component of word processing, which involves procedures, is also quite unique. Because of modern technology, the telephone is likely to be used in the dictation process. A telephone is used to transmit the word originator's dictation to the machine dictation equipment where the dictation is stored until it is transcribed. Once the typist has transcribed the material dictated by the word originator, the typed document is returned to the word originator for further action, which may include signing the document, revising the document before final typing, or approving and returning the document to the typist for final typing. In many instances, the word originator may first request a rough draft of the material. The word originator may make several changes or may ask that the document be typed as shown on the rough draft. The rough draft is then returned to the expert typist who uses the appropriate magnetic card or cassette for automatically typing the final draft of the document. Any revisions desired by the word originator at this point have to be manually typed.

In addition to transcribing dictation, the typists may also type from longhand copy or from typewritten copy.

Determining the Need for Word Processing

Because of its widespread effect on the typing and transcription function in the organization, the need for a word processing center should be systematically determined before the center is installed. To install a center without first determining its need cannot be justified. The need for installing a word processing center is determined by a **feasibility study**. In addition to helping determine the need for a word processing center, the feasibility study can also be used to help determine the types and amount of equipment needed in the center.

The feasibility study is likely to be conducted in a two-stage process. The first stage is a preliminary study that determines whether the organization would benefit from the installation of a word processing center. The second stage, which is more detailed, involves a thorough analysis of the nature of the typing and transcription processes in order to determine the type of equipment best suited for the center.

First Stage of the Study

The first stage of the feasibility study frequently involves both the word originators and the employees who type for the word originators. The word originators are asked to identify the amount of time they spend (1) dictating to secretaries, (2) using dictation equipment, and (3) giving secretaries or typists material to type that is written in longhand. The greater the amount of time the word originator spends each week dictating or handwriting material to be typed, the more feasible word processing is likely to be. The employees who type for the word originators are asked to identify the amount of time they spend each week typing broad categories of work, such as letters and reports; statistical material, like tables; and forms. In addition, the typists are asked to identify the extent to which the word originators revise material. Another factor considered in the preliminary study is the extent to which the secretary or typist types repetitive material, which consists of material that is already in typewritten format. The greater the amount of letter, report, and statistical material, the more often material is revised, and the greater the amount of repetitive typing, the more desirable word processing is. If the results of the preliminary study indicate that a word processing center may be feasible, the second stage of the study is conducted. If the results of the preliminary study do not indicate a need for word processing, no further action will be taken at this point.

Second Stage of the Study

Before the second stage of the feasibility study is conducted, it may be very desirable for the employees of the organization to receive orientation about the word processing concept, its advantages, its limitations, and to see a prototype word processing center. Because the installation of word processing is most likely to result in significant changes in the organization's typing and transcription function, employees should be made aware of the possibility of such an installation very early in the investigative stage. In fact, some organizations prefer to have the orientation take place prior to the time that the first stage of the feasibility study is conducted. Because of human nature, employees are often resistant to change; and when change is significant, a considerable amount of orientation may be necessary.

The second stage of the feasibility study, which may also be classified as a task analysis, involves the employees who type for the word originators. These employees, whether they are classified as secretaries, clerk-typists, or by some other title, keep track of their daily duties for a period of time. This phase, which may last for a week or two weeks, involves their recording the amount of time they spend performing nontyping tasks and the amount of time they spend typing. The nontyping tasks are likely to consist of filing, answering the telephone, handling mail, copying or duplicating materials, and so forth. By recording the amount of time spent typing, a detailed record of this phase of their jobs is developed. The employees are asked to record the source of material they type, which includes the following: longhand, shorthand, machine dictation, printed or typed copy, or self-composed material. For each of these sources, the employee is asked to record the number of lines typed and the nature of the material, which includes letters and memos, reports, statistical typing, forms, and other types of material. In addition, the employees are asked to record whether or not each item they type has been revised and whether or not the material is repetitive. Thus, at the end of this phase of the feasibility study, it is possible to determine the total number of typewritten lines produced by the organization in terms of the source of the material (longhand, shorthand, machine dictation, and so on), the type of material (letters, reports, forms, etc.), the extent to which the material was revised, and the extent of repetitive material.

The financial feasibility of a word processing center is determined by input, output, and equipment costs. A word processing center may be more financially feasible if considerable use is made of machine dictation for input as opposed to longhand or shorthand input. The cost of using shorthand as input is nearly three times greater for a word originator making $20,000 per year than the cost of using machine dictation for input. For the same word originator, the cost of using longhand is about five times more costly than the cost of using machine dictation. Therefore, if word originators make extensive use of machine dictation, the cost of word processing may not only be less costly but also more efficient than traditional systems.

While the input costs are determined by the salaries of the word originators in relation to the type of input they use, output costs are determined by the hourly salaries of the typists and the amount of time they spend each day in a typing activity.

On the basis of the number of lines typed and the extent of revision and repetitive typing, it is possible to determine the type and amount of equipment needed for an efficient word processing center. The traditional typing and transcription processes in most organizations require that each typist have a typewriter, no matter how much or how little the typewriter is used. In word processing systems, few, if any, typewriters will be found outside the word processing center. Even though word processing generally involves the use of fairly expensive automatic typewriters, the equipment outlay may be considerably less, since fewer conventional typewriters will be needed. Thus, a cost savings may be realized in terms of the amount of equipment needed. The word processing concept also enables an organization to make more efficient use of its equipment because it is used for a large portion of each workday. Because of the employee specialization that is characteristic of word processing, fewer employees may be needed. The organization may also be able to realize a cost savings in terms of employee salaries.

The financial cost of the present typing and transcription function should be compared with the cost of the proposed word processing center in terms of the following formula:

Input costs + output costs + cost of equipment = cost of the system

If the cost of a word processing system is considerably less than the cost of the present system, the management of the organization should seriously consider the installation of such a system.

The use of representatives of equipment manufacturers for determining the need for a word processing system should not be overlooked. Some equipment manufacturers undertake the complete feasibility study and subsequently analyze and interpret the data provided by each of the employees. Other manufacturers will assist in undertaking the study, but the organization is responsible for a larger portion of the work involved. In addition to providing assistance with the feasibility study, representatives of certain equipment manufacturers assist by determining the types and amount of equipment needed for an efficient word processing center.

Making the Decision

The financial feasibility is just one of the factors that is considered in determining whether or not the installation of a word processing system can be justified. If a word processing center is not feasible in terms of its financial cost, it is doubtful that its installation can be justified on any other basis. Therefore, no further investigation into the feasibility of a word processing system would be undertaken.

If the installation of a word processing center is financially feasible, several other factors should also be considered. One such factor is the perceived acceptance of the concept by the word originators and the employees who do their typing. Even though a word processing system may be financially feasible, the installation of a system is questionable if it is obvious that the employees will never accept the system. It is doubtful that the system would ever be effectively or efficiently utilized if the employees are adamantly opposed to the installation of the system. One reason for the early orientation of the employees to the word processing concept is to help them overcome their resistance to the new system.

Another factor to consider in making the decision is the nature of the material that is produced by the organization. For example, if a considerable amount of the typewritten work consists of typing forms, the installation of a word processing system may not be justifiable. Because the word processing equipment is especially desirable when there is a need for the frequent revision of material or when a considerable amount of repetitive material needs to be processed, it is more desirable for typing certain kinds of material than it is for typing forms. Its use for processing forms does not result in a significant advantage because the material contained on forms rarely has to be revised or be repetitively typed. Approximately 15–25 percent of the typical typing and transcription jobs of an organization are not well suited to the word processing concept.

In addition to these factors, the ease with which the duties of employees can be adjusted and revised should be considered. In most word processing systems, office employees either type the greatest portion of the day or they do not type at all. Those whose jobs involve nontyping activities perform such duties as filing, answering the telephone, receiving callers, and so forth. In traditional systems, office employees are likely to perform typing duties as well as nontyping duties. For the word processing system to work well, the office employees will have to decide which of the two types of jobs are more appealing—the jobs consisting mainly of typing duties or the jobs consisting of nontyping duties. Because employees' jobs will have to be adjusted and revised, this factor should be given serious consideration in deciding whether or not to install a word processing system.

Equipment Used in Word Processing

Word processing consists of three components, which are people, equipment, and procedures. Because some of the equipment used in word processing is rather specialized and because the efficiency of a word processing center is likely to be partially determined by the type of equipment used, this component is discussed in detail in this section.

Automatic Typewriters

Automatic typewriters, which are also referred to as automatic keyboard equipment and text-editing equipment, are very commonly found in word processing centers. This type of equipment has several basic characteristics, including the following: recording of material on a magnetic medium as the material is typed the first time; depending on the type of equipment, typing speeds ranging from 170–750 words a minute; and technology that permits the easy revision of material, including the deletion of material, the changing of words, or the addition of material. The revision capability of automatic typewriters makes their use especially desirable in word processing systems.

Figure 8–1, which illustrates the IBM Mag Card II, is an example of an automatic typewriter. As the typist types the first draft of the material, the control unit on the machine can be set so that the material is simultaneously recorded on a magnetic card. The recording of the material on the magnetic card takes place in the console unit of the typewriter. This particular typewriter is equipped with an error correction device that enables the typist mechanically to lift errors off the paper. Thus, the first draft might also be used as the final copy, provided no revisions in the material are desired. As errors are corrected on the paper, the incorrect characters are automatically erased from the magnetic card and the correct characters recorded on the card as the correction is made on the paper. On automatic mode, this particular typewriter has a nominal typing speed of 15.5 characters per second.

If the word originator wishes to delete a word on the final copy of the material, the word is circled on the first draft. When the draft is returned to the word processing center, the magnetic card on which this particular material is recorded is inserted into the console unit. The typist, by depressing the appropriate keys on the keyboard, can direct the typewriter to type automatically the material recorded on the magnetic card. The typewriter is stopped at the point at which the word is to be deleted. Using the appropriate control keys on the keyboard, the next word that is recorded on the magnetic card is automatically deleted. The typewriter continues to type automatically until the next change is to be

FIGURE 8-1   Automatic Typewriter

Courtesy of International Business Machines Corporation

made on the material. The control keys on this particular typewriter can be used automatically to delete characters, sentences, and paragraphs, in addition to words. If a word, sentence, or paragraph are to be added to the first draft of the material, the typewriter automatically types to the point at which the addition is to be inserted, and the typist then manually types the addition, which simultaneously records this material on the card. The typewriter then continues to type automatically until the next change has to be made. All changes in the material are also simultaneously made on the magnetic card. Thus, the card can be used to prepare as many copies of the revised material as are needed.

Figure 8-2, which illustrates another type of automatic typewriter, the Linolex system, produces the same end result. But the applications of this equipment and that illustrated in Figure 8-1 are quite different.

FIGURE 8–2 Automatic Typewriter

Courtesy, Linolex Systems Inc., Subsidiary 3M Company, Information Management Department

Rather than typing a first draft of the material on paper, the material typed by the typist appears on the visual display unit. As material is typed on the keyboard, the material simultaneously appears on the visual display unit. When material equivalent to one typewritten page appears on the display unit, the typist proofreads the material and makes any necessary corrections. The material is then instantly transferred to a magnetic disk. When the typist has completed recording all the material, the disk is inserted into the printer, which prepares a printed copy of the material at a rate of approximately 350 words per minute. Since the input and the output devices of this particular equipment are not integrated into one unit, the typist can be recording the material on a disk while the printer is printing the material recorded on another disk. Equipment that incorporates a visual display unit is distinctly advantageous because of the rapid location of material that needs to be revised. A full page of material appears on the display unit at one time. By means of a device called character string search, the location of the material that has to be revised can be found very quickly. After the change has been made and recorded on the magnetic disk, the typist continues to display pages on the display unit until the next change is to be made. The change is made, is recorded on the disk, and the process continues for the remainder of the changes that need to be made.

Recording Equipment

Another type of specialized equipment used in the word processing center is **recording equipment,** which is used to record the word originators' dictation. Although a variety of systems are now manufactured, one of the more common systems utilizes the word originators' telephones. To record dictation, word originators simply use a three- or five-digit telephone number to connect their telephones with the recording equipment located in the word processing center. In most cases, the recording equipment can also be activated by a telephone outside the building. Thus, the recording equipment can be used by word originators twenty-four hours a day, regardless of their location.

Figure 8–3 illustrates the Touch-Tone Telephone Input System, which carries a registered trademark of American Telephone and Telegraph Company. The Touch-Tone system is used to connect a telephone with IBM Corporation's recording equipment. Although this system illustrates the use of a pushbutton telephone, a dial telephone can also be used, but it is not as flexible. After the word originator's telephone is connected with the recording equipment in the word processing center, various numbers on the telephone can be depressed to communicate with the recording equipment. For example, the recording equipment is activated or deactivated by pushing the 1 button on the telephone. The 2

FIGURE 8–3   Recording Equipment

Courtesy of International Business Machines Corporation

button is depressed when the word originator wishes to rewind the magnetic belt in the recording device in order to listen to or review the material that has just been dictated. The 4 button is used to index instructions or corrections of material. By depressing the 5 button, the word originator can talk with an individual in the word processing center.

While the Touch-Tone system utilizes a standard telephone, other systems utilize a variety of devices, including special telephones and recording microphones. One distinct advantage of installing a system that utilizes a regular telephone is the opportunity to record dictation twenty-four hours a day from any part of the world where long distance telephone calls can be made.

Transcription Equipment

Another type of equipment required in a word processing center is **transcription equipment.** After the word originator has recorded the dictation, the magnetic medium on which the dictation is stored is removed from the recording equipment and is inserted in the transcription equipment. The typist then plays back the dictation and transcribes the material at the typewriter. Depending on the nature of the magnetic medium used in the recording equipment, the typist may not begin to transcribe any of the material recorded on the medium until the medium is filled with dictation. An exception to this occurs when a particular job is classified as high priority or a rush job, in which case the material is likely to be transcribed immediately. Figure 8–4 illustrates a transcription unit.

FIGURE 8–4   Transcribing Equipment

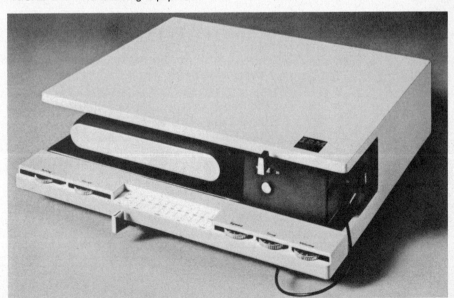

Courtesy of International Business Machines Corporation

Copy Equipment

Another type of equipment used in word processing centers is copy equipment. Fewer and fewer organizations are making carbon copies of typed material. Instead, copies of typed material are made on copy equipment. The reasons for this are several and include the following: the unit copy cost of material reproduced on a copy machine is decreasing; the typist does not know whether the first draft of material typed will be the final draft, and to make a carbon copy of material that may be revised does not represent efficiency; the extra human effort required to insert and align carbon paper and second sheets exceeds that required to make copies on copy equipment.

Advantages and Disadvantages of Word Processing

The use of word processing results in several distinct advantages. While the use of word processing is advantageous in many organizations, its use also results in some disadvantages.

Advantages of Word Processing

One of the most distinct advantages of using word processing is the increased productivity of word originators. Prior to the installation of a word processing system, many word originators compose in longhand. At a longhand writing rate of approximately fifteen words per minute, the word originator's time is likely to be inefficiently utilized. When using shorthand, the average word originator's dictation rate is approximately 35–40 words per minute. The use of machine dictation, which is a characteristic of word processing, enables word originators to increase their dictation rates to an average of 60–80 words per minute. Therefore, the use of word processing equipment reduces the amount of word origination time and increases the amount of time word originators have for performing other duties.

In addition to increasing the productivity of word originators, the productivity of those who transcribe the material can also be increased. When shorthand is used in the word origination process, two individuals are involved: the word originator and the transcriber. With machine dictation, on the other hand, the transcriber is not involved in the word origination process. Thus, this individual is able to be more productive. In addition, if the word originators speak clearly and enunciate properly when recording the dictation, the transcription process is likely to be more rapid than when using shorthand dictation. This is true because the transcriber does not have to take time to decipher poorly or incorrectly written shorthand characters.

Another advantage of using word processing is the increased efficiency with which equipment is used. In the traditional system, each secretary or typist has a typewriter. In some cases these typewriters may be used only a few hours during each work day. With word processing, on the other hand, the automatic typewriters are likely to be used nearly every minute of the working day. In addition, the recording equipment is also likely to be used more efficiently than the recording equipment in a traditional system. Even though word originators may have access to recording equipment in a traditional system, they may still make considerable use of longhand. Or if the word originators use the recording equipment, individual recording units may only be used a few minutes each day. Because the word processing concept discourages word originators from using longhand for most types of input, recording equipment is likely to be used more often and with greater efficiency.

Because of the division of labor that is characteristic of word processing, greater employee specialization is possible. Those who transcribe are expert in the transcription and proofreading functions. Those who perform the other secretarial support duties, which are likely to include filing, handling the mail, receiving office callers, performing certain tasks as delegated by the managers or administrative personnel, and so forth, are also expert in the functions they perform. Because of this division of labor, the resulting specialization enables an organization to realize greater efficiency in the production processes. The division of labor is discussed in greater detail in the next section of this chapter.

Another significant advantage of word processing is the savings that result from the need for fewer personnel and less equipment. Over a period of time, it is not uncommon for organizations to reduce their payroll costs by 15–25 percent because of word processing. Because employees are more efficiently used, fewer are needed to produce the same amount of work. Equipment costs can also be reduced because fewer typewriters will be needed. In its pure form, only the typists in the word processing center and the private secretaries to the top managers are provided with typewriters. It should be noted that some organizations do find it convenient to place a minimum number of typewriters throughout the organization.

Another advantage of word processing is the lessened turnaround time for getting material typed. Some organizations have a maximum turnaround time of two hours, with more rapid turnaround time on rush jobs. In a traditional system in which a typist is likely to be responsible to three or more word originators, the turnaround time is likely to be much longer.

The quality with which work is produced is another distinct advantage of word processing. Office employees are hired and placed in positions that take into consideration their special talents and abilities. Thus, less work is likely to have to be retyped because of a poor typing ability on the part of the typist. Those with poor typing abilities are not likely to be placed in the word processing center. Another dimension of the quality of work is the ease with which material can be revised, thus resulting in better quality work.

Disadvantages of Word Processing

In some instances, the disadvantages of word processing may outweigh the advantages. One significant disadvantage is the resistance of some word originators to accept the new system. If the system is forced upon word originators, it is very unlikely that their resistance to the system can ever be totally overcome. For this reason, it is wise to provide many opportunities to help word originators overcome their resistance to the system before it is installed. The decision to install a word processing center, knowing that most word originators are opposed to the concept, could hardly be considered a wise decision.

Another disadvantage of the concept is the lack of job satisfaction that some transcribers receive from their jobs. Although the individuals who are expert transcribers and typists and who are placed in the word processing center may derive a great amount of job satisfaction for a period of time, this does not necessarily mean that a high amount of job satisfaction will continue to be derived. The complaints of such individuals are likely to center around the pressure of the job; the routine, repetitive nature of the work; the lack of familiarity with the word originators; the lack of involvement with other employees in the organization; and the lack of promotion opportunities. Some organizations have found that some of the employees who work in the word processing center succumb to the pressure of the job after a period of time. When this occurs, the organization places the employee in another job for a period of time. After they have had a chance to relax and unwind, they return to their jobs in the word processing center. Organizations that have this rotation plan find that the attrition rate of such employees decreases significantly.

Another distinct disadvantage of word processing is the fact that not all typing tasks are appropriately processed in the word processing center. For example, the use of automatic typewriters for completion of forms is an inefficient use of the equipment because rarely would the information contained on forms need to be repetitively typed or revised. Special arrangements have to be made for the processing of work that is inappropriate for processing in the word processing center.

Effect of Word Processing on Secretarial Personnel

The installation of a word processing center in an organization usually results in a major restructuring of the secretarial function of the organization. The secretarial function is performed by two distinct classes of secretaries: correspondence secretaries and administrative secretaries. This creates a division of labor that results in greater employee specialization.

An organization utilizing word processing no longer has secretaries located throughout the building who perform both typing and nontyping secretarial functions. Rather, the typing function is performed in the word processing center by the correspondence secretaries. The tasks of correspondence secretaries include transcribing dictation, proofreading, and editing material. The administrative secretaries, on the other hand, perform the nontyping functions. Such secretaries are located throughout the building and are responsible for such tasks as mail handling, filing, receiving callers, and providing administrative support to several managers.

The utilization of the word processing concept is frequently thought to provide a variety of new career opportunities for secretarial personnel. Secretaries are classified as either **correspondence secretaries** or **administrative secretaries,** and within each classification there may be several different levels. For example, within the word processing center, an individual may be hired as a correspondence secretary, level I. After a period of time, this individual may be promoted to correspondence secretary, level II, and then to correspondence secretary, senior level. The next promotion may be to correspondence secretary, scheduler. The highest level job within the word processing center is typically the supervisor or manager of the center. In some instances, correspondence secretaries are not responsible for the proofreading of their own work. Rather, the proofreading may be the responsibility of the correspondence secretary, proofreader. Also, some centers have an executive correspondence secretary who is responsible for the transcription and typing of high-level executives' materials, much of which may be confidential.

Just as the correspondence secretary category has several different levels, so does the administrative secretary category. The different administrative secretary levels, from the lowest to the highest, may include the following: administrative secretary, level I; administrative secretary, level II; senior administrative secretary; executive administrative secretary; and administrative support supervisor. The word processing supervisor and administrative support supervisor are likely to be responsible to a manager of word processing/administrative support.

In theory, the promotion opportunities of administrative and correspondence secretaries to midmanagement positions are equal. But, in practice, the promotion opportunities are much more desirable for the administrative secretaries. This is primarily because the administrative secretaries work with managers on a daily basis. Correspondence secretaries rarely, if ever, have direct communication with the managers. Thus, the administrative secretaries have a distinct advantage because their abilities and the quality of their work are constantly noticed and observed by managers who are in a position to recommend them for high-level positions. Because the administrative secretaries are in such a strategic position for the quality of their work and their contributions to be noticed, they are typically promoted to midmanagement positions at a faster rate and in greater numbers than are the correspondence secretaries.

When correspondence secretaries realize that their promotion opportunities are not as abundant as the opportunities for the administrative secretaries, the manager of the word processing/administrative support function may be confronted with a group of correspondence secretaries who are very difficult to motivate. Unless the correspondence secretaries are given a reason to stay in the word processing center, many either seek a transfer to an administrative secretarial position or seek employment in some other organization.

Several different techniques have been successfully employed by organizations to motivate the correspondence secretaries. One of the most commonly used motivational techniques is the rate of pay they receive. Many organizations pay their correspondence secretaries rates considerably above other classifications of secretaries. Another technique successfully used is recognition of correspondence secretaries for outstanding performance. Several organizations have also found that correspondence secretaries find their jobs to be motivational if given the opportunity to work on large projects from the beginning of the project to the end of the project. To have several different secretaries responsible for only a portion of the project destroys some of the employee's motivation. Other organizations use job rotation as a means of motivating their correspondence secretaries. To rotate employees between correspondence and administrative functions allows the correspondence secretary to also be noticed by managers. This also gives such secretaries the opportunity for promotion to midmanagement positions.

Data Processing and Word Processing

Like many other office applications, word processing is being influenced by several developments in data processing. Essentially, the developments primarily consist of integrating data processing and word processing.

Many of the data processing applications that are used in word processing utilize the minicomputer. In addition to having the capability of simultaneously processing other data, the minicomputer can also print the material that is held in storage. Much of the material that is held in storage is contained on magnetic disks, which provide almost unlimited storage capacity. In some cases, terminals are located throughout the organization and everyone in the organization has a manual that contains copies of the form paragraphs that are on disk storage. The terminal operator simply enters the paragraph code in the terminal and in a very short period of time, the terminal prints the paragraph on the appropriate paper. Not only does this save time in terms of eliminating the need to dictate original letters, but also the quality of the correspondence is likely to improve since the form paragraphs can be professionally developed.

The use of minicomputers in preparing mass mailings of letters is especially useful. By coding the letter that each individual is to receive, the minicomputer is able to prepare the mass mailing. Not only is the minicomputer able to select and print the appropriate letter for each individual, but it is also able to print the individual's name and address on the letter.

Review
Questions
1. Define word processing.

2. Why is it important to determine in the feasibility study the amount of repetitive and revised material that is typed?

3. What is a task analysis and how is it used when determining the need for a word processing center?

4. How is the financial feasibility of a word processing center determined?

5. Why are most copies of materials that are typed in a word processing center made on an office copier rather than by means of carbon?

6. Why does the word processing concept result in a lack of motivation for some employees?

7. In practice, why are the promotion opportunities of correspondence secretaries less than those for administrative secretaries?

8. In what ways are word processing and data processing becoming increasingly related?

Minicases

The Barr-Wimble Corporation has expanded rapidly during the last few years, primarily because of the invention and manufacture of antipollution devices used on automobiles. Even though the corporation has expanded rapidly, most of its operating procedures are quite efficient. The corporation is now considering the installation of a word processing system, but before a vendor is contacted, the managers are interested in having someone identify for them a list of the circumstances that make word processing desirable and those that make it undesirable. What circumstances should be placed on the list that you have been asked to prepare?

*   *   *

The Davis Company is considering installing a word processing center. Financially, it appears feasible. In fact, the data indicate that the center should reduce operating costs by approximately 10–12 percent. The primary factor that is presently keeping the company from deciding to install the system is the specialization that results from classifying employees as administrative secretaries and correspondence secretaries. This troubles some of the managers. Perhaps if the managers were to see a list of the advantages and disadvantages of the employee specialization that results from word processing, they may be able to make a decision more quickly. You have been asked to prepare such a list for distribution to the managers.

Case

The word processing center in the Data Service Company has been in existence now for about three years. While the word originators are very impressed with the system, the correspondence secretaries are not as impressed. The word originators like the system because they can record dictation twenty-four hours a day, they do not have to wait for a secretary to record their dictation in shorthand, and the quality of the output has generally been quite good. The correspondence secretaries, on the other hand, have complained about the concept almost from the beginning. Their criticism centers around the following: it is a high-pressure job; they don't ever get to talk with anyone; their talents are never noticed by high-level managers, which probably prohibits their being promoted to a middle-management level position; and for the amount of work they do, in comparison to the amount of work that the administrative secretaries do, their salaries are not comparable. All of these factors have caused the turnover rate among secretaries to increase very rapidly. In addition, the level of morale of the correspondence secretaries is very low, the quality of work is just now beginning to decline, and the employees are using many of their sick days.

The supervisor of the word processing center has frequently talked with the administrative office manager about these problems. So far nothing has been done because no one in the organization really knows what to do. At one time there was talk about dismantling the word processing center and returning to the former typing/transcription system. When several of the higher-level managers heard about this, their reaction was "no way."

1. Do you think the organization should keep or dismantle the word processing center? Why?

2. What suggestions can you offer the Data Service Company to improve the plight of the correspondence secretaries?

3. After your suggestions have been implemented for a period of time, what suggestions do you have for evaluating their effectiveness?

Part
3
The
Employee

Selecting Office Employees

Chapter
9

Sources of Recruiting Office Employees
    Internal Sources
        Employee referral
        Employee promotion
    External Sources
        Unsolicited applications
        Advertising
        Educational institution placement services
        Professional organizations
        Public employment agencies
        Private employment agencies
        Temporary help agencies

The Selection Process
    Employee Requisition Blank
    Job Description and Job Specification
    Screening Interview
    Application Blank
    Employee Testing
    Background and Reference Investigation of Applicants
    Selection Interview
    Payroll Change Notice

The Testing Program
    Test Reliability and Validity
    Legal Considerations
    Types of Testing
        Performance or achievement tests
        Aptitude tests
        Intelligence tests
        Personality tests

The Interviewing Process
        The patterned interview
        The direct interview
        The indirect interview
        The stress interview

Federal Legislation
    Civil Rights Act of 1964
    Age Discrimination in Employment Act of 1967
    Equal Employment Opportunity Act of 1972

Chapter Aims   After studying this chapter, the student should be able to:

1. Discuss the various internal sources of recruiting office employees.
2. Discuss the various external sources of recruiting office employees.
3. Discuss the steps involved in a comprehensive employee selection program.
4. Explain the basic differences between test reliability and test validity.
5. Explain the basic difference between what achievement tests measure and what aptitude tests measure.
6. Identify the characteristics of patterned, direct, indirect, and stress interviews.
7. Discuss the various federal legislation acts that have an impact on employee selection.

Chapter Terms   *Unsolicited application:* applying for a position in an organization without knowing whether an opening actually exists.

USTES (*United States Training and Employment Service*): the agency which has control over the public employment agencies found in the various states.

Employee requisition blank: the blank filled out in the department in which an opening exists. The information on the form may include: date, name of department, title of position being filled, job duties, and so forth.

Job description: a written document that identifies the duties and responsibilities of a particular job.

Job specification: a written document that identifies the requirements of a particular job.

Test reliability: an evaluative technique designed to determine whether or not the results of a test are consistent from one time to another.

Test validity: an evaluative technique designed to determine whether a test predicts the performance that it is intended to predict.

Performance (*achievement*) *test:* a test designed to measure an individual's proficiency in performing certain activities or skills.

Aptitude test: a test designed to measure an individual's potential to learn.

Intelligence test: a test designed to measure an individual's mental or reasoning ability.

Personality test: a test designed to measure such factors as interpersonal relations, motivation, ability to handle pressure, self-concept, and individual needs.

Patterned interview: a type of interview in which the interviewee's responses are recorded on a form.

Direct interview: a type of interview in which the interviewer asks only those questions directly related to an interviewee's background or qualifications for a particular job.

Indirect interview: a type of interview in which the interviewee is stimulated to talk about himself or herself.

Stress interview: a type of interview in which the interviewee is put under pressure in order to determine his or her ability to cope with pressure.

Since the quality of an organization's work force is directly related to the quality of its employee selection process, the activities involved in selection are reflected either positively or negatively throughout the organization. The effectiveness of the organization is to a large extent determined by the effectiveness of the work force.

The process of employee selection involves several distinct activities, starting with the recruitment of employees and continuing through the placement of employees in appropriate jobs. Determining present and future manpower requirements, however, is generally excluded as part of the selection process. Employee selection, therefore, begins at the point where a specific opening exists within a department or functional area within an organization.

An important measure of the success of the selection process is the organization's employee turnover rate. An effective selection process can do much to reduce turnover. Inasmuch as the cost of recruiting, interviewing, testing, placing, and orienting a new office employee is very likely to exceed a thousand dollars, the necessity of an effective selection process is readily apparent.

Sources of Recruiting Office Employees

Office employees may be recruited either internally or externally. Internal sources consist of employee referral and promotion from within, while external sources are more varied and consist of the following: **unsolicited applications,** advertising, educational institution placement services, professional organizations, public employment agencies, private employment agencies, and temporary help agencies.

Internal Sources

In some instances, using an internal source for recruiting office employees has distinct advantages over the use of an external source. For example, if a new supervisor is needed in a certain department and one of the present employees would make a good supervisor, promoting that employee to the supervisory position would probably be more advantageous than hiring a supervisor from outside the organization.

Employee referral. When the employee referral method is used, employees recommend individuals for positions open within an organization. Although this recruiting source may give employees a feeling of recognition and importance to the organization, this recruiting source may also result in serious disadvantages. For instance, the employee may experience a considerable amount of embarrassment if the individual he or she recommends does not perform satisfactorily. Some organizations consider this recruiting source to be sufficiently valuable for bonuses to be given to employees recommending someone who is ultimately hired.

Employee promotion. A second internal source is promotion of an employee to a higher-level position rather than filling the position with someone recruited from outside the organization. Filling positions by promoting employees has several distinct advantages. For example, employees are apt to perform better if they know there is a possibility of their being promoted to a higher-level position. Furthermore, morale is likely to increase and turnover is likely to decrease when employees are considered for higher-level positions. Perhaps the greatest disadvantage of filling open positions by employee promotion is that new ideas are not brought in from the outside.

External Sources

Under certain circumstances, the use of an external recruiting source is preferable to using an internal source. For example, an organization should consider an external recruiting source if none of its present employees are qualified to fill an open position.

Unsolicited applications. When an individual applies for a position in an organization without knowing whether an opening actually exists, the unsolicited application is being used. Individuals using this method may apply either in person or in writing.

Unsolicited applications are viewed somewhat negatively by some individuals. In certain instances, however, the individuals who use unsolicited applications are very competent; and because of their intense interest in working for a particular organization, they perform exceptionally well. An organization should not totally discount the value of all unsolicited applications simply because this recruiting source characteristically does not produce a high number of acceptable applicants.

Advertising. This recruiting source includes classified newspaper ads, magazine and journal ads, and radio and television notices. Advertising reaches a large audience in a short period of time. Therefore, depending upon the situation, a large number of individuals may apply for only a few openings. Using this source of recruiting may also result in a large number of marginally qualified or even unqualified applicants. Consequently, the screening process may be considerably more time consuming than for some of the other recruiting sources. Advertising may be very desirable, however, when a large number of employees are needed in a short period of time, such as when a new facility opens. By restricting advertising to certain trade journals or professional magazines, recruiting can be restricted to a homogeneous group.

Educational institution placement services. Many large organizations and a growing number of smaller organizations utilize the placement services of educational institutions when seeking college graduates. Some of the larger educational institution placement services can provide important services both to the employer and to the job seeker. For example, the placement services will usually develop interview schedules and will provide the employers with copies of letters of recommendation. A potential disadvantage of this recruiting source is the tendency for some organizations to recruit at only one or two colleges or universities. In time, because of a lack of diversity in the backgrounds of employees, an organization may find that its managerial philosophy has become very narrow.

Professional organizations. A growing number of professional organizations are developing and operating placement services for their members. Recruiting primarily takes place at conventions or meetings sponsored by the professional organizations but may also take place through the organizations' professional journals and magazines. Since the members of professional organizations are primarily a homogeneous group, screening of applicants is not a great concern with this recruiting source.

Public employment agencies. Although the **United States Training and Employment Service (USTES)** has control over the public employment agencies almost always found in large metropolitan areas and sometimes in less populated areas, each agency is operated by the state in which it is found. The types of services provided by the public employment agencies help employers design testing programs, assist with wage surveys, and help with job analysis and job evaluation.

Each state stipulates that any individual who receives unemployment compensation must be registered with the public employment agency in that state. Therefore, an individual receiving unemployment compensation must be willing to accept any suitable employment offer. Neither an employer or employee is charged for the use of placement services provided by public employment agencies.

The USTES will eventually provide nationwide service so that individuals in one state can readily find out what job openings exist in another state.

Private employment agencies. Whereas public employment agencies do not charge for the placement services they provide, private employment agencies do charge for services rendered since this is their primary means of support. The fees charged by private employment agencies depend to a great extent upon the nature of the open position (higher fees are usually charged for higher-level positions), the location of the agency, and the reputation of the agency. The fees may range anywhere from a few days' salary for the position filled by the agency to a percent of the annual salary of the position—frequently 10–15 percent.

The employer will frequently pay either a portion or all of the fee charged by the employment agency. Generally, the higher the fee charged by the agency, the greater the likelihood that the employer will pay a greater percentage of the placement fee.

Certain criteria should be considered when selecting a private employment agency. For example, the reputation of a private employment agency can be determined to a certain extent if the agency is a subscribing member of the National Employment Association. Employers and individuals might also contact the agency's former clients to determine the level of satisfaction with the services provided by the agency. In addition, another criterion to consider is the agency's ability to provide the quality of employee sought by the organization.

Temporary help agencies. Many organizations use temporary help agencies as a means of obtaining office workers for a short period of time—perhaps for one day to as long as one or two months. Use of individuals placed by temporary help agencies is frequent during seasonally busy times. Temporary office workers are also frequently used to substitute for employees who are sick or who are on vacation.

Many organizations use the services of the temporary help agency primarily for economic reasons. The organization pays the temporary help agency for the service rendered, and the temporary help agency then pays the individual. Consequently, the organization is relieved of any responsibility for paying payroll taxes, social security benefits, unemployment compensation, insurance benefits, and any fringe benefits the organization provides its full-time employees. In many instances, it is less expensive for an organization to use the services of a temporary help agency than it is to hire a full-time employee. Kelly Services and Manpower, Inc., are two of the more commonly used temporary agencies for office employees.

The Selection Process

The selection process begins at the time a job vacancy exists, either because of the creation of a new position or because of employee attrition. The following is a detailed discussion of the various steps involved in a comprehensive employee selection program.

Employee Requisition Blank

The first step in a well-developed employee selection process is to notify the personnel department that an opening exists. In many instances, the manager or supervisor of the department in which the vacancy exists fills out an **employee requisition blank**, thus authorizing the personnel department to begin recruiting potential employees to fill the open position. Some employee requisition blanks contain only a minimum amount of information, including date, name of department, and the title of the open position. Other employee requisition blanks are more comprehensive and include a description of job duties and requirements expected of the job holder.

The employee requisition blank is also useful for those organizations who maintain a waiting list of interested applicants. By using the information contained in the employee requisition blank, an employer can quickly determine which individuals on the waiting list are well qualified for the open position. The individuals who have desirable qualifications can be contacted and invited to interview for the open position.

Job Description and Job Specification

Job descriptions and **job specifications,** which are discussed in detail in Chapter 16, can play an integral role in employee selection. Job applicants who are shown a job description, which discusses the duties and responsibilities of a particular job, and a job specification, which discusses the requirements of the job, can easily and readily determine whether or not they are qualified for the job or whether or not they are interested in the job. This step can provide an important screening function since individuals who decide they are not qualified for the job can terminate the employee selection process at this point. Individuals who feel they are qualified proceed to the next step, which involves the screening interview.

Screening Interview

The screening interview, although not a part of the selection process of all organizations, is used to further screen job applicants. Skillful interviewers are frequently able to determine which applicants are obviously not qualified for the positions for which they are applying. The screening interview thus conserves time and effort for the interviewer and the applicant.

In some organizations, applicants fill out only a portion of the application blank prior to the time of the screening interview. In other organizations, applicants will have filled out the entire application blank prior to the screening interview. In still other organizations, applicants will be given the application blank to complete after the screening interview.

The screening interview is usually kept very brief and the interviewer should make every effort to develop rapport with the applicant. In this way, subsequent interviews with applicants will probably be more realistic, and the information provided by the applicants will be more valid.

Application Blank

An applicant who qualifies for the position for which he or she is applying in most cases is required to complete an application blank, which is the most widely used form in the selection process.

The application blank is useful for collecting the same information for all job applicants. Therefore, the blank facilitates comparing the background of one applicant with another's background. The application is also used by some organizations as a record of employees' history of employment. Depending upon the questions or items included in the application blank, the psychological impact of certain answers provided by the applicants may also be assessed.

The content of application blanks must be closely scrutinized, since federal legislation prohibits any items that might result in unfair discrimination against job applicants. Content sections frequently found on application blanks include the following: personal data, educational background, employment history, and references. Figure 9–1 illustrates a typical application blank.

More and more organizations are designing application blanks that incorporate numerical scoring scales. Consequently, a numerical score can be obtained for each applicant, and those with scores below a certain point are eliminated from the selection process.

Applicants who are still considered by the organization to be potential employees may be asked to take one or more of a variety of tests.

Employee Testing

The use of tests in selecting office employees is very commonplace. Although many standardized tests are available for testing office employees, some organizations have developed tests to meet their own specific needs.

The use of well-designed tests results in two significant advantages: (1) test results can be objectively obtained and thus eliminate some of the human bias that may develop during the course of an interview; (2) depending upon the nature of the test, unknown talents or skills of applicants may be uncovered.

A more detailed discussion of employee testing is also presented later in this chapter. Care must be taken to assure that the testing program conforms with the Equal Employment Opportunity Act of 1972, which is also discussed later in this chapter.

Background and Reference Investigation of Applicants

If the applicant is still considered to be a potential employee after the results of the test scores have been analyzed, many organizations investigate the backgrounds and references of the applicants. Although more and more organizations are using the telephone to investigate the applicants, a written investigation is still common.

Figure 9–2 illustrates an inventory form that is useful for obtaining information from former employers of the applicants. Because of the possibility of law suits, some employers prefer to use the telephone to provide information about a former employee. In such instances, a former employer is likely to be more candid when using the telephone than when asked to provide a written evaluation.

The validity of written letters of recommendation has been challenged recently by many organizations because individuals normally ask for letters of recommendation only from those acquaintances who are certain to write positive recommendations. Therefore, the information in letters of recommendation may be somewhat distorted. For this reason, many organizations place more emphasis on information provided by former employers than on the information provided in letters of recommendation.

When an employer intends to investigate the credit background of an applicant, the Fair Credit Reporting Act of 1971 requires that an employer tell the applicant that a credit investigation is being conducted.

Selection Interview

The two or more applicants who are considered to have the greatest amount of potential as employees are now identified. These applicants are usually interviewed by the department manager or supervisor of the department in which the opening exists. The manager or supervisor will select the applicant considered to have the greatest amount of potential. Since the interviewing process is extremely crucial and is quite involved, interviewing will be discussed in greater detail in a subsequent section of this chapter.

Payroll Change Notice

After the applicant has accepted the position, a payroll change notice is completed. This notice authorizes the payroll department to start paying the new employee. A payroll change notice is illustrated in Figure 9–3.

The Testing Program

If tests are considered to be an integral part of the employee selection process, extreme care must be taken in administering tests and interpreting the test results. For this reason, organizations have had to employ individuals who have specialized training in testing and evaluation.

Test Reliability and Validity

Before any test can be used as a satisfactory measurement device, the **reliability** and **validity** of the test must be determined. A test is considered to have a reliability value if it produces consistent results. In other words, if the same test is given to matched sets of people or if the same group of people takes a slightly different version of the test, the test is reliable if the matched sets of people achieve an approximately equal score or if the individuals taking different versions receive an approximately equal score on several different test administrations.

Test validity refers to the predictive value of the test. In other words, to be valid the test must predict the performance that it is intended to predict. If a selection test is valid, the test will predict those

FIGURE 9–1 Application Blank

APPLICATION FOR EMPLOYMENT

(PLEASE PRINT PLAINLY)

The Civil Rights Act of 1964 prohibits discrimination in employment because of race, color, religion or national origin. Public Law 90-202 prohibits discrimination because of age. The laws of some states prohibit some or all of the above mentioned types of discrimination.

Date: ______

PERSONAL

Name ______ (Last, First, Middle Initial) Social Security No. ______

Present address ______ (No., Street, City, State, Zip)

How many years have you lived at this address? ______ Telephone No. (Area) ______

Previous address ______ (No., Street, City, State, Zip) How long did you live there? ______

Job(s) applied for 1. ______ Rate of pay expected $ ______ per ______

2. ______ Rate of pay expected $ ______ per ______

How did you learn of this opening? ______

Do you want to work ☐ Full-Time or ☐ Part-time. Specify days and hours if part-time ______

Have you worked for us before? ______ If yes, when? ______

List any friends or relatives working for us ______

If hired, on what date will you be available to start work? ______

Are there any other experiences, skills, or qualifications which you feel would especially fit you for work with the Company?

If hired, do you have a reliable means of transportation to get to work? ______

Do you have any physical handicaps which would prevent you from performing specific kinds of work? ______ If yes, describe the defect(s) and explain the work limitations. ______

Have you had a serious illness in the past 5 years? ☐ No ☐ Yes (describe) ______

Have you ever received compensation for injuries? ☐ No ☐ Yes (explain) ______

Have you ever been convicted of a crime, excluding misdemeanors and summary offenses? ☐ No ☐ Yes

If yes, describe in full ______

Person to be notified in case of accident or emergency

Name ______ Phone Number ______

Address ______

Re-order Form #08281 From Amsterdam Printing and Litho Corp., Amsterdam, N. Y. 12010

EDUCATIONAL BACKGROUND

TYPE OF SCHOOL	NAME AND ADDRESS	How Many Years Attended	Graduated	COURSE OR MAJOR
GRAMMAR OR GRADE			☐Yes ☐No	
HIGH SCHOOL			☐Yes ☐No	
COLLEGE			☐Yes ☐No	
POST GRADUATE			☐Yes ☐No	
BUSINESS OR TRADE			☐Yes ☐No	
OTHER			☐Yes ☐No	

MILITARY SERVICE RECORD

Have you ever served in the armed forces? ☐ Yes ☐ No If yes, what branch? ______

Dates of duty: From ______ (Month, Day, Year) To ______ (Month, Day, Year) Rank at discharge ______

What were your duties in the Service (include special training and duty station)? ______

Have you had any schooling under the G. I. Bill of Rights? If yes, describe. ______

TO THE APPLICANT:

Do not answer any *italicized* question below the double line unless the employer has checked the box next to the question. A check indicates that the information requested is needed for 1) a bonafide occupational qualification, 2) is in compliance with national security laws, or 3) other legally permissible reasons.

☐ *Are you over 21 years of age?* ☐ *Yes* ☐ *No* *If no, employment is subject to verification that you are of minimum legal age.*

☐ *When were you born?* ______ (Month, Day, Year)

☐ *How old are you?* ______

☐ *Sex:* ☐ *Male* ☐ *Female*

☐ *Height:* ______ *ft.* ______ *in.*

☐ *Weight:* ______ *lbs.*

☐ *What is your marital status* ☐ *Single* ☐ *Engaged* ☐ *Married* ☐ *Separated* ☐ *Divorced* ☐ *Widowed*

☐ *When were you married?* ______ (Month, Day, Year)

☐ *How many dependents do you have (including yourself)?* ______

☐ *Are you a United States Citizen?* ☐ *Yes* ☐ *No*

☐ *Have you registered for the Draft?* ☐ *Yes* ☐ *No*

☐ *What is your Selective Service classification?* ______

☐ *Please tell us when you attended school.*

☐ *Elementary - - From* ______ *to* ______ ☐ *College - - - - From* ______ *to* ______

☐ *High School - - From* ______ *to* ______ ☐ ______ *(other) - From* ______ *to* ______

☐ *Have you ever been bonded?* ☐ *Yes* ☐ *No* *If yes, for what job(s)?* ______

☐ *Employer may ask other bonafide occupational questions below:*

☐ ______

☐ ______

Courtesy, Amsterdam Printing and Litho Corporation

Occasionally the form of an application blank makes it difficult for an individual to adequately summarize his complete background. To assist us in finding the proper position for you in our company, use the space below to summarize any additional information necessary to describe your full qualifications.

Thank you for completing this application form and for your interest in employment with us. We would like to assure you that your opportunity for employment with this company will be based only on your merit and on no other consideration.

PLEASE READ CAREFULLY
APPLICANT'S CERTIFICATION AND AGREEMENT

I hereby certify that the facts set forth in the above employment application are true and complete to the best of my knowledge. I understand that if employed, falsified statements on this application shall be considered sufficient cause for dismissal. You are hereby authorized to make any investigation of my personal history and financial and credit record through any investigative or credit agencies or bureaus of your choice.*

Signature of Applicant: _____

*NOTE: The Provisions of the Fair Credit Reporting Act may be applicable if a credit report on the applicant is obtained and considered.

DO NOT WRITE BELOW THIS LINE

INTERVIEW ☐ YES ☐ NO   Date _____ Hour _____

Result of Interview _____

_____

Acceptable for Employment? _____ Starting Rate _____ Starting Date _____ Shift _____

Occupation _____ Dept. _____ Clock No. _____

Interviewed by _____ Employed by _____

Approved by _____

This Application For Employment Form is sold for general use throughout the United States. Amsterdam Printing and Litho Corp. assumes no responsibility for the inclusion in said form of any questions which, when asked by the Employer of the Job Applicant, may violate State and/or Federal Law.

Re-order Form #08731 From Amsterdam Printing and Litho Corp., Amsterdam, N. Y. 12010

PERSONAL REFERENCES
(Excluding Former Employers or Relatives)

Name and Occupation	Address	Phone Number
1.		
2.		
3.		

PRIOR WORK HISTORY (LIST IN ORDER, LAST OR PRESENT EMPLOYER FIRST)

DATES FROM	TO	NAME AND ADDRESS OF EMPLOYER	RATE OF PAY START	FINISH	SUPERVISOR'S NAME AND TITLE	REASON FOR LEAVING

Describe in detail the work you did.

DATES FROM	TO	NAME AND ADDRESS OF EMPLOYER	RATE OF PAY START	FINISH	SUPERVISOR'S NAME AND TITLE	REASON FOR LEAVING

Describe in detail the work you did.

DATES FROM	TO	NAME AND ADDRESS OF EMPLOYER	RATE OF PAY START	FINISH	SUPERVISOR'S NAME AND TITLE	REASON FOR LEAVING

Describe in detail the work you did.

DATES FROM	TO	NAME AND ADDRESS OF EMPLOYER	RATE OF PAY START	FINISH	SUPERVISOR'S NAME AND TITLE	REASON FOR LEAVING

Describe in detail the work you did.

May we contact the employers listed above? _____ If not, indicate below which one(s) you do not wish us to contact

FIGURE 9–2   Reference Check

Name of Applicant	
Former Supervisor	Title
Company Where Applicant Worked	Telephone Number

1. (Applicant's name) has applied for employment with us. I would like to *verify* some of the information given us. When did he/she work for your company?

From _____ 19____ To_____ 19____

2. What was his/her job when he/she started to work for you?

_____

   When he/she left?

_____

   $_____ per _____
   Is that correct?

☐ Yes, ☐ No, $_____

4. What did you think of him/her? (Quality and quantity of work, attendance, how he/she got along with others, etc.)

_____

_____

   4a. What accidents has he/she had?

_____

5. Why did he/she leave your company?

_____

_____

_____

6. Would you re-employ?

☐ Yes, ☐ No, (If not, why not?) _____

_____

_____

Additional comments _____

_____

_____

_____

_____

Date of Check _____ 19____ Made by _____

Form No. OT-203

Courtesy, The Dartnell Corporation

FIGURE 9–3   Payroll Change Form

TO: PAYROLL DEPARTMENT

Please Enter the Following Change(s) in Your Records to Take

Effect _____
          (Date and Time)

Employee _____

Social Security No. _____ Clock No. _____

THE CHANGE(S)

✓ Check all Applicable Boxes	From	To
☐ Department		
☐ Job		
☐ Shift		
☐ Rate		
☐		

REASON FOR THE CHANGE(S)

☐ Hired   ☐ Probationary Period Completed

☐ Re-Hired   ☐ Length of Service Increase

☐ Promotion   ☐ Re-evaluation of Existing Job

☐ Demotion   ☐ Resignation

☐ Transfer   ☐ Retirement

☐ Merit Increase   ☐ Layoff

☐ Union Scale   ☐ Discharge

☐ Leave of Absence From _____ Until _____
                              (Date)   (Date)

☐ Other (Explain) _____

_____

_____

_____

Change Authorized by _____ Date _____

Change Approved by _____ Date _____

Form # 08320   Amsterdam Printing and Litho Corp. Amsterdam, N.Y. 12010

Courtesy, Amsterdam Printing and Litho Corporation

who will succeed and those who will fail in a particular job or in a particular skill or task.

If properly used, and if the results are properly interpreted, many standardized tests are both reliable and valid. However, when used improperly, reliability and validity cannot be guaranteed.

A test that is very commonly used in the selection of office workers is a five-minute timed typewriting test. Although the test is reliable (applicants will be fairly consistent in their rates), the test is not at all valid. A five-minute timed test will do very little to predict a typist's performance when typing letters, statistical tables, reports, and so forth. A much more valid test could be developed to include typing tasks that applicants will experience on the job.

Legal Considerations

Special attention must be focused on the legal considerations of the testing program so that no ethnic or cultural group will be discriminated against. Section 703(h), Title VII of the Civil Rights Act, which includes the Tower Amendment, states that a test will not be considered discriminatory as long as the test is not by design, intent, or use discriminatory because of race, color, religion, sex, or national origin.

Special attention also needs to be focused on the culturally disadvantaged. Many culturally disadvantaged applicants will score lower on tests simply because of cultural deprivation. A test that is valid for one group of workers may not be valid for the culturally disadvantaged. A test may be considered to unfairly discriminate against the culturally disadvantaged if the members of the culturally disadvantaged group obtain significantly lower test results than their counterparts, provided they would be as successful on the job as their counterparts.

The Equal Employment Opportunity Act of 1972, which is discussed later in this chapter, provides legislation that prohibits using a selection test that unfairly discriminates against any applicant.

Types of Testing

Several different kinds of tests have been designed for use in screening applicants. Among the more common are: **performance** or **achievement tests, aptitude tests, intelligence tests,** and **personality tests.**

Performance or achievement tests. There is a wide variety of office positions for which performance or achievement tests provide an excellent measure of the applicants' proficiency in performing certain activities or skills. For example, an applicant's shorthand skill can be accurately measured by giving the applicant realistic dictation. A clerk-typist might be asked to type a series of letters. A file clerk might be asked to code and file a series of documents. For jobs that require a considerable amount of decisionmaking, the applicants might be asked to react to a series of situations requiring realistic decisionmaking.

Some of the well-known standardized performance or achievement tests are:

1. SRA Language Skills (Science Research Associates)
2. SRA Typing Skills (Science Research Associates)
3. SRA Dictation Skills (Science Research Associates)
4. Seashore-Bennett Stenographic Proficiency Tests (The Psychological Corporation)

Aptitude tests. Performance or achievement tests measure the proficiency of an individual in performing specific tasks or skills, while aptitude tests measure an individual's potential to learn. Therefore, if an applicant is being considered for a position in which job holders frequently move up to higher-level positions, the applicants will probably be given an aptitude test.

The following aptitude tests are appropriate for evaluating office workers:

1. General Clerical Test (The Psychological Corporation)
2. SRA Clerical Aptitude Test (Science Research Associates)
3. Minnesota Clerical Test (The Psychological Corporation)
4. Purdue Clerical Adaptability Test (Occupational Research Center)

Intelligence tests. When mental and reasoning abilities are crucial to the success of an employee, an intelligence test will most likely be administered to each individual applying for a position. Because of the specialized nature of the interpretation of the results, some organizations no longer administer intelligence tests, as the organizations employ no one qualified to interpret the results. The use of intelligence tests has been criticized recently since such tests tend to favor applicants who have had considerable verbal and numerical experience. Therefore, applicants whose verbal and numerical experiences are limited are discriminated against to a certain extent.

The intelligence tests appropriate for evaluating office workers include:

1. Wonderlic Personnel Test (Wonderlic and Associates)
2. Army General Classification Test (Science Research Associates)
3. Otis Quick-Scoring Mental Ability Test (Harcourt Brace Jovanovich)
4. SRA Adaptability Test (Science Research Associates)
5. Hemmon-Nelson Tests of Mental Ability (Houghton Mifflin)

Personality tests. Although personality tests are being used less frequently, organizations still administer the tests to applicants applying for jobs that require certain personality traits or characteristics. Personality tests measure such factors as interpersonal relations, motivation, ability to handle pressure, self-concept, and individual needs. Some feel that since individuals are able to determine which responses are most desirable, the validity of personality tests as a selection device for office workers is questionable.

Standardized personality tests include the following:

1. California Psychological Inventory (Consulting Psychological Press, Inc.)
2. Wonderlic Personality Tests (Wonderlic and Associates)
3. Cutswold Personality Assessment (Robert Gibson and Sons, Ltd.)
4. Temperament Comparator (Education-Industry Service)

A rather recent development in testing is to require individuals applying for certain types of jobs to submit to a polygraph (lie detector) test. This is especially true in jobs where confidentiality must be maintained or where large sums of money are handled. Several states have enacted legislation that restricts the use of polygraph tests, while other states have enacted legislation that requires polygraph operators to be licensed.

The Interviewing Process

The selection interview, considered by many to be the most crucial step in the selection process, serves a variety of functions.

1. The interviewer is able to ask questions to clarify any ambiguous areas with regard to the applicant's background.
2. The interviewer can emphasize areas of particular concern to the organization.
3. The self-expression, confidence, poise, and appearance of the applicant can be readily assessed.
4. The applicant can ask additional questions about the job and the organization.
5. The applicant can emphasize certain areas about his or her background that might be helpful in making an employment decision.

Anyone who has had an employment interview knows that interviewing can be a frustrating experience, as well as a rewarding one. The interviewer can do much to enhance the success of the interview. For example, the interviewer should immediately try to make the applicant feel at ease, should develop rapport with the applicant, and should avoid asking any personal questions that have no bearing on the position for which the applicant is applying.

Although many organizations utilize specialists in the testing function of the selection process, fewer organizations utilize professionally trained individuals to conduct interviews. More and more, organizations are beginning to discover the crucial role of the interview and are realizing the necessity for adequately trained interviewers.

Several different types of interviews are used in selecting office employees. Interviews are categorized by the amount or nature of control that the interviewer exerts over the interview. In some instances, the interviewer will exert a considerable amount of control, while in other interviews, the interviewer will give the applicant a considerable amount of leeway.

The most common types of interviews used for selecting office employees are **patterned, direct,** and **indirect.** Although not recommended for the selection of most classifications of office employees, the **stress** interview may be appropriately used under certain conditions.

The patterned interview. When the patterned interview is used, a form similar to the one illustrated in Figure 9–4 lists the questions to be asked by the interviewer. Sufficient space is also provided on the form for the interviewer to record the interviewee's responses.

The use of the patterned interview is especially useful under certain circumstances. For example, if many people are applying for the same position, the form facilitates comparing the interviewees' backgrounds, since they will all have responded to the same questions. Furthermore, if an organization makes a practice of inviting former applicants to apply for an open position, the patterned interview form helps determine which former applicants will be invited to apply.

Perhaps the most significant advantage of using the patterned interview, provided the interviewer follows the form, is that all crucial areas are covered. There is little or no chance that any areas will not be covered. The patterned interview also insures that the interviewee will have ample opportunities for providing information about his or her background. All too often, because interviewees discuss the organization or job in too much detail, there is too little time to get sufficient information from the applicants.

The direct interview. The direct interview is characterized as being conducted rather quickly, since the interviewer asks only those questions directly related to the interviewee's background and the qualifications he or she has for a particular job. The direct interview is also characterized

FIGURE 9-4 Patterned Interview Form

PATTERNED INTERVIEW
(Short Form)

Name _____
Address _____

Date of Birth _____ Soc. Sec. No. _____
Check your State and Federal laws as to discrimination because of age.

Rating: [1] [2] [3] [4] Comments: _____
In making final rating, be sure to consider applicant's stability, industry, perseverance, loyalty, ability to get along with others, self-reliance, leadership, maturity, motivation; also, domestic situation and health.

Interviewer: _____ Job Considered for: _____ Date _____

Why are you applying for work in this Company? _____
Is applicant's underlying reason a desire for prestige, security, or earnings?

If you were hired, how long would it take you to get to work? _____
How would you get to work? _____ Is there anything undesirable here?

WORK EXPERIENCE. Cover all positions. This information is very important. Interviewer should record last position first. Every month since leaving school should be accounted for. Note military service in work record in continuity with jobs held since that time (In New Jersey exclude Military questions).

	LAST OR PRESENT POSITION	NEXT TO LAST POSITION	SECOND FROM LAST POSITION
Name of Company			
Address			
Dates of employ.	From To	From To	From To
		Do these dates check with application?	
Nature of work		Will applicant's previous experience be helpful on this job?	
Starting salary			
Salary at leaving			
What was especially liked about the job?		Has applicant made good work progress?	General or merit increases?
What was especially disliked?		Has applicant been happy and contented in his/her work?	
Reasons for leaving	Were applicant's dislikes justified?	Is applicant chronically dissatisfied?	
	Are applicant's reasons for leaving reasonable and consistent?		

OTHER POSITIONS

Name of Company	Type of Work	Salary	Date Started	Date Left	Reasons for Leaving

Has applicant stayed in line of work for the most part?
Has applicant gotten along well on his/her jobs?
Are applicant's attitudes toward his/her employers loyal?
Was applicant interested in creative work? In work requiring activity?
Has applicant approved self and position?

Form No. OP-202

Copyright, 1975, The Dartnell Corporation, Chicago, Illinois 60640. Printed in U.S.A.
Developed by The McMurry Company

How many times did you draw unemployment compensation? _____ When? _____ Why? _____
Does applicant depend on self?

How many weeks have you been unemployed in the past five years? _____ How did you spend this time? _____
Did conditions in applicant's occupation justify this time? Did applicant use time profitably?

What accidents have you had in recent years? _____
Is applicant "accident-prone"? Any disabilities which will interfere with work?

SCHOOLING
How far did you go in school? Grade: 1 2 3 4 5 6 7 8 High School: 1 2 3 4 College: 1 2 3 4 Date of leaving school _____

If you did not graduate from high school or college, why not? _____ Is applicant's schooling adequate for the job?

What special training have you taken? _____ Are applicant's reasons for not finishing sound?

Extracurricular activities (exclude military, racial, religious, nationality groups) _____ Will this be helpful? Indications of perseverance? Industry?

What offices did you hold in these groups? _____ Did applicant get along well with others? Indications of leadership?

FAMILY BACKGROUND	FINANCIAL SITUATION	DOMESTIC AND SOCIAL SITUATION
Financial aid to family	Cost of living per month $	Group activities (Exclude military, racial, religious, nationality groups)
Leisure time activities	Any current debts?	When did you have last drink? Sensible?
Summer vacations	Savings on last job $ Net Worth $	What types of people rub you the wrong way? Bias?
Group activities	Did applicant keep busy?	
(Exclude military, racial, religious, and nationality groups)		Ever convicted of a felony?
Positions of leadership		Charges Immaturity?
	Leader?	(This does not constitute an automatic bar to employment)
How old when fully self-supporting?	Self-Reliant?	

HEALTH
What serious illnesses, operations, or accidents did you have as a child? _____ Has applicant retained any infantile personality traits due to childhood illnesses?

What illnesses, operations, or accidents have you had in recent years? _____ Are applicant's illnesses legitimate rather than indicating a desire to "enjoy ill health"?

How much time have you lost from work because of illness during past year? _____ Will applicant be able to do the job?

How are your teeth? _____

Does anyone in your home suffer ill health? _____ Are spouse, children, or family relatively healthy?

ADDITIONAL INFORMATION: _____

Do you suffer from:
☐ Poor Eyesight
☐ Poor Hearing
☐ Rupture
☐ Rheumatism
☐ Asthma
☐ Heart Trouble
☐ Diabetes
☐ Ulcers
☐ Hay Fever
☐ Flat Feet
☐ Nervousness

Courtesy, The Dartnell Corporation

as being somewhat limited in terms of the information that can be gathered.

Because of the nature of the direct interview, it is recommended only for lower-level office jobs or for use as an initial screening interview. The intended purpose of the direct interview does not make it feasible for exploring needs, attitudes, and feelings of applicants.

The direct interview is most useful when a limited amount of information must be gathered rather quickly. To use the direct interview for any other purpose is questionable.

The indirect interview. As its title implies, the indirect interview covers a much broader range of topics than does the direct interview. The indirect interview is unstructured in format, and thus the applicant has a considerable amount of freedom for areas of discussion. Many interviewers feel that the primary objective for using the indirect interview is to stimulate the interviewee to talk about himself or herself—to discuss individual needs, attitudes, feelings, and so forth.

Because of the unstructured format, the indirect interview is difficult for many interviewers to conduct. Although the interviewer is responsible for "keeping the interview on target," the interviewer has to become a good listener and should interrupt only when it is obvious that the applicant will not provide important information unless the interviewer asks specific questions related to that information.

The stress interview. Of the four types of interviews discussed in this chapter, the stress interview is the least commonly used for selecting office employees. The stress interview was developed during World War II as a means of identifying individuals who could withstand pressure-laden situations or situations involving a considerable amount of stress. The interview is typically conducted by several individuals who ask the interviewee questions in very rapid succession. The goal is to put the interviewee on the defensive as a means of assessing the interviewee's ability to cope with pressure.

Because the stress interview can actually be detrimental to the psychological ego of some individuals, not everyone should be subjected to such an interview. Individuals who during the course of the interview become emotionally distressed should have some assistance in returning to a normal state of mind before the conclusion of the interview.

The stress interview, although not appropriate for many office jobs, is used by some organizations to determine applicants' suitability for leadership positions. The interview is most effectively conducted by individuals who have had some specialized training in using interviews of this type.

Federal Legislation

Anyone in an organization who is involved with selecting new employees should be thoroughly aware of the federal legislation that might have an impact on the selection process. Specific legislation prohibits sex or age discrimination. Once an individual is employed, other legislation prohibits the use of an individual's sex as a salary determinant (see Chapter 18). Since the following acts are discussed in greater detail in Chapter 18, only a short summary of each is presented in this chapter.

Civil Rights Act of 1964

Title VII of the Civil Rights Act has significant implications for the hiring of individuals. The act states that employers or unions with twenty-five or more workers must treat all persons equally regardless of their sex, race, color, national origin, or religion. An exception to this provision allows an employer to use sex, national origin, or religion as a selection factor if justifiable as bona fide occupational qualifications.

Age Discrimination in Employment Act of 1967

This act prohibits using age to discriminate against persons who are forty to sixty-five years of age. The act forbids an employer's use of age as a basis for refusing to hire, for determining compensation, or for discharging an employee.

Equal Employment Opportunity Act of 1972

This act significantly amended Title VII of the Civil Rights Act of 1964. The Equal Employment Opportunity Act of 1972 has some significant implications for hiring, transferring, training, or retraining employees. The Equal Employment Opportunity Commission, the regulatory agency of the act, has issued guidelines that state that the test questions must be related to a bona fide occupational qualification and that test scores of applicants must be directly correlated to the important elements of job success. Also, where technically feasible, tests should be validated for each minority group. In other words, a test may be considered discriminatory if individuals protected by Title VII are disproportionately rejected on the basis of a test that has no significant relationship to success in a particular job. While test validation is feasible for large employers, smaller employers have more difficulty because there are so few employees on which to validate a test. In certain instances, when there are too few employees to validate a test, the results of validity studies conducted by other organizations, such as those cited in test manuals, may be considered acceptable if the jobs and the individuals in the two organizations are basically comparable. This regulation has resulted in some employers no longer using tests in the selection process.

Before a test is used for selecting office employees, it may be wise to obtain from appropriate authorities or officials an opinion regarding the test's validity. Individuals who work for the Equal Employment Opportunity Commission are in a position to provide valuable assistance.

If other selecting devices, such as application blanks and interview sheets, are used to discriminate against a class of individuals protected by Title VII or are discriminatory in nature, they are prohibited under the provisions of the Equal Employment Opportunity Act of 1972. It is the employer's responsibility to prove that a test or selection device is not discriminatory.

Review Questions

1. What is likely to be the greatest disadvantage of using the employee referral method of employee selection?

2. If a large number of employees are needed in a short period of time, which recruiting source would perhaps provide the greatest number of applicants?

3. In addition to providing recruiting assistance to organizations, what other types of assistance does the USTES provide?

4. What advantages are provided by using temporary help agencies when additional help is needed on a short-term basis?

5. What are the primary purposes of the employee requisition blank?

6. Of what value are job descriptions and job specifications in the selection process?

7. What advantages result from employee testing?

8. What impact does the Fair Credit Reporting Act of 1971 have on employee selection?

9. What special advantages are provided by using the patterned interview?

10. In terms of selection of employees, what are the major provisions of the Civil Rights Act of 1964, the Age Discrimination in Employment Act of 1967, and the Equal Employment Opportunity Act of 1972?

Minicases

The administrative office manager of Jameson, Ltd., has been developing a series of tests for the selection of new office employees. To measure shorthand skill, the applicants are given dictation at rates of eighty and one hundred words a minute for three minutes each. The applicants are asked to transcribe their notes. An error limit of 5 percent is allowed at each rate. Applicants who pass the one hundred word-a-minute test are eligible for higher-level jobs than those who pass the eighty word-a-minute test. To measure typing skills, a five-minute timed writing test is given. Depending on the job for which applicants are applying, they may be given other tests. The administrative office manager is now interested in determining whether or not the shorthand and typewriting tests are valid and reliable. Do you think the tests are valid and reliable? If so, why? If not, why not? How would you determine the validity and reliability of the two types of tests?

*   *   *

The Colemann Company has become increasingly concerned about the legality of some of their hiring practices. Several of the companies in the same city in which Colemann is located have had a variety of problems with some of their hiring practices which violate various provisions of federal legislation. The Colemann Company wants to avoid any similar problems. Several employees in the company have been asked to prepare a list of items that the federal legislation prohibits in hiring employees. You are one of the employees who has been asked to prepare a list. What items should be placed on the list that federal legislation prohibits in the hiring of new employees?

Case

The Ardway Corporation recently had an opening for an offset printing press operator in its printing and duplicating area of the office services department. Two people applied for the opening—Bill Jackson, a mail clerk in Ardway, and Linda Smith, who has been working for another firm in the same geographical area.

Jackson, who has worked as a mail clerk now for three years, has limited experience as an offset printing press operator. Smith, on the other hand, recently finished a printing and graphic arts program in a local vocational high school.

John Doyle, in his tenth year as administrative office manager for Ardway, is in charge of the printing and duplicating area and is therefore responsible for selecting employees for positions under his jurisdiction. Doyle, prior to being promoted to his present position, was supervisor of the printing and duplicating area. While he was supervisor, he was very opposed to hiring women to work in the printing and duplicating room. He used the following as the basis for his opposition:

1. The work involved too much physical effort for females to handle.

2. Females had only one role in an organization—to perform secretarial and clerical work.

3. It was more appropriate for most females to be homemakers than to be employees in a business firm.

Smith, after being refused the job, filed a sex discrimination charge against Ardway because Jackson was hired; she thought she was better qualified than he was.

1. What additional information do you need before you can decide if Smith was unfairly discriminated against?

2. What is your assessment of Doyle's philosophy with regard to female employees?

3. If you were the administrative office manager in this case, how would you have handled the selection process?

4. What steps should the organization take as assurance that future job applicants won't be able to charge that they were unfairly discriminated against?

Appraising the Performance of Office Employees

Chapter

10

Purposes of Performance Appraisal

Objectives of Performance Appraisal Programs

Need for Establishing Performance Standards

Methods of Performance Appraisal
    Traditional Appraisal Methods
        Graphic rating scale
        Paired comparison appraisal
        Checklists
        Simple ranking
    New Appraisal Methods
        Forced choice
        Critical incidents
        Peer rating
        Group rating
        Results-oriented appraisal

Rating Errors
    Halo Effect
    Influence of Recent Performance
    Bias

Analysis of Appraisals

Appraisal Interviews

Chapter Aims   After studying this chapter, the student should be able to:

1. Discuss the various uses of performance appraisal.

2. Explain why performance standards have to be established before an appraisal program can be developed.

3. Discuss each of the following traditional rating scales: graphic rating scale, paired comparison, checklists, and simple ranking.

4. Discuss the forced choice, the critical incidents, the peer rating, the group rating, and the results-oriented appraisal methods.

5. Explain the halo effect on performance appraisal.

6. Explain the purpose for the appraisal interview and discuss its advantages and disadvantages.

Chapter Terms   *Performance appraisal:* the formal evaluation of employees' performance, which is used to identify their strengths and weaknesses. The results of performance appraisal are used for determining the amount of salary increases, for promotions, and for transfer to another job.

Halo effect: an employee's being rated extremely high or extremely low in all areas because the rater is influenced by the rating the employee received in a few of the categories.

Appraisal interview: the interview designed to inform the employee of the results of the appraisal and to discuss ways the employee's performance may be improved.

The assessing—either formal or informal—of one individual by another is always occurring. Within organizations, the formal program designed to assess employees' performance is known as **performance appraisal.** Employees desire to have their performance appraised to confirm that they are performing satisfactorily. The absence of such knowledge results in a great amount of insecurity for individuals.

Purposes of Performance Appraisal

The purposes of the formal appraisal of employee performance are many and varied. Performance appraisal was originally developed as a means of identifying supervisors who should be promoted or who should receive salary increases. The appraisal process, no longer restricted to supervisors, is used to identify employee strengths and weaknesses. This helps employees improve the effectiveness of their performance, which in turn results in salary increases, promotions, and transfers.

A formally established performance appraisal program also provides an objective basis on which to evaluate employees, eliminating charges of favoritism and bias. The program provides motivation for individuals to work harder and to try to overcome identified weaknesses as a means of obtaining salary increases and promotions.

The results of performance appraisal are often used in manpower planning. Long-range planning is facilitated, since performance appraisal helps to determine which positions will eventually need to be filled because of employee promotion. The results of the appraisal process are also often used to determine areas suitable for training of individuals, since performance appraisal clearly identifies weak areas in employees' performance.

A by-product of the performance appraisal process is the strengthening of communication between supervisors and subordinates. By discussing the results of the appraisal, the communication lines between the supervisor and subordinate become a reality. Another by-product of the appraisal process is improved quality of supervision. Supervisors who are responsible for the appraisal of their subordinates' performance are apt to be more cognizant of the subordinates' strengths and weaknesses, which should result in more effective supervision.

Objectives of Performance Appraisal Programs

The following objectives are typical of those found in performance appraisal programs:

1. To provide an objective basis on which to appraise employees.

2. To provide a systematic basis for determining salary increases, promotions, and transfers.

3. To provide an identification of areas in which training is appropriate because of employee deficiencies.

4. To establish effective communication between supervisors and subordinates.

5. To provide employees with feedback about their performance as an incentive for them to work harder or to perform at a higher level.

Need for Establishing Performance Standards

In any appraisal process, it is crucial to determine the basis or standards against which employees are to be evaluated. With performance appraisal, these standards or criteria should be predetermined and made known to each employee at the time of initial employment. Otherwise, it would be sheer coincidence for an employee's performance to be consistent with the expectations held by an organization.

Although it is crucial to identify performance standards in all jobs, it is perhaps even more crucial to identify standards in nonproduction jobs (those jobs that involve more than a quantity or quality output). In nonproduction jobs, such factors as human relations, ability to work with others, initiative, judgment, and so forth are likely to be paramount.

With increasing frequency, organizations are utilizing appraisal techniques in which the employee's performance is compared with objectives or expected results that were established at some previous time. This concept works well not only for production jobs but also for nonproduction jobs. Although this concept is fundamental to the results-oriented appraisal, it can also be incorporated into most of the other appraisal methods that are discussed in the next section.

Methods of Performance Appraisal

Some of the methods for appraising the performance of employees have been in existence for many years. Others are more recent. In all probability, the appraisal process for employees who belong to a union will have a different emphasis. For these employees, seniority plays an important part in determining who will be promoted or who will receive a salary increase.

Traditional Appraisal Methods

The traditional appraisal methods typically evaluate employee performance on traits that are considered essential for effectively carrying out job duties. Unless these traits are observable, are fairly standard for all comparable jobs within an organization, and can be measured objectively, the effectiveness of the traditional rating method might be hampered.

Among the traditional appraisal methods are graphic rating scales, paired comparison appraisal, checklists, and simple ranking.

Graphic rating scale. The graphic rating scale, perhaps the most widely used method of performance appraisal, utilizes a scale similar to the one illustrated in Figure 10–1. The rater, in completing the scale, indicates

FIGURE 10-1 Performance Appraisal

Name _____ Social Security number _____ Present salary _____

Present position _____ Date employed _____ Date of last promotion _____

QUALITY OF WORK Refers to neatness, accuracy, completeness of work	X Quality of work is considered above average and only rarely does any have to be redone	X Quality of work is superior and none ever has to be redone	X Quality of work is improving but is still sub-standard	X Much work has to be re-done	X Quality of work is average and only some of it has to be redone
Comment:					
QUANTITY OF WORK Refers to volume of output	X Normally works at above average rate and wastes little time	X Works at a consistently high level with very little wasted time	X Is not able to produce at acceptable level	X Produces at an average rate but is steady and wastes little time	X Output is frequently below expected level. Wastes time
Comment:					
INITIATIVE Refers to ability to develop ideas and to ability to get things done	X Is capable of working without being told what to do	X Because of lack of initiative, always has to be told what to do	X Self starter. Never has to be told to do something	X Rarely does anything without first being told	X Develops new ways of doing things. Is resourceful
Comment:					
RELATIONS WITH OTHERS Refers to ability to get along with others	X Is respected by everyone, is helpful, and is looked upon by others as a "leader"	X Is disagreeable and does not get along well with others. Has few friends. Is a trouble maker	X Has a good attitude toward others and is liked and respected by others	X Is friendly and gets along well with others	X Is not friendly and is generally disliked by others
Comment:					
DEPENDABILITY Refers to trustworthiness and amount of supervision required	X Is always dependable, is completely trustworthy, and requires very little if any supervision	X Is not always dependable, cannot be trusted in all respects, and requires frequent supervision	X Is very trustworthy, is always dependable, and requires very little supervision	X Cannot be trusted, is not dependable, and requires constant supervision	X Can be trusted most of the time, is dependable, and requires only an average amount of supervision
Comment:					
JOB KNOWLEDGE Refers to the knowledge the individual has about the job	X Has average knowledge about job	X Knows about everything there is to know about the job	X Is very knowledgeable about the job	X Lacks job knowledge and is generally unwilling to learn	X Lacks job knowledge but is willing to learn
Comment:					

Summary Comments:

Overall rating: _____ Outstanding; _____ Above average; _____ Average

_____ Below average; _____ Poor

Today's date _____

Appraiser's signature _____

Employee's signature _____

the degree to which the individual being rated possesses that trait or characteristic.

The three methods commonly used in constructing the evaluation section of the graphic rating scale are: (1) descriptive phrases, (2) descriptive words, and (3) numerical scales.

The use of descriptive phrases probably provides more objectivity in rating than do either of the other two methods. For example, for the trait "Job Knowledge," the descriptive phrases might be: thoroughly understands the job, more than adequately understands the job, has sufficient knowledge of the job, etc. Some appraisal forms using descriptive phrases provide space for written comments about each trait.

When descriptive words are used (outstanding, excellent, above average, average, below average, poor, etc.), it is difficult for all raters to be consistent, since what is "outstanding" to one rater may only be "excellent" to another. Appraisal forms using descriptive words also frequently provide space for written comments about each trait. For example:

	Outstanding	Excellent	Average	Below Average	Poor
JOB KNOWLEDGE:	x	x	x	x	x

Refers to the theoretical
knowledge and practical
knowledge as related to
the present job.

COMMENTS:

When this method is used, each trait is usually defined or described as a means of getting a greater amount of consistency between raters.

Numerical scales involve a series of numbers (perhaps 1–6, 1 being low, 6 being high) for appraising the performance of each individual on each trait. Assuming that all traits are weighted equally, the numerical scores can be added to get a total value for the performance of each individual. To make this method as objective as possible, the numerical values and each trait should be defined. Appraisal forms using this method can also be designed to provide space for written comments about each trait.

More objectivity can also be achieved by randomly placing the scale values on the form. Rather than placing the highest value at the left and lowest value at the right for each trait, the values should be reordered from one trait to the next. The rater, therefore, has to be more careful in appraising the individuals, which results in a more thorough, objective appraisal.

Also commonly included on graphic rating scales is a summary section that consists of two subsections. One subsection is used for general comments about the individual being rated, and the other is used to provide an overall rating of the individual (superior, above average, average, etc.).

Although the graphic rating scale is a fairly simple and quick method for appraising the performance of a fairly large number of employees and for comparing the performance of one individual against another, it does possess some serious shortcomings:

1. Unless the traits are individually weighted, each trait is considered to be of equal performance. For example, some jobs require an extensive amount of decisionmaking, while others require very little. To treat all traits equally for all jobs is not realistic.

2. The graphic rating scale is subject to certain errors that tend to distort the rating of individuals. (These errors are discussed in the next section of this chapter.)

3. The rating scale appraises one's past performance—after it is too late to improve the quality of performance.

4. Unless special effort is made on the part of the supervisor, some employees have considerable difficulty in overcoming the types of weaknesses identified by the graphic rating scale.

5. The graphic rating scale may contain either too many or too few traits. From six to nine traits are generally considered adequate.

Paired comparison appraisal. The paired comparison appraisal involves comparing one individual with each of the other individuals in a particular work group. Specific traits might be considered in appraising the individuals, or the performance of the individual might be considered as a totality.

A chart similar to the one illustrated in Figure 10–2 is useful. Each individual within the work group is listed on the left side (vertically) and also across the top (horizontally). When the performance of the individual being rated is of higher quality than the individual against whom he or she is being compared, a check mark is placed in the corresponding square. For example, according to Figure 10–2, the performance of Employee *A* is considered to be of higher quality than Employees *B*, *C*, and *D*. Employees *E* and *F* have a higher performance level than does Employee *A*. Therefore, a check mark is placed in the corresponding square. The total number of check marks in the rows have to be determined for each individual. The employees with the greater number of check marks receive a higher appraisal than those with a fewer number of check marks.

Although the paired comparison appraisal readily facilitates the

FIGURE 10–2   Rating Grid

	Employee A	Employee B	Employee C	Employee D	Employee E	Employee F
Employee A	■	✓	✓	✓		
Employee B		■	✓	✓		
Employee C			■	✓		
Employee D				■		
Employee E	✓	✓	✓	✓	■	
Employee F	✓	✓	✓	✓	✓	■

Checkmark Tally: Employee A--3
Employee B--2
Employee C--1
Employee D--0
Employee E--4
Employee F--5

comparison of individuals within a work group, the method is characterized as possessing some of the same shortcomings as the graphic rating
scale. In addition, unless specifically identified traits are used to evaluate
individuals, their strengths and weaknesses are not readily apparent.
The number of employees that can be effectively appraised by the paired
comparison method of performance appraisal is quite small.

Checklists. Checklists consist of a series of statements about various
traits. The rater appraises the employee by responding to each statement,
which evaluates the performance of the individual being rated. A partial
checklist is illustrated in Figure 10–3.
     A distinct advantage of the checklist method of performance ap-
praisal is that specific items are evaluated—not just broad or general
traits. Although the rating errors characteristic of the graphic scale are
minimized when using the checklist, both tend to treat the traits as being
equal in weight or importance.

Simple ranking. The simple ranking appraisal method ranks employees
from the best to the poorest. The method is fairly simple and can be

FIGURE 10–3   Checklist

Trait	Yes	No
Initiative		
1. Does the individual frequently need guidance and direction from others?	—	—
2. Is the individual able to determine what course to follow without having to be told?	—	—
3. Is the individual a leader?	—	—
4. Is the individual a follower?	—	—
5. Does the individual accept work willingly?	—	—
Quality of Work		
1. Is the individual's work error-free most of the time?	—	—
2. Does a considerable amount of work have to be redone?	—	—
3. Is the individual's work completed on time?	—	—
4. Do the individual's work habits frequently disrupt the flow of work because of poor quality of work?	—	—

used for appraising a fairly large number of employees. The method is facilitated by putting each employee's name on an index card. The cards can then be easily arranged and rearranged until the proper ranking is achieved.

The advantages of this method are readily offset by its lack of specificity and usefulness to the individual being rated. Only when the rater identifies problem or weak areas for the employees do they know the reasons for their rating. Unless the rater uses some objective basis for appraising the individuals, bias and subjectivity will enter into the appraisal.

New Appraisal Methods

Although the traditional methods of performance appraisal are still frequently used in organizations, some of the newer appraisal methods are becoming increasingly popular. Among the newer appraisal methods are forced choice, critical incidents, peer rating, group rating, and results-oriented.

Forced choice. The forced choice method consists of twenty-five to forty sets of statements, and the rater chooses from each set the statement that is *most* descriptive and the statement that is *least* descriptive of the person being appraised. The following is an example of two different sets of statements:

Most	Least	
1	1	Wants to do things his own way
2	2	Is valuable in a new operation
3	3	Doesn't go outside area of authority
4	4	Is looked upon by peers as a leader
5	5	Realizes capabilities of others

Most	Least	
1	1	Needs complete information about a situation before willing to make a decision
2	2	Would be easy to replace
3	3	Is sensitive to needs of others
4	4	Stands up well under pressure
5	5	Has gone about as far as his capabilities will permit

Since the rater does not know which statement in each set is viewed as favorable and which is viewed as unfavorable, bias and subjectivity can almost be totally eliminated. Only two statements within each set affect the person being appraised (the most and the least favorable statement), while the other three are neutral statements. Should any of the three neutral statements be selected by the rater, the appraisal of the individual would not be affected. When the rater chooses the favorable statement, the individual's appraisal is affected positively. On the other hand, when the rater chooses the unfavorable statement, the individual's appraisal is affected negatively. If the rater chooses two neutral statements, the individual's appraisal is not affected.

While the use of this appraisal method has some significant advantages over the use of some of the other methods (eliminates bias and subjectivity), its use also has some serious limitations. The method is costly to develop and install since the statements for the most part have to be designed for specific job categories. What is a favorable statement for one job may be a neutral statement for another. The results of the appraisal are also difficult to use as a basis for employee counseling and developing.

Critical incidents. The critical incidents appraisal method involves formulating for each type of job a list of critical job requirements. For a secretary, for example, critical job requirements might include the ability to work with others, the ability to meet deadlines, the ability to perform at a quality level, and so forth.

After the critical job requirements have been identified, the office supervisor watches each subordinate for outstanding examples in which critical job requirements were either favorably or unfavorably met. The examples or incidents are immediately recorded on the appraisal form as a means of building an appraisal record for each subordinate. The favorable incidents are listed on one side while the unfavorable incidents are listed on the other side. For example:

Ability to Work with Others

10/16—Mary stayed after hours to help Pat finish a project	12/3—Mary asked to not be assigned to work on a particular project with Carol (for personal reasons)
10/17—When several office workers were ill today, Mary helped reorganize work so deadlines could be met	

A distinct advantage of this method is that the appraisal is based on objective facts and evidence rather than subjectively evaluated traits. Furthermore, the rater is required to list specific incidents for appraising subordinates. The method also provides the opportunity to immediately discuss favorable and unfavorable incidents with the subordinates.

A potential disadvantage of this method is the impression among subordinates that the supervisor is keeping a "little black book" in which to record unfavorable incidents. This tends to create some subordinate resentment against the supervisor.

The critical incidents method of performance appraisal was developed in Delco-Remy Division of General Motors Corporation. It was found in Delco-Remy that six minutes a day was the average time required for supervisors to record the critical incidents.

Peer rating. The peer-rating appraisal method involves using coworkers to evaluate the performance of an individual, even though the results of peer appraisal are often consistent with the results obtained by a supervisor. The fact that one's peers often see a different type of behavior than does the supervisor is what distinguishes this appraisal method from the other appraisal methods. When there is a need to fill a leadership position, it might be advantageous to select the individual who is generally appraised by his or her peers to have the greatest amount of leadership ability, for example.

Group rating. When the group rating method is utilized, a group of individuals who are familiar with the person being rated do the appraisal collectively rather than individually. The group will generally consist of the individual's immediate supervisor, the supervisor's superior, and other persons who are familiar with the individual being appraised. The results of the appraisal are probably more objective since more than one individual is involved in the appraisal process. This appraisal method is also advantageously used in organizations where individuals might have some responsibility in two departments or work units.

Results-oriented appraisal. A significant trend in performance appraisal nowadays is the use of results-oriented appraisal. The philosophical foundation of this appraisal method lies within the management by objectives concept, which is discussed in detail in Chapter 14. The method generally involves the following steps:

1. Employee performance goals that are measurable are set jointly by the supervisor and the subordinate.

2. Specific courses of action are decided upon as a means of accomplishing these goals.

3. At interim intervals, the supervisor and subordinate discuss the progress that has been made toward accomplishing these goals.

4. At the conclusion of the time period (perhaps six months to a year), the supervisor and subordinate officially evaluate the degree to which the specified goals were accomplished.

5. Goals for the next evaluation period are set.

It should be pointed out that results-oriented appraisal can be used in organizations that do not utilize management by objectives. In many organizations where MBO is used, results-oriented appraisal is likely to be linked to the objectives specified by the goal-setting process of MBO. For example, if the organization has a specific goal of increasing profit, many employees in the organization are apt to have waste reduction goals as part of their results-oriented appraisal program.

Individual objectives should be developed around the following guidelines:

1. Only measurable objectives should be used. (For the most part, behavior traits are not suitable since they cannot be measured.)

2. There is no ideal number of objectives for any one individual.

3. The objectives should be achievable within a relatively short period of time. Not all objectives have to be achieved at the same time.

4. The objectives should consist of three elements: (1) the desired results, (2) the quantity or amount of change, and (3) the day by which the objective should be achieved.

Advantages of using results-oriented appraisal are:

1. The appraisal method emphasizes the future (over which the subordinate has some control) rather than the past (over which he or she no longer has any control).

2. The method emphasizes performance rather than character traits.

3. The method helps identify areas suitable for training.

4. Subordinates are compared against their own progress rather than competing with their peers.

5. The method tends to strengthen superior-subordinate cooperation since the superior is in a prime position to help the subordinate achieve the specified goals.

6. Employees tend to work harder when they have a specific goal that they are trying to achieve.

7. The appraisal is tailormade for each employee.

8. Employees are motivated to work harder for the attainment of major organizational objectives.

The following are seen as disadvantages of using the results-oriented appraisal method:

1. Subordinates may set their goals too high or too low.

2. The work performed by some employees cannot be quantified or measured.

3. The use of this appraisal method may require some managers to adjust their managerial style. In some cases, some managers cannot or will not make the necessary adjustment.

4. Some supervisors feel that there is less need to counsel their subordinates because the subordinate can readily determine how well he or she is achieving the previously determined goals.

5. The method leads employees to work only for measurable goals and not unmeasurable goals (morale, for example).

Rating Errors

Appraisal methods that use scoring scales (whether the scale involves descriptive phrases, words, or numerical values), are subject to human rating errors that tend to distort the results of the appraisal. The rating errors usually involve judgment and occur because traits cannot be quantified or measured on an objective basis. Rating errors can be minimized to a great extent by training supervisors to appraise employee performance.

Halo Effect

The **halo effect**, which is a common rating error, results in evaluating an employee excessively high or low in all areas because the rater is influenced by the rating the employee received for a few specific traits. For example, if undue emphasis is placed on *attitude,* those employees whose attitude is judged to be above average are apt to be rated excessively high on all other traits. Employees whose attitude is judged to be below average are apt to be rated excessively low on other traits. The halo effect can be minimized if raters consider each trait individually and do not allow the rating on one trait to affect the rating on other traits.

Influence of Recent Performance

The recent performance of a subordinate is also apt to have an impact on the appraisal process. Employees whose recent performance is considerably above average (even though their earlier performance may have been below average) are likely to be rated unduly high. Likewise, employees whose performance decreases immediately before the appraisal process takes place may receive a rating that does not truly reflect the quality of performance. The critical incidents method, which involves an ongoing appraisal of each employee, is not subject to this type of rating error.

Bias

As hard as supervisors may try, it is almost impossible to overcome unconscious bias or prejudices. The appraisals of subordinates are likely to be affected by such bias, especially if subordinates' preferences are not consistent with the supervisor's preferences. A technique that is sometimes used to minimize the effect of bias is to have the supervisor appraise each subordinate two different times—perhaps two weeks apart. The results of the two appraisals are compared and any differences are resolved.

Analysis of Appraisals

Even though quality appraisal forms may be used in the appraisal process, the reliability and validity of the appraisal results should be determined. This analysis is especially important when graphic rating scales and forced choice appraisal methods are used.

As a means of determining the reliability of results, employee ratings in different work units or in different jobs should be analyzed. If significant differences are found, an adjustment may be necessary. For example, some raters feel that individuals who hold more important jobs should receive a higher rating than those whose jobs are considered to be of lesser importance. Raters should always be cognizant of the fact that appraisals are concerned with how well employees perform their jobs rather than how important the jobs are within the organization.

One way to determine the validity of the appraisal results is to make an analysis of the strictness or leniency with which each rater appraises his or her subordinates. Ratings made by overly strict or lenient supervisors cannot be fairly compared with the ratings made by supervisors considered to be neither strict nor lenient. In order that all results are evaluated on a fairly comparable basis, some adjustment factor may have to be implemented.

Ratings can be made more reliable by determining the importance of each trait to the total performance of the individual. Rarely could all traits justifiably be treated as being equal in importance. To make the results more reliable, each trait in each job category is assigned a specific weight in relation to the importance of the trait.

Another means of assessing the quality of the appraisal process is to follow up employees who have been promoted to high-level positions primarily because they received high evaluations in the appraisal process. The effectiveness of the appraisal process can be verified to a certain extent if employees who received high evaluations while filling one position continue to receive high evaluations while filling a higher-level position.

Appraisal Interviews

Although the success of the performance appraisal program is greatly dependent upon the appraisal form, the elimination of rating errors, and the analysis of results provided by the appraisal process, the program will not be totally successful unless employees are informed of the evaluation results. The **appraisal interview** is designed to inform employees of the results of the appraisal.

In many organizations, prior to the time of the appraisal interview with the employee, the supervisor completes the appraisal, which is then given to the supervisor's immediate supervisor for approval. There are several advantages of superior approval: (1) the superior, if not in agreement with the supervisor's rating, can make suggestions for modifying the rating; (2) the superior can determine areas suitable for training; (3) the superior can become more familiar with the employees for whom he or she is responsible. If the superior approves the supervisor's rating, the results of the evaluation are discussed with the subordinate during the appraisal interview.

The advantages of conducting appraisal interviews are: (1) the present performance of the subordinates can be discussed, as can areas in which improvement is desirable; (2) the interview provides an opportunity for the supervisor and subordinate to become more familiar with one another's goals, aspirations, feelings, and attitudes; (3) the interview tends to strengthen lines of communication between the superior and subordinates.

Among the disadvantages of the appraisal interview are: (1) supervisors feel incompetent in the interviewing process and therefore are reluctant to conduct the interviews unless so required; (2) if the interview is poorly conducted, it is likely to cause a considerable amount of resentment and hostility between the supervisor and subordinate; (3) supervisors feel that conducting appraisal interviews are a low-priority responsibility and therefore either hurry through the interview or fail to conduct the interview; (4) subordinates become defensive when criticized, which causes them to be reluctant to accept the negative portions of the rating.

The following are suggestions for conducting the interviews:

1. Start the interview by having the employee evaluate his or her performance.

2. Try to put the employee at ease immediately.

3. If at all possible, let the employee decide how the weaknesses will be overcome.

4. Emphasize strengths before discussing weaknesses.

5. Limit the areas of employee improvement to those that can be overcome within a reasonable length of time.

6. Substantiate ratings with specific examples of performance.

7. The individual conducting the interview must be willing to "hear out" the employee.

8. If possible, the employee should read the appraisal before the interview.

Review Questions

1. What are the objectives of performance appraisal?

2. When designing a graphic rating scale, what suggestions can you offer that will result in making the scale as objective as possible?

3. What are the advantages and disadvantages of the paired comparison, checklists, and simple ranking methods of performance appraisal?

4. Why are some employees opposed to the critical incidents method of performance appraisal?

5. When establishing the goals for the results-oriented appraisal method, what guidelines should be used?

6. When appraising employees' performance, what kinds of rating errors are likely to occur? Give examples of each type of error.

7. How can the reliability and validity of an appraisal rating form be determined?

8. What suggestions do you have for improving the effectiveness of performance interviews?

Minicases

The administrative office manager of a large company is considering the installation of a forced choice performance appraisal program. At this time, the administrative office manager knows very little about the appraisal technique, except that sets of five statements are used. You are to explain the technique in sufficient detail to enable the administrative office manager to decide whether or not the technique should be given additional consideration.

*   *   *

The Madenson Company uses the results-oriented performance appraisal technique. The following is a description of the procedures they follow:

1. The employee's immediate supervisor rates the employee, using a graphic rating scale.

2. The supervisor analyzes the results of the rating and sets goals for the subordinate.

3. In one year's time, the supervisor completes another graphic rating scale to determine whether or not the employee has accomplished the goals that were set the year before.

4. If the goals are not reached, they are again included in the next evaluation period.

The Madenson Company has had only limited success with the results-oriented appraisal program. Assess the program and make recommendations for improvement.

Case

The Johnson Supply Company, presently employing twenty white collar workers, grew rather rapidly during the 1960's. The personnel function was originally under the direction of the firm's accountant. As the company grew, the personnel function (which includes responsibility for performance appraisal) was assigned to the administrative office manager. The partial appraisal form shown below was developed by the administrative office manager. Individual employees are appraised by their immediate supervisors. Although the company is planning to hire a personnel manager in the future, several employees feel that the form presently used has some serious limitations and cannot wait for revision until the personnel manager is hired.

1. What do you consider to be the most significant limitations of the present appraisal form?

2. Considering the limitations identified in Question No. 1, develop a new appraisal form.

	High							Low
Quantity of Work	1	2	3	4	5	6	7	8
Quality of Work	1	2	3	4	5	6	7	8
Knowledge of Job	1	2	3	4	5	6	7	8
Initiative	1	2	3	4	5	6	7	8
Attitude	1	2	3	4	5	6	7	8
Promptness	1	2	3	4	5	6	7	8
Appearance	1	2	3	4	5	6	7	8

Employer-Employee Relations

Chapter
11

Labor Relations
Norris-LaGuardia Anti-Injunction Act
Wagner Act
Taft-Hartley Act
Landrum-Griffin Act

Compensation
Fair Labor Standards Act
    Minimum wage
    Overtime pay
    Child labor provisions
    Records
Equal Pay Act of 1963
Walsh-Healey Act
Fair Labor Standards Act, 1974 Amendments

Employment
Civil Rights Act
Age Discrimination in Employment Act of 1967
Equal Employment Opportunity Act of 1972

Safety and Health
Occupational Safety and Health Act of 1970

State Legislation Affecting Employer-Employee Relations
Workmen's Compensation and Disability
Unemployment Compensation
Payment of Wages
Time Off for Voting

Developing Effective Employer-Employee Relations
Job-Centered versus Employee-Centered Approach
Adequate Information
Subordinate Participation
Listening to Subordinates
Feeling of Approval
Showing Interest in Employees
Fair Treatment of Employees
Making Exceptions
Dealing with Mistakes

Chapter Aims   After studying this chapter, the student should be able to:

1. Discuss the provisions of the Norris-LaGuardia Anti-Injunction Act that have an impact on labor relations.

2. Identify the employee rights guaranteed by the Wagner Act.

3. Discuss the major provisions of the Taft-Hartley Act.

4. Discuss the provisions of the Landrum-Griffin Act that have an impact on labor relations.

5. Identify the areas with which the Fair Labor Standards Act is concerned.

6. Discuss the significance of the Equal Pay Act of 1963 as it relates to employee compensation.

7. Discuss the provisions of the Walsh-Healey Act.

8. Identify the types of employers to whom coverage of the Fair Labor Standards Act was extended by the 1974 Amendments.

9. Discuss the provisions of the Age Discrimination in Employment Act of 1967 that have an impact on employees.

10. Explain how the Equal Employment Opportunity Act of 1972 amended the Civil Rights Act of 1964.

11. Discuss the provisions of the Occupational Safety and Health Act of 1970 that have an impact on employees' health and safety.

12. Discuss the various ways in which effective employer-employee relations can be developed by the employer.

Chapter Terms   *Yellow-dog contracts:* refer to an employer's forbidding employees to join a union. Such contracts were made illegal by the Norris-LaGuardia Anti-Injunction Act.

Overtime pay: refers to an employee's right to at least time and one-half pay for working more than forty hours per week provided the employee is covered by the provisions of the Fair Labor Standards Act.

Minimum wage: refers to the minimum wage that an employer must pay an employee when the employee is covered by the provisions of the Fair Labor Standards Act. The rate of the minimum wage is raised from time to time.

Bona fide occupational qualification: a job qualification that can be justified on the basis of the nature of the job.

Employer-employee relations can be viewed from several different perspectives. One perspective is to examine the nature of relations in view of the impact that federal and state legislation has on the relations. A second perspective for examining employer-employee relations is to consider the informal interaction between an employer (or supervisor) and the employee (or subordinate). This interaction is also discussed in this chapter. A third perspective is the impact of unionization, which is the topic of Chapter 12.

The legal basis of employer-employee relations is for the most part shaped by the provisions of significant labor legislation. Many daily activities must comply with various provisions of this legislation. While much of the earlier legislation was concerned with union activities and labor relations, recent legislation is more concerned with conditions of employment. Specific areas of concern in the more recent legislation are recruiting, interviewing, testing, selecting, laying off, discharging, and retiring individuals. Salary and fringe benefits are also covered in certain of the legislative acts.

Because of the nature of this legislation, it is important for all managers, and especially those managers responsible for hourly employees, to be familiar with the provisions of some of the more important legislation. Failure to adhere to the provisions of the legislation may result in an employer's being found guilty of noncompliance with federal and state legislation, which may have a serious financial impact on the employer.

Although in larger organizations an individual other than the administrative office manager usually has primary responsibility for developing organizational practices that comply with the legislation, the administrative office manager's need for an understanding of the significant legislation is nonetheless very important.

Over the last few decades, several different legislative acts have been passed that have special significance for the administrative office manager. The more important legislation is discussed in the sections that follow.

The legislative acts discussed in this chapter are classified into the following categories: labor relations, compensation, employment, and safety and health.

Labor Relations

Several significant acts have been passed at the federal level that define the rights of employees and employers with regard to union activities. These include the Norris-LaGuardia Act, the Wagner Act, the Taft-Hartley Act, and the Landrum-Griffin Act.

Norris-LaGuardia Anti-Injunction Act

The passage of the Norris-LaGuardia Anti-Injunction Act of 1932 is significant in that the conditions under which injunctions can be issued were clearly defined. The result is that the federal courts are drastically limited as to the conditions under which injunctions can be issued. One condition is that required hearings have to be held before an injunction can be issued. Prior to the passage of this act, employers were able to get an injunction against the workers when it appeared that a strike was imminent.

This act also forbids the use of **yellow-dog contracts,** which required the employee to enter into an agreement with the employer not to join a union. Before this act was passed, yellow-dog contracts were often required as a condition of employment.

Wagner Act

This act, also known as the National Labor Relations Act of 1935, is one of two federal laws (the other is the Railway Labor Act of 1926) that outline employees' rights with regard to union activities. Section 7 of the act guarantees employees' rights "to self organization, to form, to join, and assist labor organizations to bargain collectively through representatives of their own choosing, and to engage in concerted activities for the purpose of collective bargaining or other mutual aid or protection." The act specifies which employer practices are considered to interfere with employees' rights to participation in union activities. The following employer practices are considered to be unfair:

1. To interfere with, restrain, or coerce employees in their exercise of the rights that are guaranteed in Section 7 of the act.

2. To dominate or interfere with forming or administering any labor organization or to contribute financial or other support to the organization.

3. To discriminate in the hiring or tenure of employment or any term or condition of employment as a means of encouraging or discouraging employment.

4. To discharge or discriminate against an employee because the employee has filed charges or has testified under the provisions of this act.

5. To refuse to bargain collectively with the individual or individuals chosen to represent the employees.

The provisions of the Wagner Act are enforced by the National Labor Relations Board. Some of the activities performed by the board include: determining bargaining units, conducting union representative elections, and prosecuting employers for noncompliance with the guaranteed provisions of the act.

The Wagner Act provided the mechanism by which unions grew rapidly and became very powerful in the collective-bargaining process.

This resulted in the passage of new legislation, which restricted the power of unions.

Taft-Hartley Act

The Taft-Hartley Act, which is also known as the Labor-Management Relations Act, was passed in 1947 and amended the Wagner Act. Most of the provisions of the Wagner Act, however, were incorporated into the Taft-Hartley Act. The Taft-Hartley Act applies to any private employer engaged in an industry affecting interstate or foreign commerce, with the exception of nonprofit hospitals, railroads, express companies, or airlines.

Of major significance in the Taft-Hartley Act are the following: recognition of the right of employees to refrain from union activity, broadening the employer's right of speech, and modification of procedures for election and for determining bargaining units. The following were also identified:

1. Restraint or coercion of an employee in selecting parties to bargain on behalf of the employer.
2. Restraint or coercion of employees in the exercise of their rights guaranteed by the Wagner Act.
3. Persuading an employer to discriminate against employees.
4. Refusing to bargain collectively with an employer.
5. Participation in secondary boycotts or jurisdictional disputes.
6. Attempting to force recognition from an employer when another union is the certified representative.
7. Charging initiation fees considered to be excessive.
8. Requiring the payment of wages for services not performed, which constitutes featherbedding.

The Taft-Hartley Act also utilizes the National Labor Relations Board that was authorized originally under the Wagner Act. The Taft-Hartley Act increased the size of the board and provides for a general counsel, whose function is to investigate charges and to prosecute violators if there is sufficient evidence of violation. Under the provisions of the act, the board is also responsible for prosecuting unfair labor practices by unions.

According to the provisions of the act, the following items must be included in the bargaining that takes place between management and the union: wages, hours, overtime, and work requirements and procedures to be followed with regard to discipline, demotion, promotion, discharge, recall, layoffs, transfers, suspension, grievances, health and safety practices, vacations and holidays, leaves of absence, union security, and reinstatement of workers.

Items not considered to be legal topics for bargaining are closed shop, payment for work not actually performed, and preferential hiring.

One significant provision of the Taft-Hartley Act is the checkoff of membership dues. This means that when an employer receives from an employee belonging to the union the appropriate written affidavit, the employer may deduct the union dues from the employee's pay. The written affidavit is valid for either one year's time or until the termination date of the contract, whichever comes first.

Another significant provision of the act is the right of the president of the United States, through the attorney general, to seek an eighty-day injunction against strikes that might affect the well-being of the nation. In the event that an agreement has not been reached within a period of sixty days after the issuance of the injunction, the National Labor Relations Board is required to conduct a secret vote among the union members to determine whether or not they are willing to agree to the employer's latest offer.

Landrum-Griffin Act

The Landrum-Griffin Act, which is also known as the Labor-Management Reporting and Disclosure Act of 1959, was passed after court cases and actual practice indicated that various provisions of the Taft-Hartley Act needed to be amended. Although most of the provisions of the Landrum-Griffin Act were new at the time of its passage, one section of the act amended the Taft-Hartley Act of 1947.

The provisions of the Landrum-Griffin Act apply to any private employer engaged in an industry dealing with interstate or foreign commerce, including any employer covered by federal labor relations laws.

The following are the important provisions of the Landrum-Griffin Act:

1. Each union member is guaranteed the right to:
   a. nominate candidates for the various union offices,
   b. vote in elections or referendums dealing with union affairs,
   c. attend union meetings, and
   d. participate in union meetings as well as vote on union matters.
2. Union members whose guaranteed rights are violated may seek redress in a federal court.
3. The rights of local union members are protected when trustees are appointed by the national union organization to administer the local union.
4. Annual union financial reports must be filed with the secretary of labor.
5. Loans of union funds to union officers in excess of $250 must be reported.
6. Union officers must be bonded for no less than 10 percent of the union funds for which they are responsible.

7. Expenditures of employers used to persuade employees to exercise their bargaining rights must be reported.

The following are some of the important provisions of the Landrum-Griffin Act that amended the Taft-Hartley Act:

1. A strengthening of the ban on secondary boycotts.
2. Picketing that takes place on behalf of an organization drive can be halted by the employer after thirty days if the union has failed to petition for a representative election.

Compensation

Several laws regulating various phases of employee compensation are in existence. Since administrative office managers frequently participate on wage and salary committees, it is important that they understand the major provisions of the significant legislative acts.

Fair Labor Standards Act

This act, which is also known as the Wage and Hour Law, was passed in 1938 and has been amended several times. The Fair Labor Standards Act (FLSA) is applicable in organizations whose employees are: (1) engaged in interstate or foreign commerce; (2) engaged in the production of goods for interstate or foreign commerce; (3) engaged in handling, selling, or working on goods that have moved in or were produced for interstate or foreign commerce.

If an organization is subject to the provisions of the FLSA, employees cannot be paid less than the **minimum wage,** they must receive **overtime pay** for any work week exceeding forty hours, and they must be paid on an equal-pay-for-equal-work basis. In addition, the FLSA specifies the minimum ages for employing children or young adults and requires that certain payroll records be retained for a minimum length of time.

Minimum wage. The minimum wage that must be paid employees covered by the FLSA is specified by the federal government. The rate of the minimum wage is raised from time to time. Overtime premiums cannot be included as part of the minimum rate, but the reasonable value of any benefits, such as food or lodging that are furnished by the employer, may be included as part of the minimum rate.

Overtime pay. According to the provisions of the FLSA, employees must be paid rates of at least one and one-half times their base rates if they work more than forty hours in any given week. Any bonuses or incentive payments must be included when calculating each employee's base rate. If, for example, an employee's incentive payment for a particular week increases his or her rate to $3 per hour, the employee is entitled to receive $4.50 for each hour worked in excess of forty hours. If an organization gives employees time off for working overtime, the employee is entitled to receive one and one-half hours off for each hour he or she works overtime. Even though some organizations pay employees on a piece-rate basis, the employees' hourly rates must be calculated when determining the base pay for any overtime premiums to which they are entitled.

Child labor provisions. The FLSA restricts the employment of children younger than certain minimum ages if they will be used for producing goods for interstate or foreign commerce. With certain stipulations, children of ages fourteen and fifteen may work in nonhazardous jobs in retailing, gasoline service stations, or food outlets. Employees involved in interstate or foreign commerce, manufacturing, mining, and some other business enterprises must be at least sixteen years old. Any position or occupation classified by the secretary of labor as being hazardous must be filled by individuals a minimum of eighteen years of age.

Records. According to the provisions of the FLSA, an employer is required to keep for at least three years payroll records, certificates, agreements, plans, notices, sales and purchase records.

Supplementary records—such as basic employment and earning records, wage rate tables and work schedules (hours and days of employment of individual employee)—must be kept for two years.

Equal Pay Act of 1963

The Equal Pay Act of 1963, which amended the Fair Labor Standards Act, applies to the same employers as the FLSA. Therefore, employees who are engaged in commerce or in the production of goods for interstate commerce and most employees of federal, state, and local governments are covered.

Under the provisions of the Equal Pay Act, it is illegal for an employer to have unequal pay policies or fringe benefits based on sex for employees who perform equal jobs that require equal skill, effort, and responsibility and that are performed under similar working conditions. The Equal Pay Act also makes it illegal for an employer to reduce the salary rates of one sex as a means of eliminating salary differentials.

It should be pointed out that salary differentials are not considered illegal if they are based on some factor other than sex. Therefore, according to the provisions of this act, basing salary differentials on merit or seniority is legal. Under the provisions of the act, it is not illegal to pay part-time employees less than full-time employees or to pay night shift employees more than day shift employees.

Walsh-Healey Act

The Walsh-Healey Act, passed in 1936, is also called the Public Contracts Act. The act specifically pertains to employees working on government contracts involving more than $10,000 in the purchase of materials and equipment. The act excludes those employees in an organization not directly involved in a government contract that falls under the jurisdiction of the Walsh-Healey Act.

The provisions of the Walsh-Healey Act are:

1. Employees covered by the act must be paid at least the minimum wage rate specified by the secretary of labor.
2. Employes are entitled to receive at least one and one-half times their base rates for any hours worked in excess of eight hours in any given day or any hours in excess of forty hours worked in any given work week, whichever provides the greatest number of hours in a particular work week.
3. The base rate used to calculate overtime pay must include any bonuses or incentive pay that the employees receive.
4. The act restricts the use of child labor and of convicts on covered contracts.
5. The employer is required to maintain, in addition to others, records showing the hours each employee works each workday and each work week, the wage rate, and the rate of pay.

Fair Labor Standards Act, 1974 Amendments

The 1974 Amendments to the Fair Labor Standards Act extended coverage to many more workers than were covered by the original FLSA. The Amendments cover employees in an organization not previously covered by the FLSA provided that within the organization there are other employees engaged in:

1. interstate or foreign commerce; or
2. the production of goods for such commerce; or
3. handling, selling, or otherwise working on goods or materials that have been moved in or have been produced for such commerce by any employee; and if
1. the organization has an annual gross volume of sales or does business, exclusive of certain excise taxes, of not less than $250,000; or
2. the organization is engaged in construction or reconstruction activities (no minimum dollar volume); or
3. the organization is engaged in laundering, cleaning, or repairing clothing or fabrics (no minimum dollar volume); or
4. the organization is engaged in the operation of a hospital, nursing home, or preschool; or
5. the organization is engaged in any activities of the federal gov-

ernment or of any state or political subdivision of a state, as well as any interstate governmental agency.

The 1974 Amendments of the FLSA stipulate the minimum wages that can be paid and that employees must receive overtime pay of at least one and one-half times the regular rate of pay for hours worked in excess of forty in a work week. The amendments also specify an age of sixteen as being the minimum age for most types of employment covered by the FLSA.

Employment

Several significant legislative acts that have important implications for the employment function have been passed at the federal level during the last few years. Certain aspects of this legislation are also discussed in Chapter 9.

Civil Rights Act

The Civil Rights Act of 1964 was instrumental in eliminating many forms of discrimination. Title VII of the act, which is concerned with equal employment opportunities, specifies that employers or labor organizations with twenty-five or more employees must treat all persons equally, regardless of their sex, race, color, national origin, or religion. Employment agencies serving such employers must also comply with the provisions of the act.

Unless the above-mentioned factors can be considered as **bona fide occupational qualifications,** it is illegal for an employer to:

1. Refuse to hire, discharge, or discriminate against a job applicant or employee with regard to compensation, or terms or conditions of employment, because of the individual's race, color, religion, sex, or national origin, or because the individual has opposed an illegal employment practice or has spoken out against a discriminatory employer.

2. Classify employees by their race, color, religion, sex, or national origin, if the classification deprives the employees of their employment opportunities or if the classifications affect their status as employees.

3. Discriminate against individuals because of their race, color, religion, sex, or national origin if such discrimination affects their being admitted to a training program.

4. Print or publish any advertising indicating an employment preference based on race, color, religion, sex, or national origin.

The Civil Rights Act of 1964 provided the mechanism for the creation of the Equal Employment Opportunity Commission, whose function was to help with the enforcement of the provisions of the act. The passage of a subsequent act, the Equal Employment Opportunity Act of

1972, gives the Equal Employment Opportunity Commission greater enforcement powers.

Age Discrimination in Employment Act of 1967

This act, which contains enforcement provisions similar to the FLSA, pertains to private employers of twenty or more persons; federal, state and local government units regardless of the number of employees in the unit; and employment agencies and labor organizations with twenty-five or more members.

Unless age can be justified as a bona fide occupational qualification, it is illegal to discriminate against an individual between the ages of forty and sixty-five in hiring, compensation, or in terms, conditions, or privileges of employment. It is also illegal for an employer to list age as an employment condition in an advertisement. Employees are also prevented from reducing the wage rate of any employee as a means of complying with the act.

Equal Employment Opportunity Act of 1972

The Equal Employment Opportunity Act of 1972 essentially provides a series of amendments to Title VII of the Civil Rights Act of 1964. The 1972 act provided for the first time at the federal level an independent agency (the Equal Employment Opportunity Commission) possessing the power to prohibit all kinds of employment discrimination based on race, religion, color, sex, or national origin. The EEOC, according to the provisions of the act, has the power to institute civil actions as a means of eliminating discriminatory employment practices. The 1972 act also provides coverage to employees of state and local government or governmental agencies, employees of educational institutions, and employers or labor organizations with fifteen or more employees or members.

Safety and Health

Employers are becoming more concerned about the safety and health of their employees, partially because of significant federal legislation, but also because of the increased desire on the part of employers to be more responsive to their employees' needs. The Occupational Safety and Health Act of 1970 is of major significance.

Occupational Safety and Health Act of 1970

This act sets safety and health standards for businesses affected by interstate commerce. Under the terms of this law, employers are required to provide their employees with an employment environment that is free of recognized hazards that cause or are likely to cause death or serious physical injury to employees. More specifically, the act states that employers must maintain records and post notices as required by the secretary of labor. Periodic reports on work-related deaths, injuries, or illnesses are required, as are reports outlining employee exposure to potentially toxic and harmful agents. The act also states that employees are to be notified of their overexposure to harmful agents. Under the provisions of the act, the employer is required to correct any identified hazards.

State Legislation Affecting Employer-Employee Relations

Many states have passed legislation that either complements or supplements much of the legislation that has been passed at the federal level. In some instances, the state legislation provisions are even more strict than those of the federal legislation.

Workmen's Compensation and Disability

Every state now has legislation concerned with paying injured employees with private insurance funds, company funds, and state funds. Some of the benefits include medical expenses, indemnity payments when disabled, death benefits, and burial expenses.

Unemployment Compensation

The Federal Social Security Act of 1935 and the Federal Unemployment Tax Act of 1939 are significant in that a state's unemployment compensation legislation is interwoven with these two acts. The number of individuals employed in an organization determines whether or not the organization is required to contribute to the unemployment compensation fund. The maximum number of employees permitted without having to contribute to the fund varies from state to state.

Payment of Wages

Most states have now passed legislation requiring an employer to promptly give employees who are terminating employment their earned wages. Other legislation pertaining to an employee's assignment of wages to another individual has been enacted. In addition, legislation concerned with the garnishment of wages is in effect in most states. Some states also prohibit employers' deducting union dues from employees' paychecks.

Time Off for Voting

Nearly half the states have enacted legislation that protects employees if they take time off from their jobs to vote in elections. In some of these states, the laws provide that the employees are to be paid for the time they take off to vote.

Developing Effective Employer-Employee Relations

Effective employer-employee relations are to a large extent influenced by how a group of employees feels about their employer or how subordinates feel about their supervisor. If employees and subordinates have positive feelings for their employer or supervisor, the working relationship between the two groups will be much more pleasant, cordial, and satisfying than if negative feelings prevail.

Job-Centered versus Employee-Centered Approach

Employer-employee relations can be examined by studying the approach the employer or supervisor uses in relating to employees or subordinates. For example, at one end of the employer-employee relations continuum is the job-centered approach. At the other end is the employee-centered approach. When the job-centered approach prevails, the employer or supervisor is more concerned about production levels than about employees. This means that very little attention is focused on the needs or feelings of the employees. The opposite of the job-centered approach is the employee-centered approach. The needs and feelings of employees receive a considerable amount of attention, and very little attention is focused on production levels. In terms of employer-employee relations, utilizing an approach somewhere between the two extremes of the continuum is recommended. To emphasize one end of the continuum at the exclusion of the other has obvious shortcomings.

Adequate Information

Employer-employee relations can also be improved by making sure that an employer provides the employees with adequate information about what is expected of them in their jobs and their relations with the organization. Employers who believe that employees should function with as little information as possible are forgetting that most employees have an insatiable desire to learn as much as possible about their jobs. Therefore, by providing the employees with adequate information, this basic human desire is satisfied.

Another great desire of most employees is to have knowledge regarding how they are doing in their jobs. It is only natural for humans to want to know what their supervisor thinks about their performance. Frequent positive feedback and evaluation of results provide the following advantages: greater security, increased desire to improve, greater loyalty, and more job satisfaction.

Subordinate Participation

More and more organizations are using subordinate participation in the decisionmaking process. The result has been a marked improvement in employer-employee relations. Subordinate participation is especially useful when it appears that employees are apt to resist the outcome of a decision. By encouraging subordinates to participate, they begin to feel a greater sense of responsibility for accepting the decision and, hence, become committed to the decision. Another significant advantage of subordinate participation is the possibility of their identfying other important issues or aspects of a problem being discussed. In this way, the problem can be more thoroughly studied before a final decision has to be made. Furthermore, in many instances, employees are apt to know more about a situation than others, which provides sufficient justification for their participating in the decisionmaking process.

**Listening to
Subordinates**

Employer-employee relations can be strengthened if employees have the feeling that the employer is listening to their suggestions. Listening to subordinates differs from subordinate participation in that the former is unsolicited whereas the latter is solicited from the employees.

By listening to subordinates' suggestions, the employer is often able to come to grips with a situation before major problems arise. To illustrate, many offices have become unionized as a means of solving problems that employers failed to give proper consideration.

Some employers fail to listen to employee suggestions because they feel that it is more damaging to employer-employee relations to have to reject a suggestion than it is to not listen to the suggestions. Most employees are able to readily accept the rejection of a suggestion if they are given adequate reasons for its rejection. Therefore, if an employee's suggestion is properly rejected, there is less of a chance that the relationship will be damaged.

**Feeling of
Approval**

Unless the employer is able to create throughout the organization a feeling of employee approval, employer-employee relations become strained. The impact of a feeling of approval is two dimensional. If the employer shows employees a feeling of approval, this is interpreted by the employees as the employer's desire to be loyal to them. If the employer is able to show loyalty for employees, the employees are very apt to respond with a reciprocal loyalty.

An example of an employer's showing approval is to acknowledge an employee for a crucial decision the employee was responsible for making. Another way that a feeling of approval can be shown is for the employer to give the employee moral support when needed.

**Showing Interest
in Employees**

Another way in which employer-employee relations can be strengthened is for the employer to show a sincere interest in the employees. Employees who feel that the employer has a sincere interest in their wellbeing are apt to be more productive and satisfied than employees who do not have such a feeling. Some employers are beginning to take a more active interest in employees by encouraging their involvement in community and civic activities. Some employers even support their employees' involvement either financially or by granting time off to participate in worthy community or civic activities.

One of the most unique ways of showing interest in employees is for the employer to provide the employee, when appropriate, with a letter of recognition. For example, if an employee is honored for some civic or community activity, much can be gained if the employer sends a letter to the employee regarding the employer's interest in the employee's activities.

Fair Treatment of Employees

Treating employees in a manner they consider to be unfair is likely to have a negative effect on employer-employee relations. Perhaps the most frequent type of unfair treatment is lack of consistency in dealing with personnel or discipline problems. No matter how hard an employer tries to treat employees equally and fairly, there may be charges of unfair treatment leveled by employees.

The problem of fair treatment of employees is compounded by the desire to be fair, while on the other hand trying to treat each person as an individual. The two are basically incompatible. Without a conscientious effort, many supervisors unknowingly begin to show favoritism, perhaps singling out those individuals who are most cooperative, dedicated, and loyal. If it is obvious to the other employees that a supervisor shows favoritism, the relations may suffer immensely.

Individual circumstances are likely to be a significant determinant of what is considered to be fair or unfair treatment of employees. For example, many employers tend to be more tolerant of the unsatisfactory performance of an employee who is close to retirement age than of a younger employee. Most employers also tend to give employees another chance if at all feasible.

Making Exceptions

In certain instances, unless legitimate exceptions are made, employer-employee relations will deteriorate. For an exception to be considered legitimate, employees have to be convinced that each of them would also have been entitled to the same exception under similar circumstances. Furthermore, the exception has to be accepted by each employee in order to be considered legitimate.

An example of an employer's wisely making an exception occurred when an employee was elected to a national office in a professional organization. Because the employer was supportive of employees' involvement in such organizations, this particular employee was given several more personal days than the yearly allotment of two days. To be fair, the employer had to provide other employees in similar circumstances with additional personal days. To support such employee involvement, the employer in this specific instance made a wise exception.

Dealing with Mistakes

The manner in which an employer deals with mistakes made by employees is likely to affect employer-employee relations. Conscientious employees do not expect an employer to ignore their mistakes, especially when the mistakes are obvious. An employer who ignores obvious mistakes loses the respect of the conscientious employees. An employer also loses the respect of employees if the situation is poorly handled.

Employer-employee relations are often damaged when the prevailing practice is to blame employees for their mistakes rather than to help them avoid making the same mistakes another time. Blaming rather than attempting to help employees overcome their mistakes results in several undesirable situations. For example, employees will, under certain circumstances, deny either partially or wholly any part in making the mistake. In other instances, they will attempt to find ways to cover up their mistakes. The result is that the employer is likely to be deceived about the circumstances surrounding the mistake.

When the prevailing philosophy is to help rather than to blame, the employer is more concerned with attempting to find ways to alleviate the circumstances that permitted the mistakes to be made in the first place. In other words, the situation is viewed as a learning experience rather than as a situation in which employees need to be reprimanded or disciplined.

The manner in which an employer works with employees in dealing with mistakes depends to a great extent upon the personality and temperament of the guilty individual. Because some individuals are more sensitive than others, the manner with which the situation is dealt is largely determined by the individuals and the circumstances surrounding the situation.

Because of an employee's poor human relations skills, an employer lost a valued client. Since the employee was outstanding in all other respects, the employer decided it would be more appropriate to provide this employee with special human relations training rather than discharge the employee. The employee, who willingly accepted the training, has shown marked improvement. In this instance, much was gained by helping the employee overcome the weakness that caused the problem in the first place.

Review Questions

1. What is a yellow-dog contract?

2. What types of employers fall under the jurisdiction of the Taft-Hartley Act?

3. According to the Taft-Hartley Act, what items must be included in the bargaining that takes place between management and the union?

4. According to the Fair Labor Standards Act, what kinds of records must an employer keep for at least three years?

5. Does the Equal Pay Act of 1963 make it illegal to pay part-time employees less than full-time employees and day shift employees less than night shift employees?

6. What employers fall under the jurisdiction of the Walsh-Healey Act?

7. According to the provisions of the Civil Rights Act, what employment practices are illegal?

8. What are the major differences between the job-centered and the employee-centered approach to employer-employee relations?

9. Why is subordinate participation in the decisionmaking process advantageous?

Minicases

The relations between the management and the union in the Poulman Corporation have been less than satisfactory for a long time. The union has frequently threatened the company with walkouts. When a new contract is negotiated, it frequently has to go through arbitration before it is settled. One of the vice presidents of the corporation was overheard telling another vice president that he was "sick and tired of the union always getting its way." He also indicated that it would be very helpful if the company were able to forbid its new employees to join the union. Can an employer forbid an employee to join a union? If so, what act provides this provision? If not, what act forbids this provision?

*   *   *

The Browning Corporation has thirty-two employees. The administrative office manager of the company is about to retire after eighteen years of service to the company. The vice president for corporate relations, to whom the administrative office manager reports, is in the process of preparing specifications for the new administrative office manager. Mary Jackson, a secretary in the personnel department, overheard the vice president telling the personnel manager that he would like the new administrative office manager to be around thirty-five years old, because if they are much older than that, they are very outdated, and that the new administrative office manager should be male because many of the female employees in the organization would resent having a female supervisor. Discuss the vice president's comments from the standpoint of the various federal legislation acts.

Case

The Jackson Manufacturing Company was founded in 1936 by Mr. August Jackson. The company manufacturers, among other items, ball-bearing assemblies for various automotive manufacturers located throughout the country.

The line workers became unionized in 1956. The 175 office workers are not unionized, but recently the personnel manager received a letter from a representative of an office union asking for an opportunity to speak with him regarding the very strong possibility of the office employees' becoming unionized. Since the Jackson Manufacturing Company is generally regarded as one of the most desirable employers in the community, the personnel manager was quite stunned when he received the letter from the union representative.

The personnel manager wishes to speak to you, the administrative office manager, regarding this situation.

1. What course of action will you recommend that the personnel manager take in his conversation with the representative of the union?

2. Under the provisions of the federal legislation, what rights are guaranteed the employees and the employer with regard to unionizing activities?

Office
Unions

Chapter

12

The Role of Unions
> Reasons for Unionizing
> Reasons for Not Unionizing

The Union Structure

The Functioning of Unions
> Recognition of the Union
> Collective Bargaining
> The Labor Agreement
>> Duration of agreement
>> Union security
>> Management prerogatives
>> Wages and hours
>> Promotion, layoff, recall
>> Discipline of members
>> Grievances
>> Strike clauses
> Handling Grievances
>> Definition of grievances
>> Supervisor input
>> Reasons for grievances
>> Grievance procedures

Union-Management Cooperation

Chapter Aims

After studying this chapter, the student should be able to:

1. Identify the reasons why employees join unions.
2. Discuss the structure of unions.
3. Discuss the various ways in which the collective bargaining process can be made more effective.
4. Discuss the methods by which unions become recognized.
5. Discuss the collective bargaining process.
6. Discuss the clauses typically found in labor agreements.
7. Discuss grievance procedures and how a grievance may pass through arbitration.

Chapter Terms

Business representative: the individual who is frequently responsible for the facilities or the headquarters of the local union; for collecting dues and recruiting members; for publicity; for arranging meetings; and for managing the staff of the local union headquarters.

Steward: the individual who represents union members in their place of work. The steward is usually responsible for making sure that employer practices conform with the labor agreement.

Bargaining agent: the individual who represents the unit in negotiations with the employer.

Conciliator: the individual who keeps contract negotiations moving as a means of getting the two parties to work out the differences between their two proposals.

Mediator: an individual who intervenes in the negotiation process and who attempts to keep the negotiations moving by suggesting compromises to both parties.

Arbitrator: the individual who enters the negotiation process when conciliation and mediation have failed. The arbitrator is in a position to resolve disputes by making decisions about the differences between the two proposals.

Labor agreement: a written agreement that contains proposals accepted by both parties during the negotiation process.

Union shop: a form of union security that specifies that an employee must be a member or become a member of the union within a specified period of time.

Maintenance-of-membership shop: a form of union security that requires that employees who join a union voluntarily must remain in good standing during the life of the agreement.

Agency shop: a form of union security that stipulates that employees, who are not required to join a union, are required to pay union dues since the union serves as their bargaining agent.

Dues checkoff: a written agreement between the employer and employees that allows the employer to withhold union dues from the employees' paychecks.

All managers, including administrative office managers, need a basic understanding of the role of unions in the American labor sector. Although office employees have unionized at a slower rate than other classifications of workers, administrative office managers nevertheless need to be concerned with the impact of unions on office employees.

In addition to understanding the role of unions, administrative office managers need to understand the collective bargaining process, the contract or labor agreement, and the handling of grievances. Administrative office managers also need to be familiar with the significant labor legislation that was discussed in the preceding chapter.

The Role of Unions

An important role of unions is to negotiate the labor agreement with employers and to make sure that the conditions outlined in the agreement are followed accordingly. This means that unionized employees are protected from unfair treatment or treatment that does not conform with the conditions of the agreement.

Reasons for Unionizing

The reasons employees join unions provide additional insight into understanding the role of unions. Under the terms of a union shop agreement, employees are required, as a condition of their continued employment, to maintain union membership. For this reason, some employees have no choice as to whether or not they will belong to a union.

When employees have a choice with regard to joining a union, a reason frequently cited for joining is the desire to receive more pay. This is perhaps true because employee income levels increased rapidly at the same time that union membership increased rapidly. Employees, therefore, feel that union membership has a positive effect on wage rates. Another frequently cited reason for joining a union is that employees are in a better position to negotiate for better working conditions. Although negotiating for improved working conditions does not occur as frequently among white collar employees as it does among blue collar employees, it is nevertheless an important reason for union membership.

Also related to wage rates and improved working conditions is the employees' desire for improved fringe benefits. Many union agreements now contain very substantial fringe benefits, which explains why employees cite this as a reason for joining unions.

Employees also frequently join unions as a means of obtaining greater job security. Most labor agreements contain provisions outlining the procedures to be followed when laying off employees.

Furthermore, employees often feel that by joining a union, there is a greater opportunity to express their feelings to management without jeopardizing their positions. Nonunionized employees are sometimes reluctant to express their opinions because of the feeling that management may later have the opportunity to "get even with them" for speaking out. Unionized employees who have the support of the union in most instances feel more free to express their feelings than is the case with nonunionizd employees.

Employers' failure to handle grievances to the satisfaction of employees is another reason employees desire to join unions. Upon unionizing, the union typically provides the necessary mechanism through which legitimate grievances are handled, which provides individual employees with a considerable amount of assistance in this area.

In some instances, employees have joined unions because they feel their employer does not fully recognize the importance of their work or their jobs. In this sense, the unions provide an important informational function.

Reasons for Not Unionizing

The reasons employees cite for not unionizing are quite varied. Some employees feel that if they were to unionize, they would be disloyal to their employer. Other employees feel that to unionize may cause them to have to forego some of their other benefits. For example, some employees who take time off from work for a doctor's appointment make up the time after working hours. This practice might not be possible if the employees were to unionize. Another reason some employees cite for not unionizing is their inability to accept various union practices, such as strikes, boycotts, walkouts, and so forth. Finally, some employees fail to unionize because of their aversion to paying union dues.

The Union Structure

The structure of national unions closely resembles the structure of any large organization. A national union operates according to its constitution, which clearly outlines the framework under which the union exists.

Some of the provisions found in the constitutions of national unions are: (1) process for chartering local unions; (2) conditions for maintaining an affiliation with the national union; (3) conditions that must be included in the labor agreement; and (4) regulations with regard to collection of dues and initiation fees.

National unions provide many important services for the local unions. For example, national unions often provide professional and financial assistance to local unions during strikes and during the bargaining process. National unions also sometimes provide an important service to employers by preventing a local union from following a course of action that would not be in the best interests of either the employer or the union.

It is common for local unions to have a president, vice president, secretary, treasurer, a business representative, and a steward. In instances where the local union is small, the officers are usually full-time employees who provide their services to the local union. In larger unions, one or more of the officers are likely to be full-time employees of the union, and therefore, their salaries are paid by the local union.

If any of the union officers are full-time employees of the union, it is the **business representative** that is most likely to be full-time union employee. The primary responsibility of the business representative is to negotiate and administer the labor agreement and to handle problems associated with the agreement. The business representative is also frequently responsible for the facilities or the headquarters of the local union; for collecting dues and recruiting members; for publicity; for arranging meetings; and for managing the staff of the local headquarters.

The **steward,** on the other hand, represents union members in their place of work. The steward, therefore, is usually responsible for making sure that employer practices conform with the labor agreement. In many cases, the steward's most time-consuming activity is handling grievances.

At the local level, two different unionizing patterns have emerged. One pattern is for all the individuals in the same line of work within a given geographical area to belong to one union. This pattern is found more often among blue collar workers than among white collar workers. An illustration might be having all bricklayers in a given area belong to one union. The effect is a very powerful union structure. The other pattern is for the various types of employees of organizations in a given area to belong to their own respective unions. Thus, the office employees of Organization A belong to one union, and the office employees of Organization B belong to another union.

The Functioning of Unions

The functioning of unions starts with the union's gaining recognition, proceeds through the negotiating process, and concludes with the acceptance of the labor agreement. Once the labor agreement has been accepted, there exists the possibility of employees' filing grievances against the employer. This section also includes a discussion of the methods of handling grievances.

Recognition of the Union

Before collective bargaining or negotiating can take place between two parties—the employer and employees—the union must be recognized by the employer. Union recognition comes about as a result of efforts of various individuals desiring to organize a union. In most instances, a campaign to unionize is undertaken by a group of employees who are dissatisfied with some facet of the relationship between the employer and the employees. In other instances, a union's working on its own will undertake the unionizing campaign. In some cases, members of another union will be invited by a group of employees to undertake the unionizing campaign.

The success of the union campaign will depend to a large extent on the morale level of employees within the organization. When the morale level is low because the employees feel that the employer is not adequately meeting their needs in one way or another, the union campaign is likely to be more successful than if a high morale level exists among employees. Another factor that affects the success of the unionizing campaign is the manner in which the employer is able to withstand pressures of the unionizing campaign. If the employer is able to convince the employees that to join a union may not be in their best interests, the success of the campaign will be affected. The prevailing attitude in the community toward unions also affects unionization. In communities in which unions are quite strong and where they are thought to greatly help employees, the campaign is apt to be successful. The nature of the work being performed by the employees will also have a bearing on the success of the campaign efforts. As was mentioned earlier in this chapter, white collar workers have been slower to unionize than blue collar workers.

Depending on the circumstances, a union election may have to be held. If two unions are competing to represent the employees in an organization, an election will have to be provided. If an employer is not certain that the majority of employees want to join a union, the employer may request that an election be held to determine the employees' interest in unionizing. If the employer is certain that the employees wish to unionize and only one union is interested in representing the employees, employers will sometimes agree to start the negotiating process without first having an election.

Union elections are closely regulated by either federal or state agencies. In some instances the election will be conducted by the National Labor Relations Board, which came into being as a result of the Taft-Hartley Act. In other instances, the election will be conducted by the labor agency in the state.

Union elections that are not conducted by the employer or a competing union can be held without preelection hearings. This type of election is known as a *consent election*. If the election is contested and preelection hearings must be held, the election is called a *formal election*. Employees vote by secret ballot, which lists the names of the unions desiring to represent the employees as well as the choice of "no union." When there are three or more choices on the ballot and none of the choices receives a clear majority, a run-off election is held between the two choices that received the greatest number of votes in the previous election. The union receiving a majority of the votes in the election is then designated as the bargaining unit for the employees.

The **bargaining agent** represents the unit in negotiations with the employer. The nature of the bargaining unit, which consists of the employees within an organization who desire to be unionized or who must be unionized—according to whether or not there is a union shop agreement—is significantly affected by the classifications of employees found in a given organization. For example, the bargaining unit in some organizations consists of all unionized employees—blue collar and white collar workers alike. In other organizations, more than one bargaining unit is found. Therefore, it is possible for each major classification of workers to have their own bargaining unit. In certain instances the bargaining units can be determined by the National Labor Relations Board.

Collective Bargaining

The collective bargaining process can be time-consuming and frustrating for both the employer and the bargaining agent. The process consists of negotiations between the two parties with regard to the terms of the labor agreement.

The smoothness with which the negotiations between an employer and employee proceed depends to a great extent on how well both parties prepare for the negotiation process. The quality of preparation in many instances also has a significant impact on whether one of the parties is able to get the other party to accept one of the provisions in the agreement.

Preparation for the negotiating sessions involves gathering appropriate information and planning appropriate strategies and tactics. Gathering appropriate information is an almost continuous process. Since many employers and bargaining agents nowadays start planning for the next negotiations soon after a labor agreement is accepted, both parties collect information almost continuously.

The sources for gathering information for the negotiating process are quite varied. The employer has access to a variety of records, including transfers and promotions, overtime, layoffs, grievances, and performance of individuals. Another important source of information in preparing for the negotiating process is to get feedback and suggestions from the supervisors who work closely with unionized employees. Such feedback is likely to provide some insight as to the types of demands the bargaining agent may seek for the bargaining unit. A variety of external information is also useful, especially information about competing employers in the community. External information about wage rates, fringe benefits, cost of living, etc., is the type of information with which an employer should be familiar before taking part in the negotiation process. Business publications, trade periodicals, and various union publications might also provide some insight as to the areas that the bargaining agent might try to negotiate for the bargaining unit.

Another significant factor that determines the success with which both parties are able to negotiate with one another is the strategies or tactics that are used in the negotiation sessions. One very common strategy is for one party to make greater demands than the other party can be expected to agree to. This provides a certain amount of flexibility by providing opportunities for making concessions in certain areas in order that original demands in other areas remain intact.

The collective bargaining process is regulated by the Taft-Hartley Act, which was discussed in the preceding chapter. For example, the Taft-Hartley Act states that the employer and the bargaining agent must meet at reasonable times and confer in good faith with regard to the provisions of the labor agreement.

The initial meeting between the two parties may very well set the stage for the entire negotiation process. When the initial meeting consists of a considerable amount of arguing and one party makes accusations against the other party, the remainder of the negotiation sessions will most likely follow the same pattern. A cooperative atmosphere at the first meeting, on the other hand, may set the stage for cooperative sessions to follow. The initial meeting between the two parties is used to determine the rules that will be followed in the negotiating process. The initial meeting is also sometimes used for the two parties to exchange their proposals with one another.

A considerable amount of strategy is used in the sessions when the proposals of both parties are negotiated. Both parties try to keep from one another the importance attached to the various proposals. High priority proposals could become very costly to one party if the other party discovers the importance attached to a particular proposal. Furthermore, when one party concedes too early in the negotiating process, the other party may view this as an excellent opportunity to get still more concessions out of the conceding party. The expediency with which the negotiating sessions progress is also determined to a great extent by the manner in which the two parties are able to resolve the differences between the proposals. If one party is unwilling to concede to the point that the proposal is acceptable to the other party, or if the concessions of one party are not sufficient to cause the other party to agree to the proposal, a stalemate in the bargaining process will result. Such a stalemate is often the forerunner of a union's boycotting, picketing, or striking.

Although employers do not very often use economic pressure to put an end to the stalemate, they may halt operations and lay off personnel, transfer work to another location, or subcontract the work to another organization.

If a stalemate or deadlock in the negotiations lasts for a very long period of time, the two parties may agree to work with a third party to get the negotiations moving once again. Different degrees of outside assistance are used. A **conciliator** keeps the negotiations moving, which results in the two parties' working out the differences between their proposals. If it is obvious that the services of a conciliator will not be successful, a **mediator** may be needed. The mediator, who also intervenes in the negotiating process, tries to keep the negotiations moving and suggests compromises as a means of getting both parties to agree to the proposals.

If both of the negotiating parties agree, an **arbitrator** may be used. The arbitrator considers the worth of each side's proposals and then resolves the dispute by making decisions about the differences between the two proposals.

In instances where the deadlock may result in a work stoppage that will have an adverse effect on the well-being of the nation, the government may intervene in the negotiation process. The government has the authority to issue injunctions against work stoppages and can withdraw government contracts. In some instances, fact-finding boards may be used to determine which of the two parties is responsible for the stalemate.

<table>
<tr><td>

The Labor
Agreement

</td><td>

The **labor agreement** is the written agreement that contains the proposals accepted by both parties during the negotiation process. The coverage found in labor agreements varies somewhat from situation to situation. There appears to be a trend toward longer and more detailed agreements nowadays than was the case several years ago. This is probably because both employers and employees find that more detail in the agreement results in less ambiguity and hence reduces the chance of incorrectly interpreting the clauses in the present agreement. Agreements are also becoming longer because more items are being negotiated, which results in their having to be included in the agreement. Not only does the labor agreement have to coincide with the terms that the two parties agreed upon but it also has to contain certain clauses as required by the Taft-Hartley Act.

</td></tr>
</table>

Some of the essential clauses of the labor agreement are the following:

Duration of agreement. Labor agreements exist for a specified period of time, most frequently ranging from one to five years, with two- to three-year agreements being the most common. Many agreements also provide for automatic extension of the current agreement as long as negotiations for renewing the agreement are in process.

Union security. The clauses within the labor agreement dealing with union security outline the extent to which the union is responsible for the disciplinary control of its members. Also commonly included in this section is an identification of the form of union security, which may include a **union shop, maintenance-of-membership shop, agency, shop,** and **dues checkoff.**

The most common form of union security is the union shop, which means that an employee must be a member or become a member of the union within a specified period of time; otherwise, the employee can be terminated.

The maintenance-of-membership shop, which occurs only infrequently, requires that employees who join a union voluntarily must remain in good standing during the life of the agreement. The agency shop, on the other hand, does not require employees to join a union, but does stipulate that they have to pay union dues since the union serves as their bargaining agent. The agency shop is found most often in states that have right to work laws that forbid mandatory union membership. Dues checkoff is a written agreement between the employer and employees that allows the employer to withhold union dues from the employees' paychecks.

Management prerogatives. This clause of the labor agreement specifies the rights or prerogatives that management retains. Generally, anything that is not contained in the labor agreement and is not restricted by law remains a management right or prerogative.

Management rights or prerogatives have generally eroded over the years. Items that used to be regarded as management rights—hours of work, seniority, and the like—are no longer so regarded and, therefore, they have become a part of the labor agreement.

Many of the union demands result in an increase in operating costs, which means that management has to find ways to become more efficient to offset the increase in operating costs. The result has been that unions want to have some impact in determining the ways that management can improve efficiency. Unions claim that without this input, the job security of some of their members may be threatened. The result is that when the next labor agreement is negotiated, the union is likely to bring forth proposals regarding such issues.

Wages and hours. Labor agreements are required by law to contain a section on wages and hours. Included in this section may be methods of payment, rates of pay, commissions, bonuses, and incentive pay plans. Escalator clauses, which provide for automatic adjustments in salary rates as the cost of living increases, are also common in many labor agreements today. Some agreements even provide for job evaluation, which is used to determine the monetary worth of jobs. Labor agreements also outline working hours, procedures for overtime pay, vacation time, and provisions for holidays.

Promotion, layoff, recall. Labor agreements commonly include clauses for promotion, layoff, and recall of members. Since layoff and recall may be on the basis of a seniority system, the system is also frequently outlined in the agreement. The agreement may also state that bidding on job openings has to be on the basis of the seniority system. If synthetic seniority—the practice of allowing members who are on leave to accumulate seniority—is practiced, this also needs to be outlined in the agreement.

Discipline of members. Labor agreements list the situations for which employees may be disciplined, as well as the type of discipline that may be leveled against the employee. For example, actions for which employees might be disciplined are intoxication, fighting, insubordination, dishonesty, and violation of company rules.

Grievances. Most labor agreements explain the procedures for filing a grievance, the situation in which an employee charges the employer with unfair treatment. Since the labor agreement is used as the basis for the relationship with employees, it should be worded so that the clauses in the agreement cannot be misinterpreted.

Strike clauses. Some labor agreements contain clauses that prohibit employees' striking or walking out during the time that the current agreement is in force. Some unions are becoming reluctant to allow a no-strike clause to be included in a labor agreement because of the possibility of their being sued in the event of a wildcat strike.

Much of the success of a labor agreement is directly related to the administration of the agreement. If the two parties want the agreement to work and strive toward that end, even a poor agreement can be made to work. On the other hand, no matter how carefully prepared an agreement is, it will not work well if the parties fail to try to make the agreement work.

A considerable amount of contract administration involves applying and enforcing the terms of the agreement. In some instances, administration also involves the terms of the agreement. Interpreting the terms of the agreement frequently involves trying to determine the intent of both parties at the time the agreement was accepted.

Handling Grievances

The manner in which grievances are handled is likely to have a significant bearing on the cordiality of relations between the employer and employees. Even though the labor agreement was carefully negotiated between the two parties, grievances are inevitable. The grievances quite often arise because employees feel that they are not being treated fairly and consistently. It is important that the grievances be resolved as expeditiously as possible; otherwise, morale is likely to decrease, which in turn may seriously affect the employees' desire to work efficiently.

Most labor agreements now provide a discussion of the procedures for the handling of grievances. Without definite procedures for handling grievances, the union members may discover that the only way they can get management to be concerned about the situations that precipitated the grievances is to exert economic pressure (strikes, slowdowns, etc.), against the employer.

Most would agree that the best way to handle a grievance is to avoid the circumstances that cause employees to file grievances. This means that the administrative office manager will have to be thoroughly familiar with the terms of the labor agreement and will have to make sure that the office employees are treated fairly and consistently. This also means that the personnel guidelines that the administrative office manager follows must be in conformity with the labor agreement.

Definition of grievances. A discussion about handling grievances could hardly be complete without defining what is meant by a grievance. Some define a grievance as any problem that causes dissatisfaction. As used in this text, grievance is more limited and refers to a company-related complaint that has an adverse effect on productivity.

Supervisor input. The desirability of getting input from supervisors for use in preparing a proposed labor agreement was discussed earlier in this chapter. The desirability of getting input and feedback from supervisors is desirable for another reason. If the supervisors have good rapport with the employees whom they supervise, the employees are apt to feel free to speak out and to air their complaints before they become of such significance that grievances are filed. If this is the case, the management through the supervisor might be able to rectify the situation before a grievance is filed.

Reasons for grievances. There are a variety of reasons for which employees file grievances. In some cases the stated reasons are not the real reasons that precipitated the filing of a grievance. Before a grievance can be adequately considered and handled, every attempt should be made to understand fully the true reason why the grievance was filed.

Many grievances are filed because employees either fail to function properly in a job or because they fail to gain satisfaction from performing the job. In either case, employee selection processes may ultimately be responsible for the employees' failure. There is a great need for an organization to utilize selective procedures that place individuals in jobs that they are able to perform and that are satisfying to them. If the employees' grievances do not stem from faulty selection procedures, then the reasons may be due to poor supervision or even inadequate orientation and training.

The labor agreement has also been responsible for many employees' filing grievances. Labor agreements that are either ambiguous or incomplete will require a considerable amount of interpretation. It is often the interpretation of a clause in the contract that causes an employee to file a grievance. In some cases, certain grievances have been used as a basis for revising the agreement. If the grievance is settled to the union's satisfaction, the union may attempt to include the settlement in the next labor agreement.

Grievance procedures. A well-developed labor agreement will contain an important section that explains how grievances are to be handled. Many labor agreements are so detailed that they help greatly in the day-to-day operation of the organization. In other words, by making the labor agreement quite detailed, there is only minimum need for interpretation of the agreement, which results in the filing of fewer grievances.

Labor agreements containing clauses about the filing of grievances frequently explain how the grievance may be initiated. If a cordial relationship exists between the individual's filing the grievance and the individual's supervisor, the grievance will probably be filed with the supervisor. If an individual does not have a cordial relationship with the supervisor or if the individual feels that the supervisor will not give adequate attention to the grievance, the individual may file the grievance with the union steward, who then contacts the supervisor about the nature of the grievance. In the majority of instances, grievances are settled at the initial step, without first having to appeal the grievance. The fact that most grievances are resolved before having to be appealed is indicative of the willingness of most supervisors to discuss problems with subordinates. It is for this reason that many supervisory training programs include sections on the handling and resolving of grievances.

Although the majority of grievances are resolved at the initial step, some, of course, are appealed to higher levels for resolution. Perhaps the supervisor does not have the authority to resolve the grievance, or because of the nature of the relationship between the supervisor and the employee, the grievance cannot be resolved. While many grievances at the initial level are not put into writing, it is essential that grievances be put into writing when they have to be appealed to higher levels. There are several advantages to using written grievances at this point. The employee is required to fully think through the reasons that precipitated the grievance. Unless all the facts are available, it is difficult to make a fair decision. Since the employee's success or lack of success in getting the grievance resolved may be dependent upon the wording of the written grievance, many employees seek the assistance of their steward. The services of stewards in this function should not be overlooked from either the employees' or management's point of view. In some instances, stewards who feel that the employee's grievance is not valid can convince the employee to terminate the grievance procedures at this point. The steward can also help the employee focus more sharply on the causes that precipitated the filing of the grievance, thus helping make sure that the grievance is valid.

The number of steps through which a grievance may pass if not resolvable at the initial level is likely to depend upon the size and nature of the organization. Larger organizations commonly have more appeal levels than do smaller organizations. Figure 12–1 illustrates the differences between small organizations and larger organizations in terms of the steps through which a grievance may proceed. In each case, the final step is arbitration.

Arbitration, which is used as a last resort in resolving grievances, involves a third party, who, on the basis of all the presented facts, recommends a solution for either or both parties to follow. If the labor agreement contains provisions for arbitation, and most do nowadays, it is very important that the outlined procedures be closely followed.

Arbitration proceedings may be carried out by an arbitrator or by

FIGURE 12–1   Grievance Procedures in Different Size Organizations

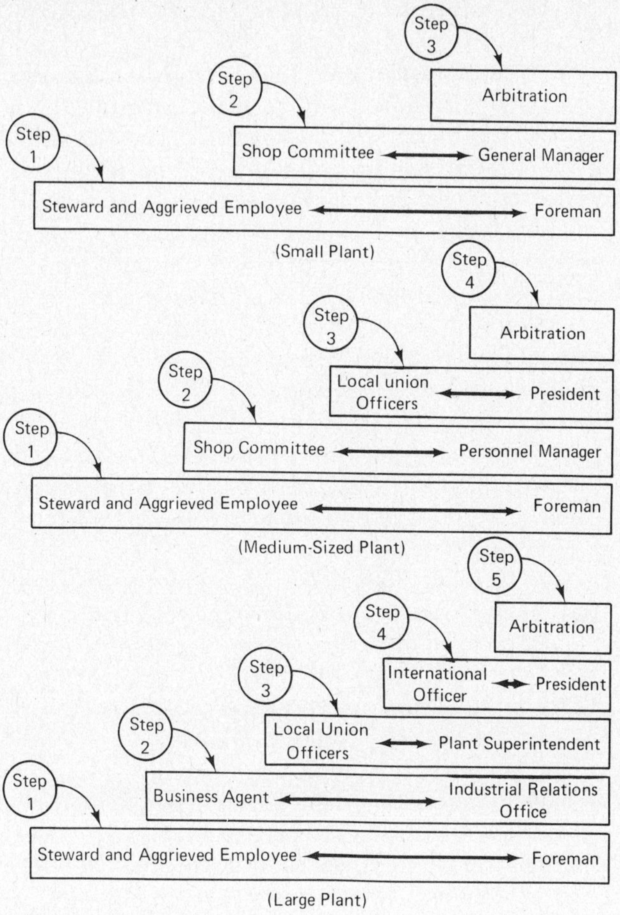

(Small Plant)

(Medium-Sized Plant)

(Large Plant)

Source: C. Wilson Randle, Collective Bargaining, *4th ed., Boston: Houghton Mifflin Company, 1966. Reprinted by permission.*

an arbitration board. When arbitrators are used, they may be hired to hear only one grievance, or they may be hired on a rather permanent basis. Although some arbitrators do nothing but arbitrate grievances, most do arbitration only on a part-time basis. The American Arbitration Association compiles a list of individuals who are qualified to serve as arbitrators. An arbitration board consists of representatives from the union and management, in addition to an arbitrator who is acceptable to both parties. Arbitration proceedings consist of two types: voluntary and compulsory. Voluntary arbitration, the most common type, takes place when both parties mutually agree to the proceedings. Compulsory arbitration, on the other hand, takes place when both parties are required to start the procedures because potential strikes would cause an economic hardship.

When the grievance is finally ready to be arbitrated, the arbitrator has primary responsibility to make sure that both sides receive a fair hearing and that all the pertinent facts are presented. In some instances, if the arbitrator is not sure that all the facts have been made known, witnesses may be asked to appear during the arbitration proceedings.

After the conclusion of the arbitration proceedings, the arbitrator usually has thirty days in which to consider the facts presented by both sides and to make a decision. To assist arbitrators in making decisions, several arbitration services are in existence that publish arbitration decisions. The American Arbitration Association and Commercial Clearing House are two such services.

Union-Management Cooperation

Developing a spirit of union-management cooperation is time-consuming, and in some cases is a very long-term process. In some instances, the union and management in organizations never develop much of a cooperative relationship.

A considerable amount of animosity between the two parties will most likely develop during the time that the union becomes recognized. It is not uncommon for an employer to resist the unionizing efforts vigorously, which in many cases is to no avail. Once the union becomes a reality and the employer recognizes the union as the bargaining agent for the employees, very little is gained by the employer's continuing to vigorously resist the union. At this point, both parties need to begin to accommodate one another. An accommodation of each other does not indicate a weakness on the part of either party—but rather, it indicates a willingness to coexist with one another. Full cooperation with one another exists when the parties accept each other as partners in terms of the union-management relations. Only rarely does this happen. Union-management cooperation may develop to the point that joint union-management committees are formed. These committees often discuss topics other than those included in the labor agreement. Thus, the discussion between the two parties involves topics of mutual benefit to one another and not just topics that have to be discussed because they are included in the agreement.

Often the cooperation between union and management is tied to the financial success of the organization. In such instances, the employers share any profits in excess of those retained by the company. It is to the advantage of both parties to become more cooperative by becoming more productive. If, for example, the union allows management to change a work process in order that greater productivity can be achieved and thus greater profits are realized, the union members share a certain amount of the excess profits. It is, therefore, to the advantage of both parties to develop a sense of cooperation.

Review Questions

1. What are the major functions of the union's business representative?

2. How do the functions of the business representative and the steward differ?

3. What is the role of the bargaining agent?

4. Prior to a negotiation session, what is the nature of preparation of both parties?

5. What are the major differences between the services provided by a conciliator, a mediator, and an arbitrator?

6. What is meant by union shop, maintenance of membership shop, and agency shop?

7. In a labor agreement, what are management prerogatives?

8. Why is it important that grievance procedures be carefully outlined in the labor agreement?

Minicases

The office employees' union of Blackwell Electronics has been negotiating a new labor agreement with the management of the firm. The labor agreement that is about to expire was judged by both parties to be quite successful except for the grievance procedures. This section of the agreement frequently caused problems because it did not sufficiently outline the grievance procedure steps to be followed. To avoid the problem again, both parties have decided that this section must be clearly outlined in the new agreement. What items should be included in the grievance procedures section of the new labor agreement in order to eliminate the problems of the present agreement?

*   *   *

The union to which the office employees of a large manufacturing plant in Chicago belong and the management of the plant have been negotiating a new labor agreement. It became apparent not too long ago that the differences between the two parties were quite extensive and that the chances of getting both parties to accept the agreement without an outside party were quite small. The management and the union have agreed to utilize the services of a third party. What are the stages through which their negotiations may pass before the agreement is accepted by both sides? What is likely to take place during each stage of this negotiation process?

Case

The Browning Company, located in a large city in the South, assembles a variety of electronic components used by a variety of manufacturers located throughout the country. The office employees recently formed a union, but have not become affiliated with a national or international union. The employees originally unionized because of poor wages, poor fringe benefits, and somewhat unsatisfactory working conditions.

At the present time, approximately 95 percent of the office employees belong to the union. A committee was recently formed to develop a list of proposals for the new labor agreement that will be negotiated very soon. Several of the union members feel that a union shop clause should be negotiated. Several also feel that the union should become affiliated with an international or national union.

1. What is your reaction to a union shop clause in a new agreement?

2. What is your reaction to the proposal that the union become affiliated with a national or international union?

Supervising
Office
Employees

Chapter

13

The Leadership Role
Leadership Styles
Leadership Orientation
Leadership Behavior

The Functions of Supervision
Planning
Organizing
Staffing
Directing
Controlling

Characteristics of Good Supervisors
Achieving Cooperation
Listening
Making Decisions
Delegating
Understanding Others
Fairness

Special Skills of the Supervisor
Human Relations Skills
Teaching Skills
Coaching Skills
Counseling Skills
Communication Skills

Supervisory Training

Special Responsibilities of the Supervisor
Tardiness
Absenteeism
Alcoholism and Drug Abuse

Chapter Aims   After studying this chapter, the student should be able to:

1. Discuss the leadership role in terms of leadership styles, leadership orientation, and leadership behavior.
2. Discuss the five functions of supervision and the typical activities involved in each.
3. Discuss the characteristics of good supervision.
4. Discuss the special skills needed of supervisors.
5. Discuss the supervisor's responsibility for tardiness, absenteeism, and alcohol and drug abuse.

Chapter Terms   *Autocratic approach:* a leadership style in which supervisors make major decisions without seeking the ideas, suggestions, and recommendations of subordinates.

Democratic approach: a leadership style in which the supervisor extensively utilizes ideas, suggestions, and recommendations of the subordinates.

Laissez-faire approach: a leadership style in which subordinates are given very little assistance, if any, from the supervisor, who allows subordinates a considerable amount of freedom.

Achievement-oriented supervision: a supervisor's orientation toward subordinates in which more concern is shown for the achievement of the subordinates than for the subordinates as individuals.

Subordinate-oriented supervision: a supervisor's orientation toward subordinates in which a greater amount of concern is shown for the subordinates as individuals than for their achievement.

Boss-centered leadership: a leadership behavior that is very autocratic in nature.

Supervisor-centered leadership: a leadership behavior that is very democratic in nature.

Supervision, which refers to the efforts of individuals who have the necessary authority and responsibility for planning, directing, and controlling the various activities of subordinates, requires leadership skills. Some supervisory positions require considerably greater utilization of leadership skills than do other positions. Among the factors having an impact on the amount of leadership skills required in a supervisory position are: the hierarchical level of the supervisory position, the number of subordinates for whom the supervisor is responsible, the nature of the work performed by the subordinates, the background of the subordinates, and the stability of the work unit. Because of the important role that leadership plays in the supervisory process, an examination of that role is necessary.

The Leadership Role

The leadership role can be examined by studying several of the different elements that comprise the role. One such element to be studied is the various leadership styles. Other elements include leadership orientation and leadership behavior.

Leadership Styles

Although leadership styles vary between an **autocratic approach** and a **democratic approach,** there are several degrees between these two approaches. This means that while some supervisors use a very autocratic approach in supervising subordinates, others utilize a very democratic approach. Other supervisors utilize various degrees of the autocratic and democratic approaches, which means that their approach is somewhere between the two extremes. The following illustrates the autocratic-democratic leadership continuum:

Autocratic └─┴─┴─┴─┴─┴─┴─┘ Democratic

The autocratic leadership approach is present when the supervisor makes major decisions without seeking the ideas, suggestions, and recommendations of subordinates. The supervisor who uses this approach tends to exert extensive control over the behavior and actions of subordinates. In many cases, subordinates are disciplined before an attempt is made to determine the reasons responsible for their misconduct. Autocratic supervisors rarely deviate from the norm or the expected course of action. Because autocratic supervisors tend to be inflexible, many subordinates are resentful of those who utilize this approach.

Supervisors who utilize the democratic approach extensively use ideas, suggestions, and recommendations of their subordinates. A cooperative relationship exists between the supervisor and the subordinates. The subordinates are very likely to be asked to participate in the decision-making process, especially if the impact of the decision will have an effect on them. It should be pointed out that even though subordinates participate in the decisionmaking process, the supervisor is ultimately responsible for the decisions that are made. In addition to utilizing subordinate participation, the democratic approach is also characterized as providing greater flexibility. A supervisor who utilizes the democratic approach is more likely to investigate the reasons for subordinate error or misconduct before deciding whether disciplinary action is appropriate.

A third leadership approach that is quite distinctive from the other two discussed in this chapter is referred to as the **laissez-faire approach.** When this approach is used, the subordinates are given little, if any, assistance from the supervisor. The laissez-faire supervisor also generally allows subordinates considerable freedom. A lack of care on the part of the supervisor may not be the only reason that a supervisor utilizes the laissez-faire approach. Another reason is the feeling of some supervisors that the only way to be a popular supervisor is to give subordinates a considerable amount of freedom.

Each of the three approaches has certain merits in certain situations. For example, when subordinates are poorly trained, when they are basically undisciplined, or when an emergency or crisis situation exists, the autocratic approach may be most desirable. On the other hand, if subordinates are trained, if they are highly motivated, or if subordinates need to work together as a team, a more democratic approach may be appropriate. In technical groups in which an extensive amount of creativity is useful, the laissez-faire approach may be most beneficial. In most office situations, a democratic approach is generally considered to be the most desirable of the three approaches.

Leadership Orientation

Another of the elements of the leadership role in the supervisory process is the supervisor's orientation toward subordinates. Some supervisors are only concerned with the achievements of the subordinates, which is referred to as **achievement-oriented supervision.** Other supervisors are greatly concerned with the surbordinates as individuals; this is referred to as **subordinate-oriented supervision.**

The supervisor who is greatly concerned with the output of the subordinates is likely to be only minimally concerned with the wants, needs, and feelings of the subordinates. In other words, the achievement-oriented supervisors expect their subordinates to maintain a high output level no matter what the impact is on the subordinates. The subordinate-oriented supervisor is also concerned with output, but not to the degree that the achievement-oriented supervisor is concerned. The subordinate-oriented supervisor feels that if the subordinates' needs are fulfilled, their output will be at a satisfactory level.

Leadership Behavior

Figure 13–1 illustrates leadership behavior. At one end of the continuum is **boss-centered leadership** while **subordinate-centered leadership** appears at the other end. Boss-centered leadership is autocratic and the

FIGURE 13–1   Continuum of Leadership Behavior

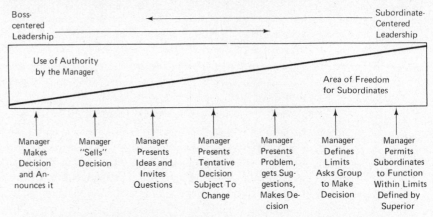

Boss-
centered
Leadership

Subordinate-
Centered
Leadership

Use of Authority
by the Manager

Area of Freedom
for Subordinates

| Manager Makes Decision and An- nounces it | Manager "Sells" Decision | Manager Presents Ideas and Invites Questions | Manager Presents Tentative Decision Subject To Change | Manager Presents Problem, gets Sug- gestions, Makes De- cision | Manager Defines Limits Asks Group to Make Decision | Manager Permits Subordinates to Function Within Limits Defined by Superior |

*Source: R. Tannenbaum and W. H. Schmidt, "How to Choose a Leadership Pattern,"
Harvard Business Review, Vol. 36, No. 2 (March–April, 1958), pp. 95–101 and Vol. 51, No. 3
(May–June 1973), pp. 162–170. Reprinted with permission.*

supervisor is achievement oriented. Subordinate-centered leadership, on the other hand, is democratic and the supervisor is subordinate oriented. An examination of Figure 13–1 reveals that as leadership behavior becomes less boss-centered and more subordinate-centered, the amount of authority exercised by the supervisor or manager decreases as the area of freedom for the subordinates increases.

An effective supervisor is able to readily determine the amount of subordinate participation or subordinate control that is appropriate for each situation. An extensive amount of subordinate participation is appropriate in some instances, while little or no subordinate participation is appropriate in other situations.

The Functions of Supervision

In Chapter 1, five functions of management were identified: planning, organizing, staffing, directing, and controlling. Supervision also consists of these same five functions.

Planning

The planning function may consume a considerable amount of the supervisor's time. The amount of time consumed by the planning function is likely to be directly related to the hierarchical level of the supervisor's position. Higher-level supervisors spend more time in the planning function than do lower-level supervisors. Furthermore, the plans developed by lower-level supervisors are usually for a shorter range of time than are the plans developed by higher-level supervisors. This is because the planning activities of the lower-level supervisors frequently involve implementing the goals and objectives developed by higher-level managers.

Organizing

Organizing, as one of the functions of supervision, involves determining which of the subordinates in the work unit are best qualified for a particular job that has to be done and subsequently assigning that job to the appropriate subordinates. Thus, organizing involves developing a manpower system as a means of effectively accomplishing the established plans. Another dimension of the organizing function is the development of an environment in which subordinates can be productive and efficient. The supervisor is also responsible for developing work procedures and processes that are efficient.

Staffing

In some instances, the supervisor's staffing activities are quite extensive, while in other instances, the staffing activities are quite limited. Higher-level supervisors frequently have a considerable amount of control over selecting new employees for their respective work units. Lower-level supervisors, especially first-level supervisors, may not have as much control. Other staffing activities of a supervisory nature are orienting new employees, training new employees, retraining employees, and counseling employees. Supervisors' jobs are made much easier if the subordinates for whom they are responsible are efficient, well-trained individuals. If such is not the case, supervisors will most likely have to be more concerned with the activities involved in the planning, organizing, directing, and controlling functions.

Directing

Some of the activities involved in the directing function of supervision include leading, motivating, developing, recognizing, and criticizing subordinates. The directing function is concerned with the manner in which the supervisor relates to a subordinate on a person-to-person basis or to a group of subordinates on a person-to-group basis. To maximize the directing efforts, a supervisor must not only be concerned with the goals and objectives of the organization but also with how well the needs of each subordinate are related to the organization's goals and objectives.

While the lower-level supervisors are generally not as involved with the activities characteristic of the planning function, the activities in the directing function are very important to lower-level supervisors. Higher-level supervisors are generally not as involved with the directing function as are lower-level supervisors.

Controlling

This function involves comparing actual results with anticipated results. For this reason, the activities characteristic of the controlling function are likely to consume a considerable portion of the supervisor's time. If the actual results are less than the expected results, the supervisor is responsible for taking corrective action to rectify the situation.

Without the establishment of standards against which actual results can be compared, controlling efforts are of little value. In addition, it is the responsibility of the supervisor to determine the validity of the standards that are implemented and to develop work measurement methods.

Characteristics of Good Supervisors

Over the years, many different characteristics of good supervisors have been identified. Because a discussion of all these characteristics would result in a discussion more extensive than the author chooses to make at this point, the discussion of the characteristics of good supervisors is limited to the following six: achieving cooperation, listening, making decisions, delegating, understanding others, and fairness.

Achieving Cooperation

One of the most important characteristics of good supervisors is their ability to achieve cooperation. Without the cooperation of subordinates, the supervisor's job becomes very difficult. Unless the supervisor has the cooperation of the employees, many of their actions are very likely to reflect poorly on the supervisor.

One way to achieve cooperation among subordinates is to show an interest in them as individuals and in the work they do. In many instances cooperation is achieved simply by the supervisor's showing concern for the quality of the subordinates' performance.

Another way to achieve cooperation among subordinates is to make them aware that higher-level management is dependent upon them for their ideas and suggestions. There are many advantages of using subordinates' ideas and suggestions, one of which is to achieve cooperation. If the organization does not subscribe to the participative management concept, there are other ways in which subordinates' ideas and suggestions can be effectively utilized. The implementation of a suggestion system is one such way. In many instances, the employees who work most closely with a given work procedure are able to provide valuable ideas and suggestions when changes have to be made. When subordinates' ideas and suggestions are accepted by higher-level management, they tend to become more cooperative. But the cooperation will not be very long-lasting unless the subordinates are able to see rather quickly that their ideas and suggestions are accepted and utilized. Accepting but not utilizing subordinates' ideas may do more to destroy cooperation than if their ideas and suggestions were not accepted in the first place.

Supervisors can also obtain cooperation by providing as much variety as possible in the daily routine. If routines are not varied, subordinates tend to become rather complacent and soon lose interest in their jobs. It is rather difficult for a supervisor to have the full cooperation of subordinates who lack interest in their jobs.

For a supervisor to be unable to justify why certain policies exist or why certain procedures must be done a certain way also tends to destroy a desire for subordinates to cooperate. A good supervisor is able to answer subordinates' questions, and if the answer is not known, the supervisor should make every attempt to learn the answer. Much cooperation is lost by telling subordinates that something "has to be done a certain way because that is the way it has always been done." Such a response does not indicate much of a willingness to cooperate on the supervisor's behalf. Subordinates are apt to react with a comparable lack of cooperation.

Listening

Another characteristic of a good supervisor is the ability to listen to subordinates. It is difficult for many supervisors to "hear out their subordinates," especially those against whom the supervisors have negative feelings. Unless subordinates are convinced that their supervisors are willing to listen, it is impossible for an effective relationship to develop between the supervisors and the subordinates.

Supervisors are often guilty of failing to listen to a subordinate who wishes to discuss a situation about which the subordinate may disagree. The supervisor gives the impression that the subordinate is not in a position to question or discuss the situation. Another fault some supervisors have is making decisions or judgments about a situation being discussed by a subordinate even before the subordinate has finished discussing the situation. Such a habit reflects negatively on a supervisor, since the subordinate is likely to have the impression that the supervisor has little concern for the subordinate. Another undesirable listening habit of some supervisors is the injection of their comments or feelings about the situation being discussed before they are aware of all the circumstances surrounding the situation. The supervisor who does this is likely to "force" the subordinate to feel the same way that the supervisor feels about a particular situation.

Listening to a subordinate is not enough. The supervisor must also pay attention to or concentrate on what the subordinate has to say if an effective relationship is to develop. Although it is sometimes difficult for a supervisor to concentrate continually on what the subordinate has to say, such concentration is crucial.

The mark of a good listener is the ability to hear what is actually being told or said, not just what the supervisor expects to hear. Supervisors who hear only what they want to hear cannot be completely objective when having to make decisions.

There are several ways the supervisor can become a more effective listener. One way is to give subordinates complete attention, which prevents their comments from being blocked out. Another way to become a better listener is to evaluate the merits of the subordinates' suggestions, rather than evaluating the suggestions on the basis of the individuals making the suggestions. The listening process can also be improved by the supervisor's summarizing what the subordinate has said. Thus, the accuracy of the supervisor's understanding of the situation can be verified. The supervisor can also become a better listener by maintaining an open mind. If emotional, biased feelings are allowed to surface, the supervisor will not be able to understand completely the full impact of the subordinate's comments. Effective listening involves more than understanding words. Facial expressions, voice inflections, and gestures are also important in understanding the full impact of the discussion.

Making Decisions

A considerable portion of a supervisory position involves making decisions. Nearly every problem with which a supervisor is confronted involves decisionmaking of varying magnitudes. Decisionmaking involves solving problems by using logical steps:

1. An identification and analysis of the problem or situation.
2. An identification of alternative solutions.
3. An analysis and evaluation of the alternative solutions.
4. Selection of the most appropriate alternative.
5. Followup on the selected alternative.

Many decisions are either poorly or inefficiently made, either because some supervisors fail to clearly identify the problems, or because the situations surrounding the problems are only vaguely identified. In some instances, supervisors fail to distinguish properly between problems and their symptoms. Unless the symptoms are clearly analyzed, decisions may be somewhat ineffective. Decisionmaking can be made more effective if those involved in decisionmaking processes are guided by the future implications of their decisions. Making a decision without considering the impact of the decision may indicate a shortsightedness on the part of the decisionmaker. Because many decisions involve taking risks, the extensiveness of the risks can be minimized by considering the future implications of decisions. The future impact should be considered especially if the decisions are likely to have a significant effect on employees, work processes, or financial resources. When selecting an appropriate alternative, the future impact of the alternative definitely needs to be considered.

Once the decision has been made, it needs to be communicated to those who will be affected by the decision. Its acceptability is likely to be greatly influenced by the manner in which the details of the decision are communicated to others. If the employees feel that certain facts, details, or implications are purposely withheld, the acceptability of the decision may be greatly diminished.

The nature of some decisions will require the utilization of certain control measures to help insure that the decisions are being properly carried out. These control devices may be in the form of progress reports, briefing sessions, or other types of followup devices. If the results show that corrective measures are needed, the supervisor will have to determine the appropriate measures.

Delegating

One of the most important characteristics of good supervisors is their ability to delegate tasks meaningfully to subordinates. Without effective delegation, supervisors either have to do much of the work themselves or have to depend upon the subordinates to assume the responsibility for a considerable amount of task completion.

There are a variety of reasons why supervisors are hesitant to delegate tasks to subordinates. Some supervisors simply cannot delegate or they are afraid to delegate. Other supervisors sometimes are hesitant to delegate because they feel they can perform certain tasks more effectively than can subordinates; because it is easier for them to do a task than to teach a subordinate how to do the task; or because they want the tasks done their way, which may not be the way the subordinates would choose to do the tasks. Some supervisors are also hesitant to delegate because the subordinates to whom they delegate tasks may be able to perform more effectively than the supervisor who did the delegating. This situation is likely to reflect negatively on the supervisor.

Several guidelines can be made to help improve the effectiveness of delegation. These guidelines include the following:

1. *Select the appropriate person to whom a task is being delegated.* Since each subordinate is not equally able to perform the same tasks with the same degree of quality, the supervisor needs to be selective in making assignments. Much of one's success in delegation can be attributed to selecting the appropriate person for each job.

2. *Select tasks that can be delegated.* A good supervisor is selective in delegating tasks. While some tasks cannot be delegated, others should be selectively delegated. Generally, those tasks that can be delegated are routine in nature, they may involve infrequent judgment, and the task steps can be easily identified.

3. *Help the person to whom tasks have been delegated.* Good supervisors help subordinates to whom they have delegated tasks. Some supervisors feel that if a subordinate is qualified to undertake a task, no assistance or help should ever be needed. Therefore, the subordinate is left alone to do the assigned tasks. While more subordinates are able to do many tasks without help from a supervisor, help should be available when needed.

4. *Make sure that work assignments are fully understood.* A good supervisor is patient with subordinates who have been delegated a task for the first time. Even though the subordinates may think they fully understand the assignment, once they undertake the assignment, certain questions may arise. Fewer questions will arise once the work is underway if subordinates understand their work assignments.

Even though a supervisor delegates task assignments to subordinates, the supervisor is usually held responsible for the completion of the assigned tasks. The subordinate to whom the task has been assigned should have commensurate authority and responsibility to complete the task. Since the supervisor is usually held ultimately responsible for the completion of the task, a supervisor cannot use task delegation to avoid responsibility.

One of the greatest difficulties for many supervisors to overcome when delegating is accepting the fact that there may be more than one correct way to do a particular task. No matter how much a supervisor would like to have a subordinate do a task the way the supervisor does the task, the supervisor-subordinate relationship may be jeopardized if the supervisor requires the subordinate to follow certain procedures when others may be just as effective.

Understanding Others

Since the supervisor is responsible for motivating subordinates, a thorough understanding of the needs, drives, interests, and attitudes of each subordinate is important. Without this understanding, it is difficult for a supervisor to inspire each subordinate to perform effectively.

There are several aspects of each subordinate's background that the supervisor needs to understand in order to effectively supervise the subordinates.

1. *Ability to think.* If a supervisor is to fully understand a subordinate, the supervisor must be aware of the subordinate's ability to think. The ability to sort the important from the unimportant and to logically organize important thoughts is also very important. It is the supervisor's responsibility to assess the subordinate's ability to think.

2. *Social traits.* For a supervisor fully to understand subordinates, an awareness of the social traits of the subordinate is needed. In other words, the supervisor needs to know whether each subordinate has a tendency to become aggressive, to withdraw, to dominate the situation, or to put others at ease.

3. *Personality traits.* An effective working relationship between the supervisor and the subordinate requires the supervisor to have a fairly comprehensive understanding of the subordinate's personality. Without

this knowledge, it is difficult for a supervisor to know how to respond to or how to supervise subordinates. An understanding of personality traits can also be used to assess the emotional needs of subordinates.

4. *Character.* An awareness of each subordinate's character is needed by the supervisor. Without this awareness, the supervisor can only guess the degree to which subordinates can be trusted. Since subordinates do not all have the same level of personal standards, the supervisor may have the right to place greater trust in some subordinates than in others.

5. *Work habits.* A knowledge of subordinates' work habits is also needed by supervisors. The supervisor needs to be aware of who is a self-starter, who needs some direction, and who needs a considerable amount of direction. The work habits of subordinates are a significant determinant of the degree of supervision that subordinates require.

6. *Relations with others.* For a complete understanding of others, the supervisor must be aware of how various subordinates relate to others. This understanding is very important in deciding which subordinates are able to work together on a given project, which subordinates can be utilized for public relations, and so forth.

Supervisors who know and understand their subordinates well can give them assignments they are sure to enjoy. Happy, satisfied subordinates make the supervisor's job much easier. Knowing and understanding subordinates also helps the supervisor know how to respond to their individual needs.

Fairness

The last characteristic of good supervisors to be discussed in this chapter is fairness to subordinates. The relationships between many supervisors and their subordinates have been damaged because of a lack of fairness on the part of the supervisor. A lack of fairness that is only imagined is often as damaging to the relationship as is a lack of fairness that is real.

Supervisors who allow their personal feelings toward subordinates to sway their decisions regarding their subordinates have difficulty in treating their subordinates fairly. Those subordinates for whom the supervisor has strong positive feelings are very likely to receive favored treatment, while those for whom the supervisor has strong negative feelings are likely to be treated unfairly.

The best practice for supervisors is to treat all subordinates equally in similar situations. Policies that exist for one subordinate should exist for all subordinates. When unjustifiable exceptions are made, subordinates are not treated equally.

In some instances, when a subordinate is involved in a situation of a serious or drastic nature, the immediate supervisor perhaps should not be involved in deciding upon an appropriate course of action. For example, if a subordinate's conduct or actions are of such serious nature that dismissal is an alternative, the final decision regarding the subordinate may be made by higher-level individuals who are neutral and, thus, objective. The subordinate is therefore not able to charge that the supervisor failed to provide fair treatment because of prior bias or negative feelings.

Special Skills of the Supervisor

In addition to possessing the characteristics discussed in the preceding section, good supervisors must also have certain skills if they are to be effective. These include the following: human relations skills, teaching skills, coaching skills, and counseling skills. These skills are often developed through supervisory training experiences made available to new supervisors or to supervisors who need or desire refresher training.

Human Relations Skills

Years ago, employees were chosen to be supervisors because of their technical competence. But as a more employee-oriented management philosophy developed, other criteria were used in selecting supervisors. One such criterion was skill in human relations. Nowadays, not only must supervisors have technical competence, but they also must be skilled in other areas, including human relations.

Without human relations skills, the supervisor is likely to alienate the subordinates. Once the supervisor-subordinate relationship is damaged, it is difficult for the supervisor to have the full cooperation of the subordinates, to motivate the subordinates, or to have their loyalty. With human relations skills, the chances of such problems arising are greatly diminished.

With human relations skills, the supervisor will have a better idea of how to treat each subordinate in each situation. Because personalities and situations vary so much, the supervisor must be able to maintain the proper amount of closeness or distance, whichever is appropriate for the situation. Supervisors who remain distant in every situation or who tend to have a close relationship with their subordinates soon find that they are considered to be either uncooperative individuals or individuals who can be easily taken advantage of. In either case, the subordinates are eventually likely to lose respect for their supervisors.

Human relations skills can be learned either through on-the-job training or through courses designed to help supervisors improve their human relations skills. Some supervisors also utilize college and university courses to help improve human relations skills.

Teaching Skills

Supervisors who are expected to teach or train subordinates need special teaching skills. Although most supervisors could probably train subordinates without ever having training in this area, a more effective job is likely to be done if the supervisor has training in the elements of teaching subordinates.

Perhaps the two most significant elements of teaching that a supervisor needs training in are demonstrating and explaining. In addition, skills in evaluating subordinates' performance are needed. Supervisory teaching skills are effectively learned through college and university courses and through supervisory training experiences developed by the organization.

Coaching Skills

Another of the skills needed by an effective supervisor is a skill in coaching subordinates. Coaching is generally thought to take place when a superior (usually the supervisor) makes a concerted effort to develop a subordinate. The development process involves the subordinate's job and the problems related to that job. The objective of coaching is to improve job skills and to increase the subordinate's understanding of the technical aspects of the job.

A distinct difference exists between on-the-job training and coaching. Whereas on-the-job training involves teaching the subordinate about the techniques of job performance, coaching most likely encompasses more than the job presently held by the subordinate. As an example, coaching may involve developing the managerial skills of a subordinate, especially if such skills are needed by an individual who is about to be promoted to a managerial position.

Coaching skills are effectively learned through organization-sponsored supervisory training programs.

Counseling Skills

Over the years, supervisors have counseled subordinates in a variety of areas. Some of these areas are generally considered to fall within the domain of the supervisor-subordinate counseling relationship, but others are clearly not within the domain of the relationship. The appropriate areas for counseling have been somewhat restricted because of this circumstance. In addition, most supervisors do not have time to counsel subordinates in all the areas in which they experience problems, which is another reason the areas of the counseling relationship have been restricted. Although the supervisor must listen to certain of the subordinates' problems in order to have an effective supervisor-subordinate relationship, the supervisor must judiciously screen the appropriate areas in which to become involved.

Larger organizations often have professional counseling staffs, in addition to utilizing the counseling assistance of supervisors. The rationale behind this practice is that supervisors do not have the time or the qualifications to counsel subordinates in certain areas. Some feel that the supervisor should not become involved in a counseling relationship. Others feel that as long as the supervisor does not attempt to perform therapy work, supervisory involvement may be useful in developing a stronger supervisory-subordinate relationship.

Several different counseling techniques exist, ranging from a nondirective technique in which the subordinate does most of the talking, to a technique in which the supervisor is responsible for a greater amount of direction in the counseling process. What is appropriate for one individual and one set of circumstances may be completely inappropriate for another individual and the accompanying set of circumstances.

Counseling skills can be learned through college and university training as well as organization-sponsored training programs. Without specialized training in counseling, supervisors should restrict their counseling activities to include only a very minimum number of areas.

Communication Skills

A considerable portion of the supervisor-subordinate relationship depends on communication. Therefore, the supervisor needs to have fairly well-developed communication skills if the relationship is to be effective.

A good supervisor should be aware of the forces that are often responsible for impeding the communication process. Among these forces are the following:

1. *Lack of knowledge or background.* A lack of knowledge or background on the part of the receiver or sender will impede the communication process. Reasons causing a lack of knowledge or background are lack of education, intelligence, or exposure to the topic being discussed.

2. *Inappropriate verbal usage.* Not everyone has the same level of vocabulary understanding. Therefore, to use vocabulary that is not understood by the receiver injects a barrier in the communication process.

3. *Use of bias or prejudice.* The use of bias or prejudice is another force that impedes the communication process. When a prejudiced comment is leveled against an individual, those who hear the comment are likely to arrive at a biased conclusion with regard to a situation involving the individual against whom the prejudiced comment was made.

4. *Impact of filtering.* As messages pass from one individual to another, the original intent of the message may become distorted or changed in meaning. This process is filtering. The impact of filtering needs to be understood by supervisors, especially when a message is conveyed through several individuals.

Communication also involves the ability to show empathy and concern for others. The communication between two individuals is often hampered because either or both of these factors are absent.

Another way the supervisor can make the communication process more effective is to avoid becoming defensive. When an open relationship between the supervisor and the subordinate exists, the supervisor may at times be criticized by the subordinate. In instances in which the criticism is warranted, the supervisor will impede the communication process by becoming defensive.

The supervisor can further strengthen the communication process by using a direct approach where appropriate and an indirect approach when the direct approach is not appropriate. In a sensitive situation, the supervisor may be wise to use an indirect approach when communicating with a subordinate. To use the direct approach may jeopardize a good working relationship between the two.

Effective communication processes are frequently taught at colleges and universities, as well as in supervisory training programs. Because so many individuals spend so much time during the working day communicating with others, they feel that their communication skills are well developed. Although this may be true in certain instances, many supervisors can and do profit from formal training experiences in this area.

Supervisory Training

Because most supervisors are promoted to supervisory positions from production-oriented jobs, many supervisors can profit from supervisory training experiences. Although most supervisors have the necessary technical competence, they are in need of training experiences that teach them how to be effective in other areas. Many different training techniques are available for such training. Because the techniques are discussed in Chapter 15, they will not be repeated in this chapter.

One of the most important factors in designing training programs for supervisors is determining the areas in which they need training. The appropriate areas are to a great extent determined by the organizations in which supervisors are employed and the duties the supervisors are expected to perform. Since not all supervisors need training in the same areas, some discretion should be used in selecting the appropriate training areas for each individual. Some of the topics frequently covered in supervisory training programs include:

1. Delegating work
2. Disciplining employees
3. Training employees
4. Hiring, orienting, and promoting employees
5. Handling grievances
6. Scheduling work
7. Quality control of work
8. Developing effective work procedures
9. Developing effective human relations skills

10. Developing effective communication skills
11. Developing effective counseling skills

Some supervisory training programs are of an intensive nature and, therefore, are conducted over a short period of time. Others are less intensive and exist for a longer period of time. The success of the training program may be significantly determined by the effectiveness of the supervisor.

Special Responsibilities of the Supervisor

Employees are frequently tardy or absent from work because of a laxness of supervision. Employees who know that they can be late to work or can be absent from work with little or no penalty will often do so. Therefore, it is the supervisor's responsibility to make sure that employees do not violate the tardiness or absenteeism policies of the organization.

Because supervisors are in close contact with their subordinates, many organizations are now asking their supervisors to be observant of employees who may have problems with alcohol or drug abuse. Many organizations are taking a paternalistic view toward alcohol and drug abuse and are attempting to help employees who may not only seek help but also may profit from such help.

Tardiness

Over a period of time, tardiness can be quite costly to an organization. The supervisor is responsible for determining which employees are tardy because of situations over which they have no control. Examples are traffic jams, automobile malfunctions, mass transportation problems, and the like.

When employees are excessively tardy because of some fault of their own, there are a variety of ways to deal with the problem. Most supervisors feel that as the problem becomes more severe, the discipline leveled against the employee should also become more severe. Employees may first receive an oral or written reprimand. If this does not help, the next course of action may be a reduction in pay according to some predetermined scale. If the problem continues, the employee may be given a week's layoff with no pay. Finally, the last course of action is to discharge the employee.

Some organizations have found that the best way to eliminate tardiness is to reward employees for being punctual. The reward system may be on an individual basis or on a group basis, such as a work unit or department. Examples of rewards are the following: time off, monetary bonus, public recognition, faster promotion, and larger salary increases.

Supervisors who are responsible for the tardiness of employees can do much by setting a good example. It is difficult to justify an employee's being punctual if the supervisor does not also have to be punctual.

Absenteeism   The absenteeism rate of their employees is of great concern to many organizations. Absenteeism is costly not only in terms of salaries, but also in terms of the productivity that is lost because an absent employee's output is another employee's input.

A supervisor may find that 10 to 20 percent of the subordinates are responsible for 75 to 80 percent of the absences. By paying particular attention to these percentages, the supervisor may be able to find ways to more effectively control the absenteeism.

As is true with tardiness, some absences are unavoidable. Examples of such absences are illness or job-related injuries, illness of a family member, and deaths of family members or close friends. Although such examples are legitimate absences, some employees will also use the same reasons as excuses for being absent. The supervisor therefore must attempt to determine when an employee's reason for being absent is legitimate and when the reason is not legitimate.

One of the most common reasons for employees' being absent from work is a lack of job satisfaction. Although the employee will generally offer some other reason for being absent, the real reason may be a lack of interest in the job. When this is the case, the supervisor may take one of several courses of action: determine ways in which the job can be made more interesting and challenging to the employee in order to increase the amount of the employee's job satisfaction; determine if the requirements of the job are considerably less than the employee's capability to fill the job; determine the reason for the employee's taking the job in the first place, besides the need for money; or determine if the working conditions are satisfactory.

Supervisors often handle absenteeism in the same way that they handle tardiness. The following courses of action are frequently used in dealing with absent employees: oral or written reprimand, pay deduction, temporary layoff, and discharge.

Providing employees with personal days has considerably reduced the number of absences for many organizations. Many organizations give employees two personal days per year. The only restriction that may be placed on the use of personal days is that they be approved several days ahead of the time that the employee wishes to use them. The organization is therefore able to plan accordingly for the employee's absence, which is less likely to be disruptive to the work processes in the organization.

Organizations have experimented with a variety of ways to reward employees for having good attendance records.

1. Adding an extra day or two to an employee's yearly vacation time.

2. Giving employees a monetary bonus.

3. Providing in-house recognition for employees who have a good attendance record.

4. Making available a "pool" in which an employee's chances of winning the pool are increased each day that the employee works.

5. Giving employees higher salary increases and faster promotions.

Alcoholism and Drug Abuse

Another of the special responsibilities of many supervisors is the detection of employees who have an alcoholism problem. In the past, many organizations discharged employees when it was discovered that they had an alcoholism problem. Because of a growing awareness about alcoholism, many organizations have developed some rather sophisticated programs designed to help the alcoholic employee and to give the employee another chance. Many of the programs have been quite successful in helping employees once again become fully productive employees.

The National Council on Alcoholism has been very helpful in getting alcoholism to be considered a disease. Individuals tend to accept alcoholics more readily when they are considered to have a disease rather than some other type of uncontrollable problem. Alcoholic employees tend to respond more favorably when they are accepted rather than rejected by their coworkers. The National Council on Alcoholism has done an outstanding job of educating the general population about the abuses of alcoholism.

Organizations that have installed programs to help alcoholics generally utilize the supervisor extensively. Because the supervisor is in an excellent position to detect the signs of alcoholism, most supervisors are given training to detect the signs of alcoholism. Because most supervisors are not in a position to help employees overcome alcoholism, the usual course of action is to refer the employee to the appropriate individual, which may be a physician or a counselor. In some severe cases, the employee may be given a choice of accepting treatment or facing discharge.

The recovery rate of alcoholic employees is approximately 60–70 percent. With this recovery rate, it is difficult to understand why some organizations feel that the recovery rate is too low to justify the development of a program to help alcoholic employees.

The use of drugs by employees is a rather recent phenomenon for many organizations. This is perhaps the reason that many organizations were slow to develop programs to help employees with a drug addiction problem. Many organizations have provided their employees with a variety of information about drug abuse. This information can be developed in-house or obtained from such agencies as the Bureau of Narcotics and Dangerous Drugs and the United States Public Health Service. In addition, many local police departments have narcotics divisions that provide information to organizations about drug abuse.

Similar to alcoholism, in many organizations supervisors are responsible for detecting employees who may be addicted to drugs. Because the symptoms of drug abuse may not be as noticeable as with alcohol abuse, the supervisor's responsibility for drug detection is more difficult. The supervisor must be especially careful not to accuse someone of drug addiction without the presence of fairly substantial evidence. To mistakenly accuse an employee of drug abuse may put the supervisor and the organization in a precarious legal situation.

If the supervisor has fairly substantial evidence that drug abuse is present, the supervisor generally refers the individual to someone who is capable of providing professional assistance. Once the individual agrees to rehabilitation, most organizations will continue to employ the individual until it is obvious that the rehabilitation is not successful. At this point, the organization may consider terminating the individual's employment.

Review Questions

1. What are the characteristics of an autocratic, a democratic, and a laissez-faire leadership style?

2. Identify the differences between an achievement-oriented supervisor and a subordinate-oriented supervisor.

3. How do boss-centered leadership and subordinate-centered leadership styles differ from one another?

4. What supervisory duties are involved in the directing function?

5. How might a supervisor gain the cooperation of subordinates?

6. What steps are frequently involved in a decisionmaking process?

7. How do on-the-job training and coaching differ from one another?

8. What kinds of topics are frequently involved in supervisory training programs?

9. Discuss the supervisor's responsibility for employee absenteeism and tardiness and for alcoholism and drug abuse detection.

Minicases

Millie Brown is an office supervisor in the Crandell Corporation, a processor of meat and dairy products. Brown has worked for the company now for thirty years, five of which have been in a supervisory capacity. As an office employee, her work was outstanding and very well done. Brown is considered by many of her colleagues to be a perfectionist. Brown's supervisory record is not as impressive as was her office employee record. One of her weaknesses as a supervisor is her desire to do many tasks that her subordinates are capable of doing. She is therefore often behind in her work. Which of the characteristics of good supervisors is Brown lacking? What suggestions can you make to help her overcome this weakness?

*   *   *

The payroll department of the Americo Oil Company needs a new office supervisor since the present supervisor, Amy Jackman, is about to retire. Jackman has been the office supervisor of the payroll department for about twenty-five years. The vice president for finance, who is ultimately responsible for the payroll department, has decided that the employees should have more participation in the selection of a new supervisor than has been the case in the past. Therefore, the vice president would like you, an office employee in the payroll department, to identify the skills you would find important in an office supervisor. What skills do you feel should be included in your list?

Case

Mary Brown, the supervisor of the word processing center in Delta Corporation, recently retired because of her age. During the years that she has been supervisor, various managers felt that Brown should be dismissed because of her laxness in supervising the ten employees in the center. Because she was approaching retirement age, however, she was not dismissed. The employees were often late to work, took longer breaks than were permissible, took advantage of the corporation in terms of sick days, and so forth. Mary was repeatedly asked to be stricter in her supervisory efforts, but no noticeable changes were ever made.

When the qualifications for the replacement for Mary Brown were developed, it was decided that the new supervisor should be more authoritarian and should require the employees in the word processing center to conform with existing company policy. The replacement, Annabell Jackson, was hired primarily because of her authoritarian characteristics. All of her former employers that were contacted regarding Jackson's performance mentioned her authoritarian personality. Because of the laxness of Brown and the hope that Jackson could improve the situation, she was offered the job.

As the administrative office manager, you are aware that the first day that Jackson is on the job will probably determine whether or not the employees in the word processing center will cooperate with her. Thus, you feel a necessity to discuss several things with her before her first day on the job.

1. Identify the types of information she should know about the employees in the word processing center.

2. Outline the approach you feel Jackson should take in winning the respect and cooperation of the employees in the word processing center.

3. What suggestions do you have to assure Jackson's success as a supervisor in the word processing center?

Motivating Office Employees

Chapter
14

Priority of Human Needs
Physiological Needs
Safety Needs
Belonging and Love Needs
Esteem Needs
Self-actualization Needs
Reasons for Differing Employee Needs
Summary

Attitude of Management

Motivation and Job Satisfaction
Motivation-Hygiene Theory
The motivators
The hygiene factors

Programs Designed for Employee Motivation
Job Enrichment
Positive Reinforcement
Management by Objectives
Suggestion Systems
Flexitime

Chapter Aims   After studying this chapter, the student should be able to:

1. Explain Maslow's priority of needs concept.
2. Explain the reasons for differing employee needs.
3. Explain the relationship between motivation and job satisfaction.
4. Explain Herzberg's motivation-hygiene theory.
5. Explain the steps involved in job enrichment.
6. Explain the steps involved in positive reinforcement.
7. Discuss the characteristics of a well-designed suggestion system.
8. Discuss the flexitime concept.

Chapter Terms   *Priority of needs:* a concept developed by A. H. Maslow that states that human needs are classified into broad categories, including the following (in ascending order of importance): physiological needs, safety needs, belonging and love needs, esteem needs, and self-actualization needs.

Motivation-hygiene theory: a concept developed by Frederick Herzberg that identifies factors that tend to satisfy employees and those that tend to dissatisfy employees. Those that satisfy employees tend to be associated with the content of the job, while those that tend to dissatisfy employees tend to be associated with the environment in which the job is performed.

Job enrichment: a motivational technique in which employees are given greater responsibility, control, and planning opportunities in job performance.

Positive reinforcement: a motivational technique that is based on the assumption that employee actions that produce desirable results tend to be repeated, while actions that produce neutral or undesirable consequences tend not to be repeated.

Management by objectives: a motivational technique in which an employee and his or her supervisor determine objectives that are to be achieved by the employee within a definite time period. In addition, the best means of achieving the objectives and the criteria for measurement are also determined by the employee and the supervisor.

Suggestion systems: a motivational technique that seeks employees' ideas and suggestions for improving various phases of the organization's operations. A financial award is generally given to those whose suggestions are accepted.

Flexitime: a motivational technique that enables employees to determine the starting time of their work days. The starting time is usually within a two- to three-hour block of the normal starting time.

To be an effective administrative office manager, an individual must have a sound knowledge of the technical aspects of administrative office management. But equally important, the administrative office manager must also have a fundamental knowledge of human needs, as well as a basic knowledge of human behavior. Since human needs must be considered in motivating employees, the administrative office manager must be aware of human needs of employees. Without such an awareness, the process of motivating office employees becomes increasingly complex.

Motivation is defined as the desire to perform effectively. Employees who are not motivated tend to be absent and tardy more frequently than motivated employees, their turnover rates are likely to be higher, the quality of their work is likely to be less satisfactory, and they tend to show less loyalty toward the organization. Furthermore, employees who are not motivated experience very little job satisfaction. Not only are unmotivated employees more difficult to supervise, but they also represent a real financial burden to the organization. The work performed by such employees is frequently of such poor quality that much of it has to be redone, thus decreasing the profits of the organization.

A variety of motivation techniques have been developed over the years. Some have worked very well, while others have not been as effective. Some of the techniques have been somewhat less than totally satisfactory because they have resulted in employee exploitation. For example, a program that ties employees' wages to production rates tends to be exploitative if the employees are compelled to perform at higher rates without their being able to achieve corresponding increases in job satisfaction.

Before an administrative office manager can effectively assess a program designed to motivate employees or before the manager can develop programs for employee motivation, a thorough understanding of human needs is crucial.

Priority of Human Needs

Human behavior is influenced by the desire to satisfy human needs. Supervisors or managers who fail to realize this psychological fact often find the behavior of employees to be somewhat bewildering or puzzling. Supervisors who know and understand the needs of each of their subordinates find supervising to be more fulfilling and rewarding. Consequently, a knowledge of the needs of subordinates enables the supervisor to provide more effective employee motivation.

Several different schemes for classifying human needs have been developed over the years. One of the most widely used classification schemes is the **priority of needs** model developed by the late A. H. Maslow.

According to Maslow, human needs can be classified into five basic categories. These categories are in a hierarchical order, which means that the higher-level needs are not important in terms of employee motivation unless or until most of the lower-level needs have been satisfied. Maslow's model consists of five categories:

1. Physiological needs
2. Safety needs
3. Belonging and love needs
4. Esteem needs
5. Self-actualization needs[1]

To illustrate Maslow's model, until an individual's physiological and safety needs are satisfied, the belonging and love needs are not important to that individual.

Physiological Needs

In order for humans to survive, their physiological needs must be satisfied. Included in this category are such needs as food, water, oxygen, rest, muscular activity, and freedom from extreme temperatures. Because these needs are basic or primary, higher-level needs in the model are not important until these needs are mostly satisfied. For most individuals in an industrial society, physiological needs are fairly well satisfied. The salaries and wages of employees are usually able to at least minimally satisfy these needs.

Safety Needs

Once the physiological needs are satisfied, the safety needs of employees become important. Safety needs include both physical and psychological elements.

The safety needs of a physical nature include such items as clothing and shelter, as well as freedom from physical danger. Like the physiological needs, the safety needs of a physical nature can be at least minimally satisfied by employees' salaries and wages.

The safety needs of a psychological nature include job security and a wide variety of fringe benefits. Because supplemental unemployment benefits, retirement benefits, and disability pay provide individuals with a considerable amount of financial and emotional security, they are classified as safety needs of a psychological nature. Their absence is apt to result in significant psychological insecurity.

Many jobs and the environments in which these jobs are performed satisfy the safety needs for many employees. In many instances, employees become very secure in their jobs. But with changes in jobs or changes in the environments in which the jobs are performed, employees become very resistant to the changes. Managers and supervisors, there-

---

[1] Based on "A Theory of Human Motivation" in MOTIVATION AND PERSONALITY, 2nd ed., by Abraham H. Maslow. Copyright © 1970 by Abraham H. Maslow. By permission of Harper & Row, Publishers, Inc.

fore, become responsible for helping such employees overcome their resistance.

Belonging and Love Needs

Once the physiological and safety needs are satisfied, belonging and love needs become important. Included in this category are the need for belonging to a group, the need for companionship, the need for love or affection, and the need for socializing.

Many employees look upon their working environments as an important means of satisfying this category of needs, especially in terms of the need for belonging to a group and the need for socializing. When barriers prevent such needs from being satisfied within the working environment, people tend either to withdraw or to become overly aggressive.

The manager or supervisor who believes that employees must use their nonworking environments for fully satisfying belonging or love needs fails to understand fully the importance of the working environment for satisfying this category of needs. Many employees nowadays, more than ever before, are using their working environments for need satisfaction. Employees, therefore, must feel that they are accepted by the other members of their work group, as well as that their supervisor accepts them as individuals. For this reason, supervisors must have a complete understanding of supervisor-subordinate relations as well as of group relationships.

Money is used to purchase the things that satisfy many of the physiological and safety needs, but money cannot be used to purchase the things that satisfy belonging and love needs. Many physiological and safety needs can be satisfied by physical and tangible objects, but the belonging and love needs are of a more intangible nature.

Esteem Needs

Once physiological, safety, and belonging and love needs are satisfied, esteem needs become important in the motivation process. Esteem needs consist of two types: self-esteem and the esteem of others. Needs of a self-esteem nature include the desire for achievement, self-respect, confidence, and mastery. The esteem of others includes such needs as recognition, attention, prestige, and status. Whereas the self-esteem needs derive from within the individual and therefore are internal, the esteem of others requires the recognition and attention of others and therefore is external.

When individuals feel their esteem needs are being satisfied, they have a feeling of worth, importance, and confidence. But when these needs are not satisfied, individuals are likely to feel dejected, incompetent, and useless. These feelings can ultimately lead to behavior of a neurotic or hostile nature.

Some of the most long-lasting, useful techniques for motivating employees capitalize on satisfying esteem needs. For example, employees who are allowed the opportunity of participating in the decisionmaking processes of the organization are given the recognition they seek. The result is motivated employees who are willing to exert more effort.

Self-actualization Needs

Inasmuch as the self-actualization needs are the highest-level needs in the hierarchy, most individuals find them to be the most difficult needs to satisfy. Of all the category of needs, this category is the least frequently satisfied. Before the self-actualization needs become important in the motivational process, the other needs in the hierarchy must be for the most part satisfied. Self-actualization refers to one's desire to become the individual one is capable of becoming. In other words, it involves being able to achieve one's maximum potential.

A variety of reasons exist that tend to thwart individuals in the satisfaction of their self-actualization needs. For example, one common reason is the job itself. Some employees perform jobs that prevent them from achieving their maximum potential. Another reason some employees fail to have their self-actualization needs satisfied results from the organization's practice of a seniority system. In such instances, employees generally have to work their way through the ranks, and until individuals with the greatest amount of seniority either resign or retire, employees with less seniority are unable to fill positions that would allow them to achieve their maximum potential. A final reason that some employees are unable to satisfy their self-actualization needs is that they aspire for positions requiring greater ability than they have. Such employees will never be able to satisfy their self-actualization needs.

Some employees find that while their jobs only minimally satisfy their self-actualization needs, the self-actualization needs of their personal lives are quite well satisfied. The fact that the self-actualization needs of their personal lives are met probably enables such employees to be more productive in their jobs.

Reasons for Differing Employee Needs

Administrative office managers need to have a thorough understanding of human needs in order to effectively motivate the employees they supervise. A thorough understanding of human needs is necessary because the needs of each employee are very likely to differ. This means that what motivates one employee may not motivate another employee. Unless the administrative office manager has a thorough understanding of human needs, it is difficult to determine how to effectively motivate each employee for whom the manager is responsible.

There are several reasons responsible for differing employee needs. The nature of the prior experiences of employees is one significant reason for such differences. For example, employees who have been fairly successful in satisfying their needs may be less concerned with esteem needs and self-actualization needs than are employees who have previously experienced only limited success in satisfying these needs. Other reasons employees differ in terms of their needs include socioeconomic levels, relations with supervisors and fellow employees, personality, aspirations, and attitude toward work.

Summary

Employee motivational programs that take into consideration the priority of needs are much more successful than those that fail to consider the various human needs. It is obvious that a motivated employee, one whose needs are for the most part being satisfied, is likely to be a more productive employee.

Some of the lower-level needs are satisfied largely through the use of money for purchasing objects, such as food, for example. Therefore, most employees work in order to earn money for use in satisfying their lower-level needs. Money, on the other hand, cannot be used to satisfy the higher-level needs in the model. These needs are primarily satisfied by the individual's relationship with others and by the degree of success experienced within the organization.

Although some of the basic physiological functions of humans occur without the individual's being motivated, most conscious behavior is motivated or caused. It is, therefore, the duty of management to seek out and stimulate employee motives toward successful task completion.

Whereas the lower-level needs pertain to the physical body, the higher-level needs are related to the mind and spirit. Another distinction can be made between the lower-level and higher-level needs. For the most part, the lower-level needs are finite, but the higher-level needs are essentially infinite.

Attitude of Management

As discussed in the preceding section, an important determinant in the process of motivating employees is the nature of the needs of employees. Another important determinant in the motivation process is the attitude of management toward employees.

The degree to which managers feel responsible for helping employees satisfy their needs is greatly determined by the attitude of managers toward employees. This is especially true with regard to satisfying the higher-level needs of employees.

Some managers or supervisors view employees simply as human machines whose sole function is to produce. The relationship between the supervisor and the subordinate is based on units of input and output. About the only human need that such managers or supervisors are concerned with is helping their employees satisfy their need to be productive.

Other managers or supervisors utilize a paternalistic approach. Such supervisors feel that they know what is best for the employees in terms of what programs, benefits, and so forth to provide. In such instances, employees have very little control over their welfare. The result is that several of their needs cannot be satisfied.

Still other managers or supervisors utilize a noninvolvement approach. The belief is that managers should not be involved and, therefore, that the employees are themselves responsible for the satisfaction of their higher-level needs. The result is that certain needs of employees remain unsatisfied.

The humanistic approach is considered by most managers and supervisors to be the most appropriate way in which to view subordinates. With this approach, not only do managers and supervisors recognize that employees have certain needs that they can help employees satisfy, but they also recognize that employees have certain needs that only the employee can satisfy. This approach recognizes individual differences among employees. Managers and subordinates work as a cooperative team in the satisfaction of employee needs. Therefore, motivation programs using the humanistic approach are generally more effective than when one of the other approaches is utilized.

Motivation and Job Satisfaction

The first section of this chapter deals with the necessity of satisfying human needs in the process of motivating employees. It has also been found that the degree to which human needs are satisfied determines to a great extent the amount of job satisfaction that employees experience.

More and more organizations are increasingly concerned about the job satisfaction of employees. The extent of this concern is reflected by the number of organizations making formal studies of the job satisfaction of employees. These studies are often made by having employees complete questionnaires. While many organizations develop their own questionnaires, others utilize questionnaires developed and standardized by outside organizations.

The questionnaires designed to assess job satisfaction of employees frequently contain items concerned with:

1. The content of the job.
2. The nature of supervision.
3. The nature of opportunities for advancement.
4. The amount of pay.
5. The nature of fringe benefits.
6. The suitability of working conditions.

Motivation- Hygiene Theory

One of the most famous studies of job satisfaction of employees was conducted by Frederick Herzberg and involved interviewing 200 engineers and accountants in nine different companies in different geographical locations. The outgrowth of this study is the **motivation-hygiene theory** developed by Herzberg and his associates.[2] The interviews with the engineers and accountants were designed to determine what

---

[2] F. Herzberg, B. Mausner, and B. Snyderman, *The Motivation to Work*, © 1959. Reprinted by permission of John Wiley & Sons, Inc.

satisfied and what dissatisfied employees with regard to their jobs. The respondents were asked to identify those critical incidents causing them to feel exceptionally good about their jobs and those causing them to feel exceptionally bad about their jobs. The researchers also probed into the reasons employees had these feelings.

The research conducted by Herzberg and his colleagues found that employees' job experiences that produced *positive* attitudes were associated with the *content* of the job. On the other hand, the job experiences producing *negative* attitudes were associated with the *environment* in which the employees perform their jobs. They also found that the experiences leading to *positive attitudes* were related to the *psychological needs* of employees but that experiences leading to *negative attitudes* were related to the *basic needs* of employees. Herzberg has labeled those experiences leading to positive attitudes as *job satisfiers* or *motivators*. The experiences leading to negative attitudes are labeled as *job dissatisfiers* or *hygiene factors*.

The motivators. The factors responsible for producing positive attitudes or job satisfaction include the following:

1. *Achievement:* the opportunity for task completion, for seeing results of effort, and for solving problems independently.
2. *Recognition:* positive acknowledgment of completion of a task or for individual achievement.
3. *Work itself:* content of the job in terms of its tasks.
4. *Responsibility:* being responsible and accountable for task completion, for individual performance, and for having sufficient control to decide how and when tasks are to be completed.
5. *Advancement:* advancement or promotion to a higher-level job or position.
6. *Growth:* opportunity for growth, as well as for new experiences.

The hygiene factors. Whereas the motivators or satisfiers are concerned with job content, the hygiene factors or dissatisfiers are more concerned with the environment in which the job is performed. The hygiene factors include the following:

1. *Company policy and administration:* the effectiveness of company organization and the effectiveness with which the company's policies are administered.
2. *Supervisors and relationships with supervisors:* the technological expertise of the supervisor, as well as the fairness with which the supervisor deals with subordinates.
3. *Working conditions:* the environment of the place of work and the adequacy of equipment and supplies.

4. *Salary:* all types of compensation.

5. *Interpersonal relations:* relationship between an employee and his or her peers.

6. *Personal life:* impact that an individual's personal life may have on job performance and vice versa.

7. *Relationship with subordinates:* refers to how well the supervisor relates to subordinates.

8. *Status:* amount of status provided by the job.

9. *Security:* amount of security provided by the job.

Herzberg's motivation-maintenance model is illustrated in Figure 14–1.

FIGURE 14–1   Motivation-Hygiene Theory

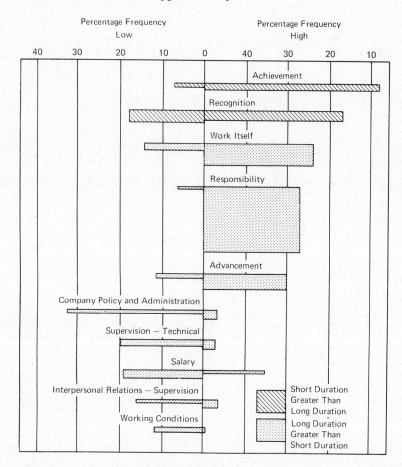

Source: The Motivation to Work, *by Herzberg, Mausner, & Snyderman. Copyright © 1959. Reprinted by permission of John Wiley & Sons, Inc.*

On the basis of his research, Herzberg concluded that the absence of various job conditions tends to dissatisfy employees. When present, however, such job conditions do not act as significant employee motivators (or satisfiers). On the other hand, another set of job conditions, when present, tend to result in employee satisfaction (or motivation). But the absence of such conditions does not result in employee dissatisfaction. Thus, according to Herzberg, the various motivators (satisfiers) and maintenance factors (dissatisfiers) are not opposite ends of a continuum, but rather, the factors are separate and distinct. In other words, the opposite of employee satisfaction is not employee dissatisfaction.

Figure 14–2 illustrates a comparison of Maslow's priority of needs model and Herzberg's motivation-maintenance model. An examination of Figure 14–2 reveals that the various factors that comprise Maslow's five needs are the same factors that Herzberg has identified in his motivation-maintenance model.

FIGURE 14–2   A Comparison of Maslow's Need-Priority Model with Herzberg's Motivation-Maintenance Model

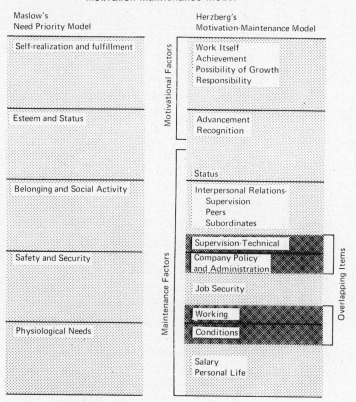

Courtesy, McGraw-Hill Book Company

Programs Designed for Employee Motivation

The importance that human needs play in the process of employee motivation has been discussed. Without the satisfaction of these human needs, employees lack motivation as well as experience very little job satisfaction. Consequently, when managers design and develop programs to motivate employees, the satisfaction of human needs becomes fundamental. Programs designed to motivate employees will be only marginally successful unless the needs of employees are satisfied.

A variety of programs has been developed over the years for the purpose of motivating employees. Some of these programs have been successful and are still being widely used. Other programs have not been as successful and are no longer used for the purpose of employee motivation.

Some of the programs that are being widely used are presented in the section that follows. Such programs include the following: **job enrichment, positive reinforcement, management by objectives, suggestion systems,** and **flexitime.**

Job Enrichment

Job enrichment involves giving employees greater responsibility, control, and planning opportunities in job performance. This results in employees having the opportunity to experience achievement, recognition, and job growth. Job enrichment is based on the premise that employees will experience greater job motivation and satisfaction if the content of the job is enriched than if the environment in which the job is performed is enriched.

Job enrichment can be differentiated from job enlargement. Whereas job enlargement provides employees with a broader range of job duties without corresponding increases in responsibility and control, job enrichment provides a broader range of duties with corresponding increases in responsibility and control. Because of its nature, job enlargement has a very limited impact on employee motivation and satisfaction.

At the turn of the century, when emphasis on job specialization prevailed throughout the country, jobs became very specialized and narrow in scope. They began to be repetitive, monotonous, and boring, resulting in very little employee motivation and job satisfaction. The results of more recent research pointed to the need for employees to experience achievement, recognition, and growth from their jobs. To do this, employees were given greater responsibility, control, and opportunity for planning.

The job enrichment process is successful for several fundamental reasons. Employees become motivated because of increased opportunities for achievement, responsibility, recognition, and so forth. Furthermore, enriched jobs have greater variety, which produces higher activation levels and greater employee motivation. Enriched jobs also result in greater intrinsic rewards, which have a positive effect on the level of employee motivation.

The success of job enrichment efforts depends to a great extent upon the nature of the planning that takes place. Since the employees are the ones who will be directly affected by job enrichment, they should be consulted when deciding how their jobs should be enriched. In most instances, employees know better than anyone else about ways to enrich their jobs.

Job enrichment is generally thought to consist of a three-step process. In enriching jobs, the first step is to identify the natural units of work. If employees' jobs enable them to complete natural units of work, they will most likely have a feeling of greater control and responsibility for task completion.

The second step in the enrichment process is to train employees to complete the natural units of their work processes. In some instances, employees can be trained to immediately assume the entire work process. In other instances, employees will assume the new work process gradually. The supervisor is responsible for deciding the pace with which employees are able to assume the control and the responsibility for their enriched jobs.

The third step is to gather feedback on the success of the job enrichment efforts once the employees have assumed their enriched jobs. Employees and their supervisors need feedback in the event that changes have to be made. When the feedback is positive, the effect on the employees is greater levels of motivation.

The following illustrates how job enrichment is utilized in American Telephone and Telegraph. Before AT & T installed a job enrichment program, employees were responsible only for specific areas of compiling a telephone book. Because of job enrichment, employees were given greater responsibility, which involved their compiling the entire white pages section for a city. In another department, keypunch operators were given the responsibility for handling the payroll for an entire department.

Positive Reinforcement

Another rather recent development designed to enhance employee motivation is positive reinforcement. The theoretical foundation for positive reinforcement is that employees perform according to the ways they find most satisfying to themselves. This means that management can improve the performance of employees by making available to them the type of rewards they find to be satisfying.

Positive reinforcement is based on the assumption that the actions of employees that produce desirable consequences tend to be repeated, while actions that produce neutral or undesirable consequences tend not to be repeated. As might be expected from the foregoing, positive reinforcement makes a maximum utilization of positive feedback and a minimum utilization of punishment. According to the assumption on which positive reinforcement is based, the desirable consequences are repeated and the undesirable consequences tend not to be repeated, which ultimately decreases the need for punishment.

Step 1: Several rather well-defined steps exist for developing a positive reinforcement program. The first step in positive reinforcement is to determine expected performance levels and to compare expectations with actual results. By determining expected performance levels, the organization has developed a base for evaluating actual performance levels in the future.

Step 2: After the performance levels have been determined, the next step is to develop reasonable performance goals for each employee. The success with which goals of employees are reached depends to a great extent upon the degree to which their individual goals can be measured. If the performance levels cannot be measured, it is difficult to determine when the performance levels have been reached.

When the performance goals of employees are set by a democratic process involving both the employee and the supervisor, the chance of employee acceptance of the goals is greatly increased. Goals that are forced upon employees are generally not entirely acceptable to them.

Step 3: The next step in the positive reinforcement program consists of each employee's keeping a log of his or her work performance. This feedback gives the employee continual reinforcement and increases employee motivation. Employee performance is reinforced in two ways: by performing at a higher level than previous performance levels, or by performing at a level that allows them to reach their performance goals. The performance goals should be assessed sufficiently often so that the efforts of employees are concentrated on reaching their established goals. Some employees find that goals assessed on a weekly basis (or even longer) are spread too far apart to be successful.

Step 4: The last step in the positive reinforcement program consists of the supervisor positively reinforcing the employee's performance when appropriate. The log of each employee is compared against the performance goals established in Step 2. When an employee has successfully reached the established goals, the supervisor praises the employee. When the goals have not been met, praise is withheld. Since actions that produce desirable consequences tend to be repeated but actions that produce undesirable or neutral consequences tend not to be repeated, the employee is then motivated to again reach the established performance goal and subsequently to receive the praise of the supervisor.

Several advantages result from the use of positive reinforcement. One significant advantage of the program is its effect in lowering absenteeism. Since employees have goals toward which they are working, they will be more hesitant to be absent. They are less likely to place themselves in a position whereby their goals cannot be reached. Second, the employees have a tendency to work harder. Because they are justly rewarded for working harder, they do not feel that they are being exploited. Finally, because employees know exactly what is expected of them in terms of performance levels, they experience greater levels of job satisfaction.

The positive reinforcement program is not without criticism. For example, the program is primarily an individual feedback system. In some organizations, a work process must be completed by the work group. Therefore, it is difficult to have the individual feedback that is so necessary for the program to be successful. The program can also be criticized because of the apparent inability of some employees to respond to the praise that is a characteristic of positive reinforcement. Such employees perhaps need to experience tangible rewards. Finally, the program can be criticized because it is difficult for some managers to feel comfortable using the positive reinforcement program. If such managers are required to participate in the program, its success will often be diminished.

Management by Objectives

Another of the developments designed to motivate employees is management by objectives. MBO has been adopted by many organizations, and the results have been quite substantial. When MBO is utilized, the employee and his or her supervisor determine the employee's objectives to be achieved within a definite time period. The employee and supervisor also determine the best means of achieving the objectives and the criteria that will be used to measure the employee's achievements. The objectives of each employee should be compatible with the objectives of the total organization.

In most instances, the objective-setting process should be a joint effort between the employee and the supervisor. Although the supervisor may not always participate in the objective-setting process, the supervisor must review the objectives with the subordinate and approve the objectives. It is important that both parties agree with the objectives that the employee is striving to reach.

Periodically, the employee and the supervisor will discuss the employee's success in attaining the previously defined objectives. If the employee has been successful, a new objective may be defined. If an objective should have been attained but has not been, the objective may be modified in consideration of the employee's current performance. The employee's progress in reaching objectives should be reviewed regularly. Some organizations have review sessions every three months, while others have them every six months. The elapsed time between the sessions should be sufficiently long so that employees can see progress but sufficiently short so that they do not lose sight of their objectives.

In theory as well as in practice, MBO is very similar to the first two steps of positive reinforcement. The fact that positive reinforcement contains two additional steps differentiates positive reinforcement from MBO.

MBO is useful for getting employees to overcome their resistance to change. By involving employees in deciding how the changes will be made, they feel more responsible for successfully making the change. Because of their involvement, employees are likely to be less resistant to making the changes.

Employees find MBO to be motivational because it gives them the opportunity to participate in decisionmaking processes. Because of this participation, employees are more motivated to work toward successful achievement of the defined objectives.

The use of MBO results in several advantages:

1. It satisfies human needs, thus providing the employees with the necessary motivation to achieve their objectives.

2. Since the employees become more involved within the organization, they feel their jobs take on added importance.

3. It provides the employees with definite objectives toward which they should work, thus eliminating any ambiguities in carrying out their work assignments.

4. Employees take considerably greater interest in the performance of their jobs when they have an opportunity to participate in defining their objectives, when they are given the latitude to achieve their objectives, and when they know that their performance will be measured against the success with which they achieve their objectives.

Among the disadvantages of MBO are:

1. The objective-setting process is time-consuming.

2. The end results are sometimes not reached because of lack of supervisory involvement in working with employees.

3. Some people do not respond to a system that does not have a definite reward system.

Suggestion Systems

Suggestion systems have also been successfully used as a means of motivating office employees. A suggestion system provides an opportunity for employees to submit their ideas for improving various phases of the organization's operations. When their suggestions are accepted and implemented, employees receive recognition, thus helping satisfy one of the basic human needs.

The use of employee suggestions is very worthwhile. Since no one in the organization is apt to be as familiar with the jobs as the jobholders themselves, they can make significant contributions by making suggestions for improvement. Suggestions will often be concerned with ways to reduce costs and waste, ways to save time, and ways to increase the quality or to improve the efficiency of various procedures.

For a suggestion system to be successful, certain characteristics should be present. For example, rather than having one individual within the organization decide on the suitability of a suggestion, a committee should be appointed to accept or reject the suggestions. In most instances those individuals serving on the committee are not eligible to submit suggestions.

Successful suggestion systems also characteristically utilize anonymous suggestions. So that suggestions receive fair treatment, suggestions are usually submitted without the name of the individual appearing on the form. In such instances, an identification numbering system might be used so that the employee can receive proper credit for submitting the suggestions.

Another characteristic of successful suggestion systems is providing immediate acknowledgment of the receipt of each suggestion. The suggestion committee should immediately notify employees of the receipt of their suggestions. If an identification number system is used, employees can be notified by having the identification numbers posted on a bulletin board.

Successful suggestion systems are further characterized as immediately notifying those whose suggestions have been accepted. The reasons for the committee's acceptance of the suggestion should be stated. Equally important to notifying those whose suggestions have been accepted is notifying those whose suggestions have not been accepted. These employees also need to be informed of the reasons that their suggestions are not accepted.

Successful suggestion systems are also characterized as being worthwhile for employees to take the time and effort to submit suggestions. Therefore, an award system is very crucial to the success of the program. A variety of awards exist for this purpose. Probably the most frequently used award is money. Depending on the organization and the projected worth of the suggestion, employees may receive as little as $10 or $20 or as much as 10 percent of the anticipated savings the suggestion provides in one year's time. Other awards consist of merchandise, trips, and company stock.

Another characteristic of successful suggestion systems is the extensive publicity they receive. Without frequently being reminded of the value of suggestion systems, employees tend to forget the usefulness and importance they provide. Therefore, a continual, high-level promotion of the system is needed. Perhaps one of the best ways to sell a suggestion system is to recognize the employees whose suggestions are accepted. Some organizations publicize the suggestion in their company newspaper. Other organizations recognize such employees at organizational meetings. Still others publicize employee's efforts through bulletin boards and other means of display.

Flexitime

Flexitime is a technique that enables employees to develop their work schedules in accordance with their individual preferences. This means that employees are able to select their starting times, usually restricted to a two- to three-hour time span. Consequently, an employee may start work as early as 6 A.M. or as late as 9 or 10 A.M. Even though the employees' starting times are flexible, they must work the required number of hours per day or per week.

When most companies implement a flexitime program, certain well-defined policies are usually adopted to guide employees in deciding when to start their working day. For example, most organizations require that their employees be on the job during certain core hours during the day—perhaps between the hours of 10 A.M. and 3 P.M. Most flexitime programs also specify the time span within which employees are to report for work. To facilitate scheduling, some organizations also specify that employees must report to work at the same time each day for a week's duration. Some organizations also have policies against the participation of certain employees in the flexitime program if their output provides input for other employees. This policy is especially prevalent in situations in which the work process might be hampered by the variable starting hours of employees.

Flexitime provides some rather distinct advantages:

1. Flexitime greatly decreases the rate of absenteeism and almost totally eliminates tardiness.

2. Levels of production increase because employees are responsible for a full working day no matter when they arrive on the job.

3. Because flexitime helps fulfill some of the human needs of employees, they experience greater job satisfaction.

4. Employees experience less frustration in going to and from work because public transportation facilities and highways are less congested.

5. Employees whose leisure activities require several hours of daylight have the flexibility to plan their work schedules accordingly.

6. Flexitime provides employees with the opportunities of easily accumulating overtime hours in order to take time off later.

7. Employees can use their own time to schedule doctor and other kinds of appointments.

Among the disadvantages are:

1. Employees whose output becomes another employee's input may not be permitted to participate in the flexitime program. In some instances, larger inventories are maintained so that the work process is not hampered when employees utilize variable starting hours.

2. Planning work schedules may become cumbersome, especially in organizations that utilize multiple shifts.

3. Employees who ride in carpools with other employees of other organizations find flexitime to be impractical.

One company implemented a flexitime program for a six-month trial. After the end of the trial period, 88 percent of the supervisory personnel wished to adopt the flexitime program on a permanent basis, because worker morale improved and productivity increased.

**Review
Questions**

1. What is meant by motivation?
2. What advantages result from employing individuals who are motivated?
3. What are self-actualization needs (Maslow) and why are such needs difficult to satisfy?
4. Why is management's attitude toward employees important in the motivational process?
5. With regard to the motivation-hygiene theory, what factors are considered to be motivators? Hygiene factors?
6. What is the relationship between the following: job satisfiers, hygiene factors, positive attitudes, psychological needs, job dissatisfiers, job content, basic needs, motivators, negative attitudes, and work environment?
7. How do job enlargement and job enrichment differ?
8. On what premise is job enrichment based?
9. What is the theoretical founding of positive reinforcement? The assumption of positive reinforcement?
10. How does management by objectives motivate employees?

Minicases

The Davis-Jackel Corporation implemented a positive reinforcement program several years ago. The program has never been considered very successful by the employees. One of the employees suggested that an outside consultant be hired to try to improve the program. The president of the corporation accepted the employee's recommendation. The consultant found the following to be the basis of the corporation's positive reinforcement program: "Positive reinforcement involves giving employees both positive and negative feedback. If the positive feedback is emphasized and the negative feedback is minimized, employees will tend to respond by working harder. Giving employees only positive feedback will soon lose its impact." What is your reaction to the statements that provide a basis for the corporation's positive reinforcement program? Do you feel the program should be revised? If so, what are your suggestions for revising the program?

*   *   *

As the administrative office manager of Blackwell, Inc., you have become increasingly interested in the flexitime concept. You feel that it has possibilities for your company. Since the management of the company is very receptive to new ways to motivate its employees, you decide to present the concept at the next administrative staff meeting. It is your feeling that if the members of the administrative staff were made aware of the flexitime concept, they would be very interested in giving its implementation some serious thought. You feel that perhaps the best way to present the concept is to design a prototype flexitime program for the members of the administrative staff group to consider. In designing the prototype program, what items or factors are you going to consider? What advantages and disadvantages of the concept are you going to point out?

Case   The Wilson Company is a wholesaler of paper stock used for printing forms, documents, and other kinds of products. The company grew from four employees in 1947 to the present seventy-eight. From time to time, the management of the company discussed the desirability of installing a suggestion system. Each department has its own suggestion system. The suggestion system was installed about seven years ago and has the following characteristics:

1. The office employees deliver their suggestions to the administrative office manager's secretary.

2. The secretary decides on the merits of the suggestion.

3. The secretary decides what portion of the $2400 yearly allocation for suggestion awards the employee should receive.

4. The employee first finds out about having a suggestion accepted when the award money is received.

What criticism can you make of the suggestion system of the Wilson Company? What suggestions can you make for the restructuring of the suggestion program?

Developing Office Employees

Chapter

15

Orientation

Training
Development of Training Programs
Responsibility for Training

Principles of Learning
Learning by Doing
Motivation
Knowledge of Results
Individual Differences

Organization of Learning Experiences
Distributed Learning
Whole versus Part Learning
Transfer of Learning

Training Techniques
Information Distribution Techniques
The lecture method
The conference method
Programmed instruction
Sensitivity training
Laboratory education
Closed-circuit television
Motion pictures and slide presentations
College-level refresher courses
Simulation Techniques
Role playing
Case method
Incident method
Business games
In-basket
On-the-Job Techniques
Education-employer cooperative training
On-the-job coaching
Job rotation

Counseling

Chapter Aims   After studying this chapter, the student should be able to:

1. Discuss the reasons for orientation of new employees and identify the topics that are frequently included in orientation programs.
2. Discuss the steps involved in developing a training program.
3. Explain the following principles of learning: learning by doing, individual differences, distributed learning, whole versus part learning, and transfer of learning.
4. Discuss the following information distribution techniques of training: conference method, sensitivity training, and laboratory education.
5. Discuss the following simulation techniques of training: role playing, incident method, business games, and in-basket.
6. Discuss the following on-the-job techniques of training: employer-employee cooperative training, on-the-job coaching, and job rotation.
7. Identify the ways in which employee counseling is made more effective.

Chapter Terms   *Employee development:* a process designed to help employees increase their job satisfaction and value to an organization. Employee development frequently consists of the following: orientation, training, performance appraisal, employee counseling, and employee motivation.

Orientation: those experiences designed to help employees adjust more quickly to their new jobs and to the organization.

Training: those experiences designed to assist employees to become more effective in performing the various tasks that comprise their jobs.

Employee counseling: a component of employee development in which an employee and his or her supervisor confer on a regular basis about concerns of the employee.

The recruiting, selecting, and placing of employees in their jobs constitutes the first phase of their employment in an organization. The second phase, which is **employee development,** increases employees' job satisfaction as well as increasing their value to the organization. Employee development must be an ongoing process, continuing throughout the duration of each individual's employment. When an organization fails to continue the development process, the result is likely to be inefficient work procedures, antiquated methods, and general operating ineffectiveness.

Employee development programs vary widely from organization to organization. Most programs commonly consist of **orientation** and **training** components. Other components that are found in employee development programs are performance appraisal, **employee counseling,** and employee motivation. The primary purpose of employee development is to enable individuals to become more efficient employees, in addition to enabling them to experience greater job satisfaction. Without at least a minimum employee development program, this purpose cannot be fully realized.

Inasmuch as performance appraisal and employee motivation are covered in other chapters in this text, this chapter consists of the remaining three commonly found components of employee development: orientation, training, and counseling.

Orientation

The orientation of employees helps them to adjust more readily to their new jobs and to the organization. Because of orientation, they make fewer errors and experience greater job satisfaction. Without adequate orientation, their production levels will be lessened because of the likelihood that they will make more errors than will employees who receive adequate orientation.

Orientation programs cover a wide variety of topics. When the individuals who are responsible for employee orientation choose the topics to be covered in the orientation phase, a primary fact to consider is that the more intensive the orientation programs, the greater the amount of employee understanding. Some of the topics frequently found in orientation programs include:

1. History of the organization and the various departments that comprise the organization.
2. Structure of the organization.
3. Policies of the organization.
4. Goals of the organization.
5. Nature of products and/or services of the organization.
6. New developments and anticipated future developments in products and/or services of the organization.
7. Employee compensation.

8. Employee fringe benefits.
9. Vacation and holiday schedules.
10. Promotion plans of employees.

If new employees participate in a general orientation program, certain specific areas should be covered by the employee's supervisors. These areas include: (1) the relation between a new employee's position and other positions in the department; (2) policies of the department; (3) expectations of the supervisor; and (4) goals of the department.

As a means of helping new employees adjust more rapidly, some organizations have a "buddy system" in which experienced employees are assigned to new employees to answer questions they may have. Psychologically, this system has some very significant advantages for some new employees. In certain instances some new employees are hesitant to ask questions of a supervisor, but they do feel free to ask questions of fellow employees. When the experienced employee is unable to answer the questions, either the new employee is referred to someone else or the experienced employee can attempt to obtain the answer from other employees.

To ensure that all new employees are exposed to each element of the orientation program, many organizations use a checklist to keep a record of what each employee has been and has not been exposed to. The checklist is especially useful when the orientation process extends over several weeks' duration. A representative checklist is illustrated in Figure 15–1.

Training

Training involves providing employees with directed experiences that enable them to be more effective in performing the various tasks

FIGURE 15–1 Orientation Checklist

	Completed by	Date
1. Summary of Company History	——	——
2. Explanation of Company Policies	——	——
3. Employment Conditions	——	——
4. Salary and Fringe Benefits	——	——
5. Explanation of Union Contract	——	——
13. Explanation of Mail Procedures	——	——

that comprise their jobs. If effective, the training experiences will result in changes in employees' attitudes, work habits, and performance levels. Ineffective training experiences will result in little, if any, positive outcomes.

Effective training results in several significant advantages. Employee morale is improved. Employee turnover is lessened. Employee errors are reduced. Employees experience greater self-confidence. Production levels increase. Employees adjust more readily to their jobs. And employees require less supervision.

Development of Training Programs

The development of training programs consists of several well-defined steps. The development should include the following:

Step 1: Determine the need for the training program. Several different factors can be considered in determining the need for a training program. The degree to which new employees are qualified for their jobs is of primary consideration. If the majority of new employees are only marginally qualified, training experiences become very important. Employees' attitudes toward the necessity of a training program might also be considered. Their attitudes are often assessed by analyzing their responses to an employee attitude survey. The feedback of supervisors is also often useful for determining the need for a training program, as are the results of employee performance appraisal. Areas of performance that are generally regarded as weak or deficient are typically considered suitable for training.

Step 2: Define objectives of the training program. This step requires that the objectives of the program be defined before the nature of the training program is determined. Some training programs provide new employees with experiences that enable them to more effectively perform their jobs. Other training experiences are of a "refresher" nature. These enable present employees to improve their effectiveness. Refresher training experiences are frequently made available to employees throughout the duration of their employment.

Step 3: Determine the type of training program. On the basis of the stated objectives and the perceived need for a training program, the type of training program should be determined. The following are the special types of training programs:

1. *Basic knowledge:* Training experiences of this type are designed to help new employees qualify for the positions they have been hired to fill. In many instances, employees who are exposed to such training programs have very little, if any, knowledge about the activities that comprise their jobs.

2. *Job exposure:* This type of training program is also frequently used for new employees. Employees for whom job exposure training programs are made available have basic knowledge about their jobs but need training in certain areas. Such training programs frequently involve

training employees to perform certain activities that comprise their jobs.

3. *Refresher training:* This is designed to help employees maintain their high level of effectiveness in performing their jobs. Because of changes in procedures, new technology, or changes in job activities, refresher training is frequently made available to employees.

Step 4: Determine appropriate training techniques. Once the need for training programs has been established and the areas suitable for training have been determined, the training techniques should be selected. Important principles of learning should be considered in selecting the appropriate training technique. Training techniques and principles of learning are presented in other sections of this chapter.

Step 5: Provide training experiences. After the training technique has been devised, the next step is to provide the employee with the training experiences. The training experiences might be presented within the organization or through some contractual arrangement outside the organization. Depending upon the chosen training technique, frequent assessment of employee progress might be desirable. In addition, achievement levels will have to be determined, as well as a means of measuring achievement. Without such information, the success of the training program cannot be fully realized.

Step 6: Conduct followup studies. After the employees complete their training experiences and return to their jobs, followup studies should be conducted, perhaps at six-month intervals. Not only should the effect of the training experience on an employee's performance be assessed, but also the employee's attitude toward the training experiences should be considered. Subjecting employees to training experiences that do not meet their expectations will have a negative impact on the effectiveness of the training program.

Responsibility for Training

Although overall coordination of and responsibility for the training program may be a function of the personnel department, the administrative office manager or designated subordinates may have specific responsibility for various portions of the training program. This is especially true for job exposure and refresher training experiences. In such instances, the managers of each department are frequently responsible for the specialized training of new employees or for training designed to upgrade present employees.

Principles of Learning

The development of training techniques should take into consideration basic principles of learning. Unless such principles are considered and are incorporated in the training techniques, the effectiveness of the training program may not be maximized.

Learning by Doing

Learning by doing results in the learner's becoming actively involved in the learning process. Active learning, in contrast to passive learning, has been found to be a much more efficient, rapid learning process. The greater the number of senses that are involved in the learning process, the better the ensuing results. Passive learning does not require full concentration on the part of the learner and thus may not have a significant impact on the quality of learning.

Motivation

In order for learning to be effective, the learners must have the desire to improve their job performance and thus to receive the promotions they seek. Learners who are involved in the training program because of the opportunity for advancement rather than because of the threat of job dismissal due to poor job performance are likely to experience greater job satisfaction from the training efforts. Greater job satisfaction is likely to result in greater motivation to succeed. The individuals responsible for the training experiences must provide opportunities for employees to want to learn and to improve.

Knowledge of Results

If employees are to receive the reinforcement they need, they should have knowledge of the results of their learning, which is also sometimes referred to as feedback. For learning to be effective, the learners must be made aware of how closely their behavior or response conforms to expected behavior or response. With knowledge of results, employees can continue to make the correct response or can modify their incorrect responses so that they conform with expectations. Informing learners of only the incorrect responses is unsatisfactory because of the frustration they experience from receiving feedback only when mistakes have been made. Human nature requires that learners be made aware of correct responses as well. To be most effective, knowledge of results needs to be made available as soon as possible after the response has been made.

Individual Differences

Because individuals vary so greatly in terms of their abilities to learn and their attitudes, motivations, initiative, prior knowledge, and so forth, the differences between individuals must be recognized in the training experiences. Some individuals learn more rapidly than others, some need greater amounts of practice than others, and individuals respond in a variety of ways to the different training techniques. Some of the training techniques presented in the next section provide for individual differences more effectively than do others.

Organization of Learning Experiences

The learning experiences are more effective if they build on one another, starting with the more simple experiences and proceeding to the more complex experiences. When experiences build on one another, the learner is able to continue to utilize previous learnings, which reduces the possibility of forgetting earlier learned knowledge.

Distributed Learning

This principle of learning has a significant impact on the design of the practice schedule. It has generally been found that training experiences spread over a longer period of time result in faster learning and greater retention than training experiences offered over a short period of time. Thus, spreading a twenty-hour training program over a longer period of time is more effective than if the same training program was offered in its entirety without intervention.

Whole versus Part Learning

Learning in wholes versus learning in parts is a fundamental factor with which the developers of the training materials have to be concerned. Some job activities simply cannot be broken down into parts or components, while others readily lend themselves to the components approach. When feasible, it is generally thought that learning by parts rather than by wholes is more effective.

Transfer of Learning

Effective learning experiences are characterized as having transfer value. This means that the substance of what employees learn as a result of training efforts transfers to what the employees need for carrying out their jobs. Training programs that consist of experiences that are not applicable to the actual jobs they perform have very little transfer value and contribute very little to employee development. Several different transfer of training theories have been developed. One theory states that in order for transfer to take place, employees must experience the same elements in the training programs as they experience on the job. Another theory states that transfer can take place even though the elements in the training program and the employees' jobs are not identical.

Training Techniques

A variety of training techniques have been developed over the years. Not all the techniques are equally suited to accomplishing the same training results. Certain techniques are better suited for training certain individuals in certain areas than are other techniques. In selecting the appropriate training technique, several factors should be considered:

1. The nature of tasks or jobs for which training programs are being developed.
2. The number of individuals to be trained.
3. The financial outlay the organization is willing to make.
4. The ease with which previously developed materials can be obtained.
5. The length of time needed to train individuals adequately.
6. The adequacy of the training facilities within the organization.
7. The abilities of the individuals for whom the training experiences are being developed.

Training techniques can be placed in three different categories: information distribution techniques, simulation techniques, and on-the-job techniques.

A primary characteristic of each of the information distribution techniques is their use for presenting information, concepts, knowledge, and facts. Because these techniques do not allow for practice opportunities, they are not useful for situations requiring learner practice in order to master the material being taught.

The lecture method. This training technique, which is unilateral communication between the lecturer and audience, generally consists of the lecturer's verbally presenting information to a group of learners. Although it is often criticized because of several shortcomings, the lecture method can be effectively used in training employees. Perhaps the most frequently leveled criticisms are that the technique does not provide for individual differences (each learner is presented the same information at the same rate) and the learners have very little provision for learner feedback. Nor is there much opportunity for reinforcement or practice.

The lecture method is advantageous for certain reasons. For example, the method is one of the most economical training techniques, a large amount of information can be presented in a short period of time, and the learners can be exposed to outstanding practitioners or experts.

The success of the lecture method is greatly dependent upon the lecturer. In many instances, even though the material being presented is relevant and crucial for the learners' understanding of their jobs, the material fails to have a significant impact because of the lecturer's delivery. The lecture can be made more effective by utilizing audience (learner) participation as well as visual devices.

The conference method. The conference method is another of the information distribution training techniques. This technique utilizes small group instruction, with a conference leader whose function is to provide guidance and feedback rather than instruction. Although this technique has been utilized more widely for training supervisors and managers, it does have a certain amount of usefulness for training office employees. Its primary function in training office employees is to develop problem-solving skills and decisionmaking abilities. The conference method can also be used to acquaint employees with new materials or to modify attitudes of employees. The conference method is especially suited to helping employees overcome resistance to change.

In the lecture method, the learner remains primarily passive. But in the conference method, the learner is placed in a very active role, typically because of the frequent verbal interaction between the conference participants. Feedback, which is usually the responsibility of the conference leader, is an important element of the conference. In some instances, feedback may be provided by the other participants or by some other individual designated with this responsibility.

The conference method has been criticized because (1) it consumes a considerable amount of time before substantive results are apparent; (2) it frequently results in considerable confusion and sidetracking of the important issues unless there is a considerable amount of organization present; and (3) it is restricted to small group instruction.

Programmed instruction. This technique, which is very useful for training office employees in certain areas, is currently receiving increased attention as a training technique. With programmed instruction, the material to be learned is clearly defined. The material is then divided into its component parts, and with this information available, the programmed instruction unit is prepared. Careful attention must be paid to the sequencing of the component parts when the instructional unit is prepared. Unless the parts are properly sequenced when the unit is written, it is likely to be confusing to the learner. The instructional unit may present the material to the learner in textbook format or teaching machine format. After presenting small units of information, the learner answers questions by writing a response (textbook format) or by pushing a button (teaching machine format). If the learner's response is correct, the learner is then instructed to proceed to the next unit of information. If an incorrect response is made, the learner is recycled through more material, after which another question is presented to check the learner's mastery of the material being studied.

The programmed instruction training technique has three distinct advantages: the learner obtains immediate knowledge of results, the learner progresses through the instructional unit at an individualized pace, and the learner takes an active role in the learning process. Among the disadvantages are high initial cost and the time consumed in developing the instructional units. Furthermore, some learners, without direction provided by a teacher, find it difficult to pace themselves properly when using programmed instruction.

Sensitivity training. This training technique, like the conference technique, also utilizes small groups and individual participation. The sensitivity training technique, which was originally used to develop learners to implement decisionmaking by democratic rather than autocratic methods, differs from the conference method in terms of the nature of the material discussed. While the material discussed in the conference method frequently facilitates developing problem-solving abilities and decision-making skills as well as presenting new material, the sensitivity training technique utilizes the behavior of the individuals in the group as a base for discussion. The technique is designed to help individuals become more sensitive to the characteristics of working groups. Individuals discuss the reasons for saying what they say and for reacting the way they do to what others say. In doing this, they are concerned with their ability to communicate, with the self-defenses they construct for protecting their egos, and with the reasons for certain individual's attacking or reinforcing others. The success of sensitivity training rests on the willingness of group members to honestly and freely communicate what they think about and feel for the other group members. Through sensitivity training, learners develop an awareness of the influence they have on others as well as the ways they may unconsciously hinder the group.

Sensitivity training can be characterized as producing various amounts of frustration and conflict because individuals attempt to use their previously established behavior patterns. The members of the sensitivity training group are likely to question some of these behavior patterns—for example, why the individual is trying to project the self-image that is being projected, why the individual becomes defensive, or why the individual is critical of others in the sensitivity group. When group members question the behavior of other group members, the result is very likely to be frustration and conflict among the group members.

When sensitivity training is used as a training technique, the role of the group trainer is very important. In many instances, the trainer serves in the capacity of a resource person or as a behavior model for the other group members. The trainer openly and honestly communicates his or her feelings but does not become defensive or withdraw because of the criticism. In some instances, the trainer may follow a very nondirective approach, which permits the group to determine the direction it follows. In still other instances, the trainer, by offering more guidance, informs the group about what is happening and interprets for the members what they are actually saying to one another.

The negative impact that sensitivity training may have on employees needs to be considered when an organization is considering its use as a training method. Some employees may become quite emotionally upset. Such employees may need special help in overcoming the distress caused by the method.

As a training technique, sensitivity training frequently involves a specific problem to be solved. The group members examine their interpersonal skills, which are used in developing a solution to the problem. Sensitivity training can enable learners to understand their actions toward one another and the ways in which each learner's behavior affects the other learners. It can provide an understanding of why other individuals act as they do, and it can promote an increased tolerance and appreciation of the behavior of others. Sensitivity training can also provide individuals with the opportunity to experiment with new ways of interacting with others and to receive feedback regarding how the new ways affect others.

As a technique for training office workers, sensitivity training is perhaps less useful than many of the other training techniques. Much of the problem solving that office employees have to do is not as effectively learned through sensitivity training as it is through some of the other training techniques. In addition, many organizations do not have the capability of providing sensitivity training for their office employees.

Laboratory education. This training technique involves sensitivity training as a primary ingredient but also includes other training techniques, such as short lectures, role playing, and the like. A laboratory design, which specifies the content of the training sessions, the duration of the sessions, the participants in the training sessions, and their sequence, is developed for each training experience. Because laboratory designs are so diverse, many different training variations can be developed. This type of training technique can be individualized because the training needs of the learners and the characteristics of the situation are considered in developing the laboratory design.

Closed-circuit television. Closed-circuit television is another of the information distribution techniques that is being used with increased frequency as a technique for training office employees. Closed-circuit television enables an organization to develop its own videotapes of various procedures, processes, or methods. The learners then view the videotapes as many times as are needed for mastery. Not only is this teaching technique useful for first time learning, it is also advantageous for refresher learning. When the videotapes are developed within the organization, the learner is able to identify more closely with the material being presented.

Compared with lectures, closed-circuit television offers certain advantages. For example, the individual presenting the information on closed-circuit television is generally very effective. The same may not be true of a lecturer. Furthermore, closeups of procedures or processes can be presented on closed-circuit television. This is not always possible with the lecture technique.

Motion pictures and slide presentations. Motion pictures and slide presentations, although not as flexible as closed-circuit television, are other techniques designed for training office employees. Closed-circuit television is more flexible because the videotapes can be erased and reused, but this is not possible with motion pictures and slide presentations. The use and end results of motion pictures and slide presentations are comparable to the use and end results of closed-circuit television.

College-level refresher courses. Some organizations either sponsor employees or reimburse employees for a part or all of the tuition for college-level refresher courses. In some instances, the course may be taught within the organization. In other instances, the course may be taught at an educational institution. Such courses cover a variety of topics. An example of a commonly taught refresher course is the review course designed for those individuals wishing to take the Certified Professional Secretary examination. Another refresher course, although not as commonly taught, is the course designed for those individuals wishing to take the Certified Administrative Manager examination.

Simulation Techniques

The training techniques that involve simulation place the learner in an artificial representation of a real-life situation. The learner is required to react as if the situation were real. Many simulations have been developed that very closely resemble a real-life situation.

Role playing. When role playing is used as a training technique, learners assume the roles of the individuals involved in a given situation. For example, to train employees how to deal with certain human relations problems, the trainer might assume the role of an angry client while the learner assumes the role of the employee dealing with the client. As the play-acting progresses, the learners who are not involved in the role-playing situation have an opportunity to assess the correctness or incorrectness of the actions of the learner involved in the role playing. The learner therefore has an opportunity to show how he or she would have handled the situation had it been a real-life problem. At the conclusion of role playing, the learners and the trainee have the opportunity to discuss the suitability of the learner's handling of the role-playing situation.

For certain areas of training, role playing is very useful, especially in areas dealing with human relations. The disadvantages of role playing are as follows: It is time consuming; only a few individuals have an active role at a given time; and because human relations problems involve so many variables, the chances are very slight that the learner would ever experience an identical situation on the job.

Case method. When the case method is used, the learners are given a description of certain organizational conditions, involving either a hypothetical organization or the organization for whom the learner works. The learners are typically required to identify problems, develop situations, or make recommendations. The case method places an emphasis on employee participation. The amount of information presented to the learner varies from situation to situation. In some instances, the information is so brief that the learner has to make some assumptions in arriving at a solution. In other instances, irrelevant information is presented in the case, thus necessitating the learner's developing an ability to sort the important from the unimportant material.

The case method is advantageous for the following reasons: the learners who actively participate are able to obtain feedback on their suggestions and recommendations, and there is often a fairly extensive amount of transfer from the case to the real-life situation. The case method is criticized because the method does not allow for the teaching of general principles and because the learners are seldomly presented with all the information they need for problem solving.

Incident method. As another simulation technique, the incident method is closely related to the case method. When the incident method is used, the learners are given a few of the details concerning a specific incident. In order to obtain sufficient details for developing a solution to the incident, the learners ask questions of the trainer. When the learners feel they have sufficient information on which to make a decision, the question-asking process is concluded and the learners then prepare a solution to the problem being considered. After the learners have presented their solution to the incident, the trainer then discloses any additional information the learners failed to obtain through the question-asking phase of the problem. The trainer also usually provides a solution that takes into consideration all the important facts—not just those that were made available to the learner—so that the learners can compare their solution with the trainer's solution.

Business games. This technique is useful for training learners for the economic processes of an industry, an organization, or a subunit of an organization. The game incorporates a set of rules that are developed from economic theory or from the financial operations of an industry or an organization. The set of rules determine how various input variables (raw materials, capital, equipment, and personnel), along with certain mediating variables (wages, finished product prices, and advertising expenditures), affect the output variables (quantity sold, amount of profit, and net worth). The game is played by the learners' deciding what product prices to charge, the amount of money to allocate for advertising, new equipment to purchase, the number of additional employees to hire, and so forth. A primary advantage of business games is their realistic nature. To provide additional realism for this training technique, many business games nowadays incorporate the use of a computer. On the other hand, business games have been criticized because of their use of "gadgetry," which tends to detract from the purpose for which the game was developed. Another potential disadvantage is the time-consuming nature of some business games.

Such games seem to be especially useful in helping employees acquire an understanding of the various interrelations within the organization and the degree to which these interrelations affect the success of the organization's operations.

Although business games are perhaps more suitable for training managers than office employees, with certain modifications the technique can be used for training office employees.

In-basket. This technique is very useful for training office employees, especially in the areas of decisionmaking and problem solving. An in-basket technique represents the type of materials that would accumulate over a period of time (perhaps two weeks) in the "in-basket" on one's desk. It consists of internal and external communications, customer or client complaints, reports, and other items that accumulate. The learner is required to decide the priority in which each situation is to be considered, as well as a solution or recommendation for each situation. After each learner completes the in-basket situation, the trainer and the learner discuss the various solutions and recommendations.

The in-basket technique can be made more realistic by using actual organizational situations rather than contrived situations. Although the technique does very little in teaching general principles, it is useful for developing the learners' decisionmaking skills.

On-the-Job Techniques

Training programs consisting of on-the-job techniques are very popular for training office employees. The on-the-job training experiences are performed within the actual jobs. Therefore, the practice that employees have during their training experiences transfers very readily to the jobs they actually perform.

Education-employer cooperative training. This training technique combines formal classes with on-the-job experience. Cooperative training, which is most often found at the high school and college levels, enables students to be enrolled in school and at the same time have part-time employment. The students learn in their school experiences how various office tasks are performed. During their part-time jobs, they have the opportunity to put their knowledge into practice. The students receive direction from both their employers and a specially trained employee of the school. Inasmuch as some organizations offer full-time jobs to the students upon completion of their educational experiences, this training technique is considered by some organizations to provide a valuable source of employees.

On-the-job coaching. When this training technique is used, the learner's supervisor is the trainer. Thus, the supervisor-subordinate relationship is also a trainer-learner relationship. While few would disagree with making the supervisor responsible for training subordinates in certain areas, the critics of this technique point out that being a good supervisor or manager may be in conflict with being a good trainer. Unless this conflict can be kept to a minimum, the effectiveness of the individual who has dual supervisory and training responsibilities may well be diminished.

Eastman Kodak Company utilizes on-the-job training. The philosophy of the company is that only at a work station can an employee experience the coaching that is needed. When it is not possible to have the training take place at the work station, Eastman Kodak attempts to keep the training location as close as possible to the work station.

Job rotation. Although job rotation is very useful in training certain individuals, it is not used often as a technique for training office employees. This is perhaps because of the length of time over which the job rotation spans, as well as its fairly high cost. With job rotation, employees rotate from one area to another, which gives them an opportunity to gain knowledge about what takes place in other functional areas. The extent to which employees perform duties in the various functional areas depends on the organization. Some organizations allow employees to actually perform tasks in each of the areas, while other organizations simply have the employees observe the operations.

Counseling

Another important component of employee development is employee counseling. In many instances, employee counseling is very haphazard. This may be due to the fact that the prevailing philosophy in many organizations seems to be that once employees are hired, their needs are all satisfied, they enjoy their work, and their jobs fully challenge them.

Although no one can predict the times when employees will need conferences with their supervisors, a routine conference schedule can be developed. This may consist of a supervisor-subordinate conference after employment of one month, three months, six months, and twelve months. Because of unpredictable situations, the opportunity must be made available for additional conferences when the need arises.

Conferences can be made more effective if they are conducted away from the employee's work station, perhaps in the privacy of the supervisor's office or in a conference room. The supervisor is responsible for setting the stage for the conference. If the employee is not made to feel at ease during the conference, its effectiveness will be hampered. The supervisor must also be willing to listen to the employee, as well as to provide suggestions and advice when sought. For the conference to be more effective, both the supervisor and the employee must have respect for one another and must be able to understand each other's viewpoints. In addition, the supervisor must display a willingness to be helpful, a sense of fairness, and general concern for the employee.

The Utah Copper Division of the Kennecott Copper Corporation, through a program called INSIGHT, provides employees with a twenty-four hour counseling service. To use the system, employees call the appropriate number to make an appointment for counseling in the employee's home, in the INSIGHT office, or at some other location designated by the employee.

Review Questions

1. What are the components commonly found in employee development programs?

2. What advantages are likely to result from employee training programs?

3. How can the need for an employee training program be determined?

4. What are the different types of training programs and how do they differ from one another?

5. Why is knowledge of results important in a training program?

6. What factors should be considered in determining which training technique to use?

7. In what ways do the lecture method and the conference method differ?

8. Compare and contrast sensitivity training and the laboratory education method of training.

9. Why is employee counseling an important part of employee development?

Minicases

A frequent complaint of the office employees of Aerensten Company is that they do not receive adequate training when they begin working for the company. This results in the employees' making frequent errors, which is becoming very frustrating to them. Up to this point, no training programs have been formally developed. Only a few of the supervisors provide any training—and it is done on a very informal basis. Most of the problems that employees experience are due to their lack of understanding of the procedures of the company. Most of the employees have adequate office skills. If the company were to develop a training program to help the employees understand the various procedures of the organization, what training technique(s) would you recommend? Who do you feel should be in charge of training the office employees?

*   *   *

The administrative office manager of Smith and Jones, Inc., has decided to use the in-basket technique to help new employees improve their decisionmaking skills. None of those presently on the market are considered to be suitable for their needs. Therefore, the company has decided to develop its own in-basket technique. The purpose of the in-basket technique is to help new office employees at all levels improve their decisionmaking skills. What suggestions do you have for those responsible for developing the in-basket technique? Which of the principles of learning are utilized in the in-basket technique?

Case

At the present time, Smith, Foster, and Brown, a moderate-sized legal firm in Lincoln, Nebraska, has no formal training program for its office employees. The firm, which is now thirty-five years old, was a rather small firm until about seven years ago. During the first twenty years of its existence, the four secretaries had worked for the firm for an average of eighteen years. Since the turnover was so low, the need for a training program could not be justified. As the firm started to expand, and as more office employees were hired, the turnover rate has increased.

At the present time, the firm employs twelve office employees. During the last five years, the turnover rate has averaged about 27 percent per year. This rate is alarming to the office administrator, who has authorization from the three partners to investigate the possibility of a training program. You have decided to prepare a report justifying the need for the training program. In this report, you decide to include the following topics: data supporting the need for a training program, steps involved in developing the program, the appropriate techniques for training office employees, and a plan for evaluating the effectiveness of the training program.

1. How are you going to collect data to support the need for the program?

2. What steps are you going to mention as being appropriate for the development of the training program?

3. What training techniques are you going to recommend?

4. How do you plan to evaluate the effectiveness of the training program once it is functioning?

Part
4
The
Job

Job
Analysis

Chapter
16

The Nature of Job Analysis

Uses of Job Analysis
    The Job Analysis Program
    Methods of Collecting Job Information
        Questionnaire method
        Interview method
        Observation method
        Combination of methods

Describing the Job
    The Job Description
    The Job Specification
    Uses of Job Descriptions and Job Specifications

Chapter Aims   After studying this chapter, the student should be able to:

1. Discuss the uses of job analysis.

2. Identify the types of information sought on a job analysis questionnaire designed for a fairly large organization.

3. Discuss the advantages and disadvantages of the questionnaire method of job analysis.

4. Discuss the advantages and disadvantages of the interview method of job analysis.

5. Discuss the advantages and disadvantages of the observation method of job analysis.

6. Identify the content found on a job description and a job specification.

7. Explain the reason for using the *Dictionary of Occupational Titles* in preparing job descriptions and job specifications.

8. Discuss the various uses of job descriptions and job specifications.

Chapter Terms   *Job analysis:* the process of collecting information about a job to identify the components involved in that job.

Job description: the written statement that outlines the duties and responsibilities of a job.

Job specification: the written statement that outlines the personal qualifications that an individual must possess in order to perform the duties and responsibilities identified in the job description.

Questionnaire method: a job analysis method in which employees complete a job analysis questionnaire.

Interview method: a job analysis method in which the job analyst interviews employees in order to gather information about their jobs.

Observation method: a job analysis method in which the job analyst observes employees performing their jobs as a means of gathering information about their jobs.

Dictionary of Occupational Titles: a publication prepared by the Bureau of Employment Security that contains descriptions of 21,741 separate jobs.

Prior to the tremendous increase in the size of organizations, managers were usually familiar with the jobs performed by their employees. In most instances, the managers were able to perform many of the jobs themselves.

The tremendous increase in the size of organizations has brought about marked changes in management procedures. Managers are no longer able to maintain a high degree of familiarity with the jobs their employees perform. Nor are managers always able to perform all the tasks assigned to their employees. This situation increases the need for each job to be clearly defined and described, which results in better control and coordination of individual effort and produces greater job satisfaction among employees.

The Nature of Job Analysis

Determining the various components of a specific job is known as **job analysis,** and the information gathered through job analysis procedures is used to prepare **job descriptions** and **job specifications.**

Job analysis refers to the formal process of collecting information about a job to identify the components involved in performing that job.

Job description is the written statement outlining the duties and responsibilities of a job.

Job specification refers to the written statement outlining the personal qualifications that an individual must possess in order to perform the duties and responsibilities identified in the job description.

Uses of Job Analysis

Job analysis, being an administrative management function, is useful for several reasons. The data collected in job analysis are used to prepare job descriptions and job specifications, and ultimately are used in the process of job evaluation. In addition, job analysis is used in recruiting, selecting, and placing employees in appropriate jobs. It is also used to determine qualifications of employees and it facilitates employee performance appraisal, employee promotion procedures, and employee transfer. Furthermore, it is used to identify areas in which new employees may need training.

Job analysis also facilitates standardizing like jobs performed by several employees. Control over employee production is improved since standardization facilitates an efficient measurement of employee output. It also serves as an important human relations function in an organization. Job analysis is used in the development of equitable salary scales since it provides information about the relative difficulty of the tasks that comprise various jobs.

Although the process of job analysis may identify inefficient utilization of time and motion in office procedures, job analysis processes should not be confused with time and motion study. While time and motion study provides data relating to specific jobs, it is primarily an industrial engineering function. Job analysis, on the other hand, is an administrative management function. The basic purpose of time and motion study is to identify waste and inefficiency, while the basic purpose of job analysis is to identify duties and responsibilities of specific jobs.

The Job Analysis Program

A successful job analysis program involves important preparatory work, including a clear identification of objectives of the program, the purposes for its existence, and the procedures to be followed in collecting the data. Prior to starting the analysis procedures, the following four items must be considered: (1) the jobs to be included in the analysis, (2) the order in which the jobs will be analyzed, (3) the nature of the information to be collected, and (4) the method to be used in collecting the information. To minimize employee resistance to the program, detailed explanation of the objectives, purposes, and benefits of the program must be communicated to the employees.

Employee cooperation and support will be obtained more quickly when the employees are familiar with the following benefits:

1. Job analysis provides a more objective basis for determining the importance of each job, determining the rate of pay for each job, and appraising the performance of each employee.

2. Job analysis enables each employee to better understand the job duties and responsibilities.

3. Job analysis facilitates the assignment of a more equitable work load to each employee.

4. Job analysis assists employees in areas where self-improvement may be appropriate.

5. Job analysis aids in supervising employees since each job is clearly defined.

Methods of Collecting Job Information

The success of the job analysis program is to a large extent affected by the reliability of the information collected. The individual in charge of the analysis program has a choice of three methods for collecting information: **questionnaire, interview,** and **observation.** In some instances, a combination of two or more methods is appropriate.

Questionnaire method. When the questionnaire method is used, those individuals who are most familiar with a particular job complete the questionnaire, which typically consists of a series of short answer questions. The success of the questionnaire method depends on the employees' ability to correctly interpret the questionnaire items and to provide accurate and easy to classify answers.

To a great extent, the design of the questionnaire is determined by the number of employees expected to complete it. In organizations with a small number of employees, a simplified questionnaire that includes the following items may be sufficient:

Title of job
Description of duties
Tasks performed daily, weekly, monthly, quarterly, annually
Special requirements (skills, experience, knowledges) for the job
Special work performed on the job

When a greater number of employees are expected to complete the questionnaire, more detail may be required. An example of such a questionnaire is illustrated in Figure 16–1.

Because of the nature of some jobs, it may be important to analyze the special methods, forms, and reports used by the employees, especially if the use of such items consumes a considerable amount of time in a particular job. Such an analysis assists in preparing the job description and job specification for that particular job.

If the job analysis program is to be successful, the information gathered on the questionnaire must be accurate. Situations to guard against are: omission of important facts, inclusion of inaccurate information, or statements that tend to inflate the importance of a particular job.

Situations for which the questionnaire method is appropriate are:

1. When the job being analyzed is not especially difficult to describe.
2. When the job being analyzed comprises mostly physical activities as opposed to human relations or personality factors. It is generally quite difficult for employees to assess the importance of the human relations or personality factors they use in their job.
3. When there are a large number of employees whose jobs are to be analyzed.
4. When the questionnaire can be precisely and clearly worded.
5. When job information has to be obtained quickly.

In comparison to the other methods of collecting information, a large amount of information can be rapidly obtained by the questionnaire method. Some organizations, however, supplement the questionnaire method with interviews and/or observations to assist in the gathering of accurate information.

A potential disadvantage of using this method involves the construction of the questionnaire. Questionnaires frequently become too complex, too confusing, and too long to be effective. This may result in inaccurate information provided by employees because of the difficulty they have in completing the questionnaire. Another disadvantage of using the questionnaire method is the tendency for employees to over- or underestimate the importance of the jobs they perform. Finally, the information gathered on the questionnaire has to be synthesized, which tends to be a time-consuming process.

Interview method. The interview method involves questioning employees —either at their work stations or in the interviewer's office—about the duties and responsibilities of their jobs. When the interview is conducted at the work station, the interviewer frequently observes the job during the interview process, thus combining the interview and observation methods of gathering job information.

As the printed questionnaire facilitates the questionnaire method, a *job information worksheet* facilitates the interview method. The items included on the job information worksheet are similar to the items included on the questionnaire. Accuracy and completeness of information can be increased by reading the employee's responses back to him or her for confirmation. Some organizations also require the employee's supervisor to confirm the accuracy of the information.

The interview method of gathering job information is appropriate in the following situations:

1. When the number of employees whose jobs are to be analyzed is quite small.

2. When the job being analyzed is quite complicated. (This method enables the interviewer to ask the employee questions until he or she sufficiently understands the job.)

3. When it is useful for the interviewer to observe the job while talking with the employee about the job.

4. When the job being analyzed largely comprises human relations and personality factors.

The primary advantage of using the interview method is that it assures the interviewer of collecting all the desired facts about a particular job. Incomplete or omitted information, which may be a characteristic of the questionnaire method, is partially overcome by the interview method.

A disadvantage of the interview method is the time-consuming task of talking with each of the employees. Therefore, it is a much slower process than the questionnaire method. Furthermore, unless rapport is readily established between the interviewer and the employee, the completeness and/or accuracy of the employee's responses may be affected.

Observation method. A third method of gathering job information involves observing the employee's performing his or her job. The observation takes place at the employee's work station or at the various locations where the employee performs the job. The analyst records the observations on a *job observation sheet*, which includes many of the same items found on a job analysis questionnaire or the job information worksheet.

FIGURE 16-1 Job Analysis Questionnaire

Your Name_____ Supervisor's Name_____
Title of Job_____ Today's Date_____
Level of Job_____ D. O. T. Number_____
Department_____ (To be filled in by analyst)

A. Description of Duties: Please describe the duties and responsibilities of your job as you understand the situation. In your
description, please be as specific as you can in telling what your
job consists of, the importance of each duty and responsibility, and
the frequency with which each is performed. The following suggestions
may facilitate your response:

1. Divide your job into specific duties and steps.

2. In describing each step, indicate from whom the work is
    obtained, explain the nature of the operation, indicate to
    whom the finished work in given, and indicate the frequency
    of the operation.

    (If the space provided below is not sufficient, please
    continue on the reverse side of this page.)

B. Educational Requirements: Please place a check mark (√) beside
the amount of education required for the job you hold.

No education requirement_____ College degree_____
High school diploma_____   Years of college work required_____
Some college work_____   Other_____ (Please specify)

C. Skills Required: Please indicate the nature of any skill requirements for the job you hold, including the level of skills required.

        Nature of skills   Level required

_____
_____
_____

D. Experience Requirements: Please indicate the nature of any job
experience requirements for the job you hold, including the number of
years required.

        Nature of experience   Years of required experience

_____
_____
_____

E. Job Knowledge Requirements: Please indicate the nature of any job
knowledge (specific or general) for the job you hold, including the
appropriate sources for obtaining the required knowledge.

     Job knowledge requirements   Source of gaining knowledge

_____
_____

F. Equipment/Tools Used: Please list the equipment and tools used in
the discharge of your job, including the frequency of usage and the
amount of skill required in using the equipment and tools.

     Equipment/Tools   Frequency of use   Skills required

_____
_____

G. <u>Materials</u> <u>and</u> <u>Forms</u> <u>Used:</u> Please list the materials and forms used
in the discharge of your job, including the frequency of use.

<u>Materials</u> <u>and</u> <u>forms</u> <u>used</u>   <u>Frequency</u> <u>of</u> <u>use</u>

H. <u>Source</u> <u>of</u> <u>Supervision</u>: Please identify, by title only, the
individual(s) responsible for supervising your work, including the
degree to which you are supervised.

<u>Supervisor's</u> <u>title</u>   <u>Degree</u> <u>of</u> <u>supervision</u>

I. <u>Contact</u> <u>with</u> <u>Others:</u> Please indicate with whom (outside your own
department) you come in contact, the nature or purpose of the contact,
and the medium through which the contact is made (phone, person,
etc.). Include only company employees.

<u>Contact</u> <u>with</u>   <u>Nature</u> <u>of</u> <u>contact</u>   <u>Medium</u> <u>of</u> <u>contact</u>

J. <u>Working</u> <u>Conditions:</u> Please indicate to what extent your work is
performed in undesirable or hazardous conditions. Consider such items
as noise, temperature, air, lighting.

K. <u>Physical</u> <u>Requirements</u>: Please indicate the nature of any physical
requirements for the job you hold.

L. <u>Responsibility</u> <u>Requirements:</u> Please indicate the nature of any
responsibility you have for exercise of judgment, direction of others,
and public relations.

M. <u>Physical</u> <u>Effort</u> <u>Requirements:</u> Please place a check mark (√) in
the appropriate columns.

	Very Frequently	Frequently	Sometimes	Seldom	Never
Walking					
Sitting					
Lifting					
Reaching					
Stooping					
Standing					
Other_____					
Other_____					

N. <u>Other</u> <u>Considerations:</u>

   1. How long does it take to become familiar with this job?
   2. What is the next job in the promotion channel?
   3. What is the present salary for this job? (Give range)
   4. Please provide any other information you care to that would
      assist in analyzing this job.

The observation method is appropriately used in the following instances:

1. When the nature of the job prohibits the employee's absence from his or her work station.

2. When, because of the complexity of the job, it is difficult for the job analyst to analyze the job on the basis of the information gathered through a questionnaire or interview.

3. When the number of jobs to be analyzed is small.

The primary advantage of the observation method is the accuracy of the information gathered by the analyst. Since the method does not depend upon employee responses, the analyst can be certain of the accuracy of the information. In addition, the analyst is able to observe the employee for as long a period as needed without interrupting the work flow.

A disadvantage of this method results from the time-consuming process of gathering the information. Although somewhat minor, another disadvantage of the method is the uncomfortable feeling some employees experience while being observed.

Combination of methods. Two or more of the previously described methods can be combined to obtain information about a particular job. Using a combination of methods usually assures accurate and complete information since verification of information is easily accomplished. Job facts omitted while using one method will usually be obtained through the use of a second method. Although using a combination of methods results in an increase in time, effort, and costs, some feel that the advantages far outweigh the disadvantages.

Describing the Job

Determining the duties and responsibilities that comprise a particular job is one of the functions of the job analysis program. When employees' duties are not officially determined or are not put into writing, management has little control over employee performance. In some cases, an employee might perform only those duties he or she is willing to perform. Formal descriptions of jobs help to insure that employees are performing their assigned duties. Such descriptions also prevent jobholders from gradually changing a job over a period of time. Futhermore, the descriptions prevent misunderstandings between employees and their supervisors as to the nature of job duties.

As previously indicated, the written statement that outlines the duties and responsibilities of a particular job is known as a job description. The job specification identifies the personal qualifications that an individual must possess in order to perform the duties and responsibilities identified in the job description. A job description may be combined with a job specification, or they may be maintained as two separate documents. Maintaining the two as separate documents is an advantage when the information in the job description and the job specification is used for different purposes.

**The Job
Description**

The use of clear, concise statements is paramount in preparing job descriptions. The following are offered as suggestions in writing job descriptions:

1. The writing style should be terse and direct, using simple sentence structure.

2. All words and phrases not contributing to the description should be omitted.

3. Each sentence should start with a functional verb, present tense, and the jobholder should be the implied subject.

4. Emphasis should be given to the skills involved as well as to particular tools and equipment used.

5. Full capital letters should be used for the job titles appearing in the description.

6. The term *occasionally* should be used to describe those duties performed once in a while, and the term *may* should be used to describe those duties which are performed only by some workers.[1]

When preparing job descriptions, every attempt should be made to have job titles and descriptions compare closely with comparable listings in the **Dictionary of Occupational Titles** (D.O.T.). The D.O.T. is a document prepared by the Bureau of Employment Security of the U.S. Employment Service. The dictionary consists of Volume 1 (Job Description), Volume 2 (Occupational Classifications), and Volume 3 (Update Supplements). The third edition, which was published in 1965, contains 21,741 separate jobs that are known by 13,809 alternate titles, making a total of 35,550 titles included in the dictionary.[2]

The D.O.T. descriptions help to standardize job titles and descriptions found in organizations throughout the country. Consequently, reporting of statistical information is enhanced, which facilitates movement of workers from one part of the country to another part of the country where job opportunities may be greater.

Figure 16–2 illustrates the D.O.T. job description for a secretarial position.

---

[1] J. L. Otis and R. H. Leukart, *Job Evaluation*, 2nd ed. (Englewood Cliffs, New Jersey: Prentice-Hall, Inc., 1954), pp. 274–76.
[2] U.S. Department of Labor, Bureau of Employment Security, *Dictionary of Occupational Titles*, vol. 1, "Definitions of Titles," 3rd ed. (Washington, D.C.: U.S. Government Printing Office, 1965), p. xv.

FIGURE 16–2   D.O.T. Job Description

SECRETARY (clerical) **201.368. girl friday; secretarial stenographer.** Schedules appointments, gives information to callers, takes dictation, and otherwise relieves officials of clerical work and minor administrative and business detail: Reads and routes incoming mail. Locates and attaches appropriate file to correspondence to be answered by employer. Takes dictation in shorthand or on Stenotype machine [Stenotype Operator] and transcribes notes on typewriter, or transcribes from voice recordings [Transcribing-Machine Operator]. Composes and types routine correspondence. Files correspondence and other records. Answers telephone and gives information to callers or routes call to appropriate official and places outgoing calls. Schedules appointments for employer. Greets visitors, ascertains nature of business, and conducts visitors to employer or appropriate person. May not take dictation. May arrange travel schedule and reservations. May compile and type statistical reports. May supervise clerical workers. May keep personnel records [Personnel Clerk]. May record minutes of staff meetings.

Source: Dictionary of Occupational Titles.

Although there is not a standard format for presenting job descriptions, they typically consist of:

1. *Job identification.* This section includes the title of the job, the level of the job, the department in which the job is found, the comparable D.O.T. number, and the date on which the job description was approved and adopted.

2. *Summary of job.* This section is a brief summary of the job. Sufficient information should be included in the summary so the job being described can be clearly differentiated from other similar jobs.

3. *Duties of job.* This section describes the primary duties and responsibilities of the job. The statements should identify the duties and responsibilities, as well as the frequency of occurence of the duties and responsibilities. Uncommon duties and responsibilities should be explained in sufficient detail and with sufficient justification to prevent any ambiguities. Although the following items may be included in other sections of the job description, they may also be included as a part of this

section: (1) identification of the tools and equipment used, as well as any forms and materials used in carrying out the job; (2) the title of the individual responsible for supervising the jobholder and the degree of supervision received; (3) the relationship of the job being described to other jobs in terms of work flow and transfer and promotion possibilities. A job description is illustrated in Figure 16–3.

The Job Specification

Like the job description, there is no standard format for presenting the material in a job specification. The writing guidelines given for preparing job descriptions are also appropriate for preparing job specifications.

Job specifications typically consist of some or all of the following parts:

1. *Job identification*. This section includes the title of the job, the level of the job, the point value of the job, the department in which the job is found, the comparable D.O.T. number, and the date on which the job specification was approved and adopted. In addition, a column is usually provided on the right side of the specification for the purpose of recording the number of points assigned each factor during the job evaluation process.

2. *Experience requirements*. This section is used to specify minimum experience requirements. In addition to specifying the nature of the requirements, the statement should include the number of years' experience required.

3. *Educational requirements*. Identified in this section are the minimum educational requirements for the jobholder. Any specific courses or technical training that is required should also be listed.

4. *Human relations requirements*. This section specifies human relations and/or personality factors required of the jobholder. Although the nature of such factors is difficult to assess, many times they are critically important in the performance of a particular job. Typically included are personality traits, initiative, ambition, resourcefulness and cooperation.

5. *Job knowledge requirements*. This section identifies any job knowledge requirements that are not covered in the experience and/or educational sections. Typically included are such items as tools, equipment, and materials.

6. *Responsibility requirements*. This section provides a description of the areas of responsibility for the job being described. The extent of the responsibility should also be included in the description. Possible areas of responsibility include the following: safety, equipment and materials, other employees, work of others, quality of work, and cost reduction.

7. *Skill requirements*. Provided in this section is a listing of the

FIGURE 16-3 Job Description

Title of Job___Secretary_____	D. O. T. Number___201.368
Level of Job___Level III_____	Date Approved_____11/30/7_
Department_____Office Services____	

SUMMARY OF JOB: The individual holding this job performs secretarial duties for the manager of the department. Since the job involves relieving the manager of some of his or her administrative duties, a considerable amount of the work is administrative in nature. The individual also supervises other office employees.

DUTIES OF JOB:

Most Frequent Duties: (Comprising at least 70 percent of work day)

1. Taking dictation and transcribing materials
2. Keeping manager's appointments calendar
3. Supervising other office employees
4. Working with office budget
5. Answering correspondence
6. Protecting confidentiality of materials
7. Acting as RECEPTIONIST for manager's callers
8. Answering telephone
9. Preparing weekly salary data
10. Allocating work among others

Least Frequent Duties: (Comprising not more than 30 percent of work day)

1. Filing documents and materials
2. Preparing reports
3. Designing interoffice forms
4. Evaluating subordinates
5. Duplicating materials
6. Maintaining petty cash

TOOLS AND EQUIPMENT USED:

Typewriter, calculator, copy machine, dictation equipment

FORMS AND REPORTS USED ON JOB:

Departmental budget, payroll forms, personnel evaluation forms, petty cash disbursements, and other office reports as called for

SUPERVISED BY: DEPARTMENT MANAGER

RELATION TO OTHER JOBS: This position is related to all other secretarial and clerical jobs in department since the individual is responsible for assigning work to other employees. Since this position is the highest secretarial position in the department, promotion possibilities include a secretarial position in the central offices or as an ADMINISTRATIVE ASSISTANT.

skills required to perform the specific job. If different skill levels are possible, the level of skill required should also be identified. Levels of skill required for typewriting, shorthand, transcription, and calculating machine operation are frequently included.

8. *Physical effort requirements.* This section of the job specification describes the nature of the physical effort requirements. Included are such factors as walking, sitting, lifting, reaching, stooping, and standing. The specification should stipulate the amount of physical effort required and the amount of time consumed by each type of physical effort.

9. *Environmental conditions.* Described in this section are the conditions and/or surroundings under which the job is performed. Factors to be included are lighting, air, temperature, and noise levels.

A representative job specification is illustrated in Figure 16–4.

FIGURE 16-4   Job Specification

Title of Job   Secretary   D. O. T. Number   201.368
Level of Job   Level III   Date Approved   11/30/7_
Department   Office Services   Point Value   270

	RATING
	Points

EXPERIENCE REQUIREMENTS: A minimum of 3 years' previous experience is required.

40

EDUCATIONAL REQUIREMENTS: A high school diploma is required and some college work is desirable.

30

HUMAN RELATIONS REQUIREMENTS: Ability to get along well with people, to meet people, to be creative, and to cope with stress situations.

40

JOB KNOWLEDGE REQUIREMENTS: Ability to perform bookkeeping functions and to use calculating equipment, in addition to regular secretarial requirements.

50

RESPONSIBILITY REQUIREMENTS: Responsibility for assuring the quality of work of others, as well as being responsible for assuring the maintenance of equipment.

50

SKILL REQUIREMENTS: Ability to type at 60 words a minute and ability to take shorthand at 100 words a minute.

50

PHYSICAL REQUIREMENTS: Must be able to sit for long periods of time.

10

Only justifiable personal requirements should be included in a job specification. It is not uncommon for specifications to include more strenuous requirements than may be necessary. For example, it is difficult to justify requiring typing rates of seventy words a minute when typing rates of fifty words a minute may be more than adequate.

State and federal laws prevent basing certain job requirements on age, sex, race, religion, and color. Job specifications should be reviewed periodically to determine if any requirements are discriminatory or ambiguous.

Uses of Job Descriptions and Job Specifications

The most carefully prepared job descriptions and job specifications will be of no value unless they are used. Job descriptions and job specifications should be readily available to jobholders and their supervisors.

Appropriate uses of job descriptions are:

1. To inform the jobholder about the duties and responsibilities of his job.
2. To assist the jobholder in improving his performance on the job.
3. To assist the jobholder in preparing for promotion and/or transfer.
4. To facilitate orientation and training of new employees.
5. To assist in the arbitration of employee grievances.

Among the uses of job specifications are the following:

1. To facilitate recruitment and selection of employees, especially in screening job applicants.
2. To facilitate the job evaluation process.

Review Questions

1. In what general ways do job analysis, job descriptions, and job specifications differ?
2. What is the relationship between time and motion study and job analysis?
3. What are the benefits of job analysis?
4. In what situations is the questionnaire method of job analysis especially suited?
5. In what situations is the interview method of job analysis especially suited?
6. In what situations is the observation method of job analysis especially suited?
7. What are the various uses of job descriptions and job specifications?

Minicases

Mr. Thomas Johnson, the administrative office manager of Seaway, Inc., was recently appointed chairman of a committee that was formed to do a complete analysis of each job in the organization. After the job analysis has been completed, it is intended that a complete evaluation of each job will also be undertaken. At the organizational meeting of the job analysis committee, Mr. Johnson indicated that the committee had a very limited scope because job analysis has only one use—and that is to determine the content of jobs. Discuss the accuracy of Mr. Johnson's statement. Do you agree? If so, why? If not, why not?

*   *   *

The Arnett Corporation has just completed a thorough job analysis program. The committee responsible for job analysis is also responsible for preparing job descriptions and job specifications. The committee was asked to prepare the descriptions and specifications, keeping in mind that the administrative group of the organization would have to approve the descriptions and specifications before they are considered to be official documents. At the meeting called to approve the descriptions and specifications, the vice president for corporate relations questioned the committee's setting the minimum typing and shorthand rates at 75 and 140 words per minute, respectively. The committee chairman replied that although the committee realized that they would rarely be able to hire someone with these skills, the committee felt it "looked good on paper." Discuss the appropriateness of this comment.

Case

The Johnson and Smith Corporation is a wholesale distributor of automotive replacement parts. The majority of their orders are received by mail. When Abigail Dunham was recently hired as the office supervisor, she proposed that the following job titles be combined into the single job title of junior clerk: verifying clerk, junior file clerk, junior clerk-typist, checkout clerk. Mrs. Dunham's proposal includes the following brief description of the new junior clerk position:

Requires little experience and training; works under direct supervision; performs elementary clerical tasks, including proofreading, counting, comparing, filing, and typing.

1. As administrative office manager, what other kinds of information will you need before deciding to act on her proposal?
2. What advantages do you see for her proposed changes? Why?
3. What disadvantages do you see for her proposed changes? Why?
4. What is your decision likely to be?

Job
Evaluation

Chapter
17

Job Evaluation Methods
Ranking
Job Grading
Factor Comparison
Point Evaluation
The point manual
Evaluating the jobs

Adopting a Job Evaluation Method

Chapter Aims   After studying this chapter, the student should be able to:

1. Explain the difference between nonquantitative and quantitative methods of job evaluation.
2. Explain the steps involved in the ranking method of job evaluation.
3. Explain the steps involved in the job grading method of job evaluation.
4. Explain the steps involved in the factor comparison method of job evaluation.
5. Explain the steps involved in the point evaluation method of job evaluation.

Chapter Terms   *Nonquantitative methods of job evaluation:* job evaluation methods that evaluate jobs as whole jobs rather than on the basis of job parts. It includes job ranking and job grading.

Quantitative methods of job evaluation: job evaluation methods that evaluate jobs on the basis of job parts rather than on the basis of whole jobs. It includes factor comparison and point evaluation.

Ranking: a job evaluation technique in which jobs are ranked in the order of relative importance and are then assigned to a specific job level.

Job grading: a job evaluation technique in which jobs are classified or grouped according to a number of predetermined classes or grades and are then ranked in order of importance in each predetermined class.

Factor comparison: a job evaluation technique in which the worth of jobs is determined by the importance of each of the following frequently used factors: skill requirements, mental requirements, physical requirements, responsibility requirements, and environmental requirements.

Point evaluation: a job evaluation technique in which jobs are evaluated in terms of subfactors that comprise the following typically used factors: job skills, efforts, responsibilities, and working conditions.

A fundamental objective of sound employee management is to pay wages commensurate with the nature of the job being performed. Another fundamental objective is to pay each employee wages that are consistent with wages received by other employees in the organization who perform similar jobs. These objectives are partially accomplished by a job evaluation program that enables an organization to determine the relative worth of a specific job in relation to other jobs. The information collected through job analysis procedures is used to determine the relative worth of each job.

A formally established job evaluation program is beneficial for several reasons. Through job evaluation procedures, the value of each job can be determined objectively. Using any other method to determine the relative value of jobs is too subjective to be valid. Furthermore, employees are more likely to accept the relative values of their positions when job evaluation is used as a basis for determining job worth. Because of job evaluation, employees typically have a greater appreciation and understanding of the relationship between the demands of their jobs and the rates of pay they receive for performing their jobs. Job evaluation should, to a great extent, reduce the number of employee complaints about wage inequities.

Another beneficial result of job evaluation is its use as a basis for determining lines of authority and patterns of advancement within an organization. It can also be used to determine appropriate areas for new employee orientation and training, as well as to facilitate employee transfer.

Job Evaluation Methods

When a job is evaluated as a whole job rather than in terms of job parts, a **nonquantitative method** of job evaluation is being used. When a job is evaluated on the basis of job parts or factors, a **quantitative method** is being used. The two most popular nonquantitative (whole job) methods of job evaluation are **ranking** and **job grading**. Of the quantitative methods (job parts), **factor comparison** and **point evaluation** are the most popular.

Ranking

The simplest and oldest method of job evaluation is the ranking or order of merit system. The job description and specification of each position are used in determining the relative importance of each job. When using the ranking method, jobs are ranked in the order of relative importance, and then each job is assigned to a specific job level. The number of job levels is predetermined by the individual or the committee doing the evaluation.

There are three steps used in the ranking method: (1) the number of different levels to be used in the job evaluation process is determined; (2) by means of a ranking device, the various jobs are ranked from most important to least important; (3) each job is assigned to one of the pre-determined job levels.

Figure 17–1 illustrates the ranking method of job evaluation by ranking the jobs (from the least important to the most important) and indicating the level into which each job is placed. After the jobs are ranked, the next step is to determine the rate of pay for each of the job levels. To remain competitive, an organization has to pay its employees a salary comparable to those rates paid by other organizations in the community. Methods of gathering rates of pay in other organizations in the community are covered in Chapter 18.

Figure 17–2 illustrates the rate of pay for each job level included in Figure 17–1. For example, Job Level 6, which includes the clerk typist II and the word processing typist II, was found to have an average monthly salary of $670 in other organizations in the community. In the organization for which this salary scale was prepared, Job Level 6 has a monthly salary range of $540 to $820, with $680 per month being the midpoint salary. The salary range between the minimum and maximum rates is used to compensate employees according to the quality of work they perform as well as their longevity with the organization.

A frequently used technique for ranking jobs utilizes index cards.

FIGURE 17–1   Ranking Method of Job Evaluation

Job Title	Job Level
Messenger	1
Mail Clerk	2
Requisitions Clerk	2
File Clerk	3
Keypunch Operator I	3
Clerk Typist I	4
Word Processing Typist I	4
Keypunch Operator II	5
Secretary I	5
Clerk Typist II	6
Word Processing Typist II	6
Duplicating Machine Technician	7
Secretary II	7
Computer Programmer	7
Computer Technician	8
Executive Secretary	8
Administrative Assistant	9
Systems Analyst	9

FIGURE 17–2   Salary Ranges

Job Level	Average Salary Paid for Job Level in Other Organizations	Salary Range		
		Minimum	Midpoint	Maximum
1	$470	$370	$460	$ 540
2	500	400	500	600
3	550	430	540	650
4	600	480	600	720
5	640	520	650	780
6	670	540	680	820
7	720	580	730	880
8	780	640	800	960
9	870	720	900	1100

Each job title is placed on a separate index card, and the cards are then arranged in the order of job importance.

The use of the ranking method is limited to situations in which only a minimum number of jobs are to be evaluated. The method becomes too cumbersome when the number of jobs to be evaluated increases beyond twenty-five to thirty jobs. The method is also appropriately used when time and financial cost are important considerations.

There are several advantages in using the ranking method. The method is readily understood by employees. It is a fairly quick and simple method to use. And it is fairly inexpensive to install.

There are also disadvantages. The method does not provide a highly refined index of the worth of the job since comparisons are made on the basis of the job as a whole and not on job parts or factors. The importance of the job may be influenced by the job holder. Job ranking may be influenced by going wage and salary rates rather than on actual importance. And, the method is difficult to implement when more than twenty-five to thirty jobs are being evaluated.

Job Grading

The job grading method (also known as job classification) of job evaluation is similar to the ranking method since jobs are evaluated on the basis of whole jobs rather than in terms of job parts or factors. The job grading method is used in the federal civil service system.

In the job grading method, jobs are classified and grouped according to a number of predetermined classes or grades. The number of classes or grades used is influenced by the nature of job duties, responsibilities, skills, and knowledges. Once the predetermined classes have been set, standard job descriptions are prepared. More objectivity can be obtained if one organization compares its standard job descriptions with the standard job descriptions of other organizations. The competitive salary ranges are developed much like those for the ranking method. Each of the actual jobs is then compared with the standard job description to determine the level of "best fit."

It is generally necessary to develop different standard job descriptions for each of the family groups found in an organization. Family groups typically found include the following: clerical, stenographic, sales, accounting, and data processing.

Figure 17–3 illustrates a *standard job description* for clerical positions. Each of the actual clerical jobs in the organization is compared with the clerical standard job descriptions to determine the appropriate level in which to place each of the jobs.

In summary, there are four steps in the job grading method of job evaluation. The predetermined classes of jobs are designated. A standard

FIGURE 17–3 Standard Job Description

Level 1—Job duties include mail sorting, simple typing, some filing. There is almost no responsibility for decisionmaking and use of judgment. The job requires no special equipment or special skills or knowledges.

Level 2—Job duties include working with records (other than indexing or coding) and typing. There is very little responsibility for decisionmaking and use of judgment. No specialized equipment is used, nor are any special skills or knowledges required.

Level 3—Job duties include indexing and coding records and filing records, as well as typing. There is some responsibility for decisionmaking and judgment, some specialized equipment is used, and a knowledge of indexing and coding rules is required.

Level 4—Job duties include typing, machine calculations, filing. There is an average amount of responsibility for decisionmaking and use of judgment. This level requires the use of various calculating machines.

Level 5—Job duties include complex typing, machine calculations, and filing. There is an above-average responsibility for decisionmaking and use of judgment. A knowledge of calculating machines is required.

Level 6—Job duties include typing and transcription. There is a considerable amount of responsibility for decisionmaking and use of judgment. This level also requires the use of dictation/transcription equipment, and special skills and knowledges required include ability to operate word processing equipment and ability to proofread and properly use punctuation and grammar.

Level 7—Job duties include typing and complex transcription. There is extensive responsibility for decisionmaking and use of judgment. The use of dictation/transcription equipment is required as is the ability to proofread and properly use punctuation and grammar.

Level	Clerical	Stenographic	Data Processing
		FIGURE 17–4 Job Grading Method of Job Evaluation	
1	Mail Clerk		
2	Requisitions Clerk		Keypunch Operator I
3	File Clerk	Secretary I	
4	Clerk Typist I		Keypunch Operator II
5	Clerk Typist II	Secretary II	
6	Word Processing Typist I		
7	Word Processing Typist II	Executive Sec.	Computer Programmer
8			
9		Admin. Assis't.	Computer Technician
10			
11			Systems Analyst

job description is prepared for each of the predetermined classes. The jobs are placed in the various predetermined classes. Each job is compared with the various levels outlined on the standard job description to determine the appropriate level in which to place the job.

Figure 17–4 illustrates the job grading method of evaluating clerical, stenographic, and data processing jobs. For example, the lowest level clerical job is assigned Level 1, whereas the lowest level stenographic and data processing positions are assigned to Levels 3 and 2 respectively. The highest data processing position (systems analyst) is considered to be more important than the highest ranked clerical and stenographic positions. The file clerk position, for example, is most comparable to Level 3 on the standard job description. For this reason, the file clerk has been graded as Level 3.

The job grading method has three appropriate uses: (1) when there are too many jobs in the organization to appropriately use the ranking method; (2) when the organization consists of several different family groupings of jobs (clerical, stenographic, data processing, accounting, for example); (3) when time and cost are of some consideration.

Using job grading is advantageous because it is rather inexpensive to install. Also, the method is quite easily explained to employees and they readily accept the method.

There are also disadvantages, however. Some jobs may overlap between two of the levels in the standard job descriptions. The whole job is evaluated without regard for the proportionate importance of specific job parts or factors. Also, the importance of a particular job may be somewhat biased by current rates of pay or by certain jobholders.

Factor Comparison

Factor comparison is a quantitative method of job evaluation, which means that the evaluation is based on job parts or factors rather than on the job as a whole. Although the factors utilized vary from organization to organization, five factors frequently used include:

1. Skill requirements
2. Mental requirements
3. Physical requirements
4. Responsibility requirements
5. Environmental requirements

The factor comparison method consists of six well-defined steps:

Step 1: Key jobs are identified.
Step 2: Key jobs are ranked factor by factor.
Step 3: Salary is apportioned among each factor and key jobs are ranked according to salary.
Step 4: Factor ranking of each job is compared with its monetary ranking.
Step 5: Monetary comparison scale is developed.
Step 6: Non-key jobs are evaluated using the monetary comparison scale as a basis.

Step 1: For factor comparison, a suitable number of key jobs is fifteen to twenty. The key jobs should be somewhat standard in nature and should be of varying difficulty and importance, and salary rates for the key jobs should be internally and externally consistent.

Step 2: This step consists of ranking the key jobs, factor by factor, using job importance as a basis for the ranking. The ranking technique discussed previously is also suitable for ranking jobs when using this method. If a committee is responsible for ranking the jobs, common definitions should be developed for each of the factors in order to provide greater consistency of results among committee members. For example, the common definition of skill might be as follows: a technical proficiency (usually physical or manual) developed through education or actual experience, or a combination of both. The factor ranking of jobs can be facilitated by preparing a chart similar to Figure 17–5. (For expediency, fewer than the normal number of jobs will be used to illustrate this method).

Illustrated in Figure 17–5 are the different factor rankings for each of the five key jobs. For example, the skill requirements are the most extensive for the executive secretary, while the skill requirements are the least extensive for the messenger.

Step 3: This step consists of apportioning the monetary worth of the key jobs among each of the factors. The importance of each factor to each of the key jobs is the basis of the apportionment. The job evaluation committee determines the relative importance of each job factor, and the

FIGURE 17–5　Factor Ranking of Key Jobs

	Factor Ranking				
	Skill	Mental	Physical	Respon-sibility	Environmental
Exec. Sec.	1	1	4	1	4
File Clerk	4	4	2	3	3
Keypch. Op.	3	3	3	4	1
Messenger	5	5	1	5	2
Secretary I	2	2	5	2	5

more important job factors will receive a greater proportion of the total salary. For example, Figure 17–6 indicates that skill is the most important factor in the executive secretary position since it receives a greater proportion of the total salary. As illustrated, the executive secretary position pays an average monthly salary of $790. Of the total monthly salary, $320 is paid for skill requirements; $130, mental requirements; $100, physical requirements; $170, responsibility requirements; $70, environmental requirements.

After the total monthly salary is apportioned among each of the factors, the factors are then ranked accordingly. The results are illustrated in Figure 17–6 under the Monetary Ranking (MR) columns. As an example, the executive secretary position, with a $320 allocation for skill, ranks first among the key jobs, while the messenger, with a $50 allocation, ranks last.

Step 4: This step involves comparing the factor ranking of key jobs with the monetary ranking of the key jobs. A chart similar to Figure 17–7 facilitates the comparison. The figures in the factor ranking column come from Figure 17–5 and the figures in the monetary ranking column come from Figure 17–6.

FIGURE 17–6　Proportion and Monetary Rank for Each Factor

	Average Monthly Salary	Skill		Mental		Physical		Responsi-bility		Environ-mental	
		Prop.	MR	Prop.	MR	Prop.	MR	Prop.	MR	Prop.	MR
Exec. Sec.	$790	$320	1	$130	1	$100	4	$170	1	$ 70	4
File Clerk	560	100	4	90	3	130	2	120	3	120	3
Keypch. Op.	610	150	3	80	4	120	3	110	4	150	1
Messenger	470	50	5	60	5	150	1	70	5	140	2
Secretary I	670	270	2	120	2	90	5	130	2	60	5

FIGURE 17–7 Comparison of Factor Ranking and Monetary Ranking of Key Jobs

	Skill		Mental		Physical		Responsi-bility		Environ-mental	
	FR	MR	FR	MR	FR	MR	FR	MR	FR	MR
Exec. Sec.	1	1	1	1	4	4	1	1	4	4
File Clerk	4	4	(3)4	3	2	2	3	3	3	3
Keypch. Op.	3	3	(4)3	4	3	3	4	4	1	1
Messenger	5	5	5	5	1	1	5	5	2	2
Secretary I	2	2	2	2	5	5	2	2	5	5

When the factor rankings and the monetary rankings do not agree, adjustments must be made to bring the rankings into agreement. The job evaluation committee must decide either to adjust the factor ranking or to change the proportion of salary that will affect the monetary ranking. In Figure 17–7, the rankings for mental requirements of the file clerk and the keypunch operator illustrate a situation in which the rankings did not agree during the preliminary evaluation procedures. The numbers in parentheses represent the new rankings. For example, the original factor ranking for mental requirements for the file clerk was ranked as No. 4 and the keypunch operator as No. 3. To bring the rankings into agreement, the factor rankings of the two positions were reevaluated, and the numbers in parentheses represent the new rankings.

Step 5: The fifth step in the factor comparison method is to develop a *monetary comparison scale* similar to the one shown in Figure 17–8. The monetary comparison scale facilitates evaluating each non-key job. After the scale has been developed, the monetary worth of each of the five factors comprising each key job is placed on the scale. This information is obtained from the Proportion column in Figure 17–6.

Step 6: The final step consists of evaluating each of the non-key jobs, using the monetary comparison scale as a reference point. The position of each key job on the monetary comparison scale serves as a guide for evaluating the non-key jobs. As non-key jobs are evaluated, factor by factor, the monetary value of each factor is entered on the monetary comparison scale. Evaluation is facilitated by examining the relationship between the job being evaluated and the jobs already entered on the scale. The monetary worth of each non-key job is determined by totaling the monetary values of each factor.

The factor comparison method of job evaluation is primarily used when job factors vary too much to use one of the whole-job evaluation methods. It is appropriately used in organizations that have a large number of different job titles.

FIGURE 17–8 Monetary Comparison Scale

Salary	Skill	Mental	Physical	Responsi- bility	Environ- mental
$330					
320	Exec. Sec.				
310					
300					
290					
280					
270	Sec. 1				
260					
250					
240					
230					
220					
210					
200					
190					
180					
170				Exec. Sec.	
160					
150	Keypch.		Messger.		Keypch.
140					Messger.
130		Exec. Sec.	File Clk.	Sec. 1	
120		Sec. 1	Keypch.	File Clk.	File Clk.
110				Keypch.	
100	File Clk.		Exec. Sec.		
90		File Clk.	Sec. 1		
80		Keypch.			
70				Messger.	Exec. Sec.
60		Messger.			Sec. 1
50	Messger.				
40					

The following are advantages of using the factor comparison method:

1. It provides more accurate results than either the ranking or job grading methods of job evaluation since it compares factors against factors.

2. Since different evaluative factors may be selected, factor comparison can be designed to readily meet the needs of the organization.

3. The accurate worth of each factor is easily determined.

4. The evaluation of non-key jobs is simplified to a great extent by using a device such as the monetary comparison scale.

Among the disadvantages of the factor comparison method are:

1. Periodic adjustment of salary rates may cause some inequities to develop in the system.

2. Inequities in salary rates of key jobs will affect the evaluated worth of non-key jobs.

3. A wrong interpretation of the importance of any one of the factors can cause a serious error in the proper evaluation of a job.

4. Because of the complicated nature of the method, it is somewhat difficult to explain the system to employees, and it is difficult for some employees to understand the system.

Point Evaluation

The point evaluation method is quantitative in nature, and therefore jobs are evaluated in terms of parts or factors that comprise the jobs. Factors typically used include job skills, efforts, responsibilities, and working conditions. The factors are divided into degrees, and each degree is then assigned a specific number of points.

As an example, Figure 17–9 illustrates: (1) the four typical job factors; (2) the subfactors that comprise each of the factors; (3) the degrees for each of the subfactors; and (4) the number of points allocated to each of the degrees. The percentages found beside each of the four primary job factors indicate the importance of each factor to the whole job.

A reasonable amount of judgment must be exercised in selecting the factors and subfactors used in point evaluation. In large, complex organizations, several different plans may have to be developed, since what is appropriate for evaluating office jobs, for example, is not appropriate for evaluating factory jobs. It is important that the chosen factors and subfactors meet the needs of the organization in addition to being representative of the jobs being performed. Generally, eight to sixteen subfactors are sufficient for this method.

FIGURE 17–9 Allocation of Points for Job Factors

Factors	First Degree	Second Degree	Third Degree	Fourth Degree	Fifth Degree
SKILL (30%)					
1. Education	10	20	30	40	50
2. Experience	10	20	30	40	50
3. Job Knowledge	15	30	45	60	75
4. Manual Dexterity	5	10	15	20	25
EFFORT (25%)					
5. Physical	10	20	30	40	50
6. Mental	10	20	30	40	50
7. Visual	5	10	15	20	25
RESPONSIBILITY (30%)					
8. Equipment/Tools	8	16	24	32	40
9. Materials/Products	10	20	30	40	50
10. Work of Others	5	10	15	20	25
JOB CONDITIONS (15%)					
11. Surroundings	10	20	30	40	50
12. Hazards	5	10	15	20	25
13. Safety of Others	5	10	15	20	25

The point manual. Like the job grading method, the point evaluation method requires the preparation of a manual describing each of the degrees into which the subfactors have been divided, as well as listing the number of points that are allocated for each of the degrees. Once the manual is ready to use, the specifications of each job are compared factor by factor with the descriptions in the manual in order to determine the appropriate point value that each job is to receive. The total of the point values for each subfactor determines the relative worth of each job.

A variety of trade associations, management consultant firms, and companies have developed point manuals. Among the more widely used manuals are those prepared by the National Metal Trades Association and the National Electrical Manufacturers Association. When adopting one of the prepared manuals, care must be taken to insure that the manual meets the needs of the organization.

Care should be taken to select only those subfactors that are significant to the jobs being evaluated. Likewise, care should be taken to eliminate subfactors that tend to overlap with one another, that are not clearly definitive, or that tend to evaluate personal rather than job factors.

Selecting the number of degrees into which each subfactor is divided is somewhat flexible. When selecting the appropriate number of degrees, the following conditions should be considered: the relative importance assigned to each subfactor and the ease of defining individual degrees. Although Figure 17–10 shows five degrees for each subfactor, some subfactors may be divided into as few as three degrees, while others are divided into as many as eight degrees.

The last step in developing the point manual is to assign the number of points to each of the degrees. Two methods are generally used: (1) the straight arithmetic method by which the points increase by a constant amount (for example, 10, 20, 30, 40, or 8, 16, 24); and (2) the geometric progression method by which the points increase by a constant percentage, such as 3, 6, 12, 24.

Figure 17–10 illustrates a partial point manual with descriptions for office jobs.

Evaluating the jobs. The last step involved in the point evaluation method is to use the point manual to evaluate each of the jobs. The job specification is compared subfactor by subfactor with the degree or level descriptions in the point manual. When the appropriate degree is determined, the actual job factor is then assigned the corresponding number of points, which are entered in the appropriate place on the job specification. After each factor has been evaluated, the relative worth of the job is then determined by adding the total number of points for each of the factors. The total points value for each job is then converted into salary rates, such as illustrated in Figure 17–11.

FIGURE 17–10   Point Manual
              (Office Jobs)

EDUCATION: This subfactor is concerned with the nature of the educational experience of the employee. High school equivalency certificates will be accepted in lieu of a high school diploma. As far as college work is concerned, community college and business and/or technical school attendance is accepted. Work taken in adult education programs does not count as college-level work.

Degree	Points	Description
1st	10	Less than high school diploma
2nd	20	High school diploma but no college work
3rd	30	High school diploma and not more than 2 years (60 semester hours) of college work
4th	40	High school diploma, at least 2 years (60 semester hours) of college work, but no college degree
5th	50	College graduate

FIGURE 17–10   (Continued)

EXPERIENCE: This subfactor is concerned with the amount of time that it takes an employee to obtain and develop skills necessary to perform a particular job. It is assumed that the individual already possesses the required job knowledge prior to starting the time element involved in the experience factor. Any previously obtained experience, either inside or outside the organization, is recognized.

Degree	Points	Description
1st	10	Up to and including three months' experience
2nd	20	Over three months but less than one year of experience
3rd	30	Over one year but less than two years' experience
4th	40	Over two years but less than four years' experience
5th	50	Over four years of experience

PHYSICAL: This subfactor is concerned with the amount of physical effort expended in carrying out the duties of the job. In determining the appropriate level to which a particular job is to be assigned, "normal" efficiency in carrying out the duties should be used as a guideline.

Degree	Points	Description
1st	10	This level involves a balance of physical effort: sitting, standing, or walking. Included in this level are those office jobs with a normal amount of physical effort
2nd	20	This level involves expending a considerable amount of physical effort through the jobholder's moving around a considerable amount
3rd	30	This level involves expending physical effort through one continuous activity, such as sitting, typing, machine operation, etc. Some lifting may be involved, the jobholder typically works for a long period of time in one position
4th	40	This level involves a considerable amount of walking or standing, especially for long periods of time
5th	50	This level involves continuous standing in one place or a considerable amount of walking or lifting for long periods of time

There are five steps involved in the point method of job evaluation. First, the factors and their relative worth are determined. Second, the factors are divided into subfactors. Third, the point manual is developed, specifying the number of points assigned to each degree in the various subfactors. Fourth, the job specification of each job is compared subfactor by subfactor with the degree descriptions in the point manual to determine the number of points to be assigned each subfactor. And finally, the points assigned to each subfactor are added to determine the

FIGURE 17–11 Salary Range: Point Evaluation

Total Points	Midpoint	Minimum	Maximum
0–300	$500	$400	$600
301–320	550	440	660
321–340	600	480	720
341–360	640	520	760
361–380	670	540	800
381–400	720	570	870
401–420	800	640	960

worth of the job, and the higher the number of points a job receives, the greater is its importance.

The point evaluation method is appropriately used in organizations that have a large number of diversified jobs. When intraorganizational problems require a high degree of sophistication in job evaluation methodology, this method is appropriately utilized.

There are several advantages of using the point evaluation method:

1. Of all the methods, it is the least easy to manipulate, and there is only minimum opportunity for pressure to be exerted on the individual or committee doing the evaluating.

2. The method has a high degree of objectivity and consistency of results.

3. It is easy to give yearly salary increases without affecting the evaluated jobs since the point values of the jobs stay the same until the components of the job are changed.

4. Because of the flexibility in selecting subfactors, degrees, and points, it is possible to develop a tailormade system.

There are also disadvantages:

1. Developing a point manual can be a difficult and time-consuming task.

2. The system takes a considerable amount of time to develop and to install, and in some cases, specially trained personnel may have to be hired for such purposes.

3. Selecting and writing definitions of degrees is not an easy task.

4. The allocation of points among each of the subfactors may be somewhat arbitrary.

Adopting a Job Evaluation Method   As was mentioned earlier, various trade associations have developed job evaluation programs for their association members. It is not recommended that other organizations adopt these programs without making certain that the program will meet the needs of the organization. A program that is succesful in one organization may be just as unsuccessful in another organization unless certain measures are taken to modify the program. In modifying the program, it is recommended that the following be closely examined:

1. The nature—specific and general—of the jobs in the organization.

2. The duties and responsibilities that comprise the jobs in the organization.

3. The procedure for determining salary rates.

4. The philosophy of the organization's management with regard to the job evaluation program.

Review Questions

1. What benefits are provided by a job evaluation program?

2. Why is job ranking considered a nonquantitative method of job evaluation while factor comparison is considered to be a quantitative method?

3. Compare and contrast the job evaluation techniques discussed in this chapter in terms of:

    a. the number of jobs for which each method is suitable;

    b. any special apparatuses required by each method;

    c. special characteristics of each method;

    d. validity of results of each method; and

    e. special conditions for which the use of each method is appropriate.

Minicases

The Dickson Manufacturing Company, which employs about seventy individuals, has been rather flexible in its operating procedures. There is now ample evidence that employees are no longer as loyal to the firm as they once were and that they are becoming greatly concerned about their welfare in the company. Some of the employees have been complaining to management that the job demands and pay are not at all in line with one another. Some employees whose jobs are more demanding earn less than those whose jobs are less demanding. The company decided to install a job evaluation program. At the present time, the employees are known by twenty-three different job titles. The company feels that the job ranking method of job evaluation would best meet its needs at this point. What suggestions could you make to help the Dickson Manufacturing Company be successful with the job ranking method of job evaluation? Do you feel the job ranking method would be most suitable? Why?

*   *   *

You recently received a call from Larry Thompson, the administrative office manager of the Farkel Corporation, seeking your help in their job evaluation program. The Farkel Corporation has previously used the job ranking technique for evaluating their jobs. Because job ranking is too cumbersome for the number of jobs in the Farkel Corporation, Mr. Thompson has decided to investigate the job grading method. Mr. Thompson called you to seek your help because he does not know how to use the job grading method of job evaluation. Explain the job grading method to Mr. Thompson.

Case

Jasimine Smith is completing her eighteenth year as a stenographer in the office services department of Jackson, Inc. She has held the position of stenographer ever since she started working for the organization. Ten years ago, the organization did a thorough evaluation of the jobs in the organization. At this time, job descriptions and job specifications were prepared for each of the jobs. Although the specifications stipulated that stenographers must possess shorthand and typing skills, nothing was done to reclassify Smith, who has only minimum typing skills and no shorthand skills. For the most part, Smith performs duties more appropriately classified as clerical rather than stenographic. She is considered to perform very well in this capacity.

Recently, several stenographers have complained that Smith, whom they feel should be classified as a clerk, is earning a higher salary than they are. Although the administrative office manager realizes that if he were to reclassify Smith, she would earn less salary (as a stenographer, she is earning a higher salary than the maximum salary for clerks), he is reluctant to reclassify her because of her outstanding long-term service to the organization.

1. What alternatives might the administrative office manager consider? Which should he take—and why?
2. What implication does this have for the evaluation of jobs?

Salary Administration

Chapter

18

The Salary Administration Program
Goals of the Salary Administration Program
Policies and Procedures of the Salary Administration Program
Responsibility for the Salary Administration Program

Determining the Salary Structure
Factors Affecting the Salary Structure
Relative worth of the job
Going rates
Cost of living index
Legislation
Collective bargaining
Developing the Wage Curve
The salary scattergram
Establishing the salary range
Planning for Salary Increases

Fringe Benefits

Federal Legislation
Fair Labor Standards Act
Walsh-Healey Act
Davis-Bacon Act
Pension Reform Act

Chapter Aims   After studying this chapter, the student should be able to:

1. Discuss the goals of a salary administration program.
2. Discuss the factors that affect an organization's salary structure.
3. Explain how a wage curve is developed.
4. Explain the development of a salary scattergram.
5. Identify several of the fringe benefits that are provided employees.
6. Discuss the important federal legislation that has an impact on salary administration.

Chapter Terms   *Relative worth of the job:* the worth of one job in relation to other jobs in the organization. The relative worth of the job is determined by job evaluation.

Going rate: the rate of pay for a particular job that firms in the same geographical area pay for comparable jobs.

Salary survey: a survey conducted to determine the rates of pay for jobs in other firms in the same geographical area.

Salary scattergram: a correlation chart that shows the relationship between the relative worth and the monetary worth of a job.

The functions of salary administration and job evaluation are closely related. The purpose of job evaluation is to determine the relative worth of jobs in an organization, while the salary administration program is responsible for determining an equitable monetary compensation for such jobs. When salaries are determined by any means other than the systematic procedures characteristic of efficient salary administration programs, many inequities in salaries are likely to develop. For example, salaries are likely to be determined by rather arbitrary procedures, employee morale is likely to decrease as a result of the alleged inequities, and eventually, the production and efficiency of the organization will suffer.

Some of the more important factors that are considered in determining an equitable salary are level of skill required by the job, working conditions of the job, responsibility of the job, employee performance and motivation, salaries paid for comparable jobs in other organizations within the community, cost of living, legislation, and the impact of collective bargaining.

The Salary Administration Program

If high levels of employee efficiency and morale are to be found within an organization, employees must feel that they are receiving an equitable salary. The salary administration program is responsible for determining equitable salaries based on the importance or worth of the various jobs. The program enables an organization to recruit, select, and retain capable employees, which enables the organization to produce higher quality services or goods more efficiently at lower prices.

Goals of the Salary Administration Program

Efficient and effective salary administration programs operate within the framework of well-defined goals.

1. *To provide a systematic determination of equitable compensation for employees.* Effective salary administration programs reduce salary inequities by providing a sound foundation for the determination of equitable employee compensation. A sound salary administration program will help reduce the number of salary-related grievances filed by employees.

2. *To help the organization conform to existing legislation pertaining to employee compensation.* Legislation affecting employee compensation is frequently modified. By making the director of the salary administration program responsible for keeping the salary administration program in conformity with recent or modified legislation, fewer violations will occur.

3. *To help the organization control its salary costs.* A well-designed salary administration program benefits the organization by helping control its salary costs. The program helps to provide balance between the

worth of each job and the salary paid for that job. Therefore, the organization is more readily able to operate within the monetary allocation budgeted for employee salaries.

4. *To help reduce employee turnover.* Employee turnover greatly increases when an organization's salary structure is not internally equitable or externally competitive. A salary administration program will help minimize problems of this nature.

5. *To motivate employees to perform at an optimum level.* Providing employees with various financial or nonfinancial incentives motivates employees to become more efficient and productive. The guidelines, procedures, and policies for rewarding employees for greater levels of efficiency and productivity are typically functions of the salary administration program.

6. *To promote employer-employee relations.* When employer-employee relations are cordial and pleasant, employees are apt to be more cooperative and supportive. A common cause of management-union disagreements is the compensation policy of the organization. A sound salary administration program will minimize disagreements, and in many instances, the disagreements can be quickly and totally resolved without going through arbitration procedures. A sound salary administration program helps to assure that employees are being paid a fair day's salary for a fair day's work.

Policies and Procedures of the Salary Administration Program

Well-designed salary administration programs depend upon certain policies and procedures that help govern decisionmaking regarding various aspects of the program. Such policies and procedures result in greater consistency and equity in making important decisions. The policies are also important to management since they provide the structure that translates management's philosophy into action. The result is that the organization is able to achieve its goals and objectives.

The salary structure of many organizations utilizes a range for each job grade or level. To insure the equal and fair treatment of all employees, policies and procedures must be developed to help determine where a newly hired employee or a recently promoted employee should be placed in the salary range. Policies should also exist that specify how employees will be advanced in one salary range or to another salary range.

Other policies and procedures should exist that specify the organization's plans for periodic review of its salary structure, the plans for periodic review of the classifications of jobs, and the appropriate steps involved in filing a grievance due to employee dissatisfaction with compensation.

If an organization provides merit increases for its employees, the policies and procedures regarding such increases need also to be clearly defined. Failure to have clearly defined policies and procedures may result in the use of factors other than individual achievement as a basis for merit increases. Policies and procedures regarding merit increases also need to be clearly communicated to the employees.

The policies and procedures regarding salary increases also need to be clearly defined. Salary increases usually consist of either (1) a flat increase of a certain number of cents per hour; or (2) a percentage-of-salary increase. When the flat increase method is used, the employees with the lower salaries actually get a greater percentage increase than those employees with the higher salaries. In time, unless adjustments are made, the salary differential between the lower and higher paid employees will diminish. Some claim that when the salary differentials diminish significantly, employees will no longer have as great an incentive to prepare themselves for the higher paying jobs or for those jobs typically involving higher skill levels. The eventual result will be a scarcity of skilled employees.

Fringe benefits, another function of the salary administration program, must be administered by well-defined policies and procedures. For example, some organizations consider paid holidays to be a fringe benefit. In the case of an employee's absence from work the day before or after the paid holiday, the organization needs to have a well-defined policy that specifies the conditions under which the employee will or will not be paid for the day he or she is absent.

Another area for which policies and procedures need to be specified is the incentive salary plan. Many organizations, for example, provide employees with certain types of bonuses. The policies and procedures for determining eligibility and the amount of the bonuses should be specified. Many organizations also provide their employees with a profit sharing or stock option plan. Policies and procedures for making such allocations should be clearly defined.

Policies regulating shift and/or overtime pay should also be well defined. Federal legislation specifies minimum rates for overtime pay, but some organizations pay more than the minimum overtime pay. If, for example, an organization has a salary differential for day and night shifts, regulating policies should be clearly defined.

In organizations in which the employees belong to a union, many of the policies regulating various phases of employee compensation are written into the union-management contract, which becomes a part of the collective bargaining agreement.

Responsibility for the Salary Administration Program

If the salary administration program is to function consistently, and if its policies are to be carried out uniformly, the program will most likely operate more smoothly under centralized control. The location, duties, and responsibilities of the director of the salary administration program are to a great extent determined by three factors: the size of the organization, the nature of goods or services produced by the organization, and the types of jobs involved. Even though in many organizations the responsibility for the salary administration program rests with the personnel department, the administrative office manager can make a significant impact on the success of the program. Many organizations appoint an advisory committee to assist the director of the salary administration program. In many instances, the members of the advisory committee may have a greater understanding of the technical aspects of the jobs and are therefore able to supply the program's director with information regarding important job requirements and compensation rates.

In extremely small organizations, the personnel director is frequently responsible for the salary administration program. The personnel director will frequently devote part of his time to salary administration, in addition to being responsible for other personnel functions.

In larger organizations, the salary administration program is sufficiently time-consuming to justify a full-time director. In some organizations, the director of the salary administration program is responsible to the personnel director, while in other organizations the personnel director and the individual in charge of the salary administration program are co-equals.

Determining the Salary Structure

Another distinction between job evaluation and salary administration can be made at this point. While job evaluation determines the basis for the salary rate, salary administration determines the rate.

Factors Affecting the Salary Structure

Determining the salary structure is not an easy process. The task is made more complex because of the variety of factors that have an impact on the salary structure. Some of the significant factors that must be considered are: **relative worth of the job, going rates,** cost of living index, legislation, and collective bargaining.

Relative worth of the job. Employees deserve and have the right to expect that the salaries they receive are properly related to the demands of their jobs and to the salaries paid to employees performing other jobs in the organization. Otherwise, salary inequities are likely to occur, which will result in a low level of employee morale. The relative worth of each job is determined by job evaluation. Four different methods of evaluating jobs are presented in Chapter 17.

Going rates. If an organization is to maintain a competitive salary position within the community, the organization will have to determine what other employers in the same locality are paying for comparable jobs. In some instances, the going rates can be obtained from prepared **salary surveys.** In other instances, the organization will have to conduct its own salary survey.

The *National Survey of Professional, Administrative, Technical, and Clerical Pay,* conducted annually since 1961 by the Bureau of Labor Statistics, provides salary data for eighty-one different occupational work levels. The survey includes nationwide data for each of the eighty-one positions, in addition to compiling data on clerical positions for a number of metropolitan areas throughout the country. The survey also includes information on a variety of fringe benefits and provides brief descriptions of jobs.

Edward N. Hay and Associates compiles *Compensation Comparisons—Industrial and Financial Management,* which is an annual update of trends in exempt executive, management, and technical employees. The information for the survey is gathered from a comprehensive sample of national and international firms. To be classified as an exempt position, at least half of the job duties and tasks have to be of an administrative or managerial nature.

The Administrative Management Society annually updates its *Directory of Office Salaries,* which includes twenty commonly found office and data processing positions. The survey includes weekly salaries for cities in which Administrative Management Society chapters are found, in addition to including regional average salaries and nationwide averages for each of the twenty positions.

Starting in 1973, the Administrative Management Society conducted its first annual middle management survey, the *AMS Guide to Management Compensation.* The survey provides salary data on twenty key exempt middle management positions. The survey also provides information on fringe benefits and on trends in company policies regarding hours of work, paid vacations, holidays, and pension plans.

Various local chambers of commerce and trade associations compile salary data for jobs found in the local communities. Using the results of such surveys will save many organizations a considerable amount of time, effort, and money.

If a published salary data listing is not available, an organization may have to conduct its own survey. Without this vital information, the organization has no way of knowing whether its salaries are competitive with other organizations in the community.

When designing a salary survey, certain criteria or guidelines should be considered:

1. If only a portion of the total number of organizations in a community are to be surveyed, special provisions must be employed to randomly select the organizations to be included in the survey.

2. The number of organizations to be surveyed must be large enough to be representative of the total number of organizations from which the sample was drawn.

3. For best results, the organizations to be surveyed should be of the same classification as the organization conducting the survey. For example, banks should survey other banks, manufacturing organizations should survey other manufacturing organizations, and so forth.

4. The questionnaire must be designed to gather the desired information. Frequently included in salary surveys are:

a. number of employees in the firm;

b. number of employees in each job category on which the salary information is based;

c. salary range for each job category;

d. number of hours per week for each job included in the survey;

e. the pay policy for employees who work on holidays;

f. the type of supplemental pay available and the monetary worth of each type (includes bonuses, profit sharing, stock options, pension plans);

g. the holidays for which employees receive pay;

h. the organization's policy regarding vacations with pay, sick leave, insurance, salary increases, overtime, incentive pay, and shift differential pay.

5. To provide some assurance that jobs are comparable, the organization conducting the survey should obtain job descriptions from the organizations being surveyed. Even though jobs in several cities have comparable titles, they may differ considerably in terms of duties and responsibilities.

After the salary information has been collected, a median or average salary for each job can be computed. The organization is then able to decide how competitive its salary structure is in comparison to the salary structures found in other organizations.

Cost of living index. During inflationary times, the cost of living index, which is calculated by the federal government, is frequently used in the development of the salary structure of an organization. The use of the cost of living index as a salary determinant means that salaries are periodically adjusted upward to enable employees to maintain their purchasing power. In other words, employees' salaries increase by the same amount as the increase in the cost of living index. Often, the salary structure is mathematically tied to the index by an escalator clause in the union-management contract. For example, some contracts stipulate that when the cost of living index increases by a certain percentage, employees' salaries will automatically increase by a specified amount. While the cost of living index is popularly used as a salary determinant during inflationary periods, it is generally not popular with unions during periods of declining prices.

Legislation. Another significant determinant of the organization's salary structure is the compensation legislation enacted at the national and state levels. Included in this legislation are such items as minimum salary rates, overtime pay, child labor regulations, and so forth. Since the time that the first significant legislation affecting compensation was passed in the 1930s, Congress has passed legislation on three different occasions that freezes salaries and controls the amount of salary increases.

Some of the more significant legislation—including the Fair Labor Standards Act, the Equal Pay Act, the Walsh-Healey Act, the Davis-Bacon Act, and the Pension Reform Act—is discussed in another section of this chapter.

Collective bargaining. When the employees of an organization belong to a union, their salaries are determined by collective bargaining processes. Although going rates, cost of living increases, and job worth will most likely be considered in the bargaining process, the salary rates finally agreed upon will reflect the degree of "give and take" between the two parties. Oftentimes, organizations with unionized employees are considered to set the salary trends. In order for nonunionized organizations to maintain a competitive position, they must follow the trends started by other organizations.

Developing the Wage Curve

After the relative worth of each job has been determined by one of the job evaluation methods discussed in Chapter 17, the monetary worth of the job can be determined. For example, when the job ranking method of job evaluation is used, the relative importance of each job is used to determine into which predetermined level each job should be placed. By using the procedures presented in this chapter, the monetary worth for each of the levels is determined. The same basic procedures are used to determine the monetary worth of jobs when the job grading method of job evaluation is used. When the factor comparison method is used, the monetary worth of each key job is first determined. The monetary worth of the key jobs is used as a basis for determining the monetary worth of the non-key jobs. When the point evaluation method is used, the point value of each job is used to determine the monetary worth of each job. Since point evaluation is the most frequently used method of job evaluation, it will be used to illustrate the salary determination process.

In addition to using the relative worth of the job in determining the salary structure, going rates, cost of living index, legislation, and the impact of collective bargaining must also be considered. For each job, either a single rate or a salary range will be established. When salary ranges are used, individuals frequently receive extra compensation for longevity of service and for quality of service to the organization.

The salary scattergram. The first step in determining the monetary worth of each job is to prepare a salary scattergram, similar to the one illustrated in Figure 18–1. The salary scattergram shows the relationship between the relative worth and the monetary worth of each job. The horizontal axis of the scattergram illustrates the points value or relative worth of the jobs, while the vertical axis illustrates the monetary worth. The relative worth (point value) and monetary worth (salary) of each job are then plotted on the salarygram. For example, if a job has a 200-point value and pays a salary of $400, a dot is placed on the scattergram at the intersection of these two values. A correlation line is drawn on the scattergram in such a position that an approximately equal number of dots are above and below the correlation line. The correlation line clearly

FIGURE 18–1   Scattergram

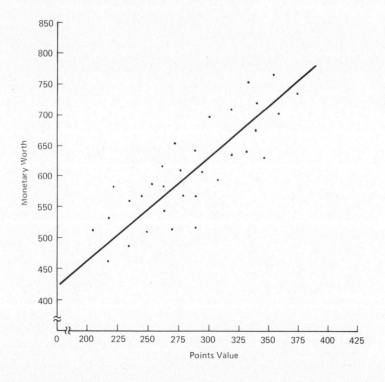

illustrates the relationship between the relative importance of any job and its monetary worth.

To provide some assurance that an organization's salary structure will be externally competitive, the correlation line of the organization should be compared with the correlation line of a composite of other organizations in the same community. If the organization's salary structure is lower than the composite of other organizations in the community, the organization should consider adjusting the salary structure. Such an adjustment is illustrated in Figure 18–2.

Establishing the salary range. Once the correlation line has been officially established, the next step in salary determination is to set the upper and lower limits of the salary range for each pay grade. This can be easily done by placing a line a fixed percentage amount (10 percent, for example) above the correlation line and another line the same percentage amount below the correlation line. Figure 18–3 illustrates the upper and

FIGURE 18–2 Salary Comparison and Adjustment

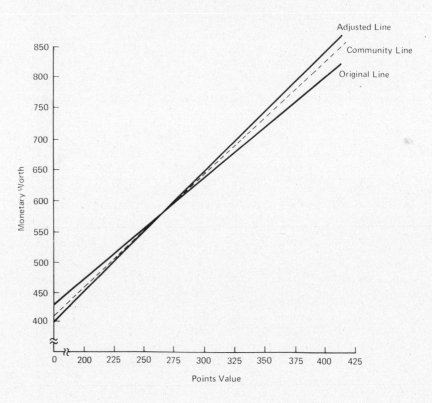

FIGURE 18–3 Salary Ranges

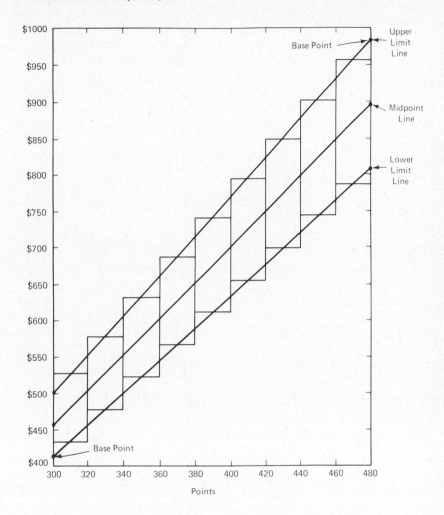

lower limits of each pay grade by using a salary range of 10 percent above and 10 percent below the correlation line. At the lowest end of the correlation line, base points that are 10 percent above and 10 percent below the midpoint are placed on the chart. At the highest end of the correlation line, base points that are 10 percent above and 10 percent below the correlation line are also identified. The upper and lower limits of the salary range can then easily be determined by drawing lines through the two base points above the correlation line and the two base points below the correlation line. For each points category, rectangular-shaped boxes that intersect the upper- and lower-limit lines are then drawn on the figure. The rectangular-shaped boxes readily identify the upper and lower limits of each salary range.

Most salary structures are designed with overlapping rates for adjoining job categories. This concept is illustrated in Figure 18–3. The jobs in the 300–320 points category receive a salary of $437 to $525. The salary range for the adjoining category (321–340 points) is $475 to $580, thus overlapping by $38. When a salary structure is designed with overlapping rates, an employee with considerable experience can be paid a salary equal to or higher than a relatively inexperienced employee in the next higher category.

When an organization undertakes a thorough job evaluation and a corresponding adjustment of its salary structure, salaries of some employees are likely to be less than the lower salary limit, while other employees will be paid more than the upper limit allows. Adjusting the salaries for employees earning less than the minimum amount is relatively simple. In most instances, the employees' salaries will simply be increased to conform to the new salary structure. Adjusting salaries is not as simple for employees earning more than the maximum amount allows. Generally, these employees receive smaller or less frequent increases until their salaries conform to the new salary structure. Two other alternatives, although neither are recommended, are to withhold all salary increases until the employees are paid the appropriate salaries or to lower the employees' salaries to the point where they are in conformity to the new salary structure.

Planning for Salary Increases

The procedures for increasing employees' salaries also have to be built into the organization's salary structure. Salary progression enables employees to move upward in their salary range as well as facilitating the promotion of employees from one job level to a higher job level. Informing employees of the organization's procedures for increasing salaries and of the amount of increases will in many cases motivate them to work harder to attain the maximum increase in the shortest possible time.

Employees' salaries are usually increased at specific time intervals, by individual merit, or by a combination of specific time intervals and merit. Using specific time intervals as a basis for increasing salaries results in automatic salary increases for all employees who come under this plan, provided they are performing at a satisfactory level. For example, employees whose salaries are increased at specific time intervals receive a certain percentage increase every six months or every year if their work performance is satisfactory.

Individual performance or merit is also a frequently used method for increasing employees' salaries. Some organizations, when granting merit increases, tie the quality of performance to the amount of increase.

Thus, employees whose work is distinctly superior receive a larger amount of merit increase than those employees whose work is considerably above average but not superior.

When a combination of both methods is used, organizations frequently increase salaries at specific time intervals until employees reach the midpoint or average salary for their respective salary ranges. To reach the upper limit of the salary range, an employee's performance must be outstanding. Thus, salary increases are automatic from the lower limit to the midpoint of the range, but merit increases are necessary for an employee to reach the upper limit of the salary range.

Fringe Benefits

Fringe benefits refer to the supplemental compensation in excess of the direct compensation an employee receives for performing a specific job. The amount of fringe benefits paid employees has increased rapidly over the years. A survey conducted in 1973 by the Chamber of Commerce of the United States of America revealed that the average amount paid by organizations for fringe benefits was 32.7 percent of the total payroll and that the average benefits per employee per year amounted to $3230. A categorized breakdown of the amount paid for fringe benefits is illustrated in Figure 18–4.

FIGURE 18–4   Employee Benefits by Type of Payment

Type of Benefit	Percent of Payroll	
Legally required payments (employer's share only)		
Old-Age, Survivors, Disability and Health Insurance	5.3	
Unemployment Compensation	1.2	
Workmen's compensation (including estimated cost of self-insured)	0.9	
Railroad Retirement Tax, Railroad Unemployment and Cash Sickness Insurance, state sickness benefits insurance, etc.	0.1	
	—	7.5
Pension and other agreed-upon payments (employer's share only)		
Pension plan premiums and pension payments not covered by insurance type plan (net)	5.1	
Life insurance premiums, death benefits, sickness, accident and medicare insurance premiums, hospitalization insurance, etc. (net)	4.6	
Contributions to privately financed unemployment benefit funds	*	
Separation or termination pay allowances	0.1	
Discounts on goods and services purchased from company by employees	0.2	

FIGURE 18-4   (Continued)

Type of Benefit	Percent of Payroll
Employee meals furnished by company	0.2
Miscellaneous payments (compensation payments in excess of legal requirements, disability insurance, moving expenses, etc.)	0.3
	10.5
Paid rest periods, lunch periods, wash-up time, travel time, clothes-change time, get-ready time, etc.	3.5
Payments for time not worked	
Paid vacations and payments in lieu of vacation	4.7
Payments for holidays not worked	3.0
Paid sick leave	1.1
Payments for State or National Guard duty, jury, witness and voting pay allowances, payments for time lost due to death in family or other personal reasons, etc.	0.4
	9.2
Other items	
Profit-sharing payments	1.1
Contributions to employee thrift plans	0.2
Christmas or other special bonuses, service awards, suggestion awards, etc.	0.4
Employee education expenditures (tuition refunds, etc.)	0.1
Special wage payments ordered by courts, payments to union stewards, etc.	0.2
	2.0
TOTAL	32.7

* Less than 0.05 percent.

Source: Employee Benefits, 1973 (Washington, D.C.: Chamber of Commerce of the United States of America, 1974), p. 8.

There are certain advantages in making various fringe benefits available to employees. Employee turnover is reduced. Employee morale is increased. Employees show more loyalty for their employers and jobs. Employees have greater job satisfaction. Employee productivity is increased. And, employees are provided greater job security.

Some of the more common fringe benefits provided employees are discussed in the paragraphs that follow.

Paid holidays. A very common fringe benefit provided by many organizations is to pay employees for national holidays that fall on a working day. For example, many employees are compensated for New Year's Day, Memorial Day, Independence Day, Labor Day, Thanksgiving, and Christmas. In many organizations, employees are paid for Fridays when holidays fall on Saturday and for Mondays when holidays fall on Sunday. Some organizations also pay employees for the following holidays: Washington's Birthday, Lincoln's Birthday, and Veterans' Day. In addition, some organizations observe special state holidays.

Paid vacations. Many organizations also pay their employees while on vacation. In most instances, the length of the paid vacation depends upon the length of time that an employee works for an organization. Exempt employees frequently receive longer paid vacations than nonexempt employees since they are not eligible to receive overtime pay.

Sick leave. Another fringe benefit frequently provided employees is sick leave. Most organizations provide a specified number of days of sick leave per year. In some organizations, employees are permitted to accumulate sick days from one year to the next. In other instances, employees can add unused days onto their paid vacations. In still other instances, organizations pay employees upon retirement for unused sick days accumulated over the years. There appears to be a trend toward rewarding employees for not taking sick days for reasons other than illnesses. Unless closely controlled, employees tend to abuse sick leave benefits.

Paid personal days. More and more organizations are giving employees a certain number of paid personal days that can be used as the employee wishes. Employees given paid personal days are less apt to use sick days for reasons other than illness. When all of the employee's personal days are used, the employee's wages are likely to be reduced for being absent from work.

Educational assistance. Many organizations pay a portion or all of the tuition costs incurred by employees who attend school part time. A majority of the organizations also help pay for the cost of books and supplies. Some stipulations that are frequently part of the employer-employee educational assistance agreement are: (1) the course must be directly related to the employee's job or to a higher-level job for which the employee is trying to qualify; (2) the employee must successfully complete the course; (3) the course must be taken at an institution approved by the organization; and (4) the employee is obligated to continue working for the organization for a specified length of time upon completing the course.

Insurance programs. Another very common benefit employees receive is life insurance paid either partially or wholly by the employer. In many instances, the amount of life insurance the employee is entitled to receive is in relation to the employee's salary. In addition to death benefits, many life insurance programs also provide dismemberment or accidental death benefits.

Medical insurance. Group medical, surgical, and dental insurance is also a fringe benefit paid either partially or wholly by the employer. In some instances, the employees can obtain coverage at a nominal cost for other family members.

Professional assistance. Many organizations of sufficient size to have full-time attorneys and accountants permit their employees to use on a limited basis the services of these professional advisors. For legal matters of a complicated nature, employees will most likely be referred to individuals outside the organization.

Pension plans. Another very common fringe benefit provided employees is a pension plan. The Pension Reform Act of 1974, which is discussed later in this chapter, provides some important regulatory mechanisms with regard to pension plans offered by organizations.

Profit sharing. More and more organizations are installing profit-sharing plans, which enable employees to share any yearly profits in excess of a certain amount the organization decides to retain for operating purposes. In some instances, employees receive a cash payment, while in other instances, employees receive stock in the organization. It is to the employees' advantage to become more conscious of their efficiency and productivity, since the organization's profit is dependent to a large part on employees' work habits.

Child care services. To accommodate working mothers, many organizations provide daycare centers for children whose mothers are employed by the organization. Certain restrictions—for example, age and health status of the child—are frequenty imposed by the organization.

Car pools. A growing number of organizations are making employees' participation in car pools increasingly attractive. Some organizations provide privileged parking places to employees who belong to car pools, while other organizations provide free parking for those employees who belong to a pool.

Cafeteria services. Eating facilities are provided by organizations for a variety of reasons. In some instances, the cafeterias in organizations operate on a breakeven basis, resulting in reduced meal costs for employees.

Federal Legislation

The provisions of federal legislation are also important considerations in the development of a salary administration program. Among the more important pieces of federal legislation are: Fair Labor Standards Act and its amended act, the Equal Pay Act; the Walsh-Healey Act; the Davis-Bacon Act, and the Pension Reform Act. The important provisions of these acts that have an impact on the salary administration program are discussed below. Several of these acts are discussed in greater detail in Chapter 11.

Fair Labor Standards Act

The significant provisions of this act that pertain specifically to salary administration state that employees who are covered by the act must be paid at least the legal minimum wage. The act contains specific provisions for overtime pay, equal pay for equal work, and minimum ages for employing children.

Walsh-Healey Act

The Walsh-Healey Act covers employees working on government contracts that utilize materials and equipment in excess of $10,000. The act stipulates that employees must receive at least the minimum wage, must be paid overtime, and child labor must not be used.

Davis-Bacon Act

The Davis-Bacon Act, passed in 1931, is also known as the Prevailing Wage Law. The act sets minimum wages for persons employed on federal public works projects worth more than $2,000. The minimum wage rate is established at the prevailing level of pay for other similar jobs in the area.

Pension Reform Act

The Pension Reform Act, officially known as the Employee Retirement Income Security Act of 1974, has a significant impact on the pension plans offered by organizations throughout the country. The act does not require an organization to have a pension plan; but if the organization does have a plan, the plan must meet the requirements outlined in the act. If an organization offers a pension plan, the organization is required to meet a minimum funding standard. This means that the organization must contribute at least a minimum amount to a qualified defined benefit or money purchase pension or to an annuity plan.

It is possible for an organization to have an exempt, fully insured plan if the plan meets certain requirements during the plan year. One such requirement is that the plan be funded exclusively with individual insurance or annuity contracts. Another requirement is that the contracts must provide for payment of level annual (or more frequent) premiums from the time an employee becomes a participant in the plan until the employee reaches retirement age or until the employee ceases participation in the plan.

If the organization has a plan that is subject to the provisions of the act, all employees who have reached the age of twenty-five and who have worked for the organization for one year (1,000 hours in industries of an intermittent or seasonal employment nature) are covered.

Let us examine some of the more important provisions of the act. Pension plans must be vested, which means that employees are entitled to the amount they contribute to their pension plans, in addition to a share of their employer's contribution, under one of the following three options: (1) fully vested after ten years of continuous service; (2) partially vested after a time—for example, after five years of service, 25 percent vested; after ten years, 50 percent vested; and after fifteen years, 100 percent vested; (3) vesting under the "forty-five rule," which means that after five years of service, the employee is entitled to 50 percent vesting when the sum of the employee's age and years of service exceeds forty-five, with added vesting for additional years of service until the employee is entitled to 100 percent vesting. (For example, an employee who has ten years of service and whose age and service equals or exceeds fifty-five is entitled to 100 percent vesting.)

In most cases, employees who are hired after a mandatory retirement age are also covered by the act. Employees changing jobs can take their vested benefits with them. If the new employer approves, the vested benefits could be transferred to the new employer's retirement program. Such transfers are limited to once every three years. The annual benefit payable to any employee covered by the act may not be greater than the lesser of $75,000 or 100 percent of the employee's average compensation for the three consecutive calendar years in which the employee received his or her highest amount of compensation.

The benefits of the plan must be communicated to the employees in a summary plan description. The description must include:

1. The name of the plan; the common name of the plan; the employer and address; the type of plan; how the plan is administered; the administrator's name and address; the date of the plan's fiscal year; the employer identification number; the name and address of the person responsible for the legal services of the organization; and the names, titles, and addresses of the plan's trustees.

2. Requirements for participation and the benefits; "normal" retirement age; description of joint and survivor benefits; service requirements for accruing full benefits; how benefits are prorated for less than a year's service; and who pays for the plan.

3. Identity of any organization that maintains the plan's funds or provides benefits; the manner in which claims are to be filed; the procedure to follow when a claim is denied; and whether or not the plan is insured under the Pension Benefit Guaranty Corporation.

Review Questions

1. What is the relationship between job evaluation and salary administration?

2. In what ways does a salary administration program help employees perform at an optimum level?

3. What types of policies should be developed with regard to the salary administration program?

4. Who is generally responsible for salary administration in a large organization? Small organization?

5. Which of the prepared salary surveys are available for determining going rates for:
   a. office or clerical employees?
   b. middle management?
   c. exempt employees?
   d. data processing employees?

6. How is the salary range for specific jobs determined?

7. How can an organization be sure that its salaries are competitive with salaries paid by other organizations in the community?

8. Why do organizations make fringe benefits available to employees?

9. What provisions of the Fair Labor Standards Act have special significance for salary administration?

10. What workers are covered by the Walsh-Healey Act? By the Pension Reform Act?

Minicases

The management of a small but rapidly growing manufacturing plant in a midwestern city feels that it is now time to examine the salary structure of the company. The last time that this was done was about eight years ago, and there is now evidence that the lower-level jobs in the company are not competitive in terms of salaries, but that the salaries for the higher-level jobs are quite good. At this time no one knows just how much the company's salary structure varies from the salary structure of other companies in the community. The management of the manufacturing plan has conducted a rather thorough community salary survey. The management is now interested in continuing by preparing an analysis of its salary structure. What device do you recommend be used to analyze the salary structure of this company? How is this device used?

*   *   *

The Manhattan State Bank, which is located in a Michigan city of about 40,000, has a fairly high turnover among its office employees. The administrative office manager and the personnel manager of the bank have been attempting to determine the reasons for the high turnover. Over the last few years, a growing number of employees have indicated, upon terminating their employment, that they can find higher-paying jobs elsewhere in the community. For a time, this fact did not bother the bank management since there was usually a waiting list of qualified applicants. During the last six months or so, the number of qualified applicants has greatly diminished, partially because a large insurance company moved its regional headquarters into the city and hired about 200 local residents. The Manhattan State Bank is now concerned about its noncompetitive salary structure. It has been decided that a community salary survey be undertaken to determine competitive salaries. (None of the published salary lists are appropriate for this city.) What suggestions do you have to assure the accuracy of results of the salary survey?

Case

The Japan Mutual Insurance Company recently moved its headquarters from a decaying urban area of Watertown to a suburban office park in Jackson, a distance of approximately fifteen miles. Shortly before the move was made, the average salary of the 179 office employees of Japan Mutual was $487 per month. Shortly after the move, the developer of the office park, as part of a promotional campaign, advertised that the "average salary of office employees in the Jackson area is $524 per month."

While the Japan Mutual Insurance Company's headquarters were located in Watertown, it had a reputation of being a "trend setter" because of salaries paid its employees. Since the management took a considerable amount of pride in paying above average salaries, the employees were always kept informed of the company's average salary. Now that the employees are aware that the average salary of the company is no longer considered to be externally competitive, some are dissatisfied, while others are talking about finding other employment in the area.

You, as administrative office manager, are a member of the company's salary committee.

1. What additional information do you feel the committee needs before a specific course of action can be recommended to the company's management?

2. Should the company increase its salary structure as a means of becoming more competitive? If so, why?

3. Should the company ignore the employees' feelings about the company's salary structure? If so, why?

4. If your committee recommends to management that the average salary should be increased, what rationale are you going to use?

Work
Measurement
and
Work
Standards

Chapter
19

Nature of Work Measurement
    Objectives of Work Measurement
    Advantages
    Characteristics of Measurable Office Activities

The Work Measurement Program

Work Measurement Techniques
    Production Records
    Work Sampling
    Time Study
    Micromotion Study
    Predetermined Standard Time Data

Performance Leveling

Work Standards
    Advantages of Work Standards
    Types of Standards
        Quantity standards
        Quality standards
        Descriptive standards

Chapter Aims   After studying this chapter, the student should be able to:

1. Discuss the objectives of work measurement.
2. Identify the characteristics of measurable office activities.
3. Explain the steps for installing a work measurement program.
4. Discuss the criteria that are used to select an appropriate work measurement technique for a particular task.
5. Discuss the production record technique of work measurement.
6. Discuss the work sampling technique of work measurement.
7. Discuss the time study technique of work measurement.
8. Discuss the micromotion study technique of work measurement.
9. Discuss the predetermined standard time data technique of work measurement.
10. Explain performance leveling.
11. Explain the differences between quantity, quality, and descriptive standards.

Chapter Terms   *Work measurement:* a system designed to determine what comprises a fair day's work from the standpoint of both the employer and the employee.

Work standards: guidelines used to compare actual output results with anticipated output results. Work measurement provides a basis for setting work standards.

Production records: a rather simple work measurement technique that utilizes employee production records to determine the amount of time needed to complete a particular job.

Work sampling: a work measurement technique that has a statistical base and that utilizes random observations to determine the amount of time consumed by each element of the total work process.

Time study: a work measurement technique in which a stopwatch is used to determine the amount of time consumed by each element of a work process.

Micromotion study: a work measurement technique that utilizes a motion picture film of the work process. The amount of time consumed by each element of the work process is determined by multiplying the number of film frames on which a particular element appears by the speed of the film as it advances through the camera.

Microchrometer: a special timing device used in micromotion study.

Predetermined standard time data: a work measurement technique in which pretermined standards are usually obtained from an external source, such as a management consulting firm.

Performance leveling: a technique that adjusts work standards to accommodate average employees.

Quantity standards: standards that are expressed in terms of units of output per unit of time.

Quality standards: standards used to measure the accuracy and acceptability of work.

Descriptive standards: standards that identify acceptable descriptive characteristics of areas or objects within an office.

Work measurement, one of the basic components of scientific management, is frequently used to determine what comprises a fair day's work from the standpoint of both the employer and the employee. More specifically, work measurement is a system designed to assess employee productivity in terms of the amount of time consumed to produce a unit of output. Furthermore, work measurement provides the mechanism for determining **work standards,** which are necessary before employee productivity can be compared with acceptable standards or levels of productivity. The methods used for measuring work vary widely. Some office activities are measured by simply counting the number of units produced or processed by office employees. Others require more sophisticated measures involving fairly complex procedures and equipment.

Nature of Work Measurement

As increasing numbers of organizations are becoming more efficiency conscious, the measurement of office activities is receiving a greater amount of attention. Many administrative office managers view work measurement as a means of controlling office operations. Using the work standards to compare actual results with anticipated results, greater control over the office operations is possible. Although standards can be developed to measure the effectiveness of most office activities, some office activities are not measurable and, therefore, standards cannot be developed.

Objectives of Work Measurement

1. An important objective of work measurement is to determine a reasonable level of productivity in order to compare what an employee is expected to produce with what the employee is able to produce. Such levels of production are expressed in terms of work standards.

2. Another important objective of work measurement is to aid in the planning and scheduling of work. Using work standards, the administrative office manager is able to determine how long a given job will take to complete. The standards can also be used to determine the number of employees that will be needed to complete a project within a given amount of time. Thus, work measurement can be used to help determine if additional employees are needed to complete a project on time.

3. Helping to determine the efficiency of work methods and processes is another objective. By comparing an employee's productivity level with generally accepted standards, it is quite simple to determine if the employee is overproducing or underproducing. If employees consistently underproduce in terms of the generally accepted standards, an attempt should be made to determine the reasons for the low production levels. If the reason is employee inefficiency, the desirability of providing additional training for these employees might be investigated.

4. Another objective of work measurement is to facilitate determining the cost of office operations. Since the unit output is determined during the work measurement process, and since the total cost of an operation

can be determined, the unit output cost can be calculated by dividing unit output into total cost. The unit output cost can then be compared with comparable figures of other organizations. The unit output cost can also be used to help in budget preparation. By projecting the total units of output that will be produced during the budget period and by multiplying this projection by the unit output cost, the amount that should be budgeted for each activity or work process can be estimated.

A final objective of work measurement is to help determine equitable work loads among employees. By using the standards to determine equitable work loads, greater equity in assignment of work can be assured. Equally important is better employee understanding of job expectations, which results in better employee morale.

Advantages

There are significant advantages of work measurement. Greater control over work processes and methods is possible. Work measurement facilities determine if a particular work unit is either overstaffed or understaffed. The efficiency with which individuals produce is readily determined. Greater efficiency in planning work is possible and bottlenecks can be avoided by using the results of work measurement in scheduling work. Finally, the results of work measurement can be used to help simplify work processes.

Characteristics of Measurable Office Activities

To be measurable, office activities must be isolated and countable. This means that the activities comprising specific office jobs must be identifiable. Measurable office activities must also be fairly consistent from one measurement to another. If a considerable amount of variation exists, accurate standards cannot be set. The office activities to be measured should also be of sufficient quantity to justify the cost involved in their measurement. Some office activities are of sufficiently low volume and are so costly to measure that the results do not justify the expense.

Office activities that are impossible to measure include those consisting of considerable amounts of judgment and decisionmaking. Since the time consumed varies so greatly with activities involving judgment and decisionmaking, the development of standards for such activities is subjective. Office activities involving a considerable amount of creativity are also difficult to measure.

The Work Measurement Program

The installation of a work measurement program involves a considerable amount of planning and investigation of the various alternatives that are possible. Organizations installing a work measurement program are likely to have to put forth a considerable amount of effort selling the program to the employees as well as seeking their support. Unless the program has the support of the employees, its success is likely to be diminished.

Several techniques have been found to be successful in selling the work measurement program to employees. Perhaps foremost on employees' minds is their trying to determine the nature of any changes they may have to make in performing their jobs. Also foremost on the minds of some employees is whether or not the results of work measurement will indicate a need for the organization to retain their positions. To inform employees about the ways in which work measurement is likely to change their jobs and to provide them with assurance that the results of work measurement will not cause anyone to be displaced on the job will do much to enhance their acceptance of the program. Other techniques that might be used are group meetings in which the merits of such a program are discussed, case studies about other organizations that found work measurement programs to be successful, and step-by-step communication of how the installation of the work measurement program is progressing. It is also recommended that once the decision has been made to install the program, the employees should receive from a top-level executive a letter or memo outlining the reasons for the decision.

The following is a step-by-step plan for installing a work measurement program.

1. *Preliminary planning.* The objectives of the program should be outlined, the work measurement techniques should be selected, and the timetable for installing the program should be determined. If professional consultants will be required to help install the program, the contracting for such services should be considered.

2. *Initial staffing.* The duties and responsibilities of the individuals responsible for the program should be determined prior to the time that individuals are selected.

3. *Gaining acceptance of and support for the program.* Those individuals who will work closely with the installation and operation of the program should be used extensively during this step.

4. *Collecting important data.* If the chosen work measurement technique requires gathering data from various work units, the individuals responsible for collecting the data should receive appropriate training.

5. *Analyzing collected data and developing standards.* Once the necessary data has been collected, the data should be analyzed, and standards should be developed accordingly. If the work measurement program utilizes predetermined standards purchased from a management consulting firm, the appropriate standards for the various office activities should be developed during this step.

6. *Training supervisors and managers.* Each supervisor and manager in the organization directly or indirectly responsible for an employee whose job is affected by work measurement should receive training on the results of work measurement and the implementation of standards.

7. *Instructing employees.* Once the standards have been set and the supervisors have received training in the implementation of such standards, employees should be informed of expected levels of production.

8. *Followup*. If the work measurement program is to be successful, the program must receive periodic followup. The followup should be more frequent during the early stages of the program. It is important for management to know how actual results compare with expected results. If the actual results do not compare favorably with the expected results, the reasons for the lack of comparison should be determined and appropriate modification of the program should be made.

Work Measurement Techniques

Several work measurement techniques are used to set work standards. In selecting the technique to use, the following criteria might be considered:

1. The intended use of the standards.
2. The degree of accuracy of the standards.
3. The cost the organization is willing to assume in developing the standards.
4. The nature of the work for which standards are desired.
5. The degree to which individuals responsible for the program understand the elements of work measurement and standards.

Among the work measurement techniques available are production records, work sampling, time study, micromotion study, and predetermined standard time data.

Production Records

The use of **production records** is a rather simple and quick technique for measuring work in order to develop work standards. The technique consists of using employee production records to determine the amount of time needed to complete a particular job.

Figure 19–1 illustrates a time log that is helpful when using the production records technique. The time log enables each employee to keep a record of the work produced and the amount of time taken to produce the work. Each task performed by the employees is entered in coded form on the time log (column 1). The units produced (column 2) and the amount of time taken to produce the units (column 3) are also entered on the time log. The time increments are usually expressed in units of five or ten minutes.

The time log should be kept by each employee for as long a period of time as is needed to smooth out or balance any unusual fluctuations. In most instances, a period of two weeks is considered a minimum amount of time. After the production records of all the employees have been accumulated, the total units produced by all employees and the total amount of time taken to produce the units are determined. By dividing the total units produced by the total time taken to produce the units, a standard can be determined. The standard represents the average of the em-

FIGURE 19–1   Time Log

Activity 1	Units Produced 2	Time 3
D	*1*	8:00 8:10
A	*15*	8:20 8:30 8:40
C	*2*	8:50 9:00
D	*1*	9:10
F	*15*	9:20 9:30 9:40
		9:50 10:00 10:10 12:00

ployees' performance. In some instances, the standard will be adjusted either upward or downward as a means of pacing an employee's performance against the average standard.

When the various components of a work process change or when the conditions under which the work process is performed change, the standards will also very likely have to be adjusted. This is the reason for routinely investigating the validity of the standards determined by this technique.

Production records kept over a period of time are also sometimes used to determine work standards. Some departments regularly maintain production records. For example, the log maintained in many word processing centers might be sufficient to set work standards. Such logs are frequently used to keep track of the time taken to transcribe the contents of a magnetic dictation belt or tape. By approximating the number of words on the belt or tape and by knowing how much time is consumed by the transcription process, a standard can be developed. Allowances have to be made, however, for variations in the dictator's speed of dictation, the complexity of the material, and so forth. Because of the nature of many uncontrollable variables, this technique may not be very accurate.

The advantages of using the production records technique to determine work standards are that the technique is simple and easily understood and it is inexpensive to use. Thus, the technique is the only one that is financially feasible for many offices. Also, it enables standards to be developed quickly and can be implemented without the use of specially trained individuals.

The disadvantages of using the production records technique are that it may result in inaccurate standards because of an employee's failure to maintain accurate time logs or that the standards developed by this technique are readily affected by changes in work processes and may frequently necessitate employees' keeping time logs so that standards can be subsequently adjusted.

Work Sampling

The **work sampling** technique, which has a statistical base, utilizes random observations to determine the amount of time consumed by each element of the total work process. The statistical base of the technique incorporates the following law of probability: If a sufficiently large sample of valid random observations of a work process are made, the data that is gathered is considered to be as reliable as if work processes were observed continuously over a period of time.

The work sampling technique, which utilizes random observations, identifies the type of activity being performed by an employee at the time of the observation. The observations are considered to be random if the employee or employees that are being observed are randomly selected and if the times of the observations are randomly determined. The random observations are made to determine the percent of the total process that each activity consumes.

The filing of insurance applications is used to illustrate the work sampling method. The filing process involves five distinct activities. A total of one hundred random observations was determined to be a sufficient number to be a reliable sample. Random observations are made to determine the percent of the total process that each activity consumes. Figure 19–2 illustrates this relationship. For example, of the one hundred random observations, Activity A was observed twenty times; Activity B, ten

FIGURE 19–2

A Activity	B Observations	C Percent	D Time	E Units Produced	F Standard (D÷E)
A	20	20	100 min	250	.4
B	10	10	50 min	100	.5
C	40	40	200 min	200	1.0
D	20	20	100 min	50	2.0
E	10	10	50 min	125	.4
Totals	100	100	500 min	725	

times; Activity C, forty times, and so forth. The total filing process consisted of 500 minutes. Therefore, if Activity A constitutes 20 percent of the total process in terms of the number of observations, Activity A should also constitute 20 percent or 100 minutes of the total time consumed by the filing process. (This is determined by multiplying 500 by .20.) Records also have to be examined to determine the number of units produced during each activity. This is illustrated in Column E of Figure 19–2. During the 500 minutes consumed by the filing process, 250 units were produced during Activity A, 100 units during Activity B, and so forth. To determine the standard for Activity A, the number of units produced (250 units) is divided into the amount of time (100 minutes). Therefore, a standard of 0.4 is derived for Activity A.

The random selection of the employees and the times they are to be observed can be greatly expedited by using a table of random numbers. Such tables and directions for using the tables can be found in statistics books.

Determining the proper number of observations is crucial, since the accuracy of the work sampling technique can be greatly diminished by too few a number of observations. The proper number of observations to be made is dependent upon (1) the portion of time that the smallest activity in the total work process consumes; (2) the degree of tolerance (or accuracy) required; (3) the reliability of results required.

To illustrate, if the smallest activity in the work process consumes 25 percent of the total process, if 90 percent accuracy is required, and if 80 percent reliability of results is required, fewer observations would have to be made than if the smallest activity consumes 5 percent of the total process, if 95 percent accuracy is required, and if 90 percent reliability is required. Statistics books also contain tables that can be used to determine the proper number of observations to make.

The advantages of the work sampling technique are as follows:

1. Provided that random observations are made, the results are very accurate.
2. The technique does not require the services of a highly trained analyst.
3. The technique is fairly reasonable in terms of the cost of installation.
4. The results can be gathered rather quickly.
5. Work sampling is well suited for long-cycle work processes.

Among the disadvantages of the work sampling technique are the following:

1. Some employees have a tendency to perform differently if they know they are being observed. If unusual performance occurs frequently, the results of work measurement could be affected significantly.

2. Work processes that consist of numerous minute activities are not suitable for work sampling.

3. To set standards, production records have to be used to determine units of output. Such output records are not always readily accessible.

Time Study

Time study is also sometimes referred to as stopwatch study or stopwatch time study because of the frequent utilization of a stopwatch in the data-gathering process. For this technique to be successful, all wasted motions should be eliminated before the work process is analyzed. Standards set on work processes consisting of wasteful motions are of little value.

The time study technique involves three steps:

1. Identify and break down into its basic elements the job being studied.

2. Record the time consumed by each element of the work process on a time study sheet, repeating this step for several cycles of the work process.

3. On the basis of the time consumed by each element of the work process, determine appropriate standards.

The time study technique is illustrated in the time study sheet in Figure 19–3. Illustrated is the work process for calculating payroll. The time study sheet is completed by entering on the sheet the amount of time consumed by each of the elements of the work process. The process is timed for several cycles. Two timing techniques are possible: *continuous* timing of the entire process or *lapsed* timing for each element of the entire process. When the continuous technique is used, the analyst simply records in the "R" (reading) column of Cycle 1 the stopwatch reading at the time each element of the process is completed. For example, in Cycle 1, the first element was completed when the stopwatch reading was fifteen seconds; the second element, thirty-seven seconds; the third element, ninety-two seconds; and the fourth, 110 seconds. The amount of time consumed by each element is then entered in the "T" (time) column. The first element consumes fifteen seconds; the second, twenty-two seconds; and so forth. The timing of the work process is repeated a sufficient number of cycles in order to give validity to the measurement process.

When the lapsed time technique is used, the analyst resets the stopwatch at "0" each time one element is completed but prior to starting the timing of the next element. These figures are immediately recorded in the "T" column. Unlike the continuous method, no subtraction is involved when the lapsed time technique is used.

The performance of the employees being timed has a direct bearing on the validity of standards. Some organizations select for timing those

FIGURE 19-3   Time Study Sheet

Work Process: _Calculating Payroll_
Date: _September 3, 1975_

Analyst's Name: _L. Davis_
Worker's Name: _Stanley Evans_

Elements	Cycle																Standard	Notes
	1		2		3		4		5		6		7		8			
	T	R	T	R	T	R	T	R	T	R	T	R	T	R	T	R		
Determine Total Hours Worked	15	15	16	176	15	734	14	342	15	451							15	
Multiply Hours Worked by Base Rate of Pay to Arrive at Gross Pay	22	37	21	147	21	755	22	364	*26	*407							22	*Put wrong value in machine—had to start over (lost 4 seconds)
Calculate Deductions	55	92	53	200	55	340	54	418	54	511							54	
Subtract Deductions to Get Net Pay	18	110	19	219	19	328	18	436	18	529							18	

employees who are most respected by their fellow workers. The reason for this is that the other employees are more apt to accept the standards. If the employees to be timed are also the most skilled workers, the standards will most likely have to be lowered to accommodate the majority of employees. Another important characteristic to consider when selecting employees to time is the consistency with which the employees being observed perform their jobs. An erratic performance is apt to have a negative impact on the reliability of the standards.

The following advantages result from the use of time study to determine work standards: (1) the standards developed on the basis of this work measurement technique are very accurate; (2) this technique is more accurate for measuring work processes comprised of minute elements than is either the production records technique or the work sampling technique; and (3) once the standards are determined, they can be readily used for measuring the performance of employees.

Among the disadvantages of this technique are the following: (1) the measurement process requires the use of a trained analyst, which adds to the cost of the work measurement program; (2) office employees tend to have a negative reaction to standards determined on the basis of stopwatch studies; (3) the technique is not useful for measuring elements of a work process that are time-consuming.

Micromotion Study

Micromotion study involves making a motion picture of the work processes being studied. Therefore, the various elements that make up the work process can be studied in detail. Micromotion study is especially appropriate for work processes involving both humans and machines. By studying the motion picture, the processes can be analyzed and inefficiency can be eliminated or various elements of the process can be simplified. In this way, micromotion study can also be used for work simplification purposes.

When the primary purpose of micromotion study is to provide data for the setting of standards, the motion pictures are analyzed to determine the amount of time each element of the work process consumes. To determine the amount of time consumed by each element of the work process, the number of motion picture frames on which each element of the work process appears is multiplied by the speed through which the film advances through the camera. The result is the standard for that particular element. To illustrate, if 2,000 frames advance through the camera per minute and if one element of the process appears on 200 frames, the standard would be one tenth of a minute (six seconds) for that particular element.

If the elements of the work process are extremely minute, a **microchrometer** may be needed. The microchrometer, which is a special timing device attached to the camera, enables the unit of time to be photographed on each frame of the motion picture. The time consumed by each element of the process can be determined by analyzing the motion picture frames. The standard for each element is determined by subtracting the time that appears on the first frame of a particular element from the time that appears on the last frame of the same element.

Because of its tendency to be an expensive work measurement technique, micromotion study is mostly used for work processes that occur frequently and that are quite costly. Unless a work process meets these criteria, many feel that the use of the technique cannot be justified.

The advantages of micromotion study are that as a work measurement technique it is very accurate; it is well suited for analysis of the most minute elements of a work process; and it can also be used as a means of work simplification since the wasted motions appear on the film.

But there are also disadvantages of the micromotion study technique. The technique is very costly in comparison to some of the other work measurement techniques. The technique is limited to those work processes that occur with a high degree of frequency and that are costly. And it requires the services of a trained analyst, which would preclude some organizations from selecting micromotion study as a work measurement technique.

Predetermined Standard Time Data

The **predetermined standard time data** technique is the only work measurement technique discussed in this chapter that most often utilizes data from external sources. When predetermined standard time data are used, the data are generally purchased from management consulting firms or from work management associations. The purchased standards are used to guide the setting of work standards within organizations using the predetermined standard time data. In rare instances an organization may develop its own predetermined standard time data, which requires the use of individuals who have extremely specialized training.

A fundamental premise must be made when using predetermined standard time data. This technique rests on the premise that if the same motions are performed under identical conditions, the time values of identical motions will be constant from one situation to another. Therefore, an organization can use predetermined standard time data to set standards for basic motions provided the motions are performed under the same conditions that were present when the predetermined standard times were determined.

When using predetermined standard time data, the analyst utilizes the following steps:

1. The work process is broken down into its most minute elements.
2. Each element is analyzed in terms of the motion involved.
3. Each motion of the work process is compared with the purchased predetermined standard time data to determine the appropriate standard for each of the motions. Figure 19–4 illustrates one of the tables found in one predetermined standard time data system.

FIGURE 19–4 Predetermined Standard Time Data

TABLE II – MOVE – M

Distance Moved Inches	Time TMU				Wt. Allowance			Case and Description
	A	B	C	Hand In Motion B	Wt. (lb) Up to	Dynamic Factor	Static Constant TMU	
3/4 or less	2.0	2.0	2.0	1.7				
1	2.5	2.9	3.4	2.3	2.5	1.00	0	A Move Object to Other Hand or Against Stop.
2	3.6	4.6	5.2	2.9				
3	4.9	5.7	6.7	3.6	7.5	1.06	2.2	
4	6.1	6.9	8.0	4.3				
5	7.3	8.0	9.2	5.0	12.5	1.11	3.9	
6	8.1	8.9	10.3	5.7				
7	8.9	9.7	11.1	6.5	17.5	1.17	5.6	B Move Object to Approximate or Indefinite Location.
8	9.7	10.6	11.8	7.2				
9	10.5	11.5	12.7	7.9	22.5	1.22	7.4	
10	11.3	12.2	13.5	8.6				
12	12.9	13.4	15.2	10.0	27.5	1.28	9.1	
14	14.4	14.6	16.9	11.4				
16	16.0	15.8	18.7	12.8	32.5	1.33	10.8	
18	17.6	17.0	20.4	14.2				
20	19.2	18.2	22.1	15.6	37.5	1.39	12.5	
22	20.8	19.4	23.8	17.0				C Move Object to Exact Location.
24	22.4	20.6	25.5	18.4	42.5	1.44	14.3	
26	24.0	21.8	27.3	19.8				
28	25.5	23.1	29.0	21.2	47.5	1.50	16.0	
30	27.1	24.3	30.7	22.7				
Additional	0.8	0.6	0.85		TMU Per Inch Over 30 Inches			

4. The standard for the entire process is found by adding the standard times for each of the motions.

Internally and externally developed predetermined standard time data are generally developed by either stopwatch time studies or by micromotion study. Since the data are developed by trained analysts, the data are very accurate.

When predetermined standard time data are obtained externally, several different systems are available. These include such systems as Motion-Time Analysis (MTA), Methods Time Measurement (MTM), Basic Motion Time Study (BMT), Universal Maintenance Standards (UMS), and Master Clerical Data (MCD). Although the same basic principles were originally used in developing each of the systems, specific details of the various systems differ significantly.

The data illustrated in Figure 19–4 represent one of the thirteen tables that comprise the MTM system. The time measurement unit

(TMU) used in MTM is one hundred-thousandth of an hour. Because the time units are so minute, MTM is not well suited for many of the typical work processes performed in many offices. For example, grasping and placing a paper in working position may involve three or four different MTM motions.

Master Clerical Data, which is an adaptation of MTM, classifies clerical work into thirteen different elemental categories. When MCD is used, the appropriate elemental categories are used to provide standard times for the various elements of clerical work processes. Figure 19–5 illustrates the standards for a portion of the MCD system.

There are several advantages in using predetermined standard time data. The technique results in very accurate standards. Once the predetermined standard time data are available, additional work measurement analyses do not have to be completed when a work process is changed or a new work process is developed.

Because of the specificity with which the standards are developed, employees accept the results more readily than when some of the other less sophisticated techniques are used.

And finally, the application of the technique is fairly rapid.

Yet there are also disadvantages. The technique is very costly to use because of the necessity of using highly trained analysts and expensive predetermined standard time data. Certain office operations, primarily those of long cycle, are not adaptable to the predetermined standard time data technique. Also, when internally developing the predetermined standard time data, the technique is very time-consuming.

Performance Leveling

The work measurement program is designed to determine what constitutes a fair day's work from the standpoint of both the employer and the employee. In order for employees to experience a fair day's work, **performance leveling** or rating may be necessary. Performance leveling is the technique used to adjust the standards to accommodate average employees.

Since most of the work measurement techniques gather data on work processes being performed continuously, the techniques may not take into consideration the individual differences between employees, the effect of fatigue on employees, interruptions, coffee breaks, rest breaks, and so forth. In order for standards to be somewhat reasonable, they must be adjusted in consideration of such conditions.

Although a 100 percent goal for attaining standards is desirable, rarely can that goal be achieved, even under the best of conditions. If the standards are set so high that even the most productive employees are unable to attain these standards, the benefits of the work measurement program will most likely be negligible. It is for this reason that performance leveling is desirable.

FIGURE 19–5　Master Clerical Data

PLACE AND REMOVE ELEMENTS			
Code	Time	Code	Time
PBP	99	PFT01	84
PBR	16	PFT02	44
PCL01	26	PFT03	128
PCL02	11	PFT11	49
PCL03	37	PFT12	37
PCL11	16	PFT13	86
PCL12	22	PG	13
PCL13	38	PKC01	43
PCT01	42	PKC02	13
PCT02	28	PKC03	56
PCT03	70	PKT01	18
PCT11	25	PKT02	16
PCT12	28	PKT03	34
PCT13	53	PMA	61
PD	75	PML	42
PFL01	35	PMP	138
PFL02	20	PMS	58
PFL03	55	PMT	86
PFL11	23	PN	54
PFL12	30	PR	45
PFL13	53	—	—

TYPEWRITING ELEMENTS			
Code	Time	Code	Time
TAC	159	TIN03	16
TAA	78	TIN04	3
TAP01	18	TKC	6
TAP02	9	TKE	4
TAS	54	TKM	6
TBC01	13	TKS01	4
TBC02	4	TKS02	2
TBT01	10	TLR	50
TBT02	2	TLP	91
TCC01	82	TOT	9
TCC02	68	TOB	13
TCL01	50	TPC	129
TCL02	29	TPP	44
TCS01	49	TPR	38
TCS02	18	TPS	48
TEF01	234	TRM	27
TEF02	226	TRE	14
TEF03	335	TRS	13
TEF04	327	TSM01	52
TEA01	198	TSM02	34
TEA02	299	TST01	15 + 4N
TEE01	79	TST02	17 + 2N
TEE02	180	TST03	51
TEP01	47	TST04	27
TEP02	36	TST05	20
TER01	75	TST06	15
TER02	78	TST07	37
TES01	62	TST08	16
TES02	57	TST09	11
TIA01	8	TTF01	12
TIA02	4	TTF02	12
TIA03	3	TTA01	5
TIN01	26	TTA02	3
TIN02	9	—	—

WRITING ELEMENTS			
Code	Time	Code	Time
WD	18	WS	61
WLL	19	WWL	15
WLU	24	WWU	22
WP	15	—	—

TIME CONVERSION TABLE

1 Unit = 0.00001	Hour
= 0.0006	Minute
= 0.036	Second

Courtesy, Serge A. Birn Company

The use of trained analysts for performance leveling is advantageous. The knowledge and experience of these individuals adds considerably to the accuracy of the leveling results. If trained analysts are not available (for instance when the production records technique is used), the individuals in charge of the work measurement program may have to level the standards several times until they are appropriate for the circumstances.

Work Standards   One of the primary objectives of work measurement is to collect data to help set standards for office work. Unless work measurement activities are reasonably accurate, the reliability of the resulting standards is likely to be affected. In addition, without some form of work measurement, the development of reliable and accurate work standards is impossible.

When work standards are set, they should not be set at a level only obtainable by the most efficient, productive employee. Nor should they be set at such a low level that each employee is capable of attaining the standards. Rather, the standards should be set at the level at which the average employee is successful in attaining the standard but also at a level that provides a sufficient incentive to perform well. To be most effective, the standards must be acceptable to the employees. In many instances, the most difficult and time-consuming step in developing work standards is employee acceptance.

Advantages of Work Standards

The utilization of work standards provides several important advantages.

1. Standards help increase the efficiency with which employees perform their jobs.

2. Standards help communicate to employees the production levels that are expected of them.

3. Standards assist managers in making personnel decisions, since the employees who are performing beyond expected levels of production can be readily identified.

4. Because employees are aware of the procedures for doing their jobs, less supervision is needed and greater control over the work process is possible.

5. Standards provide the basis for incentive wage systems.

6. Standards help to increase employee morale by making employees aware of what is expected of them.

Types of Standards

Several different types of standards are found in offices. These include **quantity, quality,** and **descriptive standards.** Although work measurement is used only to develop the quantity standards, the others are important for various kinds of office work or functions.

Quantity standards. Quantity standards are expressed in terms of units of output per unit of time. For longer work cycles, the unit of time is usually expressed in terms of hours. For shorter work cycles, the unit of time may be expressed in terms of minutes or even seconds. Quantity standards consist of two types: subjective and engineered. Subjective standards are based on an educated guess. The accuracy of the subjective standards can often be challenged. The engineered standards, on the other hand, are much more precise since they are based on the results of work measurement. While subjective standards are more arbitrary, engineered standards are more accurate and therefore are more reliable and acceptable.

Quality standards. Quality standards, although not determined by work measurement, are very important in an office. Quality standards are used to measure the accuracy and acceptability of work. For example, quality standards are used to determine the acceptability of typewritten work and the accuracy of filing, arithmetical calculations, keypunching, and so forth. Although adherence to strict quality standards may result in some work being redone, enforcement of strict standards will save money in the long run.

Descriptive standards. Like quality standards, descriptive standards are not determined by work measurement. Descriptive standards identify acceptable descriptive characteristics of areas or objects within an office. For example, descriptive standards are used to determine the amount of office space appropriate for the different levels of employees. To illustrate, a vice president is entitled to more square feet of floor space than is a clerk-typist. Descriptive standards also exist to identify the size and type of working areas or desks to which the different levels of employees are entitled. Descriptive standards also are used in purchasing office supplies, equipment, and items that may have an effect on the working environment—for example, lighting—of the office.

Review Questions

1. In what way can work measurement be used to determine the efficiency of work methods and procedures?
2. In what way can work measurement provide a greater amount of control over work processes and methods?
3. How can work measurement be used to determine equitable work loads?
4. In what ways do the production records technique and the work sampling technique of work measurement differ?
5. What is the difference between continuous and lapsed time methods of timing work for the time study method of work measurement?
6. Since predetermined standard time data frequently utilize data purchased from an outside source, how can one justify its use in another organization?
7. Why is performance leveling necessary?
8. In what ways are work standards used?

Minicases

Because of an apparent decrease in the operating efficiency of the Lunta Corporation, several managers feel that a work measurement program should be installed. These managers have become quite concerned about the decreasing production levels of the employees. They feel that if work standards are available, the standards could be used to provide the employees with acceptable production goals. Although the managers know that not all office activities can be measured, they are not exactly sure which activities can be measured and which cannot be measured. These managers would like you to provide them with a set of guidelines that could be used to determine which activities can be measured.

*   *   *

A work measurement program is about to be installed in the Donald Corporation. The company has determined that the work sampling technique will best meet its needs. This decision was made on the necessity for developing fairly accurate standards at a fairly reasonable cost. You, the administrative office manager, have been asked to prepare a list of suggestions to make the work sampling technique more successful for the Donald Corporation. What suggestions should be included on the list?

Case

The headquarters of the Harvey Insurance Company are located in a medium-sized city in the midwest. Although the office employees in the company are not unionized, there is talk periodically among the employees that a union might be desirable, primarily because of the below-average salaries that the office employees have been receiving. The company officials feel that the office employees are not performing as well as might be expected. Several officials claim that the below-average performance is due to the poorly qualified employees that the company has been hiring.

In order for the company to determine what can be reasonably expected of the employees and for the employees to know what they can be reasonably expected to produce, the management of the organization has decided to undertake a work measurement study. Immediately upon hearing about the work measurement study, many of the office employees became very upset. The office employees claim that the work measurement study will indicate a need for fewer employees, that their jobs will become so hectic that they will never get caught up, and that the study is a scheme to further "rip them off." To exert pressure on management, the office employees are again threatening to unionize.

You, as an office supervisor, have been placed on a special committee by the management to investigate the appropriate courses of action. As a committee member, be prepared to discuss the following questions:

1. Should management continue to pursue the development of a work measurement program in light of the fact that the employees may unionize as a result? Why or why not?

2. What suggestions can you offer for overcoming employee resistance to a work measurement program?

3. If the employees decide to call a union vote, what should management do?

Part
5
The
Process

Records
Management

Chapter
20

The Records Cycle

Organizing a Records Management Program
Objectives of the Records Management Program
Policies of the Records Management Program
Organization of the Program
Centralized control
Decentralized control
Filing Systems
Personnel
Records Retention
Benefits
Conducting the records inventory
Classifying the records
Scheduling retention periods
Storage and Retrieval of Records
Types of storage equipment
Records and information retrieval
Disposition of Records
Protection
Transfer
Microrecording
Destruction
Evaluating the Records Management Program

The Records Management Manual

Chapter Aims   After studying this chapter, the student should be able to:

1. Explain the steps in the records cycle.
2. Explain the meaning of centralized and decentralized control.
3. Discuss the advantages and disadvantages of centralized and decentralized storage.
4. Explain how a records retention schedule is developed.
5. Discuss the criteria that should be considered in selecting a particular type of storage equipment.
6. Explain the differences between records retrieval and information retrieval.
7. Discuss the various methods of disposition of records.
8. Explain finding and use ratios.
9. Identify the content to be included in a records management manual.

Chapter Terms   *Records management:* the activities designed to control the life cycle of a record from its creation to its ultimate disposition.

Life cycle: the stages through which records pass, including the following—creation, utilization, storage, retrieval, and disposition.

Filing: one of the activities in the records management program, which involves systematically classifying, coding, arranging, and placing records in storage.

Alphabetic filing: a filing method in which records are indexed according to names, subjects, or geographical areas.

Nonalphabetic filing: a filing method in which records are indexed according to a numerical or chronological sequence.

Computer output microfilm: computer output in the form of microfilm or microfiche, rather than in the form of paper or some other type of output.

Transfer: one of the methods of disposition of records, which involves changing a record from active status to inactive status.

Finding ratio: a ratio that determines how many requested records are actually found.

Use ratio: a ratio that determines if too many records are filed that are not used.

Rapidly increasing operating costs necessitate the need for the efficient management of records. Since the smooth functioning of an organization is greatly dependent upon the efficient utilization of information, **records management** is rapidly becoming a crucial, strategic area in many organizations. Considerable inefficiency and poor utilization of resources result when little or no control is exerted over the creation, utilization, and storage of records.

In this chapter, *records* refer to the informational documents utilized by an organization to carry out its various functions. Types of records commonly utilized include forms, letters, memorandums, reports, and manuals. Records management refers to the activities designed to control the **life cycle** of a record from its creation to its ultimate disposition. Therefore, a distinction is made between **filing,** which is one of the more familiar activities in the records management program, and records management.

The emergence of data processing has resulted in new applications in the storage and retrieval of information. Prior to the time that organizations utilized data processing, storage and retrieval of information involved tangible documents; but with data processing, a considerable amount of information is stored on magnetic tapes, drums, or disks. Consequently, new methods of retrieving information have been developed that add new dimensions to the records management function.

The Records Cycle   Records and other information documents typically proceed through the life cycle illustrated in Figure 20–1. One of the most important functions of the *creation stage* is to exert control over the development and adoption of new forms and records. New forms and rec-

FIGURE 20–1   Records Cycle

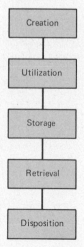

ords should be developed only when a definite need can be substantially justified; and when new forms are developed, careful attention must be given to their design. The creation stage is also concerned with developing efficient methods of entering data on documents since the accuracy and completeness of data is of utmost importance. Another important function of this stage of the cycle is determining the length of time records should be stored before their destruction.

The *utilization stage* of the records cycle is concerned with developing efficient procedures in order that desired records can be retrieved and delivered to the desired location at the desired time. Consideration is also given to developing efficient procedures through which documents will move. The effectiveness with which a document is utilized in this stage is greatly dependent upon the quality with which information is entered on the document in the creation stage.

The *storage stage* involves efficiently utilizing filing equipment and the space occupied by the equipment. For the greatest efficiency and convenience, records should be stored in a location accessible to those who utilize them. Storage is also concerned with protecting records against disaster or unauthorized use.

The *retrieval stage* involves rapidly locating requested records. In addition to "signing out" documents when removed from the files, retrieval also involves tracing documents not returned to the files within a reasonable length of time.

The *disposition stage* involves preserving valuable documents, especially those that are vital for the smooth operation of the organization. Disposition also involves the transfer of records from a high-cost storage area to a low-cost storage area, as well as the proper destruction of records no longer having any value to an organization. Microrecording of documents is also an important function of this stage.

Organizing a Records Management Program

In addition to becoming increasingly aware of the rapidly growing number of records created and the costs incurred, more and more managers are becoming cognizant of the benefits of implementing an efficient records management program. The following sections provide information about the various components of a records management program.

Objectives of the Records Management Program

One of the first priorities in developing a records management program is to clearly identify the objectives of the program. The following objectives are characteristic of many records management programs:

1. To provide control over the records cycle, i.e., the creation, utilization, storage, retrieval, and disposition of records.
2. To develop efficient procedures for each stage of the cycle.
3. To eliminate needless storage of duplicate records.

4. To reduce costs in each stage of the records cycle.

5. To develop realistic standards for employee performance and program evaluation.

6. To develop throughout the organization an awareness of and an appreciation for the value of a records management program.

7. To standardize procedures and equipment in the records management program.

Policies of the Records Management Program

Once the objectives of the records management program have been developed, general operating policies of the program should be adopted. The policies are frequently used to guide decisionmaking about various aspects of the program. The policies should be clearly worded, since vague or ambiguous policies often result in ineffective or improper actions. The following are examples of the kinds of policies frequently included in records management programs:

1. The records management program has the support of the management of the organization and is considered to be an integral organizational function.

2. Each record created in the organization comes under the jurisdiction of the records management program and, therefore, is subject to centralized control.

3. The records management program shall operate under the procedures outlined in the records management manual.

4. Records must receive adequate protection at all times.

5. The administrative office manager has primary responsibility for the records management program, but ultimate responsibility lies with the vice president for internal affairs.

6. In terms of work flow, efficiency will have precedence over cost.

Organization of the Program

The type of control and the location of the records storage determine the organization of the records management program. Some records management programs operate under centralized control, while others operate under decentralized control. The storage of records may be centralized throughout the organization, or they may be stored decentrally within the various work units.

Centralized control. When the control of a records management program is centralized, the overall authority and responsibility for the program is vested in one individual. Centralized control results in a formally organized records management program, and two alternatives for storing records are available—centralized storage and decentralized storage.

Centralized storage, which means that the records are stored in a central location within the organization, results in the following advantages:

1. The storage of duplicate records is eliminated.

2. Equipment is more efficiently utilized and, thus, fewer file cabinets are required.

3. The organization can take advantage of the cost savings that result from standardized equipment and procedures.

4. The program utilizes trained employees, which results in greater accuracy in filing records.

5. Greater control is exerted over retrieval, retention, and transfer of records.

6. Centralized storage helps to assure that all records pertaining to a particular subject are stored in one place.

7. Since the program operates continuously, it is not hampered by the absence of employees.

8. Obscure records are more quickly obtained, since their whereabouts are known.

Among the disadvantages of centralized storage are:

1. Records may become more vulnerable since they are stored in one central location.

2. Considerable time is spent transporting frequently used records to and from the central storage area.

3. If records cannot be immediately obtained, inconvenience is likely to result.

4. The confidentiality of records may be more difficult to maintain (more and more organizations are storing confidential records decentrally).

Decentralized storage means that records are kept within the various work units until time for destruction or transfer to low-cost storage areas. The following are advantages of decentralized storage: (1) confidential records are stored in work units throughout the organization and therefore are less vulnerable; (2) since the records are stored "on site," valuable time is not spent in transporting records; (3) since each work unit is primarily responsible for the storage of its own records, flexible procedures can be developed.

The following outlines the disadvantages of decentralized storage: (1) some work units are likely to develop their own procedures rather than using those of the system; (2) duplicate filing equipment may be required; (3) filing equipment may not be efficiently utilized.

Several factors should be considered when deciding whether to store records centrally or decentrally. Among the more important factors are: attitude of top management toward the storage of records, competence of personnel, size and type of the organization, philosophy of the organization with regard to centralization and decentralization, and the number and kinds of records stored.

Decentralized control. With decentralized control, each work unit assumes responsibility for the management of its own records. Decentralized control results in duplication of equipment, records, and personnel effort, as well as results in a lack of consistency in methods and procedures. In most cases, when control is decentralized, so is the storage of records.

Filing Systems

Another component of the records management program is the filing system, which involves systematically classifying, coding, arranging, and placing records in storage so that they can be quickly and easily retrieved when needed. Most organizations use standardized filing rules approved by the American Records Management Association. Cross-referencing of materials is also frequently involved in the filing process.

Two general filing methods exist—**alphabetic** and **nonalphabetic.** The alphabetic method consists of three specialized indexing systems— filing by *name*, *subject*, or *geographical* area, while the nonalphabetic method is comprised of *numerical* and *chronological* indexing systems. Many organizations use a combination of two or more indexing systems. Figure 20–2 illustrates the indexing systems.

Most organizations use one of the alphabetic indexing systems. Each of the three alphabetic indexing systems utilizes alphabetic sections (A, B, C, D, etc.), and filing rules determine the alphabetic sections under which records are filed. Each system also utilizes two types of folders— individual and miscellaneous—for each alphabetic section. When a specified number of records (usually five) are filed under a particular category, a separate individual folder is then prepared. For example, when the specified number of records pertaining to "Adjustments" are filed, a file folder labeled "Adjustments" is prepared. Until the specified number of records are filed, records are placed in the appropriate miscellaneous folder. Using the above example, until the specified number of records pertaining to "Adjustments" are filed, records pertaining to this subject are filed in the "A" miscellaneous folder, along with other records of insufficient quantity to warrant an individual folder. Records within each miscellaneous folder are filed alphabetically, with the most recent record for each category filed at the front of the category.

Both of the numeric systems utilize a number system in the filing of records. Numeric systems are used extensively for filing records numbered serially and for records on which the date is an important information item. Examples of records filed by numeric systems are purchase orders, sales slips, invoices, etc.

When the numerical indexing system is used, each category is assigned an individual number. To illustrate this system, the salesmen in an organization are the categories, and the records pertaining to each salesman are filed by their individual numbers. Cross-referencing is crucial to the numerical system. In the example used above, the name of

FIGURE 20–2   Alphabetic and Nonalphabetic Indexing Systems

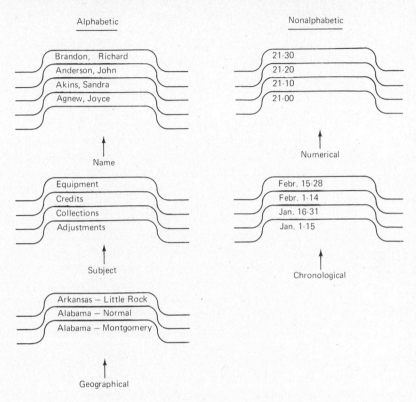

each salesman and his number are recorded on a three-by-five inch index card, and since the cards are filed alphabetically, the cross-reference index is used to determine under what number a particular individual's records are filed. Although time is consumed when using the cross-reference index, this system is useful when the secrecy and confidentiality of records must be maintained.

With the chronological indexing system, records are filed by significant dates. In some cases, this indexing system is used to follow up situations that require attention by some specific date. In other cases, the system is used for filing such records as daily reports and sales summaries. When the chronological indexing system is used, the record being filed is placed in front of all others in the file folder; thus, the file is arranged with the most recent record on top of the accumulation and the least recent record on the bottom.

Personnel   The personnel needs of the records management program are greatly influenced by two factors: the type of organization utilized in the program and the size of the organization. Centralized control utilizes personnel working with records full time; decentralized storage may result in personnel working with records part time. Some organizations have found that when converting from decentralized storage to centralized storage, more personnel are needed to staff the records management program. Over the long run, the expertise and specialization provided by the full-time personnel are apt to offset the increased labor costs.

In small organizations utilizing centralized control and storage in their records management program, responsibility frequently rests with the administrative office manager, but all day-to-day operations are performed by one employee, usually a file clerk. As organizations increase in size, greater specialization takes place. Responsibility for the program is still likely to rest with the administrative office manager, but a file supervisor manages the day-to-day operations, and the support staff is comprised of file clerks, requisition clerks, and messengers. While the file clerks are responsible for filing and retrieving records, the requisition clerks approve requests after determining whether the request is valid and whether the individual making the request has proper authorization to do so. The requisition clerks are also responsible for the followup of materials not returned to central storage after a reasonable length of time. Messengers deliver requested records and return records to the central storage area for refiling.

In extremely large organizations, a records manager—rather than the administrative office manager—assumes responsibility for the management of records, and the mechanical aspects of the program are carried out by the support staff.

As more organizations develop data processing systems, records management personnel are becoming increasingly familiar with data processing and other types of automation since such equipment is frequently used in the retrieval of information. Protection and storage of information recorded on various kinds of magnetic devices utilized in data processing systems are likely to be under the jurisdiction of the records management program.

Records Retention

Records retention, another important component of the records management program, uses retention schedules to specify the length of time that records and documents must be retained by an organization.

Benefits. Systematic records retention provides an organization with several benefits. Among the more important are the following:

1. Considerable cost and space savings result from transferring inactive status records to low-cost storage areas and from ultimately destroying records no longer useful to the organization.

2. Retrieval of records is simplified since fewer active status records are stored.

3. Systematic destruction of records prevents their being destroyed prematurely.

4. Equipment for storing records—both active status and inactive status—is more efficiently utilized.

Conducting the records inventory. Prior to developing a records retention schedule, it is important to determine the nature and volume of all records created and filed, which is the major reason for conducting the records inventory. To conduct the records inventory by sorting through the files record by record would result in considerable time consumption and effort. An overall view of what has been created and filed is usually sufficient. To facilitate the process, a records inventory form similar to the one illustrated in Figure 20–3 is useful.

If the records are stored decentrally, cooperation of each department head is essential; otherwise, the inventory is likely to be somewhat inaccurate. Often a liaison person is appointed within each department to assist the personnel conducting the inventory.

Classifying the records. After the records inventory has been completed, the next step in the development of a comprehensive records management program is to classify records according to their value to the organization. A widely used classification scheme, which was developed by

FIGURE 20–3   Records Inventory Form

Name or Title or Record	Form Identification No. (if Used)	Type of Copy (Original, Carbon Copy, etc.)	Location	Number and Location of Carbon Copies (if in Existence)	Indexing Method	Volume (in Linear Feet)	Inclusive Dates of Records	Frequency of Use and by Whom

the National Fire Protection Association,[1] uses the following four categories to classify records: vital, important, useful, and nonessential.

Vital records comprise those records needed by an organization for its continued existence. Since records with this classification must be kept permanently, their protection and storage is of utmost importance. Examples of vital records include certain accounting, personnel, legal, corporate, and production records. To guard against a catastrophe, many organizations store duplicate or photographed copies of vital records in several different locations. Much vital information is stored on magnetic devices, which creates some special problems since this information is virtually useless without the computer programs and equipment with which to access and process the information.

Important records, although no longer considered to be of current use to an organization, should be adequately protected. When such records lose their active status and become inactive, they are transferred to low-cost storage areas. Examples of records with this classification are certain kinds of financial, sales, and personnel records.

Useful records lose their value after a short period of time—perhaps after only a few months. When records with this classification are no longer useful, they should be immediately destroyed. Most general correspondence and certain data processing records receive this classification.

Nonessential records have little or no perceived value and consequently should be destroyed as soon as they have served their intended purpose. Most nonessential records are used for such a short period of time that they are never formally filed. Nonessential records frequently consist of form, sales, and advertising letters; brochures; and interoffice memorandums.

Scheduling retention periods. The records retention schedule, used with considerable frequency in a records management program, specifies the length of time that each record is to be kept prior to destruction. It does not designate when records should be transferred from active status to inactive status. This means that if the retention schedule indicates that a certain record has a life of three years, the record will be ready for destruction after three years have passed.

The development of the records retention schedule involves several well-defined steps, which include:

1. Getting authorization to develop the schedule.
2. Conducting a records inventory to determine the kinds, volume, location, etc., of stored records.

---

[1] Quoted, with permission, from NFPA 232, *Protection of Records*, Copyright, 1975, National Fire Protection Association, Boston, MA.

3. Developing a records classification scheme in order that the value of each kind of record may be determined.

4. Developing a tenative retention schedule.

5. Securing top management's approval of the schedule.

6. Distributing the approved schedule to appropriate individuals.

Generally, a committee is appointed to develop the schedule. In smaller organizations, a representative from each work unit might be appointed to serve on the committee. In larger organizations, where having a representative from each work unit would be too cumbersome, an individual should be appointed to represent several work units.

In addition to relying on the judgment of the committee members to develop the records retention schedule, several other factors should be considered. Since some records have legal significance and value for specified periods of time, the statute of limitations should be considered. The statutes, which vary from state to state, specify the legal life of certain records. *The Guide to Records Retention Requirements*, published annually by the U.S. Government Printing Office, lists retention periods of records as required by departments of the federal government. The legal life of other records is determined by federal legislative acts—the Walsh-Healey and Fair Labor Standards Acts, for example.

After the tentative records retention schedule has been developed, but before it receives final approval, the organization's tax specialist, attorney, and chief financial officer should examine the schedule with close scrutiny. The insight of these individuals is very helpful. In some instances, one or more of these specialists are appointed to serve on the committee that develops the records retention schedule.

As is true with all programs and policies, the records retention schedule should be reviewed periodically to determine if revision is necessary. As additional legislation is passed and as the use and quantity of records changes, the schedule may need to be updated.

An example of a records retention schedule is presented in Figure 20–4.

Storage and Retrieval of Records

The success of the records management program is also significantly affected by the equipment used for the storage of records and the efficiency with which the equipment is utilized. When purchasing storage equipment, every attempt should be made to assure that it will meet the needs for which it is intended.

An advantage of the centrally controlled records management program results from the standardization of storage equipment. Through standardization, equipment will be the same size and will have the same durability, capacity, and design characteristics. Of particular significance is the temperature that the equipment is able to withstand, especially for the storage of vital and important records.

FIGURE 20–4   Records Retention Timetable

Legend for Authority to Dispose	Legend for Retention Period
AD—Administrative Decision	AC—Dispose After Completion of Job or Contract
ASPR—Armed Services Procurement Regulation	AE—Dispose After Expiration
CFR—Code of Federal Regulations	AF—After End of Fiscal Year
FLSA—Fair Labor Standards Act	AM—After Moving
ICC—Interstate Commerce Commission	AS—After Settlement
INS—Insurance Company Regulation	AT—Dispose After Termination
	ATR—After Trip
ISM—Industrial Security Manual, Attachment to DD Form 441	OBS—Dispose When Obsolete
	P—Permanent
	SUP—Dispose When Superseded

Type of Record	Retention Period Years	Authority
ACCOUNTING & FISCAL		
Accounts Payable Invoices	3	ASPR-STATE, FLSA
Accounts Payable Ledger	P	AD
Accounts Receivable Ledgers	5	AD
Approvals		
Authorizations for Accounting	SUP	AD
Balance Sheets	P	AD
Bank Deposits	3	AD
Bank Statements	3	AD
Bonds	P	AD
Budgets	3	AD
Capital Asset Record	3*	AD
Cash Receipt Records	7	AD
Check Register	P	AD
Checks, Dividend	6	
Checks, Payroll	2	FLSA, STATE
Checks, Voucher	3	FLSA, STATE
Cost Accounting Records	5	AD
Earnings Register	3	FLSA, STATE
Entertainment Gifts & Gratuities	3	AD
Estimates, Projections	7	AD

* After Disposed
** Normally
† Govt. R&D Contracts

Courtesy Electric Wastebasket Corp., New York, N.Y. 10036

FIGURE 20–4 Records Retention Timetable (continued)

Type of Record	Retention Period Years	Authority
ACCOUNTING & FISCAL (CONT'D)		
Expense Reports	3	AD
Financial Statements, Certified	P	AD
Financial Statements, Periodic	2	AD
General Ledger Records	P	CFR
Labor Cost Records	3	ASPR, CFR
Magnetic Tape and Tab Cards	1**	
Note Register	P	AD
Payroll Registers	3	FLSA, STATE
Petty Cash Records	3	AD
P & L Statements	P	AD
Salesman Commission Reports	3	AD
Travel Expense Reports	3	AD
Work Papers, Rough	2	AD
ADMINISTRATIVE RECORDS		
Audit Reports	10	AD
Audit Work Papers	3	AD
Classified Documents: Inventories, Reports, Receipts	10	AD
Correspondence, Executive	P	AD
Correspondence, General	5	AD
Directives from Officers	P	AD
Forms Used, File Copies	P	AD
Systems and Procedures Records	P	AD
Work Papers, Management Projects	P	AD
COMMUNICATIONS		
Bulletins Explaining Communications	P	AD
Messenger Records	1	AD
Phone Directories	SUP	AD
Phone Installation Records	1	AD
Postage Reports, Stamp Requisitions	1 AF	AD
Postal Records, Registered Mail & Insured Mail Logs & Meter Records	1 AF	AD, CFR
Telecommunications Copies	1	AD
CONTRACT ADMINISTRATION		
Contracts, Negotiated. Bailments, Changes, Specifications, Procedures, Correspondence	P	CFR
Customer Reports	P	AD

FIGURE 20–4   Records Retention Timetable (continued)

Type of Record	Retention Period Years	Authority
CONTRACT ADMINISTRATION (CONT'D)		
Materials Relating to Distribution Revisions, Forms, and Format of Reports	P	AD
Work Papers	OBS	AD
CORPORATE		
Annual Reports	P	AD
Authority to Issue Securities	P	AD
Bonds, Surety	3 AE	AD
Capital Stock Ledger	P	AD
Charters, Constitutions, Bylaws	P	AD
Contracts	20 AT	AD
Corporate Election Records	P	AD
Incorporation Records	P	AD
Licenses—Federal, State, Local	AT	AD
Stock Transfer & Stockholder	P	AD
LEGAL		
Claims and Litigation Concerning Torts and Breach of Contracts	P	AD
Law Records—Federal, State, Local	SUP	AD
Patents and Related Material	P	AD
Trademark & Copyrights	P	AD
LIBRARY, COMPANY		
Accession Lists	P	AD
Copies of Requests for Materials	6 mos.	AD
Meeting Calendars	P	AD
Research Papers, Abstracts, Bibliographies	SUP, 6 mos. AC	AD
MANUFACTURING		
Bills of Material	2	AD, ASPR
Drafting Records	P	AD†
Drawings	2	AD, ASPR
Inspection Records	2	AD
Lab Test Reports	P	AD
Memos, Production	AC	AD
Product, Tooling, Design, Engineering Research, Experiment & Specs Records	20	STATUTE LIMITATIONS

FIGURE 20–4   Records Retention Timetable (continued)

Type of Record	Retention Period Years	Authority
MANUFACTURING (CONT'D)		
Production Reports	3	AD
Quality Reports	1 AC	AD
Reliability Records	P	AD
Stock Issuing Records	3 AT	AD, ASPR
Tool Control	3 AT	AD, ASPR
Work Orders	3	AD
Work Status Reports	AC	AD
OFFICE SUPPLIES & SERVICES		
Inventories	1 AF	AD
Office Equipment Records	6 AF	AD
Requests for Services	1 AF	AD
Requisitions for Supplies	1 AF	AD
PERSONNEL		
Accident Reports, Injury Claims, Settlements	30 AS	CFR, INS, STATE
Applications, Changes & Terminations	50	AD, ASPR, CFR
Attendance Records	7	AD
Employee Activity Files	2 or SUP	AD
Employee Contracts	6 AT	AD
Fidelity Bonds	3 AT	AD
Garnishments	5	AD
Health & Safety Bulletins	P	AD
Injury Frequency Charts	P	CFR
Insurance Records, Employees	11 AT	INS
Job Descriptions	2 or SUP	CFR
Rating Cards	2 or SUP	CFR
Time Cards	3	AD
Training Manuals	P	AD
Union Agreements	3	WALSH-HEALEY ACT
PLANT & PROPERTY RECORDS		
Depreciation Schedules	P	AD
Inventory Records	P	AD
Maintenance & Repair, Building	10	AD
Maintenance & Repair, Machinery	5	AD
Plant Account Cards, Equipment	P	CFR, AD
Property Deeds	P	AD

FIGURE 20–4   Records Retention Timetable (continued)

Type of Record	Retention Period Years	Authority
PLANT & PROPERTY RECORDS (CONT'D)		
Purchase or Lease Records of Plant Facility	P	AD
Space Allocation Records	1 AT	AD
PRINTING & DUPLICATING		
Copies Produced, Tech. Pubs., Charts	1 or OBS	AD
Film Reports	5	AD
Negatives	5	AD
Photographs	1	AD
Production Records	1 AC	AD
PROCUREMENT, PURCHASING		
Acknowledgments	AC	AD
Bids, Awards	3 AT	CFR
Contracts	3 AT	AD
Exception Notices (GAO)	6	AD
Price Lists	OBS	AD
Purchase Orders, Requisitions	3 AT	CFR
Quotations	1	AD
PRODUCTS, SERVICES, MARKETING		
Correspondence	3	AD
Credit Ratings & Classifications	7	AD
Development Studies	P	AD
Presentations & Proposals	P	AD
Price Lists, Catalogs	OBS	AD
Prospect Lines	OBS	AD
Register of Sales Orders	NO VALUE	AD
Surveys	P	AD
Work Papers, Pertaining to Projects	NO VALUE	AD
PUBLIC RELATIONS & ADVERTISING		
Advertising Activity Reports	5	AD
Community Affairs Records	P	AD
Contracts for Advertising	3 AT	AD
Employee Activities & Presentations	P	AD
Exhibits, Releases, Handouts	2–4	AD
Internal Publications	P (1 copy)	AD
Layouts	1	AD
Manuscripts	1	AD

FIGURE 20–4 Records Retention Timetable (continued)

Type of Record	Retention Period Years	Authority
PUBLIC RELATIONS & ADVERTISING (CONT'D)		
Photos	1	AD
Public Information Activity	7	AD
Research Presentations	P	AD
Tear-Sheets	2	AD
SECURITY		
Classified Material Violations	P	AD
Courier Authorizations	1 mo. ATR	AD
Employee Clearance Lists	SUP	ISM
Employee Case Files	5	ISM
Fire Prevention Program	P	AD
Protection—Guards, Badge Lists, Protective Devices	5	AD
Subcontractor Clearances	2 AT	AD
Visitor Clearance	2	ISM
TAXATION		
Annuity or Deferred Payment Plan	P	CFR
Depreciation Schedules	P	CFR
Dividend Register	P	CFR
Employee Withholding	4	CFR
Excise Exemption Certificates	4	CFR
Excise Reports (Manufacturing)	4	CFR
Excise Reports (Retail)	4	CFR
Inventory Reports	P	CFR
Tax Bills and Statements	P	AD
Tax Returns	P	AD
TRAFFIC & TRANSPORTATION		
Aircraft Operating & Maintenance	P	CFR
Bills of Lading, Waybills	2	ICC, FLSA
Employee Travel	1 AF	AD
Freight Bills	3	ICC
Freight Claims	2	ICC
Household Moves	3 AM	AD
Motor Operating & Maintenance	2	AD
Rates and Tariffs	SUP	AD
Receiving Documents	2–10	AD, CFR
Shipping & Related Documents	2–10	AD, CFR

Before deciding upon a particular kind of storage equipment, various criteria should be considered:

1. The nature of the records being stored, including size, quantity, weight, physical composition, and value.
2. The frequency with which records are retrieved.
3. The length of time that records are stored in active status and in inactive status.
4. The location of storage facilities (centralized and decentralized).
5. The amount of space allocated for storage and the possibilities for expansion.
6. The type and location of storage for inactive records.
7. The layout of the organization.
8. The degree to which stored records should be protected.

Types of storage equipment. Equipment designed for mass storage of records can be categorized as *vertical, lateral,* and *power.* Each category of storage equipment consists of a variety of different types of equipment.

Vertical equipment is the type most commonly used in records management programs; and of the various types of vertical equipment, the standard four-, five-, or six-drawer file cabinet is most common. While using approximately 2.5 square feet of floor space, additional space must be allowed for opening drawers. A distinct advantage of the standard file cabinet is the ease with which it may be moved with its contents intact.

Another type of vertical equipment often used in records management programs is the open shelf file. Although the open shelf file makes good utilization of space (the files frequently extend from floor to ceiling) and improves storage efficiency, this equipment is recommended only for records that are filed and removed with the folders intact. It is not well suited for situations where individual records are frequently removed from folders (see Figure 20–5a).

Several types of vertical rotary files have also been developed. In a comparable amount of floor space, this type of equipment holds considerably more records than does the standard file. Because of its rotary feature, retrieval is fast and easy (see Figure 20–5b).

Vertical equipment is most often used for the storage of inactive records in low-cost storage areas. Records are frequently stored in cardboard containers that are placed on steel shelves extending from floor to ceiling. The containers are often the same ones used to transfer records from high-cost storage areas to low-cost storage areas.

Lateral equipment, although vertical in structure, utilizes lateral pull-out drawers, which require considerably less space than standard file cabinets. Storing records in drawers rather than on open shelves may expedite retrieval. Since lateral equipment can be insulated and equipped

FIGURE 20–5   Filing Equipment

20–5a: Courtesy, Aurora Steel Products

with locking doors on the front, some consider lateral equipment to have distinct advantages over open shelf files that are not so constructed (see Figure 20–5c).

Power filing equipment, although not necessarily new, is being installed with increasing frequency in organizations throughout the country. Comparatively, the initial investment is considerably greater with power equipment than with other types of storage equipment. Some types of power equipment reduce the number of personnel needed in the records management function—and the resulting savings in labor costs can be used to offset the cost of the equipment.

When installation of power equipment is being considered, several factors should receive primary consideration:

1. Structurally, will the floor withstand the weight of the equipment?

20–5b: Courtesy, Acme Visible Records, Inc., Crozet, VA.

2. Since the installation of this type of equipment is permanent, have future storage space needs received adequate consideration?

3. What effect will power outages have on the system; i.e., can the system be operated manually?

4. Do the equipment and physical environment provide adequate protection and security for the stored records?

5. Are service representatives located nearby in the event of equipment malfunction?

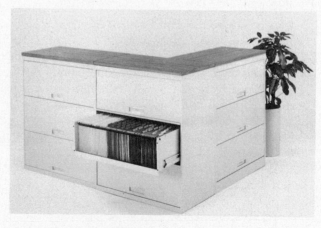

20–5c: Courtesy, The HON Company

Power equipment consists of three basic types: (1) card files specially designed to accommodate a particular size card or form; (2) structural files designed to accommodate all kinds of forms and records; (3) mobile files. Card files are frequently used by organizations to store information about customers or clients—for example, patient records in hospitals or doctors' offices. Power is used to rotate the file bins until the desired bin is accessible and the file clerk then retrieves the requested record (see Figure 20–5d).

Structural power files are typically used to store all types of records—not just one type of record as is characteristic of card files. Some of the newer heavy-duty files are equipped with an electronic eye, and at the push of a button, the transport mechanism scans and locates the desired storage container. A retrieval mechanism then connects with the storage container and moves it to the console operator who retrieves the requested record. Structural power files are often custom designed to meet the special needs of a particular records management program (see Figure 20–5e).

For classification purposes, the mobile file equipment is classified as a power unit even though some units are operated manually. Since mobile units eliminate the need for file space, they are especially useful where storage space is limited. Shelves are stored back to back against

20–5d: Courtesy, Sperry Univac, Office Equipment Division, Sperry Rand Company

20–5e: Courtesy, Supreme Equipment and Systems Corporation

one another, and a rail system allows the shelves to be readily moved either forward or backward, and thus, aisle space between two shelf units is created. When access is needed between two shelves that are back to back, the two shelves are spread apart either by power or manually to create aisle space between them. Only one aisle can exist within the unit at any one time; therefore, the remainder of the unit is nonaccessible because all other shelves are back to back (see Figure 20–5f).

Records and information retrieval. A distinction is made between records retrieval and information retrieval. *Records retrieval* refers to the activities involved in locating and removing tangible records from the files. *Information retrieval,* on the other hand, refers primarily to the activities involved in accessing information from computer magnetic media or microforms (which includes microfilm). Information retrieval involves two primary stages: (1) accessing the desired information, and (2) transforming the information into a readable state.

Although many organizations utilize computer systems and microforms, records retrieval is still very commonplace. A step-by-step outline for retrieving records stored in a central storage area involves: (1) the individual making the request fills out a request slip, which is transported to the central storage facility, (2) the requisition clerk approves the request and asks the file clerk to retrieve the record, (3) the record

20–5f: Courtesy, Lundia, Myers Industries, Inc.

is transported either by messenger or by a mechanical device to the individual making the request, (4) the record is returned to the central storage area when no longer needed by the individual making the request. The procedures for manual retrieval are very similar for both power and nonpower equipment.

The success of information retrieval is clearly dependent upon the quality of the indexing and coding systems used to identify the location of the stored information. For example, microrecording results in a size reduction of approximately 98 percent. Thus, the information stored in one hundred file cabinets can be stored in approximately two cabinets when microrecorded. This example readily illustrates the need for extremely accurate, efficient indexing and coding systems.

To make microforms readable, the forms are magnified by a reader. If a tangible or hard copy of the microform is desired, a reader-printer is used. The microrecording process will be discussed in greater detail in the Disposition of Records section of this chapter.

The format of the microform, to a great extent, determines which retrieval method will be used. The most common formats are films, reels, rolls, and cartridges (accurately called microfilm); aperture cards; microfiche; ultrafiche; and jackets. Since the latter two do not lend themselves to mechanical retrieval, they will not be discussed in this chapter. Aperture cards, microfiche, and ultrafiche are more accurately labeled microforms, since their formats are not strips of film. The various types of microforms are illustrated in Figure 20–6.

Several systems have been developed to facilitate the indexing of microfilm. One of the more extensive systems is Miracode, a system developed by Eastman Kodak Company. Adjacent to each frame on the

FIGURE 20–6   Types of Microforms

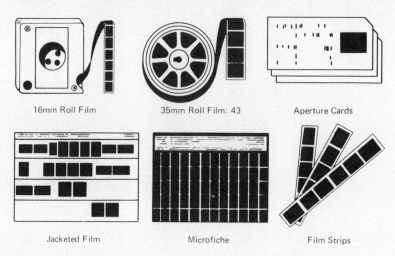

16mm Roll Film   35mm Roll Film: 43   Aperture Cards

Jacketed Film   Microfiche   Film Strips

Courtesy, Hitchcock Publishing Co.

film strip, a binary code index notation is made. To find a specific frame, the film is inserted into a reader-printer and the binary code index of the desired frame is entered into the machine by means of a keyboard. In a matter of seconds, the desired frame is mechanically retrieved and displayed on the screen of the reader.

Aperture cards resemble data processing cards, with the exception that microimages are mounted in openings (apertures) on the cards. Using keypunch equipment, the index code is punched on the card. By means of a card sorter, the desired card can be quickly retrieved.

Microfiche, a transparent sheet containing microimages, is becoming an increasingly popular type of microform. Microfiche is actually a piece of microfilm that is commonly cut into four-inch by six-inch pieces. Depending on the reduction ratio utilized and the microrecording technique, varying numbers of images can be recorded on a single microfiche. For example, if the reduction ratio being used is twenty-four to one, ninety-eight pages measuring eight and one-half inches by eleven inches can be recorded on a single piece of microfiche. If a reduction ratio of forty-two to one is being used, 325 pages can be recorded on the same sheet of microfiche. For quick retrieval of a specific image, a coordinate indexing system is used. After the microfiche has been inserted in the reader, a locating grid is used to find the index coordinates of the desired image, thus readily locating and displaying the desired image. For filing purposes, the general content of the microfiche is identified at the top of each fiche and is called the fiche title.

Several types of automated systems have been developed that rapidly retrieve microforms simply by entering the proper record index into the system by means of a keyboard located on a display unit. The system illustrated in Figure 20–7 holds thousands of microforms. Once the proper index has been entered, the desired image is automatically retrieved and projected on the unit's display screen. These systems will accommodate several display units located a reasonable distance from the system's central storage unit. The automated systems are most frequently designed to accommodate microfiche and aperture cards.

To retrieve and access information stored within a computer sys-

FIGURE 20–7   Automated Microfiche Retrieval System

Courtesy, Infodetics Corporation

tem, keyboard terminal equipment is often used. One type of keyboard terminal device resembles a typewriter. The device is connected directly to the computer. By means of the keyboard, the index code of the desired information is entered into the computer and is typed on paper rolls that move through the typewriter. In a matter of seconds, the desired information is fed back through the terminal and is typed on paper rolls.

Another terminal device, illustrated in Figure 20–8, used to retrieve information from a computer is the cathode ray tube, frequently referred to as a CRT. The CRT has a keyboard and display screen, and information is retrieved by means of a keyboard located on the unit. After the designated code for the desired information has been entered on the keyboard, the information appears on the screen in a matter of seconds. Hard copies of information can be obtained if the display unit is equipped with certain devices.

Another method of retrieving and utilizing computer prepared information is **computer output microfilm,** more commonly referred to as COM. The magnetic device on which computer readable language is

FIGURE 20–8   Cathode Ray Tube

Courtesy, Burroughs Corporation

contained (tape, disks, etc.) is used to prepare documents. Prior practice has been to pass this tape through the computer, which utilizes only a small portion of its capacity, to print the information onto paper using an impact printer capable of speeds up to 2,000 print lines per minute.

Using COM, these same documents can be produced on microfilm, or more commonly, microfiche, at speeds twenty to twenty-five times faster than printing. In addition, each microfiche is individually titled, describing the range of information it contains, and an index frame, usually in the lower right-hand corner, provides a cross-reference coordinate location for each "page" or image on the fiche. The primary advantages of COM are its speed; the increased data retrieval speed using fiche; the increased data availability, since fiche copies are easily and inexpensively created; the decreased cost of data distribution; the reduction of storage space; and the environmental advantages of disposing of the fiche as opposed to volumes of paper. It should be pointed out that the equipment costs of a COM operation are extremely high. To make COM economically feasible, many organizations contract service companies to provide COM.

Disposition of Records

Disposition refers to the ultimate fate of records. For example, some records are permanently stored. Others are transferred to low-cost storage areas where they may be either permanently stored or eventually destroyed. Still others are microrecorded, while others are immediately destroyed. The four major methods of records disposition are: protection, **transfer,** microrecording, and destruction.

Protection. The value attached to vital records is a basic factor in determining the type of protection the records are to receive. The protection afforded most vital records is in the form of insulated, fire resistant safes and vaults. If this protection is not adequate, vital records can be duplicated and the copies stored in several different locations.

Transfer. Transfer refers to changing the active status of a record to inactive status. In many instances, as soon as the status of records has changed, they are transferred from the high-cost storage areas to the low-cost storage areas. A basic factor used to determine when records should be transferred is their frequency of use. For example, records that are referred to at least three times a month should be considered active. If a record is referred to twice a month, it is still considered active but should probably be stored in the less accessible areas of the storage center (for example, in the lower drawers of file cabinets). Records that are referred to not more than once a month should be considered inactive and, therefore, should be transferred to low-cost storage areas. In all probability, most of the records found in active status will be the current year's and the past year's records.

The two most common methods of transfer are *perpetual* and *periodic*. When the perpetual method is used, records are continuously transferred to low-cost storage areas. The records are continuously examined, and those whose age render them inactive are then transferred.

When periodic transfer is used, the files are examined at frequent intervals (perhaps every four months), and the inactive materials are transferred. An adaptation of the periodic transfer method is the *duplicate equipment technique*, which requires a double set of files and equipment. The current year's records are stored in one set of file cabinets. The previous year's records are filed in the other set of cabinets, which are located beside the current year's files. After a year has passed, transfer takes place. The current year's records (now a year old) become the previous year's records. The previous records (now two years old) are transferred to low-cost storage or destroyed, and the now empty set of files are used for the current filing of records.

Microrecording. Microrecording, as a means of records disposition, is used primarily for two reasons: (1) it can significantly reduce the amount of space needed to store records; (2) it is a means of making duplicate copies of those records sufficiently important to justify keeping duplicate copies.

Several questions need to be thoroughly considered before the decision is made to install a microrecording system. For many organizations, the following question is perhaps the most important: Can and how will the high cost of the system be offset? Obviously, the greater the number of ways that the system can be made to pay for itself, the more advantageous its installation will be.

Much of the cost of a microrecording system can be attributed to the equipment. A minimum of three pieces are needed: a camera to photograph the records; a processor to process or develop the film; and a reader that magnifies the images so that they can be read. Another piece of equipment frequently used is the reader-printer, which magnifies the images and produces hard copies of the records when needed. Film duplicators produce duplicate copies, which is less expensive than photographing the records a second time. If large numbers of microforms are stored, automated retrieval equipment becomes essential. The installation of a COM system requires still more equipment. In addition to equipment costs, there are labor and supplies costs.

After the decision has been made to install a microrecording system, decisions concerning what to microrecord have to be made. The following questions should be considered:

1. *How long is the record to be kept?* Generally, records must be kept for at least four years before microrecording is financially feasible.

For each year longer than four years that records are retained, microrecording becomes increasingly desirable.

2. *Will the physical characteristics of certain records prevent their being microrecorded?* The quality of the microform will be no better than the quality of the original. Dark colors sometimes do not photograph well when black and white film is used.

3. *Will the microform be admissible as evidence in legal courts?* More and more microforms are becoming acceptable as court evidence, but before original copies are destroyed, appropriate laws should be checked.

4. *Is there sufficient volume of certain records to warrant their microrecording?* Generally, the greater the number of records, the more advantageous microrecording is apt to be.

5. *Considering the frequency of use, would it be more convenient to refer to the original record or the microform?* If efficient procedures are utilized, the original record and the microform should be about equal in terms of convenience of use.

Destruction. After records have been in existence the length of time stipulated by the records retention schedule, they should be considered ready for destruction. Several destruction methods are available. In warmer climates, the heating requirements of some buildings can be partially or wholly provided by the burning of records in incinerators. Other organizations shred records and sell the paper for packing and for other industrial purposes. For ecological reasons, many organizations are disposing of records by recycling. In any event, the destruction of confidential records must be closely regulated. When records are destroyed, a certificate of destruction is usually prepared that identifies the date on which the document was destroyed.

Evaluating the Records Management Program

Records management programs should be periodically evaluated, especially those recently developed. As programs have been in existence for longer periods of time, the evaluations can probably be conducted with less frequency, with the first evaluation being conducted after the program has been operating for six to nine months.

The **finding** and **use** ratios are frequently used to evaluate the condition of the files in which records are stored. The finding ratio is used to determine how many requested records are actually found. The formula is as follows:

$$\text{Finding Ratio} = \frac{\text{Number of records not found}}{\text{Number of records found}}$$

Thus, if 200 requested records were found and two were not, the finding ratio of 1 percent would result. The suitable range for the finding ratio is 3 percent or less. Ratios over 3 percent indicate that one or more of the following conditions may exist: (1) records are misfiled; (2) records are not properly indexed or coded; (3) records are not promptly returned to the storage area for refiling; (4) the whereabouts of records are not known because of improper checkout procedures.

The use ratio is used to determine if too many records are filed that are not used. The formula is:

$$\text{Use Ratio} = \frac{\text{Number of records used}}{\text{Number of records not used}}$$

A ratio of 20 percent or higher is generally considered satisfactory. The following situations may be responsible for a low use ratio: (1) too many records are being maintained in active status when they should be transferred to inactive status; (2) individuals are using duplicate records rather than requesting records from the central storage area.

Using performance standards is another means of evaluating the records management program. Comparing employees' performance against reliable standards will provide some evidence about employee efficiency in carrying out the mechanical aspects of the program. The comparison will indicate whether or not the employees are performing at an acceptable rate or at an above-average rate. For those employees not performing at acceptable levels, training in appropriate areas may be desirable. Figure 20–9 illustrates performance standards for filing and other related activities. It should be noted that these standards were developed under certain conditions, and unless the organization is able to duplicate the conditions under which the standards were originally developed, adjustments may need to be made.

FIGURE 20–9   Filing Standards

Tasks	Units per Hour
Type 3 x 5 inch cards, labels, or tags	100
Code one-page letters	200
Sort 3 x 5 inch cards	300
Sort indexed or coded correspondence	250
File 3 x 5 inch cards	180
File correspondence	250
File vouchers numerically	700
Retrieve 3 x 5 inch cards	180
Retrieve correspondence and prepare charge-out forms	70

Source: Wilmer O. Maedke, Mary F. Robek, and Gerald F. Brown, *Information and Records Management*, Beverly Hills: Glencoe Press, 1974, p. 160. Reprinted with permission.

Comparing the operation costs of the records management program with standard operating costs is another means of evaluating the program. Acceptable standard operating costs vary among organizations and geographical areas, but the following guidelines are typical:

Salaries—75–80 percent
Equipment and Supplies—15–20 percent
Space—5–10 percent

The Records Management Manual

Once the records management program has been implemented, the records management manual becomes crucial. After it has been prepared, the manual should be approved and then periodically updated as changes are made in the program. The manual should also be made available to each employee who works with the management of records.

Appropriate content sections for inclusion in the manual include:

1. Objectives of the records management program.
2. Statement of policy of the program.
3. Organization structure of the program.
4. Filing systems used in the program and the types of records filed under each system.
5. Personnel structure of the program.
6. Records retention schedule.
7. Procedures for records and information retrieval.
8. Disposition of records, including protection, transfer, microrecording, and destruction.
9. Procedures for evaluating the program.

Review Questions

1. Review the differences between records management and filing.
2. What is meant by records disposition?
3. In deciding whether the storage of records should be centralized or decentralized, what factors should be considered?
4. What kinds of filing systems are available for use in a records management program?
5. What kinds of employees are likely to be utilized in a centralized records storage location?
6. Identify the kinds of records that are likely to be classified as vital, important, useful, and nonessential.
7. What kinds of microform formats are now available, and what are the characteristics of each?
8. What is COM?
9. Explain the perpetual, periodic, and duplicate equipment methods of records transfer.

10. How can the effectiveness of a records management program be evaluated?

Minicases

For several years, several of the managers of the Davidson Corporation felt that the company should develop a centralized records management program. This feeling prevailed primarily because of the increasing inefficiency and inability to control the present decentralized system. Jack Daniels, who was administrative office manager for the company for twenty years, vigorously fought the centralization of the records management program. He felt that the cost of a centralized program would be far greater than the cost of a decentralized program. Upon his retirement two years ago, the managers saw an opportunity to install a centralized program, which they promptly did. The centralized program has now been functioning for one year; and while there is evidence that the program is functioning well, several managers now feel it is time to evaluate the effectiveness of the new program. What procedures might be used to evaluate the effectiveness of the program? Explain how you would use the various procedures that you selected.

*   *   *

The Manderson Company has been using the periodic method of records transfer. At the end of each three-month period, the files are searched for records whose active life has expired, which makes such records eligible for transfer to inactive storage. The employees in the central storage area frequently complain about this method. The criticism seems to be centered around the following: the interruption of their normal work four times a year to go through the files, the duplication of effort, and so forth. Several of the employees feel that the duplicate equipment method may be more advantageous, since the employees would not have to transfer records four times a year. Which method do you feel may be more advantageous? Why? What are the disadvantages of the method you recommend?

Case

Approximately five years ago, the A–1 Company, a wholesale automotive parts distributor, designed and implemented a centralized records storage system. All records other than those classified as confidential are stored centrally. The system was designed and implemented by Jackson Albert, who left A–1 about two years ago to accept a position as vice president for corporate affairs in an insurance company in a neighboring state.

Over the past several months, Thomas Cady, Albert's successor, has been hearing a growing number of complaints about the centralized system. The following complaints are most frequent:

1. Records cannot be retrieved rapidly enough.

2. Some records that have been requisitioned have never been found.

3. It is not always possible to determine the whereabouts of records that have been checked out of the central storage area.

4. Some employees keep in their offices duplicate copies of records so they don't have to wait for records to be delivered from central storage.

5. There are discrepancies as to which subject category certain records should be filed.

6. Employees who work in centralized storage find the work boring and monotonous.

The company is now thinking of returning to a decentralized storage system whereby records would be stored in the various departments.

1. On the basis of the information presented, do you feel the company should retain centralized storage or return to a decentralized storage system?

2. If the company decides to keep the centralized storage system, what courses of action would you recommend to alleviate the problems that have been cited?

3. What factors should be considered in deciding whether to keep the centralized system or to install a decentralized system?

Systems
Analysis

Chapter
21

The Systems and Procedures Concept
    Definitions
    Objectives
    Advantages and Disadvantages
    Characteristics of Systems
    A Purchasing System: An Illustration

The Systems and Procedures Staff

Designing or Modifying Systems

Systems and Procedures Tools
    Work Load Chart
    Flow Process Chart
    Office Layout Chart
    Right- and Left-hand Chart
    Operator-Machine Process Chart
    Horizontal Flow Process Chart
    EDP Block Diagram

Chapter Aims   After studying this chapter, the student should be able to:

1. Identify the components that comprise a system.
2. Explain the relationship between a system, a procedure, and a method.
3. Discuss the advantages and disadvantages of systems' utilization.
4. Explain the characteristics of a well-designed system.
5. Discuss the various staffing alternatives for the systems function of an organization.
6. Discuss the steps involved in (a) designing a new system, or (b) modifying an existing system.
7. Discuss each of the following systems analysis tools: work load chart, flow process chart, office layout chart, right- and left-hand chart, operator-machine process chart, horizontal flow process chart, and EDP block diagram.

Chapter Terms   *Integrated systems:* the interrelation of the various operating functions of an organization, including the following: sales, production, marketing, purchasing, and financial. Most integrated systems utilize a computer extensively.

System: the interrelated procedures necessary to achieve a well-defined goal.

Procedure: the related methods necessary to complete a work process.

Method: specific clerical or mechanical operations or activities.

Work load chart: a systems analysis tool that identifies the major activities performed by a given work unit, the amount of time the work unit spends on each activity, the activities performed by each employee, and the amount of time each employee spends performing the activities.

Flow process chart: a systems analysis tool designed to identify each step in a specific work process and to categorize each step as one of the following: operation, transportation, inspection, delay, and storage.

Office layout chart: a systems analysis tool that is a scale drawing of the present office layout. It is especially useful for visualizing work flow, backtracking, crisscrossing, and inefficient work flow.

Right- and left-hand chart: a systems analysis tool that is used to identify the movements of an individual's hands in processing work.

Operator-machine process chart: a systems analysis tool designed to study the relationship between an operator and the machine used by the operator.

Horizontal flow process chart: a systems analysis tool that illustrates the movement of each copy of a multicopy form set from the time of its creation until its disposition.

EDP block diagram: a systems analysis tool that is developed in conjunction with the preparation of a computer program.

As a means of controlling rapidly increasing office costs and improving operating efficiency, many organizations have developed and are utilizing the total or **integrated systems** concept. This means that the sales, production, marketing, purchasing, and financial functions of such organizations are interrelated and operate as one integrated system. When organizations utilize the total systems concept, the various functions are appropriately titled subsystems. In organizations in which the functions are not interrelated but are maintained as separate entities, each function is a distinct system rather than a subsystem. At the center or hub of many well-designed, integrated systems is the computer.

The Systems and Procedures Concept

Functional systems and subsystems (for discussion purposes, these two terms have the same meaning and can be used interchangeably) consist of several components, including employees, equipment, and forms or materials. Through systems analysis, the interrelationships between the components are studied in an attempt to simplify work processes and to provide a solid foundation for managerial decisionmaking.

In many organizations, the systems concept encompasses a broad range of activities. For example, in large organizations, it is not uncommon to find either a direct or indirect relationship between the systems function and the following activities:

Manpower planning	Budgeting
Procedures analysis	Operations research
Work scheduling	Quality control
Forms management	Administrative auditing
Records management	Systems design
Time and motion study	Job standards
Work measurement	Standardization of operating
Work simplification	produces
Office layout and design	Promotion and training

Definitions

By definition, a **system** refers to the interrelated procedures necessary to achieve a well-defined goal. A **procedure** consists of related methods necessary to complete various work processes, while **methods** consist of specific clerical or mechanical operations or activities. Figure 21–1 graphically illustrates the relationships between systems, procedures, and methods.

Objectives

The objectives for developing and utilizing systems vary from organization to organization. The following, however, identify the major objectives for using the systems concept:

1. To improve the efficient utilization of the organizational resources.

FIGURE 21–1   Systems, Procedures, Methods

PROCEDURE 1	Method A	Method B	Method C	Method D
PROCEDURE 2	Method A	Method B	Method C	Method D
PROCEDURE 3	Method A	Method B	Method C	Method D
PROCEDURE 4	Method A	Method B	Method C	Method D

SYSTEM

2. To control operating costs.

3. To improve operating efficiency.

4. To help achieve the objectives of the organization.

5. To assist in carrying out the various functions of the organization.

Advantages and Disadvantages

Among the advantages claimed for using the systems concept are: the various functions of the organization are better coordinated; systems' utilization helps to eliminate wasteful, unproductive, and uneconomical activities; systems' utilization helps to improve the operating efficiency of the organization; and more effective control can be exerted over various activities and functions.

Potential disadvantages of systems' utilization are: a certain amount of operating flexibility may be destroyed when utilizing the systems concept; inefficiency that is built into the system will disproportionately increase as work flows through the system; and a totally integrated system may be hampered somewhat when changes are made in one of its subsystems.

Characteristics of Systems

The following are characteristics of effective, well-designed systems:

1. *Flexible.* Although an effective system is structured, it should be sufficiently flexible to allow for special or unusual circumstances.

2. *Adaptable.* If a system is well designed, changes in the system can be made without destroying or hindering its functioning.

3. *Systematic.* An effective system is one that is systematic and logical.

4. *Functional.* For a system to be effective, it must serve the purpose for which it was intended.

5. *Simple.* A system does not have to be complex to be effective.

6. *Resourceful.* A well-designed system appropriately utilizes organizational resources.

A Purchasing System: An Illustration

To illustrate the systems concept, a system designed for purchasing office supplies will be presented. Figure 21–2 illustrates the various procedures and methods that comprise the purchasing system. Each of the systems' components (employees, forms, equipment) is present in the purchasing system illustrated in Figure 21–2.

FIGURE 21–2   Purchasing System

Procedure 1:   Requisition supplies
   Methods: A.   Fill out purchase requisition
            B.   Obtain necessary authorization

Procedure 2:   Obtain quotations from possible vendors
   Methods: A.   Fill out quotation forms
            B.   Send forms to prospective vendors
            C: Catalog respective bid quotations upon receipt

Procedure 3:   Order supplies
   Methods: A.   Fill out purchase order
            B.   Send purchase order to vendor

Procedure 4:   Receive order
   Methods: A.   Check order to verify quantities and acceptability
            B.   Deliver supplies to appropriate department
            C.   Notify accounts payable of receipt of order

Procedure 5:   Pay vendor
   Methods: A.   Prepare payment voucher
            B.   Prepare check
            C.   Send check to vendor

The Systems and Procedures Staff

Several alternatives are available for staffing the systems and procedures function within an organization. To a large extent, the most appropriate staffing alternative is governed by the size of the organization; the nature of the organization; the organization's commitment to the total or integrated systems approach; and the philosophy of top management toward the systems and procedures function.

The various alternatives for staffing the systems and procedures function include utilization of outside consultants (which includes the use of consultants employed in firms specializing in the design of systems, as well as the use of consultants employed as service representatives by office equipment or supplies vendors); utilization of a full-time systems staff; and utilization of a part-time systems staff.

When outside consultants are hired, they are frequently hired on a retainer basis, in much the same way that the organization's lawyer might be hired on a retainer basis. In most instances, the consultants provide recommendations but leave the final decisions to the management of the organization.

Several advantages result from using outside consultants. Perhaps the most significant is the expertise that these individuals are able to provide. Since the consultants are outsiders, they are able to be more objective in making recommendations. When outside consultants are retained over a period of years, they are able to keep their clients' systems up to date. The most significant disadvantage of using outside consultants is the high consulting cost that must be borne by the organization. Another disadvantage may result when the consultants are not readily available at all times.

Some organizations choose to have their own full-time systems staff. For some organizations, this alternative is most advantageous in terms of staffing the systems function. A full-time systems staff enables an organization to continually develop and improve all of its systems and work processes—not just the most important ones. A full-time systems staff is also advantageous when problems arise and assistance is needed immediately. But for some organizations, the cost of employing a full-time systems staff is considered to be a disadvantage. Some organizations also consider the possible conflict between line managers and the systems staff to be a disadvantage.

If an organization is too small to warrant the use of outside consultants or a full-time systems staff, the systems function is frequently assigned to an individual who functions in some other capacity. This individual is frequently the administrative office manager. The primary advantage of this alternative results from significant cost savings, which, however, might be overshadowed by the inability of the individual to effectively carry out the assignment because of insufficient time or expertise.

Designing or Modifying Systems

If a new system is being developed or if an existing system is being modified, the process will be enhanced by proceeding through a series of well-designed, sequential steps. If new systems are being developed, only steps one, four, and five of the following are appropriate. On the other hand, steps one through five are appropriate if an existing system is being modified.

1. *Define clearly the process to be studied.* Clearly defining and delineating the process will result in an analysis appropriate for the situation to be studied. In many cases, studies will be conducted because of one or more of the following problem situations: bottlenecks in work flow, crisscrossing or backtracking work flow, inefficient work flow, inefficient utilization of organizational resources (both human and non-human), and duplication of effort. In some cases, the study of work processes has to be restricted to repetitive, high-volume tasks.

2. *Outline the details of the present process.* Before the system can be modified, the present process has to be clearly outlined. The present process can be outlined in narrative form or by using one of the charts described in the next section of this chapter. Outlining the present process will involve breaking down and identifying each step on the appropriate form or chart. Outlining the present process will be facilitated by providing answers to the following: who, what, when, where, why, and how.

3. *Analyze the present process.* After the process has been clearly outlined, the next step is to analyze the process. The necessity of each step in the work process should be questioned. The analysis of the work process may involve simplifying, eliminating, or combining steps in the work process. When work processes consist of complex steps, simplifying the process may be appropriate. It may also be appropriate to either combine steps or eliminate steps in the work process. By eliminating a step in the work process, perhaps other steps that follow will be automatically eliminated.

4. *Outline the improved process.* After the present process has been thoroughly analyzed, the improved process should be clearly outlined, typically using the same type of form or chart that was used to outline the present process. Care should be taken to assure that the improved process is as simple as possible and consists only of those steps crucial to the work process. In many cases, the improved process can be tried during a "trial run" before the process is officially adopted. Modifications can be made, and it is possible to determine the degree to which the proposed process is an improvement over the present process.

5. *Install the new process.* After a decision has been made to implement the new process, it is ready for installation. In some instances, some employees may need to be convinced that the new process is actually an improvement. Such a task is largely the responsibility of the various supervisors. The new process should be subjected to periodic followup and review. In this way, portions of the process that may need to be modified can be identified.

Systems and Procedures Tools

Several tools are available to facilitate the modifying of existing systems or for developing new systems. When selecting a tool for either use, care should be taken to assure that the tool is appropriate for its intended use.

Work Load Chart

The **work load chart,** also referred to as a work distribution chart, is a useful tool for developing efficient systems and for simplifying work processes. A work load chart will identify:

1. The major activities performed by a given work unit.
2. The amount of time the work unit as a whole spends on each activity.
3. The activities performed by each employee and the amount of time each employee spends performing the activities.

When analyzing the work load chart, answers to the following questions should be sought:

1. Is the work unit performing the work it is intended to perform?
2. Are employees performing too many duplicate operations?
3. Are the tasks performed by each employee of a related nature?
4. Are the special skills and talents of the employees being utilized to the fullest extent?
5. Are the major functions of the work unit actually consuming the greatest amount of time?
6. Are the employees' work loads evenly distributed?
7. Are the employees being productive?
8. Is the flow of work efficient?

The work load chart points out areas of inefficiency—areas that should be corrected prior to developing a system. A basic purpose for using the systems concept is violated if inefficient procedures or methods are allowed to be built into the system.

The information needed to complete the work load chart should be collected over a representative work period, perhaps one to two weeks in length. Each employee records on a daily log sheet the activities he or she performs. A daily log sheet is illustrated in Figure 21–3. At the end of the information-collecting period, a summary log, illustrated in Figure 21–4, is prepared.

After each employee has completed the summary log, an activity list is compiled. The purpose of the activity list is to identify the activities performed by the work unit as a whole. A partial activity list is illustrated in Figure 21–5.

The work load chart, illustrated in Figure 21–6, is prepared from the information presented in the summary log and the activity list. Each activity is assigned a code. The activities are then entered in coded form in the "activity number code column" at the far left of the chart. The

FIGURE 21–3   Daily Log

| Employee's Name | Esther Jones | | Department | Purchasing |
| Employee's Title | Clerk-Typist | | Today's Date | 9/23/77 |

Clock Time	Time Consumed	Activities
8:00~8:30	30 minutes	Type report
8:30~8:45	15 minutes	Type quotations
8:45~9:15	30 minutes	Type purchase orders
9:15~10:15	60 minutes	Type letters (follow-up)
10:15~10:30	—	Take break
10:30~12:00	90 minutes	Compile data for report

FIGURE 21–4   Summary Log

| Employee's Name | Esther Jones | | Department | Purchasing |
| Employee's Title | Clerk-Typist | | For Period Ended | 9/27/77 |

Activities	Hours	Minutes
Type quotations	5	
Type purchase orders	21	30
Type letters (follow-up)	6	15
Compile data	1	30
Receive callers	2	
Type reports	3	
Keep vendor interview appointments	1	30
Answer phone	1	30

FIGURE 21-5 Activity List

Department	Purchasing	For period ended	9/27/77
Number of employees	5		

Activities performed	Activity code
File	A,B,C,D,E,F
Type follow-up letters	D
Review receipt of orders	C
Answer phone	F
Compile data	F
Prepare payroll	F
Type reports	F
Type purchase orders	B
Type quotations	E
Duplicate materials	F
Review purchase requisitions	B
Approve purchase requisitions	B
Handle personnel matters	F

activity column provides a brief description of the activity, and the "hours column" lists the total amount of time consumed by the various activities. A separate column is provided for each employee in the work unit. In these columns, the activities performed by each employee and the amount of time consumed by each activity are listed.

An examination of Figure 21-6 reveals that the activities in the activity column are listed in descending order as to the amount of time consumed. In the employee's section of the chart, the employees with the greatest job importance are listed at the left and those with the least amount of importance are listed at the right.

Flow Process Chart

Another systems tool frequently used to analyze and simplify work processes is the **flow process chart,** a tool especially useful for identifying each step in a specific work process. Each step in the process is categorized and identified by one of the following symbols:

o Operation: changing the physical or chemical characteristics of an object. Examples of operations are erasing, stapling pages together, typing, underlining, circling words, etc.

▷ Transportation: the movement of an object from one location to another. An example of transportation is giving a letter to the word originator for signing.

FIGURE 21-6 Work Load Chart

Activity Code	Activity	Hours	Jack Adams Purchasing Agent	Hours	Ralph Anders Buyer	Hours	Susan Brown Audit Clerk	Hours	Esther Jones Clerk-Typist	Hours	Mary Green File Clerk
A	Interview vendors	49	Interview vendors	12	Interview vendors	25			2 1	Receive vendors Keep interview appointment sheets	9	File literature
B	Review requisitions Approve requisition Prepare purchase orders	44	Review requisitions and proposals Approve requisitions Dictate memos explaining disapproval	7 2 5	Approve purchase orders	1			21	Type purchase orders	4 4	File approved requisitions File purchase orders
C	Verify receipt of orders, audit invoices, approve invoices	42			Review receipt of orders	1	15 15 3	Compare invoice with receipt of order forms and note discrepancies Audit invoices Approve invoices for payment			4 4	File receipt of order forms File invoices
D	Follow-up	12	Review major discrepancies	1	Dictate follow-up letters and review of discrepancies	3			6	Type follow-up letters	2	File follow-up letters
E	Obtain quotations	11			Request quotations	1	3	Maintain quotation forms	5	Type quotations	2	File quotations
F	Miscellaneous	42	Appointments Reading brochures Preparing reports Personnel matters Preparing payroll	2 3 5 2 1	Reading brochures Compiling data	8 1	4	Compiling data	1 3 1	Compiling data Typing reports Answering phone	2 9	Miscellaneous filing Duplicating material
TOTALS		200		40		40	40		40		40	

□ Inspection: verifying data or checking an object. A common example is proofreading.

◻ Delay: situations that cause the next step in the process to be delayed. A letter awaiting signature is an example.

▽ Storage: storing and/or protecting an object. Filing is a typical example of storage.

Each of the steps in a particular work process that is classified as an operation can also be classified as a *get ready*, *do*, or *put away* step. Special attention should be focused on the *do* steps, because, by eliminating these, the *get ready* and *put away* steps can also be eliminated. By assessing each step in terms of who, why, where, how, and when, the justification for the step can be determined. Those that cannot be substantially justified should either be eliminated or be combined with another step.

The flow process chart briefly describes the nature of each step in the process, identifies the distance that objects are transported, and identifies the amount of time consumed by each delay step. To facilitate analysis, the symbols representing each step are connected with a line and those symbols depicting *do* operations are darkened. After the present work process is outlined on the flow process chart, the chart is then analyzed to determine where simplification may be appropriate. Each step should be subjected to several questions. Is the step necessary? If so, why? Can the step be eliminated, simplified, or combined with another step? Is each step properly sequenced within the total process?

After the process has been analyzed, the right-hand part of the flow process chart is prepared to outline the proposed work process. The present and proposed processes are then summarized in the upper left corner as illustrated in Figure 21–7.

Office Layout Chart

The **office layout chart** is frequently used in conjunction with the flow process chart. Since the layout chart is especially suited for visualizing work flow, backtracking, crisscrossing, and inefficient work flow are clearly identified.

The office layout chart is actually a scale drawing of the present office layout, and the flow of work is depicted by connecting with lines the various work stations. When the layout chart is used in conjunction with the flow process chart, layout charts depicting the present and proposed work flow should be prepared.

Figure 21–8 illustrates layout charts for the present and proposed work flow that was outlined in Figure 21–7.

Right- and Left-hand Chart

The **right- and left-hand chart** is used to identify hand movements in a particular work process. Like the flow process chart, hand movements are classified into various categories, namely:

- ○ Operation: the movement of the hand at one location, such as grasping an object, stapling, writing, typing, or using a calculating machine.
- ⇨ Transportation: the movement of the hand when transporting an object from one location to another. Examples include inserting a form in a typewriter and placing an object in an out basket.
- ○ Hold: the holding of an object while the other hand is used to do something to the object. An example is holding several sheets of paper with one hand while using the other hand to operate a stapler.
- D Delay: the situation of an idle hand while the other hand is in motion. An example would be a motionless hand while the other hand holds a letter being proofread.

The right- and left-hand chart consists of four distinct sections. In the upper left corner is the layout section, which is used to illustrate the arrangement of materials involved in the work process. For example, in Figure 21–9, which illustrates the manual collating of five sheets of paper, the five sheets are identified as 1, 2, 3, 4, and 5.

In the upper right corner of the chart, space is provided for identifying the nature of the job being analyzed. The summary section appears below the layout and identification sections. Space is provided for summarizing the present process, the proposed process, and the differences between the two processes.

The lower two-thirds of the form is used to summarize the movement of the right and left hands in relation to one another. Space is provided for a brief description of each motion, and the symbols representing the various motions are connected with lines.

After the present work process has been carefully outlined, the necessity and efficiency of each step in the process is considered. After the process has been analyzed and various motions have been appropriately eliminated, combined, or simplified, the proposed process is outlined on a second right- and left-hand chart. The various motions are then summarized in the proposed area of the summary section. The differences between the present and proposed methods are also noted in the summary section.

Operator-Machine Process Chart

The **operator-machine process** chart is used to study the relationship between an operator and the machine used by the operator. The chart is primarily limited to high-volume, repetitive work processes.

As is true with the other process charts discussed in this chapter, the primary reason for using the chart is to analyze a work process, attempting to eliminate, simplify, or combine as many steps as possible. By eliminating as much idle time as possible, higher levels of productivity will be realized.

Figure 21–10 illustrates the operator-machine process chart. The

FIGURE 21–7   Flow Process Chart

	Present	Proposed	Difference
◯ No. of Operations	8	7	1
⇨ No. of Transportations	4	2	2
▢ No. of Inspections	3	1	2
◗ No. of Delays	1	1	-
▽ No. of Storages	1	1	-
Distance Traveled	149	117	32

Job __Processing Credit Applications__

Forms Used ___—___

Charted by __L. Davis__

Department __Office Services__

Date __11/30/77__

Present Method	Operation	Transportation	Inspection	Delay	Storage	Distance in Feet	Time in Minutes	Proposed Method	Operation	Transportation	Inspection	Delay	Storage	Distance in Feet	Time in Minutes
Credit application opened by mail clerk.	●							Credit applications opened by mail clerk	●						
Credit applications alphabetized	●							Mail clerk scans applications for completeness	◯		☒				
Credit application transported to credit clerk	◯	☒				17 ft		Credit applications alphabetized by mail clerk	●						
Credit clerk scans application for completeness	◯		☒					Credit applications transported to credit clerks	◯	☒				17 ft	
Credit clerks contact references	●							Credit clerk contacts references	●						
Credit clerks wait for references	◯			☒			1 week average	Credit clerk waits for references	◯			☒			1 week
Information provided by reference entered on application	●							Information provided by reference entered on application	●						
Applications transported to supervisor	◯	☒				15 ft		On routine applications, credit clerk decides on desirability and limit	●						
Supervisor inspects applications	◯		☒					Application sent to data processing	◯	☒				100 ft	
Supervisor decides on desirability of applicant	●							Information keypunched on card	●						
Supervisor assigns credit limit	●							Application stored	◯				▽		
Applications transported back to credit clerk	◯	☒				17 ft		Credit card prepared	●						
Credit clerk inspects application	◯		☒						◯						
Application transported to data processing	◯	☒				100 ft			◯						
Information keypunched on card	●								◯						
Application stored	◯				▽				◯						
Credit card prepared	●								◯						

FIGURE 21–8   Office Layout Chart

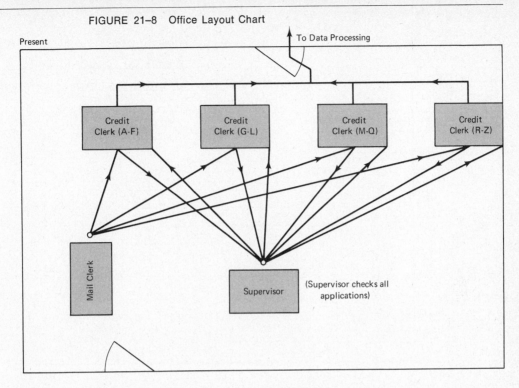

Present

To Data Processing

Credit Clerk (A-F)

Credit Clerk (G-L)

Credit Clerk (M-Q)

Credit Clerk (R-Z)

Mail Clerk

Supervisor   (Supervisor checks all applications)

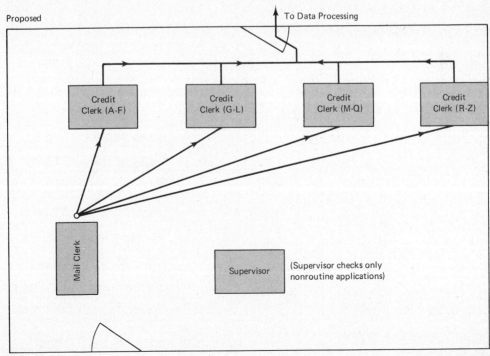

Proposed

To Data Processing

Credit Clerk (A-F)

Credit Clerk (G-L)

Credit Clerk (M-Q)

Credit Clerk (R-Z)

Mail Clerk

Supervisor   (Supervisor checks only nonroutine applications)

Scale: 1″ = 5′

FIGURE 21–9 Right- and Left-Hand Chart

Proposed

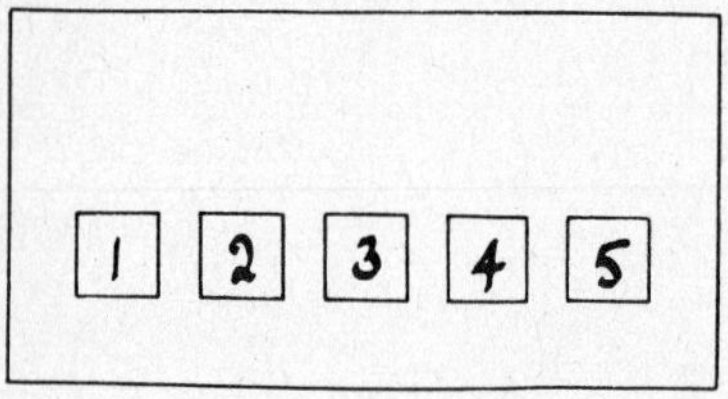

1 2 3 4 5

Job **Collating 5 pages**

Forms Used **Sheets of paper**

Charted By **D. Evans**

Date **11/30/77**

Department **Office services**

	Present		Proposed		Difference	
	LH	RH	LH	RH	LH	RH
◯ No. of Operations	6	6	4	4	-2	-2
⇨ No. of Transporations	3	2	3	2	0	0
⬡ No. of Holds	–	–	–	–	–	–
▭ No. of Delays	–	–	–	–	–	–

LEFT HAND	Operation	Transportation	Hold	Delay		Operation	Transportation	Hold	Delay	RIGHT HAND
Grasp page 1	⊗	⇨	◯	▭	1	◯	⇨	◯	▭	
Transport to page 2	◯	⊗	◯	▭	2	◯	⇨	◯	▭	
Place page 1 on top of page 2	⊗	⇨	◯	▭	3	◯	⇨	◯	▭	
Grasp pages 1 and 2	⊗	⇨	◯	▭	4	◯	⇨	◯	▭	
Transport pages 1 and 2 to 3	◯	⊗	◯	▭	5	◯	⇨	◯	▭	
Place pages 1 and 2 on top of 3	⊗	⇨	◯	▭	6	◯	⇨	◯	▭	
	◯	⇨	◯	▭	7	⊗	⇨	◯	▭	Grasp pages 1, 2 and 3
	◯	⇨	◯	▭	8	◯	⊗	◯	▭	Transport pages 1,2 and 3 to 4
	◯	⇨	◯	▭	9	⊗	⇨	◯	▭	Place pages 1,2 and 3 on 4
	◯	⇨	◯	▭	10	⊗	⇨	◯	▭	Grasp pages 1,2,3 and 4
	◯	⇨	◯	▭	11	◯	⊗	◯	▭	Transport pages 1,2,3,4 to 5
	◯	⇨	◯	▭	12	⊗	⇨	◯	▭	Place pages 1,2,3,4 on 5
	◯	⇨	◯	▭	13	⊗	⇨	◯	▭	Grasp pages 1,2,3,4 and 5
Joggle pages 1,2,3,4 and 5	⊗	⇨	◯	▭	14	⊗	⇨	◯	▭	Joggle pages 1,2,3,4 and 5
Transport pages 1-5 to pile	◯	⊗	◯	▭	15	◯	⇨	◯	▭	
Place pages 1-5 on pile	⊗	⇨	◯	▭	16	◯	⇨	◯	▭	

chart consists of a summary section, an identification section, a layout section, a parts section, and the section used to illustrate the various steps in the work process. The left-hand activity column is used for operator activities, while the right-hand activity column is used for machine activities.

The time column in the middle of the chart is used to depict the amount of time consumed by each activity. Each line in the time column represents a standard unit of time, perhaps one to six seconds. The columns on either side of the time column are darkened to clearly identify inactivity either on the part of the operator or the machine.

Horizontal Flow Process Chart

The **horizontal flow process chart** is extremely useful for illustrating work processes that involve multicopy forms (such as purchase orders, invoices, credit applications, etc.). These charts follow the movement of each copy of the form, starting with the point of origin, moving through the various steps in the flow of work, and ending with the disposition of each copy of the form. The symbols used in the horizontal flow process chart are similar to those illustrated in Figure 21–12.

Figure 21–11 is a horizontal flow process chart that illustrates a purchasing system, including the preparation of the purchase requisition and the purchase order, sending the purchase order to the vendor, and transmitting copies of the purchase order to the receiving and accounting department. The receiving department and the accounting department will also prepare horizontal flow process charts that illustrate the flow of work through their respective departments.

When designing new systems, the horizontal flow process chart is useful for outlining the various procedures in the system. The chart is also useful when modifying existing systems.

EDP Block Diagram

Since many systems are organized around the computer, a variety of computer programs must be prepared to facilitate the orderly processing of data and information.

Prior to the preparation of a computer program, an **EDP block diagram** is frequently prepared to assist the programmer in organizing ideas about solving business problems in an efficient, sequenced manner. The diagrams are also very useful when a program malfunctions or has to be modified. EDP block diagrams use standardized symbols, such as those illustrated in Figure 21–12.

Although the EDP block diagram illustrated in Figure 21–13 is not readily transferable into a computer program, the basic fundamentals of the diagram are illustrated. The diagram illustrates the process that a student may go through in getting ready to go to class, in getting ready for the class to start, and in getting ready to leave the class.

The decision steps of the diagram (depicted by the diamond-shaped symbols) involve either a *yes* or *no* decision. In the case of a *yes* decision,

FIGURE 21–10   Operator-Machine Process Chart

OPERATOR-MACHINE PROCESS CHART

Job **Opening letters by machine**

Machine Used **Letter opener**

Forms Used _____

Charted By **D. Evans**

Date **11/30/77**

Department **Mail Room**

	Operator		Machine	
	Time	%	Time	%
Work	42	58	30	42
Idle	30	42	42	58

Layout

| LETTER BIN | LETTER OPENER | TABLE |

Parts

Operator	Time*	Machine
Operator joggles handfull of letters and inserts in opener		IDLE
IDLE		Opener opens 100 letters in 30 seconds
Puts opened letters on table		IDLE

* Each Line Represents 6 Seconds

FIGURE 21–11   Horizontal Flow Process Chart

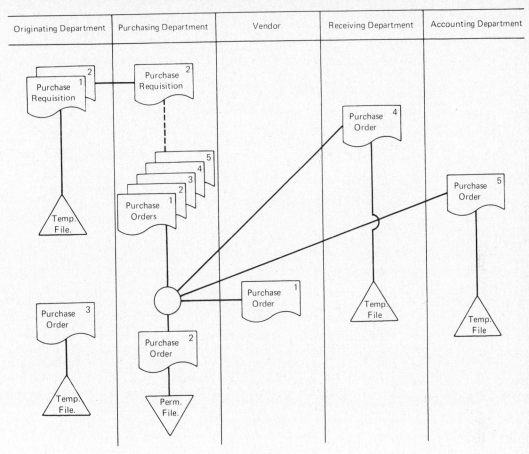

the process then proceeds to the next step in the vertical sequence of the diagram. In the case of a *no* decision, an alternative step (called branching) is utilized, until the appropriate situation is present, which will then allow the process to continue in the vertical sequence of steps. For example, in Figure 21–13, the student will continue to study until it is the appropriate time to leave for class.

Figure 21–14 summarizes some of the characteristics of each of the systems analysis tools that may have an impact on the use of the various tools.

Review Questions

1. What is meant by the integrated systems concept?
2. What are the objectives of the systems concept?
3. What are the characteristics of a well-designed system?
4. What advantages result from using outside consultants for designing a system?

FIGURE 21–12 Flowcharting Symbols

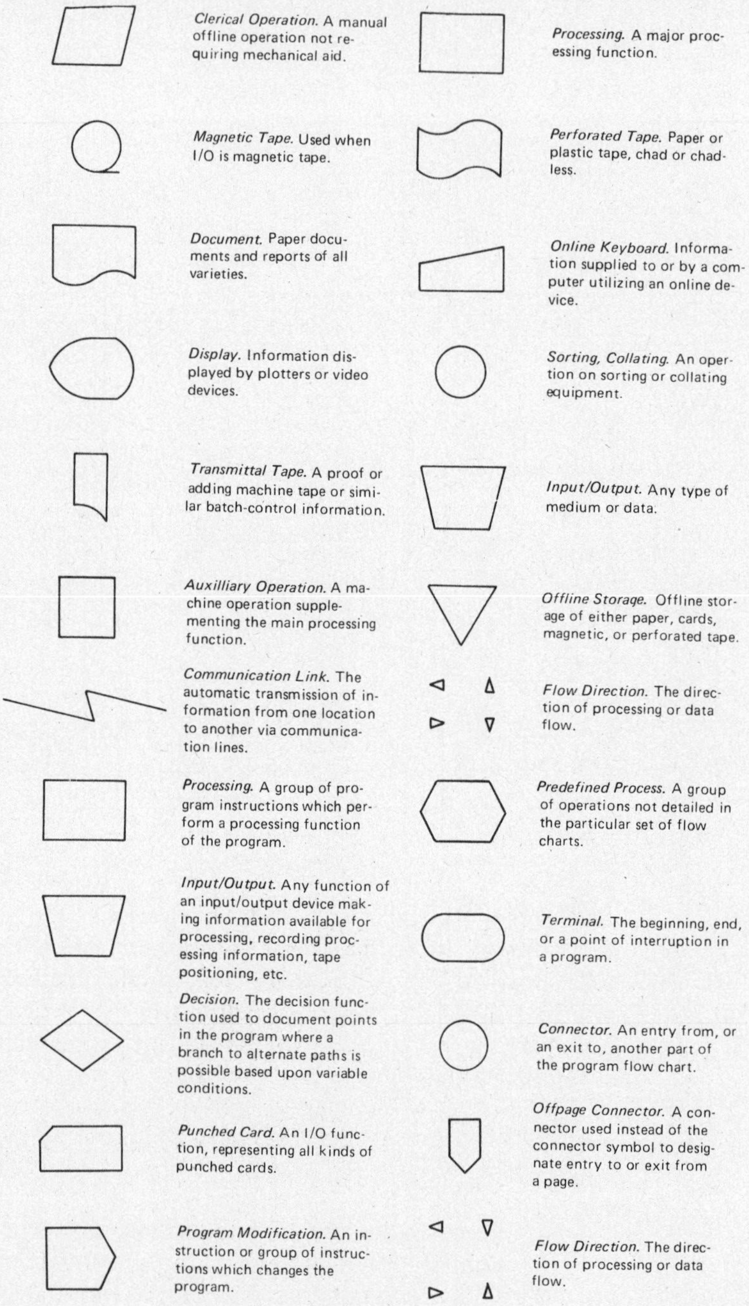

Clerical Operation. A manual offline operation not requiring mechanical aid.

Processing. A major processing function.

Magnetic Tape. Used when I/O is magnetic tape.

Perforated Tape. Paper or plastic tape, chad or chadless.

Document. Paper documents and reports of all varieties.

Online Keyboard. Information supplied to or by a computer utilizing an online device.

Display. Information displayed by plotters or video devices.

Sorting, Collating. An operation on sorting or collating equipment.

Transmittal Tape. A proof or adding machine tape or similar batch-control information.

Input/Output. Any type of medium or data.

Auxilliary Operation. A machine operation supplementing the main processing function.

Offline Storage. Offline storage of either paper, cards, magnetic, or perforated tape.

Communication Link. The automatic transmission of information from one location to another via communication lines.

Flow Direction. The direction of processing or data flow.

Processing. A group of program instructions which perform a processing function of the program.

Predefined Process. A group of operations not detailed in the particular set of flow charts.

Input/Output. Any function of an input/output device making information available for processing, recording processing information, tape positioning, etc.

Terminal. The beginning, end, or a point of interruption in a program.

Decision. The decision function used to document points in the program where a branch to alternate paths is possible based upon variable conditions.

Connector. An entry from, or an exit to, another part of the program flow chart.

Punched Card. An I/O function, representing all kinds of punched cards.

Offpage Connector. A connector used instead of the connector symbol to designate entry to or exit from a page.

Program Modification. An instruction or group of instructions which changes the program.

Flow Direction. The direction of processing or data flow.

Courtesy of International Business Machines Corporation

FIGURE 21–13   EDP Block Diagram

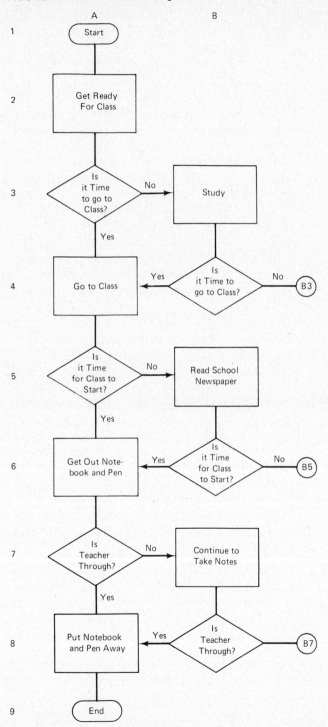

5. Explain the use of the daily log sheet.

6. In a flow process chart, why is it advantageous to eliminate *do* steps in a work process?

7. What special situations are identified by office layout charts?

8. For what type of systems analysis is the horizontal flow process chart especially suited?

Minicases

The Ajax Corporation is a small corporation that recently installed a small computer system. When the system was installed, it was intended that the computer be used for a variety of applications in the future, but it is presently being used for only a few unrelated applications. This is primarily because of a lack of technical expertise on the part of any of the present employees. Because of this lack of expertise, no one is able to develop fully integrated systems. At the last administrative staff meeting, it was decided that unless the computer was used for more applications, its continued use would be difficult to justify. Therefore, the president of the organization has decided that various systems will have to be installed as quickly as possible. In terms of staffing the systems function, what alternatives are available in this instance? Which do you recommend? Why?

*   *   *

The Arnold Corporation is interested in analyzing its present purchasing system, with the intent of improving the system. Although it is felt that the system is fairly efficient at this point, the director of purchasing is interested in making changes if they are needed. The director is primarily interested in analyzing the purchasing system in terms of (1) the five-part purchase order and (2) the steps involved in the purchasing system from the point that a purchase requisition is sent to the purchasing department until the order is received and delivered to the department making the requisition. Intermediate steps include obtaining authorization to place the order, entering information on the purchase order, and taking receipt on the order. What systems analysis tools should be used in this instance? Why?

Case

The Abraham Automobile Insurance Company has recently done some cost analysis studies and found that the cost of processing insurance claims is increasing at an alarming rate. Abraham's processing cost is the highest of any company in the area—and about 15 percent higher than the national average.

At a recent meeting, the company executives discussed the high cost of processing the claims and decided that much of the cost can be attributed to inefficient work flow. Because of the volume of claims that have

FIGURE 21–14

	Work Load Chart	Flow Process Chart	Right- and Left-hand Chart	Operator-Machine Chart	Horizontal Flow Process Chart	EDP Block Diagram
Analysis of employee or departmental activities	x					
Useful for nonintricate work processes	x	x				
Identification and analysis of steps in specific work processes		x	x	x	x	x
Identify nature of each step in work process		x	x	x	x	x
Identify distance that objects or employees move		x				
Identify amount of time of each step	x			x		
Identify ways to eliminate, combine, simplify steps	x	x	x	x	x	x
Identify hand movement in work process		x	x	x		
Identify relationship between operator and machine				x		
Identify activity of each copy of a multicopy form					x	
Identify steps of a computer program						x

to be processed, part-time help often has to be utilized to help process the backlog.

The following outlines the steps involved in processing the insurance claims:

1. The claim is received in the mailroom.

2. The claim is transported to the claims department, a distance of 371 feet.

3. The claim is opened and is assigned to a claims clerk according to an alphabetic allocation system.

4. The claim is transported to the claims clerk, a distance of about 18 feet.

5. The claims clerk briefly scans the claim and goes to the file to retrieve the customer's folder, a distance of 20 feet.

6. After checking the customer's folder for coverage, premium status, and history of claims, the claims clerk approves the claim and makes a notation on the folder.

7. The claim is transported to the supervisor for final authorization, a distance of 20 feet. (Because of the backlog, there is often a two- to three-day delay before the supervisor gives final authorization.)

8. After the supervisor has authorized the claim, it is transported to data processing, a distance of 160 feet.

9. The claims clerk refiles the customer's folder.

You have been assigned the responsibility of charting the process as it presently exists and to make suggestions for simplifying the process.

1. What other information will you need before you can chart the process?

2. What analysis tool or tools would be appropriate for charting the process?

3. Using an appropriate tool, chart the process and make recommendations for simplifying the process.

4. Chart the proposed process using an appropriate tool.

Forms
Design
and
Control

Chapter

22

Forms Control Program

Types of Office Forms
    Continuous Forms
    Unit-Set Forms
    Carbonless Forms
    MICR Forms (Magnetic Ink Character Recognition)
    OCR Forms (Optical Character Recognition)
    Mark-Sense Forms

Forms Design
    Forms Design Illustrated

Professional Forms Services

Chapter Aims   After studying this chapter, the student should be able to:

1. Explain the steps involved in designing a forms control program.
2. Identify the characteristics of the following types of forms: continuous, unit-set, carbonless, MICR, OCR, and mark-sense.
3. Discuss the background information that is needed before a form can be efficiently designed.
4. Discuss the factors that should be considered in the design of a form.
5. Discuss the functions provided by professional forms service organizations.

Chapter Terms   *Forms control program:* a program whose function includes determining whether or not a new form is needed; eliminating, consolidating, or simplifying existing forms; assisting in the design and development of new forms; and facilitating the development of efficient work procedures.

Continuous forms: forms or form sets that are attached to one another. The perforations facilitate their separation from one another.

Unit-set forms: individual forms or form sets.

Carbonless forms: a type of multicopy form that utilizes a special coating on the back of one side and the face side of the next copy. The coating enables the copies to be made.

MICR forms: a type of form frequently used by banks on which MICR numbers appear. The MICR numbers are printed with an ink that can be magnetized, which enables the numbers to be read by special processing equipment.

OCR forms: a type of form on which OCR characters appear. OCR characters can be either alphabetic or numeric, and they are read by special processing equipment.

Mark-sense forms: a type of form that involves the use of a special pencil for entering data in appropriate areas on the form. The pencil mark is read by special processing equipment.

Data entry method: the method of inserting information on a form. Two common methods are handwriting and printing by machine.

Grade of paper: refers to the quality of paper. As the cloth content of paper increases, so does its quality.

Grain of paper: refers to the fibers contained in the paper. The direction of the fibers determines how well the paper feeds through various types of equipment.

Professional forms service organizations: organizations that specialize in the design of forms, the production of forms, and inventory control and replenishment of forms.

Many business transactions involve the extensive use of forms. The majority fulfill a very useful function. Others provide a very limited function, perhaps because they are poorly designed, because they simply are not needed, or because they no longer serve the purpose for which they were originally designed.

In the preceding chapter, which deals with systems analysis, the three basic components of an integrated system are defined. These components include employees, equipment, and forms or materials. Since the forms utilized in a system must be compatible with the equipment, as well as with other forms utilized in the system, their design becomes even more crucial. The intent of this chapter is to present information pertaining to the control and design of forms.

Forms Control Program

Since the administrative office manager is frequently involved with forms design, it seems logical to also involve the administrative office manager with forms control. In some instances, the **forms control program** utilizes the advisory services of a forms control committee, while in other instances, the forms control program operates without the use of such advisory services. Whether or not the forms control program has the advisory services of a committee, the program must have the support of top management if it is to be effective.

The following objectives are typical of those under which forms control programs operate:

1. To guard against the development of unneeded forms.
2. To eliminate existing forms that are not needed.
3. To assist in the development and design of efficient forms.
4. To consolidate and simplify existing forms when appropriate.
5. To provide a continuous review of existing forms.
6. To facilitate the development of efficient work procedures.

The utilization of a systems approach necessitates the compatibility of the forms used throughout the organization. For this reason, the systems staff should work closely with the individuals concerned with forms control and design. Without such cooperation, the effectiveness of the system will be diminished.

Several distinct steps are involved in the design of an efficient forms control program. These steps are presented in the order in which they should be performed when designing a forms control program.

Step 1: Forms Cataloging. The purpose of the cataloging of forms is to enable those individuals responsible for the forms control program to determine the nature, type, and purpose of the forms that are utilized throughout the organization. The cataloging procedure consists of each department's or work unit's submitting several copies of each of its forms to the individuals responsible for forms control. The cataloging procedure will reveal:

1. The primary purpose of each form.
2. The forms utilized by each department or work unit.
3. The frequency of use of each form.
4. The number of multiple copies of each form.
5. The routing of each of the copies of a multiple-copy form set.
6. The final disposition of each copy of a multiple-copy form set.
7. The primary method of entering data on each of the forms.
8. The relationship between one form and another form.

Also during Step 1, each form is assigned an identification number. This number, which is generally found in the lower left corner, frequently appears in coded format. Generally, each department within an organization is assigned a different numerical code. Each form within a given department is then assigned a specific numerical code. To illustrate, the following identification number is coded as follows:

23-010
refers to the marketing department
refers to the tenth form developed in the marketing department

Some organizations also include in the identification number the month and year that the form was last revised and the number of forms printed the last time the supply was replenished. This would appear as follows:

23-010 Rev. 1/77 4M

"Rev. 1/77" means that the form was revised in January 1977 and "4M" means that 4,000 copies of the form were printed.

Step 2: Forms Classification. The use of a forms classification scheme facilitates the analysis of the forms assembled during the cataloging process. Forms are typically classified by function and by number.

Classifying forms by function means that they are organized according to the purpose of the form. As an example, all forms pertaining to sales are grouped together, all forms pertaining to accounts receivable are grouped together, and so forth. When completed, the functional classification enables those responsible for forms control and design to analyze the similarities and differences among the various forms.

Classifying forms by number involves assembling the various forms according to the identification number assigned to each form in

Step 1. Although classifying forms by number is typically not satisfactory for comparing forms, it does provide a master file of all forms, which is useful for cross-referencing purposes. The master file is useful when determining the identification number to be assigned to newly developed forms.

Step 3: Eliminating Forms. If the forms' cataloging indicates that certain forms are no longer being utilized or that certain forms no longer need to be utilized, their elimination should be considered. Certain forms may no longer be needed because the purpose for which they were designed is no longer being served. Perhaps the purpose of a form is now being served by another form. Another significant reason a form is no longer used is because it is not compatible with the organization's systems and procedures.

Step 4. Consolidating Forms. After the unneeded forms have been eliminated, an analysis of the remaining forms may reveal that certain forms contain similar items. In such instances, it may be possible to develop one new form that consolidates two or more presently existing forms. The result is reduced cost to the organization. When consolidating forms, a grid similar to the one illustrated in Figure 22–1 is useful for identifying the various items on several different forms.

An analysis of the grid is made after it has been completed. This

FIGURE 22–1   Data Comparison Grid

	Firm Name and Address	Ship To	Send To	Quantity	Description	Catalog Number	Price	Total Price	Suggested Vendor	Terms	Sub Total	Tax
PURCHASE REQUISITION				X	X	X			X			
PURCHASE ORDER	X	X	X	X	X	X	X	X		X	X	X
RECEIPT OF GOODS				X	X	X	X	X			X	X

analysis will reveal which forms have common items. The greater the number of common items, the easier it is to consolidate the forms.

Step 5: Design Guidelines. Before new forms are designed or existing forms are revised, design guidelines should be developed. Such guidelines will assist in making forms compatible with one another and will help standardize certain sections of various forms. The following illustrate design guidelines:

1. When the same data or information appear on several different forms, that data or information should appear in the same location on each form (for example, the name and address of the organization).

2. Information that is to be transferred from one form to another form should appear in the same order on both forms. (For example, the columns common to a purchase requisition and a purchase order should appear in the same order.)

3. When control of forms is important, the forms should be numbered sequentially. (For example, sequentially numbering the organization's checks helps to guard against their misuse.)

4. The design of the form should be guided by such characteristics as simplicity, practicality, and ease of use.

Step 6: Development of Forms. The development of forms, whether being revised or newly designed, should be in accordance with the design characteristics discussed in another section of this chapter. If a new form is being developed, it is the responsibility of those involved with the forms control program to determine whether sufficient justification exists for the development of the form.

Step 7: Printing Forms. In the past, most organizations had their forms printed by outside printers. As more and more organizations are developing extensive printing and duplication departments that have the necessary specialized equipment to print forms, the forms are being printed internally with increasing frequency.

Step 8: Perpetual Supply Inventory. The last step in the forms control program is to develop procedures for maintaining a perpetual supply inventory. The function of this inventory is to keep a sufficient supply of forms on hand. When the supply of forms reaches a certain point, the supply of forms is then replenished.

Types of Office Forms

Several different types of office forms are in existence. The following types of office forms will be presented in this chapter: **continuous, unit-set, carbonless, MICR, OCR,** and **mark-sense.**

Continuous Forms

Many of the forms used in offices today are the continuous type. Although continuous forms are attached to one another, because of the perforations separating each form, they can be easily detached from one another after being completed. Continuous forms are available in three different types: fan-fold, roll, and removable side strip. Figure 22–2 illustrates each of these three types.

Although the fan-fold type is a multiple-copy set, the removable side-strip forms may be either single or multiple copy. The roll is a single-copy form.

Fan-fold forms are distinctive in that the various copies are made by bellow folding a single sheet of paper a number of times in order to make the various copies. Carbon paper is interleaved between the folds. The

FIGURE 22–2 Types of Continuous Forms

Fan-fold

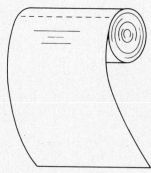

Roll

Removable Side Strip

forms are generally perforated on the sides and the top and bottom for easy separation.

The multiple copy removable side-strip type of continuous forms consists of separate sheets of paper for each copy. The strip on the side-strip type serves two purposes: the holes in the strip are used for feeding the forms through the equipment; also, the holes help hold the original and the multiple copies of the forms together until they are to be separated.

The roll type is restricted to single-copy forms because multiple-copy forms become misaligned when rolled. The most frequently used roll-type form is roll letterhead paper. Because each letterhead is perforated, they can be easily separated from one another.

Continuous forms are especially suited for automatic printing equipment, such as computer printers and automatic typewriters. A considerable amount of time is saved, because continuous forms are automatically fed through the equipment, which eliminates the task of individually inserting each form in the equipment.

Cards suitable for being processed through data processing equipment are also now available in continuous format. Such cards are most often used for customer billing. The cards are designed with removable side strips on both sides, which facilitates automatic feeding through the equipment. After the data has been entered on the cards, they are separated and are then mailed to the customers. A portion of the card is generally returned with the customer's payment. This portion can then again be processed through the data processing equipment.

Unit-Set Forms

Unit-set forms are separate forms and are not attached to another set as are continuous forms. Unit-set forms may be either single- or multiple-copy forms. Unit-set forms of the multiple copy variety frequently utilize a one-step carbon removal technique, which permits all carbons to be removed at one time. This is accomplished by having a perforated strip at the top of each copy of the form. The carbon between each copy of the form is attached to the perforated strip. The carbons attached to the perforated strip are shorter than the various copies of the form. By grasping the perforated strip with one hand and the copies with the other hand, the carbon and the copies can be easily separated in one step. The carbons remain attached to the perforated strip.

A unit-set form is illustrated in Figure 22–3.

Unit-set forms are very versatile. For example, when it is desirable to delete certain portions of the carbon copies, this can be accomplished during the manufacturing process in either of two ways: (1) by not carbonizing the portions to be deleted; (2) by omitting the section on each copy that is to be deleted. (This can be easily accomplished by reducing the size of the paper on which there are to be deleted portions.)

FIGURE 22–3   Unit-Set Form

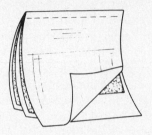

Carbonless Forms

Carbonless forms utilize a process in which the back side of one copy and the face side of the next copy have special coatings. When pressure is applied to the various copies, an impression is made, thus making a copy of what was written on the original copy.

Although the cost of making copies by this method is approximately 15 percent higher than with other methods, the carbonless process results in significant advantages. For example, portions of copies can be easily deleted by not applying the coatings to these portions. Since carbon paper does not have to be inserted between the various copies of the form, the form set is thinner. Not only can more copies be made, but also the sets consume less storage space. Furthermore, since carbon paper is not used, the process is cleaner and is less likely to result in smudged copies. The carbonless form also enables one to easily detect erasures, which decreases the possibility of unauthorized changes on the forms. Furthermore, since no carbon is used, the carbon used to make carbon copies of confidential material does not present a security problem.

MICR Forms (Magnetic Ink Character Recognition)

MICR forms are used primarily by banks to expedite the sorting and processing of numerical data found on banking documents. Equipment reads the numbers printed with a magnetic ink and then transmits the data to the computer or other processing equipment.

OCR Forms (Optical Character Recognition)

Whereas the MICR forms use only numerical data, OCR forms use both alphabetical and numerical data. As the data is read on the OCR form, the data is transmitted to the computer where it is processed. Although machines are generally used to enter data on OCR forms, handwriting can be used to a limited degree.

The nature of OCR requires considerable precision in the development of forms incorporating the OCR concept. Improper alignment can result in the equipment's misreading the data.

FIGURE 22–4 Mark-Sense Form

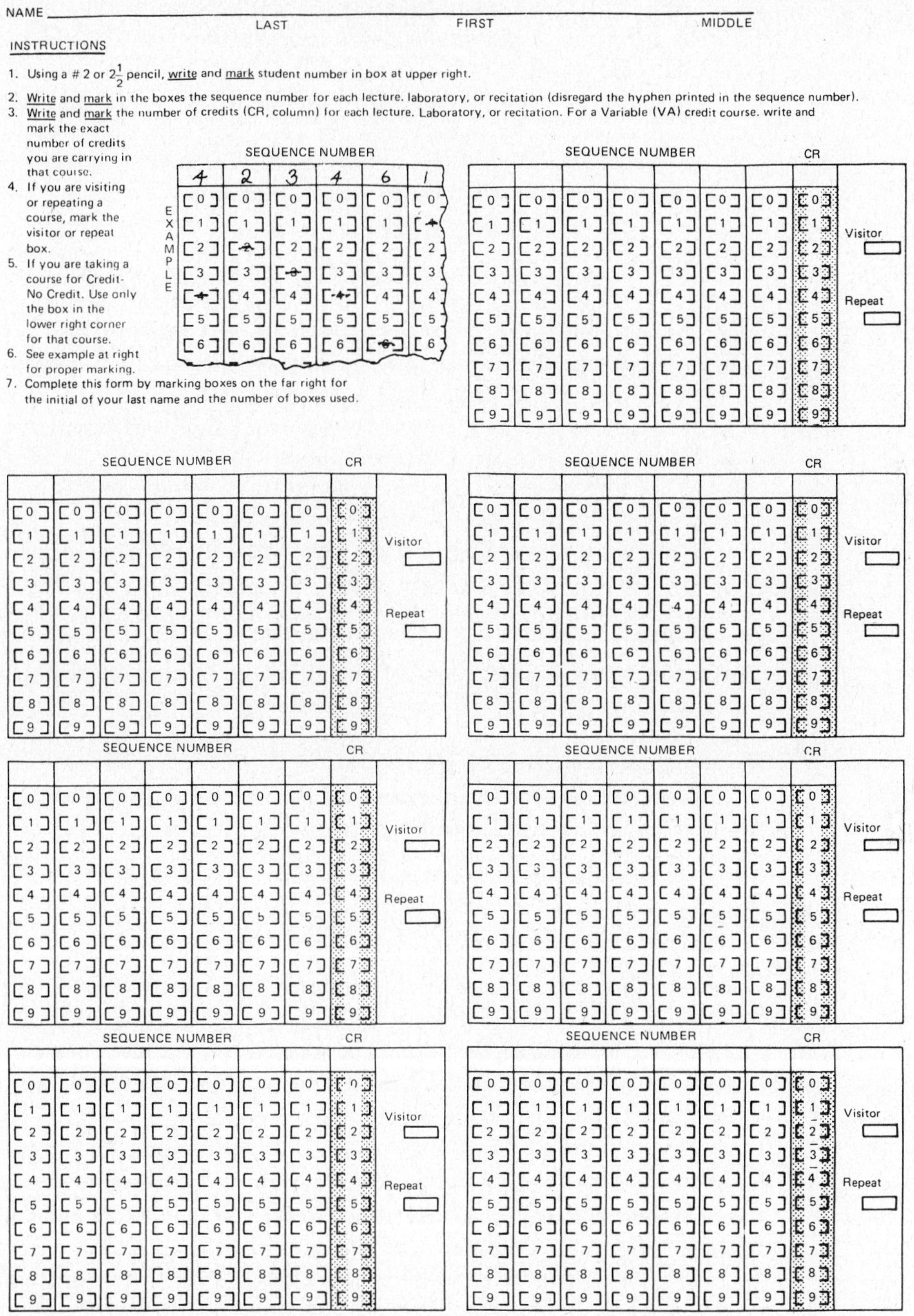

NAME _____

LAST   FIRST   MIDDLE

INSTRUCTIONS

1. Using a # 2 or $2\frac{1}{2}$ pencil, <u>write</u> and <u>mark</u> student number in box at upper right.

2. <u>Write</u> and <u>mark</u> in the boxes the sequence number for each lecture. laboratory, or recitation (disregard the hyphen printed in the sequence number).

3. <u>Write</u> and <u>mark</u> the number of credits (CR, column) for each lecture. Laboratory, or recitation. For a Variable (VA) credit course. write and mark the exact number of credits you are carrying in that course.

4. If you are visiting or repeating a course, mark the visitor or repeat box.

5. If you are taking a course for Credit-No Credit. Use only the box in the lower right corner for that course.

6. See example at right for proper marking.

7. Complete this form by marking boxes on the far right for the initial of your last name and the number of boxes used.

Courtesy, Michigan State University

Mark-Sense Forms   A mark-sense form is illustrated in Figure 22–4. Data can be entered on the form by using a special pencil to fill in the appropriate areas. The location of the mark, which is in coded form, can be read by special data processing equipment.

This type of form is especially advantageous when the data is mostly numerical rather than alphabetic. The data-entering process becomes quite cumbersome when a considerable amount of alphabetic information must be entered in the mark-sense area.

Forms Design

The efficiency with which a form is completed and processed is greatly dependent upon the design of the form. Poorly designed forms are difficult to complete, especially for individuals who are not familiar with such forms. Furthermore, poorly designed forms are apt to be responsible for the entering of inaccurate data. A greater number of errors are likely to be made on forms that are poorly designed than on forms that are properly designed. In many instances, poorly designed forms are ambiguous and are impossible to accurately complete, since the individual who enters data on the form does not know what is desired.

Extreme care must be exercised when designing forms that are part of a functional operating system within an organization. If the form is incompatible with the system or if the form is incompatible with other related forms, the efficiency of the work process will not be optimum. For this reason, many organizations often utilize the services of professional forms designers when new forms are needed. The expertise of such designers helps to assure the compatibility of the various forms within the organization's operating systems.

Depending on the qualifications of the organization's internal staff, the services of outside forms designers may not be needed. Also, because of the intended use of some forms, or the frequency with which the forms will be used, the use of professional forms designers may not be justified.

Before the actual work begins on designing the form, certain background information is needed. This information can be summarized as follows:

1. *The purpose of the form.* The purpose of the form must be defined in order to determine the type of information that must be included on the form, the number of copies that will be needed, the routing of each copy, and the nature of the directions or instructions for completing the form. In addition, the purpose of the form will determine the necessity of certain control procedures for the form—prenumbering and authorizing signatures, for example.

2. *The nature of the equipment through which the form will be processed.* This is important because the equipment may determine the minimum or maximum size of the form. The equipment will also de-

termine whether or not automatic feeding of the form is possible. Some equipment with an automatic feeding mechanism requires the removable side-strip form. In addition, the nature of the equipment will also determine certain characteristics of the paper on which the forms are printed. Finally, the nature of the equipment will also determine the amount of space needed for printing.

3. *The relationship between the form being developed and any other previously developed forms.* If the form being developed is in any way related to any previously developed forms, care must be taken to assure compatibility of the forms. The sequencing of items should be identical, especially if the information from one form has to be transferred to another form.

4. *The length of time that various copies must be legally retained.* If a certain form must be kept for a long period of time because of the statute of limitations, the paper on which the form is printed must be of sufficient durability to withstand the time element. This will have a direct bearing on the quality of paper used to print the form set.

After the four background characteristics have been considered, the actual process of designing the form may begin. The following factors should be considered:

1. *Adequate identification.* The name of the form should be clearly displayed on the form. Also, if the form is external, which means that the form will be routinely sent outside the organization, the name, address, and telephone number should also appear on each copy of the form. Other than the use of the organization's logo or trademark on the form, use of symbols or pictures should be kept to a minimum.

2. *Alignment of items.* The items on a form should be aligned so that the number of machine tab sets can be kept to a minimum. In other words, the items should be aligned so that one tab set can be used for several items. The following illustrates the incorrect and correct way of aligning items on a form:

Incorrect	*Correct*
Name:	Name:
Address:	Address:
City:	City:
State:	State:

In the incorrect illustration above, a single tab set cannot accommodate all the items; but by aligning the items shown in the correct illustration, one tab set will accommodate all the items. Aligning items will save a considerable amount of physical effort over a period of time.

3. *Preprinting.* As much information as possible should be pre-

printed on the form. This simplifies the process for the individual completing the form and perhaps enhances the completeness of the data that is entered on the form. If information can be preprinted, the individual completing the form simply checks the desired items. This is illustrated below:

	Correct
Incorrect	☐ Parcel post
Please state which shipping	☐ Land freight
method you prefer _____	☐ Truck freight
	☐ Other _____

The use of ballot-box design shown in the correct illustration is a very useful time-saving technique in forms design.

4. *Prenumbering*. Many forms today are prenumbered. It is advantageous to preprint numbers on forms that should be sequentially numbered. By prenumbering, employees' time and effort is saved; greater control can be exercised over the use of the form; and if necessary, the processed forms can be easily rearranged in numerical order. The forms are typically prenumbered in the upper right corner.

Types of forms that are frequently prenumbered are purchase orders, checks, payment vouchers, invoices, and so forth.

5. *Instructions*. Because of the complexity of some forms or because the individual using a certain form may not be familiar with the procedures for completing the form, instructions are important. Generally, external forms are the only ones on which instructions are needed. Employees, either through training or use, are sufficiently familiar with internal forms so that instructions are not needed.

Instructions should be placed as close as possible to the items to which they pertain. If this is not possible because of insufficient space, the instructions may be placed on the back side of the form or on a separate sheet. The location of the instructions should be emphasized.

6. *Identification number*. It is important for each form to have an identification number. This number is generally located in the lower left corner and might consist of a department number, the number of the form within the department, the adoption or last revision date, and the quantity of forms printed during the last printing. The following, which contains the four elements mentioned above, illustrates an identification number:

212:017 Rev. 9/75 4M

7. *Type of carbon*. Selecting the type of carbon used to make copies of a form is dependent upon several factors:

    a. The frequency of use of the form.

    b. The number of copies of the form that must be made.

    c. The confidentiality of the form.

    d. The opportunity for tampering with the data on the form (erasing and retyping, for example).

    e. The method for entering data on the form.

    f. The nature of the equipment through which the completed form may have to be processed.

Several different methods exist for making carbon copies: carbonless; one-time carbon; carbon roll fastened to the equipment; and single-sheet carbon.

If the circumstances justify it, the use of the carbonless system to make copies results in several advantages. These are outlined on page 502.

One-time carbon is the type of carbon that is used in continuous forms or unit-set forms. It is a low-grade carbon and is to be used only one time. Because the carbon is inserted between the various sheets of the form during the manufacturing process, a considerable amount of employees' time is saved.

Although not used frequently, some machines are equipped with a carbon roll device that is attached to the piece of equipment. The carbon feeds through the equipment independently of the feeding of the forms through the equipment. Therefore, employees do not have to manually insert carbon between each copy of a form each time.

Because some forms are not used frequently enough to justify one of the above methods for making carbons, the single-sheet carbon method is used. Single-sheet carbon is of a good grade and therefore can be used many times. A single-sheet has to be manually inserted between each sheet of the form each time the form is used. This process can be quite time consuming.

    8. *Data entry method.* The **data entry method** on a form has a significant impact on the spacing between items and on the design format of the form.

    a. *Spacing.* The primary method for entering data on the form should be considered in determining the amount of vertical and horizontal space to provide between items on the form. If the typewriter is the primary data entry method, the vertical spacing between items on the form should accommodate the regular spacing on the typewriter. Otherwise, employee time and effort will have to be expended in manually aligning the form in the typewriter. Double spacing (three lines to an inch) is the recommended vertical spacing when using the typewriter as the primary data entry method.

Sufficient horizontal space must also be provided when the primary data entry method is the typewriter. A sufficient amount of space should be allowed to accommodate the longest alphabetic or numerical data to be typed on the form.

If handwriting is used as the primary data entry method, greater amounts of horizontal space must be provided on the form than is the case with forms that are primarily completed on a typewriter. Three lines to an inch is also the recommended vertical spacing when handwriting is the primary data entry method.

b. *Design format.* The primary data entry method must also be considered in designing the format of the form. For example, if the primary data entry method is to be a typewriter or some other mechanical printing device, a box design is preferred. The box design simplifies to a great extent the proper alignment of the form in the typewriter. The following illustration shows the appropriate design format when data are mechanically entered:

Last Name	First Name	Middle Initial
House Number	Street	
City	State	ZIP Code

The identifying tabs should appear in the upper left corner of each box rather than below the box. By placing the identifying tabs in the upper left corner, the typist does not have to space down to read what is to be typed and then space back up and type the desired information.

Line design, which is illustrated below, is the preferred design format when the primary data entry method is handwriting.

Last Name	First Name	Middle Initial
House Number	Street	
City	State	ZIP Code

In this illustration, the identifying tabs appear below the lines.

9. *Paper.* The paper on which forms are printed must be considered for several reasons. The type of paper has a significant impact on its durability, the manner in which the paper will withstand the passage of

time, and the ease with which the paper can be handled. Paper possesses three basic qualities—weight, grade, and grain. The effect that each of these qualities has on forms design is presented in the following sections.

a. *Weight*. The weight of the paper on which forms are printed is important because it determines the durability of the form. The weight of paper is determined by the weight of 500 sheets (a ream) of paper stock measuring seventeen by twenty-two inches. If the ream weighs twenty pounds, it is referred to as twenty-pound paper. If the ream weighs sixteen pounds, it is sixteen-pound paper. The ream is then cut into different sizes, depending upon the size of the form. Forms should be printed on as light a weight of paper as conditions allow.

Since many forms nowadays are multiple-copy forms, the weight of paper becomes especially important because the weight has a significant effect on the number of copies that can be made. The weight of paper is also likely to have a significant effect on postage costs.

b. *Grade*. The **grade of paper** on which forms are printed determines how well the form will withstand the passage of time. The grade of paper is determined by the type of materials used in its manufacture. The cloth and/or sulphite content determine the grade of paper. As the cloth content increases and the sulphite content decreases, the grade of paper improves. In other words, paper consisting of 100 percent sulphite lasts only a few years, whereas paper partially or wholly consisting of cloth content lasts considerably longer.

The grade of paper on which forms are to be printed should be determined by (1) the number of years the organization is legally required to keep a particular form; (2) the frequency of use of the form (greater cloth content makes the paper less brittle); and (3) the primary data entry method.

In addition to the physical content of paper, the finish of the paper may also be an important consideration. The finish of the paper is apt to determine the ease with which erasures can be made, how rapidly ink will soak into the paper, and the overall appearance of the paper. Although several different types of finish are available, bond finish is perhaps the most commonly used. Bond paper, which has greater internal strength than nonbond paper, is relatively easy to erase because of its fairly smooth finish.

c. *Grain*. The **grain of paper** refers to the fibers contained in the paper. The fibers can run through the paper in either a vertical or horizontal direction, depending on how the paper is cut. If equipment is used for entering data on the form, special consideration should be given to the grain of the paper on which the form is printed. When forms are automatically fed through the equipment, the grain of the paper should be vertical rather than horizontal. This means that the grain of the paper should be in the same direction that the paper feeds through the equipment. If the grain is opposite of the direction that the paper feeds through the equipment, the paper is more apt to misfeed in the equipment.

10. *Color.* The use of colored paper and ink in printing forms should be kept to a minimum and should be used only when justifiable. Colored paper is justifiable for use in multiple-copy form sets, especially when different copies of the form are to be routed to different places. By printing each copy of the form set on a different color of paper, the sorting process is greatly simplified. Light colored stock should be used since it provides a better contrast between the paper and the ink.

The use of several different colors of ink is generally impractical. Not only does the cost of printing increase, but also the different colors are apt to distract from the purpose for which the form is used. Generally, black is the most desirable color of ink for printing forms. In some instances, using a different color of ink to print certain sections of the form is advisable if those sections need to be emphasized.

11. *Size.* The size of the form is basically determined by the amount of data that eventually has to be entered on the form. Forms for which a typewriter is the primary data entry method could perhaps be smaller than if the primary data entry method is handwriting. This factor must be considered in determining proper form size. Another factor to consider is the size of the type used to print the form. Also of some importance in certain instances is the size of the paper stock from which the forms are cut. To keep the trim waste to a minimum, the size of the paper stock might be considered in determining the size of the forms to be cut from the stock. Other factors to consider are possible restrictions placed on form size by the equipment in which the forms will be used.

12. *Print type size.* There are many different printing type styles available for use in printing forms. The number used should be kept to a minimum. When several different type styles are used, items of equal significance should be printed with the same type size and style. Items that are to be emphasized can be printed in a different type style to make the items more distinctive.

Some states have passed legislation setting minimum type sizes for certain portions or areas of forms. The type size will frequently pertain to items having a financial or legal significance. To illustrate, one state has passed legislation that sets minimum type sizes on conditional sales contracts.

13. *Shading.* To emphasize certain portions of forms, the areas to be emphasized are sometimes shaded. This makes the areas more distinctive, drawing the user's attention to those particular areas.

14. *Adequate margin size.* The method of data entry should be considered in determining adequate margin sizes. This is especially true when the typewriter is the primary data entry method. Because forms

tend to slip in the typewriter when typing near the bottom of the form, a sufficient margain should be left at the bottom.

Forms Design Illustrated

Figure 22–5 is presented to illustrate several of the forms design factors discussed in the preceding section. The encircled numbers on the form correspond to the numbers identifying the factors covered in the preceding discussion. Figure 22–5 illustrates a three-part unit-set form. One-time carbon is utilized for making carbon copies.

1. *Adequate information:* The name of the form (Components) is clearly presented on the perforated strip at the top of the form. The name of the organization and its phone number appear in the upper left corner, along with the organization's logo.

2. *Alignment of items:* The form illustrates the alignment of items (hospital and city), which reduces the number of tab sets that must be set on the equipment.

3. *Preprinting:* A considerable amount of preprinting (method of transporting, components, and use of components) is shown on the form. The form also makes use of ballot-box design for these two items.

4. *Prenumbering:* The sequential number of the form (01255) appears on the form.

5 and 13. *Instructions and shading:* Instructions appear in the lower left corner near the items to which they pertain. The instructions are highlighted by shading and arrows.

6. *Identification number:* The identification number of the form (LRP 5500) appears on the perforated strip in the upper left corner.

8. *Data entry method:* Since the data entry method is primarily by typewriter, this fact was considered in designing the form. The form accommodates the typical vertical spacing found on typewriters. The form also illustrates the design format recommended when typewriters are used for data entry.

11. *Size:* The size of the form accommodates the various types of equipment that will be used for completing and storing the form.

12. *Printing type styles:* Items of equal emphasis on the form are presented in equal type sizes.

14. *Adequate margin sizes:* To prevent slippage, an adequate bottom margin appears on the form.

Professional Forms Services

The use of **professional forms services** should not be overlooked, especially when an organization utilizes sophisticated systems. The use of professional forms services becomes perhaps even more crucial for designing forms that are an integral part of an organization's system.

Professional forms services provide a variety of functions for their clients. The nature of the service depends, of course, upon the forms

FIGURE 22–5 Forms Design Illustrated

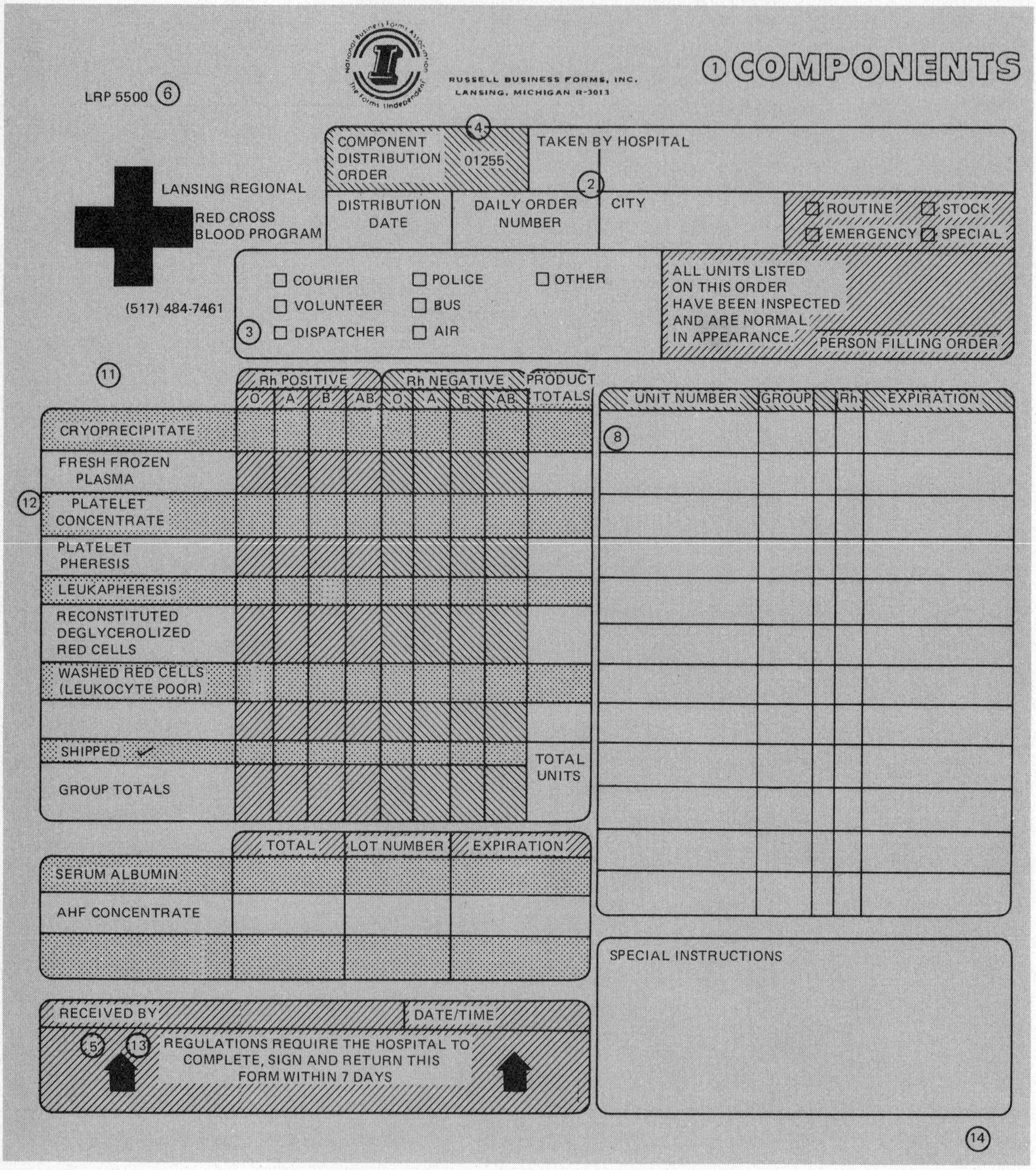

National Business Forms Association — The Forms Independent

RUSSELL BUSINESS FORMS, INC.
LANSING, MICHIGAN R-3013

(1) COMPONENTS

LRP 5500 (6)

LANSING REGIONAL
RED CROSS
BLOOD PROGRAM

(517) 484-7461

(4) COMPONENT DISTRIBUTION ORDER 01255

TAKEN BY HOSPITAL (2)

DISTRIBUTION DATE | DAILY ORDER NUMBER | CITY

☐ ROUTINE ☐ STOCK
☐ EMERGENCY ☐ SPECIAL

(3)
☐ COURIER ☐ POLICE ☐ OTHER
☐ VOLUNTEER ☐ BUS
☐ DISPATCHER ☐ AIR

ALL UNITS LISTED ON THIS ORDER HAVE BEEN INSPECTED AND ARE NORMAL IN APPEARANCE.
PERSON FILLING ORDER

(11)

	Rh POSITIVE O	A	B	AB	Rh NEGATIVE O	A	B	AB	PRODUCT TOTALS
CRYOPRECIPITATE									
FRESH FROZEN PLASMA									
(12) PLATELET CONCENTRATE									
PLATELET PHERESIS									
LEUKAPHERESIS									
RECONSTITUTED DEGLYCEROLIZED RED CELLS									
WASHED RED CELLS (LEUKOCYTE POOR)									
SHIPPED ✓									TOTAL UNITS
GROUP TOTALS									

UNIT NUMBER	GROUP	Rh	EXPIRATION
(8)			

	TOTAL	LOT NUMBER	EXPIRATION
SERUM ALBUMIN			
AHF CONCENTRATE			

RECEIVED BY | DATE/TIME

(5) (13) REGULATIONS REQUIRE THE HOSPITAL TO COMPLETE, SIGN AND RETURN THIS FORM WITHIN 7 DAYS

SPECIAL INSTRUCTIONS

(14)

Courtesy, Russell Business Forms

service. Some forms services are nationwide, while others are independent and serve a more limited geographical area.

The two most common functions provided by professional forms services are forms design and production. After the forms specialist identifies the purpose of a form and its function within an operating system, the specialist then designs the form. After the form is designed and is approved by the organization, the professional forms service makes arrangements for the production of the form. The forms specialist can also offer many suggestions for forms revision. Because of the expertise of the specialist, the organization is able to utilize forms that are compatible with one another as well as with its operating systems.

Some professional forms services also provide a variety of other functions. Because some organizations have limited storage space for their supply of forms, some forms services provide warehouse facilities for storing the supply of forms. These forms services keep the organization supplied with a sufficient quantity of forms for a given period of time. When the supply of forms stored in the warehouse reaches a certain level, the forms service automatically takes care of reordering a new supply of forms. The forms service thus assumes responsibility for the storage and perpetual supply inventory of each of its clients' forms that are under contract.

Review Questions

1. Why is forms control important?
2. What is involved in the cataloging of forms?
3. Why is prenumbering forms useful?
4. What techniques exist for making carbon copies of forms?
5. When instructions are included on forms, where should they be placed?
6. Why should the data entry method be considered when designing forms?
7. How is the weight of paper determined?
8. How do the grade and grain of paper differ?

Minicases

The employees who process the payroll records for the Dixon Company have complained about the payroll forms for a long time. The following summarizes most of their criticism: The weekly payroll card and the withholding statement have reversed columns. This means that the columns are not in the same order on these two forms. (These two forms are used in conjunction with one another in the processing of data.) In addition, the withholding statement and the attached check frequently slip out of the typewriter before the last line has been typed on the form. Another criticism is the use of a fairly good carbon paper for making a carbon copy of each form. The carbon paper has to be manually inserted and removed from each form set. The data entry method is typically by typewriter and the typist has to manually align the typewriter before each line on the form can be typed. The numbers on the checks are not preprinted. Therefore, the typist has to type the check number on each check. In consideration of the principles of good forms design, criticize the payroll records discussed above.

*   *   *

The Darnell Corporation is interested in developing a new purchase order that can be used in their new minicomputer system. Up to this time, the data entry method on the form has been by typewriter. Because of the growing amount of paperwork and because of the ability to computerize their system, the purchasing department manager has made the decision to develop a purchase order form set that can be completed on the firm's minicomputer. What type of form do you recommend? What type of carbonizing process do you recommend? What suggestions can you offer those who are responsible for designing the new form?

Case

You have been hired by the Smikie Manufacturing Company to provide consultation regarding some of their office procedures. In contracting for your services, the vice president for corporate relations indicated to you that the office area "is being plagued with increasing amounts of operating inefficiency."

After spending several hours analyzing the operating procedures of the company, you conclude that many of their problems are related to the lack of a forms control program. In fact, employees generally develop new forms at will. When you suggested to the office manager that the lack of a forms control program appears to be the source of many of their problems, the office manager become very defensive. In fact, he indicated to you that many employees now consider the unrestricted development of new forms to be a fringe benefit and that if this "privilege" is taken away from them, some of the employees will no longer be able to "show the firm's management how valuable they are to the firm." You realize that the employees will be opposed to your recommendation that they no longer have this "privilege," but you also realize that the inefficiency will continue to increase if they are not stripped of this "privilege." You, therefore, must do an outstanding job of selling the management and the employees on the necessity of a forms control program.

1. What benefits of a forms control program are you going to relate to the company?

2. What are you going to recommend to the management as being appropriate steps for developing the program?

3. What additional suggestions do you have for making the program more acceptable to the employees?

Report
Writing

Chapter
23

Preparing Informal Reports
> Short Reports
> Periodic Reports
> Progress Reports
> Staff Reports
> Justification Reports

Preparing Formal Reports
> Title Page
> Letter of Authorization
> Letter of Transmittal
> Table of Contents
> List of Illustrations
> Abstract
> Introduction
>> Background of the report
>> Purpose
>> Scope
>> Methodology
>> Definitions
>> Limitations
>> Historical background of the report
>> Report organization
> Text of the Report
> Summary
> Conclusions
> Recommendations
> Appendices
> Bibliography

Chapter Aims   After studying this chapter, the student should be able to:

1. Identify the factors that a report writer should consider when determining the appropriate type of report to use in a specific situation.
2. Discuss the characteristics of each of the following types of reports: short reports, periodic reports, progress reports, staff reports, and justification reports.
3. Discuss the characteristics of formal reports.

Chapter Terms   *Short report:* a type of informal report that contains a discussion of facts as well as conclusions and recommendations. Short reports follow a rather standardized format.

Periodic report: a type of informal report that provides information about either past or present events. Periodic reports are prepared on a regular basis.

Progress report: a type of informal report that provides information about a specific plan or program. Such reports are prepared only when there is progress to report.

Staff report: a type of informal report, generally prepared in memorandum format, that presents facts and provides conclusions and recommendations.

Justification report: a type of informal report used to justify a certain recommendation or course of action.

Formal report: a type of report, which is typically analytical in nature, that is presented to the reader in a rather formal format and consists of several fairly standardized parts.

Inductive arrangement: the presentation of information in a report in the following order: facts or findings, conclusions, and recommendations.

Deductive arrangement: the presentation of information in a report in the following order: summary, conclusions, recommendations, and facts or findings.

Report purpose: the benefits expected to result from solving the report problem.

Report problem: the reason or reasons that necessitate the preparation of the report.

Factors of the problem: either the causes of the problem or the area or areas being investigated.

Primary research: the use of information that is collected specifically for the report being prepared.

Secondary research: the use of printed information in the presentation of a report. Such information is frequently found in textbooks, periodical articles, and so forth.

The use of both informal and formal reports by managers is rapidly increasing. While most of the reports used by managers are prepared internally, some are prepared by individuals outside the organization. The reports used by managers fulfill many functions, including disseminating information, providing a basis for decisionmaking, and justifying a certain course of action. The reports used by administrative office managers are frequently prepared by someone below their hierarchical level. This, however, does not mean that administrative office managers do not need to know the fundamentals of report preparation. The administrative office manager is frequently responsible for preparing reports that are transmitted to managers at higher hierarchical levels. It is also possible that the reports used by the administrative office manager are prepared by someone of higher hierarchical rank or by someone in a lateral relationship to the administrative office manager.

The purpose of this chapter is to provide information about the various types of reports. Also included is information about the special uses of several of the different types of reports. The effectiveness of a report can be enhanced if the report writer uses the appropriate type of report in the appropriate situation. Although some situations require a certain type of report, other situations will permit the use of more than one type. In determining the type of report to use in a specific situation, the report writer should consider the intended purpose of the report; the readership of the report; the nature of the material being presented in the report; circumstances over which the report writer has no control but which tend to place limitations on the report (such as cost, time, or availability of information); and the ability of the report writer.

Reports are frequently classified as either informal or formal reports. The formality of the situation surrounding the report should be considered in determining which classification of report to use. The following types of informal reports are presented in this chapter: **short reports, periodic reports, progress reports, staff reports,** and **justification reports.** This chapter also includes a discussion of **formal reports.**

Preparing Informal Reports

Most of the reports used by administrative office managers are classified as informal reports. Typically, informal reports are shorter than formal reports, are written in a more informal style than formal reports, and make less use of graphic illustrations than formal reports.

Short Reports

Informal reports are often presented in either memorandum or letter format. When either of these two formats is used, the length of the report is limited to a few pages. When there is a need for the preparation of a longer report that does not require the use of a formal report, a short report should be considered. Several distinctions can be made between the formal report and the short report. These include the following: the short report is frequently not as lengthy as the formal report; the short report contains fewer report parts than does the formal report; and the writing style of the short report is frequently less formal than that used in formal reports.

Short reports can be used to present a variety of different types of information. For example, the short report might be used to present information about an investigation conducted by the report writer. It might also be used to present the findings of a research study that was conducted or to present the results of questionnaires that were filled out by 500 individuals.

The report writer has two options for arranging the information in short reports. When an **inductive arrangement** is used, the facts or findings are presented before the conclusions and recommendations. When a **deductive arrangement** is used, the short report begins with a short summary, which is followed by the conclusions and recommendations. The facts and findings are then presented. Because many report readers find the summary, conclusions, and recommendations to be of greatest interest and use the facts and findings only if additional information is needed, the deductive arrangement is frequently used in presenting short reports.

If graphic illustrations would facilitate the presentation of information, their use should be considered. The report writer should also consider the use of headings and side headings, which are very helpful to the report reader. In addition, if the report contains conclusions, the report writer must be sure that the conclusions are supportable by facts or other evidence. To present unsupported conclusions renders the report virtually useless.

An example of a short report is illustrated in Figure 23–1.

Periodic Reports

Periodic reports provide a very useful function in the business world. They provide on a regular basis documentation about either past or present events. Periodic reports are frequently prepared weekly, biweekly, monthly, bi-monthly, quarterly, semiannually, or annually. The need for periodic reports should be reviewed at least once a year to determine whether the use of the reports continues to be justifiable. Many organizations continue to have periodic reports prepared long after the need for the reports exists.

Periodic reports are often upward in direction. This means that they are prepared by subordinates for superiors. In some instances, the reports prepared by individuals of the same hierarchical rank are combined and a composite report is prepared, which is then transmitted to the next hierarchical level. The same process takes place at that hierarchical level, until a composite report reaches the top hierarchical level of an organization.

Because periodic reports frequently contain financial or other types of numerical information, they are often presented in tabular form. If a

Figure 23-1 Short Report

REPORT ON FEASIBILITY OF INSTALLING A WORD PROCESSING SYSTEM IN JOHNSTON CORPORATION

The preparation of this report was authorized by Mr. David Brown, Vice President of Corporate Operations, on December 12, 1975, who was given the following assignment: to determine the feasibility of installing a word processing system in Johnston Corporation.

Summary of Findings

The investigation process involved in preparing this report consisted of talking with word processing equipment vendors, reviewing appropriate literature, and observing word processing systems in other corporations. The investigator determined that the installation of such a system is not only feasible but desirable. One of the basic determinants of the feasibility of installing such a system is the need for the system. In the case of the Johnston Corporation, the need for a word processing system definitely exists.

Recommendations

On the basis of the investigative efforts, the following recommendations are presented:

1. That another study be conducted to determine the brand of word processing system most desirable for the Johnston Corporation.

2. That on the basis of that study, a decision be made soon thereafter regarding the brand of word processing system to be installed by Johnston Corporation.

3. That a representative of the vendor of the recommended system conduct a study of the needs of the Johnston Corporation to determine the exact nature of the required equipment.

4. That the individuals in Johnston Corporation who will use the system be exposed to information regarding the use of the system, the advantages resulting from the use of the system, and the potential of the system.

Conclusions

Although the present transcription system used in Johnston Corporation is efficient and the employees of the firm are quite satisfied with the system, the need for the installation of a word processing system is based on the following conclusions:

1. That the installation of a word processing

system can be justified on the present volume of work completed in Johnston Corporation.

2.   That as greater amounts of typewritten work are required in the Corporation in the future, the present transcription system will become less efficient.

3.   That the installation of a word processing system will enable the Corporation to mechanize more of its operating procedures.

Findings of the Investigation

Three different sources of information were utilized in preparing this report. The information gathered through each of the sources is presented in the sections that follow.

Information provided by word processing equipment vendors. Without exception, the equipment vendors who were contacted regarding this study reported that the volume of work is the primary factor to consider in deciding whether or not the installation of a word processing system is feasible. Several different variables have to be considered in determining the volume of work, including the following: number of employees at each of the hierarchical levels; amount of repetitive typing in comparison to the amount of typing that is done only one time; turn-around time required for various tasks, and so forth. Utilizing these variables to determine the need for such a system, the investigation revealed that the typing and transcription output of Johnston Corporation is 8 percent higher than the minimum level required to be able to justify the use of a word processing system. It is on the basis of this information that the recommendation is being made to install a word processing system.

Review of appropriate literature. The primary source of the periodical articles reviewed during the process of preparing this report was Word Processing Journal and . . .

---

narrative format is more appropriate, the periodic report may be presented in memorandum, letter, or short report format.

Figure 23–2 illustrates a periodic report.

Progress Reports

Like periodic reports, progress reports have a rather specialized function, which is to report progress about a specific project or program. One of the major differences between periodic reports and progress reports is the regularity with which they are prepared. Periodic reports are prepared on a regular basis; progress reports are prepared when there is progress to report. Progress reports are often prepared for individuals in

FIGURE 23–2   Periodic Report

Monthly Expenditures of Accounting Department
January, 1976

	Beginning Balance	Ending Balance	Expense
Salaries	$38,000	$34,800	$3,200
Equipment Rental	1,200	1,000	200
Duplicating Costs	240	210	30
Telephone Charges	600	500	100
Supplies	360	300	60

the top hierarchical levels of an organization. For this reason, they frequently facilitate the making of decisions about certain projects or programs.

The organization of progress reports generally follows a specific outline, which includes the following sections:

1. *Introduction.* This section identifies for the reader the purpose of the project or the objective of the program and the individuals who are involved in the project or program.

2. *Summary of progress reported in prior progress reports.* Because some progress reports are one of a series, this section provides a very useful function. The purpose of this section is to review for the reader the progress that has been reported in prior progress reports. If the reader is quite familiar with the project or program, this section does not have to be as detailed as when the reader is unfamiliar with the project or program.

3. *Summary of progress since last progress report.* The purpose of this section is to provide for the reader a summarization of the progress that has been made since the last progress report. In many cases, this section contains the major substance of the progress report.

4. *Progress that is not according to plan.* Because some progress reports provide a basis for decisionmaking, the report writer should decide whether or not the report should contain information about progress that is atypical. If decisions have to be made regarding progress, it is quite likely that decisions will have to be made about progress that is not typical or according to plan. For example, assume that the administrative office manager has requested reports about the progress on the installation of a new word processing system. Because of the inability of the equipment vendor to obtain the necessary equipment, the installation is behind schedule. Since this represents atypical progress, the report writer should consider presenting this fact in the progress report.

5. *Summary of uncompleted work on the project or program.* The

purpose of this section is to give the report reader some indication of the work that remains to be done on the project or program. This information is especially useful in helping the report reader assess the total status of the completion of the project or program.

Although progress reports are frequently presented to the reader in either the memorandum or the letter format, they may be presented as a short report as well. The formality of the situation should govern which format is used. Memorandum and letter formats are appropriate for less formal situations, while more formal situations may require utilizing the short report format.

An illustrative progress report is presented in Figure 23-3.

Figure 23-3   Progress Report

```
      TO:  Mr. David Brown
    FROM:  Dick Jenkins
 SUBJECT:  Status Report on the Feasibility of
           Installing the Word Processing System
    DATE:  July 7, 197_
```

Introduction
     The purpose of the project on which Mary Johnson and I are working is to determine the feasibility of installing a word processing system in Johnston Corporation.

Summary of Progress
     Up to this point, Mary and I have talked with four of the six equipment vendors of word processing equipment in this area and have completed the review of the appropriate literature regarding word processing systems.

Nature of Atypical Progress
     According to the time schedule agreed upon by you, Mary, and me, the conversations with all six vendors were to have been completed and observations of four of the word processing installations were to have been made by this date. Because of Mary's absence for a week and because of my having to assume a portion of her tasks, the project is now four days behind schedule.

Summary of Work to be Completed
     At this point, we have yet to complete two of the conversations with equipment vendors and seven of the observations of word processing systems.

Staff Reports

Whereas some of the other types of informal reports are prepared externally, staff reports are always prepared internally. Because a high level of formality is typically not required in presenting staff reports, they are often presented in memorandum format.

The nature of staff reports often determines the items or sections that are included in their presentation. Because staff reports are frequently prepared subsequent to the solving of a particular problem, the sequence of items frequently follows a problem-solving approach. Therefore, many staff reports utilize the following sequence of items:

1. *Preview*. This section is primarily utilized to give the reader a preview of what is to follow in the report.

2. *Purpose of the report*. Since some readers will not be familiar with the problem discussed in the report, a statement of the **report purpose** is necessary. The **report problem** summarizes the reason or reasons necessitating the preparation of the report, while the purpose outlines the benefits expected to result from solving the problem identified in the report.

3. *Presentation of facts*. This is the major section of the staff report. The facts are presented and discussed in this section. If graphic illustrations would facilitate the reader's understanding of the material contained in the report, the inclusion of appropriate illustrations should be considered.

4. *Conclusions*. Some readers are primarily interested in the conclusions that have been derived from the facts presented in the preceding section. In order for the conclusions to have value, they must be supportable by the facts presented in the previous section of the staff report.

5. *Recommendations*. If appropriate for inclusion in a staff report, the recommendations section is the final section of the report. Since not all staff reports require the development of recommendations, they should be included in the report only if appropriate. Although the recommendations are based upon what the report writer believes to be appropriate courses of action, they should be fairly consistent with the facts or information presented earlier in the report.

Figure 23–4 illustrates a staff report.

Justification Reports

The justification report is frequently prepared at the initiative of the report writer. It is often used to justify a certain recommendation or course of action. Because the recommendation or the course of action is considered to be the most important section of the report, the report writer frequently includes this section before presenting the facts or findings. Thus, the report reader peruses the section considered by the report writer to be the most important section.

The following sections are frequently used in justification reports:

1. *Purpose of the report.* This section outlines for the reader the major reason for the writer's preparing the report.

2. *Identification of recommendation or recommendations.* This is the section of the report that the report writer is most interested in having read. To facilitate ease in reading, the recommendations are often enumerated.

3. *Suggestions for adopting the recommendations.* Because of the nature of some recommendations, certain courses of action have to be modified upon adopting the recommendations. If this is the case, the suggestions for modification should be discussed in the report. If the adoption of the recommendations will not require a change, this section can be omitted.

4. *Discussion of facts pertaining to the recommendations.* It is often to the report writer's advantage to discuss the facts pertaining to the recommendations. Perhaps the report reader will not fully support the adoption of the recommendations until after having read this section. This is the section in which the advantages and disadvantages of adopting the recommendations can also be identified.

5. *Summary of conclusions.* The final section of the justification report is the summary of conclusions. The conclusions typically outline for the reader the reasons why the writer feels the conclusions should be adopted. Like the conclusions contained in the other types of informal reports, there must be sufficient evidence to support each conclusion.

The justification report can be presented to the reader in memorandum format, letter format, or short report format. The writer-reader relationship should be considered when determining which of the three formats to use.

A justification report is illustrated in Figure 23–5.

Preparing Formal Reports

Formal reports are typically analytical in nature, whereas informal reports are nonanalytical. Generally, formal reports are used less frequently in the business world, but they are nonetheless equally important and useful. Formal and informal reports are similar, since both are used to provide a basis for making decisions.

Because of the level of formality of formal reports, a considerable amount of the effort takes place prior to the time that the actual writing commences. This prewriting effort is necessary in order to give proper organization to the preparation of formal reports.

One of the most fundamental steps involved in preparing formal reports is the identification of the report problem when there is a problem to be solved. The identification of the problem is often made by the individual who authorized the preparation of the report. In some cases the authorization will be in writing, while in other cases the authorization will be made orally. When the authorization is made orally, the report writer must exercise a considerable amount of care in developing the

Figure 23-4   Staff Report

TO: John Crocker
FROM: David Samuels
SUBJECT: Changes in Purchasing Procedures
DATE: January 27, 197_

Preview
     As I agreed to do in our discussion of September
27, I am providing you with information outlining
my investigation of the purchasing procedures
followed by our company. This report includes a
discussion of the facts of the investigation, conclusions, and recommendations regarding the purchasing procedures.

Purpose
     An investigation of the purchasing procedures of
our organization was undertaken because of lack of
consistency between the various departments with
regard to the purchasing procedures they follow. Because of the lack of consistency, much inefficiency
has resulted, thus increasing the financial burden
on the organization. The purpose of this report,
then, is to provide suggestions for improving the
purchasing procedures.

Presentation of Facts
     At the present time, the purchasing procedures
of the organization are decentralized. This means
that each department has developed its own procedures
for purchasing. The results of the investigation
revealed the following findings:
     1.   That no two departments follow exactly the
same procedures for purchasing.
     2.   That some of the departments have very loose
procedures while others have very strict procedures.
     3.   That many of the departments purchase their
office supplies from the same vendors.
     4.   That most departments overspend their budgets
for office supplies.
     5.   That departments frequently have to wait
two to three weeks for certain supplies because
their inventory of those supplies is depleted before
the supply is replenished.

Conclusions
     On the basis of the findings of this investiga-
tion, the following conclusions are presented:
     1.   That the present decentralized purchasing
system is not efficient.
     2.   That the decentralized system results in
greater costs to the organization because it is not

```
possible to take advantage of quantity purchasing.
     3.   That greater control is needed over the func-
tion of purchasing than is presently possible.

Recommendations
     On the basis of the conclusions, the following
recommendations are presented to you for your
consideration:
     1.   That the organization institute as quickly as
possible a centralized purchasing system.
     2.   That a purchasing department be developed to
oversee the purchasing function.
     3.   That departments not be allowed to overspend
their budgets for the office supplies.
```

problem. In addition to determining the report problem, the report writer must also determine the purpose of the report. The report problem and the purpose can be differentiated as follows: the problem identifies the reason responsible for the report being prepared, whereas the purpose identifies the benefits that will result from solving the problem. Both the problem and the purpose should be stated in the text of the report.

The following identifies the report problem and the purpose of the report for a situation in which the report was problem-solving in nature:

> The purpose of this report is to provide a basis for determining the need for establishing a paper recycling program in Johnson Company.

The problem identified in the above example is the need for establishing a paper recycling program. The purpose of the report is to provide a basis for determining the need of such a program.

Formal reports that are not primarily problem-solving in nature do not require the identification of a problem in the text of the report. However, the purpose for preparing the report should be identified.

Once the problem of the report has been developed, the **factors of the problem** should be identified. In this case, factors refer to the causes of the problem. To use the example cited above, the factors are the causes responsible for the need for establishing a paper recycling program. But when the report does not call for the identification of a problem, the factors refer to the area or areas to be investigated. For example, when a formal report is prepared only to present information about a certain topic, the factors are the areas to be investigated in order to present information about the topic.

Another of the report writer's activities that adds to the effectiveness of a report involves determining who its readers will be. Thus, the report writer can be sure that the report is written at a level appropriate

Figure 23-5   Justification Report

TO: Bill Bradley
FROM: Keith Simmons
SUBJECT: Earlier Starting Time During Summer Months
DATE: June 2, 197_

Purpose of Report
   The purpose of this report is to provide you with
some information I've accumulated regarding the practice of allowing employees to begin working one-half
hour earlier during the summer months, shortening
the lunch hour to one-half hour, thus being able to
quit work one hour earlier than normal.

Recommendations
   On the basis of my investigation, I recommend the
initiation of a formal study designed to determine
the feasibility of installing a summer work schedule,
which would enable employees to begin working
one-half hour earlier than normal, condensing
the lunch hour to one-half hour, and then allowing
employees to end the working day one hour early.

Suggestions for Adopting the Recommendations
   Because of the magnitude of this recommendation,
I feel the feasibility of the summer hour schedule
should be thoroughly investigated.   Information
about this practice could be obtained from other
organizations utilizing the schedule, from pertinent
literature, and from feedback from employees.   The
investigation should perhaps be carried out by a
committee comprising various company employees.   If
you feel my suggestion has merit and that a committee
investigation is appropriate, I would be happy to
serve as chairman of the committee, if you desire.

Discussion of Facts
   Because many of our employees enjoy the summer
outdoor sports and because daylight is needed for
most of these sports, employees could take advantage
of greater participation in such sports if the company adopted the summer hour schedule.   Not only
would the employees' work performance improve because
of the greater amount of exercise, but also the
morale of the work force should improve.
   In discussing this practice informally with
several of my colleagues, without exception, they
were in agreement that the idea has considerable
merit.   They indicated that starting one-half hour
earlier than normal would not be a problem, nor would
the shortened lunch hour since most never leave the
premises for lunch.

From what I've read and heard, more and more
companies in the area are installing a summer hour
schedule. Perhaps our organization could remain more
competitive in the hiring of new employees if we too
installed such a schedule.

Summary of Conclusions
     I feel the following conclusions regarding this
suggestion are appropriate:
     1.   That a committee should be formed very soon
to determine the feasibility of a summer hour work
schedule.
     2.   That such a schedule would be feasible in our
organization.
     3.   That the advantages of installing a summer
hour work schedule would far outweigh disadvantages.
     4.   That if the summer hour work schedule is
implemented, fairly strict operating procedures would
also have to be developed.

to the readers' reading ability. In addition, the report writer can determine what information should be included in or can be excluded from the report in relation to the readers' understanding of the report problem. Some report readers are sufficiently familiar with the report topic for certain background information to be excluded, while other report readers are not as familiar with the report topic and therefore will need a greater amount of background information. Furthermore, by knowing who the report readers will be, the report writer is likely to be familiar with the uses that will be made of the report. Therefore, the writer is more certain of being able to include information needed by the reader in order to make full use of the report.

The report writer also finds the use of a preliminary outline of the development of the report to be very advantageous. The outline helps the report writer to stay on course and not become sidetracked. The outline will also help the report writer to develop the report logically.

The report may be developed using an inductive, deductive, or chronological arrangement. When the inductive arrangement is used, the facts and findings are presented before the conclusions and recommendations. When the deductive arrangement is used, the conclusions and recommendations are presented before the facts and findings. The chronological arrangement is used when presenting data that has some significant relationship to time. When the chronological arrangement is used, the conclusions and recommendations may be presented either before or after the chronological presentation of the facts or findings.

The report writer has two symbolic options available in preparing the preliminary outline. The conventional outline, which is illustrated below, uses Roman and Arabic numerals as well as alphabet letters.

```
        I. XXXXXXXXX
        A. XXXXXXXXX
           1. XXXXXXXXX
              (a) XXXXXXXXX
                 (1)XXXXXXXXXX
```

The second symbolic notation option uses only Arabic numbers and decimals. This option is illustrated as follows:

1. First degree
   1.1 Second degree
   1.2 Second degree
       1.2.1 Third degree
       1.2.2 Third degree
             1.2.2.1 Fourth degree
                     1.2.2.1.1 Fifth degree
2. First degree (second division)

Another of the decisions the report writer will have to make is to determine which method of collecting information should be used. The information can be collected using either a primary or a secondary research method. **Primary research methods** involve the use of information that is collected specifically for the report being prepared. The primary methods include the use of company records, use of people, observation, and experimentation. The **secondary research method** involves the use of printed information, such as that found in textbooks, periodical articles, newspaper articles, reports, and other types of documents. Because several of the research methods involve the use of rather specialized procedures, it is recommended that the report writer become quite familiar with the procedures before attempting to use a research method. It is not within the scope of this chapter to include a discussion of these procedures.

An important function of the report writer is the interpretation of the information that is to be included in the report. Without this interpretation, the data or information lack meaning. Unless the report writer is careful, certain errors can be made during the interpretation process. One such example of an interpretation error is the drawing of conclusions on the basis of insufficient information or evidence. This error frequently occurs because report writers feel that conclusions have to be presented if the report is to have any worth. Another type of error occurs when the report writer allows personal feelings and biases to influence the interpretation of the data. Nothing is apt to be more destructive to a formal report than to allow personal bias to influence the interpretation process.

At this point, the report writer is ready to begin the actual writing of the report. A writing style that is appropriate to the writer-reader relationship is needed. Formal reports require a more formal writing style than do informal reports.

Formal reports consist of several rather distinctive report parts. No matter what the nature of the topic or what the intended use of the report is, formal reports contain several required parts. In addition, several optional parts may be included in a formal report.

Formal reports are comprised of three main sections: The preliminary section, the body section, and the appended section. Each of these sections is composed of the following parts:

> Preliminary Section
>   Title Page
>   Letter of Authorization*
>   Letter of Transmittal
>   Table of Contents
>   List of Illustrations*
>   Abstract
> Body Section
>   Introduction
>   Text
>   Summary
>   Conclusions
>   Recommendations
> Appended Section
>   Appendices*
>   Bibliography

All of the report parts in the above list are required in formal reports, with the exception of those parts identified with asterisks. These report parts are optional and should be used when needed.

A discussion of each of the report parts follows. Several of the report parts require the use of a special format. For example, a special format is used on the title page and on the table of contents, as well as on several other pages. Since the mechanics of format are beyond the scope of this book, it is suggested that the writer utilize one of the several style manuals that are available.

Title Page

The title page typically includes four main items: the title of the report, the name and title of the individual to whom the report is to be presented, the name and title of the individual responsible for preparing the report, and the city and state in which the report was prepared, as well as the date of presentation.

Letter of Authorization

If the preparation of the report was authorized in writing, the report writer has the option of including the written authorization in the report. The authorization is typically in the form of a letter or a memo-randum.

Letter of Transmittal

Even though the letter of transmittal is one of the preliminary parts of formal reports, it is frequently one of the last report parts to be pre-pared. The purpose of the letter of transmittal is to formally transmit the report from the report writer to the report reader. The letter should in-clude the date on which the preparation of the report was authorized as well as the topic of the report and an expression of appreciation for hav-ing had the opportunity to prepare the report, along with the offer to be of assistance if needed. Several optional items may be included in the letter of transmittal. If the report writer chooses to include the optional items, they are inserted between the two items mentioned above. Some of the optional items that may be included are the following: a short summary of the major findings of the report, unusual circumstances ex-perienced by the report writer in preparing the report, and information that may add creditability to either the report or the research efforts of the report writer.

Table of Contents

The table of contents provides the reader with two significant ad-vantages: a listing of the headings and subheadings included in the re-port and the page numbers on which each of the various headings and subheadings are listed. Thus, the report reader is able not only to deter-mine quickly what is included in the report but also to locate rapidly the page on which each of the topics appears. The conventional symbolic notation option is frequently used in identifying the various headings and subheadings in the table of contents.

List of Illustrations

Although this part of the report is optional, it is suggested that a list of illustrations be included in reports containing five or more graphic illustrations. In addition to the listing of the title of each illustration, the page number of the report on which the illustration is found should also be listed. At the discretion of the report writer, the table of contents and the list of illustrations may be combined if either contains only a few items.

Abstract

The purpose of the abstract is to provide a summary of the report, including the introduction, significant findings, interpretation of data or information, and conclusions and recommendations. Depending upon the detail contained in the abstract and the trust that the report reader places in the efforts of the report writer, the reader may peruse only the abstract. In most cases, however, report readers find it necessary to read at least a portion of the remainder of the report.

The body section of the formal report consists of five different parts: introduction, text, summary, conclusions, and recommendations. The introduction may be broken down into several different subparts.

Introduction

     The purpose of the introduction is to provide the report reader with a considerable amount of background information about the report. If the report reader is quite familiar with the background of the report, less detail will be needed than if the report reader has very little familiarity. The number of introductory subparts to be included in the report should be governed by the reader's familiarity with the report topic and by the writer's interpretation of the need for including such subparts.

Background of the report. The inclusion of this subpart, which is optional, provides the reader with information regarding the authorization of the report. This subpart includes the name of the individual who authorized the preparation of the report, the manner in which the authorization was made, and the date of the authorization. The name of the report writer may also be included in this subpart.

Purpose. This subpart identifies for the reader the problem of the report, provided the report is problem-solving in nature, in addition to the purpose of the report. While the problem involves the reason or reasons necessitating the preparation of the report, the purpose provides for the reader the benefits to be derived by solving the problem. If the report is primarily informational, the problem needs not be stated. The purpose identifies the areas to be investigated in the report. If the preparation of the report will result in secondary purposes, these, too, should be identified in this subpart.

Scope. The scope identifies for the reader the areas or topics to be included in the report. If the scope of the report is not identified and if some important topics are omitted, the quality of the report writer's research efforts are often questioned. But if the report writer identifies the topics or areas intentionally omitted from the report, the research efforts of the writer are viewed more favorably.

Methodology. The purpose of this subpart is to identify for the report reader the methodology used in gathering the information for the report. If one of the four primary research methods is used, the method should be explained in detail. If the data are tested statistically, the statistical test should be identified and explained.

     If the report is comprised primarily of secondary sources of information, such as textbooks, periodical articles, and reports, the location of the majority of the sources should be mentioned in the methodology subpart.

Definitions. When the report writer uses terminology that is unfamiliar to the reader or uses words in an unusual context, the report writer will facilitate the reader's understanding of the report by defining such words. The reader of the report thus uses the words in the way the writer intended the words to be used.

Limitations. It is not uncommon for reports to be affected by circumstances over which the report writer has no control. By identifying such circumstances in the report, the reader knows to what degree the information in the report can be considered to be reliable and valid. In addition, the report reader knows that the writer is not purposely attempting to disguise such circumstances in order to improve the quality of the report. Some examples of circumstances that tend to limit reports are the following: insufficient finances, insufficient time, insufficient information, and so forth.

Historical background of the report. Although this subpart is optional, it may be helpful to provide the report reader with information about the historical background of the report. This is especially true in instances when the report is one of a series of reports. The historical background may consist of a summary of prior research, prior decisions with regard to the report problem, or other important information of a historical nature.

Report organization. An identification of the organization of the report is provided to give the report writer a preview of what is to follow. Although this subpart is also optional, it is commonly used in longer formal reports.

Text of the Report

The major portion of information is contained in the text of the report. This is the section that contains the findings of the research as well as the interpretation of the findings. In reports using secondary sources of information, this is the section in which the information is presented to the reader.

The report writer should consider the use of appropriate graphic illustrations to help illustrate the information being presented in the report. A variety of graphic aids are available, including the following: tables, pie charts, bar charts, multiple bar charts, subdivided bar charts, line graphs, and so forth. Because the preparation of such illustrations is likely to be a rather detailed process, it is suggested that the report writer become familiar with the techniques involved before attempting to prepare such illustrations. Most texts concerned with report writing contain a discussion of the techniques involved in the preparation of graphic illustrations.

When material from secondary sources of information is used in a formal report, the report writer must give credit where credit is due. Footnotes must be used when quoting material verbatim or when paraphrasing material that is not considered to be common or general knowledge in a particular field. Several different footnoting variations exist. Information concerning the proper mechanics of footnoting is presented in style manuals.

Headings and subheadings in reports are used to help the reader in perusing and understanding the report. Different degrees of headings are used, with the most important material receiving a first degree heading and subdivisions receiving second or third degree headings. The proper horizontal location and style of the three commonly used degrees are illustrated as follows:

THIS IS A FIRST DEGREE HEADING
This is a Second Degree Heading
This is a third degree heading. The third degree heading is used . . .

Summary

The summary section of the formal report is designed to recap for the reader the major findings of the report. The summary typically recaps each of the major divisions or sections discussed in the text of the report and is generally presented in the same order as the divisions or sections of the report.

Conclusions

The concluding statements regarding the facts or findings presented in the report must be based on available evidence, not on opinion or supposition. If the conclusions are not supportable by the facts presented in the report, they are virtually useless.

The conclusions are typically enumerated and presented in the order of the facts or findings from which they are drawn. Thus, the reader is readily able to locate in the text the information from which the conclusions are drawn.

Recommendations

The purpose of this section is to provide the reader with certain recommendations regarding appropriate courses of action. While the conclusions must be based on the available evidence, the recommendations are based on the report writer's understanding of the information presented in the report. The report writer has a greater amount of personal freedom in developing the recommendations than in developing any other section of the report. Because the recommendations are often based on the conclusions, they too should be enumerated and presented in the same order as the conclusions.

The appended section of the formal report consists of two subparts: appendices and bibliography. The appendices subpart is optional and should be used only if a need for its inclusion exists.

Appendices

The purpose for using appendices (appendix if only one item is used) is to include material in the report that is considered supplementary. When material is placed in an appendix, the report writer should, at the appropriate place in the body of the report, refer the reader to the appended material. Some examples of materials that are often included in the appendices are the data collection device (such as a questionnaire or interview form), raw data tables, diagrams, and so forth.

Bibliography

The bibliography is important in reports that borrow a considerable amount of information from secondary sources. The purpose of the bibliography is to provide the reader with a categorical listing of the secondary sources of information used in the report. Thus, the bibliography is comprised of all sources for which footnotes exist. The report writer may also include sources used for reference purposes even though a footnote does not exist for such sources.

Bibliography entries are arranged alphabetically in the following categories: books, periodicals, newspapers, reports, unpublished materials, and miscellaneous sources. The mechanics of preparing the bibliography are contained in most style manuals.[1]

In some instances there may be a need for the report writer to add a section to the report after the report has been printed. An addendum is commonly used for this purpose. The addendum, which may be inserted before the first page of the body of the report, should identify the page in the report to which the addendum refers.

After the report is in print, an errata can be used to identify and correct errors that appear in the report. The errata should also be included at the beginning of the report and should identify the page and line on which the error appears, as well as the correction.

Since most of the parts or subparts included in formal reports are illustrated in one or more of the informal reports included in this chapter, a formal report is not illustrated.

Review Questions

1. What are the primary differences between a short report and a formal report?

2. In presenting the information in short reports, what is the difference between the use of the inductive and the deductive options?

3. What is the primary use of periodic reports?

4. What is the primary function of progress reports?

5. Why do staff reports frequently follow a problem-solving approach in the presentation of information?

6. What is the primary difference between the problem of a report and the purpose of the report?

7. Why is the recommendation section of a justification report presented early in the report?

8. In a formal report, what are the factors of the problem when the report is concerned with a problem situation?

9. What types of primary and secondary research methods are available to the report writer?

---

[1] Two of the more common style manuals are William G. Campbell, *Form and Style in Thesis Writing* (Boston: Houghton Mifflin Company, 1969), and Kate Turabian, *Manual for Writers of Term Papers, Theses, and Dissertations* (Chicago: University of Chicago Press, 1973).

10. When preparing a formal report, what types of material must be footnoted?

11. What types of materials are included in the appendices of a formal report?

Minicases

The Arnold Company is in the process of installing its first computer system. Up to this time, either information was processed manually or the services of a data processing center were utilized. The managers of the company have stipulated that the systems staff keep them informed of the progress of the installation of the new system, especially when progress is not proceeding according to plan. The managers plan to use this information in two ways: as a basis for making decisions regarding the installation of the new system and as a means of keeping the employees informed about the progress of the installation of the new system. What type of report is appropriate for such purposes? Why? What topics should be included in each report that is prepared?

*   *   *

The Acme Corporation has recently been having problems with high employee turnover. The vice president of internal affairs of the corporation has asked several of his subordinates to prepare a short report that outlines recommendations or suggestions for reducing the high turnover. You, the administrative office manager of the corporation, are one of three subordinates who have been asked to prepare the report. The investigation into the reasons for the high turnover has been completed, and it is now time to prepare the report. In presenting the report, do you plan to use the inductive or deductive arrangement of presentation. Why? Prepare an outline of your report.

Case

Although the Davidson Company has always believed in the need for its employees to take college-level courses, it has never adopted the policy of reimbursing the employees for the tuition incurred in taking such courses. At one of the recent administration staff meetings, the topic of tuition reimbursement was discussed. Although no official action was taken at that time, you feel strongly committed to the policy of tuition reimbursement, and therefore, you decide to prepare a justification report for John Davidson, president of the company. You feel that if Mr. Davidson is made aware of some of the advantages, the likelihood of the company's adopting such a policy might be much greater.

1. What sections should be included in the report?

2. Identify the items that you plan to include under each of the major sections of the report.

Office Reprographics

Chapter
24

Organization of the Reprographics Center
  Determining the Needs of the Reprographics Center
  Centralized Control of the Reprographics Center
  Personnel in the Reprographics Center
  Layout of the Reprographics Center
  Policies and Procedures of the Reprographics Center
  Maintenance of the Equipment in the Reprographics Center
  Standards of the Reprographics Center
  Cost Control of the Reprographics Center
  Equipment in the Reprographics Center

The Copying Process
  Copying Equipment Requiring Sensitized Paper
    Diffusion transfer
    Gelatin transfer
    Stabilization
    Diazo
    Thermography
  Copying Equipment Using Plain Paper
    Xerographic process

The Duplication Process
    Spirit process
    Stencil duplication
    Offset process

The Imprinting Process
    Signature machines
    Impression stamps
    Numbering devices

Auxiliary Equipment
    Automatic collators
    Binders
    Photolettering equipment
    Direct-input photocomposition equipment
    Phototypesetters

Chapter Aims   After studying this chapter, the student should be able to:

1. Discuss the manner in which the needs of a reprographics center are determined.

2. Discuss the advantages that centralized control of a reprographics center provides.

3. Discuss the policies and procedures by which reprographics centers generally operate.

4. Discuss the ways that production standards of a reprographics center are determined.

5. Discuss the characteristics of the following types of copying processes: diffusion transfer, gelatin transfer, stabilization, diazo, and thermography.

6. Discuss how the xerographic copying process functions.

7. Discuss how the offset duplication process works.

Chapter Terms   *Reprographics center:* the center found in many organizations that provides copying and duplicating services for the entire organization.

Satellite centers: the centers found throughout an organization that provide limited copying and duplicating services. Extensive or more complex projects are completed in the centralized reprographics center.

More and more organizations are installing sophisticated **reprographics centers,** which are responsible for providing copying and duplicating services. The operation of such centers is often the responsibility of the administrative officer manager. The installation of such centers has been made possible by the development of many new types of equipment, much of which is capable of performing a variety of copying and duplicating processes at very reasonable per-copy rates. Another reason for the widespread installation of such centers is the quality of work that is produced on the new equipment. No longer do organizations have to contract with outside printing firms when professional-quality work is needed.

Organization of the Reprographics Center

Like so many of the other administrative office management functions, the efficiency of the reprographics center is likely to be determined in part by the organization of the center. It is doubtful that the operating efficiency of the center could ever be maximized unless the center is properly organized. The proper organization of the center is greatly determined by the needs of the organization in which the center is located.

Determining the Needs of the Reprographics Center

Before a reprographics center can be organized, the needs of the center have to be determined. This is frequently the responsibility of the administrative office manager and/or the supervisor who is responsible for the present duplicating department. The needs of the center are determined to a large extent by the copying and duplicating requirements of the organization. In most cases, the requirements are assessed by making detailed records of what is copied and duplicated and in what quantities. A survey may also be used to help determine the copying and duplicating requirements of the reprographics center. When determining the needs of a reprographics center, several factors should be considered:

1. The number of copies needed of each document that is prepared in the organization.
2. Special production requirements of the copying or duplicating process (color requirements, reduction or blowup requirements, types of paper on which the copies are to be made, etc.).
3. The overall characteristics of the original document (typewritten, line drawings, photographs, etc.).
4. The desired quality of the copying or duplicating processes.
5. The turnaround time needed for obtaining copies of original documents.
6. The nature of specialized production jobs.

Unless this phase of the installation of a reprographics center is carefully considered, it is doubtful that the center can be efficiently organized or that the equipment in the center will be appropriate for the various production jobs.

Centralized
Control of the
Reprographics
Center

One of the characteristics of most reprographics centers nowadays is the centralized control of the center. Typically, the administrative office manager has overall responsibility and control over the operation of the reprographics center. The day-to-day operation of the center, however, is frequently the responsibility of a reprographics center supervisor.

In most cases, reprographics centers are also centrally located in the organization for reasons of accessibility. Because most of the departments in the organization are likely to use the services provided by the center, its central location is of primary importance. In organizations that occupy several different floors of a building, it may be necessary to have **satellite centers** located throughout the building. The satellite centers most likely contain only a portion of the equipment that is found in the main reprographics center. The smaller production jobs are performed in the satellite centers but the major jobs are most likely performed in the main center.

In comparison to decentralized control, centralized control of the reprographics center has several advantages:

1. Greater control over the reprographics function is possible.
2. The center is likely to operate with greater efficiency.
3. The selection and utilization of the equipment is likely to be more efficient.
4. Fewer brands of equipment are likely to be purchased, which simplifies the equipment maintenance process.
5. The purchase and replenishment of supplies are likely to be performed more efficiently.

Personnel in the
Reprographics
Center

The quality of the work produced in the reprographics center is directly related to the care with which the personnel produce the work. Because many of the processes are quite specialized, it is important that the personnel be skilled in and knowledgeable about the various processes. Otherwise, full use of the equipment is not possible.

There are a variety of means by which personnel learn to operate the equipment found in the reprographics center. For the less sophisticated equipment, equipment manufacturers generally provide short, comprehensive training sessions on the uses of the equipment. For more sophisticated equipment, the personnel may need to complete a formal educational program in order to be able to use and understand the equipment. These formal educational programs are provided by a variety of schools, including high schools, technical schools, community colleges, and four-year colleges and universities. The participants of such educational programs frequently enroll in a printing or graphics program.

It is not uncommon for operators of heavy printing equipment to serve as a printer apprentice for several years. The use of such heavy equipment is perhaps more likely to be found in organizations that specialize in printing than in reprographics centers found in organizations.

Layout of the Reprographics Center

The layout of the reprographics center must also be given adequate consideration when developing the center. Because a considerable amount of the work that is produced in the reprographics center involves several steps, the flow of work through the center must be considered. The most efficient pattern is to have a straight-line flow of work that eliminates backtracking and crisscrossing.

The specialized nature of the equipment found in reprographics centers makes the use of the various services provided by equipment manufacturers very desirable. Representatives of such manufacturers are not only able to provide excellent suggestions for the layout of a reprographics center, but they are also able to help an organization develop efficient operating procedures for the center.

In addition to planning the placement of the equipment in the center, the layout of the center involves providing adequate storage space for the enormous amounts of supplies that are needed, providing washroom facilities, and providing photographic darkroom facilities if needed. In addition, certain environmental conditions are also very important in the reprographics center. These conditions include adequate ventilation and acoustical control, which is necessary because of the noise generated by some of the machines often found in a reprographics center.

Policies and Procedures of the Reprographics Center

In addition to (1) the organization of the reprographics center, (2) the personnel who work in the center, and (3) the layout of the center, the policies and procedures used in operating the center also influence its efficiency. The policies and procedures are mainly concerned with using the services that are provided by the center.

In order to use the services of reprographics centers, the completion of a requisition form is generally required. The form is basically a work order that may include the following items: The number or name of the document being reproduced; the desired reproduction method; the number of copies needed; special directions (such as color of paper, ink, reduction, collating, stapling, etc.); the name of the department to be charged; the name of the individual making the request; and authorization.

Another procedure of concern is the handling of confidential material. To maintain the integrity of such material, some centers assign the processing of such work to certain individuals who can be trusted and who are held responsible for the confidentiality of the material.

Reprographics centers must also establish policies that are to be used for handling high priority items. Some employees feel that every item they send to the reprographics center is high priority and thus requires immediate attention. Most centers operate on a first-in, first-out basis, except for legitimate high priority or rush jobs. In order for a job to be classified as high priority, some centers require that the job be certified as such by several different individuals. This procedure eliminates the possibility of some employees identifying all jobs as being high priority or of a rush nature.

Another procedure that has to be developed is the method for determining which copying or duplicating process should be used for making copies of the original document. The basis for determining which process to use is influenced by the number of copies that are to be made and the intended use of the copies.

Maintenance of the Equipment in the Reprographics Center

Because of the specialized nature of the equipment found in reprographics centers, equipment maintenance is very crucial. Proper maintenance not only adds to the life of the equipment but also improves the quality with which the work is produced. Improper maintenance is also very likely to increase the operating costs of the center.

Equipment operators are able to provide a wide variety of routine equipment maintenance. Much of this maintenance involves keeping the equipment clean and in adjustment. More complex maintenance is typically provided by specially trained individuals. In some cases, these individuals are employed by the organization; but in most cases, these individuals work for the equipment vendors and provide maintenance service on a request basis.

Standards of the Reprographics Center

In order for a reprographics center to be financially feasible, the efficiency of the center is paramount. One means of judging the efficiency of the center is the frequency with which production standards are attained. Such standards, which can be obtained from the various manufacturers of the equipment found in the reprographics centers, identify the per-hour number of copies that are reasonably attainable on the various pieces of equipment. Without the use of such standards, the organization has no way of knowing whether the reprographics center is considered to be operating efficiently. If the actual results are considerably below the level of expected results, the administrative office manager and/or the reprographics center supervisor must determine the reasons for the difference and take appropriate action.

It may also be possible for the reprographics center to determine its own standards rather than utilizing those available from the various equipment manufacturers. To do this, the center's output has to be recorded over a period of time. These records can then be used to determine either hourly or daily output rates for each person in the reprographics center. Such a system can also be used to determine the need for more employees in the center. As the output volume of the center increases, so does the need for more employees in the center. Each time that the volume increases to the point that one more employee is needed, the reprographics center supervisor has sufficient justification to recommend the hiring of another employee.

In addition to production standards, the reprographics center must also be concerned with cost standards. Factors that must be considered in developing cost standards are the following: cost of operating the equipment (lease or depreciation); cost of supplies; operator costs; and cost of the space occupied by the center. When the per-unit costs exceed those that are considered to be normal, the administrative office manager or the reprographics center supervisor should determine the reasons for the excessive costs.

Cost Control of the Reprographics Center

The nature of the reprographics center makes cost control not only very desirable but also very crucial. Because there are so many opportunities for waste in the center, which adds to the cost of the operations, special attention must always be given to cost control.

1. Use the most economical duplicating and copying processes for the job being performed.
2. Do not request or produce more copies than are needed.
3. Keep the equipment in proper adjustment so that very few if any pages are ruined in the duplicating or copying processes.
4. Print on both sides of the paper when possible.
5. Do not use the services of the reprographics center for a particular project if some outside organization is able to provide more economical service.
6. Take advantage of quantity purchasing of supplies.

Equipment in the Reprographics Center

Another factor that has a significant bearing on the efficiency of the reprographics center is the equipment that is used. The type of equipment found in the center also determines to a great extent the types of services that the center is able to provide. A wide variety of equipment is presently on the market, much of which varies considerably in terms of the operational processes.

The sections that follow provide a detailed discussion of the following: the copying process, the duplicating process, and the imprinting process. In addition, a discussion is also provided of some of the auxiliary equipment that is likely to be found in reprographics centers.

The Copying Process

The development of efficient copying equipment has undoubtedly been greatly responsible for the paperwork explosion taking place in organizations throughout the country. Although the development of copying equipment has resulted for the most part in significant advantages, certain disadvantages have also resulted. Perhaps the most significant disadvantage is the ease with which unneeded extra copies of documents are made. Not only does this add to operating costs, but provisions also have to be made for the storage of the extra copies.

One of the most common means of categorizing copying equipment is according to the type of paper used by the equipment. While some copying equipment requires special sensitized paper, other copying equipment uses plain paper.

**Copying
Equipment
Requiring
Sensitized Paper**

Several different copying processes require the use of sensitized paper. Among these processes are the following: diffusion transfer, gelatin transfer, stabilization, diazo, and thermography.

Diffusion transfer. This process, which is also known as a wet copy process, requires the use of two chemically coated sheets of paper for each copy that is made. One of the sheets is a negative that is coated with a gelatin containing silver halide, which makes the sheet sensitive to light. The other sheet is positive. The face of the document that is being copied is placed against the gelatin side of the negative sheet. These two sheets are then exposed to an intense light. The image areas of the original absorb the light rays, while the nonimage areas of the original document reflect light back to the negative, thus forming an image on the negative. After the negative has been exposed, it is placed face-to-face against the positive sheet, and the two sheets are then passed through a developing solution. A reaction of the developing solution with the image on the negative sheet causes the image to transfer by diffusion to the positive sheet. The two sheets are then passed through rollers that remove excess developer. The negative is discarded, and after the positive sheet has been allowed to dry for a few minutes, the copy is ready for use.

In comparison to some of the other copying processes, this method results in several disadvantages, including the following: a developing solution is needed, copies have to dry before they are usable, and the process is quite slow.

Gelatin transfer. This process, which is sometimes known as dye transfer, also requires the use of special paper and developing chemicals. When this process is used, the face of the original document is placed against the surface of the negative sheet, which is coated with a gelatin substance. The original and the negative are exposed to light, and the nonimage areas of the original reflect to and expose the negative. The negative is then passed through a chemical solution that causes the gelatin in the exposed areas to harden. The unexposed areas of the negative remain soft, and as the negative is passed through the chemical solution, these areas become a dye. As the dye areas of the negative come in contact with the copying paper, the dye transfers to the paper, thus creating a likeness of the original on the paper. Up to ten copies of the original can be made before the dye either dries or is used up.

This process has the same disadvantages as the diffusion transfer process.

Stabilization. Whereas the diffusion transfer and the gelatin transfer processes require both negative and positive sheets, the stabilization process does not require the use of an intermediate sheet. This process involves the reflection of light from the original document onto the sensitized copy paper. The copy paper is then passed through a developing chemical and then through a stabilization chemical, which permanently fixes the image on the copy paper.

This process is especially suited for copying photographs. Like the other processes already discussed, disadvantages of this process are the required use of chemicals, the fact that copies have to dry before they are usable, and the slowness of the process.

Diazo. This process, which is especially suited for making copies of architectural and engineering drawings, requires the use of an original document in a translucent state. Therefore, this process can be used to copy only documents that have printing on one side of the page. The original document is placed against a copy sheet coated with a diazonium compound. The two sheets are then exposed to light. The image areas on the translucent original prohibit the light rays from passing through, while the nonimage areas allow the light rays to pass through to the coated copy paper. When light rays pass through to the copy paper, the diazonium compound is decomposed. The copy paper is then exposed to a chemical, and while the decomposed areas remain neutral, the active areas (image areas of the original) react and cause an image to appear on the copy sheet.

Although this is one of the least expensive copying processes, the process is marked by several disadvantages, including the use of ammonia fumes in the development process and the slowness with which the process works.

Thermography. Another of the copying processes that requires the use of sensitized paper is thermography. This process works on the principle that dark areas or substances absorb heat whereas light areas or substances do not absorb heat. This process is also known as the infrared or the heat-transfer process. When this process is used, the original document is placed beneath the copy paper. As the original and the copy paper are exposed to infrared rays, the image or printed areas of the original hold the heat, which causes the copy paper to turn dark in these areas. The original document images are produced on the copy paper. This process requires the use of writing or printing substances that hold heat long enough to transfer the image to the copy paper. Some types of ink and some colors do not hold heat sufficiently long to enable the process to work.

Among the more serious disadvantages of this process is the restriction of the use of this process to heat-sensitive substances and the tendency of thermography copy papers to darken and to become brittle with age.

Copying Equipment Using Plain Paper

The only copying process presently available that uses plain paper is the xerographic process. Many feel this process is superior to the other processes that require sensitized copy paper or liquid chemicals.

Xerographic process. This process is based on the physics principle that unlike electrical charges attract each other but like charges repel each other. The process, by means of a camera, transmits the image of the original document to a selenium-coated drum that is positively charged. The nonimage areas of the original document allow light to strike the drum, which causes the positive charge in those areas to dissipate. The image areas of the document, on the other hand, hold their positive charge on the drum. A negatively charged black powder is then spread over the drum, and since unlike electrical charges attract each other, the powder adheres to the image areas on the drum. A likeness of the original document appears on the drum. A plain sheet of paper with a positive charge is then passed over the drum and the images on the drum are transferred to the paper, thus providing a copy of the original document. The black powder is permanently affixed to the paper by means of a heat process.

The xerographic process provides quality copy on plain paper and requires no chemical liquids or operator training. The choice between the xerographic process or another process is a function of volume. Generally, at higher volumes the xerographic copier is advantageous due to lower cost of supplies. However, at lower volumes, the higher unit cost of the equipment can result in higher cost per copy.

Figure 24–1 illustrates a xerographic copier.

The Duplicating Process

At one time, the differentiation between copying and duplicating was fairly distinct. The major distinction between the two was the number of copies that were made. To illustrate, a copying process was typically advantageous for making fewer than twenty to thirty copies of an original, while a duplicating process was used when more than twenty to thirty copies were needed. Because of modern technology, the differences between the two processes have become less distinct. The three major types of duplicating processes found in existence today are the spirit process, the stencil process, and the offset process.

Spirit process. This process is suitable for making fewer than 300 copies from one master. Of the three duplicating processes, the spirit process is the least expensive. The spirit process requires the use of a spirit master, which consists of two sheets—the carbon backing sheet and the face of the master. As the face of the master is either written, drawn, or typed

FIGURE 24–1   Xerographic Copier

Courtesy, Xerox Corporation

on, the carbon adheres to the backside (in reverse image) of the master face. When ready for use, the face of the master is placed carbon side up on the drum of the duplicator. The master is moistened with a special alcohol solvent, which causes a small portion of the carbon to transfer to the copy paper each time a piece of copy paper passes through the duplicator. The master continues to print until there is no more carbon left on the master to transfer to the copy paper.

In addition to manually preparing spirit masters, they can also be prepared by a thermal process. The original and a thermal master are fed through a device that causes the image areas to hold heat. The heat buildup then causes the carbon on the thermal master to adhere to the face of the master. Typically, the number of copies that can be made from thermal masters is less than the number of copies that can be made from standard spirit masters.

The spirit process is quite flexible. Several different colors of carbon can be placed on one spirit master, which enables multicolor printing in one pass through the machine. The masters can be stored and reused. In addition, it is possible to eliminate certain portions of the master from printing after the master has already been used to duplicate some copies. To eliminate certain portions from duplicating, those portions can either be cut out of the master, can be covered up with tape, or the carbon in those areas can be scraped from the master.

Stencil duplication. Like the spirit process, stencil duplication is also rather inexpensive as a duplication method. Stencil duplication is suitable for making up to 2,500 copies from one stencil. The stencil consists of a fiber substance coated with wax. When the stencil is typed, written on, or drawn on, the wax is pushed aside, which enables ink to pass through the exposed areas. The stencil is attached to a drum that is covered with an ink-soaked pad. The ink, which passes through the exposed areas of the stencil, is transferred to the copy paper as the paper comes in contact with the stencil. If properly cared for, the stencil can be stored and reused.

When color duplicating is desired, a separate stencil has to be made for each color that is desired. For example, a stencil has to be prepared to transfer the red areas to the paper, another for the blue areas, and so forth. If a duplicating job involves four different colors, the paper has to pass through the duplicator four different times.

It is possible to prepare stencils on an electronic stencil-making device. The device simply burns into the stencil the same images as are found on the original document. Electronic stencil-making devices are capable of making halftone illustrations.

The stencil duplication process is suitable for making more copies from one stencil than can be made from one spirit master. In comparison to the spirit process, the stencil duplication process is less convenient for multicolor duplication.

Offset process. Although more costly and more intricate than either the spirit process or stencil duplication, the offset process is presently used more extensively than either the spirit process or stencil duplication. Depending on the conditions, several thousand copies can be made from one master.

The offset process is based on the chemical principle that water and grease do not mix. The image areas on the printing master hold the greasy printing ink, while the nonimage areas hold water, which repels the ink. The inked images are transferred or offset to a rubber blanket or roller. As the duplicating paper comes in contact with the roller or blanket, the image is transferred to the paper.

The offset masters, which are prepared in a variety of ways, are either paper or metal. Some of the paper masters are direct image and can be drawn on, typed on, or written on. Some paper masters are also prepared photographically in a paper master maker. The metal plates are photographically prepared in a plate maker. A much greater quantity of copies can be produced from a metal plate than from a paper master.

Many offset duplicators are highly automated. Some of the automated features found on offset duplicators include the following: the ability to cut sheets of paper from a paper roll; perforating, slitting, and collating attachments; counters that cause the duplicator to stop when the desired number of copies have been prepared; automatic insertion and ejection of paper masters; and automated machine cleanup.

Of the three primary duplication processes, offset offers the best quality of work. In most cases, the quality of offset duplication is almost as high as the quality of the original. Because offset equipment is more specialized, equipment operators need to receive appropriate training in uses of the equipment. In relation to the spirit process and the stencil duplication process, the per-unit cost of offset duplication is somewhat higher.

Copy printer. Copy printer equipment, which incorporates the offset printing process, is a fairly recent development in reprographics equipment. This device is designed for high-volume, short-run, repetitive jobs. It is especially suited for situations requiring from five to a thousand copies of an original. It is also especially suited for organizations printing from 150,000 to 500,000 copies per month.

A characteristic of copy printer equipment is the number of automated features. The operator simply places the copy in the machine, dials the number of copies to be made, and the machine automatically completes the job. The machine is therefore capable of electrostatic master-making, master feeding, and offset duplicating without operator assistance. In addition, most copy printers are also capable of reducing the original to a smaller-size copy as well as sorting the copies into sets.

Figure 24–2 illustrates a copy printer.

FIGURE 24–2 Copy Printer

Courtesy, A. B. Dick Corporation

**The Imprinting
Process**

The imprinting process is used to add information to an already existing document. Several imprinting processes are available, including the following:

Signature machines. Two different types of signature machines are presently available. One type of machine imprints the signature on a document by means of a ribbon. This is the type of machine frequently used to affix signatures to checks. Another type of signature machine uses a template of the individual's signature. As the stylus follows the signature contained in the template, a mechanical pen produces the signature on the document. This device is especially useful for placing original signatures on important mass mailings, for example.

Impression stamps. These are used when there is a small amount of repetitive data to be recorded on documents. Examples are data stamps, signature stamps, name and address stamps, and authorization stamps. For small jobs, an impression stamp is generally more convenient than is the imprinting of information by means of a duplication process.

Numbering devices. It is sometimes desirable to sequentially number a series of documents. The use of a mechanical numbering device is much quicker and neater than numbering by hand.

Auxiliary Equipment

During the last few years, a considerable amount of auxiliary equipment for use in reprographics centers has been developed. While some of this equipment mechanizes the duplicating process to a greater extent, other types of equipment expand the process so that a greater variety of duplicating jobs can be produced in the reprographics center. The following provides a discussion of some of the more significant developments:

Automatic collators. This development has reduced to a considerable extent some of the manual effort involved in many offices. Automatic collators, which can be attached to offset duplicators, mechanically collate pages as they leave the offset duplicator. As each page leaves the duplicator, it is transported to the appropriate bin in the collator. At the end of the production cycle, the bins in the collator will contain one copy of each page that has been duplicated. As the collated sets are removed from the collator, they can be stapled, which completes the job.

Binders. Rather than binding documents with staples or spirally binding documents, a rather recent development is the adhesive binding of documents. This process, which is also known as "perfect binding," involves putting a thin layer of adhesive along one edge of the document that is to be bound. The adhesive holds the pages together.

Photolettering equipment. This equipment, which is a form of photocomposition, is used to place letters, one at a time, on a strip of film or on photographic paper. The photolettering process is primarily used for setting miscellaneous lines of type, typically in a large-size format.

Direct-input photocomposition equipment. This type of equipment, which is relatively new in terms of its development, consists of a photocomposition unit attached to a keyboard. As the material is typed on the keyboard, the device automatically sets the type. The design of this equipment limits its use somewhat to smaller volume projects. Other photocomposition equipment is more desirable for larger projects. Figure 24–3 illustrates a direct-input photocomposition device.

Phototypesetters. This type of equipment is designed for projects that are too large for processing on direct-input photocomposition equipment. Although these typesetters are able to perform many more functions than the direct-input equipment is capable of performing, its cost is also

FIGURE 24–3   Direct-Input Photocomposition Device

Courtesy, Addressograph Multigraph Varityper Division

considerably higher. The present phototypesetters are either classified as second generation or third generation equipment.

Second generation phototypesetters are driven or controlled by other input media, such as perforated paper tape or magnetic tape produced on some keyboard device. They generate the type images by flashing light beams through a photographic master such as a revolving disk or a strip of film. The smaller phototypsetters typically have no more than four different type styles or fonts, and they set type in a minimum number of sizes. The larger phototypesetters have more type fonts, can set type in a greater number of sizes, and are much faster than the smaller phototypesetters. Some of the newer second generation phototypesetters also incorporate a minicomputer that can be programmed to hyphenate words automatically that must be divided at the ends of lines, in addition to performing other typesetting functions.

Third generation phototypesetters differ from the second generation equipment in the manner in which the type is generated. The third generation phototypesetters generate type characters on the face of a cathode ray tube, and the images on the tubes are subsequently photographed. The third generation phototypesetters permit much faster operating speeds.

Because of the complexity of the phototypesetting process, any organization giving thought to the installation of such equipment should carefully consider all the alternatives. The cost of the equipment requires a thorough analysis of its need before a decision is made to install a phototypesetting system.

Review Questions

    1. What is a satellite reprographics center and why is such a center used?

    2. What factors need to be considered in determining the layout of the reprographics center?

    3. How might the costs of a reprographics center be controlled?

    4. Which of the various types of copying processes appears to be the most efficient? Why?

    5. What are the advantages and disadvantages of spirit, stencil, and offset duplication?

    6. Explain the use of photocomposition equipment in a reprographics center.

Minicases

    The Johnson Corporation has noticed that its copier costs have increased 30 percent over last year's costs, and that last year's costs were 25 percent greater than the previous year's costs. Part of this increase is due to the increased volume of the business of the company—15 percent for each of the last two years. Part of the increase is also due to an increase in paper and equipment rental, amounting to an increase of 5 percent in each of the last two years. What factors are likely to be responsible for the other increased costs for which the corporation has no explanation? What suggestions do you have for controlling such costs?

*   *   *

    The Tidwell Corporation recently developed a fairly extensive reprographics center. The center contains an offset process duplicator, which is owned, and a xerographic copier, which is leased from the equipment manufacturer. The firm is greatly concerned about operating costs and wishes to determine which of the two processes (duplication and copying) is more economical for a given number of copies. You, the administrative office manager, have been asked to determine the maximum number of copies that can be made on the copier and the minimum number of copies that can be made on the offset duplicator. This means that you will have to determine the number of copies that can be more economically made on the offset duplicator. To determine the per-unit cost of copies made on the copier, what factors have to be determined? To determine the per-unit cost of copies made on the offset duplicator, what factors have to be determined?

Case
Great Foods, Inc., is the second largest food-processing company in the country. Although it is considered to be an independent processor, the products of Great Foods, Inc., are sold in independent and chain supermarkets throughout the country. The headquarters of Great Foods, Inc., are located in Pittsburgh, and approximately 2,000 employees work in the headquarters building. Because of the size of the company, much of the equipment is purchased on a bid basis. In the past, the various equipment vendors have been fairly successful in underbidding one another on various purchases. The result is a wide variety of equipment, especially office copiers. Because of the nature of much of the work performed in Great Foods and because of the size of the company, there are about eighty different copiers located throughout the building. Some of these are used quite frequently, while others are used only a few times during the day. A recent survey showed that there were ten different types of copiers in the building, some requiring special paper while others use regular paper. In addition, some of the copiers require the use of a variety of other products. While some of the copiers have a fairly good maintenance record, others require a considerable amount of servicing.

Several of the managers have begun to realize that the bidding process may be producing false economies. In other words, even though the cost of the equipment may be less because of bidding, the organization ultimately spends more because of the required use of special products and because of the extensive amount of service required by some of the equipment.

You have been asked to analyze the situation discussed above. In your analysis, do the following:

1. Explain how you might determine whether or not the bidding process is producing false economies.

2. Discuss the situation from a practical standpoint.

3. Make recommendations to alleviate the situations described above.

4. Discuss the followup methods you would use to determine whether or not the situation improves after your recommendations have been implemented.

Office
Manuals

Chapter
25

Types of Manuals
> Policy Manual
> Procedures Manual
> Company Manual
> Employee Manual
> Functional Manual
> Desk Manual

Preparing Manuals
> Responsibility for Manual Preparation
> Gathering Information for the Manual
> Organizing the Manual
> Writing the Manual
> Presenting the Manual
>> Illustrations
>> Page size
> Binding
> Use of Different Colors of Paper
> Use of Special Features
> Selection of Appropriate Printing Process
> Distributing Manuals
> Revising Manuals
> Employee Use of Manuals

Chapter Aims   After studying this chapter, the student should be able to:

1. Discuss the characteristics of the policy manual.
2. Discuss the characteristics of the procedures manual.
3. Discuss the characteristics of the company manual.
4. Discuss the characteristics of the employee manual.
5. Discuss the characteristics of the functional manual.
6. Discuss the characteristics of the desk manual.
7. Discuss the various aspects involved in preparing manuals.

Chapter Terms   *Policy manual:* a manual that provides a written record of the policies by which an organization operates.

Procedures manual: a manual that outlines the steps in various work processes.

Company manual: a manual designed to provide information about a company or organization. It may contain the following types of information: history of the organization, information about the organization's products, and the organization chart.

Employee manual: a manual that frequently consists of pertinent sections found in other manuals and that is used by employees as they carry out their jobs.

Functional manual: a specialized manual that contains information about one specialized area or function of the organization.

Desk manual: a manual prepared by individual employees that is designed to help them perform their jobs.

The manuals found in organizations serve a variety of purposes, including the establishment of uniform operating policies and procedures and the orientation of employees to the organization. The different manuals provide written documentation of pertinent information with which the employees should be familiar. Therefore, the contents of the manuals are frequently used by employees as a device to guide their actions.

Types of Manuals

Although the types of manuals used by office employees are quite variable, the following encompass the types of manuals frequently found in organizations: **policy manual, procedures manual, company manual, employee manual, functional manual,** and **desk manual.** Each is explained in the sections that follow. In some organizations, each manual is a separate, self-contained document. In other organizations, some of the information from two or more manuals is consolidated as a means of developing a special-purpose manual.

Policy Manual

The policy manual serves a very useful function in organizations since it provides a written record of the policies by which organizations operate. Generally, the policies contained in the policy manual are in the form of rules and regulations that the employees are expected to follow. Because certain policies must exist in the organization if its operating efficiency is to be maximized, the policies are more likely to be understood and adhered to if they are in writing. The end result is more consistent treatment of employees in like situations, which reduces the likelihood of unfair treatment. In addition, policy manuals provide a time-saving advantage. Since the policies are in writing, employees do not have to take the supervisor's or manager's time to learn about the routine policies of the organization. The supervisors and managers are therefore able to concentrate more effectively on the nonroutine or complex situations for which policies do not exist or on situations requiring the interpretation of existing policies.

While several significant advantages result from the development and use of policy manuals, certain disadvantages may also result. Specifically, when policies exist and are expected to be followed, a certain amount of flexibility is destroyed. In some instances, it may be desirable to make an exception to the policy, but if the philosophy of the organization is to treat all employees equally in like situations, a deviation from the policy cannot be logically justified. Another disadvantage of the use of policy manuals is the fact that policy statements often contain loopholes. The amount of inconvenience that results from the use of policies containing loopholes typically outweighs the amount of convenience resulting from the existence of such policy statements. Most organizations may find it more desirable to have no written policies than to have policies containing loopholes.

The types of policies found in policy manuals frequently consist of two levels of policies: policies that govern organizationwide actions and policies that govern the actions of individual employees. Examples of the former include the organization's policy regarding a commitment to environmental problems, a definition of the concern for social responsibility, and a discussion about the necessity for the organization to be supportive of community affairs and development. Examples of the types of employee policies that are commonly found include the following: absenteeism and tardiness, sickness, injury on the job, overtime, alcohol consumption on the job, gambling, and so forth. A portion of a policy manual is illustrated in Figure 25-1.

FIGURE 25–1 Policy Manual

This policy manual explains the policies by which the organization operates. The policies should be used to guide your actions. If you have any questions regarding any of the policies, please discuss the matter with your supervisor. The policies are intended to facilitate the equal treatment of employees in similar circumstances.

Absenteeism: Employees are expected to be on the job unless they are ill or have been approved for a personal business day or have been approved for absence without pay. (See section below pertaining to the use of personal business days.) The following policies exist for unexcused absences:

1. Employees will lose a day's wages for each day they are absent without proper excuse.
2. Employees who accumulate more than three days' absences without proper excuse will lose two days' wages for each day they are absent.
3. Whenever an employee accumulates a total of seven or more unexcused absences during the time of employment with the organization, the employee will be subject to immediate discharge.

Tardiness: Employees are expected to be on the job at the time the working day begins. Employees who are late to work will be penalized in the following manner:

1. Up to 15 minutes of tardiness will result in employees' losing three minutes of wages for each minute late to work.
2. When tardy from 16 to 30 minutes, employees will lose five minutes of wages for each minute late.

3. When tardy 31 or more minutes, employees will lose seven minutes of wages for each minute tardy.

Sick Days: Employees are given ten paid sick days each full year they are employed by the organization. Except for major illnesses, these days cannot be accumulated from one year to the next. The vice president for corporate relations will determine whether the sick days can be accumulated from one year to the next. Employees will lose a day's wages for each day they are ill after they are no longer entitled to sick days. Notification of illness should be provided no later than five minutes after the beginning of the work day.

Personal Business Days: Employees are given two (2) paid personal business days for each year of full employment with the organization. These days are primarily for the purpose of conducting personal business, although employees are not required to provide a reason for wanting to use their personal days. At least two days' notice is required for requesting a personal business day. Requests are to be made through the supervisor. Employees may not take personal days the day prior to the organization's observance of a legal holiday.

Procedures Manual

The procedures manual, which outlines existing procedures for performing various duties, is likely to have a significant impact on the operating efficiency of the organization. The manual should contain a detailed explanation of the steps involved in performing various work processes.

The use of a procedures manual is especially useful for outlining the steps in the work processes that comprise the organization's operating system. In many instances, operating systems consist of work processes comprised of steps that must be completed in a certain order. If the steps are completed out of order, a malfunction in the system is likely to occur, which hampers the organization's operating efficiency.

The use of a procedures manual results in other advantages as well. Because the appropriate procedures for completing a work process are frequently simplified and are made as efficient as possible before inclusion in the procedures manual, employee efficiency can be improved by utilizing the written procedures. In addition, employees can use the steps outlined in the procedures manual when they have to undertake a task about which they are not familiar. Consequently, the supervisor or other employees do not have to spend valuable time explaining the task to the employee.

Examples of procedures frequently included in procedures manuals are the following: completing a purchase requisition, completing a payment voucher, obtaining authorization for tuition refund for college-level courses, requesting unpaid time off, and so forth. A section from a procedures manual is contained in Figure 25–2.

FIGURE 25–2   Procedures Manual

This procedures manual is designed to provide consistency in the operating procedures of the organization. It is to be used to determine the step-by-step procedures for completing various work processes. Any deviation from the steps outlined in the procedures manual should be discussed with your supervisor prior to the time you begin the work process.

Preparation of the Employee Requisition Form: Employee Requisition Forms are prepared by the department needing additional employees or replacements. The purpose of the form is to request the Personnel Department to obtain the required personnel. Two copies of the Employee Requisition Form must be prepared for the Personnel Department; one copy must be prepared for the originating department. An Employee Requisition Form is illustrated in Exhibit 1. The number of each of the items presented below corresponds with the identical number on the form.

1. The date the form is prepared.
2. The name of the department needing the employee.
3. The title of the open position.
4. The job number corresponding to the position title.
5. The total number of employees needed.
6. The date the employees should report for work.
7. The base rate of pay to be received.
8. The qualifications required or preferred, as well as other remarks which might aid the Personnel Department in their selection of applicants.

The copies are routed for the signatures of the department or division head, the unit head, and if required, the appropriate vice president. After the appropriate signatures are obtained, the original and one copy of the completed Employee Requisition Form are sent to the Personnel Department. One copy is retained by the originating department.

Exhibit 1
EMPLOYEE REQUISITION FORM

Current Date _____ (1) _____   Department Name _____ (2) _____

Job Title _____ (3) _____   Job Number _____ (4) _____

No. of Openings _____ (5) _____   Report Date _____ (6) _____

Base Rate _____ (7) _____

Recommendations and Remarks:
_____
(8)
_____

_____

Department Head   Unit Head   Vice President

Company Manual

The purpose of the company manual, sometimes referred to as an organizational manual, is to provide information about the company or the organization. The manual also includes information about the functions of each of the departments or divisions that comprise the organization or company. Also frequently included in the company manual is historical information about the company, information about the products manufactured by the company or services provided by the company, and an organization chart depicting the managerial hierarchy of the company. In some instances, a separate organization chart is also included for each of the company's departments or divisions.

The company manual is used for a variety of purposes, including orientation of new employees, providing prospective employees with important information about the company, and providing interested parties with the reference material about the company. Figure 25–3 illustrates a portion of a company manual.

FIGURE 25–3   Company Manual

The Johnson Corporation was founded in Pittsburgh, Pennsylvania, in 1920 by Ernest and David Johnson. The two Johnson brothers had worked for several years in managerial and administrative capacities for other local firms prior to the time they founded the Johnson Corporation. Their prior experiences proved to be very valuable in the founding of the new company.

At the time the Johnson Corporation was founded, its production consisted primarily of shovels, hoes, rakes, and spades. Throughout the years, the Corporation has expanded its line to include all types of gardening tools, including gas-powered lawn mowers, garden tractors, tillers, tree and shrub trimming equipment, and fertilizers and sprays.

During the last ten years, the Johnson Corporation has experienced substantial growth in sales volume. The 1976 gross sales volume of $3,792,487 was five times greater than the gross sales volume ten years earlier.

Departments of the Johnson Corporation

The Johnson Corporation consists of eight functional departments. Each of these departments has a department head directly in charge of the day-to-day operations of the department. The following identifies the functions of each of the departments:

Personnel: The Personnel Department is primarily responsible for the recruiting and hiring of new employees. Its functions include the following: listing vacancies in appropriate media sources; explaining job duties to applicants; providing applicants with application blanks; interviewing applicants; administering appropriate screening tests; selecting most desirable applicants to be interviewed by the manager or supervisor for whom the applicant will be working, notifying payroll of the hiring of the new employee; coordination of periodic employee performance appraisals; maintaining integrity of the personnel folder of each employee; determining future manpower requirements; and coordination of salary administration program.

Purchasing: The Purchasing Department is the central purchasing authority of the organization. All purchases must be processed through the purchasing department. Some of its functions include the following: Completion of purchase orders; transmittal of purchase orders to vendors; inventory of supplies on hand; release of orders for payment, notifying vendors or shippers of damaged items; notifying vendors of long or short orders; obtaining bid quotations from vendors; and talking with sales representatives of vendor firms.

Receiving: The Receiving Department takes receipt of all orders received by the organization. The functions of the Receiving Department include the following: accepting orders; verifying accuracy of orders; inspecting orders for damage; notifying Purchasing Department of discrepancies in orders; delivering orders to departments.

Employee Manual   The employee manual is typically a composite of pertinent sections of other manuals, in addition to information that appears nowhere else. The employee manual, frequently distributed to employees at the time their employment begins, provides vital information with which employees should be familiar, which helps eliminate misunderstanding. Some organizations consider their employee manual to be a "contract" between the organization and each employee.

The information contained in employee manuals varies widely from organization to organization. Some of the more common types of information contained in the employee manual that may also appear in other manuals developed by the organization include important policies affecting employees and information about the historical development of the company or the organization. Other information contained in the employee manual that is not likely to appear in another manual includes the following: an open letter from the president or chairman of the board; information about the use of the manual; terms or conditions of employment, including promotion, salary increases, layoffs, discharge, overtime, sick days; fringe benefits; and organization activities or associations for employees, as well as other information of interest to employees.

Because the employee manual is very likely to contain many different types of categories of information, its organization becomes very crucial. Poorly organized employee manuals are very difficult to use. Depending upon the amount of information contained in the employee manual, a detailed index may be desirable. A portion of an employee manual is illustrated in Figure 25–4.

FIGURE 25–4   Employee Manual

Use of Your Employee Manual

This employee manual has been prepared with you in mind. It is hoped that the use of the manual will help you better understand the various policies of the organization as well as increase the satisfaction you experience in working for us.

The manual is as complete as we can make it at this time. In fact, many of the revisions contained in this manual stem from suggestions you provided us. From time to time, additional materials will be prepared or sections will be revised. We suggest that you immediately insert such additions or revisions in this manual.

Although we think the manual is written in such a way that there is very little room for interpretation, we suggest that you contact your supervisor if you wish an additional interpretation of some section included in the manual.

We are certain that the use of this manual will make your employment with us more pleasant.

Employment Practices

Selection: Johnson Corporation is an equal opportunity employer. Therefore, no applicant or employee is discriminated against by reason of race, religion, creed, political affiliation, sex, marital status, or national origin.

Evaluation: At the end of the first three months of your employment, you will be evaluated by your supervisor. If your performance is satisfactory, the supervisor will recommend continued employment. If your performance is less than satisfactory, the supervisor will recommend either that you be given another chance to improve your performance or that you be discharged. Other evaluations will take place after you have been employed for six months and for one year. Thereafter, you will be evaluated once a year.

Classification: The classification of the job you hold determines your salary rate. Therefore, the higher the classification of the position you hold, the higher will be your salary.

Promotions: You will be considered for promotion as soon as your supervisor feels that you are qualified for a promotion. Most job openings are filled by promoting employees rather than by hiring new employees from outside the organization. Your performance is a basic determinant of how rapidly you are promoted.

Salary Increases: The amount of yearly salary increases is influenced by two basic factors: the ability of the organization to provide salary increases and the quality of your performance. Higher performance means greater salary increases.

Work Hours: The work day begins at 8 a.m. and ends at 4:45 p.m., Monday through Friday. You are entitled to one 15-minute rest period in the morning and one in the afternoon. In addition, you are also entitled to a 45-minute lunch period.

Employment Policies

Absenteeism: The policy for unexcused absenteeism is as follows:

1. Unexcused absenteeism will result in an employee's not being paid for the days absent without prior authorization.
2. At the time that an employee accumulates a total of seven days of unexcused absences, the employee will be subject to dismissal.

Tardiness: The policy for tardiness is as follows:

1. When an employee is late not more than ten minutes, the employee will lose three minutes of wages for each late minute.

Fringe Benefits

The management of the organization believes that providing employees with certain fringe benefits is very worthwhile. Therefore, the following fringe benefits are provided:

Group Health Insurance: Full coverage is provided the employee. For a small fee, the employee may also obtain coverage for a spouse and any children under the age of 20 years. Details are outlined in a policy you will receive at the time you start your job with us.

Functional Manual

A variety of functional manuals are being developed and used in organizations. Functional manuals are quite specialized and usually contain information about one specialized area or function. An example of a functional manual is the records management manual, which explains in detail the operation of the records management program. Included in the records management manual are various operating procedures of the program. Other examples of functional manuals are filing manuals that outline the filing rules utilized by an organization and typing manuals that outline mechanics of presenting various typewritten documents.

Functional manuals are more specialized than procedures manuals. While functional manuals may outline the appropriate procedures for one specialized area, procedures manuals typically contain the appropriate procedures for performing a variety of tasks or work processes. It is very likely that a procedures manual will contain information about work processes in each of the organization's departments and divisions.

An example of a functional manual is illustrated in Figure 25–5.

FIGURE 25–5   Functional Manual

Filing Rules Manual

In order to have a consistent filing system throughout the organization, those employees whose jobs consist of filing duties are asked to utilize the filing rules contained in this manual. When a variety of different filing systems are used, it becomes very difficult for an employee who is not familiar with the system to locate requested documents. This frequently happened in the past when the employee who developed the filing system in a particular department terminated employment with the organization. That employee's successor would subsequently find it very difficult to locate rapidly the desired documents.

Filing Rules

1. Each part of an individual's name is a filing unit. An individual's last name is the first filing unit, the individual's first name is the second filing unit, and the individual's middle name or initial is the third filing unit.

2. The second filing units are considered only when the first filing units are identical. Thus, in the case of John R. Jones and John Richmand Jones, the second filing units (John in each case) are considered.

3. The third filing units are considered only when the first and second filing units are identical. In the case of John R. Jones and John Richmand Jones, the third filing units (R. and Richmand) have to be considered because the first two filing units are identical.

Desk Manual

The desk manual is not an official publication of the organization. Rather, a desk manual is prepared by employees as the need for such a manual arises. The desk manual, although varying considerably from one employee to another, frequently contains information that would assist employees in performing their jobs. The information contained in the manual is typically not found in other documents in the organization.

Some of the types of information contained in the desk manual includes the following: important days to remember (birthdays, anniversaries, etc.), procedures for completing work processes that are not contained in the procedures manual, copies of form letters used, names and addresses of individuals with whom the employee's supervisor frequently deals, instructions for processing certain forms, and style guidelines for certain documents (itineraries, summary reports, etc.).

Most employees who develop desk manuals are constantly revising and adding to their manuals. Thus, the contents of most desk manuals are placed in loose-leaf notebooks that facilitate the easy removal and addition of information.

The desk manual is very useful not only to the employee who develops it but also to the employee's successor or to temporary employees. To provide a successor with the desk manual facilitates rapid familiarization with the job.

Figure 25–6, which was adapted from a document entitled "Making Your Own Desk Manual," provides the reader with additional information about the preparation and use of a desk manual.

FIGURE 25–6   Making Your Own Desk Manual*

1. *What it is*
   a. *A blueprint* of all the work that flows across your desk or that is a part of your job.
   b. *A compilation* of materials that you handle or that apply particularly to your job, *some of which* may be scattered throughout various other types of manuals—
      General information handbook
      Handbook on employment
      Standard practice handbook
      Job information handbook
   c. *A sure-fire and indispensable tool* for increasing efficiency and understanding of procedures, systems, policies, as they relate to a particular "position."
   d. *An excellent aid* in cost analysis relating to level of pay for level of task performed.
2. *What it should contain—whatever it takes* to give a complete and clear picture of your work and its relation to other work (this will vary with every job)
   a. *Brief statement* of overall scope, purpose, and duties of job.
   b. *Daily breakdown* of duties performed.
   c. *Special duties*—those that come at stated intervals.
   d. *Forms section*—include samples of each, with information concerning how filled in, number of copies, from whom, to whom, when, where kept, when recorded, why used, etc.
   e. *Special terminology*—on some jobs this will include shorthand outlines and spellings as well as definitions.
   f. *Key to your filing system*—indexing, coding; how done and who does it; who has access to the files; when and how are materials actually filed; when and how charged out.
   g. *Who's who*—in department, in company or organization, in related or allied businesses, in suppliers', dealers', or customers' firms.
   h. *Lines of authority*—to whom are you responsible and for what?

to whom are they responsible, etc.?
i. *Correspondence*
   Samples of letter styles
       Kinds of letters (content),
       (Various stationeries used)
   Notations about number of carbons
   Mail—collection and delivery times
   Who answers what
   Who sees what
j. *Telephone*—including etiquette, taboos, long distance charges, etc.
k. *Travel*—vouchers, manner of computing mileage, expenses, etc.
l. *"Fringe" duties*—when performed, for whom.
m. *"Bottleneck" areas*—a little study and attention given to these might work wonders.
n. *Policies.*
o. *Machines and Equipment*—including repairman's telephone number.
p. *Supplies*—who reorders, when, where kept, etc.
q. *Miscellaneous*—when this section gets too full, make a new section.

3. *How it is compiled*
   a. *Start* with overall statement of job, if possible.
   b. *Keep* a twenty-minute check for a few days.
   c. *Assemble* notes, forms, ideas.
   d. *Sort* into categories.
   e. *Ask* for suggestions from your superior.
   f. *Incorporate* suggestions for improvement.
   g. *Set-up* the desk manual in a loose-leaf binder.
   h. *Keep* the manual up to date.

---

* Adapted from "Making Your Own Desk Manual" prepared by Helen H. Green, Michigan State University.

Preparing Manuals

    Much of the success of the various manuals found in offices is greatly dependent upon the ease with which the manuals are used. Manuals that are difficult for employees to use are generally a waste of financial and human resources. The ease with which a manual is used is determined by several factors, including writing style, indexing, illustrations, completeness, format, and accuracy of information. The purpose of this section is to provide the reader with information regarding the preparation of the different types of manuals.

Responsibility for Manual Preparation

Except for the preparation of desk manuals, the responsibility for preparing manuals is frequently assigned to a committee, with one of the higher-level managers having responsibility for chairing the committee. The advantages of using a committee for preparing a manual are numerous. Because the manual has a wider input base, the employees are more apt to accept and utilize the manual. In addition, the use of a committee helps to assure that all important areas are covered in the manual. Third, there is greater likelihood that possible shortcomings or areas of misunderstanding will be more readily identified by the committee than is possible when a manual is prepared by only one individual.

Although the use of a committee in manual preparation results in some significant advantages, certain disadvantages also result. One disadvantage is the slowness with which some committees work. Another disadvantage is the inability of some committees to come to quick agreement about certain aspects of the preparation of the manual.

Gathering Information for the Manual

The information used in preparing a manual can be gathered from a number of different sources. In fact, the greater the amount of sources used, the greater the likelihood that the manual will be complete. The committee members responsible for preparing a manual should consider the following sources of information: similar manuals prepared by other organizations; official minutes of the organization's board; union contracts; pertinent publications of the organization; employee suggestions; and external sources of information (such as publications from freight companies, post office, telephone company, and so forth). The variety of sources of information is limited only by the creativity of the committee charged with the responsibility of preparing the manual.

Organizing the Manual

After the information to be included in the manual has been gathered, the next step in the preparation of the manual is to organize the information. The organization of the information is likely to have a significant impact on the ease with which the manual is used once it is distributed to employees. The following suggestions are appropriately used in organizing the information:

1. *Organize the information according to broad categories.* For example, all the information pertaining to the policies of the organization should be grouped together, the information pertaining to fringe benefits grouped together, and so forth.

2. *After the information has been grouped into broad categories, arrange the information according to the most appropriate sequence.* In some instances, the most appropriate sequence is the arrangement of information according to order of importance. If there is no order of importance, the information should be arranged according to the alphabetic sequence of the topics or perhaps according to some chronological sequence.

3. *Organize the information in a manner that will make the information useful to the employees.* For example, several different policies could be discussed in the same paragraph. But since this organization pattern makes it difficult for the employee to use the information, a more useful pattern is to discuss each policy in a different paragraph.

Writing the Manual

As most organizations are aware, the success of a manual is quite often governed by the manner in which the manual is written. For example, if the writing is unclear and requires a considerable amount of interpretation, it is doubtful that the manual will have much success. The following are suggestions for writing the manual.

1. The writing should be clear, concise, straightforward, and in a writing style that is easily understood by the readers of the manual.
2. When possible, the use of enumerated sentences should be considered, especially in identifying steps or procedures.
3. Important words, phrases, or sentences should be highlighted by underlining, italicizing, capitalizing, or some other mechanical means.
4. When appropriate, the definition of words is recommended.

Once the rough draft of the manual has been completed, some helpful feedback may be obtained by allowing certain individuals to read the rough draft. Changes in the wording or content of the manual can be made before the manual is printed and distributed throughout the organization.

Presenting the Manual

Another factor influencing the extent to which a manual is used is its presentation. Manuals presented in a manner and style considered to be helpful to the employee will be used more extensively than manuals that are difficult for employees to use.

Illustrations. The use of illustrations in presenting information in a manual is recommended. Not only can employees visualize what is being discussed but also the illustrations typically facilitate their understanding of the topic being discussed. Examples of illustrations frequently included in manuals are photographs, line drawings, sketches, and diagrams.

Page size. The size of the pages on which the information in the manual is printed may have a significant impact on the cost of the manual. Pages measuring eight and one-half by eleven inches eliminate trimming waste. But unless most of the pages are completely filled with information, a smaller size page may be more economical even though there may be some trimming waste. The type of binder in which the pages are placed may also have a significant impact on the size of the pages. If the pages are placed in a loose-leaf binder and if smaller or uncommon size binders are not readily available, pages measuring eight and one-half by eleven inches may be less expensive.

Binding

If frequent changes in the information contained in a manual are anticipated, the use of some type of loose-leaf binding is recommended. Thus, pages can be easily removed or inserted as changes are made. Several different types of loose-leaf bindings are available in a variety of different price ranges.

Use of Different Colors of Paper

Using different colors of paper for printing the manual may be recommended if the manual is quite long and consists of numerous sections. By printing each section on a different color paper, it is obvious when replacement sheets have been inserted in an incorrect section of the manual. If pages are rarely replaced, the use of different colors of paper may not be justifiable.

Use of Special Features

Several different special features can be added to the manual to facilitate its use, including a table of contents, an index, and a coding system if the manual is quite extensive. The coding system facilitates the removal of certain pages and the addition of other pages. The coding system may utilize a combination of alphabetic letters, Roman numerals, and Arabic numerals.

Selection of Appropriate Printing Process

A considerable amount of the expense involved in printing the manual results from the type of printing process used. The selection of the printing process should take into consideration the number of copies needed, whether or not complex illustrations are to be included, and the quality of printing needed in relation to the intended use of the manual.

Distributing Manuals

If the preparation of a manual is to be considered worthwhile, the manual must be distributed to the individuals for whom it was prepared. Generally, the nature of the manual will significantly determine which individuals are to receive the manual. For example, the employee manual should be distributed to all employees in the organization. In some instances, the employee manual is given to employees at the time of the selection interview. This course of action is based on the assumption that employees are more likely to read the employee manual when they are attempting to learn about the organization than once they are on the job.

If most of the policies affecting employees are outlined in the employee handbook, a comprehensive policy manual is often distributed only to managers or supervisors. If an organization has a procedures manual that contains the steps involved in performing many different work processes, the development of several different procedures manuals may be more efficient. Employees receive only the procedures that are most relevant to the individual jobs they perform. This practice considerably reduces the costs involved in printing the manuals.

When most of the information contained in an organization manual is also contained in the employee manual, employees usually do not receive the organization manual. Therefore, the organization manual may be distributed only to supervisors, managers, or other interested persons.

Because the functional manuals are typically specialized, such manuals are generally distributed only to the employees whose jobs pertain to the information contained in the manuals. To illustrate, a filing manual would be distributed only to individuals responsible for filing. Depending upon the nature of the various functional manuals, they may be presented to each of the managers or supervisors in the organization.

Since most desk manuals are prepared by employees for their own use, they are not produced in volume for distribution to other employees. They are, however, frequently made available to the successor of the employee who initially prepared the desk manual.

Revising Manuals

Over a period of time, as organizations change, their manuals become out of date. Therefore, provisions need to be made for the revising and updating of manuals.

The responsibility for revising manuals may be assigned to the individual originally responsible for the preparation of the manual. The revision process is greatly simplified if a list of the needed revisions is maintained as the changes take place. In addition, if employee suggestions are utilized, the process of revision will be greatly simplified and is very likely to be much more efficient.

The process of manual revision is facilitated when the manuals are placed in loose-leaf binders. As pages need to be revised, the pages containing outdated information can be easily replaced with pages containing the revised information.

Employee Use of Manuals

Once the organization has invested a considerable amount of time, effort, and financial resources in the development of various manuals, every attempt should be made to cause the employees to want to use the manuals. No matter how useful and well developed the manuals are, some employees will use the manuals reluctantly. Some of the employee reluctance can be overcome if the employees are shown how to use the manuals and the benefits derived from the use of the manuals.

The employees can be encouraged to use the manuals. The manuals should be utilized in the training programs. Employees who become familiar with the use of the manual are more apt to use the manual in performing their jobs. When new manuals are developed, conduct orientation sessions. If employees are required to attend the orientation sessions and are able to see the advantages of using the manuals, there is a greater chance that the employees will continue to use the manuals. "Write up" employees who fail to follow existing procedures or policies outlined in manuals. When employees are officially notified by their supervisors that they failed to follow organization policies or procedures as outlined in existing manuals, most employees feel more compelled to use the manuals thereafter. Utilize employee participation in the development of new or revised manuals. Generally, employees who have participated in the preparation of manuals are more likely to extensively utilize the manuals they helped prepare. Have employees "sign" for the manual as proof that they did receive the manual.

Review Questions

1. What are some of the advantages of using policy manuals?
2. Why is the use of a procedures manual helpful?
3. What types of information are included in a company manual? Employee manual?
4. What is the primary purpose of a functional manual?
5. What types of information are included in a desk manual?
6. How should a manual be prepared if it is to be used by more than one employee of the organization?
7. What are some of the sources from which information can be gathered to include in a company manual? A functional manual?
8. What ways can be used to get employees to make better use of the manuals provided them by the organization?

Minicases

Several of the executives in the Browning-Day Company were meeting to discuss the feasibility of developing a policy manual. The company has a series of policies that the employees are expected to follow. These policies have never been put into writing, and each manager or supervisor verbally explains the policies to each new employee. In several instances, the policies have been interpreted differently by different managers. At the meeting, several of the individuals who were present spoke against the development of a policy manual because it would destroy some of the flexibility they now have. What do you think of the rationale cited for not developing a policy manual? What suggestions can you make to convince those who are opposed to a policy manual that a manual is not only needed but would also be very helpful and useful?

*   *   *

One of the vice presidents of Jackman, Inc., a furniture manufacturer, is working on a masters degree in business administration at a local university. The vice president was talking one day with another MBA candidate, who is presently the administrative office manager in a regional insurance office. The administrative office manager explained to the vice president that his company had just completed revising their employee manual. The more the vice president heard about the employee manual, the more he was convinced that their organization should also have an employee manual. Shortly thereafter, the vice president assigned the preparation of an employee manual to the administrative office manager. The administrative office manager indicated that she didn't know how to proceed with the preparation of such a manual but that she would be willing to prepare a manual if she knew how. What suggestions can you offer that might help the administrative office manager prepare an employee manual?

Case

The Browning Corporation, now about twenty years old, began with four employees. Because the firm manufacturers a very popular line of electronic products, including radios, television sets, and stereo equipment, the Browning Corporation grew very rapidly. While the corporation was able to cope very well with certain areas of its expansion, other areas have been totally neglected. Since most of the top managers of the firm are electronics experts rather than professional managers, several significant areas have been overlooked, including the development of various manuals. At the present time, the operating procedures of the corporation are not formalized. Thus, employees develop many of their own procedures. Employee policies vary from department to department, with some departments having quite lax policies while others have very strict policies. Since new employees do not participate in an orientation program, they learn about the company's fringe benefits through talking with other employees or with their supervisors.

Now that the corporation presently employees about 250 persons, some thought has been given to the development of one or more manuals. As the administrative office manager of the corporation, you have been asked by one of the vice presidents to share your feelings about the feasibility of such manuals.

1. What type of manuals do you feel can be justified? Why?
2. What content should be included in the manuals?
3. What procedures should be used for preparing the manuals?

Integrated Data Processing

Chapter

26

Punched-Card Systems
>   Equipment Used in Punched-Card Systems
>   Keypunch machine
>   Verifier
>   Interpreter
>   Reproducer
>   Sorter
>   Collator
>   Calculator
>   Tabulator
>   The Components of Punched-Card Systems
>   Input
>   Processing
>   Output
>   A Punched-Card System Illustrated

Integrated Data Processing
>   Equipment Used in Integrated Data Processing
>   Teletypewriter
>   Tape-punching typewriter
>   Card-punching typewriter
>   Accounting machine
>   Tape-reading equipment
>   Card-reading equipment
>   Conversion equipment
>   Designing Integrated Data Processing Systems
>   An Integrated Data Processing System Illustrated
>   Benefits of Integrated Data Processing
>   Limitations of Integrated Data Processing

Chapter Aims   After studying this chapter, the student should be able to:

1. Discuss the characteristics of integrated data processing.
2. Discuss the punched-card system concept.
3. Discuss the function(s) performed by each of the following types of equipment: keypunch machine, verifier, interpreter, reproducer, sorter, collator, calculator, and tabulator.
4. Discuss the three components of integrated data processing and identify the types of equipment utilized in each component.
5. Discuss the functions performed by the following types of equipment used in an integrated data processing system: teletypewriter and tape-punching typewriter.
6. Discuss the steps involved in designing an integrated data processing system.
7. Identify the benefits and limitations of integrated data processing.

Chapter Terms   *Integrated data processing:* the recording of original data in machine language, mechanically processing the original data, and subsequently generating new data that are also recorded in machine language.

Punched-card system: a data processing system in which data are recorded on punched cards that are then mechanically processed.

Unit-record system: a system that is also known as a punched-card system.

Keypunch machine: a machine whose primary function is the punching of holes in cards as a means of encoding data on the cards.

Verifier: a machine whose primary function is to verify the accuracy of punched cards.

Interpreter: a machine whose primary function is to print on the top of punched cards the meaning of each hole punched into a card.

Reproducer: a machine that is used to duplicate the holes found in cards by punching identical holes in another set of cards.

Sorter: a machine that is used to sort punched cards according to the punches in the cards.

Collator: a machine that merges two decks of cards according to some predetermined order.

Calculator: a machine that is capable of performing the four arithmetic functions as well as capable of punching the results of the functions on cards.

Tabulator: a machine that is capable of performing addition and subtraction functions, in addition to printing information on paper and punching summary information on cards.

Teletypewriter: an integrated data processing machine that is capable of preparing perforated paper tapes. One teletypewriter is also capable of communicating with another teletypewriter via telephone lines.

Tape-punching typewriter: a typewriter with a paper-punching attachment that prepares perforated paper tape.

Card-punching typewriter: a typewriter with a card-punching attachment that prepares punched cards.

Although data have been manually processed for centuries, the mechanical processing of data is of rather recent origin. To a great extent, mechanical data processing techniques have revolutionized many office operations. During the last two decades, new techniques for the processing of data have been developed and implemented at a phenomenal rate. Each of the functional areas of the modern organization has been affected in varying degrees by the use of mechanical data processing techniques.

Integrated data processing, although not as sophisticated as electronic data processing (discussed in Chapter 27), is nonetheless still widely used by many organizations. Some organizations utilize only an integrated data processing system while others primarily use an electronic data processing system but may also utilize some integrated data processing techniques.

The characteristics of integrated data processing are as follows:

1. It uses a machine language common to all machines or equipment used in the system.

2. The data are processed mechanically.

3. Once the data are put into machine language, there is only minimum human effort involved in the processing of the data.

4. A considerable amount of repetitive effort is eliminated, since the data typically need to be manually recorded only one time.

5. In comparison to the manual processing of data, integrated data processing is much more rapid and accurate.

To facilitate the rapid understanding of integrated data processing, the **punched-card** or **unit-record system** is discussed first. Most integrated data processing systems utilize punched cards to a certain extent.

Punched-Card Systems

The backbone of a punched-card data processing system is the punched card, which is illustrated in Figure 26–1. The card can be used to record alphabetic information, numerical information, and special symbols including $, & / – and %.

An examination of Figure 26–1 reveals that the punched card has eighty columns and rows 0 through 9. Above the 0 row are two additional rows, which are the 12 or y punch and the 11 or x punch rows. The 12 punch and 11 punch rows are used for recording on punched cards alphabetic information and some of the special symbols. Numerical data require only one punch in a column, alphabetic data require two punches, and the symbols require one, two, or three punches, depending on the symbol being punched. A close examination of the card reveals that the 12 punch is used for letters A–I, the 11 punch for letters J–R, and the 0 row for letters S–Z. Therefore, an A on the card will require punches in the 12 row and in the 1 row; a B, punches in the 12 row and the 2 row, and so forth.

FIGURE 26–1   Punched Card

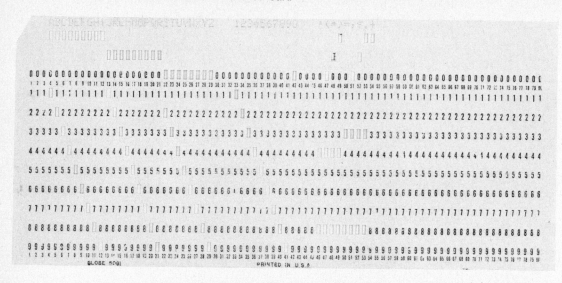

The data punched on cards are frequently obtained from a variety of source documents, including purchase orders, invoices, payment vouchers, inventory cards, and so forth. When only one unit of information that appears on a source document is to be recorded on a single card, the system is sometimes referred to as a unit-record system. To illustrate, assume that a small manufacturer uses a punched-card system, and whenever an order is received from a customer, each item on the purchase order is entered on a separate punched card. Thus, the system is appropriately referred to as a unit-record system.

When the information on a source document will ultimately be entered on one or more punched cards, this fact should be taken into consideration in designing both the document and the punched-card system. The columns on both the source document and the punched card should be arranged in identical sequences. For example, if the first column on a purchase order is used for recording the catalog number of the item, the catalog number should also be the first item to be entered on the punched card. This is illustrated in Figure 26–2.

The information, when being transferred from the source document to the punched card, is placed in the appropriate fields on the card. For example, if the longest catalog number contains eight digits, the catalog number field on the card will also have to contain eight digits. Therefore, columns 1–8 are reserved for the catalog number, digits 9–13 are reserved for the quantity field, and so on.

Equipment Used in Punched-Card Systems

In addition to a **keypunch machine,** several other types of equipment may be used in punched-card systems. The functions of each, as well as illustrations of several, appear in the following sections.

FIGURE 26-2 Sequence of Items on Source Document and Punched Card

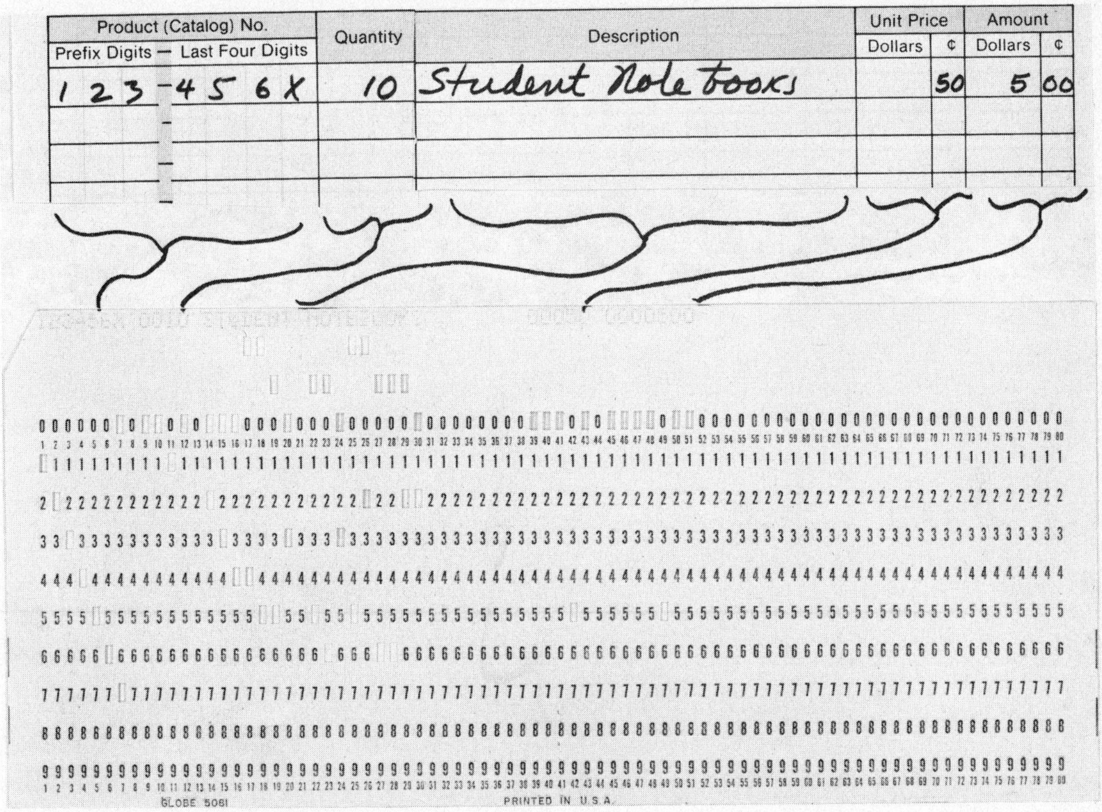

Product (Catalog) No.		Quantity	Description	Unit Price		Amount	
Prefix Digits — Last Four Digits				Dollars	¢	Dollars	¢
1 2 3 - 4 5 6 X		10	Student Note books		50	5	00

Keypunch machine. A keypunch machine is used to punch the holes in the punched cards. The machine, which is illustrated in Figure 26–3, has a keyboard similar to a typewriter keyboard. The operator simply reads the information contained on the source document and enters the identical information on the card, making sure that the appropriate information is placed in the appropriate fields.

The keypunch machine has several distinctive features, including a feeding mechanism that permits the automatic feeding of a new card in the machine's punching mechanism once the previous card is completely punched. The keypunch machine is also programmable, which means that several operating functions can be performed automatically. One such function is the automatic skip from one column on the card to another without the operator's having to use the space bar. To illustrate, if columns 37 to 78 were to be left blank, the machine can be programmed to automatically skip from space 36 to 79.

Some keypunch machines do not permit the correction of errors, which results in ruining cards when errors are made. The buffered keypunch, which is a significant improvement over earlier keypunch machines, allows the correction of errors before the card is punched. Since

FIGURE 26–3   Keypunch Machine

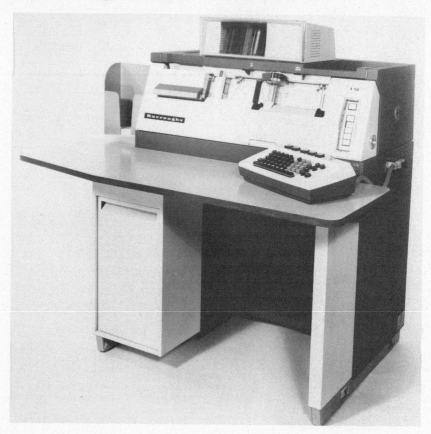

Courtesy, Burroughs Corporation

the buffered keypunch contains a memory or storage unit, a card is not punched until all the information that is to be placed on the card is in the storage unit. When an error is made, the operator simply back-spaces, which erases the error from the magnetic device in the storage unit, and then depresses the correct key or keys to enter the correct information in the storage unit. As the information is being put into the storage unit for one card, the previous card is being punched. The buffered keypunch machine is very advantageous since the operator can make sure that all the information that is stored in the memory is correct before the card is actually punched. Buffered keypunch helps to reduce costs and to increase production.

The keypunch machine can also be used to interpret the information contained on the card. Interpreting means that the letters, numbers, or symbols are printed at the top of the card, such as illustrated in Figure 26–1. Under certain circumstances, this can be used to verify the accuracy of the information punched in the cards. Other types of equipment, which are discussed in the following sections, can also be used to verify the accuracy of the information or to interpret the information.

Verifier. Since one punching error is likely to multiply in severity several times when the data are processed, the accuracy of the data contained on cards is essential. When the accuracy of the data on a few cards must be determined, verification is sometimes done manually. But when many cards must be verified, mechanical procedures must be used. The purpose of the **verifier** is to verify the accuracy of the information contained on the cards.

When the verifier is used, the operator, using the keyboard, simply enters the same information into the machine a second time. The verifier locks when there is a discrepancy between the punch already in the card and the key the operator just depressed on the keyboard. To determine whether the card contains the error or whether the verifier operator depressed the incorrect key, the correct key is again punched. If the verifier remains locked, the error is on the card; if the machine unlocks and spaces forward, the incorrect key was depressed on the keyboard. If an error exists on the card, the verifier makes a mark in the column in which the error was made, and a new card will have to be punched. If the card is correctly punched, the verifier makes a notch on the side of the card. This makes it very easy to determine whether or not all the cards in a deck have been verified.

Interpreter. The function of the **interpreter** is to print on the card the data that are contained in the punches on the card. This is referred to as interpreting the information contained on the card. Since some keypunch machines do not have a printing mechanism, the interpreter is necessary. In some instances, it may be desirable to have certain columns of cards interpreted but not other columns. Without an interpreter, the keypunch operator would have to continually switch the machine's printing mechanism on and off. When an interpreter is used, the machine can be wired to interpret either a portion or all of the columns, depending upon what the circumstances of the situation require.

Reproducer. The **reproducer** is used to duplicate the data contained on one set of cards onto another set of cards. If a certain set of cards have had so much use that they are showing wear, a new set of cards can be made on the reproducer. Badly worn cards can result in the frequent malfunction of data processing machines.

The reproducer can also be used to transfer the information contained in one field on a set of cards to another field on another set of cards. Assume that the design of a new order form necessitated the movement of the quantity field from columns 8–12 to 1–5 and the movement of the catalog number from columns 1–7 to columns 6–12. The reproducer can be wired to reverse the location of these two fields on cards. The reproducer can also be used to reproduce only certain columns on cards rather than all the columns.

Duplicate cards can also be made on a keypunch machine. But since the process is much slower on the keypunch machine than on the reproducer, the use of the latter is recommended when more than a few cards have to be duplicated.

Sorter. It is often necessary to arrange punched cards in some sequence, most often an alphabetic or numerical sequence. The sorter is designed to arrange cards according to some predetermined sequence.

When the sorter is used, cards are sorted column by column. If the operator wishes to arrange the cards according to the numbers that appear in columns 51, 52, and 53, the cards will have to pass through the sorter three times. The first time through the sorter, the cards are sorted according to the punches in the units column (in this case, column 53). The cards with nines punched in the units column fall into the nine pocket of the sorter, the cards with eights fall into the eight pocket, and so forth. During the second pass through the sorter, the cards are sorted according to the numbers that appear in the tens column (in this case, column 52). Again, the cards fall into the appropriate pockets according to the punches in column 52. The last pass through the sorter arranges the cards according to the punches that appear in the hundreds column (in this case, column 51). Upon passing through the sorter the third time, the cards will be numerically arranged from the smallest number to the largest number. The same basic process is used to sort cards according to an alphabetic sequence.

The sorter can also be used to count or tally the number of cards with a certain punch in any of the columns on the card.

Collator. The **collator** is designed to merge two sets of cards into some predetermined order or sequence. To illustrate, assume the names, addresses, and account numbers of customers are punched in one set of cards, and that the other set includes separate cards for each purchase that each customer made during the billing period. At the end of the billing period, the cards with the names, addresses, and account numbers have to be merged with the deck of cards on which the purchases appear. After the two decks are merged, the information is printed on the customer billing statement. After the printing is completed, the cards are again sorted, and the deck with the names, addresses, and account numbers is stored until needed at the end of the next billing period. The cards containing the purchases are stored and ultimately destroyed. This process is followed for each of the billing periods.

Calculator. The **calculator** is capable of performing four arithmetic functions: Addition, subtraction, multiplication, and division. The calculator performs the required arithmetic functions and punches the results of the arithmetic process in a card. To illustrate, the calculator can be used to multiply the number of units purchased by the unit price, in order to determine the extension. The results of the arithmetic function can be punched in the individual cards on which the data appear or on separate summary cards.

Tabulator. The **tabulator** is also known as an accounting machine. The tabulator consists of three different units: the reading unit, the calculating or processing unit, and the printing unit. Whereas the calculator and the tabulator are similar in some instances, there are also differences between the two machines. The calculator is capable of performing all four arithmetic functions, while the tabulator is capable of performing only addition and subtraction. Whereas the calculator is capable of punching the arithmetic results on cards, the tabulator is capable both of punching summary information on cards and of printing summary or original information on forms, paper, and so forth.

Small minicomputers have replaced the use of tabulators in many organizations. Although tabulators are no longer in production, reconditioned tabulators can be purchased or leased.

The Components of Punched-Card Systems

Punched-card systems comprise three components: input, processing, and output. Each of the machines discussed in the preceding section may be utilized in one or more of the components.

Input. In a punched-card system, the input into the system is made by punched cards, which are prepared by the *keypunch machine*, and in some circumstances, by the *calculator* and the *tabulator*. The *reproducer* is also considered to be part of the input component since it may be used in the preparation of cards.

Processing. The processing component consists of processing the information contained on the punched cards. Before the data can be processed, the cards may have to be sorted and arranged in a certain sequential pattern. The *sorter* is used to perform this function. After the cards have been sorted, they may be merged with another deck of cards, which requires the use of a *collator*. If arithmetic functions have to be performed, either the *calculator* or *tabulator* will be used, depending upon which arithmetic function is needed in the processing of the data.

Output. The input and processing components make the output component necessary. Therefore, without the input and the processing components, the output component is not needed. In a punched-card system, output is generally in the form of punched cards, printed reports, or printed forms. The *calculator* and the *tabulator* punch the cards, whereas only the tabulator can be used for printing.

A Punched-Card System Illustrated

To illustrate the use of a punched-card system, consider the situation of an organization that pays its employees on a piece-rate basis. In this particular organization, each employee is expected to produce a minimum amount each day, for which the employee receives a base wage. For each day that the employee is able to produce more than the minimum amount, the employee receives a wage bonus, which is calculated by multiplying the excess units produced by the amount the organization pays the employee for producing an excess unit. Therefore, the greater the number of excess units produced, the greater is the employee's bonus.

In designing a punched-card system to compute the payroll for this organization, three decks of cards are used. The employee deck consists of separate cards for each employee. Each card contains the employee's name, social security number, and other pertinent data necessary for calculating the employee's payroll. Another deck consists of cards on which each employee's name and social security number are punched, as well as the base wage for the pay period. The third deck is the excess production deck, which is updated each day. Whenever an employee's daily production record results in excess production, a card is prepared consisting of the employee's name and social security number, the number of excess units produced by that employee that day, and the wage allocation for each excess unit produced.

The steps involved in this payroll system are as follows:

1. Prepare the employee file card on the keypunch machine (these are stored and used again each pay period).

2. Prepare daily on the keypunch machine the excess production cards.

3. At the end of the pay period, use the sorter to arrange the excess production cards by employee social security number.

4. Using the keypunch machine, prepare the base wage cards, which include the total number of hours worked during the pay period and the hourly wage.

5. Process the base wage cards through the calculator by multiplying the hourly wage by the number of hours worked to arrive at a base wage for the pay period. Wire the calculator to also punch the wages earned on the base wage card.

6. Process the excess production cards through the calculator to add the total number of excess units produced for the pay period and to multiply this number by the wage allocation for producing each excess unit. Wire the calculator to punch this result on a summary card that contains only the employee's name and social security number and the wage addition for producing excess units.

7. Using a sorter, sort the summary cards from the excess production cards.

8. Using a collator, merge the employee file card with the wage base card, and then merge these two sets of cards with the summary excess production cards.

9. Using a calculator, add the amount of wages found on the base wage card to the amount of wage addition due to producing excess units, which is found on the summary excess production card. This is the amount of the employee's gross wages.

10. Using a calculator and the information contained on the employee file card, determine the amount of payroll deductions for the employee and subtract this amount from the gross wages. Wire the calculator to punch the net wages due the employee.

11. Sort the base wage cards, the employee file cards, and the excess production cards.

12. Process the base wage cards through the tabulator in order to print the employee's check and the withholding statement.

13. Store the employee file cards for use for the next pay period, and store all the other cards for future reference.

Integrated Data Processing

Integrated data processing refers to the recording of original data in machine language, mechanically processing the original data, and subsequently generating new data that are also recorded in machine language. Most integrated data processing systems utilize two types of data input media: punched cards, such as those discussed in the preceding sections, and perforated tape, such as that illustrated in Figure 26–4.

Perforated paper tape can be prepared on a variety of equipment, including teletype machines and tape-punching typewriters. Perforated paper tape is available in five, six, seven, and eight channels. Five-channel tape, for instance, will have five rows of holes, in addition to the small feed holes near the middle of the tape. On a five-channel tape, thirty-two combinations of letters and machine operations are possible, but by using the shift mechanism on the machine, a total of sixty-two combinations are possible. While twenty-six are assigned to the alphabetic letters, the remainder are assigned to punctuation marks, numbers, and machine operations, such as spaces, carriage return, and so forth.

FIGURE 26–4   Perforated Paper Tape

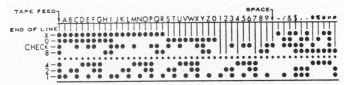

When an integrated data processing system utilizes both punched cards and perforated tape, certain data are more appropriately entered on the perforated paper tape, while other types of data are more appropriately recorded on the punched cards. Since punched cards are limited as to the number of columns available for recording data, their use for certain kinds of data is somewhat impractical. For example, if the integrated system utilizes eighty-column punched cards, and some of the types of data consumes more than eighty columns, perforated paper tape may be more appropriate for the recording of that data. Perforated paper tape is continuous and, therefore, is not restricted as to the amount of information that can be recorded thereon.

Equipment Used in Integrated Data Processing

In addition to the equipment used in punched-card systems, integrated data processing systems may use several additional types of equipment, including the following:

Teletypewriter. The **teletypewriter** is frequently used in integrated data processing systems to prepare perforated paper tapes. In addition, teletypewriters may be used by an organization that has branch offices located throughout the country. Each branch has a teletypewriter that is used in a variety of ways to communicate with the home office. For example, orders may be transmitted to the home office by a teletypewriter. As the data are entered into the teletypewriter in the branch office, the data are transmitted through telephone lines to the teletypewriter in the home office.

Tape-punching typewriter. In addition to using a teletypewriter to prepare perforated paper tapes, a **tape-punching typewriter** can also be used. This machine closely resembles a typewriter, with the punching attachment located on the side of the machine.

Card-punching typewriter. **Card-punching typewriters** are now available that punch cards in much the same way that keypunch machines punch cards.

Accounting machine. Accounting machines can be attached to a paper-punching device. As data are recorded on records or forms, the same data can also be subsequently recorded on perforated paper tape for later use.

Tape-reading equipment. Several different machines are now available into which perforated paper tapes can be inserted. The data on the tape activate the printing mechanism of the machine. Two examples are specially equipped typewriters and teletypewriters.

Card-reading equipment. Just as several machines are available to read perforated paper tape, machines are also available that print from the data recorded on cards.

Conversion equipment. Equipment can be used to convert perforated paper tape into punched cards and punched cards into perforated paper tape.

Designing Integrated Data Processing Systems

Before a decision is made to install an integrated data processing system, a considerable amount of study and investigation is necessary to determine the feasibility of the installation of such a system. Without this preliminary study, an organization may find that after a system has been installed, it cannot be afforded or that the system is not properly designed. The feasibility study discussed in a subsequent chapter can be modified and used to determine whether or not the installation of an integrated data processing system is feasible.

Once the feasibility of the system has been determined, the next step is to design efficient procedures. Much of the benefit of an integrated data processing system will be lost if the system utilizes inefficient procedures. Those responsible for designing integrated data processing systems typically find the use of flow process charts, such as the one illustrated in Figure 21–7, to be quite useful. The flow process chart is used to outline present work processes as a means of identifying steps that can be simplified, eliminated, or combined with other steps. Once the work process has been revised, the revised process is outlined on the right-hand side of the same flow process chart.

Once the flow process chart is prepared, the next step in the design of an integrated data processing system is to prepare a horizontal flow process chart, such as the one illustrated in Figure 21–11. At this point, the individuals responsible for the design of the system may find it advantageous to utilize the services of professional forms designers and vendors of integrated data processing equipment. The use of professionally trained people in the design of integrated data processing systems cannot be emphasized enough. Quite often the professionals are able to identify inefficient procedures that the employees of the organization are not aware of. The professionals can often provide suggestions for the design of forms to make them more compatible with the system. The vendors of the machines are also able to make suggestions regarding the amount and type of equipment needed. In addition, the professionals can make recommendations for the expansion of the system when such need arises. Another advantage of using the assistance of professionally trained individuals in designing integrated data processing systems is their ability to modify a newly installed system until all the "bugs" in the system are eliminated. Because this requires an extensive understanding of integrated data processing, most individuals who are not specially trained are not able to provide this function.

An Integrated Data Processing System Illustrated

An integrated data processing system is illustrated by examining an organization's purchasing system for the replenishment of supplies. The integrated system utilizes both punched cards and perforated paper tape as input media. The fact that the system is integrated means that as original data are processed, new data are generated and recorded on another input medium for later use.

The purchasing system in this particular organization utilizes purchase requisitions, purchase orders, and receipt of goods forms. The modified typewriter that is used in the system reads and prints from punched cards and perforated paper tape. In addition, the typewriter is also used to manually print data or information. The typewriter is also attached with a device that prepares a second perforated paper tape as the information is printed on the purchase order. The typewriter therefore has simultaneous reading, printing, and tape-punching capabilities.

At the time that this system was designed and installed, perforated paper tapes containing the constant information were prepared. The constant information, which is the same from one order to the next, includes the vendor's name and address, the method of shipment, the terms of payment, and the customer number that the vendor has assigned to the company. In addition, the first time that an item is ordered from a vendor, a punched card is prepared that contains the following: the vendor's catalog number for the item, the description of the item, and the unit price of the item. Both the perforated paper tape and the punched cards are kept on file for later use.

The purchasing system for the replenishment of supplies involves the following steps:

1. A purchase requisition is completed in the originating department. The requisition identifies the suggested vendor, the catalog numbers of the items to be ordered, descriptions of the items, and the desired quantity of each item. In addition, the individual completing the purchase requisition must obtain the department head's authorization to send the purchase requisition to the purchasing department. A separate purchase requisition is prepared for each vendor.

2. A clerk in the purchasing department processes the purchase requisition and multiplies the unit price by the number of units to be ordered. This extension is entered on the purchase requisition.

3. The clerk determines whether or not the originating department's budget has a sufficient balance to cover the cost of the order.

4. The processed purchase requisition is then transmitted to another clerk in the purchasing department who retrieves from the files the following items:

   a. The perforated paper tape that contains the constant information about the vendor that must be printed on the purchase order.

   b. The punched cards for each item being ordered from the vendor. If an item is being ordered for the first time, the clerk is responsible for preparing a punched card containing the vendor's catalog number of the item, the description of the item, and the unit price of the item.

5. The perforated paper tape and the punched cards are transported to the processing area of the purchasing department. The processing area contains the typewriters that are capable of reading and printing from perforated paper tape and punched cards, as well as printing data that are manually entered by the clerk.

6. The clerk in the processing area inserts a purchase order and manually types on the purchase order the current date and any special instructions that should be printed on the purchase order.

7. The mechanism on the typewriter that reads perforated paper tape is engaged, which activates the typewriter to read and print the information contained on the perforated paper tape.

8. The clerk, using the purchase requisition as a source document, manually types on the purchase order the quantity of the first item listed on the purchase requisition. At this point, the mechanism on the typewriter that reads punched cards is engaged, which activates the typewriter to read and print the information contained on the first punched card. The clerk manually types in the appropriate column on the purchase order the amount of the extension.

9. The clerk repeats Step 8 for the second item on the purchase requisition, the third item, and so forth, until all items have been printed on the purchase order.

10. After all the items have been printed on the purchase order, the clerk manually types the net amount of the order, sales tax, shipping charges, and the gross amount of the order on the purchase order.

11. The second perforated paper tape is removed from the machine. This tape contains all the information that has been printed on the purchase order.

12. The second perforated paper tape is used to prepare a receipt of goods order form for the receiving department. The form contains the same information as the purchase order except for the unit prices of the items, the extensions, and the totals.

13. The second perforated paper tape is sent to the accounting department, which uses selected portions of the tape to prepare the check for the vendor once the order has been received.

14. The second perforated tape is filed and is later used for preparing a variety of monthly summary reports.

The integrated data processing is classified as an integrated system because the originally recorded data are subsequently used for generating new data, which are also recorded in machine language. Thus, the data, although recorded only one time, are used for a variety of purposes.

Benefits of Integrated Data Processing

Since integrated data processing results in the one-time recording of data that are subsequently used for several different purposes, office operations are completed much more rapidly. This results in a significant advantage. In addition, if the data are accurately recorded on the input media, the output resulting from the input will be as accurate. Thus, the only data that have to be verified are the data that are manually entered on forms, reports, and so forth. Another advantage of integrated data processing is the reduction of the work force, which enables an organization to realize savings on labor costs. In fact, many organizations find that the lower labor expenses more than pay for the specialized equipment needed for the operation of the system.

Another significant advantage of integrated data processing is its capacity to transmit data between two locations that are a great distance from one another. To illustrate, a teletypewriter located in California can be used to transmit data to a location in New York.

Limitations of Integrated Data Processing

The value of an integrated data processing system is directly related to the efficiency of the system. If an organization utilizes an integrated data processing system comprised of inefficient mechanical procedures, the value of the system is likely to be greatly reduced. Another limitation of integrated data processing is that it does not allow for exceptional or problem situations. The routine, typical situations are handled very well by the integrated system, but such is not the case with problem situations. To illustrate, assume that in the system illustrated in the previous section, the purchase requisition contained items that had to be ordered from two different vendors. Since the system was designed to process purchase requisitions containing items to be ordered from only one vendor, a purchase requisition containing items to be ordered from more than one vendor could not be processed through the system.

Although generally considered to be an advantage, the flexibility that integrated data processing eliminates may also be a limitation. For example, it is impossible to complete steps out of order in most integrated data processing systems, even though in some cases it may be more expedient to complete steps in a different order.

Another limitation of integrated data processing is likely to result when attempting to mechanize all the operating systems in an organization. Even though greater efficiency will result from the mechanization, it is sometimes nearly impossible to mechanize all the operations in order to develop a totally integrated system.

Review Questions

1. Why is a punched-card system also referred to as a unit-record system?

2. How do keypunch machines and verifiers differ in the functions they perform?

3. How do calculators and tabulators differ in the functions they perform?

4. How do punched-card systems and integrated data processing systems differ?

5. What equipment is likely to be used in an integrated data processing system?

6. What tools are frequently used in designing integrated data processing systems? How are they used?

The Continental Textiles and Supply Company, a Chicago-based firm, is interested in developing an integrated data processing system. Presently, all information processing functions are performed manually. The president of the company is interested in utilizing equipment that is capable of reading punched cards as well as perforated paper tape. Assuming that the installation of an integrated data processing system is feasible, what suggestions can you make to assure the development of an efficient system? What tools do you recommend be used in the design of the new system?

*   *   *

The Scranton Corporation has hired you as an administrative office management consultant to determine the reasons for its increased operating inefficiency. Your analysis revealed that the firm has grown to the point where the manual processing of information is no longer feasible. You suggested to the president that the company install an integrated data processing system. The president replied that he didn't have much use for "all that gadgetry." How can you convince the president that the installation of an integrated data processing system would be advantageous for his company?

Case

Continental Distributors is a wholesale distributor of auto parts. Although the firm is not as large as many of its competitors, the firm does have a fairly sizeable number of customers who frequently place at least two orders a month with Continental. Approximately 90 percent of the customers order at least thirty times a year. About 75 percent of the orders contain the same items time after time.

Serious consideration is now being given to the installation of an integrated data processing system. As administrative office manager, you have been asked to provide input into the design of an integrated data processing system for the preparation of invoices. The vice president who is chairing the committee responsible for investigating an integrated data processing system has suggested that for reasons of flexibility, equipment be obtained that accommodates both punched cards and paper tape, in addition to having an attachment that is also capable of preparing perforated paper tape. In addition, the equipment is to be capable of manual entry of information.

1. Design the system for the preparation of invoices, explaining what types of information are to be contained on the various input media.

2. Explain what uses could be made of the perforated paper tape that is punched by the equipment as other media are being processed through the equipment.

Electronic
Data
Processing

Chapter
27

Classifications of Computers
    Digital Computers
    Analog Computers

Components of Electronic Computer Systems
    Input
        Punched cards
        Perforated paper tape
        Magnetic ink character recognition (MICR)
        Optical character recognition (OCR)
        Magnetic tape
        Magnetic disk
        Magnetic cassettes
        Magnetic cards
        Magnetic drums
        Keyboard terminals
        Console terminals
        Visual display terminals
        Point-of-sale terminals
        Touch-tone phone
        Voice communication
        Summary
    Storage
        Magnetic core
    Arithmetic-Logic Unit
    Control Unit
    Output
        Impact printers
        Nonimpact printers
        Printer-plotters
        Computer output microfilm (COM)

Computer Instructions

Chapter Aims   After studying this chapter, the student should be able to:

1. Explain the differences between digital and analog computers.
2. Identify the five components of electronic data processing.
3. Discuss the various devices that are used for input of data into a computer.
4. Discuss the functions of the storage component of a computer.
5. Explain the binary code system.
6. Discuss the functions performed by the arithmetic-logic unit.
7. Discuss the functions performed by the control unit.
8. Discuss the various devices that are used for output of data that has been processed by the computer.
9. Explain the differences between an assembler program and a computer program.

Chapter Terms   *Electronic data processing:* the use of computers for the processing of data.

Digital computer: a type of computer designed to count numbers.

Analog computer: a type of computer that is primarily used as a measuring device to process continuous values, such as voltages, temperatures, speeds, and so forth.

Input: the computer component that is used for the input of data into the computer.

Storage: the computer component (also known as memory) used to (1) store data until it is processed or converted to output and (2) hold the program instructions until needed.

Arithmetic-logic unit: the computer component in which the addition, subtraction, multiplication, and division operations are performed.

Control unit: the computer component that performs three basic functions: selection, interpretation, and execution of the program instructions.

Output: the computer that converts processed data, which is in coded form, into a form capable of being read.

Central processing unit: the unit of the computer that is comprised of the control, storage, and arithmetic-logic components.

Buffered data: the putting of data in storage to compensate for the differences in operating speeds of the computer equipment.

Binary code: the code into which data, including numbers, letters, and symbols, are converted prior to being processed by the computer.

Electronic data processing involves the use of such electronic devices as computers to process data. The impact of electronic data processing is felt in every phase of American society, from medical care, to matching individuals considered to be compatible dates, to the monitoring of pollution levels in large cities. Without the availability of computer applications, it is very probable that life in general would not be as convenient as it presently is.

Rarely has the invention of new equipment had such a revolutionary impact on work processes and procedures as has the computer. Nowadays, even the smallest organizations are likely to utilize computer applications by installing minicomputers or by contracting with service organizations for the processing of data.

The first electronic computer, which was called the ENIAC (Electronic Numerical Integrator And Computer), was completed at the University of Pennsylvania in 1946. Work on the ENIAC was begun in 1943. The computer was developed to solve complex ballistic firing problems of guided missiles and artillery shells. The first commercial electronic computer was the Remington Rand Univac I. It was dedicated on June 14, 1951, at the U.S. Bureau of Census and was assigned the task of completing the 1950 census. The first business enterprise to install and utilize computer applications on a daily basis was the General Electric Company at Appliance Park, Kentucky, which installed a Remington Rand Univac computer in 1954. Since that time, literally hundreds of thousands of computer applications have been developed for utilization in business organizations.

Computer technology has progressed through three identifiable phases and is presently in a fourth generation or phase. Distinct characteristics of each can be identified.

The first generation of computers, often thought to span the years 1952 to 1958, utilized vacuum tubes. Data input was generally restricted to punched cards, and internally stored programs were limited to magnetic cores or rotating drums. The first generation computers were used primarily by organizations for the mechanical processing of various clerical and accounting procedures.

The second generation of computers, which were built from 1958 through 1963, utilized solid state transistor cards, as opposed to the vacuum tubes that were characteristic of the first generation of computers. Because of the use of transistors, the physical size of computer equipment was greatly reduced. It was during the second generation that magnetic tape drives were developed, and the magnetic core memory devices became much more functional. In addition, the second generation saw the development and utilization of the symbolic computer languages, as well as the use of random access storage devices, such as magnetic cards and disk files. The second generation of computers enabled many organizations to develop a systems approach for the processing of data.

The era of third generation computers lasted from 1964 to 1969. During this time, miniature integrated circuitry chips were used in the construction of electronic computers. Other developments of the third generation include the following: unlimited random access storage capability, such as disks; real-time access; time-sharing capability; total-organization systems approach; greater equipment compatibility; electronic display devices; and many prewritten computer programs. The impact of the third generation computers on business applications was most significant in the development and refinement of the total systems approach for the processing of data.

The current generation of computers, which appeared in 1970, has resulted in the further simplification and refinement of the systems approach. In addition, fourth generation computers make greater use of microprogramming, which involves the rapid assembly and use of complex control and processing operations. The fourth generation computers also utilize microscopic integrated circuits, which make greater operating speeds possible. Another characteristic of fourth generation computers is the associative memory capability, which means that storage locations are identified by their content or subject matter rather than by their positions. With the earlier computers, storage locations were identified by their positions.

The data processing field has gone from computations per second, to milliseconds (one thousandth of a second); to microseconds (one millionth of a second); to nanoseconds (one billionth of a second); and to picoseconds (one trillionth of a second). There are many computer systems that are now processing in nanoseconds.

Classifications of Computers

The backbone of electronic data processing systems is the electronic computer. In order to fully understand the electronic data processing concept, an understanding of electronic computers is necessary, including the classifications of computers.

Electronic computers are classified as either **digital computers** or **analog computers.** Each has distinct characteristics and uses.

Digital Computers

The primary function of digital computers is to count numbers. Data are represented by strings of numbers, which, in turn, are expressed by electrical impulses. Therefore, this type of computer is most often used for processing business data. The digital computer is capable of calculating and manipulating discrete variables. The accuracy of the digital computer is determined by the number of decimal positions available for the manipulation of data. To increase the accuracy of the answer, more decimals in the answer can be used.

Analog Computers

While digital computers are used to count numbers, the analog computer is primarily used as a measuring device. The analog computer operates on continuous values, such as voltages, temperatures, speeds, and so forth. Analog computers are most appropriate for use in scientific research. While the digital computer is capable of calculating answers with 100 percent accuracy, the analog computer is not as accurate. The analog computer measures continuously. The accuracy of the analog computer is limited by the precision with which the continually variable physical quantities can be controlled.

In some instances, it is desirable to combine the features of both digital and analog computers to create a hybrid computer. Digital computer equipment is also available that converts analog data into digital form for processing.

Components of Electronic Computer Systems

Electronic computer systems consist of the following components: **input, storage, arithmetic-logic, control,** and **output.** These components are known as the computer hardware. The computer software, which is discussed in another section of this chapter, consists of computer programs and instructions. The relationships between each of the hardware components are illustrated in Figure 27–1.

Figure 27–1 depicts the flow of information and/or electric pulses between the various components. The **central processing unit (CPU)** consists of three of the hardware components: control, storage, and arithmetic-logic. Input and output are not part of the CPU of the computer. Each of the five components of electronic computers is discussed in detail in the following sections. Some of the input media and devices are also used for storing data and/or as output media or devices. The media or devices with multiple functions are discussed in detail in the input section of this chapter. When these same media or devices are also used for either storage or output, the media and devices are listed but are not discussed in the storage or output sections of this chapter.

The central processing unit (CPU) is able to process data much more rapidly than the computer is capable of reading the data from one

FIGURE 27–1   Components of Electronic Computers

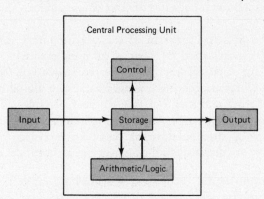

of the input media or devices. The CPU is also able to process data much more rapidly than the data appear in output form. To compensate for the difference between input and processing rates and between processing rates and output rates, the data may be **buffered.** This means that the data may be put into storage to compensate for the differences in the operating speeds of the equipment.

Input

In order for the computer to function, the letters, numbers, and symbols that humans are capable of reading must be converted into data that the computer is capable of reading. Input into electronic computers is made by paper media, magnetic media, and electronic devices. The following list identifies the types of media and devices that comprise each of the three main categories of data input:

Paper	*Magnetic*	*Electronic*
Punched cards	Magnetic tapes	Keyboard terminals
Perforated paper tape	Magnetic disks	Console terminals
Magnetic ink character recognition	Magnetic tape cassettes	Visual display terminals
Optical character recognition	Magnetic card cartridges	Point-of-sale terminals
	Magnetic drums	Touch-tone phone
		Voice communication

Punched cards. Of all the types of input, punched cards are probably the most familiar type. In addition to being used for data or instruction input, punched cards are also used as output and as a means of storing data and instructions. The cards are typically prepared on a keypunch machine, although equipment is now available that transforms data contained on mark-sense documents into punches on punched cards. Cards are also available that contain perforated punches. A pointed object, such as a stylus, is used to punch the desired holes in the cards. Such a process is not very satisfactory if more than a few cards have to be punched. This type of card is mainly associated with business inventory functions.

After the cards have been punched and verified, the data are fed into the CPU by a card reader, such as the one illustrated in Figure 27–2. The card reader functions by sensing the presence or absence of a hole in each location on the card. This information is then converted into coded electrical pulses that the computer is capable of interpreting. Some card readers are also capable of punching cards. Thus, the card reader is used for data input and output purposes.

There are certain advantages and disadvantages to using punched cards as a computer input medium. It is possible to sort the cards, to delete cards that are no longer needed, and to replace certain cards with

FIGURE 27–2   Card Reader

Courtesy of International Business Machines Corporation

other cards. This is not possible with some of the other types of input media. In addition, while it is possible to read the information contained on punched cards, it is not possible to read the information contained on other input media, such as magnetic tapes or disks. Another advantage of punched cards is their use as an external storage medium.

   Just as there are distinct advantages for using punched cards, there are also distinct disadvantages for using punched cards as an input medium. Punched cards contain eighty, ninety, or ninety-six columns. If more characters are needed than the maximum number of columns available on a card, additional cards have to be used. Another disadvantage is that, since cards are bulky, they require greater amounts of storage space than some of the other types of input require. Also, cards will warp if not stored properly. Another significant disadvantage of the use of punched cards is the ease with which they can be lost or misplaced.

Perforated paper tape. Like punched cards, perforated paper tape is used three ways in computer applications: input, output, and storage. Similar to integrated data processing, perforated paper tape is often prepared in electronic data processing as a by-product tape during the processing of other business data.

Data are usually recorded on perforated paper tape by punching round holes into the tape. Letters, numbers, and symbols are represented by one or more punches in a vertical column.

A paper tape reader, which is illustrated in Figure 27–3, is used to feed data into the central processing unit. In the same way that card readers sense the presence or absence of holes, paper tape readers also

FIGURE 27–3   Paper Tape Reader

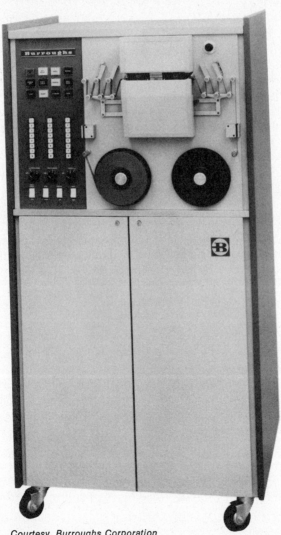

Courtesy, Burroughs Corporation

sense the presence or absence of holes. In comparison to some of the other input media and devices, paper tape readers are very slow.

The use of perforated paper tape has certain advantages over some of the other types of input. One significant advantage results from the fact that paper tape is continuous. Therefore, the amount of data that can be recorded on tape is not restricted as it is with punched cards. In addition to this advantage, paper tape is not wasted like punched cards are when they are not completely filled with data. On a punched card, if only columns 1–40 are used, the remainder of the card is essentially wasted. Perforated paper tape is also much less expensive than punched cards, perhaps as much as one-third less costly.

There are several disadvantages of perforated paper tape, including the following: it is difficult to verify the accuracy of the data recorded on perforated paper tape and tape is difficult to correct, especially when data have been omitted from the tape. To insert data on a tape that has already been punched, the tape must be either spliced or repunched. In addition, it is more difficult to delete information from tapes than from a deck of punched cards. Lastly, perforated paper tape is quite easily mutilated or torn.

Magnetic ink character recognition (MICR). This type of input medium is classified as one of the paper input mediums, since the magnetic numbers that are characteristic of the medium appear on paper. MICR is used by banks and other financial institutions as a means of processing the millions of checks that are written each day. The numbers imprinted on the bottom of checks contain iron oxide magnetizable particles. Blank checks are already imprinted with the routing symbol, the transit number, and the individual's account number. The first bank to receive a check after it has been written imprints the amount of the check in MICR numbers on the bottom of the check. Figure 27–4 illustrates the meaning of the MICR numbers that appear at the bottom of checks. The check is now ready to be processed through the regular banking channels. The first bank to receive the check may transfer the check to the Federal Reserve Bank, which transfers the check to the bank on which it was written, and finally the amount of the check is subtracted from the account on which it was written.

Magnetic ink character recognition reader-sorter units read the imprinted numbers on checks and sort the checks by bank number and by account number. Sorting rates range from approximately 180 to 2,000 documents per minute. Before the numbers are read into the reader-sorter, the checks pass through a strong magnetic field that causes the iron oxide particles to become magnetized. As the read-heads sense the characters, the characters are fed into the central processing unit of the computer or are transferred to another input medium for later processing.

FIGURE 27–4   MICR Numbers

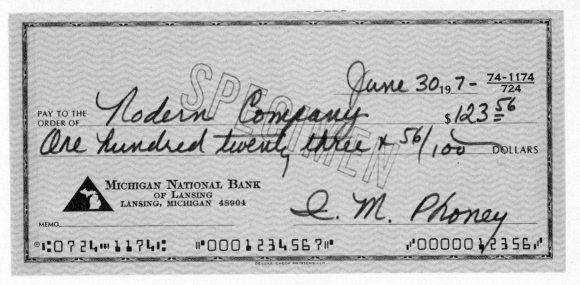

↑	↑	↑	↑
Routing Symbol	Transit Number	Account Number	Amount of Check

Courtesy, Michigan National Bank

MICR results in several advantages. A very significant advantage is the high degree of accuracy with which the checks are read. Even though they are often folded, contain staple holes, and are covered with a variety of stampings, they are read with a high degree of accuracy. Another advantage of the MICR system is that it is possible for humans to read the characters, which is not possible with some of the other types of input media. In addition, the use of MICR has eliminated the use of courtesy checks on which customers were able to fill in the names of their banks and account numbers. When courtesy checks were available, it was possible for a check to be fraudulently written on a bank that did not exist or on a bank in which a customer did not have an account. Consequently, the use of the MICR system has reduced the number of bad check losses.

Among the disadvantages of the MICR system are the following: since MICR was developed primarily for the banking industry and since only the fourteen characters needed by the banking industry have been developed, the system is not useful for other purposes. Alphabetic characters are not available in the MICR system. Second, clerical effort is sometimes needed because the preprinted numbers do not have a sufficient amount of iron oxide particles for magnetizing. Therefore, the check has to be reprocessed. In addition, the magnetized numbers on checks are sometimes printed in the wrong location, which requires reprinting before the numbers can be read by the readers.

Optical character recognition (OCR). The final paper input medium to be discussed in this chapter is OCR. Whereas MICR consists of only fourteen numbers and symbols, OCR consists of all the printed characters. In addition, OCR does not require the use of special magnetic ink that is required by MICR. In time, OCR will be sufficiently developed so that hand-printed characters can be easily read by OCR readers. Figure 27–5 illustrates the OCR letters, numbers, and symbols approved by the American National Standards Institute.

OCR is frequently used in credit card billing. When a customer charges a purchase, the customer's account number that appears on the plastic credit card is imprinted on the charge slip. If the customer's account number and the total amount of the transaction shown on the charge slip are OCR numbers, the document can then be directly read into the computer's central processing unit or transferred to another input medium for later processing.

Like the other types of input media and devices, certain advantages result from using OCR as an input medium. Among these advantages

FIGURE 27–5 OCR Numbers

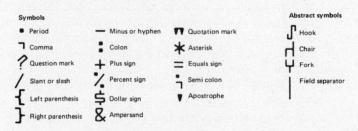

This material is reproduced with permission from American National Standard Character Set and Print Quality from Optical Character Recognition (OCR-A), X3.17–1974, by the American National Standards Institute, copies of which may be purchased from the American National Standards Institute at 1430 Broadway, New York, N.Y. 10018.

are the following: the original source document can be used for data input into the computer without first having to transfer the data onto some other input medium or device; it cuts down on the amount of human effort involved in processing data electronically; OCR data is easily read by people; and only a limited amount of rather inexpensive equipment is needed to imprint OCR characters on documents.

OCR is limited to a certain extent because of rather strict type fonts and character sizes that must be used. If an incorrect type font is used or if the characters are larger or smaller than those the reader is capable of reading, the system will not work. In addition, when OCR characters are imprinted on paper by means of a typewriter with a special type font, extreme care must be exercised when correcting errors. Another limitation is the high cost of OCR readers.

Magnetic tape. In high-speed, large-volume computer applications, magnetic tape is the most widely used type of input. Magnetic tape, which is the most widely used external data storage medium, is used as an output medium as well. The iron oxide coating on one side of the magnetic tape receives the electromagnetic pulses, which enables data to be recorded on the tape. Because the pulses can be erased and new pulses stored on magnetic tape, this input medium is useable many times.

Data are entered on magnetic tapes either directly or indirectly. For example, data that are transferred by a data converter from punched cards or perforated paper tape to magnetic tape are transferred indirectly. Several devices are available for entering data directly on magnetic tapes.

a. *Key-to-tape units.* These units utilize a keyboard similar to a typewriter keyboard. The information contained on the source document is keyed into the unit, and as each key is depressed, two things simultaneously occur: the electromagnetic pulse is recorded on the tape and, second, the letter, number, or symbol keyed into the machine appears on a screenlike display unit that facilitates verifying the accuracy of the data. Key-to-tape units prepare either standard size magnetic tape or smaller size magnetic tape found in special cartridges or cassettes. Before the data on the smaller size tape can be fed into the central processing unit, it may be necessary to use a converter to convert the data to standard size magnetic tape.

b. *Key-to-disk units.* Instead of keying data onto magnetic tape, data are sometimes keyed first onto magnetic disks that resemble thin 45 rpm records. In some instances, before these data are fed into the central processing unit, they are transferred onto magnetic tape.

Magnetic tape units are used for data input (reading) and for output (recording or writing). Such units, which are referred to as tape drives, must contain as many read-write heads as there are tracks on the magnetic tape being used. If the magnetic tape contains nine tracks, the tape drive must also contain nine read-write heads. As the electromagnets in the read-write heads pass over the pulses recorded on the tape, the data are fed into the CPU. A tape drive is illustrated in Figure 27–6.

There are several advantages in using magnetic tape, including the following: unlike punched cards, magnetic tape is not limited as to the number of characters that can be recorded on the tape; magnetic tape is relatively inexpensive to purchase; the storage of the tape consumes much less space than the quantity of cards required to store a comparable amount of data; magnetic tape is one of the fastest input mediums; and the likelihood of misplacing a magnetic tape is small in comparison to the likelihood of misplacing punched cards.

The use of magnetic tape results in certain disadvantages, one of which is the inability of humans to read the data recorded on the tape. In addition, the environmental conditions for using magnetic tape are more strict than the conditions required for using punched cards and

FIGURE 27–6   Magnetic Tape Reader

Courtesy, Burroughs Corporation

paper tape. For example, minute specks of dust can cause the data on the tape to be misread. Furthermore, there is sometimes the necessity of humidity control, as well as the chance that tapes can be mistakenly erased. When the data that are needed for a certain processing operation are at the end of a magnetic tape, all the data that are recorded on the tape up to the point of the needed data must pass through the tape drive. Therefore, information recorded on magnetic tape cannot be accessed randomly because of the sequential nature of the data on the tape. Before self-locking tape systems came into being, tapes were sometimes stretched, often crinkled, and frequently contaminated by computer operators. If care is not exercised, it is possible to erase or distort data on the tape with a magnet.

Magnetic disks. Like several of the other input media already discussed, magnetic disks are used for input, storage, and output. Unlike magnetic tape, which requires sequential accessing, magnetic disks permit random accessing of data. This means that it is possible for the computer to access data from a disk without having to read all the data on the disk up to the point where the desired data are stored. In terms of computer operations, random accessing is much faster than sequential accessing of data on a magnetic tape.

Data can be entered on a magnetic disk by means of a key-to-disk unit that utilizes a keyboard similar to the keyboard found on typewriters. By means of a converter, data can be converted from magnetic tape to magnetic disks and vice versa. Data can also be entered on a magnetic disk by means of a direct-access storage device. This device utilizes disk packs composed of several disks that resemble $33\frac{1}{3}$ rpm long playing records.

Magnetic disks are made of thin metal plates that are covered on both sides with a magnetic recording material. Several of these disks are contained in a disk pack. Data are accessed from the disk pack by arms that, upon command from the computer, move to the location of the data that are to be accessed. The read-write heads located on the arms then read and transfer to the computer the electromagnetic pulses contained in the tracks on the disk. This procedure can be likened to a record player operation. The records are comparable to the disks, the arm on the turntable is comparable to the accessing arm, and the needle on the arm is comparable to the read-write heads.

While some disk drives contain only permanent access arms with multiple read-write heads for each disk contained in the disk pack, others contain an access arm with an attached read-write head for each disk surface. When a disk drive has multiple access arms, they move simultaneously. If the computer directs an access arm to the seventh track on the fourth disk, all the arms move to the seventh track of their respective disks. The read-write head on No. 4 access arm would then read and transfer to the computer the data to be processed. A disk drive is illustrated in Figure 27–7.

The use of magnetic disks results in several advantages. One of the most significant advantages is its random-accessing capability, which shortens accessing time. Another advantage is that disks in several disk packs can receive data from one input operation. Thus, one input operation can simultaneously update the data stored on several different disk

FIGURE 27–7   Disk Drive

Courtesy, Burroughs Corporation

packs. In addition, related data stored on several different disk packs can be accessed as needed when the data are required for a processing operation.

The most significant disadvantage of magnetic disks is their cost. In relation to the cost of storing a comparable amount of data on magnetic tapes, magnetic disks are considerably more expensive. However, the cost of storing data on disk packs has decreased from one generation of equipment to the next. In addition, magnetic disks are not as practical as magnetic tape when updating data. When data are updated on magnetic tape, the old tape remains unchanged and therefore is available in the event of malfunctions or errors. But when data on magnetic disks are updated, the old data may be erased as the new data are entered on the disk. Therefore, the old data are lost and are no longer available. Another disadvantage of this input/output (I/O) is the important fact that the temperature and humidity must be controlled so that the device operates properly.

Magnetic cassettes. Another of the magnetic input media are magnetic cassettes, which resemble the tape cassettes used in cassette tape recorders. Magnetic cassettes are prepared on key-to-cassette machines. When the operator keys the data into the machine, the data appear on a screenlike display device that facilitates verification of the accuracy of the data. At the time each key is depressed on the keyboard, a coded electromagnetic pulse is recorded on the cassette tape. Cassette tapes are either fed directly into the computer or are transferred onto full-size magnetic tape prior to being fed into the computer.

Among the advantages of magnetic cassettes are their low cost, their capability of being reused, and the small amount of space required for their storage. Although the small size of cassettes is an advantage, the size may also be a disadvantage, especially if the cassettes are misplaced or lost. In addition, the data on cassette tapes occasionally need to be converted to full-size magnetic tapes before being fed into the computer. Furthermore, unless care is exercised, valuable data can be erased, which destroys the needed information.

Magnetic cards. The use of magnetic cards adds another dimension to the flexibility of the various types of magnetic input media. The magnetic cards used for input are pieces of plastic on which magnetic tape has been fastened in a side-by-side arrangement. Data are recorded on the tracks contained in the magnetic tape. The cards, which are placed in cartridges, permit the random accessing of data. Upon command, the desired card is released from the cartridge and is transferred to a rotating drum on which it comes into contact with the read-write heads for either reading or recording data. After the card is used, it is automatically returned to its proper location in the cartridge.

The National Cash Register Company is credited with developing the magnetic card system. IBM has a comparable system, called the Data Cell, which uses strips of magnetic tape rather than the cards characteristic of the NCR system.

Magnetic cards are rather low in cost and have a fairly high storage capacity. Magnetic cards are especially useful for on-line storage of large quantities of data (which means that the data are under the control of the central processing unit) for a few transactions. A significant disadvantage of the magnetic card input medium is the slowness with which the cards move from the cartridge to the rotating drum and from the rotating drum back to the cartridge.

Magnetic drums. The final magnetic input medium to be discussed in this chapter is the magnetic drum, which is a cylinder with a magnetized outer surface. Like several of the other input media already discussed, the magnetic drum is also used for storage and output. As the drum rotates, data are either read from or recorded onto the drum by means of read-write heads. Magnetic drums are erasable, and as new data are being recorded on the drum, the data previously stored in that location are erased. As data are recorded on the drum, they are assigned a specific storage location. When data have to be retrieved, the read-write heads move to the appropriate location of the stored data and the reading process begins.

A distinct advantage the magnetic drums have over disk packs is that drum devices have faster access time. In relation to the cost of storing data in the internal memory of the computer, which is discussed in another section of this chapter, the use of magnetic drums for data storage is less expensive. It can generally be said that drum devices have less storage capacity than disk devices. Another disadvantage of magnetic drums is that the old data may be erased as the new data are recorded on the drum.

Keyboard terminals. Specially equipped typewriters and teletype units can be used as data input devices. The terminals, which are connected to the computer, are capable of transforming the letters, numbers, and symbols that humans are capable of reading into codes that the computer is capable of reading. This type of terminal is not designed for the mass input of data since data are entered only as rapidly as the operator is capable of typing.

Typewriter and teletype terminals may be located in the same room as the computer or hundreds of miles from where the computer facility is located. In such cases, telephone lines are used to connect the typewriter terminal with the computer. Typewriter terminals are used for making hotel or motel reservations. To determine whether or not a room is available, the operator enters the data into the computer by means of the keyboard on the typewriter terminal. The data concerning the hotel or motel are accessed from the computer's storage facility and are transmitted back to the operator by means of the typewriter terminal. If a room is available and if reservations are then desired, the operator communicates the appropriate data to the computer by means of the typewriter terminal.

The use of the typewriter and teletype terminals have several distinct advantages. As input devices, they are rather inexpensive. In addition, these terminals can be used to communicate with a computer over a distance of many miles. Another advantage is that hard copies of input and output of data are available. The use of typewriter and teletype terminals to communicate with the computer is extremely slow. Therefore, neither is suitable for massive amounts of data input, which presents another disadvantage. Because the terminals have moving parts, a certain amount of noise is generated.

Console terminals. Another of the electronic devices used for the input of data into a computer is the console terminal, which is physically located near the central processing unit (CPU). Figure 27–8 illustrates a console terminal. The terminal is actually connected to the CPU by a cable. Like the typewriter terminal, the console terminal can be used to enter data directly into the storage unit and to receive data from the storage unit. In addition to functioning as an input device, the console terminal also functions as an output device. Console terminals are also used by the computer operator to instruct the computer to alter com-

FIGURE 27–8   Console Terminal

Courtesy, Burroughs Corporation

puter programs, to change the priority of jobs, to reassign output devices, and to identify the data stored in certain areas of the storage unit in order to change the location of data. However, it mainly functions as an input/output (I/O) device for console commands.

A distinct advantage of the console terminal is that it allows the computer operator to communicate with the computer, and vice versa, as well as to give instructions to the computer. In addition, hard copies are prepared, which often provide a convenient audit trail about the activity of computer jobs. Because the console terminal is a manual input device, it is slow and is not designed for the input of massive amounts of data. Another disadvantage is the amount of noise sometimes generated by this device.

Visual display terminals. As an input/output (I/O) device, visual display terminals, which utilize cathode ray tubes (CRT), are being used with increasing frequency. An examination of Figure 27–9 reveals that visual

FIGURE 27–9   Visual Display Terminal

Courtesy, Burroughs Corporation

display units have a televisionlike screen and a keyboard. The keyboard is used for data input into the computer and the screen functions as an output unit. Many central processing units (CPUs), instead of being equipped with console typewriters, are equipped with visual display console terminals.

It is also possible to have visual display terminals located quite a distance from the computer facility. Some of these terminals may be used as input devices (on-line update) or as inquiry-response devices (that is, the data are displayed for inquiry purposes only).

Two main types of visual display units are now available. One type displays only alphanumeric information, such as letters, numbers, and symbols. The other type displays graphs, drawings, and charts, as well as alphanumeric information. This type of terminal is illustrated in Figure 27–10. The visual display terminal that is capable of displaying graphs, drawings, and charts requires the use of special equipment in order to transmit the illustration to the computer. In some cases, an input tablet is used, which consists of a grid comprised of hundreds of copper lines connected to the computer. The copper grid is covered with a glass or plastic shield. To transmit the illustration to the computer, a special pen is required. The paper on which the illustration appears is placed on the glass or plastic shield and the special pen is used to trace over the lines on the paper. The special pen causes the copper lines to transmit electrical impulses to the storage unit of the computer. To change a line, the special pen is used to erase the original line prior to moving the new line to the desired location.

FIGURE 27–10   Graphics Visual Display Terminal

Courtesy, Control Data Corporation

An electronic light pen may also be used to transmit illustrations to a computer. The light pen, which contains a photocell, is used to trace the illustration directly onto the screen of the visual display terminal. Electric responses between the screen on the visual display terminal and the photocell in the light pen are transmitted to the computer. The light pen can also be used to add, delete, or modify lines on illustrations or tabular information.

The use of visual display terminals results in several distinct advantages, including the following: it is a noiseless system, and output is very rapidly displayed on the screen. In addition, it is the only input device suitable for the input of illustrations. Another advantage of the visual display terminal is the ease with which illustrations can be modified. Disadvantages of the visual display terminal are its inability to produce hard copies and the slowness with which data are entered through the keyboard. As an input device, the visual display terminal is not suitable for the input of large volumes of data.

Point-of-sale terminals. Terminals of this type are used in many stores and businesses in place of cash registers. In addition to performing the same functions as cash registers, point-of-sale (POS) terminals do the following things: provide computerized inventory control; provide credit information about a charge customer; print credit card charge slips; and by means of a sensing wand, read and transmit to the computer the price found on the magnetized price tags that are attached to merchandise. Calculations are performed by the computer and the results are automatically printed by the terminal on a sales receipt.

Figure 27–11 illustrates a point-of-sale terminal.

The POS terminal is especially useful for maintaining up-to-date inventory records. Other advantages of the terminal are the speed and accuracy with which the terminal operates. Significant disadvantages result from the required use of special price tags and the inoperability of the system when the computer is not functioning.

Touch-tone phone. The use of a touch-tone phone is likely to increase as a data input system. When the various keys on the phone are depressed, tone signals, which are transmitted through telephone lines, are received by a machine that punches cards or prepares perforated paper tape, which is then fed into the computer. Although still in the experimental stage, this system will undoubtedly be used extensively to conduct banking transactions, to pay bills, to place orders, and do accountinglike arithmetic.

There are two very significant advantages of using this type of data input device. One is the convenience of the device and the other is its low cost. Perhaps the most significant disadvantage is that errors can be easily made, especially if people are not completely familiar with the uses of the system.

FIGURE 27–11 Point-of-Sale Terminal

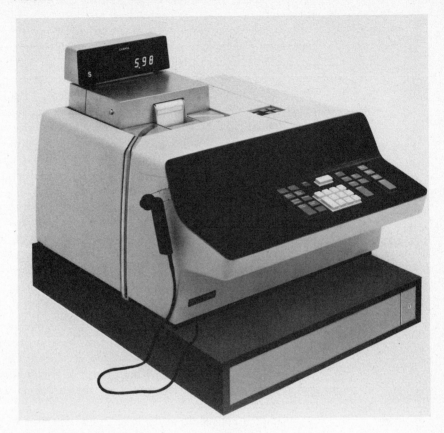

Courtesy International Business Machines Corporation

Voice communication. The final input device to be presented in this chapter is voice communication, which transforms a standard telephone into a data terminal. To illustrate, the portable audio terminal onto which the telephone receiver and mouthpiece are placed is capable of making contact with the computer. The terminal is usually battery-operated and it transmits the data through telephone lines to a receiving unit, which ultimately feeds data into the central processing unit (CPU) of the computer.

To communicate with the computer, the individual depresses the keys on the keyboard of the terminal in order to enter data into the computer. Output is in the form of prerecorded voice responses that are transmitted through the telephone lines to a speaker in the portable audio terminal.

The portable audio terminal is especially useful for traveling salesmen who, for example, need to communicate with the home office regarding the availability of certain products that a customer wishes to order.

If the products are available, the portable audio terminal is used to place the order.

Voice communication is also used by telephone companies in certain regions of the United States. When a call is intercepted by an operator, perhaps because the number that was dialed has been changed or an unassigned number was dialed, voice response units are used to communicate with the individual making the phone call. In the case of a changed telephone number, the operator uses a small keyboard to key into the computer the number that the individual dialed. The entering of the old number activates the computer, and, through a voice response unit, the new number is communicated to the individual making the call. The operator does not have to take time and expend effort to look up the new number.

Voice communication, utilizing the portable audio terminal, is advantageous for several reasons. Electronic equipment can be used to communicate information that individuals have had to communicate. The system is convenient, since any telephone can be transformed into a data terminal. Data can be kept up to date, and data can be readily obtained. The portable audio terminal is not designed for mass input of data, which limits its use to a certain extent.

Summary. While some of the input media and devices discussed in this section are used only for data input purposes, others are also used for output purposes, while others are used for input, storage, and output. The media and devices that are multipurpose are identified in the sections that follow, in addition to the devices that are used in only one of the computer components.

Other input media or devices or modifications of present ones will undoubtedly be developed by the time this book is printed. Since computer technology is rapidly changing, new developments occur at a very fast rate. This makes the data processing field extremely competitive.

Storage

The storage component of the computer, which is part of the central processing unit (CPU), is also known as the memory of the computer. After the data have been converted into a code that the computer is capable of reading, the coded data are fed into the CPU by means of one of the input mediums or devices discussed in the preceding section. When the data are fed into one of the input devices, they are transferred into storage until needed. Therefore, the storage component provides a very useful function. In addition to storing data until needed, the storage unit performs other functions, including the following: it holds the data being processed, including the intermediate results of the data being processed; it often holds the final processed results until they are converted into output; and it holds the program instructions that are needed for the processing of data. There are also many occasions when the data, while being processed, enter or exit storage but never maintain a holding pattern in the unit.

Data, in order to be read by the computer, have to be converted into a code the computer is capable of reading. The coded data, which are converted into electrical pulses, are based on the **binary code** system, which converts all letters, numbers, and symbols into combinations of 0s and 1s. To illustrate, the decimal number 9 is converted to a combination of 0 and 1 codes, and the letter C is converted to a combination of 0 and 1 codes, and the symbol representing a comma is converted to a combination of 0 and 1 codes.

Computers are comprised of several electronic components that operate in binary mode. An electric switch is either closed (0) or open (1). Electric pulses are either absent (0) or present (1). Transistors are either not conducting (0) or they are conducting (1). A magnetic core is magnetized to represent either a 0 or a 1. On a magnetic tape, the presence of data is represented by a 1, while the absence of data is represented by a 0.

Data that are converted into binary code are represented by a combination of 0 and 1 codes. Binary counting involves a right-to-left direction, starting with a 1 and each position to the left of the 1 doubles in value. In a right-to-left direction, the following illustrates binary counting:

$$128, \ 64, \ 32, \ 16, \ 8, \ 4, \ 2, \ 1$$

By using a combination of 0 and 1 codes, decimal numbers are converted to binary code. The binary code of 1 is used to represent a *yes* or *on* position, while 0 is used to represent a *no* or *off* position. The following illustrates the binary code for decimal numbers 1 through 0:

Decimal	*Binary*					
	32	16	8	4	2	1
1	0	0	0	0	0	1
2	0	0	0	0	1	0
3 (2 + 1)	0	0	0	0	1	1
4	0	0	0	1	0	0
5 (4 + 1)	0	0	0	1	0	1
6 (4 + 2)	0	0	0	1	1	0
7 (4 + 2 + 1)	0	0	0	1	1	1
8	0	0	1	0	0	0
9 (8 + 1)	0	0	1	0	0	1
0 (8 + 2)	0	0	1	0	1	0

The number 13 is represented by a binary code of 001101; 15, by 001111; 19, by 010011, and so on. Figure 27–12 illustrates the binary codes for letters A through Z.

Data may be stored or held internally within the computer or held externally on one of the various storage mediums or devices. Internal storage consists of primary and secondary storage. The list on p. 629

FIGURE 27–12   Binary Code—Alphabetic Characters

A	11 0001
B	11 0010
C	11 0011
D	11 0100
E	11 0101
F	11 0110
G	11 0111
H	11 1000
I	11 1001
J	10 0001
K	10 0010
L	10 0011
M	10 0100
N	10 0101
O	10 0110
P	10 0111
Q	10 1000
R	10 1001
S	01 0010
T	01 0011
U	01 0100
V	01 0101
W	01 0110
X	01 0111
Y	01 1000
Z	01 1001

identifies the various types of primary internal storage, secondary internal storage, and external storage.

Asterisks are used to identify the storage media that are also used as input media. Additional discussion of the media with equal input and storage functions are included in the previous section.

The amount of data that can be held in primary storage is limited by the amount of primary storage equipment available. Because primary storage equipment is very costly and because the amount of storage space available in primary storage is limited, data have to be stored either externally or in secondary storage devices. Before the data held in secondary storage can be processed, they first have to pass through a memory device. Thus, data held in secondary storage cannot be accessed as rapidly as that held in primary storage. Although its cost is quite reasonable, externally stored data is quite slow to access. For example, before data stored on magnetic tape can be accessed, the tape reel has to

Internal Storage	*External Storage*
Primary	*Punched cards
Magnetic core	*Perforated paper tape
Magnetic thin film	*Magnetic tape
Plate-wire storage	*Magnetic cassette
	*Magnetic disk pack
Secondary	*Magnetic card
	*Magnetic strip
Fast core mass memory	*MICR
Laser mass memory	*OCR
*Magnetic tape	
*Magnetic disk	
*Magnetic drum	
*Magnetic card	
*Magnetic strip	

be manually retrieved from the tape rack and then manually placed on a tape drive machine.

This discussion of storage components is limited to the magnetic core. Comprehension of this device does not require an extensive technological understanding of computer operations.

Magnetic core. The magnetic core, which is about the size of a pin head, is doughnut shaped. A magnetic core storage unit consists of thousands of these cores strung on wires. In a fraction of a second, the cores can be magnetized by electrical current flowing through the wires. The direction of the current flow through the wires determines whether the magnetic core is charged with a 0 or a 1. The 0 depicts a *no* or *off* charge while the 1 depicts a *yes* or *on* charge.

Figure 27–13 illustrates the magnetizing of a core as a means of storing data in binary code. One-half of the current needed to magnetize the core passes through the vertical wire. The other half of the current to magnetize the core passes through the horizontal wire. A binary code of 0 causes the core to be magnetized in a counterclockwise direction, while a binary code of 1 causes the core to be magnetized in a clockwise direction. Since the core illustrated in Figure 27–13 is magnetized in a counterclockwise direction, the core holds a binary code of 0.

A magnetic core plane, which is illustrated in Figure 27–14, consists of thousands of the magnetic cores strung on the wires. By stacking a certain number of magnetic core planes on top of one another, a memory array is created. The number of magnetic core planes contained in the memory array is determined by the amount of storage space needed in the computer. The fewest number that can be stacked on one another is seven, which is the number of planes illustrated in Figure 27–15.

Once the data have been converted into binary code, they can be stored internally. Figure 27–15 illustrates the storing of the letter A

FIGURE 27–13   Magnetizing of a Core

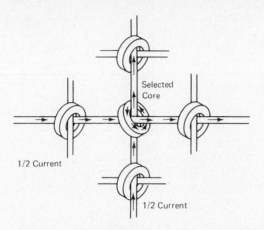

FIGURE 27–14   Magnetic Core Plane

FIGURE 27–15 Memory Array Showing Codes for Characters A and 7

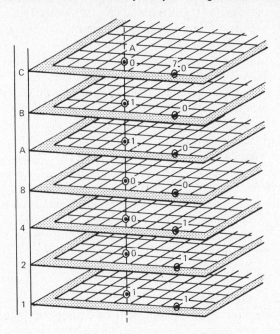

(110001) and the number 7 (000111) in binary code in magnetic cores. The topmost plane in Figure 27–15 is used for parity checking, which enables the computer to automatically check the validity of the data. Although some computers use even parity, most use odd parity. When odd parity is used, a 1 is added to the top or parity plane on the memory array whenever the six-bit binary code for a letter, number, or symbol contains an even number of 1 codes. Thus, a 1 is added in the parity plane for the following numbers: 3, 5, 6, 9, and 0. The 0 is added in the top plane for letters, numbers, or symbols that contain an uneven number of 1 codes. Therefore, a 0 is used in the parity plane for numbers 1, 2, 4, 7, and 8.

The amount of magnetic core storage is determined by the number of interconnected memory arrays that comprise the primary internal storage.

The distinct advantage of core storage is the speed with which data can be accessed. Since read-write heads are not involved, data access time is not slowed by rotational delay of a drum or disk, for example.

Arithmetic-Logic Unit

The arithmetic-logic unit (ALU), another of the components of the central processing unit (CPU), is capable of performing addition, subtraction, multiplication, and division operations. In addition to performing these operations, the ALU is capable of comparing the size of the data.

During processing operations, data are transferred upon command from storage to the ALU, manipulated, and transferred back to storage. During one processing operation, data may be transferred back and forth several times from storage to the ALU.

As data are transferred from storage to the ALU, the data are held in registers while being manipulated. To illustrate, if the computer is being used to calculate payroll, the computer may transfer the number of hours worked to a register known as the accumulator. The hourly rate of pay is also transferred to a storage register. At this point, the amount in the accumulator (hours worked) and the amount in the storage register (hourly wage) are transferred to the adder, which multiplies the hours by the wage rate in order to determine the amount of gross wages. This figure is then transferred back to the accumulator, where it is held until again needed. Eventually, this figure will have to be transferred back to the adder, which subtracts the amount of deductions to determine the net wages. The amount of net wages is stored until the output operation is performed. The adder is capable of performing all four arithmetic operations.

Control Unit

The control unit, which is another of the components of the central processing unit of the computer, performs three main functions: selection, interpretation, and execution of the program instructions. The control unit performs the following:

1. It instructs input devices to read data into storage.
2. It locates data held in secondary storage and transfers them to memory.
3. It instructs the arithmetic-logic unit to perform certain operations on the data.
4. It informs the arithmetic-logic unit of the location of the data stored in memory.
5. It informs the output devices which information is to be printed, punched, or transferred to some other medium for storage.

The control unit can be easily recognized because of its vast array of blinking lights and assorted dials. The flashing lights are used primarily to indicate that the computer is working. When the lights are not flashing, there is a problem. These flashing lights are important to the customer engineer who services the computer. In addition, the control unit typically contains either a console typewriter or a visual display terminal. These two devices are used to communicate with the computer and can be used for the input of small amounts of information.

Output

Many of the input media and devices are also used for output purposes. The input media and devices that were discussed in the input section of this chapter that are also used for output purposes are not discussed again in this section. Rather, the media and devices with a dual function are only listed, and the discussion in this section is limited to output devices that are not also used for data input.

The following input media and devices can also be used for output purposes:

Punched cards	Magnetic drums
Perforated paper tape	Keyboard terminals
Magnetic tape	Console terminals
Magnetic disks	Visual display terminals
Magnetic cassettes	Point-of-sale terminals
Magnetic card cartridges	Voice communication devices

The discussion of output devices in this section includes impact printers, nonimpact printers, printer-plotters, and computer output microfilm (COM).

Impact printers. The impact printer is very commonly used as an output device. After the data have been processed in the central processing unit, the data are transformed by means of the impact printer into characters that humans are capable of reading. In comparison to some of the other types of output devices, the impact printer is relatively slow. Some of the newer impact printers are now capable of printing up to 2,000 lines of 132 characters per minute. The impact printer functions by pressing a typeface against paper. A ribbon between the typeface and paper causes the character to print. The impact-printing process, although much faster, is similar to the typewriting process. Most impact printers are now capable of printing a line at a time. The typefaces are either on drums or on continuous chains.

Figure 27–16 illustrates an impact printer.

Nonimpact printers. Nonimpact printers, which function without typefaces, are much faster than impact printers. Some of the nonimpact printers are capable of printing at rates in excess of 13,000 lines per minute at eight lines per inch with 136 to 204 characters per line. Nonimpact printers use small jets through which electrostatically charged squirts of ink are forced. Nonimpact printing is much quieter than impact printing since there are no typefaces striking paper. With nonimpact printing, it is not possible to make multiple copies. Another disadvantage of nonimpact printers is the nonuniform characters that the system sometimes produces.

Printer-plotters. This type of output is used to prepare graphic illustrations, such as scientific and engineering drawings. Printer-plotters are also capable of printing characters, in addition to the drawings. This type of equipment is very valuable to a small segment of the data processing market. The equipment is quite costly.

FIGURE 27–16 / Impact Printer

Courtesy, Control Data Corporation

Computer output microfilm (COM). When COM is used, output is in the form of microfilm rather than paper. Either of two methods are used for preparing COM. One method utilizes output data in the form of magnetic tape that is then processed through equipment that decodes the data found on the tape. Microfilm is prepared from this operation. The other method involves a microfilm recorder. Most microfilm recorders contain a cathode ray tube (CRT) similar to the screen found on visual display terminals. As data are processed through the central processing unit (CPU), the characters are projected onto the CRT and subsequently are photographed by a microfilm camera. In terms of output speed, COM is much faster than printers.

Figure 27–17 illustrates a very large-scale computer.

Computer Instructions

Up to this point, the content discussed in this chapter has pertained to computer hardware—the physical devices, machines, and equipment needed in a computer installation. But unless software is also used, the

FIGURE 27–17   Large Scale Computer

Courtesy, Burroughs Corporation

computer hardware has nothing with which to function. Software, as used in this section, refers to the application programs and the systems programs that are supplied by the computer manufacturer. Software simplifies the programmer's job to a great extent.

The first step in developing a computer program is to define the problem. In defining the problem, the means of arriving at a solution have to be determined. Identifying the input data that are needed to solve the problem and determining the proper ways of processing the data are involved in arriving at a solution to the problem.

The second step in developing a computer program is to prepare a flow chart, such as the one illustrated in Figure 27–18. Flow charts are sometimes also referred to as decision tables. Flow charts outline what has to be done with the data in order to accomplish the desired output. The information on the flow chart is then usually converted into written instructions or coding sheets that the computer is capable of understanding.

Many of the programs use words that have meaning to humans, but before they are meaningful to the computer, they have to be trans-

FIGURE 27–18   Flow Chart

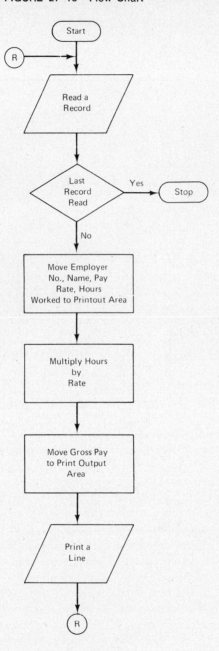

Courtesy, Methods Research

lated into instructions the computer is capable of understanding. This involves, by means of a compiler, translating the source program that humans are capable of reading into an object program the computer is capable of understanding.

Three different types of programming languages have been developed, including symbolic languages, procedure-oriented languages, and problem-solving languages. When a symbolic language is used, the translation of the source program into an object program is performed by a program referred to as an assembler. When either a procedure-oriented language or a problem-oriented language are used, a compiler is used to translate the source program into an object program.

The following outlines the steps involved in reading a program into the computer and in processing the data:

1. The compiler program is read into the central processing unit in order to translate the source program into an object program. The compiler program, which may be recorded on such media as punched cards or magnetic tape and stored on a disk pack, is usually supplied by the computer manufacturers.

2. The source program, which is recorded on an input medium, is read into the CPU.

3. The compiler program translates the source program into an object program, which is recorded on an output medium or device (tapes, disks, and cards, for example).

4. The object program is read into the CPU.

5. Using one of the input media, the data to be processed are read into the CPU.

6. The data are processed according to the object program's instructions and are stored until the control unit directs an output device to record the processed data.

Symbolic languages are characterized as resembling machine instructions. Thus, mnemonic codes are used to identify various operations. Examples of symbolic languages are AUTOCODER and SPS (Symbolic Programming System). Symbolic languages and procedure-oriented languages differ from one another in that procedure-oriented languages involve descriptions of a set of procedures to be used in solving the problem. Some examples are BASIC (Beginner's All-purpose Symbolic Instruction Code); COBOL (Common Business-Oriented Language); FORTRAN (Formula Translation); and PL/1 (Programming Language 1). Problem-oriented languages describe the nature of the problem. The language used in the program is similar to the language of the problem that is to be solved. An example of a problem-oriented language is RPG (Report Program Generator).

Although it is not the author's intent to provide a detailed discussion of program language in this chapter, a short discussion of COBOL is presented to aid the reader's understanding of computer processes.

COBOL was designed primarily for the processing of business data and is now one of the most widely used program languages for processing business data. Rather than use codes or symbols to represent processing functions, COBOL uses English words to represent processing functions. Thus, a source program written in COBOL will contain such words as ADD, SUBTRACT, CALL, and FILE. A compiler is then used to translate the source program into the object program, which enables the computer to understand the instructions contained in the program.

A COBOL program contains four divisions: identification, environment, data, and procedure. The identification section of a program written in COBOL typically includes the following types of information: the name of the program, the author of the program, the date on which the program was written, and the date on which the program was compiled.

The environment division is used to identify for the compiler the types of equipment available for compiling the source program and for processing the object program. The computer doing the translating may or may not be the same one used to run the object program. The environment division also describes the input/output devices that are to be used in the processing of the data.

The data division describes the files from which the program is to draw data on which the calculations are to be performed. Therefore, the data division is used to identify the characteristics and format of the data to be processed.

The procedure division is where the actual programming of the problem takes place. This is the part of the program that appears in the flow chart prepared earlier.

Review Questions

1. What are the characteristics of the current generation of electronic computers?
2. What is the difference between computer hardware and computer software?
3. Compare and contrast punched cards and magnetic tape as input media.
4. How do OCR and MICR differ as input media?
5. Explain how portable audio terminals function.
6. What is COM?
7. How do source programs and object programs differ?
8. What are the four main divisions of a COBOL program and what is contained in each?

Minicases

The Effingham Company is a very large supplier of automobile replacement parts. The traveling salemen, when receiving an order from a customer, telephone the order to the appropriate regional warehouse. It is not uncommon for the warehouse to be out of stock on certain items that a customer may desire. A minimum of two days pass before the salesman learns that an item is temporarily out of stock. By that time, there is always the chance that several other customers have also ordered the same out-of-stock items. Because the company is greatly concerned about customer relations, several of the managers feel that if the customers were to know immediately that an item is out of stock, the negative impact would be less than when the customer finds out two weeks later that the item is out of stock. Therefore, the company desires to provide its salesmen with a device that would enable them to communicate directly with the computer when placing orders and when determining inventory levels. What input device do you recommend? How is the device used?

*   *   *

The Dunsworth Corporation, a medium-sized office products supplier, is located in Atlanta. The present computer system is not large enough to handle the current processing needs of the company. The present system, which was installed eight years ago, utilizes punched cards for data input. Although punched cards have worked very well for the computer system of the Dunsworth Corporation, several of the employees feel that the use of magnetic tape for data input would be more advantageous than the use of punched cards. In comparison to punched cards, what advantages would the use of magnetic tape provide? What disadvantages would result from the use of magnetic tape for data input?

Case

You are the administrative office manager of the Dickson Company and have been placed on its investigation committee to conduct a feasibility study. The purpose of the feasibility study is to provide valuable information for helping determine whether or not the company should expand its present computer facilities. The present facilities are no longer adequate, primarily because of a move toward total systems integration and because of the rapid expansion of the company.

As a member of the investigation committee, it is your responsibility to investigate the various magnetic input media that are presently available. The management of the firm has specified that a magnetic medium or media are to be given primary consideration. Although some data will continue to be recorded on punched cards, this data will be converted to a magnetic medium prior to being fed into the computer.

1. What types of magnetic media might be appropriate for utilization by the company?

2. What are the advantages and disadvantages of the media that might be appropriately used?

3. Of the media that are appropriate, which is your preference? Why?

Managerial
Involvement
in
Computer
Systems

Chapter
28

The Feasibility Study
    Preliminary Survey
        Appointment of investigation committee
        Determination of the scope of the study
        Orientation of the investigation committee members
        Identification of objectives
        Development of a time schedule
        Analysis of the present system
        Analysis of present equipment
        Analysis of present personnel
        Determination of projected growth and expansion of the
            organization
        Determination of costs of present system
        Determination of alternative systems
        Preparation of the feasibility study report
        Making the decision
    Systems Design
        Determination of specifications for the new system
        Design of the new system
        Preparation of the final flow charts for the new system
    Selection of Equipment
        Request for bids
        Evaluation of the vendors' bids
        Selection of the equipment vendor
        Preparation for the installation of the new system
        Conversion to the new system
        Evaluation of the new system

Alternative Processing Systems
    Computer Service Bureaus
    Timesharing Services
    Computer Utilities

Computers and the Human Element

Chapter Aims

After studying this chapter, the student should be able to:

    1. Discuss the activities that comprise each of the three phases of the feasibility study.

    2. Discuss the services provided by a computer service bureau.

    3. Explain the timesharing concept and discuss how an organization might utilize timesharing.

    4. Explain the computer utilities concept.

    5. Discuss the various ways in which an organization may improve employees' reaction to the installation of a computer system.

Chapter Terms

Hardware: the equipment components that comprise a computer system.

Software: the computer programs and instructions that are needed to process data on a computer.

Computer service bureau: a bureau that an organization contracts to process a portion or all of its data. Some organizations use this as an alternative to installing a computer system.

Timesharing: an arrangement in which one organization purchases computer time from another organization whose computer system is more extensive. Some organizations use this as an alternative to installing a computer system or as an alternative to installing a more extensive computer system.

Computer utilities: enterprises that sell a variety of services to subscribers. Computer utilities, which are characteristically able to generate huge amounts of computer power, maintain extensive data banks and data communication systems.

PERT chart: a chart frequently used in the installation of a computer system. The chart identifies critical and noncritical subprojects. The critical subprojects must be completed in sequence and on time if the computer is to be installed on schedule. The noncritical subprojects can be completed at any time without having a negative impact on the installation of the computer.

Batch processing: a data processing technique in which several similar transactions are accumulated before being processed through the computer.

The installation of a computer system involves a considerable amount of investigative and exploratory effort. In addition to determining the need for a computer installation, the **hardware** and **software** needs of the system also have to be determined. Both of these tasks are likely to consume a considerable amount of time and effort on the part of managers. If the need for a computer installation cannot be justified or if certain equipment cannot be justified, the use of various alternatives should be investigated. Three alternatives that are discussed in this chapter are the use of **computer service bureaus, timesharing,** and **computer utilities.** It is also the responsibility of an organization's managerial team to make decisions regarding the alternative means of processing data. In addition, the installation of a computer system may have a significant impact on employer-employee relations. Again, it is the responsibility of management to determine how to lessen employees' negative feelings about the utilization of a computer system. Each of the points mentioned in this paragraph involve decisions with which the organization's managerial team must be concerned.

The Feasibility Study

Without the information provided in a feasibility study, the decision to install a computer system is very likely to result in a considerable amount of wasted time, effort, and financial resources. The enormous outlays for a computer system—equipment, programs, conversion from the present system to a new system, and the multitude of related activities—require an extensive amount of investigation. This investigation takes place during the process of conducting a feasibility study. In smaller organizations in which electronic data processing is not presently utilized, the feasibility study is conducted to determine whether or not the installation of a computer system is feasible. In organizations that already have a computer system, the purpose of the feasibility study may be to (1) revise the present system, keeping the same hardware; (2) develop new applications for the present system; or (3) revise the present system to accommodate new hardware. Feasibility studies frequently encompass the following phases: preliminary survey, systems design, and selection of the equipment. Each of these phases is discussed in detail in the sections that follow.

Preliminary Survey

The preliminary survey, although likely to be very time consuming, is essential to the success of the feasibility study. If the preliminary survey is hastily or carelessly conducted, the chances are quite good that a series of incorrect, costly decisions will be made. Perhaps the impact of these decisions will not surface until after a computer system has been installed. The seriousness of an incorrect decision is readily felt once the computer system is functioning.

Appointment of investigation committee. A feasibility study is usually conducted by an investigation committee comprised of several employees of the organization. The investigation committee, which is usually selected by top-level managers, typically consists of computer specialists, as well as representatives from the organization's functional areas, such as accounting, sales, purchasing, production, and so forth. As soon as the investigation committee has been formed, a top-level manager, perhaps the president or chairman of the board, should notify all employees that a feasibility study is underway. The notification is typically made by means of a memorandum that announces the names of the employees appointed to the investigation committee, the purpose of the committee, and possible outcomes of the study. If it is perceived that the impact of the recommendations contained in the study will result in changes in employees' jobs, the memorandum should discuss this possibility. The memo should mention the possibility that some employees may need to be retrained or placed in another job but that none will be laid off or asked to resign. It is also advantageous for a top-level manager to keep the employees informed of the progress of the investigation committee. Employees are likely to accept change more readily if they are kept informed of developments.

Determination of the scope of the study. Once the investigation committee has been formed, the scope of the study should be determined, which is often the responsibility of top-level management. If the investigation committee feels that a more effective job could be done by either expanding or contracting the scope, it is not uncommon for the investigation committee to ask for the scope to be changed.

Orientation of the investigation committee members. The investigation committee, which is typically comprised of functional managers as well as individuals with specialization in electronic data processing, needs to be fully oriented to the problem being studied. If the functional managers are not familiar with computer operations, serious thought should be given to their receiving intensive orientation in this area. Orientation can be obtained through courses offered by computer manufacturers, colleges, and universities, as well as obtained from representatives of various vendors of computer equipment. On the other hand, those who have specialization in electronic data processing but who are not familiar with the functional areas of the organization should also become properly oriented.

Identification of objectives. Before much work of any significance can be undertaken by the investigation committee, the objectives of the feasibility study must be identified. The identification of those objectives is generally the cooperative responsibility of the investigation committee and the top-level managers of the organization. Different objectives are frequently identified for different levels of the organization. For example, the objectives of top management might be to improve by having more timely information readily available for decisionmaking. At the department level, the objectives might be to increase the efficiency of various department operations, to reduce the cost of performing various departmental operations, and to improve the utilization of personnel. At the employee level, the objectives might be to mechanize routine work processes and to increase employee productivity. A broad, overall objective for the study is to help the organization increase its net profit.

Development of a time schedule. Because of the detailed nature of a feasibility study, most investigation committees feel that it is advantageous to develop a time schedule for undertaking the study. Inasmuch as a feasibility study is likely to take anywhere from several months to several years to complete, the development of a time schedule is very important. By knowing what phase of the study is likely to be completed at any time, the organization is able to do a more effective job of long-range planning and budgeting. Time schedules are usually broken down into the steps involved in each of the three phases of the feasibility study. Unless the schedule is quite specific, its use it most likely quite limited. The amount of time to be allocated to the various phases, is, of course, determined by the amount of work involved in each step.

Analysis of the present system. This step of the preliminary study involves undertaking a systems analysis, which is very time consuming in comparison to several of the other steps involved in the preliminary study. Because systems analysis involves many different aspects of the organization's operations, the interactions between the equipment, personnel, and information generated by the organization must be analyzed. The overall purpose of analyzing the present system is twofold: to determine whether or not a new system is justifiable, and if so, to provide valuable input for designing a new system.

There are several devices that can be used to analyze the present systems of the organization. The various charts discussed in the chapter dealing with systems analysis (Chapter 21) are most helpful. Such charts outline or diagram the flow of work, the processing of forms and records, and so forth. In addition, valuable input may be provided by talking with the employees who are responsible for the processing of work that is part of a system. Information that cannot be obtained from the systems analysis charts can perhaps be obtained from the employees who process the forms or who are responsible for certain phases of the work flow.

One of the primary functions of systems analysis is to provide information about the methods and procedures involved in the organization's work processes. Since a system is comprised of procedures, and since each procedure is comprised of a number of methods, this aspect of the study will undoubtedly be quite detailed. Diagramming or outlining on the appropriate charts the methods involved in carrying out a particular task not only provides information for systems analysis but also determines the efficiency of the methods. If the analysis of the methods identifies inefficiency, corrective measures should be taken before a new system is installed. It is difficult to justify the installation of a new system comprised of inefficient methods.

An analysis of the organization's procedures and methods will, of necessity, involve an analysis of its source documents. Such documents are generally considered to be output, since they contain the compilation of certain information. For example, a purchase order is a source document because it provides information for preparing a receipt of goods form. It is also output because it is the compilation of information obtained from purchase requisitions, vendors' catalogs, and so forth. In addition to determining what information is being generated, the analysis of procedures and methods should also investigate where the information is being generated and how the information is being generated. Unless clear-cut answers to these questions are readily available, it is difficult to thoroughly analyze the present system. Providing answers to these questions may indicate that a certain form or report is not needed or that certain forms can be combined or consolidated. Not only will such findings be helpful in making the present system more efficient but this information is also crucial to the development of an efficient new system.

In some instances, output provided on one form may serve as input for another form. When such is the case, it is important that the efficiency with which output becomes input be determined. The design of a form determines to a great extent how efficiently data can be entered on the form. For example, when output on one form becomes input on a subsequent form, it is desirable to arrange the identical items on the two forms in the same order.

Another important aspect of systems analysis is the volume of work produced by each work unit, as well as the costs involved in producing the work. Without the availability of such information, it is difficult to determine if a new computer system is justifiable. While it may be easier to justify mechanizing the high-volume, routine procedure, mechanization of low-volume procedures of a nonroutine nature is more difficult to justify.

Analysis of present equipment. Because systems are comprised of equipment, personnel, and forms or documents, an analysis of the present equipment must also be made. Perhaps some of the present equipment could be utilized in the new system, while other pieces will not be needed. Before identifying the types of new equipment that may eventually be needed, it is important to first determine what equipment is already available. An analysis of the cost of the present equipment will also help determine whether or not a new system is financially feasible.

Analysis of present personnel. Several characteristics of the present personnel need to be examined, including the qualifications of the present personnel for data processing positions. If the organization does not employ personnel who are qualified for data processing positions, the hiring of qualified personnel and/or the retraining of present personnel will add to the cost of installing a new program. Another characterstic of the personnel that has to be determined are present labor costs. It is possible that the qualifications and present labor costs of the personnel make the installation of a new system financially unfeasible.

Determination of projected growth and expansion of the organization. Unless the investigation committee has a fairly precise picture of the projected growth and expansion of the organization, the impact of the feasibility study cannot be fully realized. Perhaps the installation of a new system cannot be justified in terms of the present outlook for the organization, but when the projected growth and expansion of the organization are also considered, the installation of a new system may be justifiable. In addition to helping determine the feasibility of installing a new system, an examination of the projected growth helps determine the size of the system that will be needed. It is impractical to install a system capable of meeting only today's needs when the organization's growth projections are not only favorable but are quite extensive.

Determination of costs of present system. Before the investigation committee is in a position to recommend whether or not a new system should be installed, the costs of the present system should be determined. These costs are typically determined on a departmental basis. In addition to determining the costs of the present system, the benefits derived from the present system should also be determined. When the various alternatives for installing a new system are identified, it will be possible to compare the costs and benefits of the present system with the anticipated costs and benefits to be derived from each of the alternatives. It is thus possible to eliminate those alternatives that are not advantageous when compared with the present system.

Determination of alternative systems. At this point, the investigation committee is ready to identify suitable alternative systems. The alternatives are based on the findings of the committee. After the various alternative systems have been developed, it is possible to compare each alternative with the present system in order to make a decision regarding the feasibility of installing a new system.

After each of the alternatives has been identified, the investigation committee is responsible for accumulating data for each of the alternatives. For example, the costs and expected savings of each of the alternatives must be determined. Costs include both one-time costs and recurring costs. Types of one-time costs are as follows: the cost of the feasibility study, the costs involved in converting from the present system to the new system, the costs involved in either constructing or remodeling the computer room to meet the needs of the new system, and the costs involved in preparing the various computer programs. Costs of a recurring nature deal with the rental or purchase of equipment, salaries of personnel, supplies, equipment maintenance, and so forth.

The costs of most computer systems during the first few years of their operation exceed the savings that are realized. To determine whether the installation of a computer system is financially feasible, the costs should perhaps be calculated for a five-year period. In addition, the savings that each of the alternatives is expected to produce also have to be determined. These savings frequently result from the need of fewer personnel, the elimination of certain pieces of equipment, and so forth. It is now possible to compare the anticipated long-term savings of each alternative with the long-term cost of each alternative. Generally, the longer period of time the system is in operation, the greater is the amount of savings that will result from the installation of the new system.

After the total net savings have been determined for each of the alternatives, it is possible to determine whether or not each alternative provides the amount of return on the investment that the organization considers essential. Alternatives that provide a lower return are probably eliminated from future consideration. Alternatives that provide returns that exceed the minimum level are given additional consideration. The benefits to be derived from each of the alternatives should also be considered.

Preparation of the feasibility study report. Generally, the investigation committee is able to identify among the alternatives one alternative that is more feasible than the others. If this is the case, and if the top-level managers desire a recommended alternative, the feasibility study report should be centered around this alternative. Unless top management expressed a desire to have detailed information about the alternatives that were not chosen, little may be gained by providing such detailed information. It may be more appropriate to include only summary information about each of the alternatives that were not recommended.

Several of the steps involved in the preliminary study should be summarized in the feasibility study report. Since those who will read the report are most interested in the alternative being recommended by the investigation committee, the discussion of that alternative should perhaps be placed at the beginning of the report. Two types of information are considered most important by those who will make the decision: the cost of the new system and the benefits to be derived from the new system.

Making the decision. Once the feasibility study report has been transmitted to the top managers who are responsible for making a final decision regarding the installation of a new system, several courses of action are possible: (1) keep the present system and revise inefficient procedures that were uncovered during the systems analysis; (2) accept the recommendation provided in the feasibility study report but modify as deemed necessary; or (3) accept without modification the recommendation provided in the feasibility study report. After the decision has been made to install a new system, either as presented in the feasibility study report or in a modified form, the next step is to develop the specifications for the new system.

Systems Design

Systems design consists of several well-defined steps, including the following:

Determination of specifications for the new system. If the investigation committee is comprised of systems design specialists in addition to specialists in the various functional areas, the investigation committee may also be charged with the responsibility for developing the specifications for the new system. At any rate, the group responsible for developing the specifications for the new system should be comprised of both systems design specialists and specialists in the functional areas.

By nature, the development of the specifications for the new system is a fairly technical process, and a detailed discussion of the process is beyond the scope of this text. The following are some of the factors that will be considered in developing the specifications: new input needs, new output needs, new operating methods and procedures; constraints with regard to finances, work flow, and personnel; anticipated future developments of the organization that will be affected by the system; the language of the present system; and means of establishing internal control of the system.

Design of the new system. Once the specifications of the new system have been determined, it is now possible to design the new system. Typically, the component parts of the system are identified, which, when put together, comprise the new system. Before the new system is made final, tentative flow charts of the new system should be reviewed in detail by each of the departments affected by each phase of the system. It is much easier to change a system at this point than after the equipment has been selected and conversion to the new system has been initiated.

The design of the new system is also a very technical process and is considered to be beyond the scope of this text.

Preparation of the final flow charts for the new system. After the tentative flow charts of the new system have been reviewed at the departmental level and suggestions for changes have been considered, the next step is to prepare the final flow charts of the new system. These flow charts, along with certain detailed specifications regarding input needs, output needs, methods and procedures, and so forth, are made available to the equipment vendors who desire to submit bids on the system.

Selection of Equipment

The final phase of the feasibility study is the selection of the equipment that is needed to meet the requirements of the new system. Because this phase is also quite technical and is considered to be beyond the scope of this text, this phase is discussed only in general terms.

Request for bids. Most organizations find that it is financially advantageous to request bids from more than one equipment vendor. In addition, more flexibility is gained by requesting bids from several vendors. When vendors are requested to submit bids for the installation of a new system, several different types of information are made available to the vendors, including specifications of the new system, flow charts outlining the new system, plans for future expansion of the new system, and any other information that may be helpful to the vendors in their bid preparation process. In addition, the request for bids frequently describes the information that the vendors are to include in the bids they submit to the organization.

Evaluation of the vendors' bids. Once the bids have been received by the organization, a system must be developed to facilitate the objective evaluation of each bid. Unless a system is developed, it is doubtful that the bids can be evaluated objectively. Some of the criteria that are considered in the evaluation of the various bids are proposed equipment, special operating characteristics of the equipment, rental or purchase cost of the equipment, equipment delivery dates, programs for training employees to use new equipment, the extent of the software available to make the equipment operable, the vendor's plan for providing technical assistance in converting to the new system, and the vendor's equipment maintenance program.

Selection of the equipment vendor. After each of the bids has been evaluated on an objective basis, the next step is to select the vendor or vendors of the equipment and, subsequently, to sign a contract with each. The organization's return on its investment is generally an important determinant in selecting the vendors of the equipment for the new system.

Preparation for the installation of the new system. After the contracts with the various vendors have been signed, the next step is to start preparing for the installation of the new system. This can be a very detailed, time-consuming process that includes the following activities: selecting an installation time; selecting and training the personnel needed to operate the new system; remodeling the facilities as needed; making provisions for the vendor's testing of the equipment once it has been installed; developing and testing computer programs; and if necessary, converting the stored data from the present media to the media required by the new system. Because of the complexity of the activities involved in this step, a **PERT chart** is frequently used to help assure that critical steps are completed in sequence and on time. PERT charts are discussed in greater detail in Chapter 29.

Conversion to the new system. Once the new equipment has been fully tested and the new programs have been prepared, tested, and debugged, the new system is ready to become operable. In some cases, organizations use parallel processing of data as a final means of assuring the accurate functioning of the new system. Parallel processing involves the processing of data on the old system and the new system and then comparing the results of both systems. Identical results indicate that both systems are functioning properly. Different results may or may not be due to problems with the new system, since it may be possible that the old system is responsible for some of the differences. The reasons for the differences should be determined, analyzed, and corrected before total conversion to the new system takes place.

Evaluation of the new system. Once the system has been functioning for a period of time, an evaluation of the system should take place. Included is an analysis of the new system as well as an evaluation of the suitability of the new equipment. At this point, changes in systems are easier to make than changes in equipment, although the latter should not be ruled out.

Alternative Processing Systems

In some instances, the data contained in feasibility studies do not support the installation of a computer system or the upgrading of a present system. Several reasons are responsible for either of these courses of action. One reason is the financial cost of a new system. Another reason is the lack of demand for a more extensive system. Still another reason may be the lack of projected growth or expansion of the organization. Organizations that do not presently have a computer system may find it advantageous to contract with another organization to utilize their computer facilities. Organizations whose present computer facilities are no longer adequate may also find it more advantageous to utilize the computer facilities of another organization than to expand the present system. In addition to utilizing the computer facilities of another organization, several other alternatives may be appropriate, including the purchase or rental of a minicomputer. Minicomputer technology is expanding at a very rapid rate. Another alternative may be for several small organizations, in a cooperative effort, to install a computer system. Still another alternative is for organizations to purchase from other organizations their unused computer time. This arrangement makes the utilization of computer systems financially feasible for many organizations. Three other alternatives are the utilization of computer service bureaus, timesharing services, and computer utilities. Since each of the latter three alternatives are being used more widely, each is discussed in detail in the sections that follow.

Because of the significance of the alternative processing systems, top-level managers should be involved in making decisions about which of the alternatives to utilize. Without the involvement of top-level managers, this vital area does not receive the attention it deserves.

Computer Service Bureaus

Computer service bureaus are especially advantageous for small organizations that do not have computer installations. Such organizations typically do not employ persons with sufficient knowledge to develop computer systems. Such organizations, therefore, find it more advantageous to use the expertise as well as the equipment provided by computer service bureaus.

A computer service bureau may be organized in several different ways, including the following: a subsidiary of a computer equipment manufacturer, an independent bureau, a subsidiary of a large organization, or part of a national computer service bureau chain. The following are factors to consider in choosing one alternative over another: reputation of the computer service bureau, services provided by the bureau, the cost of the services provided, the accessibility of the bureau, and the procedures used to safeguard the clients' data.

A variety of services are provided by computer service bureaus. Among the more common are analysis of the processing needs of the client, development of computer programs to accommodate the processing needs of the clients, conversion of each client's data into an acceptable data input medium, and conversion into output form the results of the processed data. The types of data that computer service bureaus process for clients vary considerably but may include payroll and payroll records, accounts payable, accounts receivable, order processing, inventory, cash disbursements, and sales analysis.

One of the most useful services that computer service bureaus provide for small organizations is the conversion of their input data. If the input data are recorded in some machine language, the computer service bureau can convert the input data into a medium that is capable of being read into its computer system. Rather than having to supply the computer service bureau with data already recorded on punched cards or magnetic tape, for example, a variety of other input media can be used. To illustate, assume the organization's cash registers prepare a perforated paper tape of each transaction. The perforated paper tape can then be converted to magnetic tape for input into the computer system. Other types of input media frequently used by small organizations are optical character recognition data and magnetic strip ledger cards.

**Timesharing
Services**

Another of the alternatives to installing a computer system or expanding a present system is the use of timesharing. The services provided by computer service bureaus and timesharing services differ in several ways. When computer service bureaus are used, **batch processing** is typically used. This means that a number of similar business transactions are grouped for processing during a single continuous machine run. In other words, the clients' transactions are processed after a "batch" accumulates. With timesharing, on the other hand, each client organization has at least one data input device on its premises. This arrangement is considered to be on-line since the input device in each organization is under direct, continuous command of the central processing unit of the computer to which the input device is connected. When timesharing is used, data can be fed into the computer and processed, and output received at any time the computer is functioning. In summary, with timesharing, data are read into the computer at all times of the day, but when computer service bureaus are used, a group of similar transactions are likely to be processed at only one time during the day.

Computer service bureaus and timesharing services also differ with respect to the form of data input. Whereas computer service bureaus will convert the data for the subscriber, timesharing requires that subscribers' data be transmitted in a medium that can be immediately read into the computer. Whereas computer service bureaus provide several types of services for clients, timesharing services typically provide only computer processing time.

Another difference between using computer service bureaus and timesharing services is the extent to which each is used for processing clients' data. When a computer service bureau is used, most clients have the bureau process all of their data. When a timesharing service is used, the clients may use their own facilities for processing some of their data but use the service for processing other types of data.

Furthermore, the amount of time it takes to receive output is another significant difference between computer service bureaus and timesharing services. A period of several hours may pass before output is received from computer service bureaus, but timesharing services typically provide immediate output.

Another difference between the two alternatives is the types of jobs processed by each. While computer service bureaus are frequently used to process data for record keeping purposes (payroll, inventory, sales, etc.), timesharing services are frequently used to process data that are used by managers for decisionmaking purposes.

Most timesharing services store the clients' data files and programs. When a certain job is to be processed, the client's terminal is used to notify the computer operator which tapes are to be used. The computer operator then places the appropriate tapes on the appropriate machines.

Because most timesharing services utilize large computers capable of processing several programs simultaneously, multiprogramming is a characteristic of most timesharing services. Therefore, the lapsed time between data input and data output is minimal.

Computer Utilities   The services provided by computer utilities, which are growing in number and popularity, are more extensive than the services provided by computer service bureaus. A primary characteristic of computer utilities is the powerful computer facilities they provide. Generally, computer utilities are able to generate much more computer power than are computer service bureaus. In addition, computer utilities offer extensive data banks and data communication systems. The extensive data banks provided by most computer utilities are very advantageous for subscribers. Rather than having to generate the same data that other organizations have already generated, the data is stored in data banks shared by other subscribers.

Many of the computer utilities are part of a vast communications network. An example of a communications network is CYBERNET, which has been developed by Control Data Corporation, a large computer manufacturer. CYBERNET connects thirty metropolitan areas in the United States with twelve large computer systems. The services of CYBERNET are provided to subscribers in government, education, and business fields. Another example of a computer communications network is TYMNET, which connects fifty-four cities on two continents with thirty-seven large computers. TYMNET provides services to the same types of subscribers as CYBERNET. Another is ARPA Net, which connects the computing facilities of fifteen universities.

Computers and the Human Element   Managers, of necessity, must be concerned with the effect of a computer system on the human element since the success or failure of the computer system is very likely to be determined by the human element. If managers ignore the human element, the success of the computer system is very likely to be lessened. Not only are human relations problems likely to emerge, but also employee turnover and absenteeism are likely to increase, and employee morale is likely to decrease.

For a variety of reasons, employees tend to resist the installation of a new computer system or the expansion of a present system. One significant reason is the fear of employees that some of their job responsibilities will be taken over by the computer. Other resistance centers around the fear of total job displacement, job insecurity, and employees' feelings of an inability to cope with the new work procedures. Because many people find their present routines to be comfortable, change is uncomfortable. In addition to being responsible for making major decisions regarding the type of computer system needed and the type of equipment needed in the system, top management is also responsible for determining how to minimize the negative feelings of employees.

The installation of a new computer system or the expansion of a present system does not mean that certain employees will no longer be needed. At the time that employees are informed of the possibility of changes in this area, they should also be assured that none will lose their jobs. The types of jobs most often affected by computer applications are lower-level, routine jobs. Since the individuals who fill such jobs generally have a higher turnover rate than individuals in higher-level jobs, normal attrition will usually take care of overstaffing. In fact, the installation of a computer system is often responsible for creating more jobs than the system eliminates.

The importance of keeping employees informed cannot be over-stressed. A lack of information is often responsible for the circulation of unfounded rumors. Not only should employees be immediately informed about the investigation committee's undertaking of the feasibility study, but they should also be kept informed of the progress being made on the study. In addition, employees should be made aware of the opportunities the new system will create, as well as the time schedule with which the new equipment will be installed.

Another aspect of the human element about which managers must make decisions is the extent of the training or retraining experiences that will be made available to employees. A variety of training techniques are available. While some training programs provide in-depth experiences, others provide more superficial experiences. Employees whose present jobs are not directly affected by the new installation but who desire to participate in the training program should be allowed to do so. The advantages of this practice far outweigh the disadvantages.

First-line supervisors can be immeasurably helpful in improving employees' reactions to either the installation of a computer system or the expansion of a present system. Supervisors who have the confidence of their subordinates can do much to sell their subordinates on the changes that will take place. By emphasizing shortcomings of the present system and explaining how these shortcomings will be overcome by the new system, employees are more likely to accept the new system. In addition to using supervisors to sell the new system, many organizations have also found the leaders of informal groups to be very helpful in selling the new system.

Another practice that the management of certain organizations have found effective in reducing employees' negative reactions is to have orientation meetings on a departmental basis. The purpose of such meetings is to inform the employees in each department about how the new system will affect the department and more specifically how the new system will affect them individually. If the individuals who preside at such meetings are able to answer employees' questions to their satisfaction, this technique can also be very helpful.

In addition to having to deal with individual employees when a new computer system is installed, the union that represents the employees will also have to be dealt with. If the employees are not presently unionized, but if certain conditions are present to make unionization desirable, the installation of a new computer system may be sufficient to trigger unionizing activities. If serious unionizing efforts are being made, it is not uncommon for the negative effects of increased automation to be exaggerated to the point that employees find unionizing to be even more desirable.

Historically, many organizations have found that the concealing of facts and data from union officials eventually helps the union's cause. This is because facts and data that are intentionally concealed will eventually surface—and often at the company's expense. Therefore, it is recommended that the union be dealt with openly, honestly, and in good faith.

If the union officials are made aware of employee benefits that are expected to result from the installation of the new system, the union officials are often in a position to support the organization. In some cases, union officials are in a better position to reduce employees' negative feelings toward the installation of the new system than are the top-level managers of the organization.

No matter how appropriate the computer applications are or how efficiently the procedures are performed, the total effectiveness of the computer system cannot be fully realized unless concern is also shown for the human element. As is true of so many other aspects of the computer system, the amount of concern shown for the human element is at the total discretion of management. Unless management is concerned with the effect of the computer system on the human element, little or no concern will be shown.

Review Questions

1. What employees frequently serve on the investigation committee whose function is to conduct a feasibility study?

2. Why is it important that the announcement of the appointment of an investigation committee to conduct a feasibility study be made at the top levels of the organization?

3. What means are available for the analysis of an organization's present system?

4. How do most organizations determine whether or not the investigation committee's recommended alternative for the installation of a new system is feasible?

5. What uses are made of the specifications of the new computer system?

6. Why is the parallel processing of data advantageous when converting to a new computer system?

7. How do computer service bureaus and timesharing services differ?

8. In what ways do computer utilities and computer service bureaus differ?

Minicases

The Andleson Publishing Corporation is a relatively small book publishing house. The corporation has doubled its sales in the last three years. Because of its increased sales volume, the corporation investigated the feasibility of installing a computer system. The analysis indicated that the installation of a computer system is not yet feasible. Therefore, the management of the company is investigating the possibility of using an alternate processing system. Most managers feel that the use of a computer service bureau may be more appropriate than a timesharing arrangement. Which alternative do you feel would be more appropriate? Why? What services are likely to be provided by the computer service bureau? By the organization with whom the Andleson Publishing Corporation would enter into a timesharing arrangement?

*   *   *

The Excello Plastics Corporation is in the process of investigating the possibility of installing a new, larger computer system. The present system will not permit further expansion. An investigation committee was appointed, and they have done some of the typical preliminary work. The committee is now ready to undertake an analysis of the present system. What devices are available for analyzing the present system? What suggestions can you offer to help improve the effectiveness of the present system?

Case

The Bronson Distributing Company, now about fifty years old, started out as a family business specializing in the wholesale distribution of candy, gum, and tobacco products. The firm has now grown to the point that it is the largest distributor of its type in the state.

The company moved from integrated data processing to electronic data processing in 1964. At the time of the conversion to EDP, many employees became very anxious about the company's motives for installing the computer system. Although none of the employees were laid off and less than twenty percent experienced changes in their jobs, the employees did not readily accept the installation of the new computer. In fact, the closest the employees have ever come to unionization was at that time. An assessment of the situation a few months after the computer was installed revealed that the employees were inadequately prepared for the conversion to the new system.

Because the firm is still growing quite rapidly, and because the present computer system has been expanded to the point where further expansion is now nearly impossible, the firm's management is giving serious thought to the installation of a new computer system. The man-

agement plans to proceed in the same manner as before—that is, undertaking a complete feasibility study.

1. What suggestions can you offer to make the possible installation
of a new computer system more acceptable to the employees than was
the installation of the first system?

2. Who should be primarily responsible for carrying out each of
the suggestions you provided?

Quality and Quantity Control

Chapter

29

Objectives of Control

Advantages of Control

Elements of Control
Factors to Control
Identification of Anticipated Results
Assessment Devices
Application of Corrective Measures

Quality Control
Quality Control Techniques
Total inspection
Spot checking
Statistical quality control
Zero Defects

Quantity Control
Controlling Fluctuations
Short-Interval Scheduling

Work Scheduling
Work Scheduling Devices
Schedule log
Work chart
Work schedule calendar
Gantt Chart
PERT

Chapter Aims   After studying this chapter, the student should be able to:

1. Identify the steps involved in quantity or quality control.
2. Discuss the objectives of control.
3. Discuss how an individual determines what factors to control.
4. Discuss the following quality control techniques: total inspection, spot checking, statistical quality control, and Zero Defects.
5. Explain the various ways that an administrative office manager might control fluctuations in the quantity of work that must be done.
6. Explain the short-interval scheduling concept.
7. Discuss the following work scheduling devices: schedule log, work chart, work schedule calendar, Gantt Chart, and PERT.

Chapter Terms   *Control:* one of the functions of management that is necessary because actual results do not coincide with anticipated results.

Quality control: a technique designed to determine the quality of an employee's work.

Quantity control: a technique designed to determine if an employee's actual output conforms with expected output.

Total inspection: a quality control technique that involves the complete and total inspection of every unit of work produced by every employee to determine whether or not the work reaches minimum quality standards.

Spot checking: a quality control technique that involves periodically checking the quality of employees' work.

Statistical quality control: a quality control technique that has a statistical base and that uses random sampling to determine which work units are to be inspected.

Zero Defects: a quality control technique that concentrates on the prevention of errors because employees do their work correctly the first time.

Short-interval scheduling: a quantity control technique designed to help employees monitor on a short-interval basis the extent to which their actual output conforms with anticipated results.

Schedule log: a work scheduling device on which is recorded such information as tasks that are to be completed, the date by which the tasks are to be completed, the individual(s) to whom the tasks are assigned, and the time that the tasks are begun and completed.

Work chart: a work scheduling device on which the supervisor or manager works backward from the project completion date to determine the date on which the project must be started and when each part of the project must be completed.

Work schedule calendar: a work scheduling device that consists of a day-by-day schedule for the duration of one week. It lists the jobs or projects that are to be started on each day.

Gantt Chart: a work scheduling device that is similar in many respects to the work schedule calendar, but is used for longer, more complex projects than is the work schedule calendar.

PERT: a work scheduling device that identifies all the subprojects that comprise a project. Each subproject is identified as either a critical or a noncritical subproject. The critical paths or subprojects must be completed on schedule in order to complete the project on time. The noncritical subprojects may be completed at any time.

Control, as a function of management, is necessary because actual results do not always coincide with anticipated results. Used in this sense, control is a followup process that identifies unsatisfactory results that require the application of certain corrective measures. Control, which is one of the five functions of management (the others are planning, organizing, staffing, and directing), becomes important when the results of certain activities fail to meet minimum expectations. When a new program is developed, devices for controlling the program should be developed during the planning phase of the program. A delay in developing the control devices until after the program is functioning may result in considerable operating inefficiency.

The administrative office manager, who is responsible for many different types of office tasks, as well as for office employees, generally finds that control is very crucial for successful office operations. Without control, the operating efficiency of the office function is likely to be hampered, the quantity and quality of the work cannot be maximized, and office employees are likely to question certain management practices.

There are several different types of control with which managers have to be concerned. This chapter deals with two of the more important areas of control: **quality control** and **quantity control.**

Control, when used for quality and quantity evaluation, involves the following five-step process:

Step 1: Define the parameters of the work being subjected to the control process.
Step 2: Determine expected results.
Step 3: Evaluate actual results.
Step 4: Compare actual results with the expected results.
Step 5: Apply corrective measures when needed.

Work scheduling, although not a component of quality or quantity control, is equally important as a function of control. Unless certain control measures are applied to the completion of projects, there is no assurance that the projects will be completed according to schedule. Work scheduling is also included in this chapter.

Because the control process results in the application of corrective measures, control is considered by some to have disciplinary or punitive overtones. Of the five functions of management, the control function is perhaps the most negative function. Since the administrative office manager frequently has to apply corrective measures, such personal qualities as tact, empathy, and helpfulness are very important.

Objectives of Control

As one of the functions of management, control has several important objectives:

1. To increase the operative efficiency of the organization.

2. To assess the degree to which anticipated results and actual results conform.

3. To coordinate the various elements of a program or a task.

4. To increase the likelihood that the objectives of the organization will be achieved.

5. To assist the office employees in performing their jobs more efficiently.

6. To maximize the profits of the organization by decreasing the amount of work that has to be redone and by reducing the misuse of supplies and materials.

Advantages of Control

The use of control in office operations results in several distinct advantages.

1. Control helps to maximize the profits of the organization.

2. Employees' efficiency improves because they are cognizant of quantity and quality output requirements.

3. The organization has a yardstick by which to measure its operating efficiency.

4. Because control identifies the areas in which actual and anticipated results do not coincide, the various work processes can be modified to result in greater operating efficiency.

5. Scheduling deadlines can be met more frequently.

Elements of Control

Unless certain elements of control are present, the control process will most likely be somewhat ineffective. The elements, which should be considered when determining the means of controlling various office operations, include factors to consider, identification of anticipated results, assessment devices, and application of corrective measures.

Factors to Control

Before an office operation can be controlled, those responsible for the control process must be aware of which factors within the operation to control. Since certain factors are too insignificant to be concerned about, the individuals responsible for control will have to use their judgment in selecting the control factors. When insignificant factors are selected, the control process will likely become too cumbersome. On the other hand, the control process will be very inefficient if the significant factors are not selected.

In many office operations the control factors are crucial documents or forms utilized within specific operations. For example, in a purchasing system, the purchase order is likely to be the critical factor that should be controlled. By applying control to the purchase order, conformity exists between the actual results and the anticipated results of all the other components of the system.

Identification of
Anticipated
Results

Without clearly identifying the anticipated results, those individuals responsible for the control process have nothing against which to make a comparison of the actual results and the anticipated results. In addition to identifying the anticipated results, those responsible for the control process should be certain that the anticipated results are appropriate and are neither greater nor less than should be reasonably expected.

Once the anticipated results have been identified, the results must be communicated to the employees whose performance is expected to coincide with the anticipated results. If employees are unaware of the expected performance levels, for example, it is obvious that they cannot be held accountable for failing to reach them. A primary responsibility of managers and supervisors is the communication of the anticipated results.

Assessment
Devices

If the actual results are to be compared with the anticipated results, the actual results will have to be assessed in some way. In some instances, the assessment will be a technique that facilitates measuring the quantity output of an office operation. In this instance, the assessment device will very likely be performance standards such as those discussed in Chapter 19. In other instances, the assessment device may involve determining the degree of accuracy with which data are entered on a form.

Application of
Corrective
Measures

When actual results do not conform with anticipated results, corrective measures become necessary. For example, if an office employee fails to produce at the anticipated or expected rate, the manager or supervisor will have to judge whether or not corrective measures should be taken. It is important that the manager or supervisor who is responsible for the employee also have the commensurate authority to carry out the necessary corrective measures. Without this authority, the effectiveness of the manager or supervisor will be greatly diminished.

Quality Control

Because employees sometimes fail to produce work that is error-free, quality control is utilized by organizations as a means of increasing their operating efficiency. Without some form of quality control, errors are likely to go unnoticed, which affects the image of the organization, increases the amount of work that has to be redone, and which over a period of time, has a negative impact on the profits of the organization. In addition, errors in materials used for managerial decisionmaking may result in incorrect decisions, which may also have a negative impact on the well-being of the organization.

Both quality and quantity control use standards as a basis for evaluation. Whereas quality standards involve evaluating the accuracy with which work is produced, quantity standards in most instances are more quantifiable. To illustrate, the neatness with which a letter is typed is an example of quality control. If the letter is very poorly typed, it most likely will not be mailable. But since not all individuals have the same mailable-nonmailable standards, quality control can be rather subjective in certain instances. Quantity standards, on the other hand, are more clear-cut. The employee's output either coincides or fails to coincide with expected output levels.

A quality control program involves determining minimum standards of acceptability. Once the standards have been determined, the acceptability of the actual work can be compared with the expected standards. If there is a serious lack of conformity, corrective measures may be necesssary.

Quality Control Techniques

Several different techniques have been developed for maintaining quality control. Among these are **total inspection, spot checking, statistical quality control,** and **Zero Defects.**

Total Inspection. As a quality control technique, total inspection involves complete and total inspection of every unit of work produced by each employee to determine whether or not the work reaches minimum quality standards. If not, corrective measures will perhaps have to be taken against the employee.

Total inspection is desirable for certain types of office work. Perhaps the most frequent example of total inspection is the proofreading of typewritten work, especially in instances when total accuracy is crucial. Other examples of office work that frequently receive total inspection are the verification of important arithmetical calculations and the compilation of statistical data.

Because of the nature of some types of office work, total inspection may not be necessary. In some instances the work is of limited importance. In other instances, there is very little chance that errors have been made. An example is the filing of clients' correspondence. Although most of the correspondence would be accurately filed, this situation does not warrant the complete and total inspection of the files to insure that all correspondence has been properly filed.

Spot checking. This technique involves periodically checking the quality of an employee's work. Because the work is spot checked and no use is made of statistical processes to determine how much, who, and when the checks are to be made, the desirability of this technique is frequently challenged. By adding the statistical dimension, which is a characteristic of statistical quality control, more valid results are possible.

Statistical quality control. Because total inspection of work is not always desirable nor is spot checking sufficiently accurate, statistical quality control is used. Statistical quality control produces accurate and reliable results because of the statistical sampling base that is a characteristic of this technique.

Since statistical quality control has a statistical base, certain fundamental statistical elements are utilized. These elements include sampling, normal distribution, and control limits. Sampling, which is based on laws of probability, is used to determine what percent of the total output needs to be examined in order to be relatively certain that total output is as error-free as is the sample. In other words, if proper statistical procedures are used, the quality of the sample should be representative of the quality of the whole.

Statistical tables, which are available for determining the appropriate sample size, take into consideration the following two elements: the total number of units from which the sample is being drawn and the minimum accuracy level that is required. If the total output consists of one hundred units and an accuracy level of 90 percent is acceptable, fewer samples would have to be drawn than in the situation of an identical number of output units but an accuracy requirement of 95 percent. To illustrate, if the total output consists of one hundred units and it is determined that 96 percent accuracy is required, the statistical tables indicate that fifteen of the units should be randomly selected for inspection. If no errors are found within the fifteen units that are randomly selected, the assumption is then made that the one hundred units are also free of errors. But if one error is found within the sample of fifteen units, according to the law of probability, seven of the one hundred units would contain an error. If errors are found in two of the fifteen samples, approximately fourteen of the one hundred units could be expected to contain an error.

Depending upon the type of office work on which the quality control analysis is being made, 90 percent accuracy may be sufficient. In other instances, 100 percent accuracy may be required.

Normal distribution is another of the elements involved in statistical quality control. Normal distribution is based on the principle that randomly observed occurrences of a sufficient quantity tend to be distributed around the mean or average of all the occurrences. For purposes of illustration, assume that the average or mean number of errors that file clerks make is two errors per one hundred units of work. While some clerks will make more than two errors in filing one hundred units and others will make fewer than two errors per one hundred units, the majority will make two errors in filing one hundred units.

The number of errors per total output is important because this factor has a bearing on the number of errors or deviations that can be reasonably expected to occur within a given number of observations. Deviation refers to the amount of deviation from the mean and is calculated by using the formula for standard deviation. In any normal distribution, 68.3 percent of the total will fall within one standard deviation above and below the mean of the distribution; 95.1 percent will fall within two standard deviations above and below the mean of the distribution; and 99.7 percent will fall within three standard deviations above and below the mean of the distribution.

In the foregoing example, it was assumed that the file clerks made an average of two errors per one hundred units filed. When using the appropriate formula to calculate standard deviation, assume that a standard deviation of 0.53 is found. According to the normal distribution, 68.3 percent of the number of errors made by each file clerk will be within one standard deviation above and below the mean, thus ranging from 1.47 to 2.53 errors (2.0 $\pm$ 0.53). Two standard deviations above and below the mean (from 0.94 to 3.06 errors) will encompass 95.1 percent of the number of errors made by each file clerk. Three standard deviations will encompass 99.7 percent of the errors, which means that all but 0.3 percent of the number of errors made by each file clerk will be between 0.51 and 3.59 errors per one hundred units filed. This is illustrated in Figure 29–1.

Control limits are the third element of statistical quality control. These limits must be established in order to determine at what point the errors are considered to be due to chance and at what point the errors are attributable to some identifiable cause. For instance, in the foregoing example, if the control limits are set at two standard deviations above and below the mean, chance is responsible for employees whose errors range from 0.94 to 3.06 errors per one hundred units. Because these

FIGURE 29–1   Normal Distribution

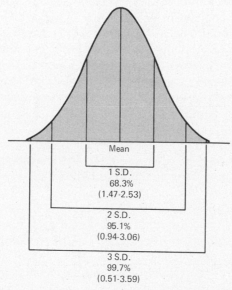

Mean

1 S.D.
68.3%
(1.47-2.53)

2 S.D.
95.1%
(0.94-3.06)

3 S.D.
99.7%
(0.51-3.59)

errors are due to chance, reasons cannot be identified for employees making such errors. On the other hand, some attributable cause is responsible for employees whose errors exceed 3.06 per one hundred units. In this particular example, the errors may be due to poorly trained employees. Figure 29–2 illustrates the control limits for this particular example.

With the exception of sample 4 in Figure 29–2, all samples fall within the control limits. Therefore, these errors were due to chance. Since the number of errors in sample 4 exceeds the maximum for the upper control limit, some factor other than chance is responsible. One speculation is that the sample was taken at the end of the work day and can be attributable to employee fatigue.

Zero Defects. The last of the quality control techniques presented in this chapter is Zero Defects. The fundamental characteristic of the Zero Defects technique is the prevention of errors because employees do their work correctly the first time. Thus, there is more to Zero Defects than identification and correction of errors. There must also be some motivation on the part of the employees not to make the errors in the first place.

In utilizing the Zero Defects technique, employees make a pledge to management that they will support the concept and will produce error-free work. Because some errors are caused by improper work procedures, faulty equipment, and the like, employees make suggestions to management regarding ways to eliminate the errors. The employees are subsequently rewarded on the basis of the quality of the suggestions they submit, on the basis of the improvement they make, and on the basis of their error-free work. In some instances, errors are attributable to management rather than the employees themselves. If nothing is done to

FIGURE 29–2   Control Limits

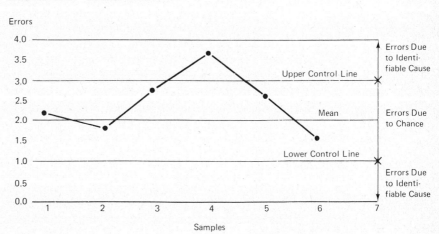

eliminate the errors attributable to management, the effectiveness of the Zero Defects program cannot be fully realized.

Quantity Control

Like quality control, quantity control utilizes standards that facilitate the comparison of anticipated results with actual results. Unless the standards are fairly accurate, the base for quantity control is not valid.

Quantity standards are developed on the basis of the data gathered during work measurement processes. The various work measurement techniques and the setting of quantity standards are discussed in Chapter 19. Work measurement is designed to determine what comprises a fair day's work for both the employer and employee. Therefore, employees have some assurance that their anticipated output levels do not exceed what is reasonably expected. Employers have some assurance that the employees are being paid for doing a reasonable amount of work.

In the normal operations of most organizations, the amount of work that needs to be done fluctuates from time to time. There will be times when employees will have more work to do than can be reasonably expected. At other times they will have less to do than what the standards indicate is a reasonable output. It is, therefore, the responsibility of management to develop ways to compensate for these fluctuations.

Because Chapter 19 explains the various techniques for measuring work and setting standards, these topics will not be repeated in this chapter. Rather, since a considerable amount of the manager's or supervisor's time may be consumed by the process of controlling the inevitable fluctuations in the amount of work that has to be done, several ways for controlling these fluctuations are presented in this section. In addition, the **short-interval scheduling** technique is presented. This technique is useful for monitoring how closely actual output levels conform with anticipated results. In the event of a serious lack of conformity, corrective measures may be appropriate.

Controlling Fluctuations

Much of the manager's or supervisor's time in controlling output will consist of determining the most effective way to handle fluctuations that result in employees' having either too much or too little work to do in a given amount of time. There are several different ways of handling these fluctuations.

When fluctuations result in too much work to be done in a given amount of time, one or more of the following may be utilized:

1. *Employee overtime.* Many organizations utilize employee overtime as a means of controlling situations when there is too much work to be done. If the situations can be remedied by a few hours of employee overtime, this method may result in significant advantages. If, on the other hand, a large number of overtime hours would be required, one of the other methods of controlling the fluctuations is recommended because of the possibility of the organization's having to compensate the employees at a rate of one and one-half times their regular rates. Rather

than compensate employees for overtime hours, another possibility is to allow employees to take time off for the hours they previously worked overtime. If the employees take time off when there is not a sufficient amount of work to be done, the organization has a very satisfactory method for controlling the "too little work" situation.

2. *Temporary help.* Another solution for controlling situations when there is too much work to be done is to use temporary help. In many cities nowadays, temporary employment agencies exist from which office help can be obtained for as short a time as one day or as long a period as several weeks. Temporary employment agencies are discussed in greater detail in Chapter 9.

3. *Part-time help.* If the fluctuations occur with a fairly consistent degree of regularity, perhaps part-time help may be most advantageous for an organization. If the fluctuations occur once a month, for instance, part-time employees may be hired to work only at the times when the work load is excessive. Such a practice is recommended because new employees do not have to be trained each month, which is likely to be the case if temporary employees are utilized.

4. *Floating work unit.* Some organizations have developed a floating work unit as a solution to instances when work loads are excessive. Employees who work in these floating units work wherever they are needed in the organization. Unless such employees are fairly competent in many different areas, they may find working under such circumstances to be very frustrating.

5. *Cycle billing.* When this technique is used, one-twentieth of the customers' accounts are due each working day. Instead of having all the customers' payments due on one day, which makes staffing difficult, the receipts are spread over a full month. Such a system is advantageous for controlling work fluctuations.

Where there is too little work to be done, the following practices may be utilized:

1. *Time off.* To compensate some employees for having worked overtime, some organizations allow them to take time off when there is a very limited amount of work to be done.

2. *Work backlog.* Because of the nature of some work, it can be postponed indefinitely. If this is possible, the work can be postponed until the time when there is too little work to do.

3. *Maintenance projects.* Some organizations have employees do maintenance projects when they have too little work to do. Examples of maintenance projects include the following: reorganization of files, cleaning of files, review of work procedures, and the like.

Short-Interval Scheduling

As a control device, short-interval scheduling assures that a given amount of work is completed in a given amount of time. Short-interval scheduling also provides the mechanism for determining whether or not the work is completed according to schedule. Short-interval scheduling, which is also helpful for the efficient scheduling of work, helps managers or supervisors determine whether or not the output standards are being consistently attained.

The basic assumption involved in short-interval scheduling is that when employees are attempting to reach obtainable short-range goals, there is a much greater chance of their being successful than if the goals are long range. Because the goals are short range, and because the status of employees in reaching their goals is determined frequently, employees are motivated to perform at higher levels.

The following illustrates how short-interval scheduling works. If an employee is expected to produce 400 units per eight-hour work day, the employee's output could be determined at the end of the work day. Unfortunately, the employee may not know until the end of the day whether or not the production goal has been achieved. With short-interval scheduling, the employee makes frequent checks throughout the work day to determine how closely production rates conform with accepted standards. These checks are typically made each hour of the work day. In the above illustration, the employee would have to produce an average of 50 units per hour to be successful in reaching the predetermined goal. If, upon checking, the employee finds that 120 units were produced during the first three hours, the employee then knows that if the 400-unit goal is to be reached, the thirty-unit shortage (150 minus 120) will somehow have to be made up during the work day. When supervisors discover that employees are failing to meet their expected hourly production levels, corrective measures can be taken. But when failure to meet the expected production levels is not discovered until the end of the work day, it is too late to take corrective action at that point.

Before short-interval scheduling can be implemented, expected production levels must be determined. Such production levels, which are presented as work standards, identify the acceptable amount of time needed to produce one unit of output.

Once the standards have been determined and the supervisor is aware of the reasonable expectations of the employees in the work unit, the work assignments can be made. To keep a record of how closely employees' actual results conform with expected results, each work assignment is accompanied by an assignment record such as the one illustrated in Figure 29–3. This information is also entered on the summary sheet, which is illustrated in Figure 29–4. After the work assignment is completed, the employee returns the assignment record, along with the completed work, to the supervisor, who then compares actual results with anticipated or expected results.

The number recorded in the "expected" column parallel to each employee's name is the production level the employee is expected to achieve during the span of one hour. For example, M. Smith was expected to produce six units of output from 8 A.M. to 9 A.M. But when the em-

FIGURE 29–3   Assignment Record

Name: *M Smith*

Supervisor: *Iyana Brown*

Job Number: *127*

Assignment: *Type form letters to our six clients in Buffalo. Form letter is attached.*

Other Comments:

Scheduled Time: *1 hr.*

Started	Completed	Elapsed Time
8.00	9.00	1 hr.

Comments: Because of machine failure, I was able to complete only 5 of the letters in 1 hour's time. MS

ployee completed the assignment and returned the assignment record to the supervisor, the supervisor discovered, because of machine failure, that only five units were produced. Therefore, "5" is entered in the "actual" column parallel to M. Smith's name. When an employee's actual performance fails to coincide with expected performance, an asterisk is entered in the appropriate place on the summary sheet.

By maintaining the summary sheet, the supervisor is able to readily determine at any point during the day if an employee's production level is ahead of or behind schedule. If the output is consistently behind schedule, corrective measures may be appropriate.

Work Scheduling

In this chapter, work scheduling is considered to be one of the functions of control. Without work scheduling, administrative office managers have very little if any control over the completion time of a

FIGURE 29–4   Summary Sheet

Employee	Results	8-9	9-10	10-11	11-12	12-1	1-2	2-3	3-4	4-5
M. Smith	Expected	6	7	10	8	9	15	20	13	7
	Actual	5*	7	10	8	8*	15	21	13	7
N. Green	Expected	3	5	3	6	10	13	14	7	6
	Actual	4	5	3	7	11	12*	14	8	6

Department: *Office Services*

Supervisor: *I Brown*

Today's Date: *11/15*

project. With work scheduling, greater control is possible, which helps assure the successful completion of a given project.

Work Scheduling Devices

A variety of devices are used for the scheduling of work to be completed within a given amount of time. Some of the devices are rather simple and can be used for scheduling rather complicated projects. On the other hand, several of the devices are rather sophisticated and are appropriately used in scheduling more complex projects.

Schedule log. As a means of scheduling office work, **schedule logs** are perhaps the most frequently used device for scheduling the completion of a given project. An example of a schedule log is illustrated in Figure 29–5. Although the schedule log illustrated in Figure 29–5 is quite simple, other more complex logs might be developed that are appropriate for the project being scheduled. The schedule log is generally completed by the project supervisor who is able to provide greater insight and direction into the successful completion of the project.

Work chart. Another of the more simple work scheduling devices is the **work chart,** which is illustrated in Figure 29–6. When using this chart,

FIGURE 29–5   Schedule Log

Name of Project:	Prepare proposal		Completion Date:	11/19
Project Supervisor:	Janice Otter			

Task	To be Completed By	Assigned to	Time Started	Time Finished
Gather data	11/01	Bill Green	8.00	4:30
process data	11/07	Mary Smith	8:00 (11/2)	2:30 (11/6)
draft proposal	11/17	Bill Green	8:00 (11/7)	4:00 (11/15)
revise proposal	11/18	Bill Green	8:00 (11/18)	3:00 (11/18)
type proposal	11/19	Diane Brown	8:00 (11/19)	4:15 (11/19)

the project supervisor works backward from the completion date. For example, in Figure 29–6, the project is to be completed by November 17. To determine the starting time of the project and the days on which each subproject must be started, the work chart is developed. Figure 29–6, which deals with the writing and submitting of a report, indicates that in order for the project to be completed by November 17, the data must be compiled by November 4, the report must be written by November 10, and so forth. By determining the completion date of a project and by determining the amount of time it will take to complete each phase of the project, the date on which each subproject must be started can be readily determined.

Work schedule calendar. Another of the more simple work scheduling devices is a **work schedule calendar,** such as the one illustrated in Figure

FIGURE 29–6   Work Chart

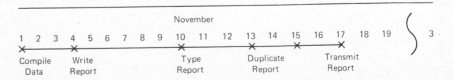

FIGURE 29–7 Work Schedule Calendar

Employee	Monday	Tuesday	Wednesday	Thursday	Friday
Sally B.	Type form letters _Type invoices_ _File correspondence_				
Jane d	Type report ↓				
Diane	Type manuscript for Mr Jones _Sort_ File cards				
Mary	On vacation				

29–7. The calendar is a day-by-day schedule for a week's duration and contains jobs or projects that are to be started on any given day. Quite often the work schedule calendar also provides a listing of the names of the employees, so that as jobs or projects are accepted by the work unit, the employee who is responsible for completing each project can be designated. As an employee completes one project, the next one can be started without the supervisor's having to make the assignment at that time.

Gantt Chart. This work scheduling device, although used for longer durations and perhaps useful for more complex projects than is the work schedule calendar, is similar in concept to the work schedule calendar. The work schedule calendar and the **Gantt Chart** are similar in that both indicate the jobs or projects that are to be completed on any given day. Figure 29–8 illustrates a Gantt Chart.

The Gantt Chart, which was developed by Henry Gantt, an early management authority, illustrates on a daily basis the jobs that are to be completed, as well as the estimated amount of completion time. Many Gantt Charts are now magnetized, which facilitates the movement of the tabs on which the various items are listed.

FIGURE 29–8   Gantt Chart

The Gantt Chart, although used for scheduling the work found in many offices, is especially useful in scheduling work to be completed on the organization's computer.

Program Evaluation Review Technique (PERT). This scheduling device was originally developed during the Polaris missile program and has been modified for use in scheduling complex projects, such as might be found in the office function of certain organizations. Because of its nature, **PERT** is most suitable for projects comprised of many parts or components. Its use in scheduling simple projects cannot be justified.

A PERT chart, which is illustrated in Figure 29–9, is developed to help schedule the component parts of the project. Each component must be identified, as must the estimated amount of time for completing each component. The numbers within circles on the chart refer to the various components that comprise the total project. The network of lines indicate the various paths that may be followed in completing the project. In preparing the PERT chart, a critical path must be determined. The critical path, which is also the longest path, consists of the components that must be completed before the project is finished. Each component or activity on the critical path must be completed on time and in the order in which the activities appear on the chart. If each component is not completed

FIGURE 29-9   PERT Chart

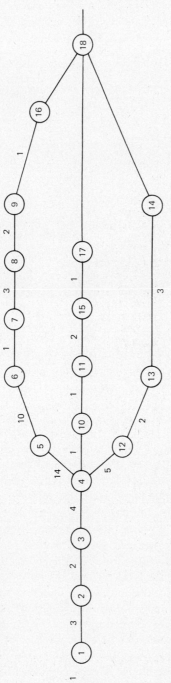

Legend:

1. Set convention date
2. Set convention location
3. Select convention chairman
4. Select convention facilities
5. Develop convention program
6. Select convention speakers
7. Set convention cost
8. Notify members of the convention program
9. Print program
10. Notify convention facility of desired setup of each meeting room
11. Select banquet menu
12. Determine recipient of outstanding member award
13. Prepare citation for outstanding member award
14. Determine honorarium for speakers
15. Arrange for registration booth
16. Make overnight lodging arrangements for members who desire to stay overnight
17. Arrange for transportation of members (from airport)
18. Await convention

on time, the project cannot be completed on time. All the other components must also be completed before the project is completed, but because these components are not on the critical path, they can be completed at any time during the course of the project without hampering the completion of the project. Noncritical components can be completed at any time.

For illustration purposes, Figure 29–9 is a PERT chart outlining the various components involved in planning a convention. The critical path consists of components or activities 1, 2, 3, 4, 5, 6, 7, 8, 9, and 16. The paths consisting of activities 1, 2, 3, 4, 10, 11, 15, and 17, and 1, 2, 3, 4, 12, 13, and 14 are not critical. Therefore, the components represented by numbers 10, 11, 15, 17, and by 12, 13, and 14 can be completed at any time prior to the opening of the convention. The components on the critical path, on the other hand, must be completed within the scheduled time if the convention is to be planned on time. The numbers above each line represent the estimated number of days needed to complete each component.

Review Questions

1. Why is control needed in office situations?

2. What are the objectives of control?

3. What advantages result from implementing control procedures?

4. What is the evaluation basis for both quality and quantity control?

5. As control techniques, how do total inspection and spot checking differ from one another?

6. What steps are involved in developing a statistical quality control program?

7. How does a floating work unit help an organization control fluctuations in its work processes?

8. When used as work scheduling devices, how does the work chart differ from the work schedule calendar?

9. When PERT is used as a work scheduling device, how is the appropriate network to be used chosen?

Minicases

The administrative office manager of the Hucksby Corporation is responsible for supervising several employees who, for one reason or another, seem to be having difficulty with the quantity of their output. The administrative office manager feels that a lack of motivation on the part of these employees may be the prime reason that their production is at a substandard level. To help such employees, the manager feels that the short-interval scheduling technique may be desirable for these employees. The administrative office manager knows that short-interval scheduling involves dividing expected output into small units so each employee knows whether or not the actual output level is close to expected output levels. The administrative office manager would like you to identify the steps involved in short-interval scheduling so that the technique can be installed at Hucksby Corporation.

*   *   *

The Daum Corporation is a fairly large, well-established farm equipment manufacturer. The operating processes of the firm are generally considered to be quite efficient. This is probably because of the firm's practice of financially supporting their employees' educational endeavors. At the present time, however, the firm is experiencing a problem that needs immediate attention. Lately, because of the installation of a centralized accounting system, several of the departments seem to be having difficulty at certain points of the month. Whenever data need to be assembled at the department level for input into the centralized system, it takes several employees several hours to assemble the data. It is surmised that as the "bugs" in the system are eliminated, several of the time-consuming processes will also be eliminated. On days when the data have to be assembled, the employees are often unable to perform their regular jobs, which creates a backlog of work. What alternatives can you make to help the employees overcome the inability to have their work completed on time? Explain why you chose the alternative that you did.

Case

The Blackmun Publishing Company is a new subsidiary of Walton Publishers, Inc. Although the subsidiary is only six months old, most of its office procedures are considered by the parent company to be quite efficient. Much of this is attributed to the fact that the publisher and the editors had a considerable amount of foresight in planning and organizing the new subsidiary. The company is now expanding at a faster rate than was previously anticipated. Because of this rapid expansion, the work backlog in the general office of the subsidiary is beginning to cause some concern throughout the organization.

Although the company is fairly certain that the output of its employees is fairly standard, there is no evidence to support this claim. Up to this point, the company has not been overly concerned about either the quantity or quality of the work produced by its employees. Work that was poorly produced could be redone, and in most cases, deadlines could be met.

Because of the rapid expansion and because of the current general disregard for quantity and quality control, it is felt by some that the installation of a quantity and quality control program should be investigated.

1. What are the pros and cons of installing a quantity and/or quality control program?

2. How should the installation of such a program be undertaken?

3. When selecting appropriate quantity and quality control devices, what factors should be considered?

4. How can the employees of the organization be sold on the merits of a quantity and/or quality control program?

Budgetary and Cost Control

Chapter
30

Budgeting
>
> Purposes of Budgeting
> Advantages of Budgeting
> Limitations of Budgeting
> Prerequisites for Successful Budgeting
>> Proper organization
>> Financial data
>> Commitment of top management
>
> Budget Preparation
>> Budget period
>> Developing the budget
>>> Responsibility for the budget
>>> Initiating the budget
>>> Types of costs and expenses
>>> Principles of budget preparation
>> Budget revision
>>> Periodic review
>>> Progressive review
>>> Moving review
>
> The Budget Manual

Budgetary Control

Cost Control
>
> Techniques for Controlling Office Operating Costs
>> Cost breakdowns
>> Standard costs
>> Cost analysis studies
>
> Taking Corrective Action
> Suggestions for Controlling Office Costs
>> Personnel costs
>> Supplies and materials costs
>> Equipment costs
>> Work process costs
>> Overhead costs

Chapter Aims

After studying this chapter, the student should be able to:

1. Discuss the purposes of budgeting.
2. Discuss the prerequisite conditions for successful budgeting.
3. Explain the various elements that are involved in the preparation of a budget.
4. Discuss the principles of budget preparation.
5. Explain the following methods of budget revision: periodic review, progressive review, and moving review.
6. Discuss the following techniques for controlling office operating costs: cost breakdowns, standard costs, and cost analysis study.
7. Discuss the various ways of controlling the following types of costs: personnel costs, supplies and materials costs, equipment costs, work process costs, and overhead costs.

Chapter Terms

Budgetary control: the process of regulating the operating budgets of the organization.

Cost control: the process of regulating the operating costs of an organization.

Budgets: a financial blueprint of an organization or a work unit within an organization.

Departmental budget: the budget of a department.

Master budget: the organization's total budget, which is a composite of departmental budgets.

Fixed costs: those costs that remain constant no matter how many units are produced.

Variable costs: those costs that vary proportionately in relation to output levels.

Semivariable costs: those costs that increase as production increases but not in direct proportion to increases in production.

Periodic review: a budget revision method in which the budget is revised at predetermined times for the remainder of the fiscal year. Budget revision periods are unequal in length.

Progressive review: a budget review method in which the budget is revised at predetermined times for equal length periods.

Moving review: a budget revision method in which the budget is revised each month, and as one month is completed, a new month is added twelve months hence.

Budget manual: the document that contains the written instructions for those involved in the preparation of the budget.

Cost breakdown technique: a technique for controlling office operating costs in which each cost is categorized as a salary cost, a supplies or service cost, or an overhead cost.

Direct salaries: the salaries paid to those individuals directly involved in the production of office work.

Indirect salaries: the salaries paid to those individuals who help make the production of office work possible but who are not directly involved in the production process.

Direct supplies: the actual supplies used in the production of office work.

Indirect supplies: the supplies used in producing office work that are not part of the work being produced.

Standard cost technique: a technique for controlling office operating costs that involves determining the unit cost of various office operations.

Cost analysis study: a technique for controlling office operating costs that involves comparing costs of a current period's operations with the operational costs of a prior period.

The administrative office manager, in addition to being concerned with quality and quantity control, needs to be concerned with **budgetary control** and **cost control.** In theory as well as in practice, the absence of quality, quantity, or budgetary control will result in increased costs of office operations. The utilization of quality, quantity, and budgetary control should greatly assist the administrative office manager in controlling office costs.

Budgetary and cost control are in many ways similar to quality and quantity control. For example, budgetary and cost control are similar to quality and quantity control because both are likely to result in regulatory action. Another similarity between budgetary and cost control and quality and quantity control is the constant attention the administrative office manager must give to each area. Without this constant attention, it is doubtful that the effectiveness of the control function can be fully realized. Another similarity is the reason for the necessity of each of these areas of control. Each is necessary because actual results sometimes fail to conform with anticipated results.

Budgeting

Budgets, which provide the organization with a financial blueprint, appear at several different levels in the organization. Budgetary control, which is discussed in the next section, is the process of regulating the operating budgets of the organization. Without budgetary control, the preparation and use of budgets results in futile effort.

Purposes of Budgeting

An important purpose of budgeting is to help an organization perform its operations more efficiently, which helps increase the profits of the organization. Another important purpose is to assist management in maintaining a program of cost effectiveness with regard to the organization's operations. If the operations are allowed to become ineffective because of improper budgeting, the efficiency of the operations cannot be maximized. Another significant purpose of budgeting is to provide a general sense of direction for the future. When the management of an organization plans for future developments and progress, the budget will provide assistance in achieving the goals and objectives of the organization.

Advantages of Budgeting

The process of budgeting results in some significant advantages:

1. Budgeting requires management to give adequate consideration to the policies of the organization.

2. Budgeting requires departmental-level managers to develop practices that facilitate the attainment of budgetary goals.

3. Budgeting requires management to identify the resources necessary for accomplishing the goals of the organization.

4. Budgeting helps determine which functions are not operating efficiently.

5. Budgeting helps management make accurate, timely decisions regarding various organizational operations.

6. Budgeting helps determine which functions are having difficulty achieving their objectives and goals.

Limitations of Budgeting

Although budgeting results in some rather significant advantages for the organization, there are certain limitations about which the administrative office manager needs to be aware.

1. Since the budget is based on estimates, the validity of the budget is to a large extent determined by the accuracy with which the estimates are made.

2. The success with which an organization is able to operate is clearly dependent upon how well management is able to motivate the employees to operate within the budgeted allowances.

3. The effectiveness of the budget is to a large extent dependent upon the accuracy with which budget revisions are made.

Prerequisites for Successful Budgeting

Successful budgeting does not simply happen. Without the presence of certain prerequisite conditions, the budgeting efforts will most likely be in vain. Although the prerequisite conditions will not automatically insure success in budgeting, their presence will improve budgeting efforts. The prerequisite conditions include the following: proper organization, financial data, and commitment of top management.

Proper organization. Certain organizational characteristics must be present if the budgeting process is to be successful. The organizational characteristics include the proper grouping of tasks within functions, definitive lines of authority and areas of responsibility, and lines of communication. The absence of any of these characteristics is likely to result in ineffective budgeting. For example, the absence of authority will make it impossible for a manager or supervisor to take the necessary corrective action when the costs of various operations exceed the budgeted allowances. Furthermore, if areas of responsibility have not been assigned to various individuals, they cannot be held accountable when various operations exceed their budgetary allowances.

Financial data. The development of a budget requires the utilization of financial data. Without the availability of financial data, the base for budget development does not exist. The necessary types of financial data include the number of units sold during the previous financial period, the relationship between the units sold and the cost incurred in producing these units, and emerging financial trends. Much of the financial data that are needed can be obtained from the financial records of the previous fiscal period.

Commitment of top management. Top management must be committed to the utilization of the budget as a control mechanism. Without commitment, the budgeting efforts are likely to produce only minimum worthwhile results. Furthermore, without the commitment from top management, lower management levels are also not very likely to be committed to the attainment of the budgetary allowances.

Budget Preparation

Budget preparation consists of several distinct elements, including determination of the budget period, development of the budget, and revision of the budget.

Budget period. The length of time covered by the office budget generally coincides with the fiscal period of the organization. Thus, if the organization's fiscal period starts in January of each year, so does its budget. In determining the length of the budget period, the length of time should be sufficiently long to compensate for any seasonal fluctuations. Since most organizations operate on a yearly budget, the office function of most organizations also operates on a yearly budget.

Developing the budget. Because of the planning that must go into developing a budget, the planning process is likely to consume a considerable amount of time. Employee participation in the planning process is very advantageous.

The office budget, which is part of a larger budget, is categorized as a **departmental budget.** The **master budget,** covering the entire organization, is a composite of the departmental budgets.

After the organization's projected amount of income has been determined, a monetary allocation can be made to each of the departments. It is from this monetary allocation that each department develops its operating budget. The departmental budgets are then consolidated to provide the basis for the organization's master budget.

Figure 30–1 illustrates a portion of a departmental budget.

Before the actual work starts on budget preparation, responsibility for budget preparation will have to be assigned. In many larger organizations, overall responsibility is assigned to the controller or treasurer of the organization. In other organizations, responsibility may be assigned to the vice president who is concerned with the financial affairs of the organization. In smaller organizations, the administrative office manager may have overall responsibility for the preparation of the budget. Regardless of the size of the organization, the administrative office manager, in most instances, is responsible for the preparation of the budget for the office function.

FIGURE 30–1   Budget

	January		February		March	
	Estimated	Actual	Estimated	Actual	Estimated	Actual
Salaries	$3,250	$3,140	$3,250	$3,250	$3,250	$3,300
Utilities	80	73	80	84	75	78
Telephone	120	150	120	110	120	125
Postage	50	73	50	75	50	80
Equipment Rental	120	120	120	120	120	120
	3,620	3,556	3,620	3,639	3,615	3,703

Many organizations currently utilize a budget committee to provide input into the development of the budget. At the organizational level, the budget committee, which is headed by the chief budget official, usually consists of departmental managers. In larger functional departments, a budget committee chaired by the departmental manager and consisting of the various supervisors in the department may be utilized. In most cases, budget committees are advisory in nature, and, therefore, their primary function is to provide suggestions to the chairperson of the budget committee on which they serve.

Although the chief financial officer is primarily responsible for the budget, it is of necessity prepared by several different individuals. The prevailing philosophy is that those managers and supervisors who are responsible for various functional areas throughout the organization should have extensive involvement in the preparation of their departmental budgets. This is because the departmental managers and supervisors are responsible for organizing their departments in such a way that the resources are efficiently utilized. Therefore, the budget is typically initiated by the chief budget officer who seeks assistance from other employees in the organization.

The president or the chairman of the board frequently gives the chief budget officer the authority to start the development of a budget. This authorization is typically received in a letter in which the president or chairman may summarize the condition of the national economy, the projected outlook for the industry of concern to the organization, and the anticipated growth trends of the organization.

Since the office function generates no direct income for most organizations, the budget of the office function contains only expenses or costs. But before reasonable allocations can be made for each type of expense or cost, an estimate of the cost of producing each type of unit output will have to be made. An estimate of the number of units of output the office function is projected to produce during the budget period is needed. These estimates are used to determine the monetary allocations for each type of expense or cost found within the office function.

The common types of expenses or costs found in the office function are:

1. Salaries and payroll
2. Fringe benefits
3. Equipment rental or purchase
4. Equipment depreciation
5. Furniture rental or purchase
6. Furniture depreciation
7. Telephone charges
8. Materials and supplies
9. Postage and mailing
10. Utilities
11. Rent charges
12. Taxes
13. Insurance
14. Maintenance costs
15. Training costs

Office costs or expenses can be divided into three groups: **fixed costs, variable costs,** and **semivariable costs.** Fixed costs are those that remain constant no matter how many units are produced. For example, rent, insurance, and taxes are examples of fixed costs, because they are constant and do not fluctuate in relation to the output levels.

Variable costs, on the other hand, vary proportionately in relation to the output levels. Examples of variable costs are materials or supplies. Generally (except when discounts are offered for quantity buying), the cost of materials or supplies increases in direct proportion to the amount used. For example, two purchase orders cost twice as much as one purchase order.

Semivariable costs increase as production increases, but not in direct proportion to production increases. An example of a semivariable cost is the rental of copy equipment. The rental of such equipment is frequently based on the number of copies made during the given period. As the number of copies increases, the per-unit cost generally decreases. To illustrate, if 500 copies are made on a copy machine during a given time, the per-unit cost may be 4.8 cents. But if 750 copies are made during the same period, the per-unit cost may be 4.2 cents.

To facilitate budget preparation, certain guiding principles should be followed.

1. *Employee participation in budget preparation is very advantageous.* When employees are allowed to participate in the preparation of the departmental budget, they are given an opportunity to participate

directly in the affairs of the department in which they work. By giving employees an opportunity to participate, they generally develop a feeling of greater commitment and are more likely to show greater concern for the budgetary allowances.

2. *The budget should reflect realistic estimates of operating costs.* Some individuals, in preparing budgets, believe that the mark of a good manager is to keep operating costs at a very low level. While this is theoretically desirable, the practical results of this situation are not always as desirable. In some instances, the amounts budgeted for certain operating costs are so minimal that operating efficiency is actually impeded. The budget should reflect estimates that are realistic and that take into consideration increases in operating costs because of inflation, greater volume of work, and the like.

3. *The budget must provide for unforeseen circumstances.* Because the budget is prepared in advance, sometimes as much as one year prior to the time of its application, unforeseen circumstances that may have an adverse effect on the budget cannot be predicted. For this reason, the budget must have built-in devices to compensate for circumstances having an adverse effect. To illustrate, a special fund may be set aside for such purposes.

4. *The employees should feel committed to the budget.* Unless employees have committed themselves to use the budget as a guide for certain of their actions, there can be only minimum assurance that the budget will be successful. A lack of commitment is likely to result in employees' being wasteful, their misusing organization facilities, and their failure to exert the amount of effort for which they are being paid.

Budget revision. Even though a considerable amount of effort may be involved in the preparation of the budget, a variety of uncontrollable circumstances may require that the budget be revised from time to time. For example, costs of materials may change, which is very likely to have an impact on the profit an organization is able to realize. In addition, operating costs may increase, which makes it difficult for an organization to continue to produce output at the same level over a period of time.

Among the different methods of budget revision are **periodic review, progressive review,** and **moving review.** The review technique that will be used by an organization will depend on the policies of the organization, the organization's financial picture, and the emphasis the organization places on budget revision.

When periodic review is utilized, the budget is revised at predetermined times for the remainder of the year. Depending on the organization, the budget may be reviewed each month for the remainder of the year, every two months for the remainder of the year, or perhaps every quarter for the remainder of the year. Figure 30–2 illustrates periodic review.

FIGURE 30–2   Periodic Review

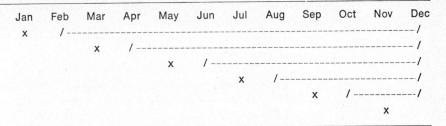

The progressive review technique differs from the periodic review technique in that the progressive review technique has definite length time spans. For example, with the periodic review technique, each time the budget is revised, it is for a shorter period of time. But with the progressive review technique, time spans are constant, perhaps six months in length. When the progressive technique is used, the budget is revised at definite times for a constant length of time. Figure 30–3 illustrates the progressive review technique.

FIGURE 30–3   Progressive Review

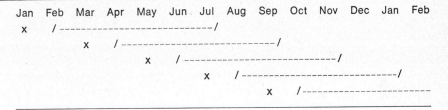

When the moving review technique is used, the budget is revised each month, and as one month is completed, a new month is added twelve months hence. Therefore, when the moving review technique is used, the budget is revised each month for the following twelve months. The moving review technique is illustrated in Figure 30–4.

FIGURE 30–4   Moving Review

Jan	Feb	Mar	Apr	May	Jun	Jul	Aug	Sep	Oct	Nov	Dec	Jan	Feb	Mar
x	/ -- /													
	x	/ -- /												
		x	/ -- /											

The Budget Manual

The **budget manual** contains written instructions for those involved in the preparation of the budget. The use of a budget manual will enable an organization to prepare the budget in a more orderly, efficient manner.

The typical contents of a budget manual include:

1. Objectives of the budget preparation process.
2. Identification of the various individuals who have authority and responsibility for budget preparation, as well as the nature of the authority and responsibility.
3. Instructions for those individuals at the various hierarchical levels who have responsibility for budget preparation.
4. Length of the budget period.
5. Procedures for budget approval.
6. Procedures for budget revision.
7. Required budget reports.
8. Procedures for taking corrective action.

Budgetary Control

After the budget has been prepared and approved, budgetary control becomes important. While budget preparation takes place once during the financial year, budgetary control is an ongoing process that takes place continually.

The budget report is a frequently used mechanism in budgetary control. The reports are used throughout the fiscal period to coordinate, assess, and control various office operations.

The detail needed in the budget report of the office function will be determined by its intended use. Since the department reports are frequently consolidated to make a larger budget report, less detail will perhaps be needed than if such a consolidation does not take place.

A fundamental purpose of budgeting is to enhance the profit of the organization. In many instances, the organization's profit is improved because of the use of skillfully written, carefully prepared budget reports. Several different types of budget reports might be prepared by the administrative office manager for use in budgetary control—for example, summaries of actual and budgeted expenses; divisional or departmental summary cost reports; and daily or weekly labor reports comparing actual and standard man hours.

When preparing budget reports, the following guidelines are suggested:

1. *Exception situations should be pointed out.* As managers and executives have an increasing number of job responsibilities, they have less time to devote to operations that are functioning smoothly and according to plan. Therefore, much of their time has to be devoted to those operations that are not progressing according to plan. In terms of budget reports, the operations that exceed budgetary allowances should be pointed out for the manager's or supervisor's immediate attention.

2. *When presenting figures in a report, a comparison base should*

be given. To present figures in a report without also presenting a base against which to compare the numbers renders the figures virtually useless. For example, to indicate in a report that the monthly telephone cost was $83.74 is meaningless. But to indicate that the budgeted amount was $70.00 or that the last month's bill was $67.29 provides a base against which comparisons can be made.

3. *Assist the reader by summarizing as much report information as possible*. The report writer can help the busy executive or manager considerably by summarizing much of the information presented in the report. Generally, as reports are presented to higher management levels, less detail and more summary is appropriate. Therefore, as reports move up the hierarchical levels, increasing amounts of information can be summarized.

4. *When appropriate, reports should include interpretative information*. To assist the reader as much as possible and because the report writer may have greater insight into specific situations than does the report reader, interpretative information may be very useful. Perhaps the report writer is aware of the reasons why a particular expense exceeded the budgeted allowance. Unless the report reader is quite familiar with a particular situation, it is doubtful that a valid explanation for the overrun could be offered.

5. *Reports should be standardized as much as possible*. To assist those who will read the reports, like reports should appear in the same format from one time to the next. By standardizing the format, the reader is able to recall more rapidly important facts or information regarding like situations in earlier reports. Furthermore, by standardizing the format of the reports, the reader is able to compare the information contained in one report with comparable information contained in other reports.

Depending upon the nature of the budget report and the use for which it is intended, sections that may be included in the budget report are: purpose of report; presentation of financial data; summary; conclusions; and recommendations.

In some instances, the summary is presented first, followed by the recommendations and the three remaining sections. Therefore, if the report reader feels that the first two sections contain a sufficient amount of information on which to make a decision, the remaining sections do not need to be read. If additional information is needed, however, it is available for the use of the report reader.

Cost Control

In an office, cost control is concerned with the cost involved in performing various office operations. In addition to determining the cost of operations, cost control is also concerned with ways of keeping costs as low as possible. A considerable amount of the administrative office manager's time will involve cost control activities.

Cost control provides several important objectives:

1. To develop standard costs for various office operations.
2. To develop within the employees a desire to be cost conscious.
3. To assist in the development of efficient operating procedures.
4. To allocate the costs of operations to the appropriate functions.
5. To identify operations that are not efficient.

Concern for controlling the costs of some office operations is not warranted. For example, spending many dollars to determine that the cost of a particular operation could be reduced only a few cents is evidence of poor management. In identifying the operations for which the costs should be determined, the administrative office manager should take into consideration the following: the volume of the operations, the degree to which the operations are standardized, the number of tasks involved in the operations, the efficiency with which the operations are performed, and the level of cost incurred in performing the operations.

The information used in determining the operating costs can be used in a variety of ways:

1. Identifying how closely the costs of office operations conform with accepted operating costs.
2. Identifying ways in which various operations are inefficient.
3. Helping determine which work methods should be revamped or revised.
4. Helping determine the type of new equipment needed when mechanizing office operations.
5. Identifying which alternative office procedures are the most efficient in view of the costs involved in performing the operation.

Techniques for Controlling Office Operating Costs

Several different techniques are available for use in controlling office operating costs. While some of these techniques are rather simple to use, others are more complex and require certain prerequisite knowledges on the part of the administrative office manager.

Cost breakdowns. A very easy-to-use technique for controlling office costs is the **cost breakdown technique.** This technique involves determining what percent of the total cost of an operation is a salary or labor cost, a materials or supplies cost, and an overhead cost. The following percentages are generally regarded as being standard for most office operations:

Salaries, including fringe benefits: 60–70 percent
Supplies and/or services, including forms, postage, stationery, telephone, telegraph, etc.: 15–20 percent
Overhead, including maintenance and depreciation of equipment, rent, utilities, taxes, and insurance: 15–20 percent

Some administrative office managers believe that the salaries and supplies categories should be further broken down into direct and indirect costs, such as the following:

Direct salaries: the salaries paid to those individuals directly concerned with the production of office work. Examples include the typists and secretaries.

Indirect salaries: the salaries paid to those individuals who help make the production of office work possible, but who are not directly involved in the production process. An example is the janitorial staff.

Direct suppliers: the actual supplies used in the production of office work. Examples include stationery and forms.

Indirect suppliers: the supplies used in producing office work that are not part of the work being produced. An example is the typewriter eraser.

To control office costs, the actual costs of operations are compared with standard cost breakdowns. If the actual costs exceed the cost breakdowns, the administrative office manager should make an attempt to determine why the actual costs exceed the breakdown percentages. Once the reasons for the excessive costs have been determined, the administrative office manager can develop a plan for reducing the costs.

Standard costs. The **standard cost technique** for controlling office costs involves determining the unit cost of various office operations. As long as the operation can be broken down into the various component parts and the cost of each part can be determined, the unit cost of the operation can be determined.

The following example illustrates the use of the standard cost technique. Assume that the standard cost for processing claims in the health insurance industry is $2.56 per claim. In a particular insurance company, the financial data revealed that the processing of one hundred claims cost $310. Therefore, the unit cost incurred by the company was $3.10. Since this amount is significantly greater than the industry's standard cost, an investigation should be made to determine why the insurance company's cost exceeded the standard cost by 54 cents.

Cost analysis studies. The last cost control technique to be discussed in this chapter is the **cost analysis study.** This type of study assists in comparing costs of a current period's operations with the operational costs of a prior period. For example, the office salaries for the current month might be compared with the office salaries for the same month a year ago. If the current figure is considerably higher than the previous figure, the reason for the increase should be determined.

Because this technique is greatly influenced by inflation and increases in operating costs, certain adjustments may have to be made when this technique is used during inflationary times. For example, the consumer price index may be utilized to adjust the figures in order to have a comparable base.

Taking Corrective Action

Control is necessary because actual results fail to conform with anticipated results. In the case of cost control, corrective action is necessary when the cost of the office operations exceed what is considered to be an appropriate cost.

When corrective action is appropriate, the administrative office manager or the supervisors in the office function are responsible for undertaking the appropriate course of action. Because many employees consider control to be a punitive measure, the individual who is responsible for taking the corrective action must use a considerable amount of discretion and judgment. Not all individuals respond in the same way to the corrective action.

The following is a composite of the situations responsible for actual costs exceeding anticipated costs:

1. Work procedures are not efficient.
2. Employees are not properly trained to perform the tasks that they are assigned.
3. Equipment does not function properly.
4. Supplies are not the appropriate quality for the situation.
5. Employees are not cost conscious.
6. Employees lack motivation to perform at acceptable levels.

Suggestions for Controlling Office Costs

Determining whether or not actual costs exceed anticipated costs is an important element of cost control. If the actual costs do exceed anticipated costs, another important element involves taking corrective action. But perhaps the most expedient way of controlling office costs is to implement practices that will not result in excessive costs. The following suggestions are offered.

Personnel costs. Because salaries of personnel account for the major portion of the costs of office operations, it is likely that greater flexibility exists here for controlling office costs than exists in other areas.

Personnel costs can be controlled in several ways. One suggestion is to make sure that the number of personnel is appropriate for the amount of work. If outside employees are needed because of a shortage of personnel in the organization, it may be less expensive in the long run to hire additional full-time, permanent employees. Because turnover is likely to increase if employees feel that their output expectations are too great, the cost of frequent selection, placement, and training of new employees may actually exceed the cost of hiring additional help.

Another suggestion for controlling office personnel costs is to determine the appropriate number of employees needed in relation to the projected amount of work that needs to be completed in a given amount of time. By using the standards developed during work measurement processes and by projecting the amount of work that will need to be done, an estimate of the number of personnel can be made.

Additional suggestions for controlling the cost of office personnel are:

1. Hire employees who are qualified for the jobs they are expected to perform.

2. In the event that employees are not qualified for the jobs they perform, provide training experiences for such employees.

3. When the amount of work to be completed occasionally exceeds the amount of manpower available for completing it, determine which of the following alternatives results in the greatest cost savings to the organization: employee overtime, part-time employees, employees from temporary help agencies, or floating work units.

4. Inform employees of the output levels they are expected to maintain. Employees who are aware of expected output levels are more likely to reach their levels than are employees who are not aware of the expected output levels.

Supplies and materials costs. Because most office work involves the use of supplies, forms, and materials, there are several ways in which such costs can be controlled. One of the most significant ways in which operating costs can be reduced is to keep the waste of supplies to a minimum. Waste occurs because employees are careless, because they make uncorrectable errors, or because they do not know how the supplies are to be used. In most instances, a very desirable way to control waste of supplies is to hire properly trained employees.

Another way to control costs of supplies, and more specifically the cost of forms, is to keep the number of forms used to a minimum. Before the use of a new form is approved, there should be ample justification for the use of the form.

Office costs can also be controlled to a certain extent by using equipment that utilizes supplies that are interchangeable with other equipment rather than supplies that accommodate only a particular piece of equipment. With the exception of copy machines, most office equipment uses supplies that are interchangeable.

The cost of office supplies can also be controlled by implementing an efficient inventory system. Without an inventory system, the chance is greater that the stock of some supplies will be excessive while other supplies will not be stocked in sufficient quantity. By reordering supplies before they are all consumed, the extra cost of rush orders can be kept to a minimum.

Equipment costs. Because some office equipment is not as reliable as other equipment, maintenance costs are greater. Before purchasing an expensive piece of equipment, the administrative office manager should investigate the dependability of several types of equipment. After a piece of equipment has been purchased, maintenance records should be kept. In the event that a particular piece of equipment has a considerably higher maintenance record than other machines, its trade-off should be considered even if the equipment has not been used the minimum number of years as specified by company policy.

Equipment costs can also be controlled by purchasing equipment that is appropriate for its intended use. Some office equipment is rather sophisticated, and if extra features are not needed to efficiently process the work, the purchase of the more sophisticated equipment should be discouraged. If, however, there is a possibility of needing the more sophisticated equipment at some point in the future, its purchase is more justifiable.

Work process costs. Not all work processes are developed with the same amount of efficiency. Because some work processes are inefficient, their revision should be considered. Some of the inefficiency of work processes can be identified by work measurement, by work simplification, and by systems and procedures analysis. Rather than controlling costs on an inefficient work process, greater economy may result from revising the work process before any costs are controlled.

The nature of many work processes results in their inefficiencies multiplying during each step of the process. Any work process in which this occurs should be given immediate attention.

In developing work processes designed to keep costs to a minimum, one should consider:

1. The cost of smooth-flowing work processes is less than erratic work processes.
2. The cost of controlling work processes involving as few employees as possible is less than those processes involving a greater number of employees.
3. Work processes involving a considerable amount of backtracking and crisscrossing will result in greater costs than those that are straight flowing.

Overhead costs. Since some of the overhead costs are variable, for example, heating, lighting, air conditioning, and electricity, these costs can be controlled by making employees more conscious of their excessive use.

As more and more organizations are becoming energy conscious, they are developing specific programs designed to result in energy conservation. In many instances, all that is needed is an energy conservation awareness on the part of the employees.

Some organizations have brought about energy conservation by establishing contests in each department of the organization. The employees in the department that experience the greatest net reduction in energy consumption over a period of time receive special recognition. In certain instances, financial awards are made.

Review Questions

1. Why is budgeting important in budgetary control?
2. What are the advantages and limitations of budgeting?
3. Who is generally responsible for the preparation of the office budget?
4. What are the differences between fixed variable and semi-variable costs?
5. Why is employee participation in budget preparation so useful?
6. Why must a budget provide for unforeseen circumstances?
7. Why should exception situations be pointed out in the budget report?
8. What advantages result from cost control?
9. As cost control techniques, how do cost breakdowns, standard costs, and cost analysis studies differ from one another?

Minicases

The Amsterdam Company was founded about ten years ago. At that time, the various managers were very cost conscious, and detailed records of expenditures were kept. The company hired a new president five years ago, when the firm's first president retired. The second president was vitally concerned about market expansion and did not place as much emphasis on the control of costs as did the first president. Because of the astute leadership ability of the second president, he was offered and accepted another position as president of a company somewhat larger than the Amsterdam Company. Like the first president, the third president is also very cost conscious. In fact, when he saw the cost of office supplies, he became quite alarmed. He has asked that you, the administrative office manager, submit to him your suggestions for controlling the cost of office supplies. What suggestions do you plan to include in your report to the president?

*   *   *

The Data Services Company is a new company in a fairly new field, which is the electronic processing of information for various clients. When the company was founded, only limited attention was given to the area of cost control. The company is doing very well financially, but it is felt by various managers that the company should be able to improve its financial picture if its operating costs are reduced. You have been hired by the company to install a cost control program. Which cost control alternatives are feasible? Which alternative are you going to recommend? Why?

Case

The executives of the Greater Merriman Medical Association have recently been made aware of increases in the operating costs of the office function of the association. For example, in two years' time, payroll costs have increased about 30 percent, the cost of supplies has increased about 40 percent, and the overhead costs have increased approximately 20 percent.

Although not heretofore considered necessary, the installation of a cost control program is being given some very serious thought. For example, there are several times during each month that some of the employees do not have a sufficient amount of work to do, the office manager has reported an increase in the amount of wasted supplies, and attempts have been futile in getting employees to be more concerned about electrical consumption. These are all considered to be reasons for the substantial increase in operating costs.

You have taken it upon yourself, as a committee of one, to try to convince the executives of the Greater Merriman Medical Association that a cost control program is greatly needed.

1. What benefits are likely to result from the installation of such a program?

2. What guidelines can you suggest to help make the installation of such a program more effective?

3. What problems are likely to result from the installation of such a program?

4. How can the association evaluate the effectiveness of the program once it is operational?

Index